BARAK RAVID

TRUMP'S PEACE

THE ABRAHAM ACCORDS AND THE RESHAPING OF THE MIDDLE EAST

Trump's Peace
by Barak Ravid

Translation into English: Sahar Zivan
Editor (English edition): Sofia Kouropatov
Editor (Hebrew edition): Yiffat Givon
Design & Layout: Studio Noam Tamari
Index: Exter Indexing
Cover Image: Hanoch Piven

To Adi, Yuval and Uri

Contents

Foreword

In April 2021, I headed north from Miami to Palm Beach to meet the person who had, up until three short months prior, been the most powerful man in the world. I spent the 90-minute drive to his Mar-a-Lago estate on the Atlantic coast replaying the four years I had dedicated to covering the changes Donald Trump had brought about in the United States, Israel and around the world—the good and the bad. It was the single most dramatic and intense period of my journalistic career, and the interview with Donald Trump, the 45th president of the United States, was set to be its climax. The Secret Service agent standing at the entrance to the estate glanced at my passport and waved me through. It was a Sunday afternoon and the place was quiet. When I entered the lobby, there was not a soul to be seen, but clues that this was the home of Donald Trump were visible everywhere. Two golden statuettes, received in recognition of his resort being awarded six stars, were perched on a table in the corner. The walls and the high ceiling of the main hall sparkled in shades of gold. Huge crystal chandeliers hung overhead and flower arrangements with dozens of large roses adorned the tables. An engraved white wooden piano stood silent at one end of the room. After a few minutes of waiting, Trump came in, dressed in a black suit and white shirt, no tie, with the familiar red MAGA hat on his head. He shook my hand and sat down. "Would you like something to drink?" he asked, and ordered his favorite beverage, Diet Coke (in a small glass bottle), from the waitress who hurried over to us as soon as we had settled onto the soft couch cushions.

When I requested the interview from Trump's chief spokesman, Jason Miller, the affirmative answer came quickly. The outgoing president granted interviews to over a dozen journalists who were writing books about his presidency at that time. I was the only Israeli among them. It was Trump's first interview with an Israeli journalist since February 2018, in fact.[1] The events at the Capitol on January 6 were still fresh in the public's mind. Holed up in his mansion, I could sense how keen the former president was to talk about other, more positive aspects of his legacy. Trump was very popular in Israel. His relationship with Netanyahu was often described as one long honeymoon. So nothing prepared me for what I heard from him that day. That meeting would change everything I thought I knew about the four years Trump spent in the White House and the relationship between the president of the United States and the prime minister of Israel.

Only seven months before I interviewed Trump, on September 15, 2020, I had seen him on the White House balcony at the signing ceremony of the Abraham Accords. The skies were clear and hundreds of white chairs—rows upon rows, like soldiers on parade—had been arranged on the grass, which looked greener than usual. In every direction, the Stars and Stripes waved alongside the flags of Israel, the United Arab Emirates and Bahrain. In America, everything is dazzling and grandiose—especially the celebrations. A perfect world painted in bright colors. And nowhere more so than in Donald Trump's White House.

I have visited the White House dozens of times on journalistic assignments throughout my career. The first time, I was very nervous. After that, it became routine. But there is one feeling that never goes away. When you stand in the White House, you can feel the power that emanates from it. It is the center of the world, the place with the greatest concentration of wealth, power and influence. That was true on this occasion as well. On a small stage on the South Lawn stood the historic wooden table around which President Truman conducted his cabinet meetings and discussions on the Marshall Plan in the aftermath of the Second World War. Truman was the same president who recognized the State of Israel 11 minutes after David Ben-Gurion declared its independence, on May 14, 1948.

The guests filtered in slowly, received by Vice President Mike Pence. They shook hands and engaged in pleasantries. Secretary of State Mike Pompeo spoke in hushed tones with Mossad Director Yossi Cohen, who minutes later had his photo taken embracing Sarah Idan, Miss Iraq 2017, who had fled to the United States after threats to her life following a photograph she had taken with Miss Israel. The president's daughter, Ivanka Trump, mingled alongside her husband, senior advisor to the president, Jared Kushner. Compositions by the American composer John Williams played in the background. Those with sharp hearing would have been able to pick out the famous opening bars of the Star Wars and Indiana Jones themes. "So many songs can be sung about America," wrote the Israeli singer-songwriter Rami Fortis, "Hollywood no longer remembers."

The senior figures in the US administration were easy to pick out in the crowd: they were the only ones not wearing masks. In the divided America of the time, two months out from the presidential election, masks had become a political statement. If you wore one, you were a Biden-supporting Democrat. If you walked around defiantly without one, you were a "Trump" Republican. Even those among the president's inner circle who were afraid of catching the coronavirus did not dare be caught wearing a mask in his presence. In the days that followed, it became clear that for many staff members at the White House, the ceremony had been a bona fide pox party. Two weeks later, President Trump himself caught the coronavirus and was taken to Walter Reed Medical Center. He recovered, but the virus played a significant role in his subsequent electoral defeat.

At a signal, Trump emerged from the Oval Office, followed by Israeli Prime Minister Benjamin Netanyahu, UAE Foreign Minister Sheikh Abdullah bin Zayed Al Nahyan and Bahraini Foreign Minister Abdullatif bin Rashid Al Zayani. Within moments, the attention of the dozens of photographers at the event moved from the crowd to the president. The only sounds to breach the silence were the rapid clicks of the cameras, like machine gun fire. Trump marched slowly with his three guests along the wooden walkway that led from his office to the site of the ceremony, pausing to admire every bush and flower bed on the way, enjoying every moment, basking in the attention, posing for every photograph. After a few minutes of walking, he stood on the balcony that overlooks the White House lawn, with James Sanderson's familiar anthem, "Hail to the Chief," playing in the background. The crowd gave him a standing ovation.

"We are here this afternoon to change the course of history. After decades of division and conflict, we mark the dawn of a new Middle East," Trump announced. "These agreements prove that the nations of the region are breaking free from the failed approaches of the past. And there will be other countries very, very soon that will follow."

Netanyahu, who stood up to speak after him, appeared emotional. He declared that this was a significant step on the way to resolving the Israeli–Arab conflict. "The blessings of the peace we make today will be enormous," he said. "The great economic benefits of our partnership will be felt throughout our region, and they will reach every one of our citizens." He did not make any mention of the Palestinian issue, nor of the fact that this celebratory event was a substitute for the initiative that he had devoted a large part of the previous year to advancing: annexing large swathes of the occupied West Bank to Israel. As part of the accords, Netanyahu committed to nixing his annexation plan for at least three years. The issue was raised at the ceremony by Foreign Minister bin Zayed. "Today, we are already witnessing a change in the heart of the Middle East, a change that will send hope around the world," he said, before turning to Netanyahu. "I also thank the prime minister of the State of Israel, Benjamin Netanyahu, for halting the annexation of the Palestinian territories, a decision that reinforces our shared will to achieve a better future for generations to come."

That moment on the stage, with the smiling leaders putting their signatures to the pages of history, was built on years upon years of clandestine relationships, secret pacts, moments of peril, an emboldened enemy, breaking points and turning points. I knew then that I wanted to tell the story of the Abraham Accords and to be the first person to do so. I sat down to write this book in December 2020, two months after the ceremony.[2] At the time, my main thought was that the agreements that had brought about the peace and normalization of relations between Israel and the four Arab countries involved represented the biggest diplomatic story I had covered in my career as a journalist since 2005. They were also the single biggest breakthrough in the Middle East peace process in over 25 years. In 1994, Prime Minister Yitzhak Rabin and King Hussein bin Talal of Jordan signed a historic peace treaty between the two nations. In 1997, Netanyahu oversaw the withdrawal from Hebron, and in 1998 he signed the Wye Accords (which were never fully implemented) with Yasser Arafat. In the more than two decades since, we have had one and a half intifadas, a unilateral Israeli disengagement from the Gaza strip, three rounds of failed negotiations with the Palestinians, two rounds of failed negotiations with Syria, war with Lebanon, three wars with Hamas in Gaza and thousands of casualties on all sides.

This book describes the negotiations behind the Abraham Accords themselves, but also the quarter century in which the secret relationship between Israel and the Gulf states developed. As is the way with most diplomatic stories, this one also involves a whole world that exists in the shadows, which is home to less familiar figures—diplomats, businesspeople, spies, foreign mediators and anonymous messengers—without whom none of this would have happened. Most of them were sitting in the chairs on the South Lawn of the White House on the day the accords were signed. The names and pictures of some of them have not been cleared for publication to this day.

But it goes deeper than them: the story of the Abraham Accords grants us new and clearer insights into the nature of the relationship between Israel and the United States during the Trump administration, and the changes that took place in the Middle East over his four years in the White House. Revealing details of the events that occurred behind the scenes also serves as a useful myth-busting exercise about the relationship between then-Prime Minister of Israel Benjamin Netanyahu and the former president of the United States. When I first heard some of the stories described in these pages, my spine tingled. When I listened to the way Trump spoke about Netanyahu, I could feel my ears burning—not only because of the new details I was hearing for the first time, but also because of the gulf between the image projected to the public and the goings-on behind closed doors. The first two chapters of this book also cover the rapid deterioration of the relationship between the Palestinian Authority and the United States during the Trump administration. You will read about Israeli, American and Palestinian steps and missteps, and how these brought the Palestinian national movement to the brink of collapse.

The book outlines a few central arguments:

- Despite the idyllic public image provided for domestic public consumption in the United States and Israel, the relationship between Donald Trump and Benjamin Netanyahu was poor. Like Bill Clinton and Barack Obama before him, Trump ultimately concluded that Netanyahu had no interest in peace with the Palestinians and reached the end of his term in office frustrated and angry with him.
- The Abraham Accords between Israel and the Gulf states, as well as the normalization agreements with Morocco and Sudan, were the single biggest breakthrough in the Middle East peace process in over 25 years.
- These agreements would never have been possible without Donald Trump and his Middle East policy.

Trump may be incredibly popular in Israel, but in many countries around the world he has an overwhelmingly negative image. Liberals in North America and Europe saw in him the realization of all their fears. With that in mind, there will undoubtedly be some readers wondering why I chose to name the book "Trump's Peace."

To call the former president "controversial" would be a great understatement. Trump was the most divisive president in the history of the United States and his legacy will forever be stained by his supporters' assault on the Capitol—the bastion of American democracy—two weeks before the end of his term. But, as is often the case, a close examination of Trump's tenure reveals that it cannot all be painted with the same brush. The president's legacy is more complex than that, and includes within it also the Abraham Accords—perhaps his signature foreign policy achievement. Intellectual honesty compels both his supporters and his detractors to recognize his failures and his successes. The same recognition should similarly be applied to the defenders and opponents of Netanyahu when it comes to the legacy of the former prime minister, who has been charged with fraud, bribery and breach of trust, divided the nation, spread hatred, encouraged incitement and tore at the democratic fabric of Israel. On the other hand, he also boasted some achievements—the normalization process with Arab countries that he led since 2009 is perhaps the most noteworthy of these.

Donald Trump was not familiar with the details of the accords that were signed in the White House on that day. But the president of the United States is a symbol. He sets the tone. He is the sum of his political capital. Trump opened the road and enabled others to drive along it. The accords were also not planned. Rather, they were a creative solution to a diplomatic crisis that arose around Netanyahu's West Bank annexation initiative. Nonetheless, they happened under Trump's watch and were brought to fruition by the people closest to him, his advisors Jared Kushner and Avi Berkowitz, with his full support. The accords were made possible by the changes taking place in the Middle East as a result of Trump's policy. Withdrawing from the 2015 nuclear agreement and the "maximum pressure" campaign on Iran strengthened the alliance between Israel and the Gulf states against the regime in Tehran. Moving the US embassy to Jerusalem exposed the fatigue and apathy toward the Palestinians within parts of the Arab world. The trust Trump was afforded in Israel and a few key Arab capitals and the offers he was willing to make in exchange cleared the way for unprecedented diplomatic breakthroughs. Last but not least, the unveiling of the Trump peace plan—which envisaged a Palestinian state with limited sovereignty and a capital city in parts of East Jerusalem—and its unequivocal rejection by president of the Palestinian Authority Mahmoud Abbas gave a string of Arab nations the pretext they required for the normalization of relations with Israel.

Benjamin Netanyahu did not plan for the Abraham Accords either, and they were not his preferred path. This book reveals to what extent that was the case. The way events leading up to the accords unfolded left him with no choice, his attempts to secure the White House's go-ahead for annexation of parts of the West Bank meeting a brick wall. However, the accords were ultimately made possible by a decade of diplomatic groundwork that Netanyahu himself had laid. Like his predecessors, he continued to develop and significantly expand clandestine relationships with the Gulf states. Unlike his predecessors, he promoted a new policy direction of peace with the Arab world before peace with the Palestinians. Many people over many years considered this to be a hopeless endeavor. But slowly and methodically, Netanyahu took steps that paved the way to this point. The Israeli ambassador to Washington at the time, Ron Dermer, who negotiated the Abraham Accords on behalf of Israel almost single-handedly, was Netanyahu's number one confidant throughout his career as prime minister. Ultimately, Netanyahu's decision to step back from the plan to annex parts of the West Bank was far from trivial. Netanyahu's attempt to portray the agreement as "peace for peace" was political spin with no basis in reality. However, his opponents, who argued that his talk of annexation was all bluster and empty threats, were equally mistaken. Over the course of dozens of interviews that I conducted as part of my research for this book, I have reached the conclusion that Netanyahu was serious in his plans for annexation and was even preparing to carry them out. It's unlikely that any other prime minister would have survived such a sharp reversal on a promise that had been championed through four election cycles without paying a political price.

The most significant individual behind the Abraham Accords was also the one who boasted about them the least. The crown prince of Abu Dhabi and de facto ruler of the United Arab Emirates at the time, Sheikh Mohamed bin Zayed, advanced normalization with Israel as part of his strategic plan.[3] The only question for him in recent years was not whether to normalize relations with Israel, but rather when to do so. It did not take much courage for Netanyahu to say yes to normalization with the UAE. For bin Zayed, this step was fraught with greater risks. As a result, it resembles in certain aspects the strategic decision by the former president of Egypt, Anwar Sadat, to make peace with Israel by any means necessary in the 1970s. It is doubtful whether the Abraham Accords would have come to pass without the UAE's initiative in early July 2020. Moreover, with this action, bin Zayed achieved several strategic goals: normalization with Israel, thwarting annexation, safeguarding the possibility of a two-state solution and significantly deepening ties with the United States.

This book is a product of interviews with dozens of American, Israeli, Emirati, Bahraini, Moroccan and European stakeholders with direct involvement in the events described. The key interviewee is the former president of the United States, Donald Trump, whom I interviewed on several occasions for over two hours. His words regarding the process that took place, the people around him and the various leaders involved have been incorporated into the different chapters, and are also explored in a standalone chapter at the end of the book.

Benjamin Netanyahu, the former prime minister, turned down my request for an interview for the book. Netanyahu has attacked the media on numerous occasions for not providing what he believes to be sufficiently favorable coverage of his diplomatic achievements with the Arab world. When I offered him the chance to discuss them at length, however, he rejected it out of hand. His two closest confidants—Ron Dermer and former Director of Mossad Yossi Cohen—likewise refused to be interviewed.

The book runs along three parallel tracks: the first is chronological, telling the story of how events unfolded from Donald Trump's victory in the 2016 election until his departure from the White House in disgrace in January 2021. The second is subject-specific and addresses the core areas of discussion in the US–Israel relationship, such as the Israeli–Palestinian conflict, the Iranian nuclear program and relations with the Arab world. The third is historical, seeking to contextualize the Abraham Accords within a broader and longer-term perspective. The combination of these three tracks offers a more comprehensive picture of these fascinating and historic events. It is my hope that this book will answer questions, arouse interest and help those in the future who were not even born when these accords were signed to learn the full story of those momentous days.

This book was published in Hebrew in December 2021. Many things have happened since then in the US–Israel–Gulf triangle. The Abraham Accords became even more relevant during this period.

I decided to update the book and add another chapter that will focus on what the Biden administration and the Israeli government which was formed after the ouster of Benjamin Netanyahu did to strengthen and expand the accords. This chapter also summarizes what has been achieved and what hasn't been achieved in the two years that passed since the Abraham Accords were signed.

Our journey begins in December 2016, with a declaration from President-elect Donald Trump that things were about to change.

Trump Enters the Arena

My phone buzzed in my hand as a tweet notification popped up on the screen. It was the afternoon of December 28, 2016 in Israel, early morning in New York. "Stay strong Israel, January 20th is fast approaching!" wrote incoming president of the United States Donald Trump from his bed in the penthouse of his famous tower on Fifth Avenue. A few hours later, US Secretary of State John Kerry was due to go in front of the cameras in the US Department of State in Washington, DC and deliver a speech in which he would present the Obama administration's guiding principles to resolving the Israeli–Palestinian conflict. The US–Israel relationship was at an unprecedented low. Trump's tweet suggested that, across the ocean, a new friend was coming with a sympathetic ear for the prime minister, Benjamin Netanyahu.

Contacts between Netanyahu's people and Trump's had been ongoing for a long time by this point. In March 2016, a few days before then-candidate Trump was due to give a speech to the pro-Israel lobby group AIPAC (American-Israel Public Affairs Committee), Ambassador Ron Dermer spoke to Trump's son-in-law Jared Kushner, who wrote the speech, and briefed him on the different facets of Netanyahu's policy. That might go some way in explaining why Trump's speech sounded like it had been lifted from a list of the Israeli prime minister's personal talking points. Netanyahu had also planned to host Trump in Jerusalem before the elections, but the presidential candidate canceled his visit after Netanyahu condemned statements he had made about Muslims that had been widely criticized in Israel. Trump did not harbor resentment toward Netanyahu, however.

His subsequent electoral victory sent shockwaves not only through Washington, but also Jerusalem. It was clear that Trump had no intention of sticking to the usual presidential transition script. Proof of this came on November 17, only nine days after his victory, when he held an unorthodox meeting with Dermer. Up until that point, the United States had maintained a tradition of "one president at a time," i.e., the president-elect and his team refrained almost entirely from initiating diplomatic contacts in the transition period. But Trump was not a man of tradition. During the meeting, which took place in Trump Tower, Dermer met with the president-elect and his close advisors, Jared Kushner, Steve Bannon and General Michael Flynn. After the initial pleasantries, discussions began with the primary subject of concern for the Israeli government at that time: a parting shot by the Obama administration in the form of a diplomatic move on the Palestinian issue. Netanyahu sought to close ranks with Trump at the earliest opportunity in order to thwart such a possibility. At the end of the meeting, Dermer went downstairs and addressed the cameras in the lobby of the building. "President-elect Trump is a true friend of Israel," he said.

A few weeks later, in early December, Mossad Director Yossi Cohen and National Security Advisor Jacob Nagel went to Washington for an unpublicized meeting with General Flynn. As the days passed, Israeli concerns began to increase. The scenario considered most likely was that the Palestinians would bring an anti-Israel resolution to the Security Council of the United Nations that the Obama administration would not veto. Three weeks later, that scenario began to take shape. On the evening of Wednesday, December 21, 2016, in New York, Egypt distributed a draft resolution condemning Israeli settlements in the West Bank and declared that it would bring it to a vote at the Security Council the very next day. In the early morning in Jerusalem, the Israeli government machine went into overdrive. Netanyahu convened the State Security Cabinet, held an alarmed phone call with Secretary of State Kerry and tweeted immediately afterward: "The US should veto the anti-Israel resolution at the UN Security Council on Thursday." Netanyahu's advisors called the White House and demanded of Obama's advisors that they veto the resolution and not change long-standing policy. The Americans refused to make any commitments. "We will have no choice but to turn to Trump," Netanyahu's aides said to their American counterparts. And so it played out. "Dermer called us and said it is happening. He said that on the way out the door Obama wants to kick Bibi (Netanyahu) in the face," a former senior White House official who was involved in those conversations told me.[4] Trump, meanwhile, was not going to pass up an opportunity to take a jab at Obama. "This sounds like a big deal," Trump said when informed of the outgoing president's intentions. He asked his advisors to draft a statement in his name to underscore that an outgoing administration was not supposed to implement such a drastic policy shift in its final days. Trump also put out a public statement calling on Obama to veto the resolution. During his questioning as part of the investigation into Russian attempts to influence the US election, General Michael Flynn— who would become Trump's national security advisor three weeks later—told the investigators that the president-elect's team saw the effort to thwart the vote as an important matter.[5] According to Flynn, the president-elect and several of his advisors called senior officials of numerous foreign governments on the day of the vote in an attempt to coalesce opposition to the resolution. General Flynn was in charge of speaking with the Russians. He called the Russian ambassador to Washington, Sergey Kislyak, and told him that Trump was asking the Russians to delay the vote or to vote against it, thereby vetoing it. At the same time, Kushner told me, Trump's team spoke to representatives of the Egyptian government and asked them to put the brakes on the move. The Prime Minister's Office in Jerusalem also applied significant pressure on Egyptian President Abdel Fattah al-Sisi, who was dependent on Israel's cooperation in his battle against the Sinai faction of the Islamic State. The Egyptian president ultimately caved in to the pressure. On that Thursday evening, an hour before the vote, Egypt announced that it would be suspending the resolution indefinitely. After Egypt's climbdown, Trump called al-Sisi to thank him.[6] The Egyptian president apologized and blamed the situation on a breakdown in communication with the Egyptian ambassador to the UN, who he said had advanced the resolution without discussing it with the government in Cairo first. "We want a good relationship with the new administration," the Egyptian president told Trump.

A collective sigh of relief could be heard in Jerusalem, but it would not last long. The following day, the battle at the Security Council picked up once more when New Zealand, Malaysia, Senegal and Venezuela declared that they would use their status as members of the Security Council to bring the draft the Egyptians had pulled to a vote. Netanyahu's people and Trump's team continued their efforts to block the resolution. Flynn spoke with Ambassador Kislyak, who made it clear that if brought to a vote,

Russia would not veto the resolution.[7] Netanyahu then called the president of Russia, Vladimir Putin, personally and asked him to veto it. The Russians refused, but nonetheless sought to take a conciliatory step toward Netanyahu and Trump. Moments before the vote, there was drama at the UN headquarters in New York. As the ambassadors were making their way to the Security Council Chamber, Russian ambassador to the UN Vitaly Churkin asked to hold a closed discussion, during which he expressed surprise at the urgency with which the process was being pushed forward and proposed delaying the vote until after Christmas. He explained that they had a problem with the timing of the move—three weeks before a new president was due to enter the White House. However, Churkin was unable to convince the other ambassadors, who demanded to hold the vote immediately. The Russian ambassador summarized the proceedings by saying he had "never seen so many people rushing to embrace an orphan."[8] The debate ended. Minutes later, representatives of 14 countries raised their hands in favor. By order of President Obama, the US ambassador to the United Nations, Samantha Power, did not use her veto and the decision passed. "The United States has been sending the message that the settlements must stop—privately and publicly—for nearly five decades," said Power in her speech to the Security Council. "One cannot simultaneously champion expanding Israeli settlements and champion a viable two-state solution… One has to make a choice." Netanyahu was furious like never before.

That Saturday night, with the smoke yet to clear after the events surrounding the vote, I drove to the central Israeli city of Ra'anana to attend the bat mitzvah of Meirav Shapiro, daughter of the US ambassador to Israel, Dan Shapiro. Dan and his wife Julie had become close friends of my wife Adi and I. The family's joy came in the midst of the greatest diplomatic crisis they had faced in their six years in Israel. "He looks worried. I wouldn't want to be in his shoes," said Yael Feldboy, the legendary spokeswoman of the US embassy in Israel who was sitting at my table.[9] The following morning, Shapiro received a telephone call from the Prime Minister's Office. He was astonished to hear that he was being "summoned" for a reprimand from Netanyahu. Moments later, the story was already in the headlines of news websites. This was the only time in Netanyahu's 12-year reign as prime minister that he did such a thing. Shapiro told me that the conversation was brutal, and that he had never seen Netanyahu so angry.

At the same time, Ambassador Ron Dermer was dispatched to media outlets in the United States. He held a round of interviews in which he claimed that the Obama administration had collaborated with the Palestinians behind Israel's back to push the anti-settlements resolution at the Security Council. He even claimed that Israel had intelligence to this effect that would be delivered to the new administration as soon as it entered office. Obama's aides denied Israel's accusations at the time, but a few years later a senior official from the Obama administration told me that there had indeed been such behind-the-scenes coordination between the United States and the Palestinians. Suspicions of Netanyahu ran so deep that, following Trump's election victory, two of Obama's advisors requested that Saeb Erekat—a senior official in the PLO—travel to the US embassy in Riyadh, Saudi Arabia, to hold a video call with them on a secure line that was safe from Israeli interception. During the conversation, the two told Erekat that Obama was looking favorably upon withholding the veto on an anti-settlements Security Council resolution, if its language was not too extreme. The day after Dermer's interviews about American coordination with the Palestinians, the Egyptian news outlet *Youm7* published a document it claimed was the summary of a meeting between Erekat, Secretary of State John Kerry and National Security Advisor Susan Rice, which had taken place 10 days before the UN vote. According to the document, the meeting had been convened in order to coordinate positions ahead of the vote, and Kerry and Rice had asked Erekat to keep the content of the meeting "top secret." After the document was published, the State Department issued a denial, but Netanyahu claimed that it was merely "the tip of the iceberg" of the trove of evidence that Israel had gathered.

On December 28, a few hours after Trump tweeted the promise that American policy on Israel was about to change, Secretary of State Kerry began his speech at the State Department in Washington. For over an hour, he summed up four years of unsuccessful attempts to advance peace between Israel and the Palestinians and outlined the Obama administration's principles for ending the conflict—including a Palestinian capital in East Jerusalem. Netanyahu did not mince his words. He recorded a video in English, attacking Kerry in no uncertain terms. "Israel looks forward to working with President-elect Trump...to mitigate the damage," he said. Three weeks before the end of the Obama administration, it appeared that there was nothing and nobody left that could prevent the relationship between Washington and Jerusalem from falling into an abyss. On January 15, 2017, my colleague Gal Berger and I flew to Paris to cover the Middle East peace conference that was being attended by dozens of foreign ministers from around the world. The Israelis and Palestinians had not been invited, and we were the only Israeli journalists present. In the days before the conference, Trump's advisors asked the French to push it back until after the new president had taken office. The French refused. Donald Trump was the elephant in the room. Many of the speeches delivered by the various foreign ministers suggested concern about the policy direction that the new president might adopt, in particular surrounding the question of the relocation of the US embassy to Jerusalem. "This conference is among the last twitches of yesterday's world. Tomorrow's world will be different—and it is very near," said Netanyahu at the cabinet meeting that had been called that morning. The Netanyahu government's countdown calendar had only five days left to cross off before January 20.

A New President

The Israeli ambassador to Washington, Ron Dermer, made his way to Capitol Hill to attend Donald Trump's inauguration ceremony. For him, a new day was dawning. Information released by the White House showed that there had been almost no meetings between the ambassador and the president's advisors during Obama's term in office.[10] Now, he was all set to go from persona non grata to part of the furniture in the Oval Office. He mingled with the many ambassadors in attendance, as excited as a kid on Christmas Eve. During Trump's first days in the White House, the president planned to sign a wave of executive orders that would reverse several of the policy decisions made by his predecessor and signal the start of a new domestic and foreign policy agenda. Word reached Israel that Trump was planning to announce the relocation of the American embassy from Tel Aviv to Jerusalem on his first or second day in office. The billionaire Sheldon Adelson, who had donated tens of millions of dollars to Trump's campaign, leaned hard on the president-elect and his advisors to push the move through. On the other hand, two of Trump's most senior appointees—Secretary of State Rex Tillerson and Secretary of Defense James Mattis—were reticent about taking such a step without a formal discussion about the potential consequences. The latter even said in his Senate confirmation hearing that as far as he was concerned, the capital of Israel was Tel Aviv, as that was where he met with Israeli government officials. Netanyahu and Dermer were unable to predict on which side Trump would come down. A few days before the swearing-in ceremony, the prime minister convened a meeting with a few of his ministers and senior officials from the IDF, Shin Bet (Israel's domestic security agency) and the police to discuss the potential implications. The meeting was marked by uncertainty, and the security establishment put forward various possible scenarios of escalation in Jerusalem, the West Bank and the Gaza Strip. Netanyahu closed the meeting by noting that a statement regarding the embassy could come at any moment once Trump entered the White House, and he ordered the security chiefs to prepare accordingly. Two days before the ceremony, Mossad Director Yossi Cohen and National Security Advisor Jacob Nagel visited Washington, where they met with the president-elect's advisors. They left those meetings none the wiser regarding whether a declaration was imminent. In Ramallah, the uncertainty surrounding Trump and his intentions was greater still. The Palestinian president, Abbas, and his advisors—who had been holding out for a Hillary Clinton victory—had no open channels of communication to Trump or those around him. A few weeks before the inauguration, Susan Rice, President Obama's national security advisor, urged the Palestinians to take Trump's statements on the embassy relocation seriously and to reach out to the president-elect before he took his place in the Oval Office. In the Mukataa, the administrative headquarters of the Palestinian Authority, complacency reigned. Their assessment was that Trump's talk on Jerusalem was empty campaign promises. It was only a meeting between Abbas and a Jewish-American businessman that shook them out of their inertia. Daniel Arbess, founder of the Xerion hedge fund, was an unknown quantity within the Palestinian Authority and among expert observers of the Israeli–Palestinian conflict in general. When Arbess asked for a meeting with Abbas, claiming to be a close contact of the president-elect's advisors, those in the Mukataa jumped at the opportunity.[11] Arbess's proximity to Trump and his people was questionable and seemed to extend no further than the fact that he sat next to Jared Kushner at the Kehilath Jeshurun synagogue in New York's Upper East Side. But that was good enough for Abbas's advisors. An Israeli source told me at the time that Arbess warned Abbas that Trump was serious about his intentions to move the embassy to Jerusalem, and that he might announce the move in his first days in office. His words served as a wake-up call and left the Palestinian president and his staff speechless. They launched a public campaign warning of the consequences of such a move and appealed to Arab leaders to deliver messages to Trump and his advisors; Abbas even sent the president-elect a personal letter urging him not to take such a step. Trump's first day in office ended without a word on the subject of Jerusalem. The second day too. On the third day, minutes before the first telephone call between Trump and Netanyahu, the White House spokesman declared that discussions on the subject were still very much in their infancy. Netanyahu, Dermer and Adelson were disappointed. Abbas and his staff breathed a sigh of relief.

"There were many important people who the president liked and trusted who pushed him to take the step on Jerusalem on day one," Jason Greenblatt, Trump's Middle East envoy, told me.[12] "I also supported recognizing Jerusalem as the capital of Israel, but I thought it would be improper to bring your personal opinions from home and to take such a step without first looking into it, without taking counsel, without a formal and structured process within government. People think Trump shoots from the hip—but he doesn't really do that kind of thing with decisions that have the potential to lead to violence. In hindsight, I'm glad we waited and took time for formal deliberations and consultations before we decided."

"The Ultimate Deal"

Every US president from 1967 onward has engaged with the Israeli–Palestinian conflict to various extents. A few of Trump's predecessors, such as Bill Clinton, George W. Bush and Barack Obama, devoted intensive efforts to this issue—holding peace conferences and negotiations on a final-status agreement between Israel and the Palestinians—but none of them were able to reach a deal. Donald Trump was no less determined. On numerous occasions during the election campaign, he stated his desire to secure a peace treaty between Israel and the Palestinians should he win. His interest appeared to only grow after the election. On one occasion, he declared that peace between Israel and the Palestinians was "the ultimate deal"; on another, he referred to it as "the mother of all deals." Trump's motivation appeared to stem from his desire to succeed where all his predecessors had failed, to prove his superiority in the art of the deal. "Everybody told me that the Israeli–Palestinian conflict was the most difficult deal to make," Trump told me.[13]

A few days before his inauguration, Trump announced that he would be appointing his son-in-law, Jared Kushner, to lead the diplomatic efforts to secure peace in the Middle East. Kushner told me in one of our conversations that he had not planned to focus his efforts in this direction at all, and that he first heard of his involvement through the media. In his first meeting with his team, Kushner said jokingly that he suspected his father-in-law had given him this task because he didn't like him.[14] "This is a mission impossible, but the president has asked that we give it a shot," Kushner told them. "Let's give this everything we've got, present the solution that we think has the greatest chance of success, and then we will see whether the wall we're banging our head against is made of concrete or papier-mâché." Alongside Kushner, Trump also appointed the chief legal officer of the Trump Organization, Jason Greenblatt, as his Middle East envoy, and his personal attorney, David Friedman (the man who had resolved Trump's bankruptcy filings) as ambassador to Israel. "Trump saw a peace agreement with the Palestinians as something that would help Israel," Greenblatt told me.[15] "He had time to devote to it because there was no COVID-19. He handed the reins on this issue to people he trusted. More than that, it was a piece of the puzzle in his regional strategy—pushing back against Iran, rehabilitating relationships with Israel and the Arab world after the Obama years and bringing Israel and the Arab world closer together." Trump made the Israeli–Palestinian conflict a top priority, but his personal views on the subject remained unclear. On the one hand, the people he appointed to address it were Orthodox Jews with a clear right-wing perspective, but on the other hand, all throughout the election campaign and beyond he had repeatedly stated that he would be "neutral." It was clear that Trump was unpredictable and that he would not be a "status-quo" president—but in January 2017, few could have predicted the scale of the impending earthquake.

Netanyahu spent a few days preparing for his first call with Trump. His most pressing priority was to defuse the threat of draft legislation put forward by the Jewish Home party—led at the time by Naftali Bennett[16]—calling to annex the settlement of Ma'ale Adumim near Jerusalem. Convening a meeting of the State

Security Cabinet, Netanyahu told the ministers in attendance that Trump's advisors had asked him not to take any far-reaching steps ahead of his first meeting with the new President. He also told those present that all the Obama-era restrictions on construction in East Jerusalem would be lifted immediately. In exchange, the draft legislation proposed by Jewish Home was removed from the agenda. The call between the two leaders took place on Trump's third day in office, at the same time as the evening news broadcasts in Israel. Trump asked Netanyahu whether he was interested in a deal with the Palestinians. "I'm interested, but the Palestinians are uncooperative," Netanyahu told him, and rattled off all the obstructionist moves the Palestinians had made over the years. "They will want to do a deal, they will compromise," Trump replied.[17] At the end of the call, Netanyahu received what he was after: an invitation to a meeting with the new president at the White House. In the weekly faction meeting of Netanyahu's Likud party the next day, he seemed pleased with the conversation, but emphasized that, despite the fact that the new president was no Barack Obama, they would still need to exercise caution. "I am not in favor of a Palestinian state, I'm in favor of a 'state-minus,'" he told the members of his faction when they called on him to work on taking the two-state solution off the table under Trump. "We now have opportunities after eight years of pressure. But if we make mistakes now, we risk losing the moment and tipping the relationship in a direction that is unfavorable to us. This is not the time to spring surprises or shoot from the hip."

On February 14, 2017, Netanyahu arrived in Washington for his first meeting with Trump at the White House. Because of his disastrous relationship with Obama, Netanyahu had not visited the US capital for over 15 months. He sought to be welcomed back to Washington with a White House honor guard and a red carpet beneath his feet. Trump was happy to provide him with this victorious shot. They both wanted to show the world that the past was in the past. Despite this, Netanyahu was uneasy. In the State Security Cabinet meeting ahead of his trip, he spoke with the attendees about the "character" of the new president. "He wants a deal," Netanyahu told his ministers. "We have to tread lightly. We must not fight with him." As soon as he touched down at Andrews Air Force Base, Netanyahu learned that while he had been over the Atlantic Ocean, a storm had engulfed the White House, with National Security Advisor Michael Flynn—who had been the Israelis' point of contact in most of the preparatory calls for the meeting—forced to resign in the wake of an FBI investigation into his conduct. I had visited the White House more than 20 times before. I attended meetings between Prime Minister Ehud Olmert and President George W. Bush and between Netanyahu and Obama, among others. But on the morning of the meeting with Trump, the energy was completely different. Netanyahu felt it too. He knew he was walking into a White House in complete turmoil, and had no idea if any of the arrangements they had made ahead of time would hold.

Behind the scenes, Netanyahu's staff tried to ask one thing above all of Trump's advisors—that the president not say the words "Palestinian state" or "two-state solution" during the press conference that preceded the meeting. Netanyahu's advisors told Trump's people that everyone interpreted it differently and so it would be preferable not to use that terminology. The Americans were won round. "We didn't want to back ourselves into a corner with these terms without being able to describe what they meant, so we preferred to say that we wanted to achieve peace," Greenblatt told me.[18] Kushner viewed things differently to Greenblatt but accepted his position. "For several years we avoided using the term 'two state solution.' It drove people crazy, but it created a bigger surprise because nobody expected it to be part of our plan." he told me.[19]

With the ever-unpredictable Trump, however, things did not go to plan. "I am looking at two-state and one-state," said Trump. "I thought for a while the two-state looked like it may be the easier of the two, but I like the one that both parties like." Some of those present in the Briefing Room erupted in laughter, others were stunned—for the first time since 1967, a sitting US president had expressed a willingness to consider the idea of a one-state solution between Jordan and the Mediterranean Sea; not autonomy, not Netanyahu's "state-minus," but one Jewish-Arab state.

Trump emerged from that first meeting with Netanyahu unconvinced that the prime minister of Israel was interested in making any progress with the Palestinians. He needled Netanyahu on a couple of occasions during the press conference. "Both sides will have to make compromises. You know that, right?" he told Netanyahu. A few moments later, he added that he was confident a deal between Israel and the Palestinians was possible. Netanyahu mumbled something to which Trump—with his reality show timing—turned to the audience in the hall and added, "Doesn't sound too optimistic," eliciting laughter from the assembled press. In my interview with Trump four years later, he said that he instantly recognized that Netanyahu was stalling. "I think Bibi didn't want to make peace. He never did," he told me.[20]

One of Netanyahu's advisors from that period who was there with him at the White House said that the more significant moment came during the private meeting between the two leaders, when Trump asked Netanyahu to freeze settlement construction. "You can refrain from building in the settlements for four years and nothing will happen," Trump said to Netanyahu.[21] In the first week of Trump's term, the Israeli government had announced plans to move forward with planning and building no fewer than six thousand housing units in existing settlements in the West Bank, as well as a whole new settlement on the site of the Amona illegal outpost—something that had not happened for many years. It took the White House a few days to respond and to underline that settlement construction was not conducive to peace. A few days later, President Trump repeated the message in an interview with the *Israel Hayom* daily, where he called on Israel to "act reasonably." Netanyahu was starting to feel an uncomfortable sense of déjà vu, reminded of his first days with the Obama administration, eight years previously. He gave Trump the same answer he had given to his predecessor. He claimed that he was unable to freeze construction and proposed reaching an understanding on the matter. With Obama, this had concluded in a 10-month freeze on construction in the settlements. With Trump, the outcome could not have been more different.

A few weeks after the meeting between Trump and Netanyahu, the president's envoy, Jason Greenblatt, arrived for his first visit in Jerusalem and Ramallah. Trump's demand for a complete freeze during his meeting with Netanyahu had disappeared. The new message was that the president would like to find a way forward that includes minimal construction in the settlements, done in such a way as to avoid derailing his efforts to make progress on the peace process. Greenblatt made it clear that the president was expecting to see gestures that would signal Israel's desire for peace. One of Netanyahu's advisors who was in the room for those meetings told me that Greenblatt came to his first meeting armed with maps and assorted paraphernalia that he used to outline the White House's primary concern. He called it "hill jumping." When Netanyahu feigned ignorance, Greenblatt unrolled an aerial photograph of the

Itamar settlement, deep inside the West Bank, and pointed to the houses scattered on the hilltops surrounding it. "Why do we need this sprawl? You're trying to capture more and more territory and it's not acceptable," Greenblatt told Netanyahu.[22] One of the proposals Greenblatt raised was that Israel would freeze all construction in the isolated settlements in the heart of the West Bank and pursue construction only in the so-called "settlement blocs" close to the Green Line. Netanyahu refused. He attempted to erase the distinction pursued by a series of American and Israeli governments—including those he himself had led—between blocs that would remain part of Israel and isolated settlements that would be removed in the framework of a future agreement. Four meetings and almost 10 hours of discussions later, there were no understandings on the horizon. As midnight approached on Thursday, after Greenblatt had departed for the airport, Netanyahu called in his chief of staff, Yoav Horowitz, Deputy Cabinet Secretary Ronen Peretz and Foreign Policy Advisor Jonathan Schachter, and asked them to head to Washington immediately to continue the talks. He ordered them to keep it confidential, even from the other advisors in the office.

When Netanyahu's advisors reached the White House, there was another person by Greenblatt's side: Scott Leith, the number one expert on the settlements within the US government. One of Netanyahu's advisors told me that they were taken by surprise by the depth of Leith's knowledge of the situation on the ground in the West Bank, and that it was impossible to mislead him. Netanyahu's advisors got the impression that the Americans thought the Israelis would attempt to outmaneuver them. "We understood that we had to act with complete transparency with them in order to build trust," he told me. As talks in Washington progressed, the two sides began to formulate preliminary understandings. A few days later, these were finalized. Israel promised to restrict construction in a way that would minimize the urban expansion of the settlements without cutting off Palestinian territorial congruity. They further agreed that any decisions regarding settlements would be made in batches on a trimonthly basis, instead of once a week, in order to minimize the media noise around the subject, which was straining the White House's relationships with the Arab world. The result of this agreement was a significant reduction in planning and construction processes in the settlements. For their part, the Americans agreed to tolerate a new settlement for the settlers evicted from the Amona illegal outpost. The two sides agreed to keep the question of Jerusalem deliberately ambiguous. "There are no restrictions on construction in East Jerusalem, but we will have to act prudently," Netanyahu told the ministers in the State Security Cabinet when he presented the decisions to them. In practice, Netanyahu often delayed or froze construction plans in Jerusalem at the behest of the White House. The question of illegal outposts was left unresolved. The Americans demanded that Israel evacuate dozens of outposts that were defined as illegal under Israeli law. Netanyahu refused, but promised to prevent their expansion. The prime minister, concerned about criticism from the right wing and the settlement lobby, explained to his ministers that Trump was determined to achieve his deal and that Israel could not allow itself to be perceived as the side that was standing in the way. "We must not attempt to double-cross Trump. The Americans know about every house that is being built in the settlements," he told them. Netanyahu's primary justification was that coordination with Trump on Iran was the top priority, and that this would require compromises on the settlements. "Common sense won the day, and in hindsight those understandings on the settlements went a long way to improving relations with Trump," one of Netanyahu's advisors told me. "Coordinating with them on this issue removed a major source of tension. Instead of talking only about the settlements, we had time to talk about other things."

Over the first months of Trump's administration, the Americans kept a close eye on the implementation of the agreement. The Prime Minister's Office would report the list of construction plans that Israel was seeking to develop, and the Americans would examine each one and give their response. One of Netanyahu's advisors told me how, in one case, Israel wanted to move forward with the construction of 800 new residential units in Ariel. A White House staffer called Ronen Peretz in the middle of the night. "Why do you need 800 new units all at once? Split it into two parts," he asked/ordered him. Peretz responded that this was in Ariel, which was in a settlement bloc that would be part of Israel in any future agreement. "So now there is such a thing as blocs," Trump's advisor responded sarcastically. Peretz got the message and agreed to split the plan in two on the spot.

Within a few months, however, American supervision over settlement construction began to lapse. One reason for this was a change in approach by Jared Kushner. Trump's senior advisor realized that constant involvement in the Israeli–Palestinian issue was creating endless distractions, as he observed his team getting dragged into daily disputes over settlements instead of working on the bigger picture of the peace plan. Instead of tackling the disease, they were tackling the symptoms. He decided that the only way to resolve the question of the settlements was through a plan that would outline a vision for a permanent solution that clearly delineated areas where construction would and would not be permitted. "Stop chasing rabbits," Kushner told Greenblatt and Friedman when they approached him with news of the latest routine crisis. "These are not rabbits, they're elephants," the two responded. Kushner laughed. "We'll deal with the elephants last," he said. David Friedman's appointment as US ambassador to Israel was another reason for the change in tactics. Friedman, who was a kindred spirit of the settler movement, became the prime minister's point of contact for approval of settlement construction plans. The cat had been put in charge of the cream. The White House attempted to keep an eye on Friedman, but with very limited success. One of Netanyahu's advisors described one absurd case in which the head of the settler movement bypassed the Prime Minister's Office entirely and met with the US ambassador directly in an attempt to convince him to approve certain construction plans. The net result of this was a more than two-fold increase in settlement construction over the four years of Trump's tenure compared to the previous four years under Barack Obama. According to figures provided by the Peace Now activist group, under the Trump administration, plans were approved for 26 thousand housing units in the settlements, compared to only 10 thousand during Obama's second term.[23] Approximately 80 percent of these housing units were in isolated settlements deep within the West Bank, and not in the large settlement blocs. Over 30 new illegal outposts were established in the West Bank, compared to fewer than 10 in the previous four years. In addition, the Netanyahu government moved forward with strategic construction plans that had been frozen under Obama, such as the E1 plan to connect the settlement city of Ma'ale Adumim to Jerusalem and bisect the West Bank, the Givat HaMatos plan to split Bethlehem off from East Jerusalem and the plan to double the size of the Jewish settlement in the heart of Hebron. The goal of all of these moves was to restrict Palestinian territorial congruity in the West Bank and to further integrate the two populations until it was no longer feasible to separate them, ultimately preventing any viable future Palestinian state.

While the relationship between the Netanyahu and Trump administrations bloomed, the Palestinians found themselves unable to establish any channels of communication with the new president and his team. Help came from none other than the president of the World Jewish Congress, Ronald Lauder. Previously one of Benjamin Netanyahu's close confidants, investigations into the prime minister aired by Channel 10—owned by Lauder—led to a complete breakdown in the relationship between the two men that lasted for several years. Lauder knew both the US and Palestinian presidents very well. He served as an advocate for the Palestinian leader with Trump during the latter's first weeks in the White House. Two months after he entered office, Trump called Abbas. The conversation lasted only 10 minutes. Trump told Abbas that he wanted to "make a deal" and asked whether Abbas would be willing to return to the negotiating table with Netanyahu. The Palestinian president stated that he would be willing but emphasized that the end goal had to be a Palestinian state. Both sides came out of the conversation happy. Trump figured that he had been given the go-ahead by Abbas to proceed with his initiative, and Abbas concluded that Trump supported a Palestinian state. He was even rewarded with an invitation to a meeting at the White House. "The conversation was positive. Abbas is experienced and knows how to say the right things, and Trump was happy," one of the president's advisors who was on the line during the call told me.[24]

A few days after the phone call, Jason Greenblatt came to the Mukataa in Ramallah for his first meeting with Abbas.[25] "Under Trump's leadership, a peace agreement is possible," Abbas told Trump's emissary. Greenblatt mostly listened as Abbas said everything he wanted to hear, including delivering a Palestinian commitment to fight terrorism and prevent incitement against Israel. The Palestinian president described how the Palestinian security services protected Israelis who accidentally entered Palestinian cities and escorted them safely back to Israel. Greenblatt left Ramallah feeling positive. The joint readout published after the meeting was the first time the Palestinians had felt at ease since Trump entered office. "Abbas can be persuasive. He knows how to play the game," Greenblatt recalled.[26] "I was still pretty inexperienced at that time. What he was saying sounded great to me, but when I started to look into it a bit deeper, I understood that it was not the full picture. Nonetheless, my impression at the time was that he wanted to move forward with the peace process."

On May 3, 2017, Abbas stepped foot inside the White House for the first time under the Trump administration. When the two stood in front of the cameras, the US president reminded everyone that 24 years previously, it was Abbas who had signed the Oslo Accords at the White House. "I want you to be the leader who signs the peace treaty between Israel and the Palestinians," Trump said to Abbas, and heaped praise on him. Abbas in turn lavished Trump with compliments. "I believe that we are capable under your leadership…your courageous stewardship and your wisdom, as well as your great negotiating ability…of bringing about a historic peace treaty," he said, and turned to address the US president in English: "With you, we have hope." During the meeting itself, Trump demanded that Abbas crack down on anti-Israel incitement and take steps to facilitate a revival of the peace process, such as ending the welfare payments that the Palestinian Authority made to terrorists in Israeli prisons and their families. Abbas tried to offer explanations, but the issue was a significant chink in his armor. Despite this, both sides hailed the meeting as a success. One of Trump's advisors who was present at the meeting described it as very constructive, partly because Abbas said all the things the president wanted to hear. In our interview, Trump told me that

Abbas had made an excellent impression on him, and that the two men had bonded. "We spent a lot of time together, talked about many things. And he was almost like a father. I think he was so nice. Couldn't have been nicer," Trump said. After meeting with both Netanyahu and Abbas, he said, his entire perspective on the peace process flipped. "Before I met with both of them, I thought it was the exact opposite. I thought the Palestinians were impossible, and that the Israelis would do anything to make peace. I found that not to be true," he told me.

A Change of Direction

Donald Trump did not enjoy flying abroad. During his four years in office, he made a total of 19 trips to 24 countries, less than half of the foreign visits undertaken by his predecessors Obama, Bush Jr. and Clinton, and even fewer than Bush Sr., Ronald Reagan and Jimmy Carter. Trump did not like international summits and failed to get along with many of his fellow world leaders. He flew only when compelled to do so, and on several occasions he even cut short foreign trips to return to the United States.

Trump's first visit abroad was to Saudi Arabia, Israel, Belgium and Italy. This was a departure from the protocol established by his predecessors, whose first visits abroad had always been either to one of the United States' neighbors or to its allies in Europe. His visit came at a time when the United States was in uproar over a series of scandals that had erupted around him. Less than two weeks prior, he had fired the director of the FBI, James Comey. Five days before the trip, reports emerged claiming that he had revealed secret Israeli intelligence regarding a planned ISIS attack to the Russian foreign minister, Sergei Lavrov.[27] Two days before the trip, former head of the FBI Robert Mueller was appointed as a special prosecutor to investigate suspicions of collusion between Trump and the Russians during the 2016 election campaign.

The visit to Saudi Arabia provided a clear indication of Trump's intended foreign policy position in the Middle East and the world, and represented a sharp break from the Obama years. Obama had begun to put some distance between the US and Saudi governments over the human rights abuses in the kingdom. At the same time, he pursued a thaw in relations with Iran following the nuclear agreement. Trump made it clear on his visit to Riyadh that, as far as he was concerned, the Saudis were once more the preferred partners in the Middle East, while the Iranians were to return to their previous position—one they held for over four decades— as sworn enemies of the United States. The decision to make Saudi Arabia his first overseas destination also carried a symbolic message regarding his values. Throughout his term, Trump regularly cultivated ties with populist or autocratic leaders and snubbed the leaders of Western liberal democracies. He expressed admiration and respect for Russian President Vladimir Putin, yet dismissed and disparaged German Chancellor Angela Merkel. He was wowed by the golden palaces and deep pockets of the kings and princes of the Gulf states, and got on well with dictators such as Egyptian President Abdel Fattah al-Sisi. Complaints over human rights were of no interest to Trump. For him, politics was purely transactional— especially where money was concerned. Lots of money. On his visit to Riyadh, he signed perhaps the largest ever agreement of its kind for military equipment, estimated at 110 billion dollars. The Saudis bestowed every honor imaginable upon him. King Salman came to receive Trump at the airport, danced the traditional Ardah sword dance with him, awarded him the kingdom's highest honor, organized a summit meeting for him with 54 leaders of Arab and Muslim countries and arranged for them to open a new Global

Center for Combating Extremist Ideology together. A photograph of Trump standing alongside King Salman and President al-Sisi, the three leaders bathed in a dim light from the glowing orb on which their hands were placed, quickly went viral on social media. Trump was widely derided for the strange image, but it perfectly encapsulated the new alliance he was trying to build in the region. In the weeks after, Trump spoke reverentially and at length about his new friend, King Salman. Another, no less important, new relationship was forged in that visit—between Trump's son-in-law, Jared Kushner, and the Saudi crown prince, Mohammed bin Salman. This relationship would go on to be pivotal in several meaningful diplomatic achievements, as well as cause the White House significant headaches along the way.

Air Force One took off from Riyadh and headed northwest. It crossed over Jordan and entered Israeli airspace minutes later. This was the first time the plane of a US president had flown directly between Saudi Arabia and Israel and was likely the first ever official flight between the two countries, which had no diplomatic relations. It was a symbolic indication of the way that Trump sought to reshape relations between Israel and the Arab world. The day before, in his speech to dozens of Arab and Muslim leaders in Riyadh, Trump emphasized his desire to achieve peace between Israel and the Palestinians. In every one of his meetings in Israel, Trump told the people in the room that all the Arab leaders he had met had encouraged him and expressed a willingness for a thaw with Israel should progress be made on a peace process with the Palestinians—and none more than King Salman.[28] "The nuclear agreement with Iran pushed many countries in the Arab world closer to Israel," Trump said in his meeting with then-President of Israel, Reuven Rivlin, in Jerusalem. "During my visit to Saudi Arabia, I could feel that those countries that until recently had held a negative position regarding Israel were starting to shift. That's a very positive thing…You have a big opportunity."

Trump landed in Israel on May 22, 2017. I was waiting for Air Force One at Ben Gurion Airport alongside hundreds of other journalists and dozens of politicians who jockeyed for position on the red carpet. Through no fault of his own, the welcome ceremony for Trump rapidly spiraled into a theater of the absurd. The presidential visit brought out the worst in Israel's politicians. The minister of internal security, Gilad Erdan, informed Trump that an incident in Tel Aviv that morning, in which a driver without a license had hit several people, was likely to have been a terrorist attack, even though by that point the police had already established that it was a traffic accident. The minister of education, Naftali Bennett, took the brief window of opportunity of the handshake to ask Trump to move the embassy to Jerusalem and quickly put out a press release to that effect. But the nadir came when the deputy Knesset speaker, Oren Hazan, who had snuck into the ceremony uninvited, stepped onto the red carpet and took a selfie with the president when he came over to shake his hand—then rushed to tweet out the image. As the president and first lady began to walk down the red carpet toward the helicopters that were due to take them to Jerusalem, the TV cameras present picked up a disdainful comment by Sara Netanyahu, the prime minister's wife. "The majority of the people of Israel, they love us, unlike the media… we have something very much in common," she said and promised to continue the discussion over dinner. In a shameless moment in front of the cameras as the Trumps were welcomed into the official residence of the prime minister on Jerusalem's Balfour St., the Netanyahus informed them that it was only thanks to the visit of the leader of the free world that they had been granted the necessary funds to repaint the walls.

If the visit to Saudi Arabia represented a break with the Obama years, marked by a thaw with Shi'ite Iran and cooling relations with the Sunni Gulf states, Trump's visit to Jerusalem represented the start of a break with half a century of US presidential policy on the Israeli–Palestinian conflict. From the welcome ceremony at the airport, Trump headed straight to the Western Wall. This was the first ever visit by a sitting US president to the sensitive holy site that stood at the center of every attempt to achieve peace between Israel and the Palestinians over the previous 25 years. The image of Trump standing at the Western Wall was the most significant moment of his visit, above and beyond any meeting, press conference or speech. At that time, the United States did not yet recognize Jerusalem as the capital of Israel, the embassy was still in Tel Aviv and not a single representative of the Israeli government joined Trump on his visit to the Wall. This moment represented the first seeds of the change in policy that would come six months later. When Vice President Mike Pence visited Israel in January 2018, Netanyahu was there alongside him to place a note in the cracks between the giant stones of the wall.

In the Palestinian Authority, preparations had also been made for the visit of the president of the United States. The presidential compound in Bethlehem was gleaming. The red carpet had been rolled out and, at its end, two children stood in traditional dress, holding bouquets for the US president and awaiting the arrival of the "Beast"—the armored presidential limousine that travels with the US president even on trips abroad. The atmosphere was festive, but also heavy with concern. The night before, Salman Ramadan Abedi, a British citizen of Libyan heritage, had blown himself up outside the Manchester Arena in the UK as people were leaving a concert by the young pop star Ariana Grande. Twenty-two people lost their lives in the attack and more than

100 were wounded. ISIS claimed responsibility. President Trump, who had been informed of the bombing late at night in Jerusalem, arrived at his meeting with the Palestinian president still highly agitated. "I will call [terrorists] from now on losers because that's what they are," said Trump at the end of his meeting with Abbas. "Peace can never take root in an environment where violence is tolerated, funded and even rewarded." Trump also took a moment in front of the cameras to praise Abbas for his willingness to move forward with a deal with Israel, but his confrontational tone at the press conference hinted at the earlier drama behind closed doors. During their meeting the day before, the Israeli prime minister had delivered a presentation that included claims of Palestinian incitement against Israel. Netanyahu, who knew that Abbas had made a positive impression on Trump at their meeting at the White House, painted a picture that placed the blame for the incitement squarely on the shoulders of the Palestinian president himself, in an attempt to blacken his name in the eyes of the US president. The famed American journalist Bob Woodward wrote in his book on Trump that he was reasonably successful, at least in the short term. Trump was shocked at the video Netanyahu showed him. Even the attempts by his secretary of state, Rex Tillerson, to assure Trump that it had been misleadingly edited failed to assuage the president. Two and a half years later, at a conference at Harvard University, Tillerson stated that on several occasions during his term as secretary of state, Netanyahu had attempted to use disinformation to bring Trump round to his view.[29] A former senior official at the White House told me that the person who had coordinated the move with Netanyahu was the US ambassador to Israel, David Friedman, who had only taken up his post two weeks earlier.[30] "He arranged the video together with the Israelis, to show how Abbas spoke, and showed it to the president at the meeting

with Bibi [Netanyahu]," a former senior White House official who was present at the meeting told me. Following the meeting with Netanyahu, an angry Rex Tillerson confronted Friedman. "That is not serious and it is not fair," Tillerson said, referring to the clips that the US ambassador had shown to Trump. "What about them was not true? I wanted the president to see what [Abbas] says in Arabic," Friedman replied. The video clips did indeed sway Trump. "He had come out of the meeting with Abbas at the White House a few weeks earlier with the impression that the Palestinian president was a harmless grandfatherly type and was surprised to hear him speaking that way against Israel," a former senior White House official who was also present at the meeting with Abbas in Bethlehem told me.[31]

The day after his meeting with Netanyahu, a very tired Trump arrived in Bethlehem. According to a former senior White House official, "He was very concerned about the negative headlines back home on Russia and was in a very bad mood." As a consequence of all of this, in their meeting, the US president unleashed fire and brimstone on his Palestinian counterpart, accusing him of deception at the White House three weeks earlier when he had presented himself as a man of peace. The Palestinian president attempted to defend himself and claimed that the video had been misleadingly edited, but the incident created significant tensions and wiped out any optimism that Abbas had brought back with him from his meeting with Trump at the White House. In that meeting, Abbas more or less rattled off his usual talking points. He was inflexible and did not indicate any meaningful desire to move forward.[32] At one point, Abbas told Trump that he did not want Israeli forces within the territorial borders of a future Palestinian state, only international forces. "Israel is doing a great job on security," Trump replied. "I spend a ton of money on the

US military. Look at it another way—you'll be able to put all your money into the economy and infrastructure and become a very rich state. You should take this offer." Abbas had no idea how to respond to this argument. Meanwhile, the US president left the meeting frustrated and feeling like both sides were leading him on. A former senior White House official claimed that the president's advisors hoped that the feeling that Trump was losing his patience would cause Abbas to budge. That did not happen.

Despite the strained meeting in Bethlehem, Trump did not cast Abbas aside and did not crown Netanyahu as a prince of peace. From Abbas, he heard an immediate readiness to return to negotiations with Israel. From Netanyahu, he heard stuttering and stammering. Despite this, when the US president spoke at the Israel Museum, just before he left for Italy, he said that both leaders had stated their desire to move forward with a peace process. "Both sides will face tough decisions. But with determination, compromise on both sides and the belief that peace is possible, Israelis and Palestinians can make a deal," Trump said. By the end of his visit, Trump recognized that the scale of the task at hand was far greater than he had anticipated. He came out of his conversations with Netanyahu and Abbas realizing that both of them would make life difficult. Trump's visit did not bring about any diplomatic breakthroughs, but it did re-introduce the word peace to the political discourse in Israel, many years after it had seemingly become taboo.

A Frustrating Reality

It was only after Trump's visit to Israel that work began in earnest on what was already then being referred to as "the deal of the century." The expression was coined by Egyptian President al-Sisi, during a visit to the White House a few weeks earlier.

"Egypt supports your attempts to find a solution to the issue of the century with the deal of the century," al-Sisi told Trump in front of the cameras. The phrase took off throughout the Middle East, initially in a positive context—and later in mockery and derision.

When the internal discussions on the Israeli–Palestinian question began, the assessment by Trump's advisors was that, ever since the failure of the Camp David talks in 2000, and even more so since the failure of the Annapolis Conference in 2008, Israel had been emboldened, building more and more settlements and taking control of more and more of the West Bank.[33] The Palestinians, meanwhile, had weakened in the interim. The Palestinian Authority had lost control of the Gaza Strip and the Western and Arab worlds had grown weary of engaging on the issue. On the other hand, whether through inertia or for fear of being accused of treachery and abandonment, both Western and Arab countries had continued to direct a steady flow of money to the Palestinian Authority. As time passed, Kushner grew increasingly convinced that the Palestinian president had no genuine interest in changing the status quo, and that he had elevated trips to foreign capitals to raise money into an art form. He felt that the way European and Arab countries had lined up behind the Palestinians had encouraged Abbas to build up unrealistic expectations regarding his international standing.

As a first step, Kushner, Greenblatt and the rest of the White House team assigned to the peace process decided to look at what had been done over the previous 25 years. They met with a long line of predecessors in the role, including Martin Indyk, Aaron Miller, Dennis Ross and Elliott Abrams, to hear their thoughts and conclusions. "The general message Kushner and Greenblatt received from these conversations was that they were wasting their time," a former official in the Trump administration told me. They asked the US Department of State to provide them with all the previous peace plans and the positions each side had adopted. Approaching it like a business plan, Kushner and Greenblatt prepared a list of all the points of dispute between the Israeli and Palestinian sides that would require resolution.

After that, Kushner met with the prime minister's special envoy, Yitzhak Molcho, and with the Palestinian chief negotiator, Saeb Erekat. The former had been Netanyahu's point of contact for Palestinian affairs for eight years, and his Palestinian counterpart had held the equivalent position for 25 years. Kushner had first delved into this issue only six months prior. Kushner's first encounter with the full frustrating force of the situation that all his predecessors had warned him about took place in his separate conversations with the two men. He pulled out the list of disputed topics and asked each of them how they would solve each of the items on it. Molcho and Erekat gave similar answers. They took him back to the 1917 Balfour Declaration, the 1947 Partition Plan, the 1967 Six-Day War. "I don't want a history lesson, I want to talk about the present day," Kushner told them. "Now, in 2017—what do you think the solution should be?" Neither Molcho nor Erekat gave him clear answers. Instead, they talked about setting up covert channels for talks, or a meeting in Europe with representatives of the two sides or an international summit. Kushner felt that he wanted to talk about peace, while the Israelis and the Palestinians preferred to talk about the process. He concluded that Molcho and Erekat primarily excelled at giving non-answers and in negotiating for the sake of negotiations. Kushner realized after his meetings with the two that they were playing a game, and he quickly lost his patience. President Trump's most senior advisor decided to take a stand. He informed Netanyahu that he was no longer interested in holding talks with Molcho. The prime minister accepted the decision and transferred the responsibility for communicating with

Kushner and his team on the "deal of the century" to his ambassador in Washington, Ron Dermer, and another of his inner circle, Dore Gold. Things were not so straightforward on the Palestinian side. Abbas informed Kushner and Greenblatt that he could not sideline Erekat, due to his senior status in the Palestinian Authority.

In mid-June, Kushner had his first visit to the region as part of the process of moving forward with the peace plan. Over the course of one week, he hopped between Riyadh, Abu Dhabi, Doha, Cairo and Amman to obtain a clearer picture. He asked the Arab leaders he met what an Israeli–Palestinian peace treaty should look like. In those countries he visited, he discovered a desire to support the Trump administration in driving the Israeli–Palestinian peace process forward. He also identified real frustration with the Palestinian president, Abbas. More than anything, however, he saw that the answers he was getting were very broad. When he came to Jerusalem and Ramallah, he made it clear to Netanyahu and Abbas that Trump was determined to achieve a deal. He received contrasting responses from the two men. Netanyahu was unenthusiastic, to say the least, and was cautious and hesitant in his words. The Israeli prime minister still bore the scars of his battle over the Palestinians with the previous president, Barack Obama, and his secretary of state, John Kerry. Moreover, Netanyahu had recently become the subject of an investigation into gifts he had received from businessmen and accusations that he had furthered their interests in exchange. Netanyahu told Kushner that he was concerned that if he started negotiations with the Palestinians, it would look as though he was attempting to deflect attention away from the investigation. Kushner responded sardonically that there was a strong correlation in Israel between prime ministers who engaged in negotiations with the Palestinians and prime ministers who were under investigation. "The impression we got was that Netanyahu was thinking to himself—I have enough problems already, I don't need this shit hanging over me," a former Trump official said. Abbas, on the other hand, demonstrated great enthusiasm. Abbas told Kushner, "I will give you something I have never given before, and I will be more flexible than ever before," according to a former American official who was at the meeting. Despite this, Abbas did not dive into specifics regarding his views. Kushner got the impression that the Palestinian president was deeply concerned about potential leaks that could further undermine the shaky political ground beneath his feet.

Upon their return from the Middle East, Trump's advisors debated the contours of their peace plan. Should it be a document outlining general principles, of the kind John Kerry had attempted to formulate, or a far-reaching and more detailed plan? Kushner took the view that general principles would not really represent an American attempt at mediating between the two sides and bridging their gaps. He decided that the Trump Plan would be detailed. "I thought that if the two sides were going to argue, it would be better for them to argue over details and not principles," he told me.[34] The work on the plan was highly restricted and secretive. Greenblatt wrote it up on an air-gapped computer in his office in the Eisenhower Building, the building adjacent to the White House where the National Security Council is located. The initial document was 20 pages long, but in the months that followed more and more details were added, and it swelled up to 50 pages. By the time the Trump Plan was published, two and a half years later, it had reached 180 pages.

"A Tinderbox"

On the morning of Friday, July 14, 2017, the sound of gunfire ripped through the silence at the Temple Mount in Jerusalem.[35]

Three Arab youths, Israeli citizens from the city of Umm al-Fahm, collected firearms that had been secreted in one of the buildings on the mount and opened fire on a group of Israeli Border Police officers who were standing by one of the gates. Two officers were killed in the attack, and the terrorists were killed in the subsequent shootout. This incident was the precursor to the first major crisis between Israel and the Palestinians during Trump's term. It's unlikely that any of the US president's advisors or Netanyahu's people fully appreciated how far the shockwaves of that morning's assault would travel. In the immediate wake of the incident, the police closed off all access to the Temple Mount. Netanyahu, who set great store in his ability to be "the first to identify" any crisis as it emerged, failed to grasp the severity of the situation. The following Sunday, he took off for a scheduled visit to Europe. In a brief conference call a few minutes before takeoff, he authorized the police to set up metal detectors at the entrance to the Temple Mount. This immediately fanned the flames. The Jerusalem Islamic Waqf—the religious trust responsible for overseeing the site—declared the decision a breach of the status quo and ordered worshippers not to enter the Al-Aqsa Mosque compound until the metal detectors were taken down. Thousands of Palestinians went to pray by the police barricades, and violent clashes broke out soon after. Abbas came out in support of the protesters and announced the suspension of security cooperation with Israel. The unrest spread to the West Bank and the Gaza Strip. The White House was following the proceedings from afar, and initially offered its full support to Israel. It took a while for the true extent of the crisis to hit home. On Wednesday night, after Netanyahu returned to his hotel in Budapest following an event with the local Jewish community, he held a half-hour conference call with Kushner and his team in an attempt to find a way to restore calm. The next day,

Kushner called Abbas. The Palestinian president told Kushner that the US government must intervene and order Israel to take down the metal detectors. "The situation risks spiraling out of control if Israel does not walk back its measures at the Al-Aqsa Mosque," Abbas told Kushner.

A few days later, his prediction came true. On July 23, a young Jordanian man came to repair the furniture at the apartment of one of the security guards of the Israeli embassy in Amman. Exactly what happened next remains unclear, but an argument broke out between the two men, during which the Jordanian man stabbed the guard. The guard opened fire and killed him. The landlord—a Jordanian doctor by the name of Bashar Hamarneh—was also seriously injured and later died of his wounds. In the immediate aftermath of the incident, the guard rushed to the adjacent Israeli embassy compound. Jordanian security forces, who arrived on the scene following the sounds of gunfire, surrounded the embassy. The incident raised tensions around the Israeli embassy in Amman to new heights after two days of heated protests over the events at the Temple Mount. The Jordanians demanded an inquiry and refused to allow the Israeli diplomats to leave the embassy compound. With hundreds of Jordanian protesters streaming into the area, the Jordanian security forces surrounding the embassy and the Israeli diplomats trapped inside, Netanyahu attempted to reach King Abdullah of Jordan by phone. He was unsuccessful. The king, who was on vacation in the US at the time, didn't pick up. The Prime Minister's Office called Kushner to ask for help. Trump's most senior advisor reached out to the king, and finally managed to get through to ask him to call off the Jordanian security forces and to allow the diplomats and the guard to evacuate to Israel. The director of the Shin Bet, Nadav Argaman, was dispatched urgently to Amman to resolve the crisis. Upon his return, the State Security

Cabinet convened and announced that the metal detectors at the Temple Mount would be removed. A short while later, all the Israelis were evacuated from the embassy compound and returned to Israel. As part of the compromise that Argaman reached with his Jordanian counterparts, the Israeli guard provided his account of events to the Jordanian investigators in the presence of Israeli diplomats. It seemed as though a larger crisis had been averted, but the following day things took a turn for the worse. Once the diplomats were safely back in Israel, Netanyahu embarked on a media crusade. In a string of posts, tweets, videos and press releases, he portrayed himself as the prime minister who had freed the Israeli diplomats from the clutches of the Jordanians, as if the situation was a worthy successor to the great Mossad operations of the past—another Operation Entebbe. Netanyahu's spin campaign reached its peak when he invited Einat Schlein, the Israeli ambassador to Amman, and the security guard to a meeting and shared photographs and videos of it as if it were a victory tour, along with captions in Arabic, so that the Jordanians would be left in no doubt whatsoever as to the intended message. The Jordanians saw all of this and went berserk. Netanyahu painted a picture in which they had been on the verge of lynching Israeli diplomatic staff, as opposed to being unwilling to let the deaths of two Jordanian civilians be swept under the rug. The Jordanian minister of foreign affairs, Ayman Safadi, went on CNN and attacked Netanyahu in no uncertain terms. The next day, when King Abdullah returned from his vacation, he convened his cabinet and accused Netanyahu of exploiting the embassy crisis—and Jordan—for domestic political capital. He accused Netanyahu of provocation and claimed that his behavior was destabilizing regional security.

The July 2017 crisis felt like a combined rerun of two of Netanyahu's greatest traumas from his first term in office as prime minister—the Western Wall Tunnel riots of September 1996 and the unsuccessful assassination attempt of Khaled Mashal, a senior figure in Hamas, in Amman a year later. For Trump's advisors, however, this was new ground. Greenblatt, who had been urgently dispatched to the region in an attempt to pressure Abbas to calm tensions, found the door to the Palestinian president's office closed to him. He had to make do with meetings with his assistants. Kushner, in the meantime, found himself on the phone with the Jordanians in an attempt to bring things back under control. For Netanyahu, the strategic lesson here was not new, but in the Trump administration, realization began to sink in that as long as Israel held control over the Temple Mount, whoever led the country would have to think a thousand times before taking any step within that tinderbox. In the worst-case scenario, careless steps at the Temple Mount could lead to another intifada, while even in the less-worse case, it would likely result in a round of violence and bloodshed, as well as damage to Israel's international standing.

Pressing Home a Deal

The Temple Mount crisis did nothing to diminish Trump's desire to push a deal between Israel and the Palestinians. In a way, it only spurred him on even more. On the Palestinian side, emotions were running high, and Abbas and his close circle were beginning to exhibit advanced signs of discontent. His advisors began to brief journalists that the White House's peace team was biased toward Israel and was even parroting Netanyahu's talking points. A few weeks after the metal detector crisis, Abbas met with representatives of the Israeli left-wing Meretz party and expressed his frustrations to them. "I've met Trump's advisors 20 times," he said. "In person, they tell me that they support a two-state solution and oppose the settlements, but they refuse to say it in public." On August 24, Kushner visited Jerusalem again, after stopping off in Egypt, Saudi Arabia and Jordan. He tried to persuade the leaders of these Arab countries to apply pressure on the Palestinians. He was only partially successful. The Saudi crown prince, Mohammed bin Salman, was all too happy to come on board. Unlike his father, he did not see himself as being bound to the traditional Saudi policy of predicating their position on that of the Palestinians. As far as Kushner was concerned, bin Salman was a strategic ally for the American peace plan. When he met with Netanyahu in Jerusalem, Kushner discovered once more that the prime minister of Israel was unenthusiastic about engaging with him on the Palestinian situation. A few weeks previously, in a meeting in Paris, Netanyahu had told the French president, Emmanuel Macron, that "it will be difficult to make quick progress on the American initiative." A senior French official who was in the room for the talks told me at the time that Netanyahu greatly preferred to move forward with diplomatic initiatives with the other Arab countries rather than with the Palestinians. In his meeting with Abbas, Kushner found himself facing a frustrated Palestinian president. Abbas even threatened that, without progress, he would initiate steps against Israel at the UN. Kushner invited Abbas for a meeting with Trump on the sidelines of the UN General Assembly in New York in September in exchange for the Palestinian president withdrawing the threat and allowing a bit more time for diplomacy.

Netanyahu came to the General Assembly with one goal in mind: to persuade President Trump not to declare that Iran was upholding its side of the nuclear agreement before the US Congress on October 15, and to start putting back in place the sanctions that the Obama administration had lifted. Trump was legally obligated to deliver an update to Congress on the matter every six months, and likewise on the issue of the embassy relocation. Both of these issues touched on campaign promises he had made. Trump's advisors told me that he felt great discomfort whenever it came time to re-certify the nuclear accord with Iran or to waive the relocation of the embassy to Jerusalem. Netanyahu planned to turn all his fire in his meeting with Trump on September 18 in New York on the Iran deal, but the US president had other plans. A few minutes before the meeting was due to begin, with the journalists (myself included) waiting in the hallway of the New York Palace Hotel for a joint statement, Trump used his Twitter account to send a clear message on where his priorities lay. "Peace in the Middle East would be a truly great legacy for ALL people!" tweeted the president.

Trump did not leave his meeting with Netanyahu happy. He felt that the prime minister was not taking his attempts to make progress on a peace process with the Palestinians seriously. "Working on this subject really got Trump excited—occasionally too excited. Netanyahu, on the other hand, was less enthusiastic, to put it mildly," said a former White House official who had participated in that meeting. The next day, in a brief meeting with UN Secretary-General António Guterres, Trump revealed his opinion on Netanyahu. "He's the bigger problem in the peace process," said the US president. When I published this quote a few days later, Trump's advisors tried to convince me to drop the story, or at least to soften it. The national security advisor himself, H. R. McMaster, called me and pulled out all the stops to explain that that was not exactly what Trump had said. But the report had been verified by numerous other sources; therefore, it was published. "I didn't know if Trump spoke like that about Abbas and Netanyahu because this is how he really saw things or because he was trying to motivate us to press Bibi more,"

Kushner told me. When I met Trump three and a half years later, he confirmed the story and added a lot more thoughts in the same vein on Netanyahu. The negative impression Netanyahu had left on Trump meant that his meeting with Abbas the following day was far more successful than had been anticipated. "I certainly will devote everything within my heart and within my soul to get that deal made," Trump told Abbas, but asked him for more time and that he refrain from taking any steps that might complicate matters in the meantime. The meeting between the two ended positively. On his way to the door, Abbas approached Greenblatt, placed a hand on his head, kissed his forehead and wished him a happy Jewish New Year. The report on Trump's complaints about Netanyahu was one of the last ones I published in my 10 years as a diplomatic correspondent for *Haaretz*. Three weeks later, I walked into the Channel 10 newsroom and set out on a new adventure.

When Netanyahu returned to Israel from the UN General Assembly, he was all too aware of the trouble in which he found himself. The first thing he did was to convene a meeting of the State Security Cabinet, where he told the assembled ministers that Trump was hard at work on a peace plan. "Trump is very determined, and he wants to achieve the ultimate deal," he told them. Two days later, he met with the heads of the settler movement. He repeated his impressions to them from the meeting with Trump and explained that this president too was setting out restrictions on Israel. The prime minister quoted a Yiddish expression to them that the US ambassador had used when he asked Netanyahu's advisors not to push their luck with the settlement expansion. "You can be a pig but don't be a swine," Netanyahu quoted Friedman. Netanyahu and his team sought ways to dampen Trump's enthusiasm toward the peace plan or, at the very least, to negatively alter his perception of the Palestinians. In mid-October, they were presented with an opportunity when Fatah and Hamas announced that they had signed a reconciliation agreement brokered by Egypt. Under the terms of this agreement, the Palestinian Authority would resume control over the Gaza Strip. Netanyahu passed a resolution in the cabinet meeting a few days later that stated that Israel would not conduct negotiations with a Palestinian national unity government, should one be formed. To Netanyahu's disappointment, the White House supported the Egyptian mediation efforts and saw them as an opportunity to restore the Palestinian Authority to Gaza and to bolster Abbas's legitimacy. Netanyahu, who had worked for years to create a separation between Gaza and the West Bank and to weaken the Palestinian Authority, saw things the other way round. A senior White House official told me at the time that the reconciliation between Fatah and Hamas would serve Israel's interests, and even added that although the Trump administration believed that Hamas should be disarmed, "there is no expectation that this will happen by tomorrow morning." This did not go down well in Netanyahu's office.

After all the conversations that Trump's team held with Netanyahu and Abbas over his first year in office, a feeling had gradually formed that both sides had retreated into immutable positions over the years, and that these had then become talking points to be repeated ad nauseam. Neither Netanyahu nor Abbas dared to move an inch from these for fear of incurring the wrath of their respective political bases. Trump's advisors tried time and again to dig them out of the holes they were trapped in and to build trust, but were only partially successful. "I thought that Bibi would be willing to engage seriously with someone like Trump in office, and that a Palestinian leader would understand that this represented an opportunity," Greenblatt told me. The Americans saw that the two sides were still very far apart but hoped that they would be able to put together a package that, once presented to them, would be sufficiently appealing to convince them to compromise, or at the very least would shift public opinion in the Israeli and Palestinian streets, which would then put pressure on their leaders to act. In one of our conversations, Kushner told me he got the impression that the younger generation in Israel and the Palestinian Authority cared more about paying their mortgage than the question of where the border is drawn in Jerusalem.

The Historic Declaration

One of the first things that Trump did upon his return to the United States from the Middle East in early June 2017 was to sign the waiver that deferred the decision to move the US embassy to Jerusalem by a further six months. Trump made the decision following an internal power struggle among his senior advisors. Those who supported moving the embassy to Jerusalem were led by Trump's far-right chief strategist, Steve Bannon. Moving the embassy to Jerusalem was one of the top items on the to-do list for Trump's first few months in the White House on the whiteboard in Bannon's office. Bannon saw this as fulfilling a campaign promise to the president's base, and especially to the evangelical voters who would be a critical part of his re-election campaign. Also pressing as hard as he could to move the embassy was the US ambassador to Israel, David Friedman. Friedman had pushed the matter of the embassy non-stop ever since the day Trump first entered the White House on January 20. He also had some powerful allies—among them Vice President Mike Pence and the US ambassador to the United Nations, Nikki Haley. Leading the opposing camp were Secretary of State Rex Tillerson, Secretary of Defense James Mattis, National Security Advisor H. R. McMaster, and even the director of the CIA, Mike Pompeo.[36] Tillerson was primarily concerned that moving the embassy would deal a terminal blow to any hopes of the peace initiative that Trump had begun to promote only weeks earlier. Mattis and McMaster worried that such a step could ignite the Middle East and result in attacks on American troops in the region. Trump's peace team—Kushner and Greenblatt—were torn. On the one hand, they supported moving the embassy. On the other hand, they were concerned that the timing was wrong and could damage their efforts to set a peace plan in motion. After Trump signed the deferral waiver, the White House put out a statement declaring that it wished to focus its efforts on achieving a deal between Israel and the Palestinians, and that the embassy would be moved at a later date.[37]

Target dates are the bane of diplomats and politicians. They very quickly become ticking time bombs that are difficult to disarm, and any attempt to do so often presents politicians with a difficult dilemma: whether to prioritize their own narrow political interest or the wider public interest. December 1, 2017, was one such case. President Trump had to make a decision on whether to enable the Jerusalem Embassy Act to come into force, thereby fulfilling a campaign promise, or whether to follow all his predecessors in signing a waiver to defer the decision by a further six months. Former senior officials in the Trump administration described a pressure cooker atmosphere in the White House at the time. Those who opposed the move (and who had come out on top six months earlier) once more attempted to repel the challenge of its supporters, who were determined not to come up short again. At the center of the attempts to persuade Trump not to delay the decision again stood two people: the first was the casino magnate and Jewish-American billionaire, Sheldon Adelson. He had poured hundreds of millions of dollars of his own money into getting

Trump into the White House, and was determined to see a political return on his investment. The second was David Friedman, who planned to use his long-standing personal connection with Trump to implement his right-wing ideology. In the six months since Friedman had taken up his role, his influence had steadily grown stronger. He managed to successfully sideline and weaken Jason Greenblatt, get close to Netanyahu and form a political coalition within Washington that he could use to influence Trump. "David employed a full-court press to make it happen," a former senior White House official told me.

The battle between the two camps in the White House continued almost to the last minute. In the discussions, Pompeo conveyed the view of the US intelligence community, which was strongly opposed to relocating the embassy. The camp opposed to the embassy relocation understood that they were losing ground and attempted to persuade Trump to adopt a more cautious approach to the relocation, one that would not blow up his peace initiative. It was to no avail. "The whole team supported moving the embassy. If there were differences, they were about the timing," Kushner told me.

In mid-November, two weeks before the verdict, the president held a meeting on the initiative to restart negotiations between Israel and the Palestinians. As the meeting was drawing to a close, the president raised the question of Jerusalem and the embassy. "What do you think?" asked Trump. Kushner and Friedman said it should be done immediately. The question caught Tillerson off guard. He was not expecting the subject to come up for discussion— he thought Trump would just go ahead and sign another waiver. "I want to do it," Trump said at the meeting. McMaster told the president that he would start preparing the groundwork. "No, no. I really want to do it now," he told his national security advisor.

"Call a meeting with everyone. Don't waste time. I want it done now." A week later, another meeting was held in the White House Situation Room. Chief of Staff Kelly refused to allow Greenblatt and Kushner to participate. A former senior White House official told me that Kelly made the case that this decision could lead to an outbreak of violence and potential harm to American citizens, and therefore the participants in the meeting should only be people who had been confirmed by the Senate. "Kelly did not want the protocols of the meeting to show that Trump's Jewish advisors were present, as they were not considered impartial on the question of Jerusalem," the official told me. "It was part of an effort to avoid any appearance that it had all been done against the professional opinion of the US defense establishment." During the discussion, a heated argument broke out between Tillerson and Friedman in front of the president. Tillerson again insisted that moving the embassy to Jerusalem would be a grave mistake that would destroy any chance of renewing the peace process under Trump. "On most things you understand more than me—on this subject I understand more than you and you are wrong," Friedman responded. Secretary of Defense Mattis intervened. "I don't understand why we should move the embassy to Jerusalem—every time I visit Israel I go to the Ministry of Defense, and that's in Tel Aviv," he said. Friedman interjected immediately. "Where is the Pentagon?" he asked Mattis. "Virginia," conceded the secretary of defense. "You got a point." Trump was convinced, and the discussion ended with a decision to move forward with a statement recognizing Jerusalem as the capital of Israel and approving the relocation of the embassy. According to a former senior White House official, Tillerson appealed to the president time and again over the following days, to no avail.

While the moment of truth was drawing closer within the White House, Vice President Pence delivered a speech at the ceremony to mark 70 years since the historic vote in the UN General Assembly on the Partition Plan. In his speech, he stated that Trump was strongly considering if and when to relocate the US embassy to Jerusalem. Two days later, the most dramatic meeting between Trump's White House peace negotiation team and Abbas's advisors took place. It was also to be the last meeting between the sides for the next three years. Erekat, who had come to the White House together with the Palestinians' intelligence chief, Majed Faraj, and the Palestinian envoy to the United States, Husam Zomlot, described the meeting as a full-on shouting match.[38] "Jared, the president is supposed to sign the waiver not to move the embassy," Erekat told Kushner. The response from Trump's senior advisor stunned the Palestinian team. "We're not going to sign," Kushner replied. Erekat responded: "What do you mean we're not going to sign? The president promised us in the White House that he would not take any step that may preempt or prejudge Jerusalem, not before negotiations." Kushner did not back down and told Erekat that it was none of the Palestinians' business, and that the United States would act in its own best interest. "If you do this, you will have disqualified yourself from any role in the peace process," replied Erekat. Kushner cut him off. "Don't threaten me," he told Erekat, who responded in kind. "Read my lips—you will have disqualified yourself from any role in the peace process." Kushner told Erekat that the facts had changed. "You don't know the changes that are happening around you in the Arab world," Trump's advisor told the advisor to the Palestinian president. "The best thing for me is to be a student—so teach me," Erekat replied witheringly. Kushner went on the attack. "Don't be sarcastic!" he replied. Erekat did not back down, and told Kushner that the Arab states would never accept the relocation of the US embassy to Jerusalem. "What do you mean by changes?" he asked Kushner.

"To them Jerusalem is a red line—all of them! Saudis, Qataris, Egyptians, Jordanians, Bahrainis." Kushner repeated that it was none of Erekat's business. "If you do this, you will bring Israelis and Palestinians to the brink of disaster," Erekat said. The meeting blew up—and the Palestinian delegation left the White House in a rage. Two days later, I met the Palestinian ambassador at the Saban Forum in Washington. He sounded utterly despondent, but even he did not anticipate how far the crisis would escalate over the following months.

In the days after that meeting at the White House, the Palestinians used every means at their disposal to dissuade Trump from making the statement on relocating the embassy to Jerusalem. Abbas called the presidents of France, Turkey and Egypt, the king of Jordan, the emir of Qatar and numerous other leaders and asked them to pressure Trump. The primary focus of his efforts were the Saudis. He called Mohammed bin Salman, who had a close relationship with Kushner. Bin Salman promised that he and his father, the king, would act. They followed through on their promise and called the White House, but it was no use. President Macron, who had a good relationship with Trump at the time, also signed up to the cause. He spoke with the president twice a day to ask him to reconsider his decision, warning him of the consequences. Trump told me how, at one point, he stopped taking phone calls from foreign leaders and asked his advisors to say that he would get back to them later. At the same time, Kushner, Greenblatt and Kushner's assistant, Avi Berkowitz, invested most of their efforts in conversations with foreign ministers and leaders of Arab countries. The message they conveyed was that if those Arab countries liked Trump's policies in other areas, such as on Iran, then they would have to act to prevent violence against Americans in the wake of the decision on Jerusalem.[39]

Trump spoke with Prime Minister Netanyahu several times in the days before the decision. Jared Kushner wrote in his book, *Breaking History,* that when Trump notified Netanyahu on December 5 about his upcoming announcement on Jerusalem, the latter wasn't enthusiastic. "If you choose to do that, I will support you," Netanyahu told Trump, according to Kushner. Trump thought Netanyahu hadn't heard him correctly. He told Netanyahu again that he is going to recognize Jerusalem as Israel's capital and move the embassy and stressed that he expects that Israel will agree to sit at the negotiation table with the Palestinians when the time comes. Netanyahu's response was once again less enthusiastic than expected. Trump became frustrated and didn't hide it from Netanyahu. "Bibi, I think you are the problem," he said, according to Kushner. Netanyahu pushed back and claimed he was part of the solution. "Trump began to second-guess his decision…and wondered aloud why he was taking this risk if the Israeli prime minister didn't think it was that important," Kushner wrote.[40]

Netanyahu denied Kushner's account, claiming that he asked Trump several times to move the embassy and that, when the president told him of his decision, he voiced his appreciation for the move.[41] "We were supportive of that throughout," said the Israeli ambassador to Washington at the time, Ron Dermer, who is one of Netanyahu's closest advisors to this day.[42] Netanyahu and Dermer laid out a different narrative about what happened in the year leading to Trump's Jerusalem announcement. Dermer said that in Netanyahu's first meeting with Trump at the White House in February 2017 and in their meeting in Jerusalem in May 2017 the former prime minister told Trump he supported moving the US embassy to Jerusalem. Dermer claimed the December 2017 phone call focused on intelligence about a possible outbreak of violence as a result of an announcement about Jerusalem. "Some people in the administration said it will lead to World War III," he said. According to the former Israeli ambassador, the intelligence Israel had at the time didn't show that a US announcement on Jerusalem would lead to an escalation. "In the call with the president, the prime minister gave a very cold assessment of the intelligence," Dermer said. "[Netanyahu said,] 'If there is a problem, I take responsibility for it and I support this.'" The former ambassador admitted that the phone call was "business-like" and that Trump thought Netanyahu "wasn't fulsome enough in the praise." When Netanyahu heard about Trump's impression, Dermer remembered, he sent him to make sure the White House understands he does support the move. According to another Netanyahu aide, the former prime minister told Trump several times that he had no reason to fear the response of the Arab world, and even promised that, after the decision, Israel would not take any steps that would change the status quo in the holy sites in Jerusalem.

The day before the declaration, Trump called Abbas. It was a difficult conversation. Abbas warned Trump that relocating the US embassy to Jerusalem or recognizing Jerusalem as the capital of Israel would have dangerous and far-reaching consequences for the security and stability of the Middle East. He also repeated that the Palestinians would no longer see the United States as an honest broker in the peace process. Trump tried to reassure Abbas. He promised that the Palestinians would be compensated and that he was still committed to the "deal of the century." Abbas was due to visit the United States for medical tests a few weeks later, and Trump offered him a meeting at the White House. Trump talked and talked, and Abbas did not respond. A few minutes passed before the US president realized that the call had been disconnected and that the Palestinian president had not even heard him. The two would never speak again.

There were a few reasons why Trump decided not to bow to the warnings and international pressure. Friedman and the other supporters of the move exploited the fact that the president hated signing off on decisions that went against his campaign promises—such as moving the embassy and canceling the nuclear accord with Iran. Despite the fact that he held a more positive impression of Abbas than he did of Netanyahu, ultimately his desire to keep his promise won out. Kushner and Greenblatt believed that there was still some positive momentum to be found in their communication with the Israelis and Palestinians. Their conversations with Abbas, on the other hand, never went into great detail and they were frustrated that they were unable to present Trump with any meaningful progress. Many of Trump's advisors, who were opposed to the existing schedule for the relocation of the embassy, were wary of saying as much in the open discussions for fear of being perceived as stalling a move that enjoyed the president's support. Unlike Friedman, they had no direct access to the president that would allow them to raise their concerns in a more intimate environment. And then there was the seemingly never-ending cycle of controversies afflicting the White House, which made Trump and his advisors desperate for meaningful achievements to tout—such as fulfilling the campaign promise on Jerusalem. "It had a strong wind at its back—and it had become impossible to stop," a former official in the Trump administration told me.

On December 6, 2017, some six months after he signed the waiver deferring relocation, Trump stood in front of the cameras and gave a historic speech in which he recognized Jerusalem as the capital of Israel and announced the relocation of the US embassy to the city. It was one of the most consequential decisions Trump would make during his term of office. "Today, we finally acknowledge the obvious: that Jerusalem is Israel's capital. This is nothing more, or less, than a recognition of reality. It is also the right thing to do," said the US president. Trump made it clear that he was still determined to finalize a deal between Israel and the Palestinians and emphasized that the boundaries of Israeli sovereignty in Jerusalem would be determined solely through negotiations between the two sides. "Jerusalem is one of the most sensitive issues in those talks. The United States would support a two-state solution if agreed to by both sides," he said. But the damage was done. Following up on their threats from a few days earlier, the Palestinians declared that they were cutting off all communication with the White House and that Trump would no longer be accepted as an honest broker between them and Israel. Far from his self-proclaimed "deal of the century," Trump's statement was in fact "the slap in the face of the century," Abbas said. In the hours that followed, condemnation came from almost every corner of the Arab world. At the same time, the thousands of Marines who had been deployed to bolster security at US embassies in the Middle East were left twiddling their thumbs. Protests took place in Amman, Cairo, Baghdad and a few other capitals, but the doomsday scenarios put forward by the opponents of the move failed to materialize. "We realized that all the fears over this conflict came from the past—but it's not so clear that they're still relevant today," a former White House official told me. The president and his advisors concluded that the Arab world had grown weary of the Palestinian issue, and that the concerns were being raised by a legion that was all generals and no foot soldiers. A few weeks after Trump's speech on Jerusalem, Kushner met the foreign minister of one of the Arab countries. "You know, nobody in our circles is talking about the Jerusalem thing anymore," he told Kushner.[43]

Although Trump's move did not lead to an outbreak of violence, it was almost universally rejected by the international community. Two weeks after the speech, the United States found itself isolated at the UN Security Council, having to use its veto power to strike down a resolution condemning Trump and pronouncing his declaration "null and void." Four days later, the UN General Assembly convened and passed a strongly worded condemnation that called on Trump to rescind his decision. Shortly before the vote, Trump threatened to cut US aid to any country that voted in favor of the resolution. That did not help. One hundred and twenty-eight countries voted in favor. The only countries to take Trump's side were Israel, Guatemala, Honduras and a few island chains in the Pacific Ocean. Trump and Netanyahu had hoped that the US decision would create a domino effect that would result in other countries moving their embassies to Jerusalem, but at the time of writing, only three had: Guatemala, Honduras and Kosovo.

During the discussions that took place at the end of November, Trump quizzed Kushner, Greenblatt and Friedman on the likely impact of the embassy relocation on his peace initiative.[44] "It will disrupt it in the short term," Kushner replied. "I don't know if it will take a month or a year, but in the long term this move will serve your interests, because you will come across as a man of his word, it will give you a lot of credit within the Israeli public—and it's also the right thing to do." In real time, Kushner and Greenblatt thought any fallout from the embassy relocation would be no more than a bump on the road. They both significantly underestimated the consequences. It's difficult to say whether Trump's peace initiative ever had a realistic chance of success, but his decision on Jerusalem was the initial trigger for the most significant breakdown in communication between the United States and the Palestinians since President Bush's speech in June 2002 in which he called to replace Yasser Arafat.[45] The Palestinian Authority cut off almost all communication with the Trump administration, with the exception of certain security and intelligence cooperation. When Vice President Pence visited Israel in late January 2018, he was declared persona non grata by the Palestinians.

Trump did not appreciate the Palestinian response to his declaration on Jerusalem, and he publicly threatened to cut US aid to them if they did not return to the negotiating table. At a gathering of the leadership of the Palestinian Liberation Organization (PLO) in Ramallah, Abbas delivered a speech that was unprecedented in its venom. In a lengthy monologue laden with historical conspiracies against the Jewish people, he declared that he would no longer agree to US mediation in the peace process. Echoing an Arab epithet, he bade the US president, "may your house come to ruin." In response, Trump followed through on his threat and froze 125 million dollars' worth of aid that had been earmarked for the United Nations Relief and Works Agency (UNRWA), which is tasked with supporting Palestinian refugees. Over the following months, the Trump administration gradually cut almost all aid to the Palestinians, close to a billion dollars a year. First it was projects run by the United States Agency for International Development (USAID), then all aid to UNRWA and finally even a sum of 20 million dollars for cancer treatments in four Palestinian hospitals in East Jerusalem. At Israel's behest, the only US aid to survive intact was the support for the Palestinian security forces.

Trump's peace team made two decisions in response to the Palestinians' stand. The first was not to chase after them to bring them back to the negotiating table. "They took a drastic decision, boycotted us and tried to show us they are strong. But actually, they just isolated themselves even more and didn't gain anything out of it," Kushner told me. The second decision was not to grant Abbas a veto over the ongoing American diplomatic initiative. Kushner set about laying out a new agenda, and on March 13, 2018, he brought representatives from 20 countries—including Israel and six Arab nations—to the White House to discuss the situation in Gaza. This was a rare sight: representatives of the government of the State of Israel were sitting at the same table as diplomats from Saudi Arabia, the United Arab Emirates, Bahrain and Qatar—none of whom had official ties with Israel. The stated goal of the meeting was to put forward suggestions for the reconstruction of Gaza as part of Trump's peace plan. No less importantly, Kushner was hoping to bring Israel and the Arab world closer together. The Palestinians were invited to the summit but rejected the offer out of hand. "In our view, if the Palestinians came it would be a win for us, and if they boycotted it that would also be a win for us, because they would be seen as intransigent," a former senior White House official said. Kushner's takeaway from the summit was that the global consensus saw Gaza as a humanitarian issue, and that they were all too ready to pour money into rebuilding a desalination plant only to see it bombed by Israel in the subsequent round of fighting, but were not willing to tackle the root of the problem. Kushner preferred to focus on resolving the situation in Gaza within the scope of a comprehensive peace deal. "We were not looking to just add a new coat of paint over the problem," Kushner told me in one of our conversations.

The American attempt to portray the Palestinians as intransigent in the eyes of the Arab world was successful to no small extent and exposed the reservations that many Arab leaders had regarding Abbas and the rest of the Palestinian leadership. In June 2018, Kushner gave a rare interview to the East Jerusalem-based *Al-Quds* newspaper. In it, he leveled harsh criticisms at Abbas.

In a conversation a few weeks later at the White House, Kushner told me that many Arab leaders had called him after they read the interview and told him that they agreed with every word he said about the Palestinian president.[46] The most outspoken Arab leader in this regard was the Saudi crown prince, Mohammed bin Salman. At the time, he was seen as the poster boy for a new Saudi Arabia, and many in the west had pinned their hopes on him. He was young, English-speaking, well-educated and willing to carry out far-reaching reforms in Saudi Arabia and weaken the religious and conservative establishment in the country. The crown prince also took a different line on the Palestinians to the previous generations of Saudi leaders. Freed from the constraints of the policies of the past and without any sentimental or emotional attachments, bin Salman did not hesitate to deliver an unsparing assessment of the Palestinian president and to take the side of the Trump administration. Two weeks after Trump's declaration on Jerusalem, the prince met with Abbas in Riyadh and the two held a blunt conversation regarding the Palestinian boycott of the White House. "The Trump Plan is the only game in town," bin Salman told Abbas, according to reports in the Arab and international press at the time. The Palestinians were stunned by the sudden shift in the Saudis' position. In March, following the White House summit on Gaza, the Saudi crown prince traveled to New York, where he met with the heads of several Jewish organizations. Bin Salman explained to those present in the room that Iran was the number one priority for the Saudis in terms of foreign policy and public opinion, and not the Palestinians. At one point, the Saudi crown prince even appeared to channel the legendary Israeli foreign minister, Abba Eban—who famously said of the Palestinians that they "never missed an opportunity to miss an opportunity." "In the last several decades the Palestinian leadership has missed one opportunity after the other and rejected all the peace proposals it was given," said the crown prince. "It is about time the Palestinians take the proposals and agree to come to the negotiating table or shut up and stop complaining." One of those who had attended the meeting told me afterward that the leaders of the Jewish organizations present almost fell out of their seats at bin Salman's words. Reports regarding the details of that meeting traveled quickly to both the White House and the Prime Minister's Office in Jerusalem. When I published the quotes, they were carried by media outlets across the Arab world. The combination of Trump's move regarding Jerusalem and bin Salman's dismissive approach to the Palestinians sparked a wave of criticism of the next-in-line to the Saudi throne within the wider Arab world and the Saudi royal family itself. The pushback was so intense that his father, King Salman, decided to take the Palestinian affairs portfolio out of his hands and to restore the traditional policy of the royal house. A few weeks later, King Salman organized the so-called "Jerusalem Summit" in Riyadh and invited many Arab leaders. He condemned Trump's recent moves and emphasized that the Saudi position on the Israeli– Palestinian conflict remained the same as it had always been.

Throughout the first year of Trump's term in office, the members of the White House peace team believed that despite his lack of enthusiasm for progress with the Palestinians, Netanyahu would ultimately cooperate. The Americans decided to deal with Netanyahu by embracing him and showering him with political gifts, reasoning that the stronger Netanyahu's political standing was at home, the easier it would be for him to make the compromises that they intended to demand of him as part of the peace plan. This was only a partial success. Abbas, on the other hand, had seemed willing to cooperate with the new president's peace process and had demonstrated far more goodwill than Netanyahu. Until Trump's embassy decision, Kushner and Greenblatt believed that Abbas would be willing to entertain compromises that extended far beyond his official talking points. Despite all of this, and especially after Trump's declaration on Jerusalem, his advisors opted to engage with the Palestinian president via pressure and threats. That backfired. Kushner believed that time was on the side of the United States and against Abbas, and that as soon as the Palestinian president realized that he was stuck with Trump for a long time and that the Palestinian situation was deteriorating in the interim, he would return to the negotiating table. That did not happen. When I met him at Mar-a-Lago a few years later, Trump admitted that the economic pressure applied on the Palestinians did not produce the intended results. He struggled to explain why he had acted against his gut instinct and offered Netanyahu the carrot and Abbas the stick.

Following Trump's statement on the embassy relocation, the received wisdom in the United States and in Israel was that it would take a long time before the decision was implemented on the ground. Secretary of State Tillerson and his team even briefed journalists immediately after the statement that the process may take three to four years.[47] The US ambassador, David Friedman, had other ideas. He looked for any means possible to open the embassy at the earliest opportunity. In the end, he found a solution: converting the existing consulate at 14 David Flusser St. in Jerusalem's Arnona neighborhood into a temporary embassy.[48] Almost four years later, Trump repeated to me at length the story of how Friedman told him that instead of spending hundreds of millions of dollars on building a new embassy, he would instead spend only a few hundred thousand on renovating the existing building. "And it's all built out of Jerusalem stone," Trump told me, his eyes shining. The new embassy was, in effect, Friedman's office, along with a few other offices for his staff. The vast majority of the US diplomats remained in their previous offices in the gray building on Tel Aviv's HaYarkon St., which became a branch office of the embassy in Jerusalem.

The ceremony to officially inaugurate the embassy in Jerusalem was scheduled for May 14, 2018—70 years to the day since Israel's first prime minister, David Ben-Gurion, declared Israel's independence on Rothschild Boulevard in Tel Aviv. Close to a thousand people filled the small courtyard of the new embassy. The guest of honor, David Friedman, shaped the event—and the guest list—in his image. Prominent among the invitees were Israelis and Americans closely identified with the religious right. The best seats in the house were reserved for the patrons of the event, Sheldon and Miriam Adelson, whose pressure on Trump had played a pivotal role in his decision. Not a single member of Congress from the Democratic Party attended.[49] There were three speakers at the ceremony besides the official officeholders, all of whom were messianic religious figures with close ties to Friedman.[50] The first was Rabbi Zalman Wolowik—an ultra-Orthodox Jew from the Chabad movement who had been Friedman's teacher in Torah studies for the better part of two decades. The second was the extremist pastor Robert Jeffress, who was primarily known for his repeated remarks targeting Muslims, Mormons, homosexuals and even Jews. With his eyes closed in front of the hundreds of guests in attendance, he gave thanks to God for delivering Donald Trump into the White House. The third was the evangelist preacher John Hagee, who had attracted controversy for antisemitic statements in the past, including claiming that the Holocaust happened as a result of the Jews failing to recognize the one true God. "Can we all shout 'Hallelujah,'" said Hagee as he closed his remarks, and the hundreds in attendance, Christians and Jews alike, responded like congregants at the pastor's own Texas mega-church. Religion and prospective signs of the Messiah's arrival were littered throughout every minute of the ceremony. "The other main absent-yet-present figure at the ceremony, alongside Trump, was God," wrote Noa Landau in an op-ed in *Haaretz*.

While the ceremonial festivities were taking place in Jerusalem, a few dozen miles to the south, tens of thousands of Palestinians were protesting on the Gaza Strip border fence. It was the climax of a wave of protests that Hamas had instigated two months earlier under the banner of "The Great March of Return." The embassy ceremony, coupled with the fact that it was the eve of Nakba Day—meant the number of participants at the protest reached new heights. In Israel and around the world, the media provided split-screen coverage with the images of the speeches and prayers at the embassy in Jerusalem alongside the chaos and violence unfolding on the border of the Gaza Strip. It was the most turbulent day since the start of the protests. Sixty-one Palestinian protesters, mostly unarmed members of Hamas, were killed by IDF gunfire, and some 1,200 protesters were wounded. Condemnation was not long in coming. Turkey recalled its ambassadors to Israel and the United States and expelled the Israeli ambassador from Ankara. The UN Security Council convened for an emergency session and the Human Rights Council declared it would be setting up an international commission of inquiry. From that day of tension onward, the situation in the Gaza Strip began to heat up, the protests continued, incendiary balloons and kites set fire to the fields on the Israeli side of the border and every few weeks mortars and rockets were fired from the Strip toward Israel. For almost three years, escalation followed escalation, and repeated attempts to restore calm were unsuccessful. Things came to a head in May 2021, with Operation Guardian of the Walls.

While this was going on, relations between the Trump administration and the Palestinians continued their long downward spiral. If the embassy relocation and the cuts to aid were not enough, in September 2018 the Trump administration ordered the closure of the PLO offices in Washington, which had served as the Palestinians' diplomatic presence in Washington since the 1990s. The administration argued that the purpose of the office was to assist in making progress with the peace process, but if the Palestinians were refusing to engage with the United States on its peace plan, well, then there was no further justification for its presence. In an act of spite, the Trump administration also revoked the visas of the wife and two young children of the head of the Palestinian mission, and they were forced to leave the country on a few days' notice. A few weeks later, Rex Tillerson's replacement at the Department of State, Mike Pompeo, announced the closure of the US consulate in Jerusalem that had served as the United States' diplomatic mission to the Palestinians for over 25 years. The driving force behind all of these steps was Ambassador David Friedman. The consulate closed its doors for good in March 2019. Its staff merged into the embassy in Jerusalem and started reporting to Friedman instead. As well as the fact that—for the first time since the Palestinian Authority was founded—there were no independent and direct diplomatic channels between the United States and the Palestinians, this was also a symbolic statement, removing all suggestions of Palestinian sovereignty and implying support for their annexation to Israel. The euphoria in the Prime Minister's Office in Jerusalem and the corresponding despair in the Mukataa in Ramallah reached unprecedented levels. Relations between the United States and the Palestinians collapsed to their lowest point ever, and the White House in those days appeared to be little more than an extension of the Yesha Council—the umbrella group for Jewish municipal settler councils in the West Bank.

The Deal of the Century

In June 2017, I arrived in Washington to participate in a conference hosted by the American Jewish Committee (AJC)—one of the oldest and most influential Jewish organizations not only in the United States, but anywhere in the world. I was the diplomatic correspondent for *Haaretz* at the time. An assignment to Washington in my job was like the journey of Kal-El from the planet Krypton to Earth, whereupon he is transformed into Superman. If that sounds like a joke, then it is at least one with a grain of truth. In Israel, *Haaretz* is an important, respected and influential media outlet, but it is small and not widely read. In the wide avenues of Washington, *Haaretz* is a powerhouse—especially thanks to its English-language edition, which is read by anyone in the US capital with an interest in Israel and Middle East affairs. Time and again, I was taken aback by the doors that being from *Haaretz* opened.

These were the first months of the new administration and, like many other journalists, I was still feeling my way through the shroud of uncertainty that surrounded the Trump White House. For a few days, I tried unsuccessfully to arrange meetings for myself. More than anything, it wasn't clear who to approach for an invitation to the most famous house in the world, at the end of Pennsylvania Avenue. On my last evening in town, I finally received an email from the deputy spokesperson of the National Security Council at the White House, inviting me for an introductory meeting. He also mentioned that he was trying to arrange a brief chat with the US envoy to the Middle East, Jason Greenblatt, whom I had already met during Trump's election campaign. When I came to the White House, however, I was met by someone else. "Hi, I'm Josh Raffel. I believe we have a mutual friend," he said. I was surprised to learn that Raffel was a childhood friend of Daniel Sobelman, the former Arab affairs correspondent at *Haaretz* and a fellow graduate of the IDF's famed 8200 intelligence unit. Raffel, the Jewish son of an Israeli mother from central Israel, had grown up in the United States and worked in PR in Hollywood for a few years. It was there that he met Jared Kushner and Ivanka Trump. When the power couple started working at the White House, they recruited him as their media advisor. "Jared wants to say hello," Raffel told me. Surprised by the sudden turn of events, I went with Raffel to Kushner's office, a few short steps away from the Oval Office. The office was almost entirely empty, save for a computer and a small conference table. Kushner, a man my age, was thoroughly good-natured. "*Haaretz* is like Israel's version of *The New York Times*, right?" he asked. I pondered my response for a few seconds. Eventually, I replied in the affirmative. "I need to go in and see the president and I want to keep talking, are you in a rush?" Kushner asked after a few minutes of conversation. "I have all the time in the world," I answered. While I was waiting for Kushner, a lean, smiling young man came over to introduce himself in fluent Hebrew tinged with an American accent. "Hi, I'm Avi. Nice to meet you," he said.

The Peace Team

Most of the senior officials in the White House are people who have spent their whole lives dreaming of the moment they get to brief the president in the Oval Office; some of them start working toward it from high school. Avi Berkowitz was not one of these people. He was born into an ultra-Orthodox family in a New York suburb. After high school, he went to Israel and spent two years studying at the Kol Torah yeshiva in Jerusalem's Bayit VaGan neighborhood. When he returned to the US, he went to college. In Passover 2011, at a pickup basketball game during a family retreat in Phoenix, Arizona, he met a young Jared Kushner.[51] At the time, Kushner was a rookie businessman and the heir to a New York real estate empire. He and Berkowitz became close friends. The next step after finishing his degree was Harvard Law School. Berkowitz was not politically active during his studies. Instead, he passed the time tutoring younger students. One of the courses he tutored was called "The Road to the White House." In 2016, a few months before he graduated, Kushner offered him the opportunity to join the presidential campaign that few thought had any chance of ending up in the Oval Office.

Berkowitz was no political expert. Far from it. But, at 28 years old, he proposed an idea that would transform the campaign's fortunes and secure him a place of honor in Trump's inner circle. At that time, candidate Trump was holding campaign rallies around the United States. Thousands of people (and sometimes even tens of thousands) participated in every rally. "Why don't we stream these rallies live on Facebook? That way we will be able to reach far more people," suggested Berkowitz. His suggestion was accepted, and within a few weeks, hundreds of thousands of people were tuning in to Trump's rallies through his Facebook page. By

October 2016, a month before the election, millions of Americans had watched Trump's rallies on Facebook. At this stage, Berkowitz came forward with a new idea: streaming a nightly interview show featuring advisors and supporters on Trump's Facebook page. The goal was to reach millions of young voters who no longer watched traditional cable news.

Berkowitz spent the 2016 election night in Trump Tower in New York. He watched together with Kushner as the stunned cable news hosts declared Trump's victory. Two and a half months later, Berkowitz entered his new office in the West Wing of the White House—a few short steps away from the Oval Office. He began shadowing Kushner, always by his side, acting as his right-hand man and assisting him with every task. In a profile piece on Berkowitz published in April 2017, Trump's advisor, Hope Hicks, described him as the guy who organized Kushner's schedule and made him coffee. This was an unfair and inaccurate characterization.

As time passed, Berkowitz's role in the Trump administration expanded. As part of his work, he was heavily involved in shaping Trump's Middle East policy, especially with drafting the White House peace plan and later on also the Abraham Accords. In my conversations with him, I was impressed by how intelligent and sharp he was. Unlike many others in the Trump administration who were involved in Israeli–Palestinian affairs, Berkowitz was not an ideologue. He refrained from getting involved in tiresome arguments about who was right and who was to blame, and instead focused his attention on making sure things got done. His pleasant demeanor and composure under pressure made him one of the only people in the administration not to make enemies—within the US or abroad. His most notable attribute was a complete lack of ego. He kept a low profile, avoided publicity and often actively refrained from taking credit for successes. You could count the number of interviews he has given over the years on one hand and still have fingers left over.

When Jared Kushner retired back to his room, we spoke for another 45 minutes, mostly about the Israeli–Palestinian situation and their two leaders—Netanyahu and Abbas. At the time, Kushner and his team were still putting out feelers and building up a preliminary understanding of the situation. Kushner's own experience bore no resemblance to that of any of his predecessors in the peace industry who had taken on the mantle during the Clinton, Bush and Obama administrations. He understood that he would have to start from scratch. Kushner began reading every book that had been written on the peace process since 1995 and met with many of those same predecessors. His unique standing within the White House made up for the gaps in his knowledge. He was not only the president's senior advisor, but also his son-in-law. The fact that he and his wife, Ivanka, worked in the White House generated a lot of criticism within the United States. But in the Middle East, it gave him an advantage. It enabled him to conduct a more open and intimate dialogue with the leaders of Arab countries that went beyond rehashing talking points with foreign ministers or diplomats. Within the Arab world, it was known that Kushner was the president's envoy as well as his family. Many of the Arab states, especially those in the Gulf, are run like family businesses. "It made sense to them that Jared was the president's son-in-law," a former senior White House official told me. In that same meeting, in June 2017, Kushner left a very positive impression on me, first and foremost because he knew what and how much he didn't know, and he was willing to learn from the experience of others and to hear their perspectives, even if he ultimately decided to go down a different road. In the first year of Trump's term, Kushner's approach to the Palestinians was too strict and businesslike, and failed to take into account the emotional aspects of the conflict. "Don't allow your grandparents' conflict to determine your children's future," Kushner said in an interview with the Palestinian *Al-Quds* newspaper in June 2018. It was a message he repeated often. Among some parts of Palestinian society, especially the educated middle classes, it was effective. But for another, larger group, the Nakba in 1948 and the occupation in 1967 were still very much part of the present day, even 70 years later.

In addition to Avi Berkowitz, Kushner also brought in other people who would become key players and leave their mark on the White House's approach to the future of the Israeli–Palestinian conflict and to Israel's relationship with the Arab world. One of these was Dina Powell. In Trump's first year in office, Powell served as deputy national security advisor. She was born in Egypt to Coptic Christian parents. Her father was an officer in the Egyptian military. The family emigrated to the United States when she was young and settled in Dallas, Texas. Her first government position was in the George W. Bush administration. For two years, she held the title of assistant to the president for presidential personnel, which gave her influence over many of the president's appointments. Later on, she became the assistant secretary of state for educational and cultural affairs. She had no prior connection to Donald Trump or his inner circle. After the November 2016 election, she received a telephone call from Ivanka Trump. Powell held a senior position at Goldman Sachs at the time, and the president's daughter sought her advice on an economic initiative she was planning to promote under the new administration. That conversation resulted in a job offer in the White House; Powell subsequently became a central figure in setting Trump's Middle East policy in the first year of his term. More than anything, she was a moderating influence when it came to the Palestinians. In early 2018, after a year in her role, she left the government and returned to the private sector.

Greenblatt and Friedman were among the more notable figures in the peace team. While both were Orthodox Jews with a conservative, right-wing political outlook, they came from different backgrounds. Greenblatt was a graduate of the Har Etzion yeshiva in the Alon Shvut settlement founded by rabbis Yehuda Amital and Aharon Lichtenstein, both believers in a moderate-humanist approach and in compromise with the Palestinians. Friedman, on the other hand, was the president of the American Friends of Beit-El Yeshiva Center organization, led by Rabbi Zalman Melamed, which is associated with the settlement lobby and the uncompromising right. I spoke with Greenblatt and Friedman on several occasions during the presidential election campaign. Greenblatt adopted a moderate and cautious tone, while Friedman had no hesitation in declaring, even during the campaign, that Trump would support annexation of parts of the West Bank to Israel if he won. Friedman even attacked the pro-Israel left-wing J-Street lobby group, calling them "worse than the kapos" in the Nazi concentration camps during the Second World War. When I traveled with Netanyahu to the United States for his first meeting with Trump, it was at the same time as Friedman's confirmation hearing in the US Senate ahead of his appointment as ambassador to Israel. It was a fascinating event, with Friedman retracting under oath almost everything he had said over the previous months. The senators on the committee were astonished to hear him expressing support for a two-state solution, opposing annexation and declaring his willingness to hand over Beit El to the Palestinians as part of a peace agreement. "You are here today having to recant every single strongly held belief that you have expressed almost. …This is fairly extraordinary," the chairman of the committee, Republican

Senator Bob Corker, noted wryly. In the vote in the Senate a month later, Friedman's appointment was confirmed by the 52 Republican senators who voted in favor, with 46 Democratic senators voting against. The close result was unprecedented. Previous ambassadors had enjoyed overwhelming support from across the aisle.

Greenblatt's first visit to the region was unusual, and surprised even those who were thoroughly familiar with the habits of US government envoys. On the one hand, it was the first time that a White House envoy met with representatives of the settler movement. On the other hand, he also visited the Palestinian Jalazone refugee camp near Ramallah. He used his Twitter account to share with his followers both his prayers at the Western Wall and his visit to a Palestinian family in the heart of Jerusalem's old city. Most of those who met Greenblatt on both the Israeli and Palestinian sides came away with a good impression, including on a personal level. At the same time, in Israel there were those who did not like his balanced approach. "I came into the job with conservative views, but my perspective changed during my time in the role," Greenblatt told me. "I came with a bias, but I quickly realized that the Israeli–Palestinian conflict is not black and white. I understood that I needed to talk to every stakeholder on this subject that we call the Israeli–Palestinian conflict in order to emphasize to everyone the need for compromise."

When David Friedman entered his role as ambassador to Israel in May 2017, the dynamic began to change. He gradually pushed Greenblatt aside and became the point man for all day-to-day Israeli–Palestinian affairs. The settlement advocate had become the man tasked with talking to the Israelis about the settlements. He also tried to assume responsibility for communication with the Palestinians, but the Palestinian leadership in Ramallah viewed him as a settler rather than a US ambassador and refused to meet with him. In March 2018, Friedman appeared before the Conference of Presidents of Major American Jewish Organizations when they visited Jerusalem. One of the participants told me they were astonished to hear him talking like a lobbyist for the settler movement and not like a US ambassador. "Evicting hundreds of thousands of settlers from their homes would lead to a civil war in Israel," Friedman said in his speech. "The IDF is increasingly being led by those from a religious Zionist background. These are people who are committed to this country as a land delivered unto them by God. I believe that a large-scale eviction will lead to civil war. That is my opinion."

From the moment he took up the role, Friedman had set himself a goal to materially change the terms of the Israeli–Palestinian conflict and to make changes on the ground that would be impossible to reverse on all matters that dated back to the 1967 war.[52] His individual crusade was an overwhelming success. The relocation of the embassy to Jerusalem was the most significant of these changes. Friedman not only pushed Trump to make the decision on recognizing Jerusalem as the capital of Israel, but also worked to open an improvised embassy in record time, within half a year, as a way to establish facts on the ground. Friedman also pushed to sell the ambassador's residence, located in the affluent part of the central city of Herzliya, near Tel Aviv, to make life more difficult for any future government seeking to turn back the dial on Trump's actions.[53] He secured the closing of the consulate for the Palestinians in Jerusalem, which had served as the Americans' diplomatic mission to the Palestinian Authority since the days of the Oslo Accords, and transferred its duties to under the watchful eye of the ambassador to Israel.[54] He also successfully sought to strike the term "occupation" from official US Department of State documents during Trump's term of office, as well as to revoke the State Department's Carter-era legal opinion stating that the settlements were illegal under international law. Friedman took more than one of these steps almost unilaterally, without waiting to receive the go-ahead from the White House. For example, on June 30, 2019, a few days after Kushner presented the economic aspects of the peace plan at the summit in Bahrain, in the presence of representatives from many Arab countries, Friedman attended a ceremony organized by a settler organization to inaugurate a new tunnel beneath the Palestinian village of Silwan in East Jerusalem, a stone's throw from the Al-Aqsa Mosque. Grasping a large hammer, Friedman enthusiastically broke through the drywall that had been installed for the occasion, thus breaking open a symbolic entrance to the tunnel. The event, which was live-streamed and quickly shared around social media, was harshly criticized in both the United States and in the Arab world and gave the White House a significant headache to deal with.[55] In the wake of Trump's electoral defeat in November 2020, Friedman, alongside Secretary of State Pompeo, took one final opportunity to twist the knife. On a visit to a winery in the Psagot settlement, Pompeo declared that the United States would label settlement products from the West Bank as "made in Israel." This was a position even more extreme than the one adopted by Israel itself. White House officials, who only heard of the move through media reports, were furious with Friedman.

During his stint as ambassador to Israel, Friedman spent the bulk of his time working with the Prime Minister's Office, the heads of settlement groups and officials in the ultra-Orthodox community. His relationship with Netanyahu was remarkable— for better and worse. On the one hand, he had a unique ability to push Netanyahu into doing things that he didn't want to do. On the other, he shared an almost complete ideological affinity with the Israeli prime minister, which sometimes led to blunders such as in January 2020, when Friedman led Netanyahu to believe that he could begin annexing parts of the West Bank to Israel, despite the fact that this had not been cleared with the US president. "He could enter the prime minister's residence at any time of day and sit for a face-to-face chat with Bibi. When we wanted Bibi to do something, Friedman was like a psychologist who knew how to lead him there," a former senior White House official told me. "On the other hand, sometimes he would go off and do things of his own accord and cause miscommunications. But for all his faults, we would not have achieved everything we achieved without him." In contrast to his predecessors, Friedman had almost no communication with Israeli government officials other than Netanyahu, and he had limited relationships with the opposition in the Knesset or with civil society organizations not affiliated with the political right. After the April 2019 Israeli elections, Friedman even tried to help Netanyahu in his domestic politics. Friedman wrote in his book that he met the leader of the Israel Beiteinu party, Avigdor Lieberman, to see if he could "break the logjam" in the coalition talks between him and Netanyahu. "I told him that we were prepared to launch a vision for peace, which I believed he would support," Friedman wrote.[56] "But we wanted Israeli buy-in and that just couldn't be achieved while the government remained this unstable. He didn't care. He wanted Netanyahu out. In a heavy Russian accent, he said it was a "mission impossible." It was clear to me from the conversation that it was his strong anti-Bibi sentiment that was the real impediment to his joining the coalition."

If Friedman was the "representative" of the settlers in the American peace team, Scott Leith was the "representative" of the Palestinians. Leith, a colonel in the US Rangers and a former infantry brigade commander, had been following proceedings in the West Bank and Gaza Strip since 2009, when he joined a team at the US Department of Defense that was tracking the situation on the ground and coordinating security affairs between Israel and the Palestinians. In 2013, he joined the team of US Envoy Martin Indyk at the US Department of State, and when Kushner set up his peace team, he brought Leith on board. Leith was the US government's number one expert on settlements and borders in the negotiations between Israel and the Palestinians. He knew every nook and cranny in the West Bank, and for Kushner, Greenblatt and Berkowitz, he acted as a kind of guardian and counterweight to Friedman. Admittedly, the balance of power was nowhere near equal, but on more than one occasion Leith halted moves that Friedman had approved. When the question of annexation was brought to the table, Leith assumed even greater responsibilities. Over his objections, he was designated the health inspector of any Israeli annexation proposal, and he had no intention of letting any violations slide.

The Battle over the Narrative

At the end of 2017, after President Trump recognized Jerusalem as the capital of Israel, the Palestinians cut off communication with Washington. A few weeks later, in early January, Abbas delivered his famous "may your house come to ruin" speech. At that time, there was a 92-page report on his desk delivered by the head of the Palestinian negotiating team, Saeb Erekat. The report offered a pessimistic outlook that the Palestinians had pieced together from conversations with senior officials in Saudi Arabia and Jordan regarding the US president's imminent peace plan to resolve the Israeli–Palestinian conflict. In his report, Erekat described the

Trump Plan as part of a strategy he referred to as "forced diktats." He wrote to Abbas that the American approach was that anyone who wanted peace must submit to the White House's diktats and anyone who disagreed was immediately defined as "an obstacle to peace and a terrorist to be fought."

According to Erekat's report, the broad parameters of the US plan included the following points:

- A Palestinian state would be established on 90 percent of the West Bank territory, with the remaining 10 percent being annexed to Israel.
- The capital of the future Palestinian state would be on the outskirts of Jerusalem along the 1967 lines.
- Israel would commit to freedom of worship for all religions at the holy sites in Jerusalem and to maintaining the status-quo.
- The solution for the Palestinian refugees' right of return would be within the Palestinian state, with no right of return to Israel.
- Israel would retain the overriding security responsibility and authority in all areas of the future Palestinian state, which would be demilitarized, with a strong police force.
- Israel would retain security oversight of border crossings, airspace, maritime territory and the connection between Gaza and the West Bank.
- The world would recognize Israel as the national home of the Jewish people and Palestine as the national home of the Palestinian people.

Erekat claimed at the time that Trump would present his plan by mid-2018 and green-light Israeli annexation of the West Bank. He recommended to Abbas not to give the Trump plan the time of day. "There is no reason for us to wait for the American plan, which would legitimize the settlements and establish Palestinian autonomy in perpetuity," wrote Erekat in his report. Erekat was wrong regarding the timetable, but the details of the plan that he outlined in his report were accurate for that point in time. Abbas and Erekat believed that their boycott of the White House would cause Trump to abandon his efforts to formulate a plan to end the Israeli–Palestinian conflict. They were wrong. Kushner and his team continued to work on the plan, but the Palestinians lost any ability to influence its contents. The Palestinian boycott strengthened David Friedman's position within the peace team and, as a result, the plan became increasingly favorable to the Israeli side over time. When it was finally presented in late January 2020, two years after Erekat's report, the plan was even worse than the Palestinians had expected. Had Trump won a second term, the Palestinians would have found themselves facing their biggest diplomatic disaster since the Nakba in 1948.

In every conversation Kushner and Greenblatt held with the Palestinians in the first year of the Trump administration, they heard the same talking points and positions on borders, Jerusalem, refugees and other issues. They were unable to get a sense of where there might be some flexibility, if at all. Once the Palestinian Authority boycotted the White House, Kushner and his team attempted to reach out through unofficial Palestinian channels instead. Palestinian experts at research institutes, journalists and businesspeople would come to the White House in secret to meet with Kushner, Greenblatt and Berkowitz. They gave their thoughts on what a deal between Israel and the Palestinians might look like and answered questions that were put to them by the Americans. But these meetings were of limited use, as the people involved had no formal authority to speak on the subject. In mid-2019, before the Bahrain summit where the economic component of the

Trump Plan was first introduced, the former British prime minister, Tony Blair, tried to set up a covert and unofficial communication channel between the Palestinian president and the White House in an attempt to bring about a thaw. Blair arranged a meeting for Kushner in London with Tareq Abbas, the president's youngest son. Trump's senior advisor was unable to make it in person and sent his deputy, Avi Berkowitz, in his place. Berkowitz brought with him a copy of the economic section of the peace plan that discussed pumping tens of billions of dollars into the Palestinian economy in exchange for reaching a peace agreement. Abbas was unimpressed and, according to a former senior White House official, responded arrogantly. "We have already been offered that in the past," said the young Abbas. The meeting ended with an agreement to keep talking, but it was the last time that the two would speak.

After the Bahrain summit, the White House began to internalize that the Palestinians would reject any proposal outright. Kushner and his team prepared for a battle over the narrative with the Palestinian president. The prevailing question was how to turn his rejection into an opportunity to push forward with other goals, such as furthering normalization between Israel and the wider Arab world and turning the proposal into a blueprint for negotiations for future American governments. "Our assessment was that Abbas would adopt an irrational position and, in doing so, demonstrate to others that he had no ability or desire to make a deal," Kushner told me. The head of the White House's peace team therefore decided that the plan would be subject to change and that, even after it was published, the United States would make it clear to the Palestinians that they could still influence its contents at any time should they choose to return to negotiations.

Netanyahu was also less than thrilled with the prospect of engaging with the American efforts to draft a solution to the Israeli–

Palestinian conflict. He saw it as a fly in the ointment, but he also had no choice: if he was to push for an American withdrawal from the Iranian nuclear agreement, then the Palestinian peace process was the price he would have to pay. Much like with the negotiations with Syria over withdrawing from the Golan Heights during his first term and the talks with the Palestinians over a state based on the 1967 borders in his third, Netanyahu did not want any direct involvement. "I want to be able to maintain plausible deniability over your peace plan," he told Kushner in one of their meetings in early 2018.[57]

Netanyahu asked Kushner to work through a team of external advisors from a right-wing think tank who did not have a formal arrangement with the Israeli government. The team was led by his former foreign policy advisor and former director general of the Ministry of Foreign Affairs, Dore Gold. Greenblatt met with Gold and his team dozens of times. The ministers in the State Security Cabinet and the heads of the security establishment were kept completely in the dark about these contacts, and the only person apart from Netanyahu who was fully informed about them was his ambassador to Washington, Ron Dermer. "I knew that Dore Gold was involved but I didn't know exactly in what capacity," Netanyahu's national security advisor, Meir Ben-Shabbat, told me.[58] Ben-Shabbat, who took up his role in August 2017, mostly concerned himself with the security implications of the plan Trump's advisors were working on. He was shut out from the other elements of the plan—whether willingly or not. "On my first day in the office, the prime minister said to me, 'Meir, your first task is to draft our security policies for the negotiations with the Palestinians,'" he recalled. "It was important for us to make sure the lessons were applied from the disengagement in Gaza, in terms of control over our borders, demilitarization, changes that might occur after the agreement, etc. The Americans told me, 'That will mean daily arrests of terror suspects.' I said, 'Yes. But if the Palestinians do the job themselves, I won't need to get involved.' Our aim was to make sure Israel's security needs were addressed in the Trump Plan—and we achieved that in full."

In one of the meetings, Kushner wanted to update Netanyahu on the progress of the talks, but the prime minister refused and implied that he would prefer not to know. He was aware that he was likely to be going into new elections toward the end of 2018 and was concerned about politically damaging leaks. "If you don't want to know then I will just move ahead without you," Kushner told him. Netanyahu was trapped. He understood that the train was leaving the station, with or without him. Throughout 2019, talks with Dore Gold gradually wound down, and the Americans increasingly worked with Netanyahu and Dermer directly. Every time the Americans formulated a policy on one of the issues, they presented it to Netanyahu for his input. Netanyahu was cooperating by this point, but he did not believe for a second that anything would come of it. At the same time, the prime minister was hopeful that, by the end, he would receive the White House's blessing for moves that would establish permanent Israeli control over parts of the West Bank.

Former White House officials told me that many of the steps Trump took in his first two years were intended to build trust with the Israeli public. The decisions on Jerusalem, UNRWA and later the recognition of the Golan Heights as part of Israel were all moves that Trump and his team wanted to make anyway. At the same time, they stored up the resulting goodwill they gained among the Israeli public until the moment the president planned to demand that Netanyahu agree to his plan, which included territorial concessions on the part of Israel. During one of Kushner's meetings with al-Sisi in Cairo in early 2018, the Egyptian president told him how the US secretary of state under the Obama administration, John Kerry, used to ask him to pressure Netanyahu to make progress with the Palestinians. He wondered why Kushner was not doing the same. "I don't need you to pressure Netanyahu for me," Kushner replied. "The polls show that Donald Trump is the most popular politician in Israel. If he presents a peace plan, Netanyahu will have no choice but to accept it."

The Jordanians were also following the progress of the plan. Kushner had been introduced to King Abdullah a few years before he took up his position in the White House. In May 2010, he visited Jordan with Ivanka to attend a baptism ceremony for the daughters of the Australian-American media mogul Rupert Murdoch (the owner of Fox News, among other outlets). Jared and Ivanka were part of a celebrity guest list that included Hollywood stars Nicole Kidman and Hugh Jackman, as well as Google co-founder Larry Page. Queen Rania and King Abdullah hosted the group in their palace in Amman for a dinner celebration. This meeting would lay the foundations for Kushner's relationship with the king seven years later. As part of his White House role, Kushner visited Jordan on five separate occasions. During each visit he would meet the king in private and brief him on the latest updates to the Trump Plan. "The king didn't help us in putting together the plan, but he also didn't sabotage it. Whenever we needed his help, for example during the Temple Mount crisis in July 2017, he was there," a former senior White House official told me. King Abdullah really didn't like what he was hearing about the American plan, especially toward late 2019, when Netanyahu began talking increasingly openly about the possible annexation of the West Bank. Hints of this tension flared up every few months throughout Trump's tenure in the form of media reports claiming that the Jordanians suspected that the US, Israel and Saudi Arabia were planning to remove the king from his role as the custodian of the Muslim holy sites in Jerusalem—specifically, the Al-Aqsa Mosque. In early 2021, a big domestic political crisis arose in Jordan. Prince Hamzah, the former crown prince, was placed under house arrest following allegations that he and his supporters had attempted to lead a coup against the king. A few months later, the American journalist David Ignatius, who was close with the Jordanian royal family, wrote an article in *The Washington Post* claiming that the Jordanians suspected Hamzah of being part of a plot involving Israel, the Trump administration and Saudi Arabia. A former senior White House official told me that Kushner had never attempted to undermine King Abdullah's legitimacy or diminish Jordan's role in Jerusalem. The matter never came up in the meetings Kushner had with Netanyahu and MBS. The Jordanian king was the one who raised the issue in the first place during Kushner's very first visit to the region. "The king told Jared that he wanted to see a solution to the Israeli–Palestinian conflict, and if that meant giving up on Jordan's custodianship of the holy sites in Jerusalem, he would be willing to do that in exchange for peace," said the former White House official. The king asked Kushner in that meeting whether he had a better alternative to Jordanian custodianship of the Al-Aqsa Mosque. The former White House official added that Kushner replied that he had spoken with all the leaders in the region— including Netanyahu and Mohammed bin Salman—and they had all told him that Jordan was doing an excellent job with the Al-Aqsa Mosque, that the kingdom was respected by all and that there was no desire to change the arrangement. "The question was never discussed again between Kushner and King Abdullah," said the same official. "The Saudis supported leaving the Jordanians in charge of the Al-Aqsa Mosque because they wanted to maintain the status of their own holy sites of Mecca and Medina."

In early 2019, a year before the American plan was unveiled, the White House carried out a public opinion poll on the Palestinian issue within the region. They set up four focus groups—in Ramallah, Cairo, Amman and Dubai. The goal was to identify the most sensitive issues among residents of the Middle East in order to enable the administration to fine-tune the PR campaign that was to accompany the plan. Kushner told me that none of the focus groups raised the issue of sovereignty in Jerusalem. The subject that did come up was concern over Israeli desecration of the Al-Aqsa Mosque or restrictions on Muslim prayer at the site. Following these findings, the articles that addressed the status quo in Jerusalem and freedom of worship for Muslims were afforded a more central role in the plan. When it was unveiled, freedom of worship was underscored in several places. It was also one of the key talking points in every interview senior officials gave on the plan.

The American plan was subjected to countless changes. Many of the core issues, such as the status of the Jordan Valley and Jerusalem, remained open until two months before it was unveiled, and were only finalized by the White House very close to the publication date. A former senior White House official told me that Kushner and his team attempted to reach what they saw as a compromise between the Israeli and Palestinian positions. "Our plan will not be the Bibi Plan," Greenblatt told me in one of our conversations in 2019. In practice, however, the plan was far closer to the Israeli mainstream view—and much further from the Palestinian one. In several of my conversations with Kushner during Trump's term of office, he repeated that he saw the plan as a way to stop Israel's creeping annexation on the ground. He was less interested in where the border was drawn, which he saw as being largely arbitrary anyway, but thought the Palestinian interest was to hear from Israel which lands it would be willing to set aside for a future Palestinian state, so that these would be kept untouched for the day when such a state could be established. In Kushner's view, every day that the Palestinians spent waiting for a better deal to come along, Israel was taking over more and more land in the West Bank. His assessment of the facts on the ground was that the moment Israel sent people to live in a settlement in the West Bank, they would never be evicted from there. "Kushner thought that the best way to stop this process was to put a map on the table," a former senior White House official told me.[59]

The Annexation Campaign

For years, Netanyahu strongly opposed the unilateral annexation of parts of the West Bank. He recognized that such a step could lead to an outbreak of violence and a harsh international response and carried the long-term risk of transforming Israel into a binational state. However, starting in 2015, his dependence on the settlement lobby began to increase. His governing coalition at the time consisted entirely of right-wing parties. The settlers and their supporters had bought themselves a foothold in Likud's internal institutions, and Naftali Bennett's Jewish Home party, which had made annexation its raison d'être, was constantly applying pressure on him from the right.[60]

The settlement lobby's pressure on Netanyahu for annexation led to one of the biggest crises of communication with the Trump administration. In February 2018, Member of Knesset (MK) Yoav Kisch of Netanyahu's own Likud party and MK Bezalel Smotrich of Bennett's Jewish Home put forward a draft bill for the annexation of the settlements. Their proposal enjoyed a large majority in the coalition, but Netanyahu opposed it and had it removed from the agenda. In an attempt to defuse the anger against him, the prime minister announced in his weekly Likud faction meeting that he was discussing the annexation of parts of the West Bank with the Trump administration, and that he wanted to finalize an agreement with them before taking such a consequential step. His words reached the White House, where they were received with disbelief. When I called Ambassador Friedman for comment, he was convinced I was pulling his leg. He was after two days of almost no sleep, discussing military coordination with the Israeli army in the wake of the heightened tensions along the northern border. The day before, the Israeli Air Force had shot down an armed Iranian unmanned drone that had been en route to carry out an attack in Israel, an Israeli F-16 fighter jet had been shot out of the sky by a Syrian rocket and Israel had carried out an unprecedented wave of attacks against Iranian targets in Syria. "I came home and poured myself a glass of wine to calm my nerves, and when you told me about what Netanyahu had said I was stunned," Friedman told me a few days later. The US ambassador's primary concern was that the finger of blame would be pointed at him, as he was thought to be a big supporter of annexation.

Officials at the State Department in Washington rushed to deny Netanyahu's claim. The Americans demanded that he issue an immediate clarification that no such talks had taken place. Netanyahu put out a prevaricating and ambiguous statement that failed to satisfy the White House, which decided to drop a bombshell. A few minutes before the eight o'clock evening news, when I was already in place at the Channel 10 studio, White House spokesman Josh Raffel sent myself and other journalists a statement asserting that Netanyahu was lying. "The claim that the United States is discussing an annexation plan of the West

Bank with Israel is false," he wrote. The drama dominated the headlines in Israel, and Netanyahu was forced to put out an additional clarification. Ambassador Dermer called Kushner and his team and protested the use of the term "false." His complaint only served to increase the fury within the White House. "If the prime minister doesn't want us to call him a liar, he shouldn't lie," Raffel told Dermer.

Netanyahu's flirtation with the annexation initiative grew more serious during the April 2019 elections, after President Trump recognized Israeli sovereignty over the Golan Heights.[61] Two weeks before the elections, Netanyahu visited Washington to attend a celebratory ceremony with the president. A Hamas rocket that hit a home in the central Israeli village of Mishmeret forced him to cut his visit short and return home. Before boarding his flight at the Andrews Air Force Base near Washington, Netanyahu was visibly irate, bitter and upset. He snapped at the press pool, whom he accused of not providing sufficient coverage of the White House ceremony. "The fact that you don't give it more than a minute's coverage is something you will be held accountable for," said Netanyahu, waving his arms. A few hours later, he had calmed down and came to talk to us at the back of the plane. "Trump established a principle that occupied lands can be held if they were captured in a defensive war," he told us with a smile on his face. A few days later, his intentions became clear. In TV interviews two days before the elections, Netanyahu promised that if he were to win, he would gradually begin to annex parts of the West Bank.

On September 5, 2019, Jason Greenblatt announced his intention to step down from his role of White House envoy to the Middle East within a few weeks. The decision was a consequence of the toll that working in the White House had taken on his family life, as well as the ongoing domestic political crisis in Israel (then days away from its second elections in six months), which forced delays to the publication of Trump's peace plan. Netanyahu heard of Greenblatt's resignation while on a visit to London, two weeks before the election. That evening, I sat in the conference room of a hotel in London, listening to Netanyahu talk about his conversations with the British prime minister, Boris Johnson, with one ear, and to Greenblatt explaining his decision in a conference call with journalists with the other. "I hope to remain in the role until the publication of the president's peace plan," said Greenblatt. "We want to do it shortly after the elections in Israel." Kushner, who spoke after him, announced that Greenblatt's replacement would be Avi Berkowitz. The man who had, up to that point, been familiar only to those in the know, was suddenly thrust to the front of the stage.

Five days after Greenblatt announced his resignation, Netanyahu convened a press conference at a minute's notice. With the Likud MKs and ministers arranged in front of him like extras in a play, Netanyahu declared that, should he win the elections, he would coordinate with the Trump administration to green-light the annexation of the Jordan Valley and all the settlements in the West Bank. Netanyahu even showed a map of the territories he intended to annex.

Netanyahu's talk of annexation before the April 2019 elections was treated dismissively by a skeptical settler movement. The September 2019 press conference in Kfar HaMaccabiah was likewise dismissed as political spin. There is a large degree of truth in the move being a borderline desperate gambit by Netanyahu—who was stalling in the polls—to bring the settlers and their supporters into his column. Netanyahu informed the White House of his intentions a few hours before the statement. Trump's advisors accepted the move as a pre-election political maneuver and didn't seek to block it. "Netanyahu would often go too far in his statements regarding annexation, and then he would call us and say, 'I'm sorry, please don't condemn me,'" a former senior White House official told me.[62] "We approached this as domestic political maneuvering and didn't take these statements too seriously, because we knew that nothing would happen without our approval, so let him play his politics. These were frustrating moments, but we didn't start fights."

Those who did take Netanyahu at his word were the heads of the Israeli security establishment. The national security advisor at the time, Meir Ben-Shabbat, told me that on September 10, 2019, when news started breaking about Netanyahu's plans to deliver a statement on annexation of the Jordan Valley, IDF Chief of the General Staff Aviv Kochavi and Shin Bet Director Nadav Argaman were dumbstruck. They were afraid that Netanyahu was not interested only in campaign spin, but rather that he was seriously considering making such a move before the elections. They requested an urgent conference call with the prime minister. They stressed that there had not been a single meeting to discuss such a far-reaching step and warned Netanyahu that the consequences could be disastrous. His speech ultimately did not lead to annexation, either before the elections or after. A decade after he took office for the second time, Netanyahu suffered his most painful defeat. The pro-Netanyahu bloc in the Knesset secured only 55 seats, with the remaining 65 going to the bloc that opposed him. Two days after the Israeli elections, Trump was asked in a short conversation with journalists about the possibility that Netanyahu would be removed from power. In response, Trump distanced himself from Netanyahu. "I'm not worried, our relationship is with Israel," he said.[63] A month after the elections, Kushner came to Israel and met with Benny Gantz, the leader of the Blue and White party that had secured one seat more than Netanyahu's Likud in the elections. This was the first time the White House had been in direct contact with one of Netanyahu's political rivals. Gantz told me how, at the end of that meeting in the American ambassador's residence in Jerusalem, Kushner pulled a piece of paper with the White House letterhead from his pocket, wrote his phone number on it and asked Gantz to keep in touch with him. "I gave him my number and since then we have had a direct line of communication," Gantz told me.[64] After his meetings with Netanyahu and Gantz, Kushner offered me an exclusive interview. "I hope they manage to form a government," he told me. "There are a lot of opportunities for the United States and Israel, but there has to be a government." But that was not how things panned out. Netanyahu's political opponents—Benny Gantz, Yair Lapid, Moshe Ya'alon and Gabi Ashkenazi—were unable to exploit their historic achievement to form a government and refused Netanyahu's offer to form a national unity government with him serving as the first prime minister in a rotation agreement. Israel was forced into a third consecutive election cycle, in the greatest political and constitutional crisis since its founding.

One Step Forward, Two Steps Back

The endless election cycles led to huge frustration within the White House and delayed the publication of the president's plan for ending the Israeli–Palestinian conflict by almost a year. In late December 2019, less than a year from the US presidential election, Kushner called an internal discussion with the White House peace team and told them that he did not intend to wait any longer. "We didn't want to present the plan in the midst of an election campaign," Avi Berkowitz recalled. "But we waited a year and there was another election and another election. And at the end of the day, we only had four years and we didn't know if we were going to have another four and we wanted to release the plan already." Kushner instructed his team to prepare for the launch of the plan within a few weeks. He gave the envoy, Berkowitz, two tasks: to go to Israel to make sure Netanyahu and Gantz were not opposed to the move, and to start a briefing round for a list of countries that they hoped would issue statements of support for the plan as soon as it came out. When the plan was published, it felt like another "gift" from Trump to Netanyahu ahead of the elections, but behind the scenes in the weeks leading up to it, the picture was the exact opposite. When Berkowitz came to the Prime Minister's Office on January 7, 2020, accompanied by Ambassador Friedman, he found Netanyahu in a foul mood. A former senior White House official recalled that the meeting did not go well and that Netanyahu was dismissive and disrespectful toward Berkowitz.[65] "It really was not a gift to Bibi. He was really opposed to unveiling the plan at that time," said the official, who was privy to the details of the meeting. "Netanyahu was worried about the elections and possible opposition to the plan from the right, and how this might affect turnout among his right-wing base." During the meeting, Friedman informed him that President Trump was considering inviting the head of Blue and White, Benny Gantz, to the launch event too. When he heard this, Netanyahu recoiled. He started asking whether the president would meet with Gantz separately and whether photos would be shared from the meeting. "Bibi was afraid that if Gantz was there too, he would not be able to claim it as a personal political victory," said the former White House official. "He bitched and moaned, but in the end he cooperated."

Berkowitz and Friedman exited the meeting with Netanyahu straight into a meeting with Benny Gantz. The two updated the former IDF chief of the general staff that the president intended to unveil his plan within the next few weeks. "I will support anything that is good for Israel, but I will not act as a backdrop in Netanyahu's show," Gantz told them. He demanded a separate meeting with Trump and for photos to be shared of it. The White House had no problem agreeing to this gesture, in exchange for approval of the plan from the two biggest parties in the Knesset, who together represented 60 percent of the voters. The meeting ended on the understanding that Gantz supported the move. Shortly afterward, however, Berkowitz and Friedman were stunned by a statement from Gantz denouncing the decision to unveil the plan shortly before the elections in Israel as outside interference in the democratic process. "That was the opposite of what he had said in the meeting," said a former senior White House official. The Americans were furious, and Friedman called Gantz to demand an explanation. Further conversations took place over the following days, during which the Americans made it clear that they expected Gantz to clarify that he was not opposed to the president's plan. On January 21, during a visit to the Jordan Valley, Gantz retracted his previous statement and declared that he supported the Trump Plan. There were two reasons behind his change of heart. First, the Americans agreed to brief him on the key points of the plan. The US ambassador sat with Gantz himself four or five times, as well as a few more times with his advisor, the former commander of the Israeli Air Force, General (Res.) Amir Eshel.[66] The second reason was that Gantz understood that the plan would be launched with or without his support, and that Netanyahu would exploit it for his election campaign either way. He didn't want to be left behind. "I understood the principles behind the plan, and Amir Eshel also drew me the general contours of the Americans' map," Gantz recalled.[67] "My only disagreement with the Trump Plan was with the isolated settlements that the plan kept in place. But at the end of the day, I didn't want to argue with the Americans. I wanted a positive working relationship with them."

Gabi Ashkenazi, the former foreign minister, told me that senior officials in Blue and White felt it was important for the Americans to hear them as an alternative voice of government. "We knew that plans were being made to unveil the peace plan," said Ashkenazi.[68] "It was important for us to say that we supported the Trump Plan but opposed unilateral annexation. I can't say whether our dialogue with them at that stage affected the American plan in its final form, but we wanted to build a relationship between Benny [Gantz] and Trump, because we thought it was important for the election campaign."

Despite Gantz's flip-flop, Avi Berkowitz called Jared Kushner from Israel and told him they could proceed. The next day, the foreign minister of the United Kingdom, Dominic Raab, came to dinner at Kushner's home in Washington. Raab brought with him the director general for political affairs at the Foreign & Commonwealth Office, Richard Moore, who was appointed head of the UK's foreign intelligence service, MI6, a few months later. Over dinner, Kushner presented the administration's plan to solve the Israeli–Palestinian conflict to his high-ranking British guests. This was the first time the plan had been shown in full to another country. Until that point, the Americans had been very careful about volunteering any details for fear of leaks, but now they wanted as full-throated support as possible from the British. The British foreign minister told Kushner that he wanted the Israeli–Palestinian expert in the Foreign Office to examine the plan before the United Kingdom adopted a position on it. Kushner sent Berkowitz to London to brief him. The UK government disagreed with large parts of the plan but were satisfied by its embrace of the two-state solution and were willing to put out a message of support. The Moroccan foreign minister, Nasser Bourita, was also in London at the time. Bourita and Berkowitz, who had an excellent relationship, met at the home of the Moroccan ambassador. Not for the first time, Bourita raised the question of American recognition of the Western Sahara region as part of Morocco. The Moroccans had discussed the matter with the Americans a few months previously. Berkowitz promised to look into it again. He presented the broad outline of the Trump Plan to Bourita and asked Morocco to put out as positive a message as was politically feasible once it was launched. Ten days later, Kushner and Berkowitz joined Trump on his trip to the World Economic Forum in Davos, Switzerland. There, they met the president of the European Commission, Ursula von der Leyen, and presented the broad outline of the Trump Plan to her. They knew that the European Union would not come out in favor of it but wanted to make sure that it would not come out against it either. At the time, Trump's attention was directed elsewhere. A book by his former national security advisor, John Bolton, was due to be published any day, and impeachment proceedings against the president were underway in Congress. Kushner and Berkowitz sensed that the peace plan was the last thing on Trump's mind. They were concerned that their whole initiative was about to fall apart. From Davos, Kushner was supposed to carry on to Israel to meet with Netanyahu and Gantz and to participate in a conference at Yad Vashem, Israel's official Holocaust memorial. On January 22, on their way to the airport, Kushner decided to cancel his trip to Israel and to board Air Force One back to Washington together with Trump instead. He wanted to utilize the flight to convince him to move forward with the plan in the following week. During the flight, Kushner had a private, one-on-one meeting with Trump. "I wanted to make sure that the president feels comfortable with the plan and with releasing it in the next few days," Kushner said.[69] "I updated him that we are going to get several positive statements from Arab countries. I told him it will also be a PR battle. But I stressed it is important to release the plan now as a preparation for a second term that will reframe the debate and anchor down the principles of the plan."

A former senior White House official admitted that Trump was only familiar with the general outline of the plan. He asked a few questions, especially whether the Palestinians were getting a fair deal, and gave Kushner permission to proceed. Over the following five days, Kushner checked in time and again to make sure that Trump hadn't changed his mind, and that the preparations for the plan's launch were heading into the home stretch.

The week before the plan was published, the White House peace team decided to make one final effort to reach out to the Palestinian president, Abbas, and to see whether he would be willing to talk. Over the previous two years, there had been almost complete radio silence between the Palestinian leadership and the White House, and the few remaining points of contact were primarily for security coordination, or through unofficial channels or mediators. Kushner told me several times during our meetings during those years that the policy was not to chase after Abbas or attempt to lure him back into the fold. He remains convinced to this day that the decision was the right one. "It was never personal," Kushner told me. "We had communication with Abbas's people the whole time. We had back channels and front channels. But there was nobody around him who was willing to challenge him and get him to shift his position. Abbas was like the person holding a plastic knife and threatening to slit his own wrists. Everyone knew it was a plastic knife, but he kept doing it, time after time."

Kushner conveyed a message to Abbas through the CIA, offering him a phone conversation with President Trump. Abbas did not reject the offer outright, but said he wanted to read the plan before he spoke with Trump. Kushner drafted a letter from the US president for him with the details of the plan. A former senior White House official told me that in the letter, Trump noted that last time he and Abbas had met, in September 2017, the Palestinian president had said that he trusted him to be an honest broker. "I did things for Israel, but I told you that I would also do things for you, and I mean to keep my promise and get you a great deal. This is your best opportunity," Trump wrote. The official in question noted that Trump's key message to Abbas was that he was asking him to read the plan and highlight any points he had problems with, and they could then meet to discuss them and see what needed to be done to reach a deal. The CIA offered to deliver the letter to Abbas, but for several days was unable to do so. Abbas refused to receive it. "It was a big mistake for Abbas not to take the president's call," claimed Kushner. "If he asked to meet the president to talk about the plan and to hold on releasing it Trump would have done it. He would pause the rollout and meet him."

The Home Stretch

Saturday evening, January 25. After the Sabbath, Benny Gantz convened a press conference and announced that he would be flying to Washington to meet with President Trump on the day before he was due to unveil his peace plan. Gantz's statement followed a few days of negotiations with the White House team, during which Gantz had received assurances that he would be treated as a dignitary and afforded a meeting with the president. When Netanyahu heard that his political rival was indeed coming to Washington, he was angry. A heated fight broke out that lasted for several days over who would meet with the president first, whose meeting would be longer, who would receive video footage and who would only receive stills. It was very important to Trump that both major parties supported the plan, and the White House appreciated Gantz's readiness to come to Washington despite the potential political price, with the elections only a few weeks away. "Gantz knew that it wasn't in his political interest and that it would look like a gift to Netanyahu, but he agreed to go along anyway," Avi Berkowitz told me. "On the other hand, he wanted to show he has a good relationship with the president too and he got it." Kushner also praised Gantz. "He was a perfect gentleman. Every time he faced a difficult decision, he always did what was best for Israel and not what was best for him."

But even before Netanyahu and Gantz boarded the plane to Washington for the ceremonial unveiling of the peace plan, the political battle in Israel thrust the question of annexation back into the spotlight. During the election campaign that Netanyahu had launched a few days before he took off for the United States, the annexation of the West Bank was at the top of his agenda. "Soon we will apply Israeli sovereignty to the Jordan Valley and northern Dead Sea, without delays," said Netanyahu in his speech. "We will apply Israeli law to every settlement, without distinction." Netanyahu knew that President Trump was days away from presenting his plan, and he hoped to be able to follow through with annexation before the elections in March.

"I remember that in January, Friedman gave us a copy of the plan and we sat down and read it," Gabi Ashkenazi told me.[70] "We were pleasantly surprised because we thought it would be far more one-sided. What we found was a plan that was supposed to bring about a separation from the Palestinians. We saw the gap between what Netanyahu was selling and what was actually in it. Netanyahu emphasized the 30 percent that he would supposedly be getting, but hid the price that Israel would pay, such as a Palestinian state, the territory in the Negev desert and the transport link between the West Bank and Gaza. He hid that and played up the part about annexation for the public. He was pretty successful with that. We tried to tell the public that the plan was part of a broader context—and were unsuccessful. We didn't want to be perceived by the public as being like Peace Now [the left-wing activist group]. We are in favor of retaining the settlement blocs and the Jordan Valley, but we are against unilateral annexation. Go make that case in the TV studios, where you're either for it or you're against it. If you're against it—you're on the left. It was not an easy trap to escape."

A week before his trip, Netanyahu summoned the IDF chief of the general staff, Aviv Kochavi, the head of the Shin Bet, Nadav Argaman and the head of the Mossad, Yossi Cohen, for a secret meeting. He informed them about the possibility that the government would move ahead with a decision to annex parts of the West Bank immediately after the Trump Plan was unveiled and ordered them to prepare for an escalation in the security situation. The IDF and the Shin Bet warned of the negative consequences of such a move, but Netanyahu rejected their concerns outright. "The heads of the security establishment do not set policy. They are there to implement the policy of the elected government," Netanyahu said in a meeting with journalists at the time, setting to one side the fact that he stood at the head of a transition government that had been leading the country for a year with no mandate from the public.

On January 26, I joined Netanyahu on his flight to Washington for the ceremony to launch the plan. The atmosphere in the prime minister's inner circle was one of anticipation mixed with euphoria. Yariv Levin, a government minister and the only politician Netanyahu kept in the loop regarding the talks with the Americans, came to the back of the plane to talk with the press pool and hinted that Netanyahu was expecting to receive the go-

ahead from the US president to annex parts of the West Bank.
"The 'deal of the century' was known only to the prime minister,
to Ambassador Dermer and to myself," Meir Ben-Shabbat told
me.[71] "There were others who came on board at various stages,
such as Levin. But Dermer was the go-to man and the coordinator
with the Americans."

The day before the plan was set to be unveiled, Netanyahu
was awarded the first meeting with the US president. In front
of the cameras, it was all warmth and affection between the two
men, but inside the room, the atmosphere changed. A former senior
White House official who was present at the meeting spoke about
how Netanyahu surprised the president by barely talking about
how he planned to push the plan forward and restart negotiations
with the Palestinians. "The president wanted to hear about how
Netanyahu intended to address the Palestinian issue, but he only
talked about Iran and what he expected to receive from the United
States under the plan," a former senior White House official told
me. An hour and a half after Netanyahu, it was the turn of the
head of the Blue and White party, Benny Gantz, to enter the Oval
Office. Right up until the last moment, Gantz's team feared that
they were walking into a trap of a joint photo with Netanyahu.
Gantz assigned one of his team members to watch over the gates to
the White House, and only when he reported back that Netanyahu's
motorcade had left did Gantz leave his hotel for his meeting with
the US president. "The meeting with Gantz was outstanding—and
the president really liked him," said a former senior White House
official. "Gantz said, 'I know the Palestinians well. If we win the
elections and I will be the prime minister, I will work hard to make
peace with them.' That was exactly what the president wanted
to hear." During our interview, former President Donald Trump
confirmed this version of events. "I liked the general (Gantz) a

lot. I said to Jared (Kushner) and David (Friedman) that if he became the guy, if he won, I think it would be a lot easier to make peace (than with Netanyahu)," he told me. In the days before the meeting, Gantz debated what to say to Trump. Ashkenazi told me how, in an internal Blue and White meeting, it was decided that Gantz would tell the president that he was in favor of the plan but would ask that it be implemented only after the elections in Israel, working in tandem with the other countries in the region and not unilaterally. "In the meeting with Trump, I congratulated him on the plan and told him that it was the first one that took into consideration the reality on the ground, but it was also clear to him that I was opposed to unilateral annexation," Gantz told me.[72] Trump and his team agreed with Gantz during the meeting that the plan would not be implemented before the Israeli elections. That was the first indication that Netanyahu's intention to move forward with a smash-and-grab annexation ahead of the elections would encounter difficulties.

As the day of the unveiling drew nearer, the euphoria among Netanyahu's supporters grew. In the days before his trip, a few commentators who were favorable toward Netanyahu shared his talking points in TV studios and highlighted everything that the prime minister claimed that Israel was set to receive from the US president. A few media representatives who joined the trip to the White House, such as Shimon Riklin (an avowedly pro-Netanyahu TV anchor on the right-wing Channel 14), filmed themselves in the hotel in Washington breaking into dance ahead of the imminent announcement on the annexation of the West Bank. The awkward videos spread quickly over social media, and only served to further heighten the sense of anticipation among the settler lobby. Netanyahu tried to recruit as many heads of the settler movement as possible to express public support for the president's plan. Many of them even came to Washington to follow the events from up close. The evening before the plan was set to be unveiled, Netanyahu met with them at Blair House—an official US residence and guest house for visiting dignitaries—and tried to sound them out about how they would respond if the Trump Plan were to include the establishment of a Palestinian state. Netanyahu knew why he was asking. The next day, the prime minister discovered that the then-head of the Yesha Council (the primary settler lobby group), David Elhayani, along with a few other regional settlement council heads, was leading the group that was opposed to the US plan on the grounds of the territorial compromise it demanded.

At the same time as Netanyahu was meeting with the settlers, I was sitting at the bar in the Mayflower Hotel in Washington. My phone rang. A senior White House official was on the other end. A few hours earlier, I had received reports from two sources that the White House had explicitly told Netanyahu that it was opposed to any immediate unilateral steps following the unveiling of the Trump Plan, such as annexation of the Jordan Valley or other parts of the West Bank. The official I had on the line confirmed the information. The main reason the Americans opposed annexation was the administration's desire to receive support for the plan from as many Arab countries as possible. A few Arab countries had already told the White House that they would issue favorable statements in response to the plan and would define it as "a good start," so Trump's advisors felt that any Israeli moves toward annexation would collapse Arab support for the plan. The second reason was the Palestinians. Kushner knew that the Palestinians would reject the plan outright, but he calculated that, were Trump to win a second term in November 2020, Ramallah might reconsider and agree to come back to the negotiating table. The White House wanted to give them room to maneuver and to change their minds over time, without taking any irreversible steps. The third reason for the US opposition to annexation was the position of King Abdullah of Jordan, who vehemently opposed it and had even threatened that annexation of the Jordan Valley would lead to the termination of Jordan's peace treaty with Israel. The king's position received support from other Arab countries, such as the United Arab Emirates, whose ambassador to Washington, Yousef Al Otaiba, was very close with Kushner. The next day, at 10am in Washington—just two hours before the ceremony was due to begin—I reported on the US opposition from the White House Briefing Room, together with my colleague Gil Tamari. The headline that went out to hundreds of thousands of Israeli phones through the *Channel 13 News* push notification sent an immediate shockwave through the political system. Netanyahu's assistant, Topaz Luk, came up to me a few minutes later and told me that the ambassador to Washington, Ron Dermer, had asked him to deliver a message to me that I had shared fake news. At the same time, Ariel Kahana, a journalist with the right-wing *Israel Hayom* tabloid, published a contradictory report stating that the White House would give Netanyahu the green light on annexation immediately after the plan was unveiled. On social media, battle lines were drawn behind these opposing headlines among supporters and opponents of annexation. Members of the settler lobby in the media gave me both barrels and viciously attacked me on Twitter, slinging mud, curses and death threats. As the hours passed, it became clear that both reports were accurate: they represented an internal power struggle that was taking place at the heart of the US administration on the day itself over the policy on annexation.

A Wedding Without a Bride

Soon after I published the story about the Trump administration's opposition to unilateral annexation of the West Bank by Israel, dozens of journalists and around 100 guests gathered in the East Room of the White House for the official ceremony to unveil the Trump Plan. The festive atmosphere felt like a pre-wedding reception, albeit one where only one side had shown up. The bride had stayed back in Ramallah and was boycotting the event. The overwhelming majority of the people in the room were Republicans who were firmly aligned with the Israeli and American political right. The late Casino magnate Sheldon Adelson, Texas Senator Ted Cruz, evangelist preacher John Hagee—everyone was there. Seeing people of their political persuasion on their feet to applaud a plan which called for a Palestinian state with its capital in East Jerusalem—the irony was tangible. Among the guests were also several whose presence was a first sign of things to come: a group of ambassadors from Gulf states. One of them was the ambassador of the United Arab Emirates to Washington, Yousef Al Otaiba. When he contacted his higher-ups in the Abu Dhabi foreign ministry a few days before the ceremony, he was instructed not to show up. But on the morning of the ceremony, Al Otaiba received a call from Abu Dhabi. Something had changed. "Go to the ceremony," he was told. Al Otaiba called Avi Berkowitz to inform him of the change in plan. "Is the invitation still open?" He asked. "Of course, we saved you a seat," Trump's envoy replied. Al Otaiba hurried to tell a few of his colleagues. As a result, the ambassadors of the Kingdom of Bahrain and the Sultanate of Oman also called Berkowitz and informed him that they were planning to attend. For the White House, this was excellent news. When the ceremony began, the three ambassadors received a special welcome and the acclamation of the other assembled dignitaries. The next day, the Egyptian ambassador, Yasser Reda, called the White House to complain that he had not been invited to the ceremony. "We actually did send Egypt an invite. Must have got lost in the e-mail," a former senior White House official told me with a wink.

The plan, which was published concurrently with the start of the ceremony, was the most favorable proposal to Israel—and the least favorable to the Palestinians—put forward by any US government since 1967. On the one hand, it had an unambiguous pro-Israel slant and shifted the terms of the debate in several areas of policy that had remained constant in every round of peace talks since the Madrid Conference in 1991. On the other hand, it was still based on a two-state solution with a Palestinian capital in parts of East Jerusalem. However, there were several notable and difficult to reconcile contradictions between the published plan, the speech that Trump gave at the ceremony and the accompanying White House press release that summarized the main points. And if that were not enough, there was a further gap between all of those and the private understandings between Israel and the United States. The resulting confusion left a lot of room for interpretation, which ultimately led to a flare-up between Trump and Netanyahu.

These are the main points of the Trump Plan, as published on January 28, 2020:

- Borders: The plan included a conceptual map which set aside 70 percent of the territory in the West Bank for a Palestinian state and 30 percent (17 percent in the Jordan Valley and 13 percent in the settlements) to be annexed to Israel as part of a future peace agreement.[73] In the map that was included alongside the plan, the Israeli and Palestinian parts of the West Bank were entangled and intertwined, with almost no territorial congruity for the Palestinian state and various parts of the West Bank connected by bridges and tunnels.

- Land swaps: Israel would compensate the Palestinians with land totaling 15 percent of the territory of the West Bank; land located in the western part of the Negev desert, along the Egyptian border, as part of an expansion of the Gaza Strip. The plan included a provision that would enable the transfer of the Arab communities in the so-called "Triangle" area[74] from Israel to a future Palestinian state as part of the land swap. This clause was not mentioned in Trump's speech or in the White House press statement, and senior officials in the Trump administration later distanced themselves from it.

- The settlements: The plan did not call for eviction of settlements, and it emphasized that not a single Palestinian or Israeli would be forced out of their home. It did, however, leave 15 isolated settlements as enclaves within the Palestinian territory, which would have made their future prospects extremely tenuous.[75] According to the plan, some 70 outposts, smaller unofficial settlements that were defined as illegal under Israeli law, would be evicted.

- Jerusalem: According to the plan, Jerusalem would remain united under Israeli sovereignty. The plan called for "Al-Quds" to become the Palestinian capital, and for it to be established in a few of the neighborhoods and villages in East Jerusalem, such as Abu Dis, Shuafat and Kafr Aqab, which are within the municipal territory of Jerusalem but on the other side of the separation barrier. The US even committed to opening a US embassy there.

- The Temple Mount/Haram al-Sharif: The holy sites in Jerusalem were to remain under Israeli sovereignty, with Israel guaranteeing freedom of access and worship in the Al-Aqsa Mosque for

Muslims. This section of the plan contained an irreconcilable internal contradiction: on the one hand, it emphasized that there would be no changes made to the status quo at the holy sites; on the other, it declared that members of every religion would be guaranteed freedom of worship on the Temple Mount—a significant change to the status quo, which currently states that Muslims may pray at the site and non-Muslims may only visit it. Jordan's role as the guardian of the Muslim holy sites in Jerusalem was not mentioned in the plan, but in his speech at the ceremony, Trump said that Israel would work with King Abdullah to maintain the status quo. This point was further reinforced in a statement published by the White House minutes after his speech ended.

- Security: The Palestinian state would be demilitarized from all heavy weaponry and would have a strong police force. Israel would retain overriding responsibility for security in the West Bank and Gaza Strip in a future peace treaty. Israel would also continue to control the border crossings, airspace, maritime territory and the tunnel that would connect Gaza and the West Bank. At the same time, the plan incorporated a pathway for Israeli security control to gradually decrease over time, subject to the capability of the Palestinian security forces.

- Refugees: According to the plan, there would be no right of return to Israel for Palestinian refugees. Instead, they would be entitled to either return to the Palestinian state, to receive compensation and citizenship of the country they were living in at the time—such as Jordan or Lebanon—or to receive compensation and move to a third country.

- Mutual recognition: Israel would recognize a Palestinian state as the national home of the Palestinian people and the Palestinians would recognize Israel as the national home of the Jewish people. The statement issued by the White House a few minutes after the ceremony emphasized that in addition to the question of recognition, all citizens of each of the two countries would be entitled to full equality under the law.

• The economy: The Trump Plan dedicated an extensive section to economic affairs, promising an investment of 50 billion dollars in the Palestinian economy in exchange for peace.

The most sensitive and talked about political issue on January 28—the day the plan was unveiled—was noticeably absent from the document that set out Trump's vision for a solution to the Israeli–Palestinian conflict. Words such as "annexation," "applying Israeli law" or "applying sovereignty" were not mentioned—even in passing—anywhere in the 180 pages of the plan. President Trump's speech included an ambiguous reference to the subject, but this too was confusing and full of internal contradictions. Trump claimed that a joint committee would be formed that would translate the conceptual map in the plan into a "more detailed and calibrated rendering" so that recognition "[could] be immediately achieved." He immediately followed this up by saying that the United States would recognize Israeli sovereignty over the territories that the plan envisioned as being part of Israel—but did not give a timeframe. After all that, he added that the Palestinians would be given four years to return to negotiations based on his plan. During this period, said the president, Israel would not expand its settlements into the territory that had been set aside for a Palestinian state. This part also did not appear anywhere in the plan, only in the letter that the American president sent to Mahmoud Abbas on the eve of the unveiling, a letter that the Palestinian president likely never read.

Netanyahu did not take the Trump Plan seriously. As with previous American peace initiatives, he played along out of respect or hope that the Palestinians would torpedo any progress by rejecting or running away from it. On every occasion so far, this gamble had paid off. With the Trump Plan, he saw an opportunity to receive the goods up front—but to pay for them in credit. For example, Netanyahu was asked by the White House to transfer land from the Negev to the Palestinians—an unprecedented request—in exchange for the territory he sought to annex in the West Bank. A former official in the American peace team told me that Netanyahu expressed no interest in the land Israel was supposed to hand over, as he figured the plan would never get to that stage. On the other hand, Netanyahu was very interested in those lands that the plan stated would remain part of Israel, seeking to move as fast as possible to annex them.

The American side took a similar view. The White House treated the peace plan as an almost arbitrary starting point. It was skewed toward Israel to ensure Netanyahu's cooperation and to lay the foundations for Trump's second term. The status of the Jordan Valley was the best example of this. In interviews with senior officials in the Trump administration, I was surprised to learn that despite the president's plan explicitly stating that the Jordan Valley would remain in Israeli hands—as shown on the conceptual map— the White House had no intention of allowing Israel to annex the area as part of any scenario, and even saw it as land that would ultimately form part of the Palestinian state. The same was true to a certain extent of East Jerusalem; the White House anticipated a larger area being set aside for the capital of the Palestinian state in a peace agreement than had been allocated in the plan as presented on January 28, 2020.

"I left the Jordan Valley for the second Trump term," Kushner told me.[76] "The Palestinians would have had no choice but to go back to the table because the Arab world and international community more broadly recognized the plan as realistic. We knew we wanted to leave meat on the bone for the day the Palestinians were willing to negotiate. We didn't want to present the full plan while they were refusing to negotiate. The plan wasn't supposed to be a bottom line, but a basis for negotiations. It was only the first stage. I think Netanyahu knew this was our position. He thought he wouldn't give more concessions but if there was a counterpart and real chance for peace, I think we could have convinced him. We thought the Trump plan makes Israel safer and gives the Palestinians a better life. We laid the ground and filled the pool with water so that both sides could jump into it in the second term."

I then asked Kushner, if the Jordan Valley was "the meat left on the bone" for the Palestinians, why did he allegedly support its annexation to Israel? "It was important politically for Netanyahu that the plan include the Jordan Valley as part of Israel," he told me. "I thought Israel needed security control in the Jordan Valley. I believed Netanyahu could have made more concessions if the Palestinians came to the table. We could have gotten an arrangement that would have worked for the Israelis and Palestinians in the Jordan Valley. It would have given Abbas a big win. In East Jerusalem too it was possible that Israel might make concessions in some of the Palestinian neighborhoods, although we didn't know how many of the Palestinians in these areas would actually want to live in the Palestinian state."

Netanyahu, who spoke at the ceremony immediately after Trump, hailed the president's "deal of the century" as "the opportunity of the century." For his part, he was not referring to the whole plan, rather to the part of it that he saw as giving Israel the green light to annex 30 percent of the West Bank. He said he would be willing to negotiate on the basis of the plan and promised that Israel would uphold the status quo in those areas of the West

Bank that had been set aside for a Palestinian state for the next four years. As for the rest of the territories, Netanyahu made his intentions unmistakably clear. "Israel will apply its laws to the Jordan Valley, to all Jewish communities in Judea and Samaria and to other areas that your plan designates as part of Israel and which the US agrees to recognize as part of Israel," he said.

As Netanyahu spoke, the US president's advisors began to regret not asking the Israeli ambassador, Ron Dermer, for an advance copy of the speech. Trump, who stood next to Netanyahu with a fixed smile on his face, did not enjoy the experience. As soon as the prime minister left the White House, Trump turned on his advisors. "What the hell was that?" Trump yelled.[77] Besides the content of the speech, he also did not appreciate standing there for 20 minutes while someone else spoke. "The president was not at all happy with Netanyahu's speech," a former senior White House official told me. "Netanyahu gave an election campaign speech at the White House and made the president look like a potted plant. He was also not generous to the Palestinians in his speech and did not really make any effort to extend a hand." Trump's advisors were frustrated. Far from being the triumphant climax to three years of work on a plan to resolve the Israeli–Palestinian conflict, the event instead marked a low point in the relationship between the US president and the Israeli prime minister. That was the point at which their relationship began to deteriorate.

A Breakdown in Communication?

A few minutes after the ceremony at the White House, while Trump was letting off steam about Netanyahu's conduct, US ambassador David Friedman held a conference call with journalists to brief them on the next steps in the US president's plan. The journalists and the other members of the White House peace team on the call were astonished when Friedman claimed that the Israeli government was free to move forward with annexing parts of the West Bank, effective immediately. "Israel does not have to wait at all.... If they wish to apply Israeli law to those areas allocated to Israel, we will recognize it," Friedman said.[78] While Friedman was holding his conference call, I was on my way with the other Israeli journalists to Blair House, on the other side of Pennsylvania Avenue, to join a press briefing being held by Netanyahu. The prime minister was in animated and ebullient form. He wasted no time announcing that he would bring the decision to apply Israeli law to the settlements in the West Bank forward for government approval at the very next cabinet meeting, five days later. I had to leave the briefing just as things were getting serious and return to the State Department building to interview the secretary of state, Mike Pompeo. As the cameraman, Yuval Sayag, and I were making our way in a taxi to Washington's 23rd St., my mind was a whirlwind of emotions. Just a few hours earlier, I had delivered a piece to camera confidently stating that the White House was opposed to annexation. The statements I had just heard from Friedman and Netanyahu, combined with the overbearing social media frenzy against me, left me with a crushing sense of professional failure. I called my friend, the veteran Israeli journalist Amnon Abramovich, and told him that I was considering resigning upon my return to Israel. Amnon thought I'd lost my mind and tried to talk some sense into me, with no great success. During my interview with Pompeo, the US secretary of state confirmed that the United States was giving the green light for annexation as long as it was done in accordance with the map published in the Trump Plan. All the negativity I had brought into the interview only grew worse.

An hour later, the picture began to change. After I had finished sharing the major points from the interview with Pompeo for the Channel 13 nightly news program, I went to meet a close friend—an Israeli diplomat who was serving at the embassy in Washington at the time. We were sitting at the Bistrot Du Coin, one of my favorite restaurants in Dupont Circle, when he received a message about an interview that Jared Kushner had just given to CNN journalist Christiane Amanpour. We watched the clip of the interview together and were taken aback by Kushner's answer to a question from Amanpour regarding Netanyahu's stated intentions to bring the annexation proposal up for government approval the following Sunday. "I don't believe that's going to happen this weekend, at least not as far as I know," he said, directly contradicting what Ambassador Friedman had said only two hours previously. I tried to get hold of a few people in the White House to carve some semblance of order out of the supreme chaos. At close to midnight, one of the senior White House officials called me back. "Don't think we haven't seen the attacks against you," he told me. "Don't worry. You were not wrong." When I asked for further explanations, he refused to go into any more detail. "Wait until tomorrow morning," he said.

It wasn't until a year later that I started understanding what had happened on that terrible and turbulent evening. Kushner had strongly disapproved of Ambassador Friedman's comments and Netanyahu's declarations. As far as Kushner was concerned, President Trump had never given any kind of approval for immediate Israeli annexation. He called Friedman and gave him a dressing down, demanding to know why he had announced that Israel could immediately begin annexing parts of the West Bank. Friedman claimed that the matter had been on the table the entire time, and that this had been his understanding of the president's plan.[79] Kushner forcefully rejected his claims. "I don't recall ever talking to Netanyahu about annexation or about doing it immediately," he told Friedman. "Let's go over all the meeting summaries and see if they include anything like that. David, this is not what I explained to the president will be happening—and we're not doing it." With that, Kushner ordered him to deliver the unwelcome news to Netanyahu himself. The ambassador, who only a few hours earlier had been celebrating what he considered to be his crowning achievement, had no choice but to cross the road to Blair House, head bowed in defeat. At the same time, a few of Netanyahu's senior advisors were sitting in a nearby restaurant to celebrate their historic achievement. No sooner had the steaks landed on their table than their phones started going off, their boss summoning them back to Blair House. The steaks were quickly packed up to take away, but they had lost their appetites. "It was the toughest all-nighter ever," one of Netanyahu's senior advisors, who had been by his side at the time, told me. "There was a genuine, deep crisis. We were convinced that annexation was going ahead, we had already started drafting the decision, then Friedman came in and slammed on the brakes. Bibi went crazy." Netanyahu, Yariv Levin and Ron Dermer sat with Friedman in the conference room of the official guest residence. Throughout the days and weeks leading up to the unveiling of the plan, they had been hearing from him that they would be able to go through with annexation, and now they were trying to understand what had changed. Friedman struggled to explain. He returned to the White House for a talk with Kushner, then back to Blair House, but the bottom line remained the same. The immediate annexation that Netanyahu had promised a few hours earlier was dead in the water. President Trump was far away by the time all this drama unfolded, at an election rally in New Jersey. He was blissfully unaware of the fierce internal struggle underway, between the advisors who were trying to push him to allow the prime minister of Israel to annex parts of the West Bank and the others who were trying to stop the maneuver. Every US administration has its internal disagreements, but the intensity of this one stood out.

For its part, the White House was not yet done showing up its ambassador to Israel. In the early morning hours, the press corps received an email inviting them to a conference call with Friedman, with no explanations or further details provided. I cast my mind back to my conversation with the senior White House official the night before, and it was clear to me which way the winds were blowing. Friedman surprised those present by immediately walking back everything he had said the day before. He stated that before any annexation could take place, Israel and the United States would have to establish a committee that would draw up the precise map. "I cannot say how long that will take," he said. A few minutes after he finished, I received a call from a senior White House official, concerned that the ambassador had perhaps not been clear enough. "President Trump could not have been any clearer—a committee must be set up to discuss annexation, and this is a process that will take time," he told me. Friedman's independent line on annexation, not coordinated with the White House, did not cost him his job, but he did emerge from it diminished. The embarrassment within Netanyahu's entourage was incalculable. The "opportunity of the century" that Netanyahu had talked about the day before had quickly disintegrated into the farce of the century. In the Prime Minister's Office, the backtracking began. First, Yariv Levin explained that the vote might have to be pushed back from Sunday to Wednesday. Then, Netanyahu's office put out a statement saying that annexation was a complex process that involved significant planning work "that includes maps and aerial photographs." A few hours later, Kushner delivered the coup de grâce when he announced that the administration would not support immediate annexation. "I think we'd need an Israeli government in place in order to move forward," he said in an interview with the journalist Ian Bremmer.[80] The next day, when we went from Washington to Moscow, Netanyahu wanted nothing more than to put the non-annexation story behind him. "There was a breakdown in communication with the White House," he told us.

Netanyahu's description came up in several conversations I held with senior Israeli and American officials involved in the events. Even today, neither side is able to pinpoint exactly what happened and the war of narratives continues. "Ambassador Friedman told us before we had even left for Washington that we would be able to begin annexation as soon as the Trump Plan was unveiled," one of Netanyahu's senior advisors told me. "Our plan was to go back to Israel and move ahead with annexation and our understanding was that the president would agree. Ron Dermer was also convinced it would be possible and that we were going to do it." Fifteen months later, when I met Jared Kushner at his home in Miami Beach, he was still wondering whether it was a genuine misunderstanding or an attempted smash-and-grab by Netanyahu. "I assume Netanyahu really thought he had a green light for annexation," Kushner told me. "I don't know why he felt that, but he was 100 percent convinced. Maybe they convinced themselves, maybe this is what David [Friedman] understood. Maybe they would have never agreed to come if they didn't think they could annex. In any case, we put the genie back in the bottle. I told them—this wasn't the deal. No way you are doing this."

After this book was published in Hebrew in December 2021, David Friedman denied that he promised Netanyahu behind the White House's back that the Trump administration would support Israel swiftly annexing parts of the occupied West Bank. In his book, *Sledgehammer*, which was published in February 2022, Friedman downplayed the efforts he made with Netanyahu to push for a swift annexation move and said everything he did was coordinated with Kushner. When Kushner's book came out in August 2022 he denied Friedman's account and stressed that the former US ambassador assured Netanyahu that he would get the White House to support annexation more immediately. "He had not conveyed this to me or anyone on my team," he wrote.[81] Friedman told me he stands by my recollection of events. "Jared and I had a misunderstanding on the timing, but not the substance, of the sovereignty deal with Israel," he said. "We had some heated discussions commensurate with the stress of the moment. In the end, however, we resolved our differences in a manner that best served the interests of both the US and Israel."[82]

Netanyahu backed Friedman and said Kushner's allegations are completely false. He even revealed an exchange of letters that had taken place between him and the US president a day before the January 28, 2020 ceremony that launched the Trump plan. In the letter Trump gave him, Netanyahu claimed, the president made it clear that the US would support Israeli annexation of 30 percent of the West Bank that was envisioned in the plan as part of Israel. Netanyahu's letter of reply made clear that Israel would move forward with a declaration regarding annexation "in the coming days," Netanyahu's said.[83] Dermer said it was clear to Netanyahu from Trump's letter that the US was going to back his annexation move and that it was clear from Netanyahu's response that he would move within days. "If Trump was surprised, he shouldn't have been, because he should have been informed what he was signing," the former Israeli ambassador added.[84]

Dermer stressed that the letters were the basis for Netanyahu's coming to Washington shortly before a crucial election. "Netanyahu is the leader of Likud. He took a huge political risk. A lot of people on the right thought the plan wasn't good...what got him to the dance was that he was going away with something. I can assure you that without those letters Netanyahu wouldn't have come to Washington," he said.

But Netanyahu's and Dermer's representation of the letters was misleading. Trump's letter never mentioned dates and doesn't set a timetable for annexation. It does, however, lay down a series of steps the Israeli government needs to take in order to embrace the US plan and prepare for its implementation. Most of these steps hadn't yet been taken when Netanyahu announced his intention to start annexing parts of the West Bank. Former White House officials who were directly involved in the events stress that there was a big gap between the importance Netanyahu ascribed to the letters and the way Kushner saw them. "In retrospect, our biggest mistake was that we didn't read Netanyahu's letter carefully enough," one former White House official noted.

Kushner and his team were frustrated after the January 28 fallout with Netanyahu because they felt like they were thinking long-term while Netanyahu was focused only on his short-term interests. Kushner was not ideologically opposed to annexation, but he wanted to do it in a measured way, to first finish transforming the conceptual map in the Trump Plan into a detailed and precise one. This would also give the Palestinian public, the Arab world and the international community more time to let the plan permeate. More than that, he wanted a stable government in Israel that represented a broad swathe of the public. "We had very difficult conversations with Netanyahu and his people," Kushner recalled. "We told them that we released a detailed plan that showed that Israel was flexible and the Palestinians were rejectionists. Arab and European countries released positive statements. But then Netanyahu's annexation statements made it all look like a land grab."

White House Middle East Envoy Avi Berkowitz, who also found himself in the eye of the storm, told me that the relationship with Israel went south fast from that moment on. When Ron Dermer asked to speak to Trump directly, Berkowitz advised him against it. "The president doesn't like you too much right now," he told Dermer. The relationship grew so sour that at one point, Dermer threatened Kushner and Berkowitz with leaking the alleged secret understandings between the sides on annexation that had not been published at the time the plan was unveiled. Trump's advisors warned him of the serious repercussions of such a move.

The debate between Trump and his advisors and Netanyahu and his team over who surprised who and who backtracked from his commitments is not going to end with an agreed-upon narrative any time soon. Each side firmly believes its side of the story and its interpretation of events. Historians will likely continue to analyze this issue.

On February 1, following a Palestinian request, the foreign ministers of the Arab League convened for an emergency discussion. "I will not go down in history as the man who sold Jerusalem," Mahmoud Abbas said in his speech. The public discourse around annexation led numerous Arab countries to line up behind the Palestinians and against the Trump Plan, but at least four Arab countries held their fire. In the meeting, the United Arab Emirates, Bahrain, Oman and Morocco took the position that the Trump Plan had some positive elements and that it could serve as a starting point for negotiations. Despite their attempts, the meeting ended with a statement that condemned and rejected the plan. "The plan does not meet the most minimal rights and aspirations of the Palestinian people," they wrote in the resolution. The White House was disappointed by the decision but were encouraged that a few countries had chosen to take a dissenting position. Blinded by the favorable outcome of the meeting, the Palestinians failed to heed the warning signs. Ten days later, they suffered one of their most striking failures in the international arena.

The UN's institutions are home turf for the Palestinians. It is the primary international arena in which they are almost guaranteed an automatic majority. Buoyed by the Arab League meeting, the Palestinians decided to press ahead with a UN Security Council resolution condemning the Trump Plan. The goal was to isolate the United States using a similar maneuver to the December 2017 General Assembly resolution on Trump's recognition of Jerusalem. Mahmoud Abbas even planned to attend the special session of the Security Council himself to deliver a speech before the vote. The Palestinians needed at least nine countries to vote in favor, but, as the day drew closer, they realized the challenge was greater than they had anticipated. Some of the UN Security Council members were far less enthusiastic than they had been with previous attempts. Jared Kushner and Avi Berkowitz worked behind the scenes to pressure the Security Council members not to support the resolution. Initially, the Palestinians were compelled to moderate the language in the resolution to avoid any direct criticism of the Trump Plan. Then, they delayed the date of the vote to give them more time to drum up support. Finally, when they realized they didn't have the necessary votes in favor, they decided to pull it from the agenda. The Palestinian president, who was already in New York when this was happening, had to make do with only delivering a speech. For the Palestinians, this was an almost unprecedented defeat. Berkowitz told me that the Trump administration tried to deliver a message to the Palestinians that there was no point appealing to the UN institutions, and that their best course of action was to return to holding a dialogue with the United States over the president's plan. "Our plan is not set in stone," said the US ambassador to the UN, Kelly Craft, who delivered a speech laden with empathy toward the Palestinians. "It is an opening offer. It is the beginning of a conversation, not the end of one." The White House considered the Security Council session to be a success, and they hoped it would further encourage the Palestinians to accept that their boycott of the US administration was an error in judgment.

Relations between Israel and the United States were better at almost every stage of Trump's term in office than they had been under Obama. But former senior White House officials told me that in February 2020, after the unveiling of the Trump Plan and up until the declaration of normalization with the United Arab Emirates in August, the relationship between Trump and Netanyahu reached its nadir. Kushner claimed in his book that Trump even considered taking the unusual step of endorsing Netanyahu's political rival Benny Gantz in the March election.[85]

A month after the Trump Plan was unveiled, Ron Dermer came to see Kushner at the White House. The third consecutive elections in Israel were just around the corner. All the frustration and tension that had built up between the sides over the previous weeks burst into the open during that meeting, details of which are revealed here for the first time. Dermer claimed that the farce surrounding the events of January 28 would hurt Netanyahu at the ballot box. "You brought the prime minister to the White House, and he agreed to all sorts of things in front of the whole world in the middle of an election campaign," he told Kushner, according to a former senior White House official. "He agreed to all this because he knew he had an American promise on annexation." Kushner hit back and tempers began to flare. "We have done more for you than any US administration in history," he told Dermer. "Don't get confused and think that everything that happened in the last three years was thanks to you. We did it because we wanted to." The Israeli ambassador in turn claimed that Netanyahu no longer knew whether he could trust the word of the Trump administration. "For you to say that about us is disgusting. Get the hell out of here!" Kushner yelled, and he threw Dermer out of his office. A former senior White House official told me that Kushner was usually kindly disposed to Dermer and saw his cool temperament as a calming influence on Netanyahu in times of division. "This time, Kushner felt like he went too far," noted the former White House official. "Dermer said things he should not have said, and Jared was not in the mood to take it."

Kushner was very different from any other US official to hold the Israeli–Palestinian portfolio before him. He was not a diplomat or an academic, nor was he a DC-based think tank expert. He was a businessman who adopted a transactional and practical approach. He was not ideologically committed to the right wing, neither a man of the Greater Israel movement driven by religious sentiment like Mike Pompeo nor a devoted ally of the settler movement like David Friedman. Equally, he was not emotionally invested in the arguments proposed by the other side, neither unduly troubled by the Israeli occupation of the West Bank like John Kerry nor seeing parallels between the Palestinians at the border crossings and Rosa Parks on the bus in Alabama like Condoleezza Rice.[86]

When it came to the Israeli–Palestinian conflict, Kushner sat firmly in the center ground. A liberal in a Republican administration. A conservative in a Democratic city. He understood that even though the Palestinians might not be the biggest concern for the Middle East, they were certainly the biggest issue facing Israel. He believed that Israel's interests, and its long-term Jewish and democratic balancing act, would be best served by separating from the Palestinians. He understood that the settlements were a tool to prevent such a separation. On the other hand, he did not adopt the Palestinian narrative and had neither time nor tolerance for debates on history, justice, refuge and Nakba. His detachment from the emotional responses to the conflict was to his detriment among the Palestinians.

Kushner understood Trump's political base, their priorities and the president's promises to them, and acted accordingly. He conducted himself as a realist seeking practical solutions. His perspective on the conflict was shaped not exclusively through conversations with Israelis and Palestinians, but also to a large extent through conversations with leaders in the wider Arab world. He listened to them, examined the changes taking place in the region and concluded that financial well-being, job opportunities, free trade and quality of life were higher priorities for the ordinary people on both sides of the conflict than symbols and never-ending wars over land. In some parts of the Middle East, this was an astute reading of the picture. In Israel and Palestine—not yet. Those who sanctify the ground between the Jordan River and the Mediterranean Sea are still more than a match for those who prioritize the well-being of those living on it.

Despite the differences from his predecessors when it came to the emotional hurdles surrounding the conflict, when it came to offering a practical roadmap, the plan Kushner formulated and his vision for resolving it was very similar to previous proposals from the Clinton, Bush and Obama administrations. Like them, Kushner too ultimately concluded that the most practical way to resolve the conflict was by dividing the territory into two states for two peoples. He too envisioned establishing a Palestinian state over the entire Gaza Strip and around 90 percent of the West Bank, with its capital in parts of East Jerusalem.

Kushner and Berkowitz hoped to continue to rally international support for the Trump Plan, but Netanyahu had other ideas. Relations with Israel deteriorated further, and the frustration among Trump's advisors increased as the Israeli elections in early March approached. Netanyahu waged an entire campaign around annexation, including photo ops around the West Bank with the US ambassador, David Friedman, who wanted it even more than Netanyahu himself. The harder Netanyahu pushed the idea of annexation, the further into the abyss Kushner and Berkowitz felt their achievements and progress within the Arab world and the Security Council victory over the Palestinians slipping. Many of the countries which had initially indicated an openness to the Trump Plan began to scale back their support, and other countries even began to appeal to the White House to stop Netanyahu. "From the point that the whole world was talking about Palestinian rejectionism, we moved within days to the whole world talking about Israeli annexation," Berkowitz told me. "Netanyahu didn't care. He was focused on his election and not on the international consensus we were trying to build in favor of Israel." In March 2020, everything changed. Not because of the Israeli elections, but because of COVID-19, which had appeared in the Chinese city of Wuhan a few weeks previously and quickly spread around the world. From that point on, the Trump Plan, the Middle East, Israel and the Palestinians were all old news. "The deal of the century" may have been relegated to the sidelines, but this dead end would also lead Trump's peace team to seek another way into the history books in the Middle East. There to open the door for them was the de facto ruler of the United Arab Emirates, Sheikh Mohamed bin Zayed.

Sheikh Mohamed

In December 2016, a few weeks after Donald Trump's election victory, his son-in-law Jared Kushner and his advisors, Steve Bannon and Michael Flynn, came to the Four Seasons Hotel on Manhattan's 57th St, a three-minute walk from the president-elect's headquarters in Trump Tower on Fifth Avenue. In a suite overlooking Central Park on one of the upper floors, a powerful and influential Arab leader was waiting for them: the crown prince of Abu Dhabi, Sheikh Mohamed bin Zayed Al Nahyan, and the de facto ruler of the United Arab Emirates. The meeting had been arranged by Rick Gerson, a friend of Kushner's who worked for the UAE government. Bin Zayed tried to keep the meeting hidden from the eyes and ears of the outgoing president, Barack Obama, arriving in New York in secret. He was unsuccessful; US intelligence found out about his visit and promptly informed the White House. When Obama's advisors made inquiries regarding the purpose of the visit, they were shocked to learn that bin Zayed had come to meet Trump's team behind their backs. During Obama's first term, his ties with bin Zayed had been good—even excellent. The two found a common language and would speak regularly on the phone. But during Obama's second term, their relationship ran into difficulties. The primary trigger was Obama's secret negotiations with Iran. One of the crown prince's advisors told me that bin Zayed felt personally betrayed and offended. Following the signing of the nuclear accord with Iran, bin Zayed, like Netanyahu, was determined to ensure that the new administration changed the prevailing policy toward the regime of the Ayatollahs in Tehran. This meeting with Trump's advisors before he entered office was intended to build a relationship with the new administration as quickly as possible and to shape its priorities. The initiative, the ambition and even the daring that resulted in this unusual meeting encapsulate how the Al Nahyan family has successfully shaped the United Arab Emirates into one of the most important countries in the Middle East in less than 50 years, and bin Zayed himself into one of the most powerful leaders in the region (and one of the most influential within Washington). "I had an excellent relationship with Mohamed [bin Zayed]" Trump told me when we met at Mar-a-Lago a few months after the end of his term. "He is a great leader and a wonderful person. He's very strong with his military and people really respect him."[87]

The United Arab Emirates is nestled below the Strait of Hormuz that connects the Gulf of Oman to the Persian Gulf. Iran lies across the strait to the north. For centuries, this naval passage has been a strategic and economic asset for whoever controlled it. Two hundred years ago, it was the sheikh of the Qawasim tribe from his seat of power in Ras Al Khaimah. Then the British Empire spotted its potential. By the end of the 19th century, the British had established a protectorate in the area.

The Al Nahyan family—the forefathers of Crown Prince bin Zayed—had ruled in Abu Dhabi since before the British arrival. They migrated from the Najd region of Saudi Arabia to the Liwa desert oasis. From there, they extended into Abu Dhabi along the Gulf coast and east toward the Al Ain oasis, in the shadow of the Jebel Hafeet mountain. The family's standing in the region shot up after Sheikh Zayed bin Khalifa, also referred to as "Zayed the Great," signed an agreement with the British that made Abu Dhabi the hub of regional political power. Under his reign, by the end of the 19th century Abu Dhabi had become the largest, wealthiest and most powerful city in this part of the Gulf. Sixty years after his passing, his grandson, Sheikh Zayed bin Sultan, became the founder of the United Arab Emirates and the father of the nation.

But one of the most consequential figures in the history of the United Arab Emirates was neither sheikh nor prince, nor even an Arab or Muslim. He was a young British diplomat named Julian Walker. In 1953, Walker was posted to the British diplomatic office in Sharjah. Fresh-faced and energetic, he quickly bonded with the local sheikhs, and especially with Sheikh Zayed bin Sultan. Walker took it upon himself to map out the borders between the different sheikhdoms in order to resolve the disputes between them—except he decided to do it together with the local leaders. Over many months, he drove around in his Land Rover and occasionally marched on foot to delineate the borders between the sheikhdoms.[88] In 1967, the British declared their intention to leave the area. In doing so, they spurred the establishment of a federation of emirates. On December 2, 1971, when Sheikh Zayed declared independence, six emirates—Abu Dhabi, Dubai, Ajman, Sharjah, Umm Al Quwain and Fujairah—signed up to join the fledgling union. Walker boarded a Royal Air Force helicopter and flew between each of the emirates to obtain the signatures of all the sheikhs on the federation agreement. Three months later, Ras Al Khaimah also joined the federation.

"Sheikh Zayed bin Sultan was the ruler of Abu Dhabi, which was the largest, wealthiest and most powerful of the emirates, but he was also a man of vision, with a unique personality," Dr. Moran Zaga, a researcher at the University of Haifa and an expert in the United Arab Emirates, told me. "After years of wars between the sheikhs, he managed to unite them. No leader had managed to do it before him. He wanted to build a federation that would survive after the British departure, and that above all would be able to protect itself against the two regional hegemonies: Saudi Arabia to the southwest and Iran to the north."

The Saudi invasion in August 1952 was a seminal event in the collective historical conscience of the United Arab Emirates, and it ultimately led to the formation of the Emirati military. With only 80 troops, the Saudis were able to cross the border into Abu Dhabi and claim the village of Hamasa. The sheikhs of the various emirates, who each possessed their own small and divided forces, were unable to beat back the invaders. It took British military intervention for the Saudis to retreat. Following this incident, Sheikh Zayed and his British advisors realized there was no alternative to building a unified Emirati military. The Emirati army, which grew powerful and well-drilled over the years, was also the melting pot that brought together young people from the individual emirates and forged a common national vision.

A strong army and a flourishing economy elevated the United Arab Emirates to its present-day status. For hundreds of years, the local economy was based on pearl diving, fishing and shipbuilding, which made the Emirates a hub for maritime trade. The discovery of oil in the 1960s, a few years before the declaration of independence, changed all that. Up until that moment, its most important economic asset had been the sea. Now, that was unexpectedly surpassed in value by the desert sands. Oil was first discovered in Abu Dhabi in

1958. Within four years, the first barrels were ready to be shipped. A few years after that, the Emirates had been transformed from a poverty-stricken region to a land of wealth and plenty. "The Emirati leadership saw that there was big money to be made in exporting oil," Dr. Zaga told me. "It became a focal point of the country's life. The United Arab Emirates went from a traditional economy to one based on oil profits, and from that point on, its development began to accelerate significantly." Today, Abu Dhabi holds approximately 6 percent of the world's oil reserves, making the Emirati capital one of the wealthiest in the world. As of 2021, its wealth fund controls assets valued at 1.5 trillion dollars. Furthermore, the Emiratis have diversified their economy, transforming their country into a financial, logistical, shipping and international air transport hub.

The UAE also has a migrant worker industry that dates back centuries. Several of the emirates were centers of slave trading, especially for the pearl-diving industry. The British protectorate significantly reduced the slave-trading activities in the region. But the oil drilling and the urgent need for working hands to keep it going brought a new wave of migrants and foreign workers— first for the oil industry, then for infrastructure and finally for construction. Foreign workers can be found in every sector of the local economy. According to the government, foreign workers from 200 nationalities and ethnic groups live in the UAE today. According to the International Labor Organization of the United Nations, as of 2021 there were approximately 8.5 million foreign workers in the country, out of a total population of 10 million. The migrant worker industry is estimated to be worth in excess of 30 billion dollars for their countries of origin. However, it has also led to discrimination and human rights abuses. While 1.5 million Emiratis are citizens afforded full rights under the law, foreign workers are recognized only as residents. For many years, foreign workers were employed under a system known as "*kafala*": the government held the Emirati employers to be sponsors of the foreign workers, and the employers were allowed to terminate employees' contracts without having to prove good cause, resulting in the employee's immediate expulsion from the country. This weakened the position of the employees and exposed them to regular withholding of wages, exploitation, abuse, confiscation of their passports by their employers and failure to receive rest days, and all with almost no legal protections. In 2017, in the wake of criticism by human rights organizations, the government of the UAE passed a law that aligned labor standards with those of the ILO's Domestic Workers Convention and required employers to provide the same labor rights to their foreign workers as they do to their local workers.[89] The 2021 US State Department human trafficking report noted that the UAE had increased efforts to address human trafficking, but reported that it still failed to meet minimum standards in several key areas, primarily prosecution of traffickers.

There are many explanations as to why the UAE has maintained its stability and flourished above and beyond several of its neighbors. Dr. Zaga suggests that the secret to its success lies in the country's hybrid model: a single federation that maintains the unique character of the individual emirates and tribes; a system of monarchy with islands of democracy; a liberal autocracy characterized by cognitive flexibility and a light-footed decision-making mechanism within a country that remains fundamentally traditional and conservative. Sheikh Zayed bin Sultan, the founding father, was an unwavering man of faith, yet in the same breath he was also highly pluralistic compared to his contemporaries within the Arab world. It was his vision to establish the United Arab Emirates as a monarchy with secular roots. The ruler was not envisioned as a religious figure. While the constitution does decree that Sunni Islam is the official religion of the state and Sharia law is the foundation for the legal system, religion is broadly viewed as a private matter and not a part of the political sphere. "If you ask an Emirati woman why she wears an *abaya* [traditional dress], she will say that it is part of her cultural identity and for historical reasons, not religious ones," said Dr. Zaga. "In the Emirates, clothing is tied to identity and culture. It distinguishes the locals from the foreigners."

The constitution also divides up the political power among the individual emirates based on their size and population. The common political practice since the founding of the UAE was that the president would always be from Abu Dhabi and the prime minister from Dubai. The constitution determines that significant decisions brought before the Federal Supreme Council can be ratified by a simple majority of the leaders of each of the emirates, but once approved, they are treated as if they were passed unanimously and are binding for all. In the first decade of the nascent state, positions in the government were divided up by tribal affiliation. Today, appointments are based on a combination of family affiliation and professional considerations.

On November 2, 2004, TV and radio stations in the Emirates cut away from their scheduled programming and displayed a recital of verses from the Quran. Every citizen of the state immediately understood what had happened. A short time later, the official statement came through from the palace: the founding father of the United Arab Emirates and its president for the 33 intervening years, Sheikh Zayed bin Sultan Al Nahyan, had passed away. The government declared a period of 40 days of mourning. Shops and government offices were closed, all the decorations and colorful lamps that festooned the market stalls and the walls of people's homes for the month of Ramadan were taken down and the advertising hoardings and bright displays around Abu Dhabi were covered with black fabric.[90]

Sheikh Zayed was 86 at his passing, but his health had been failing him for several years already. Ten months before he died, he made a decision that would have a profound impact on the future of his country. In a presidential decree, he appointed his third son, Mohamed bin Zayed, as the deputy to his eldest son, Khalifa bin Zayed, who was the crown prince of Abu Dhabi at the time. Sheikh Mohamed had been earmarked by his father as a future leader of the country, and the decree moved him ahead of Prince Sultan, the sheikh's second son, who struggled with alcohol dependency.

Sheikh Mohamed was born in 1961 in Al Ain's Oasis Hospital, which was built by an American missionary couple. The city was the power base of the Al Nahyan ruling family. His mother, Fatima, was the fifth of Sheikh Zayed's nine wives. He saw her performing a traditional dance at the age of 15 and decided to take her as his bride. At 16, she gave birth to Mohamed—her eldest son and the third among Sheikh Zayed's 29 children. Fatima was widely considered to be Sheikh Zayed's favorite wife. Then-US ambassador to the UAE, Michele Sison, described her as a humble, modest and generous woman, but as a powerful and influential political figure at the same time.[91] She was the only one of Sheikh Zayed's wives to be mentioned in the local press. In her early twenties, she set up the first women's organization in the UAE and has dedicated much of her life to promoting women's education and participation in state politics. Sheikh Mohamed was very close to his mother—as were his five brothers, and they were collectively referred to as *Bani Fatima*, "the sons of Fatima." Through smart political maneuvering, she persuaded Sheikh Zayed to appoint her son, Sheikh Mohamed, as deputy crown prince, paving his way to the top. She has also helped promote her other sons into many of the senior positions in the country over the last 20 years. Hamdan was the minister of state for foreign affairs and deputy prime minister. Mansour was appointed minister of presidential affairs and later also deputy prime minister. Hazza was appointed chairman of the State Security Service and later national security advisor. Tahnoun succeeded him as national security advisor, and the youngest child, Abdullah, was appointed minister of culture and later minister of foreign affairs.

Sheikh Mohamed stood out from a young age and over time became the most dominant and successful son. His father assigned him an Egyptian-born personal tutor, Izz ad-Din Ibrahim, who was closely affiliated with the Muslim Brotherhood. It is possible that Ibrahim's attempts to impose his own beliefs and opinions on the young prince contributed to Mohamed becoming among the most prominent opponents of the Muslim Brotherhood later in life. At age 14, Sheikh Zayed sent Sheikh Mohamed to study in Morocco. According to one version of the story, he entered the country under an assumed identity and worked in a restaurant to support himself, which was part of his father's approach to education. He completed his education at the Gordonstoun boarding school, where the European elite sent their children. After graduating, at the age of 19, he attended the British Royal Military Academy Sandhurst. It was at this stage of his life that he picked up his fluent English. When he returned to Abu Dhabi, he completed the pilot training course and became a helicopter pilot in the UAE Air Force. He quickly rose through the military ranks to become commander of the air force and deputy commander-in-chief. The former US ambassador to the UAE, Richard Olson, wrote that the Gulf War in 1991 shaped bin Zayed's perspective on the United States. He was astonished that the Americans were willing to see their own soldiers' blood spilled on behalf of a country in the Middle East.[92] At age 31, bin Zayed was appointed chief of staff of the United Arab Emirates' Armed Forces. His close connections to the United States—and to Israel—started here. As chief of staff, Sheikh Mohamed redesigned the UAE military along American lines. He was obsessed with military technology, buying anything that came to hand, and was personally involved in numerous deals. One of his advisors told me that bin Zayed often reads military magazines such as *Janes* before he goes to sleep, and that he takes pictures of new weapons systems on his phone and sends them to his advisors for them to find out more information.[93] In the years since he was appointed chief of staff, the UAE has purchased billions of dollars' worth of American weapons. Putting the vast wealth of the UAE to work, bin Zayed created the most expertly trained, disciplined and equipped military anywhere in the Arab world—a modern-day Middle Eastern Sparta.

Bin Zayed pinpointed his country's relationship with the United States as a key facet of its national security. He met with almost every member of Congress, US military official and diplomat who visited the UAE, and he was not averse to arranging meetings with experts from Washington-based think tanks who came to his country. After serving as chief of staff, he was appointed deputy supreme commander of the armed forces. He has therefore in effect been the UAE's primary decision maker on all aspects of national security since the late '90s.

Following the death of Sheikh Zayed in 2004, the new president, Khalifa, transferred more and more powers to his brother, Mohamed. In his first years in power, Khalifa kept the Supreme Petroleum Council—tasked with making decisions about the United Arab Emirates' most precious economic resource—in his own hands. Very quickly, however, Sheikh Mohamed began to overshadow his older brother. "Charismatic, savvy and very comfortable in the West, he possesses many of the qualities Khalifa lacks," Ambassador Sison wrote to the State Department in Washington.[94] When Sheikh Mohamed was appointed crown prince of Abu Dhabi in 2004, he became the de facto ruler of the largest and wealthiest emirate in the federation. In 2014, President Sheikh Khalifa suffered a stroke and his health deteriorated. He retained the title of president, but Sheikh Mohamed took over the day-to-day leadership of the country.

In 2004, Mohamed bin Zayed launched a pioneering vision to modernize Abu Dhabi—and later the United Arab Emirates as a whole—by transitioning to a knowledge-based economy and transforming the education of its population, while retaining its Bedouin cultural heritage and its moderate and tolerant interpretation of Islam.[95] He began to develop the education system, opened state-of-the-art hospitals, and brought in US advisors for its institutions and companies. One of his key reforms was to rebuild the public sector along meritocratic lines, overhauling an overwhelmingly nepotistic system. He sought to promote talented young people, and especially women, into key roles in government. He brought institutions such as New York University and the Louvre and Guggenheim museums to Abu Dhabi. His goal was to introduce locals to Western culture, expanding their knowledge and advancing the cause of tolerance.

When I came to Abu Dhabi on the first direct El Al flight (the Israeli national carrier) in August 2020, I was invited to dinner with a group of Emirati elites: scientists, engineers, government ministers and senior officials. Most of them were around 40 years old, and some even younger. At that dinner, an engineer in one of the government agencies told me about an event at which Sheikh Mohamed gathered representatives of the younger generation in the Emirati public sector and demanded they stop purchasing technology abroad and start developing local technologies instead. The best example of this was the United Arab Emirates Space Agency, which launched a space probe that reached Mars in February 2021. "He has a clear vision of how the country should look in 10- or 20-years' time. He is a patriot who is proud of his country, but also a pragmatist and a moderate," one of his senior advisors told me.

The social contract that bin Zayed offered young people in the United Arab Emirates was a tempting one: the promise of a quality education, regular employment, housing, healthcare and financial stability in exchange for political loyalty. The Emirati authorities monitor their citizens closely and public criticism of the regime is not tolerated. In 2019, the Reuters news agency exposed the details of "Project Raven," a team of former American National Security Agency operatives who set up an advanced hacking system, ostensibly to spy on terrorists on behalf of bin Zayed—but also on opponents of the regime, civil rights activists and journalists. "The Western democratic model has a very poor reputation in the UAE," said Dr. Zaga. "That's part of the message the regime sends out. The way they see it, loyalty to the ruler and what the citizens get in exchange is more important [than democracy]."

Those in Mohamed bin Zayed's inner circle describe a private and humble individual. He speaks openly and freely with his advisors, almost without any formal distance. He'll discuss details of policy or assign tasks to them and in the same breath talk about family, sports or a film he watched recently. His advisors say he is an incredibly easy-going boss who looks after his team. "His father told him—you give your employees something that to you is relatively inconsequential like money, but in exchange they give you the most important resource of all—their time. For that, you must treat them with respect," one of his assistants told me.[96] His daily routine is largely consistent. He starts his morning with a fitness session, holds two or three work meetings, then returns home for lunch with his wife and a few of his children. After lunch, he returns to the office for a few more meetings and in the evening spends his time with family or watching television. He maintains a low public and media profile, avoids the limelight and almost never gives interviews or delivers big public speeches. Neither does he enjoy flying abroad on state visits or to international summits. Even for the signing of the Abraham Accords—a historic event by any standard—he decided to send his younger brother and foreign minister, Abdullah bin Zayed, who is considered the face of the United Arab Emirates in the West, in his place. He and his brothers are very close to their mother—and to each other. They speak with Fatima on a daily basis, and one of them accompanies her on every trip abroad. One of Sheikh Mohamed's assistants, who knows his mother and brothers well, told me that they bear a far closer resemblance to a normal family than they do to a royal family in the British mold.

The "Arab Spring" may not have started in the United Arab Emirates, but the images from Egypt, Bahrain and Tunisia pushed the UAE authorities into action, clamping down on the Muslim Brotherhood with one hand while relaxing political freedoms a fraction with the other. Before 2006, there were no elections at all in the United Arab Emirates. The 40 members of the Federal National Council—the Emirati parliament—were appointed by the government. Since 2006, half of the members of the council have been chosen by the public. Those political freedoms have expanded slightly with every election since, and the number of people entitled to elect and be elected has grown. However, as of 2021, political parties are still banned, electoral candidates run as independents and there are still many UAE citizens who are not entitled to vote or stand for election.[97] One of the ways for the rulers of the United Arab Emirates to hear from their citizens is through the "Majlis," a Bedouin tradition that provides a space for the public to put their problems to their leaders in person. It is a tradition that survives to this day, an opportunity that comes around a few times a year to "book an appointment" for a short conversation with the ruler, Mohamed bin Zayed, and to raise any complaints with him.

The former US ambassador to Abu Dhabi, Richard Olson, said that one of the worst insults Mohamed bin Zayed could employ was to call someone a supporter of the Muslim Brotherhood.[98] Since 2004, he has waged an aggressive campaign against religious extremism—and especially against the Muslim Brotherhood—both within the UAE and outside its borders. He changed the educational curriculum, especially regarding the teaching of Islam in primary school, and ensured that Saudi teachers or those perceived as extremist or affiliated with the Muslim Brotherhood were replaced. Mosque sermons must be approved in advance by the Ministry of Justice to ensure they do not contain incitement to violence or extremist content. Soldiers in the military are allowed to grow facial hair, but not the thick beards identified with Islamic extremists. At a meeting with a senior US official in April 2004, Sheikh Mohamed mentioned that the military had recently identified dozens of Muslim Brotherhood supporters within its ranks, and that the men had been arrested and subjected to "reverse brainwashing." Only after that were they released from jail. "We are having a (culture) war with the Muslim Brotherhood in this country," bin Zayed told the US counterterrorism coordinator, Cofer Black, during a 2004 meeting.[99] Bin Zayed also felt like the clash of cultures was taking place inside his own family. He told a US delegation to Abu Dhabi in 2009 that his son had begun to take an interest in books on Islamic fundamentalism, and that, in response, he had sent him on a humanitarian mission to Ethiopia. But instead of the Red Crescent, bin Zayed sent his son to volunteer with the Red Cross. His son returned from the experience with a completely changed and far more positive perspective on the West.[100] In 2017, bin Zayed founded the Ministry of Tolerance to continue promoting a more moderate Islam. He declared 2019 as the year of tolerance and opened it by welcoming Pope Francis to the country for a historic visit. One of the most important projects he pursued in Abu Dhabi as part of this agenda was the Abrahamic Family House—which included a mosque, church and synagogue, designed to convey a message of religious tolerance.

Mohamed bin Zayed's loathing of the Muslim Brotherhood has had a far-reaching impact on the foreign policy of the United Arab Emirates. He sees Qatar, the UAE's northern neighbor, as the primary supporter of the Muslim Brotherhood, alongside Recep Tayyip Erdoğan's Turkey.[101] Bin Zayed believes that not only does Qatar fund the Muslim Brotherhood and its regional affiliates, but that it also disseminates their religious and political ideology through its propaganda outlets, first and foremost the Al Jazeera media network. He was the primary driver behind the decision by the Gulf states to cut ties with Qatar in 2017 and to institute a naval and aerial blockade of the small, independent emirate. Over the following years, the Emirates invested tens of millions of dollars in lobbying efforts against Qatar in Washington. Dozens of lobbyists and PR officers grew wealthy off the back of this move, but Qatar's standing within the US capital remained stubbornly resolute. The Trump administration brokered a resolution to the crisis between Saudi Arabia and the other Gulf states and Qatar in January 2021, an agreement bin Zayed accepted only grudgingly.

He did not believe that relations with Qatar could be rehabilitated, and sent the prime minister and ruler of Dubai, Mohammed bin Rashid, to the signing ceremony in Saudi Arabia in his place.

The Arab Spring was a wake-up call for Sheikh Mohamed. The US-backed overthrow of the Mubarak regime in Egypt and the subsequent rise of the Muslim Brotherhood, led by Mohamed Morsi, the Shia uprising in Bahrain and the revolution in Tunisia against President Zine El Abidine Ben Ali that ended with an Islamic party coming to power—all of these set alarm bells ringing for the leadership of the United Arab Emirates. Bin Zayed made it his mission to bring down the Muslim Brotherhood regime in Egypt. He supported the secular "Tamarod" movement, which led protests against Morsi's government, and the 2013 military coup led by General Abdel Fattah al-Sisi. When the latter won the presidential election, bin Zayed poured billions of dollars into the country in an attempt to revive the Egyptian economy and asked his close friend, the former British prime minister Tony Blair, to mentor the new Egyptian president. Despite all of this, the Egyptian economy has struggled to recover from the events surrounding the Arab Spring, and its current regime is even more restrictive and authoritarian than Mubarak's was.

But the Arab Spring also presented opportunities for Mohamed bin Zayed. The fall of the secular republics in Egypt, Syria, Libya and Tunisia raised the stock of the Arab monarchies in the Gulf— and especially of the United Arab Emirates, which remained stable and wealthy throughout. Bin Zayed used his economic and political capital to become a regional leader and attempt to expand his influence beyond his borders. He was not always successful. In 2015, together with his protégé, Saudi Crown Prince Mohammed bin Salman, he declared war on the Houthi rebels and their Iranian backers in Yemen. The war, which was declared the largest humanitarian disaster in the world by the UN in January 2021, resulted in the deaths of more than 230 thousand people, half of them from famine and disease. Human rights organizations across the board accused Saudi Arabia, the United Arab Emirates and the Houthi rebels of carrying out war crimes against innocent civilians. The war in Yemen became the Saudis' and Emiratis' Vietnam. In February 2020, after five years of fighting and hundreds of casualties—including his own nephew and son-in-law—Sheikh Mohamed pulled his troops out of the Yemeni quagmire. And yet, in those same years, he also took a side in the civil war in Libya, supporting the rebel commander, Khalifa Haftar, in his battle against the Qatari- and Turkish-backed Libyan government. The UAE set up bases in Libya and pumped tons of weapons and ammunition into the region, only to withdraw in early 2021.

On Friday, May 13, 2022, the presidential office in Abu Dhabi published a brief statement announcing the passing of President Khalifa bin Zayed. The UAE entered its second succession process in modern history, 18 years after the passing of Sheikh Zayed. The 40 days of mourning were the same as in 2004 but politically the process was less traumatic. The path was clear, and the transition was smooth. The next day, Sheikh Mohamed bin Zayed was elected to the presidency by the rulers of the individual emirates. MBZ's ascent was complete.

A former senior Mossad official who visited Abu Dhabi and met with Sheikh Mohamed on many occasions painted an evocative portrait of him: "He is a cat who looks into the mirror and sees a lion," he said. "He knows he's a cat, but he also knows that he's doing very well for a cat. He understood that from a young age, but through that determination he has changed his country from top to bottom."[102] Beyond his domestic reforms, Sheikh Mohamed's vision had one more important dimension: covert relations with Israel.

Jeremy and Jamal

Jeremy Issacharoff landed in Washington in the summer of 1993. The Israeli diplomat had just spent a year and a half as an assistant to the foreign minister, Shimon Peres, with a ring-side seat to the historic negotiations of the Oslo Accords. When he was appointed counselor for political affairs at the Israeli embassy in Washington, DC, it was the realization of a long-held dream. For Israeli diplomats, a posting in Washington is a career highlight; the equivalent of a soccer player being called up to play for the national team, and being appointed to the counselor for political affairs post was an achievement on a similar scale to famed Israeli attacking midfielder Eyal Berkovich scoring the winning goal against France in a World Cup qualifying match that same year.

It was a golden age for Israel on the soccer pitch and in the international diplomatic arena. Two years earlier, in the global shakeup that followed the Gulf War, the end of the Cold War, the collapse of the Soviet Union and the US's rise to becoming the sole superpower in a unipolar world, the Madrid Conference for the Middle East peace process got underway. For the first time since the founding of the State of Israel, Israelis, Syrians, Lebanese,

Jordanians and Palestinians sat around the same table discussing a diplomatic solution to the conflict and starting direct negotiations.

In addition to the direct talks with Israel's biggest enemies, the Madrid Conference also served as the launchpad for multilateral talks. Here it was possible to discuss matters of shared interest and general agreements: cooperation on water, agriculture, healthcare and the environment. The talks included representatives of countries that Israel had previously only dreamed of having contacts with— Saudi Arabia, the United Arab Emirates and Tunisia, among others.

The Madrid Conference and the launch of the peace process in 1991 led to diplomatic breakthroughs the likes of which Israel had not experienced since its founding. Two weeks before the conference and two months before it collapsed, the Soviet Union renewed the ties with Israel that had been cut in 1967 following the Six-Day War. Three months after the conference, a newly awakened and Western-facing China initiated diplomatic relations with Israel for the first time. A week after the Chinese, India also declared that it would be normalizing relations with Israel and engaging in full diplomatic relations.

Following Yitzhak Rabin's election victory in June 1992, he appointed a particularly big name to the Ministry of Foreign Affairs: Shimon Peres, who brought with him an equally high-profile deputy in Israeli domestic politics, Yossi Beilin. Peres, Rabin and Beilin inherited the peace process that had started with the Madrid Conference and ran with it. Direct talks took place in Washington between Israel and Syria, Lebanon and a Jordanian delegation that included Palestinian representatives from the West Bank.

Behind the scenes, however, another process was being set in motion; covert, dramatic and extraordinary in the historical context. Even before the elections in Israel were over, representatives of the Norwegian government and the director of a Norwegian research institute, Terje Rød-Larsen, reached out to Yossi Beilin with an offer to mediate talks with representatives of the PLO. Following the election, when Beilin was appointed deputy foreign minister, those proposals began to take shape.

Beilin said[103] that in September 1992, two months after he took up his new position, the Norwegian deputy foreign minister, Jan Egeland, traveled to Israel together with Larsen. During the visit, the two held a secret meeting with Beilin and a close associate of his, the historian Dr. Yair Hirschfeld. The four agreed to open a backchannel between Israel and the PLO. In December, negotiations began in Oslo. Hirschfeld was joined by Dr. Ron Pundak, and the Palestinians were represented in the talks by Ahmed Qurei (Abu Alaa).

At this stage, Beilin was acting in an unofficial capacity and did not inform Peres. He was afraid the foreign minister would immediately tell the prime minister, Yitzhak Rabin, who would scuttle the talks. At first there were only unofficial contacts, but progress was quicker than expected. Abu Alaa agreed to Israel's demands in exchange for Israeli recognition of the PLO, and a draft agreement was already on the table during the talks with Hirschfeld and Pundak in Oslo. At this stage, Beilin informed Peres, who passed the message on to Rabin, who ultimately gave the talks his blessing.

In May 1993, representatives of the Israeli government joined the talks, making them official—but the veil of secrecy remained. A breakthrough came on August 20, when Peres and the secretary-general of the PLO's Executive Committee at the time, Mahmoud Abbas, secretly signed the first of the Oslo Accords (known as Oslo I). A few days later, the news was announced, taking the Israeli public and the world by surprise. On September 9, Rabin and Arafat exchanged letters of mutual recognition, and four days later the Declaration of Principles was signed on the lawn in front of the White House. A new dawn was breaking over Israel and the Middle East.

Jeremy Issacharoff watched the events from his office in the Ministry of Foreign Affairs. He had been brought on board as negotiations moved into their final stages. When he reached Washington in the summer of 1993, he knew that a historic breakthrough with the Palestinians would define his diplomatic career, but he didn't realize the extent of it. After 15 years in the foreign service, Issacharoff's career scaled new heights. Despite his British manners and accent, he was hungry for success and ready to take on the world of Washington, DC: the Disneyland of international diplomacy and politics. "When I started out in Washington, new diplomatic opportunities had come up. At this critical moment, I hoped—much like any journalist—to be the one to be able to send the top-secret and confidential cables back to Jerusalem," he told me.[104] "Unlike a journalist, however, my target audience was very small, albeit informed and influential."

Washington, DC is a small town. Almost everyone who lives and works there is involved in politics, diplomacy, security and intelligence. Everyone knows everyone. Every few years, whenever the administration changes hands, everyone moves around. There is an unspoken revolving door policy. Today's member of Congress is tomorrow's lobbyist. The think tank expert becomes the deputy secretary of state overnight. The seasoned public relations officer from the consulting firm moves in to become the new White House spokesperson the day after the inauguration ceremony.

Barack Obama spoke of Washington as a bubble; his successor, Donald Trump, preferred the term "swamp." He also promised to drain it—and did the exact opposite. They were both right. Anyone who walks one block from the White House during lunchtime and steps into the Old Ebbitt Grill will find themselves surrounded by presidential advisors, lobbyists, policy experts, diplomats and spies. Anyone who heads to Cafe Milano in Georgetown in the evening will recognize members of Congress, cabinet secretaries, journalists, ambassadors and foreign leaders. Everyone talks to everyone. They gossip with and about each other and cut political and business deals.

Issacharoff learned about this side of the system a few weeks after he arrived in Washington. He was due to meet with the American diplomat, David Satterfield, for lunch at a Georgetown restaurant. Satterfield had recently been appointed director for Near East and South Asian affairs at the National Security Council by President Bill Clinton. While the two were chowing down, an elegant woman of around 40 made her way to their table. "Jeremy," said Satterfield, "this is Sandra, my predecessor."

Sandra Charles is the typical DC story. She was born into a military family and obtained a master's degree in international relations from Johns Hopkins University in Washington. From there, she successfully applied for an internship in the Office of the Secretary of Defense before moving on to a string of positions in the Pentagon, specializing in the Middle East. She kept climbing the ladder until she reached the position of head of Middle East affairs at the White House in the last two years of the Reagan administration and the first year of the Bush Sr. administration.

Then, in August 1991, she left the public sector. Like many of her colleagues, within a year she had founded a strategy and consulting firm that provided services to foreign governments seeking to open doors in Washington. Her clients were the same Middle Eastern governments she had previously worked opposite in her Pentagon and White House roles. The "revolving door" system has serious consequences for the political culture of the United

States. For foreign diplomats, journalists and spies, however, it's heaven. Issacharoff introduced himself politely and the two exchanged business cards. "As a diplomat, you don't always know who the people you're meeting are and how things will go with them, but I had a hunch about this woman," Issacharoff told me. "What I can say is, that lunch cost a few dollars, but the return on it and the breakthroughs that came from it were almost incalculable."[105]

Following that chance encounter in the Georgetown restaurant, Issacharoff and Charles began to speak on an almost weekly basis. At the time, she was interested in the negotiations between Israel and Syria, while he wanted inside information on the goings-on within the halls of power in Washington. Sometime in early 1994, the telephone in Issacharoff's office rang. On the other end was Charles, and what she had to say would forever transform Issacharoff's diplomatic career. "The United Arab Emirates wants to close a deal with the US to purchase F-16 fighter jets, and they'd like to avoid any conflict with you guys over it on Capitol Hill," she said.

The reason for her call on behalf of the Emiratis was all to do with QME—an acronym that is instantly familiar to Middle East experts and Washington bubble insiders with a keen interest in the region. QME, or Qualitative Military Edge, is a bedrock principle of the US's Middle East policy; a commitment to maintaining Israel's military superiority in the region. This principle was first put into practice by the United States in the wake of the disastrous Yom Kippur War in 1973. In 2008 it was enshrined in US law. The reasoning behind the QME principle is that Israel should have the most advanced military technology in the region to compensate for its smaller size (both territorially and demographically) in comparison to its enemies.[106]

That is why the US government has traditionally allowed Israel to be the first country in the region to receive its newest weapons systems. Israel received its first F-15 jets in 1976—six years before Saudi Arabia—and F-16 jets in 1980—three years before Egypt. When Arab countries purchased the same weapons systems, the Americans made sure they were inferior versions to the model in Israeli hands. Whenever Israel objected to the sale of a piece of tech to an Arab country, the US compensated it with a generous support package of its own.

In 1992, two years before Sandra Charles's call to Issacharoff, President Bush Sr. approved the sale of 72 F-15 jets to Saudi Arabia. The deal was a gesture of appreciation to the Saudis for their support in the Gulf War the year before, but it raised concerns within Israel. The thought that an enemy country would receive advanced fighter jets and station them in bases only a few minutes' flight from the nuclear reactor in Dimona led Prime Minister Yitzhak Rabin to raise objections to the deal with President Bush Sr.[107] AIPAC—the pro-Israel lobby—went to work on Capitol Hill to oppose it, and Democratic Congressman Mel Levine delivered a letter to President Bush (co-signed by 237 fellow lawmakers) calling on him to cancel it. It was all to no avail, and the deal went ahead. In exchange, however, and to uphold Israel's QME, the US supplied Israel with Apache and Black Hawk helicopters and placed stockpiles of thousands of bombs and rockets in Israel that the IDF could use in case of emergency.

The Emiratis were concerned about a rerun of the Saudi controversy. They had no desire to be dragged into a public political dispute with pro-Israel members of Congress and the potential for a long-term fallout. They wanted to find a way to reach a quiet understanding with the government in Jerusalem. The message they sent to the diplomat in the Israeli embassy in Washington was the first swallow of the summer of Israel and the UAE's ties. "That sounds interesting," Issacharoff told Charles about their desire to avoid a disagreement between the countries. "Tell them to send it to me directly so that I can see what it is exactly that they want." Issacharoff did not seek authorization from above. It was the spirit of the age; anything felt possible. Two weeks later, Charles invited him to a meeting. When he arrived at her office in Georgetown, a young Middle Eastern man in a suit was waiting for him. "Meet Dr. Jamal Al Suwaidi," Charles said to Issacharoff.

A year before Issacharoff received that first call from Charles, significant changes were coursing through Abu Dhabi. The president of the United Arab Emirates and the country's founding father, Sheikh Zayed bin Sultan Al Nahyan, had appointed his third son, Mohamed, as chief of staff of the armed forces—a significant stepping-stone on his way to the top.

After a few years as head of the air force and deputy chief of staff, Mohamed bin Zayed swept into his new role with revolutionary zeal. One of his first moves was to establish the Center for Strategic Studies and Research, a body that would provide him with situation reports and professional intelligence assessments on the Middle East as well as global trends.[108] He placed his foreign policy advisor, Dr. Jamal Al Suwaidi, an expert in political science with a PhD from the University of Wisconsin, in charge of the new center. At the time, Al Suwaidi was almost unknown within the Israeli diplomatic and security community, but he would quickly become a linchpin in the covert backchannels between the two countries.

After a quick introduction and exchange of pleasantries, Charles left the room. "Talk. Close the door behind you when you're done," she said. The conversation went on for several hours. The first subject of discussion was the fighter jet deal, but from there they quickly moved on to discussing Iraq and Iran, the Oslo Accords and the peace process with the Palestinians. The two hit it off almost immediately. As the conversation drifted from one subject to the next, it became increasingly clear they had very few areas of disagreement. "Israel is a small country surrounded by enemies, but one that knows how to cope with and tackle its security problems. We are the same," Al Suwaidi said to Issacharoff. At the end of the meeting, Issacharoff hurried back to the embassy to report to the ambassador, Itamar Rabinovich, who passed his report on to Prime Minister Rabin. "Keep talking with him," Rabinovich encouraged Issacharoff. And he did. The backchannel blossomed into a personal friendship. Issacharoff and Al Suwaidi would continue to stand at the heart of the ties between the countries for the next two decades.

But the Emiratis were not satisfied with the single backchannel they had opened through Issacharoff and the Israeli embassy in Washington. By thinking outside the box, they were able to establish an additional backchannel, one in which a man by the name of Shimon Sheves played a leading role. At the time, Sheves was one of the most powerful figures in Israel. Yitzhak Rabin's long-time right-hand man, in 1994 he was the director general of the Prime Minister's Office. One morning, a businessman and senior military reserves officer from a top-secret unit in the Israeli Air Force got in touch with Sheves and asked him for an urgent meeting. He told him about a fellow businessman by the name of Yousef Abbas who had approached him with a request. Abbas was a former officer in the UAE Air Force who now divided his time between Abu Dhabi and Lausanne in Switzerland. Abbas was well-connected with Sheikh Zayed, who knew about his business dealings with Israeli businessmen and asked him to find a way to deliver a message to Rabin. The subject: the F-16 deal with the United States. "We had the same interests then as we do today.

They were concerned about Shia attempts to take over the region. They wanted to be prepared for an Iranian attack—and they were putting together an army," Sheves told me.[109]

Sheves told Rabin about the unexpected message. The prime minister was enthusiastic. "Meet with him and see what he wants," he said. The two men arranged to meet in Munich. Sheves came to the Four Seasons Hotel by himself. Aside from Rabin and the Israeli officer who had acted as the go-between, nobody knew about the secret trip. He and Abbas had a long conversation over dinner, talking about the fighter jet deal and discussing economic cooperation. Sheves was delighted. "Until that point, there had been no communication with the UAE. Not even through the Mossad," he said. Sheves went back to Jerusalem and reported to Rabin, who told him to keep going and moving forward.

Only three people knew about the secret talks on the Israeli side: Rabin, Sheves and the head of the Mossad, Shabtai Shavit. A few weeks later, Sheves flew abroad for another meeting, this time in Zurich. For this meeting, Abbas brought along another man: Omar, from the UAE intelligence agency. The two were very anxious about the possibility of the meeting being revealed. They emphasized over and over again the sensitivity of the matter and the imperative to treat it with the utmost confidentiality. "I told them that anyone around Yitzhak Rabin knows how to keep a secret," Sheves recalled. The meeting in Zurich ended with a remarkable breakthrough: a date was set for a meeting between Sheves and the minister of state at the foreign ministry of the United Arab Emirates, Sheikh Hamdan bin Zayed, the president's fourth son.

For this momentous occasion, Sheves was accompanied by a high-ranking Mossad official. The two boarded an El Al flight to Paris. A business jet belonging to the UAE government picked them up at Le Bourget Airport and took them to Geneva. After dinner with the minister's entourage, one of his advisors unexpectedly told them that the sheikh had asked to meet with Sheves alone. The Mossad official attempted to object but was left with no choice but to stay behind, disappointed. Sheves had attended countless meetings with senior Palestinian, Jordanian and Egyptian officials over the years—some in the open and some in secret—but that short trip to meet with the Emirati sheikh in Geneva's Intercontinental Hotel felt completely different. "They received me outside the hotel in their white *Kanduras* [traditional Emirati robes] and swords," Sheves remembered. "It felt like something from Ali Baba and the Forty Thieves. There were no smart phones back then, so I couldn't ask them for a selfie, but it was incredible."

The meeting with Sheikh Hamdan was the first time that an official representative of the State of Israel had ever met with a member of the Emirati royal family. Sheves presented the sheikh with a gift: a woodcut of Jerusalem and the Al-Aqsa Mosque. The sheikh gave him a traditional Emirati *khanjar* dagger which still holds pride of place in his office. "He told me that this meeting was made possible by the Oslo process and the diplomatic contacts with the Palestinians," Sheves told me.[110] Bin Zayed told Sheves that the UAE was interested in opening a backchannel with Israel both because of the close relationship between Israel and the United States—and their respective leaders, Rabin and Clinton—and because of the Iranian threat. As the meeting drew to a close, he made a formal request to Sheves that Israel refrain from objecting to the fighter jet deal. Sheves told him there and then that Rabin had agreed in principle and that he would say as much to the Americans. "Rabin saw a shared interest between the UAE and Israel when it came to Shia Iran," said Sheves. "That potential conflict was a concern even back then. The more things change, the more they stay the same."

The meeting, which had only started at 10:30 PM, ran into the early hours of the morning. When Sheves returned to his hotel, he found the disgruntled Mossad officer waiting for him in the lobby. After a short debrief, Sheves heard there was an urgent message waiting for him at reception: "Call Amnon Lipkin-Shahak, no matter the time." The number of people who were privy to Sheves's trip could be counted on one hand. Sheves had no idea how Lipkin-Shahak, the deputy chief of staff of the Israeli military and a close personal friend, had learned that he was in Geneva. At six o'clock in the morning, Sheves called Lipkin-Shahak from his hotel room, waking him up and receiving a volley of abuse for his trouble. "You miserable creature, you go to meet with a prince from Abu Dhabi and you don't tell the deputy chief of staff of the IDF?! Your friend who was head of the Intelligence Directorate?!"

Sheves tried to apologize awkwardly. "Amnon, I'm really sorry. Rabin asked that nobody other than me and the head of the Mossad learn about this trip. You know that I keep my secrets. You've known me since I was a soldier in your battalion. But how did you find out?" The story Lipkin-Shahak told him in many ways sums up the early days of the peace process in 1994. President Sheikh Zayed of the UAE, King Hassan II of Morocco and Yasser Arafat's deputy and successor, Mahmoud Abbas, used to be neighbors in Rabat. Ever since, they would meet once a year for a weekend in the countryside and go hunting. At breakfast, Sheikh Zayed had told King Hassan and Abbas that his son was due to meet Yitzhak Rabin's advisor in Geneva that evening. The first thing Abbas did after breakfast was call his friend, Amnon Lipkin-Shahak. "You son of a bitch," Abbas said to the Israeli deputy chief of staff. "How could you not tell me that Shimon Sheves is on his way to meet with Sheikh Zayed's son in Geneva?"

In May 1995, Yitzhak Rabin came for what would be one of his last visits to Washington. One of his first meetings in the city was with the secretary of defense, William Perry. Jeremy Issacharoff sat behind Rabin and took notes. He waited on tenterhooks for the Americans to raise the fighter jet deal with the Emirates—and even more so for Rabin's response. Finally, it came. "We won't fight you over the deal," Rabin told Perry. Later on in the visit, in his meeting with President Clinton in the White House, Rabin repeated the message.

"During those months, with the renewal of the peace process and the energy it was generating, I remembered the quote from Star Trek, about space being the final frontier. I felt like expanding our ties with the Arab world had become one of Israel's most significant foreign policy goals," recalled Issacharoff. He had no idea how right he was. The next day, in the Four Seasons Hotel in Washington, a short, secret meeting took place between Rabin and the son of the Emirati ruler, Sheikh Hamdan bin Zayed. The sheikh shook Rabin's hand and thanked him for agreeing to the deal.

Six months later, Rabin was assassinated. In the wake of the assassination, Sheves fielded numerous calls from senior Emirati officials. "They were distraught," he said. "They understood that the peace process would never be the same again." Nonetheless, the ties with the United Arab Emirates survived the assassination. Rabin's gesture on the fighter jet deal led to another breakthrough soon after—the first Israeli government presence in the United Arab Emirates.

Bruce

He sat facing me in his small, nondescript office at the Director General's Office in the foreign ministry in Jerusalem. With his blue eyes, bashful smile, beard and cotton button-down shirt open at the collar, he looked far younger than his 75 years. His unremarkable features gave no indication that this man was one of the most distinguished and successful diplomats in Israel's history. In 30 years of secret trips around the Middle East, establishing covert backchannels between Israel and the Gulf countries, Bruce Kashdan had never once briefed or been interviewed by a journalist. His face was forbidden for publication and, with the exception of a few stray articles that escaped from under the watchful eye of the Israeli Military Censor, his name was known to very few people; Gulf royalty, Arab business leaders, American diplomats and Iranian spies.

As a medical student at SUNY Upstate Medical University 55 years earlier, he could never have anticipated where life would take him. When he wasn't studying anatomy, Kashdan devoted most of his time to supporting the local community. On one such occasion, he signed up to help local farmers who had been ripped off by the large retail stores they sold their milk to. He proposed that the farmers protest by driving their milk tankers into the center of the village of Canton, NY and dumping their milk in the streets, and he invited the press to attend the scene. His efforts carried a localized protest in a small village in the far corner of New York State into the national press. Two weeks later, he was invited to a White House meeting with advisors of President Richard Nixon. The White House was looking to establish a national volunteers' organization, and Kashdan seemed like a fitting candidate for the initiative. Not long after, he was already working full time at the White House.

Word of the young Jewish social activist working in the White House soon reached Israeli diplomats in the embassy, who invited him to lunch with Shimeon Amir, the head of Mashav—the Agency for International Development Cooperation in the Israeli Ministry of Foreign Affairs. Over lunch at the Hilton Hotel in Washington, Amir turned Kashdan's life on its head. "I want you to come to Israel and work for the foreign ministry," he told the young man. Kashdan was bewildered. He had never been to Israel before, and most of what he knew about Jerusalem he had picked up from his bar mitzvah. "I looked at the map and I saw that 'Jerusalem' appeared in letters so large that they extended over the whole country," he told me. Deciding to seize the opportunity for an adventure that had been dangled before him, he took unpaid leave from the White House and flew to Israel. After completing an intensive Hebrew course in a school in Kibbutz Givat Haim, the foreign ministry sent him on a three-month-long embassy-hopping trip across Africa, Asia and Latin America so that he could offer suggestions on how Israel could improve its global aid distribution. When he returned, he was offered a permanent position. Having barely found his feet in Israel, he was confused.

He had thought he was being offered a temporary change of scenery. It was only after he signed the forms that he realized his superiors had different intentions.

When Dave Kimche was appointed director general of the foreign ministry, he took Kashdan under his wing. Kimche, a former senior Mossad official, reminded the younger man of many of his colleagues from his White House days, and Kashdan soon became his protégé. In 1982, when IDF forces invaded Lebanon and began to advance northward through the country, Kimche asked him to go to Beirut and open an extension of the foreign ministry there. Kashdan didn't ask questions. He got into his private car and pointed it north until he caught up with the IDF forces. He set himself up in the Baabda District on the outskirts of Beirut and started building connections with local power brokers. He lived in Beirut for almost two years, until he was forced to leave when the Syrian intelligence services placed a bounty on his head. Years later, waiting in line for coffee at the UN headquarters in New York, he found himself standing behind the deputy foreign minister of Syria at the time, Walid Muallem. The two struck up a conversation, and Kashdan revealed his identity to Muallem and brought up his previous encounter with Syrian intelligence. "I get that you put a bounty on my head, but really, am I only worth 80 thousand dollars?" He asked the stunned Syrian official.

Following his return from Beirut, Kashdan was dispatched to the United Kingdom. At the time, neighboring Ireland was refusing to allow Israel to open an embassy in the country. Kashdan met with Irish diplomats in quiet corners of dimly lit London bars, building relationships over pints of beer and long conversations into the small hours. Later, he started hopping across to Dublin in an attempt to establish direct channels of communication with the government. "There too, I learned that the most successful approach to diplomacy is through trust and personal relationships," he told me.[111] A period of secret talks finally yielded a breakthrough, and the Irish agreed to allow Israel to open an embassy in Dublin. "The fact that [Israeli President Chaim] Herzog had an Irish background was very helpful. I arranged a visit for him and that helped to move things forward," Kashdan said.

The next stop for Kashdan was the Madrid Conference. In 1991, he was assigned as the point of contact for the Gulf state delegations to the conference. When diplomats from the Gulf approached him for help with logistical matters, he seized the opportunity to build relationships with them. He met them again when he was the assistant to the cabinet secretary, Elyakim Rubinstein, in the multilateral talks that emerged from the Madrid Conference. A few weeks after those talks began, a Qatari diplomat reached out to him, wanting to know whether Israel would be interested in procuring gas from Qatar. Kashdan reported the conversation to the foreign minister, Shimon Peres, and asked for his permission to fly to Doha to discuss the matter further. Peres approved a 24-hour lightning visit. In Doha, Kashdan met with the foreign minister and future prime minister, Hamad bin Jassim, who would become one of Israel's most important contacts in the Gulf. The foreign ministry and energy ministry in Jerusalem gave their support for the move and a few months later Kashdan returned to Doha with the minister of energy, Gonen Segev, to sign a memorandum of understanding.

No gas flowed from the meeting, but Kashdan's name did start to make its way around the offices of Gulf leaders. He increasingly found himself the go-to man for all manner of requests originating in the region, until eventually the foreign ministry appointed him as its envoy. Despite the opaqueness that surrounded his visits, the business cards he produced in the meeting rooms were Israeli. His approach was always the same. First, he would open a discreet channel of communication with a senior figure in the state who knew he was Israeli. After that, he would start working on putting together small projects—in water, agriculture, healthcare and similar sectors.

Kashdan told me that his connections in the Gulf came through the chairman of one of the Arab airlines, whom he had befriended. "He said that he supported the peace process and wanted to help," Kashdan recalled. "He suggested that I accompany him to places in the Gulf where he had meetings. Once there, I would go off to my meetings and he would go to his." In the evenings, the same businessman organized dinners that went on late into the night. He invited business leaders, senior government officials and intelligence officers who came for the food, but also for quiet conversations far from prying eyes. Kashdan used these meals to expand his network of contacts in the region. This contact opened doors for Kashdan in at least three Arab countries. Then, once he had built up sufficient connections within one country, he would ask those new connections to open doors in others.

For a few years, he traveled solo around the Gulf. In 1998, backup arrived. Josh Zarka was a young diplomat at the time. He had graduated from the foreign ministry's cadet course for new diplomats only a few months previously and had received his first posting in the North America office. He met Kashdan one day in the halls of the foreign ministry. Zarka was curious as to what it was exactly that Kashdan did. When he asked, the latter replied, "I'm involved in peacemaking." Zarka told Kashdan that he was also interested in doing exactly that. A few weeks later, Zarka was transferred to the Office of the Director General of the foreign ministry, working alongside Kashdan. At first, Zarka sat in the ministry headquarters and received updates from Kashdan as he traveled around the Gulf. But the director general soon decided that Zarka should join Kashdan on his trips. "It was all very basic. They issued me with a foreign phone, a precise sum of money in cash for daily expenses and a warning to be careful around the Arabs," Zarka told me.[112]

At home, a veil of secrecy continued to surround Kashdan and Zarka's journeys around the Gulf. Most of the employees of the foreign ministry were none the wiser—and the same was true for most other government offices. The fact that the two men were discreet and unassuming helped. The upper echelons of the Israeli business community, on the other hand, were in on the secret. Kashdan and Zarka's entire modus operandi revolved around building business and commercial ties as a stepping-stone to diplomatic ties. The first meetings were always with unofficial or business contacts in Oman, Qatar, Bahrain and the United Arab Emirates. Meetings with more official officeholders grew out of those initial contacts. On their trips, Kashdan and Zarka brought senior doctors, CEOs of large companies and, above all, tech entrepreneurs. They briefed the Israeli businesspeople on how to conduct business in the Gulf, how to set up international branches of their companies to avoid drawing attention to themselves and how to find employees who were eligible to fly to these countries.

The pair spent two weeks of every month in the Gulf— arranging meetings with businesspeople in Dubai and government officials in Abu Dhabi, then hopping over to Qatar or Bahrain when they were done. To an extent, they were making it up as they went along—"like in the days of the Palmach [pre-Israeli independence fighting force]," as one senior official in the foreign ministry put it. If anything went wrong, they didn't really have anyone to talk to. On one of their visits to Bahrain, the border police held Zarka at the airport for several hours, releasing him only a few minutes before his flight was due to take off. In hindsight, the two admit, there was more than a touch of naivety and recklessness in their approach. A sign in Kashdan's small office in the Ministry of Foreign Affairs reads "Never Never Quit," and that was exactly how he and Zarka worked. "Every time someone closed the door on us, we managed to get in through the window," they told me.

Several business deals were signed in this way over the years, and they were almost always kept secret. "We never had a case where someone from the business sector leaked," said Zarka. At the height of his operation, Kashdan had close to 2,500 contacts in the Gulf states. Throughout those years, he and his team were directly or indirectly involved in 600 business deals involving Israeli companies in the Gulf. "A lot of people were in on the secret, but despite that it was kept quiet," he told me. "I told them that if they succeeded in doing business there, it would help the State of Israel diplomatically." These business projects were not always successful. On one occasion, they discussed a deal with the CEO of a large company to set up a factory that never went through. On another, they took senior officials from the Ministry of Agriculture to Dubai to set up a farm. It is unclear to what extent the project bore fruit. Even so, every deal and every discussion allowed Kashdan and Zarka to improve their diplomatic standing in the Gulf. "We didn't get that many deals out of it, but ultimately it got us into meetings with the foreign ministers of Bahrain and the UAE," Zarka told me.

Kashdan's secret project was also very convenient for the governments in the Gulf states. They wanted ties with Israelis, as long as they could be kept under wraps. "Anyone who needed to know that I was Israeli knew, and anyone who didn't—didn't. I wanted them to know I was Israeli because the diplomatic aspect was integral to the process, so during the meetings I would hand out an Israeli business card," Kashdan recalled. On one of those trips, he attended a meeting in the palace with a senior advisor to one of the Gulf rulers. Kashdan came bearing a message from the government in Jerusalem regarding the ties between the countries. "As long as it benefits you and it benefits our people and it's done quietly—you are welcome here and you can stay for as long as you like," the senior advisor told him. This was the approach in all the Gulf states, Kashdan said: shared interests and secret contacts.

Countless foreign ministry officials I spoke to told me that Kashdan was different to any diplomat who has ever served in Israel's foreign service. They put it down to his unique blend of infectious charisma and boundless energy, combined with a reputation for being unfailingly trustworthy and possessed of an inspiring vision—and no ego. "None of the foreign ministers over the years have ever known quite what to make of him, but every one of them understood that he was an asset they could not afford to do without. He had zero formal authority or power—everything he did was purely down to his individual charm and powers of persuasion," Zarka told me. "He used his talents to do things that others could not have done," added the Israeli ambassador to Japan, Gilad Cohen, who worked with Kashdan when he was head of the coordination department at the Director General's Office.[113] "Leaders throughout the region knew him—and every door was open to him." The director general of the foreign ministry, Alon Ushpiz, told me that Kashdan's main gift was an unswerving commitment to making things happen. "He's hugely determined, creative and good at connecting with people—and that's what brought him so much success," Ushpiz said.[114]

In a way, Kashdan and Zarka's connections in the United Arab Emirates were a byproduct of the discussions that had taken place in Washington a few years earlier over the F-16 deal. Jeremy

Issacharoff, the diplomat at the embassy in Washington, knew about Kashdan's secret assignments and put him in touch with his Emirati contact, Dr. Jamal Al Suwaidi. Every time Kashdan came to Abu Dhabi, he would meet with Al Suwaidi at his research institute, which was under the authority of Sheikh Mohamed bin Zayed.

The whole time, the specter of the Israeli–Palestinian conflict hovered over this delicate, fragile relationship. When the Second Intifada broke out in 2000, the communication channel appeared to be on the verge of being discontinued. In May 2001, the Israeli Air Force bombed Palestinian Authority buildings in the West Bank in response to a suicide bombing in Netanya. Kashdan, who was in Abu Dhabi at the time, was informed by his Emirati hosts that he should leave and not return. Al Suwaidi, who did not want to see the ties broken off, asked to speak to Issacharoff as a matter of urgency. A few weeks later, Issacharoff came to Abu Dhabi together with Kashdan. The conversation with Al Suwaidi in his research institute lasted for seven hours. Issacharoff decided to direct the discussion toward the situation in Iraq, which was of grave concern to the Emiratis at the time. They went their separate ways—and Al Suwaidi went to update Sheikh Mohamed. In the evening, the three met once more at the Israelis' hotel. "The net result was that instead of expelling Bruce, the Emiratis began to hold bi-monthly strategy meetings with us," a senior official in the foreign ministry told me. Over the months that followed, Issacharoff continued to visit Abu Dhabi with Kashdan. In one of their sessions discussing Iraq, Sheikh Hazza bin Zayed—the head of the national security apparatus—showed up. In another, they were invited to the home of Sheikh Abdullah bin Zayed, the minister of information at the time. Even in those days of heightened tensions, the strategic threats in the region created shared interests that allowed them to continue their backchannel discussions despite the disagreements over the situation with the Palestinians.

The disengagement from the Gaza Strip in August 2005 led to another step forward in the secret ties between Israel and the UAE. Six months before IDF forces began to evict the Jewish residents of Gush Katif from the Gaza Strip, Mohamed Alabbar, the chairman of Emaar Properties, the largest real estate company in Dubai, visited Israel. Alabbar's trip was sanctioned by the ruler of Dubai and prime minister of the United Arab Emirates, Sheikh Mohammed bin Rashid Al Maktoum, and the crown prince of Abu Dhabi, Sheikh Mohamed bin Zayed, going ahead with their blessing.[115] The goal was to launch a new economic and diplomatic initiative which would include the construction of modern, Dubai-style residential neighborhoods in the areas where Israeli settlements in the Gaza Strip were located at the time. He met with the Palestinian president, Mahmoud Abbas, and the Israeli prime minister, Ariel Sharon. Both sides were enthusiastic about the idea, but the Israeli side rushed to leak to the press that Alabbar had offered to "buy" the settlements in Gush Katif. The story raised a public outcry in the Emirates. Alabbar came under attack—and the proposal fell through. This move by the Emirates may have been unsuccessful, but it was another data point in the trend of closer ties with Israel. In September, a few weeks after the last IDF soldier had left the Gaza Strip, Sheikh Mohamed met with a group of US generals who had come for a visit to Abu Dhabi. "The Gaza disengagement was a brave move by the Israelis," he told them.[116] The disengagement did not bring Israel's ties with the UAE out into the open, but it did solidify their covert coordination.

In late 2005, Kashdan and other senior officials in the foreign ministry reached out to the United Arab Emirates with a proposal: to establish an unofficial Israeli "embassy" in Dubai. Kashdan told the Emiratis that he was already spending a lot of time in Dubai, and everyone who needed to know about the arrangement already knew, so why not allow him to open an office dedicated to promoting trade between the countries? The Emiratis knew that the office would also serve other purposes, but the trust that had been built up over the years and the credit generated by the Israeli withdrawal from Gaza led them to reason that they would benefit significantly from such an arrangement. They agreed, and in 2006 a new company opened in Dubai under the trading name, "The Center for International Trade and Development." All the board members and employees of the company were Israeli diplomats who reported directly to the Office of the Director General in Jerusalem.

No sooner had the secret office in Dubai opened than the foreign ministry encountered an immediate problem: how to recruit suitable candidates for a role that required the utmost discretion and the psychological fortitude to cope with the solitude of life undercover. The initial batch of candidates for the new office were mostly very junior diplomats, some of them straight out of the cadet course. Diplomatic training for a foreign ministry cadet involves learning to give interviews, make public appearances, deliver speeches and conduct themselves in formal meetings as representatives of the State of Israel. Almost none of which was transferable to a secret office. "We looked into which of our young candidates had a suitable profile and called them into the Director General's Office," recalled Gilad Cohen, who was responsible for the secret diplomatic mission in Dubai within the office. "When they came in, we offered them to become diplomats of a completely different sort." Many of the candidates were unwilling, and unlike other postings, this one they were allowed to turn down. Liron Zaslansky was one of those young diplomats. In 2008, she was in the middle of her first posting, in Costa Rica, when she received the call from the Office of the Director General. "They asked if I wanted to go to Dubai," she told me.[117] "At first I said no, and then a few days later I said yes."

Those who agreed to go to the Gulf were made to sign a draconian non-disclosure agreement that forbade them from discussing their posting, including the location, with anyone other than their partners and the 20 or so people in the Israeli government who knew about the arrangement. That number grew over the years, but most of the government remained unaware of the mission in Dubai. The years-long presence was only finally revealed several weeks after the Abraham Accords and the normalization agreements between Israel and the UAE were announced. The names and photographs of the Israeli diplomats were not even cleared for publication at a ceremony in their honor, attended by Foreign Minister Gabi Ashkenazi a few months after the agreements. The Israeli diplomats interviewed for this book were not always enthusiastic to do so. For most of them, talking to a journalist about that period was the ultimate sin. They never imagined the day would come when they would be allowed to tell their stories.

The life of Zaslansky and the other diplomats in Dubai was different to that of Israeli diplomats anywhere else in the world. The office itself was managed like any other Israeli diplomatic mission, right down to the pictures of Israeli landscapes that adorned the walls. Away from the office, however, the diplomats conducted themselves like Western businesspeople. They were forbidden from speaking Hebrew under any circumstances—on the phone to each other, on the street, in social gatherings at cafés or in business meetings. One of the team, an observant Jew, had to consult with a rabbi (who worked with the intelligence community and had security clearance) to find ways to maintain a religious

Jewish lifestyle in a place with no kosher food, no ritual baths and no synagogues.

Few matters were more complicated to arrange than security. Eventually, the foreign ministry introduced dedicated security-related courses for diplomats assigned to secret postings that went beyond the scope of the regular cadet program. Unlike diplomats whose work was conducted in the open, in Dubai there was no possibility of stationing Israeli security officers in public. A senior foreign ministry official told me there were only around 10 people in on the secret within the UAE government. In the early days, one of the diplomats serving in Dubai while the secret diplomatic mission was being set up reported to the foreign ministry that she had been under surveillance for a whole day. The foreign ministry's chief security officer called his contacts in the local security forces. "Don't worry," they told him, "That's us."

Gilad Cohen, who was in charge of the mission, told me that for years, he struggled to sleep at night. "It was extremely dangerous," he said.[118] "Our assessment was that even if the office was working undercover, eventually the Iranians would find out about it. At the end of the day, our people there were building contacts with locals to promote Israeli interests, whether that meant business deals or agricultural cooperation. When you think about it, this diplomatic mission was a pretty amazing operation."

On one occasion, an Israeli diplomat posted to Dubai was even a little too successful. He built up an extensive network of contacts and became a highly prominent member of the business community in Dubai. He also left a digital footprint that showed up almost instantly in any simple internet search. Eventually the Emirati authorities intervened and asked him to reduce his presence over concerns that he would expose the Israeli mission and cause a diplomatic stir. "I had friends there who were expats working in Dubai, but they didn't know who I really was," Zaslansky told me.[119] "Whenever they asked me about my life, I told them the truth about my family or my hobbies—but without mentioning Israel. As soon as I left, I cut off contact with them. Most of them never found out who I really am." The majority of the diplomats who went to Dubai did so either alone or with a partner. Diplomats with children were forbidden from serving there. The isolation and the double life came at a significant social and psychological cost. Every two or three months they would be sent back to Israel to relax and recharge their batteries. Unable to share their experiences and their stories with almost anyone else, that didn't always make things easier. "The offices in the Gulf occupied most of my time," said Dor Shapira, the Israeli ambassador to Portugal. Shapira spent a few years as head of the Department of Coordination within the Office of the Director General at the foreign ministry, directly responsible for the offices in the Gulf.[120] "You sit in the office and you're essentially the surrogate mother and father for the diplomats out there—part boss and part psychologist. They need support and encouragement, and that requires a lot of patience."

When it came to building covert relationships with the UAE, the foreign ministry took the lead within the Israeli government. Three senior officials in the foreign ministry who were closely involved in these efforts over the past three decades told me that it was the foreign ministry that opened the doors in Abu Dhabi for the Mossad in the early '90s and helped them open communication channels with the Emirati intelligence agency. The diplomatic discussions in Abu Dhabi in those days always started with the Palestinians, with the Emiratis emphasizing their commitment to the Palestinian cause. From there, talk would quickly turn to subjects that were of more interest to both sides: Iraq, Iran, the Muslim Brotherhood and fighting terrorism. "People emerged from conversations in the UAE astounded," one senior official in the foreign ministry told me. "You really had to make an effort to find any areas of disagreement." The Israeli diplomats serving in Dubai devoted a significant chunk of their time to economic efforts, but every week or two they would travel to Abu Dhabi for discussions on diplomatic affairs. One of their key contacts in Abu Dhabi was Yousef Al Otaiba, the senior advisor to Sheikh Mohamed bin Zayed. Before the Abraham Accords, Al Otaiba held the "Israeli affairs" portfolio within the UAE. Most of the meetings with him took place in the gym where he worked out in Abu Dhabi.

Al Otaiba was born in 1974 to one of the wealthiest and most well-connected families outside of the royals themselves. Starting as traders, they rose to become the most important family in the "administrative" class: senior public servants outside of the royal family. The Al Otaiba sons and daughters forged marital bonds with the Al Nahyan tribe of the state's founder, Sheikh Zayed. They hold many of the senior public service roles in the United Arab Emirates today. Yousef was an only child to his mother—an Egyptian citizen and one of the wives of Mana Saeed Al Otaiba, the first minister of petroleum and mineral resources of the UAE and a member of the founding generation of the state. Yousef spent his childhood with his mother in Cairo. He attended the American High School in the city and grew up in very different surroundings to those in Abu Dhabi. After high school, he went to study international relations at Georgetown University. When he returned to the UAE, he was appointed as deputy general manager of the automotive division of his family's company. At age 26, he met Sheikh Mohamed bin Zayed at a social gathering. Sheikh Mohamed, the armed forces chief of staff at the time, was very impressed with the young man. "Would you like to work for me?" he asked him. Al Otaiba agreed without a second thought. The first task assigned to him by Sheikh Mohamed was to return to the United States for further academic studies, this time to spend a year at the National Defense University in Washington, DC. When he returned to Abu Dhabi after his studies, Sheikh Mohamed appointed him as his foreign policy advisor in charge of the US portfolio—the sole civilian among many military figures. He took up his new role only a few months before the 9/11 attacks. Two Emirati citizens were among the hijackers of United Airlines Flight 175 that struck the South Tower of the World Trade Center. Some of the money that financed the attacks had gone through banks and facilitators in the UAE. Al Otaiba found himself firmly in the eye of the storm. "It was a baptism of fire," Al Otaiba told me as he struggled to express how traumatic those days had been for him. He quickly became Sheikh Mohamed's right-hand man and a key player in the Emirati–American relationship. "A combination of loyalty, savvy and smarts have propelled Yousef's quick ascension once he got his foot in the door," wrote Martin Quinn, charge d'affaires of the US embassy in Abu Dhabi.[121] As Mohamed bin Zayed's power and influence grew, so too did Al Otaiba's standing, both men increasing in prominence until Sheikh Mohamed was appointed crown prince upon the death of his father, Sheikh Zayed, in 2004.

Al Otaiba grew so close to Sheikh Mohamed that it was eventually widely accepted that his pronouncements were the closest vocalization of the crown prince's own thoughts. The voice was entirely Al Otaiba's, but the words were those of Sheikh Mohamed. When he took up his ambassador's post in Washington, it was an unrivaled opportunity, and one that opened all manner of doors. Al Otaiba's years at the American High School and universities in DC had given his English a perfect American twang. He adopted American etiquette and developed a profound understanding of the local culture, society and politics. He is pleasant, kind and friendly but also sharp and no-nonsense. In his many years in Washington, he shied away from media interviews and maintained a low profile. He used his reserves of personal charm to build relationships with politicians on both sides of the aisle, as well as senior figures in research institutes in the US capital and journalists whom he would meet with regularly for background conversations. Al Otaiba's network of connections in Washington soon made him one of the most influential people in the city.

When he had worked for Sheikh Mohamed in Abu Dhabi, he had been entrusted with the Israeli affairs portfolio. He was the primary point of contact for the head of the secret Israeli diplomatic mission in Dubai, Bruce Kashdan, and the other Israeli diplomats serving undercover in the country. "The conversations with Yousef were open and frank. We knew that with him, yes meant yes and no meant no," Israeli diplomat Liron Zaslansky told me.[122] Al Otaiba continued to hold the Israeli affairs portfolio even after his posting to Washington. A meeting with him became a regular fixture for many Israeli officials on their visits to the US capital, including the former director of the Political-Military Affairs Bureau, Amos Gilead, the former head of the IDF Military Intelligence Directorate, Amos Yadlin and the former heads of the Mossad, Tamir Pardo and Yossi Cohen. Those who met him were regularly struck by the depth of his knowledge on Israel and its domestic politics.

In late June 2021, I boarded El Al Flight 975 to Abu Dhabi. This was to be my second visit to the Emirates since the peace treaty with Israel was signed. This trip was also noteworthy within a historical context as the first time an Israeli foreign minister had set out on an official and public visit to the UAE. In the 10 months that followed the declaration on the Abraham Accords in August

2020, Prime Minister Netanyahu had vetoed any and all visits to the Emirates by government ministers. He wanted to be the first to visit and made no fewer than five attempts to organize a trip to Abu Dhabi. Three times he had to delay the trip at the last minute, an additional attempt was thwarted by the Jordanians after they failed to respond to a request for permission to use their airspace and the final attempt, a few days before the March 2021 elections, was turned down by the Emiratis. Netanyahu remained like Moses, within sight of the promised land but unable to enter it. Instead, it was Yair Lapid who received the red-carpet treatment and who cut the ribbon on the Israeli embassy in Abu Dhabi. As I waited to board the plane in Israel, I saw a familiar face slowly making its way over to me. Bruce Kashdan flashed me his quiet, endearing smile and gave me a big hug. Netanyahu had not wanted him there for the signing ceremony at the White House in September 2020. In the end, he attended as a guest of the government of the United Arab Emirates. For Lapid's visit, he was a guest of honor. It felt like closure. He received the recognition he so richly deserved.

The Dubai Scandal

On January 20, 2010, Mahmoud Abdel Rauf walked into the Al Bustan Rotana Hotel in Dubai. The security cameras on the second floor tracked him out of the elevator and as far as the door to room 230, where he was staying. And where he died. His body was discovered the next day, lying on his bed in his pajamas. At first glance, he appeared to have passed away in his sleep, perhaps from a heart attack. For nine days, his death was kept quiet. The only ones who knew were the assassins, the investigators in the Dubai Police Force and the senior leadership of Hamas. On Friday, January 29, the day after his body was taken to Damascus, Hamas spokesman Izzat Al Risheq revealed that the full name of the man assassinated in Dubai was Mahmoud Abdel Rauf al-Mabhouh. He claimed that the Mossad was behind the hit and warned that Hamas would exact revenge.

Al-Mabhouh was born in the Jabalia refugee camp in the Gaza Strip and was among the founders of the military wing of Hamas in the late 1980s. He was involved in two of the most notorious terrorist attacks at the time: the kidnapping and murder of soldiers Ilan Saadon and Avi Sasportas. Al-Mabhouh had spent most of the two decades preceding his assassination at Hamas's headquarters in Damascus. From 2004 onward, he served as the organization's head of logistics and weapons procurement. He communicated with Iran and Hezbollah to transfer rockets, mortars and technological knowhow into the Gaza Strip. "When it came to weapons smuggling, al-Mabhouh was to Hamas what Qasem Soleimani was for the Islamic Revolutionary Guard Corps in Iran and Imad Mughniyeh for Hezbollah,"[123] a former Mossad official who was closely involved with the incident told me.[124] "Al-Mabhouh was a one-man show, and he managed all of Hamas's weapons procurement and stockpiling with a little notebook. He ticked all the boxes for an assassination target: a man whose actions caused Israeli casualties, who held a unique position that Hamas would struggle to fill and someone whose assassination would increase the deterrent effect and send a message to the leadership of Hamas." Other members of the Israeli security establishment and intelligence community felt differently, but that was only in hindsight. At the time, nobody raised any objections.

In the fortnight that followed the discovery of his body, speculation ran rife. Numerous reports with varying degrees of credibility were published covering the background of the story. Eventually, on February 15, the commander of the Dubai Police Force, Dhahi Khalfan, convened a press conference that resembled a police procedural drama, one that gripped the whole world. In painstaking detail, Khalfan presented the findings of the investigation that his force had conducted and shared the passports of 11 people suspected of involvement in the assassination. The passports were Irish, French, British, Australian and German. Khalfan showed video footage from security cameras across Dubai, in particular from the airport and the hotel, that showed how the hit squad had tracked al-Mabhouh, duplicated his room key using advanced technology and finally assassinated him—most likely using poison to give the appearance of death by natural causes. A few days later, Khalfan convened another press conference and revealed the names, passports and images of 16 additional members of the group. "The Mossad is standing behind this murder," said Khalfan. Israel didn't respond to the allegations. Very quickly, however, it became clear that some of the fictitious identities that the hit squad had used belonged to Israelis who held dual citizenship, and Israel's silence became immaterial. In those countries whose passports had been used in the killing—and even more so in the UAE—Israel was guilty as charged.[125]

Bruce Kashdan was sitting in the Israeli secret diplomatic mission in Dubai when he first heard about al-Mabhouh's assassination on the news. He knew the hotel where the assassination had taken place. In an ironic twist, an Israeli company with business contracts in Dubai had installed the security cameras at the Al Bustan Rotana Hotel. As soon as news of the incident hit the press, Kashdan received a phone call from the Emirati foreign minister. "We think your people killed al-Mabhouh," Sheikh Abdullah bin Zayed told him. "Please leave the country within 10 days." The call was expected, and Kashdan was not surprised. Over the course of a long career, he had been thrown out of several Gulf states, escaped Beirut with the Syrians on his heels and survived a plane crash in a Gulf state Israel does not have diplomatic relations with to this day. "I was used to this kind of thing—and at the end of the day, these countries didn't close the door on us," he said.[126] In neighboring Bahrain, they were keeping abreast of the latest developments and receiving updates from the Emiratis. At the height of the storm, a senior Bahraini official called Josh Zarka and delivered an unequivocal warning. "Don't you dare try something like that here," he said.[127]

Alon Ushpiz also heard about the al-Mabhouh assassination from the news—to be precise, from a breaking news segment on the radio as he was getting his hair cut in his hometown of Modi'in. At the time, he was the head of the Department of Coordination at the Ministry of Foreign Affairs—one of the most delicate and consequential roles in the ministry. One of its duties was acting as a point of contact for the intelligence services and security establishment. "That was…not a pleasant moment," he recalled.[128] A few hours later, he held a conference call with the team at the diplomatic mission in Dubai, who had gathered at Kashdan's house. They faced a difficult decision: to close the diplomatic mission following Kashdan's expulsion, or to leave the young diplomat, Liron Zaslansky, there on her own. "There was a real sadness in the air," Ushpiz said. "We were doing our job and paid a terrible price for something that had nothing to do with us, something that tarnished a project we had spent more than a decade building. We knew the Emiratis were furious with us, but we didn't know the extent of it. This operation was Bruce's baby, and now Liron was there by herself. We decided to cling on with our fingernails. *Tzumud* [an Arabic expression for holding firm] until it passed."

With Kashdan gone, his deputy was left alone at the mission in Dubai. The rift caused by the incident ran deep, and it was unclear whether they would be able to recover from it. She tried to reach out to her contacts and was met by a wall of silence. "My orders were to push forward—to knock on every door and see who answered," Zaslansky told me.[129] "Not many did. There was a lot of anger and hurt, but nothing terminal. This incident set us back years because the bond of trust had been broken. There was a sharp decline in the workload in the diplomatic mission after al-Mabhouh. But the important thing is that we didn't quit. We kept calling everybody, and that told them that we hadn't given up on them."

In the Office of the Director General at the foreign ministry in Jerusalem, they tried to put out the fire and to salvage the embers of the relationship with the United Arab Emirates. The task fell to Jeremy Issacharoff. He was on sabbatical from the foreign ministry that year, spending his days happily carrying out research for the Institute for National Security Studies in Tel Aviv. In April 2010, Issacharoff received a phone call from the director general of the foreign ministry, Yossi Gal, asking him to come for an urgent meeting. "Everything has dried up—the Emiratis don't want to talk to us," Gal told him, and asked Issacharoff to try and leverage his personal connection with Ambassador Al Otaiba, to re-open the channels of communication. Issacharoff called Al Otaiba, told him that he was coming to Washington and asked to meet with him. "If you are asking me for a formal meeting, my answer is no. But we are friends, so of course I will meet with you," Al Otaiba told him. It was a casual encounter between two old friends. Issacharoff didn't have much to say. It was clear he had not been authorized to apologize on behalf of the State of Israel. The only thing he could do was talk about the shared interests between the two countries and the ties they had built up over many years. "You don't understand how deeply you offended us," Al Otaiba responded. Issacharoff did not return to Israel with good news, but even a first meeting between the sides since the al-Mabhouh killing was something.

In my interview with him, Al Otaiba told me that the crown prince, Sheikh Mohamed bin Zayed, was furious and deeply offended about the assassination. He gave an order to close all channels of communication with Israel. "We saw this as a big insult and a slap in the face," Al Otaiba told me.[130] "This showed us that you don't really know us and appreciate who we are. It was a big deal for us."

And that was not the only diplomatic crisis to darken the skies between Israel and the UAE. Senior officials in the Obama administration and the Israeli government at the time told me about an incident in 2009, after Netanyahu entered the Prime Minister's Office. The head of the Mossad, Meir Dagan, and the organization's head of external relations, David Meidan, contacted him with a proposal. The offer that Dagan put before him sounded like it had been ripped from the pages of a political thriller: a secret deal to sell attack drones manufactured by the Israeli company Aeronautics to the United Arab Emirates in exchange for Emirati cooperation on Iran. According to one version, Netanyahu recognized the new options this proposal would unlock against the Iranian nuclear program and gave the green light. According to another version, the Israeli company first signed the deal with the Emirates and only later informed the relevant authorities, leaving Israel trapped. Whichever version is true, ultimately the deal went ahead. The United Arab Emirates even made a down payment of tens of millions of dollars to Aeronautics. But that was where things started getting complicated.

The Ministry of Defense, the sole entity permitted to authorize such arms deals, had been left out of the loop and only found out about the deal by chance at a relatively late stage in the proceedings. When the news reached the head of the Political-Military Branch at the Ministry of Defense, Major General (Res.) Amos Gilead, he put his foot down and refused to sanction the deal—partly over concerns that sensitive military technology would make its way from the UAE into the wrong hands and partly over American misgivings over the sale of this kind of advanced weapons technology from Israel to the Emirates. "Amos fought this deal and even warned the minister of defense, Ehud Barak, that it could lead to a commission of inquiry," a Western diplomat involved in the affair told me at the time.[131] "He didn't see any reason to pay the Emiratis in military technology for them to talk to Israel." A senior figure in the UAE who was also involved told me that Gilead explained to his counterparts in Abu Dhabi that the discussions surrounding the deal had taken place behind his back and that the company had sold them the drones without receiving authorization. "It was a huge mess. That was not one of the finest hours in our relationship," Gilad Cohen, who was working in the Office of the Director General in the foreign ministry at the time, told me. The deal was canceled and Sheikh Mohamed bin Zayed was outraged, taking it as a personal affront. "He felt that the Israelis had betrayed him," said Dan Shapiro, who at the time served as the senior director for Middle East affairs at the White House National Security Council.

Between the al-Mabhouh scandal and the canceled drone deal, from 2010 until 2012, the relationship between Israel and the UAE fell off a cliff. The breakdown in communication also impeded Israel's efforts to confront the Iranian nuclear program that was underway at the time. "For the first year, there was almost no direct communication between the two sides," Shapiro recalled. "Each side told us their position...and how terrible the other side was." A year and a half after al-Mabhouh's assassination, in the summer of 2011, only a few months into his new position, the director general of the foreign ministry, Rafi Barak, flew to Abu Dhabi. These were the first contacts between the foreign ministries of the two countries since the al-Mabhouh affair. A senior official in the foreign ministry who took part in the visit told me that the atmosphere was incredibly tense. Barak met with his Emirati counterpart, Dr. Anwar Gargash. "It was not an easy conversation, and Gargash made it clear that they had neither forgiven nor forgotten," the foreign ministry official told me. Despite the tensions, the meeting did touch on other topics too—most importantly, Iran. The Israelis listened to Gargash as he talked about the Iranians and recognized that his message was absolutely identical to the one that they had intended to raise in the meeting themselves. "I remember thinking to myself—either Gargash received a copy of the papers we prepared ahead of the meeting, or our viewpoints are perfectly aligned," the foreign ministry official said.[132] This part of the meeting gave the foreign ministry team something to cling onto upon their return to Israel: a reason for cautious optimism. Diplomatic incidents aside, the alignment of political interests between the two countries remained as strong as ever.

It was at around that point that another figure joined the efforts to rehabilitate the relationship between Israel and the United Arab Emirates: Terje Rød-Larsen, the Norwegian diplomat behind the Oslo Accords, who would later serve as a UN special coordinator and a power broker in leaders' offices around the Middle East. Larsen's relationship with the United Arab Emirates was a relatively late bloomer. He first met Sheikh Mohamed bin Zayed on a visit to Abu Dhabi in his capacity as the UN special coordinator in 2007 (before the prince became a leading regional figure), ostensibly for a meeting on Syria and Lebanon. They sat together on the beach at the Hilton Hotel in Abu Dhabi and enjoyed a barbecue. Someone who was at the meeting described how Larsen wanted to talk about Syria and Lebanon, but Sheikh Mohamed asked him questions about Israel instead. "Israel is not our enemy, Iran is our enemy," the sheikh said. Larsen realized that here was a different kind of Arab leader, a pragmatist who was not in thrall to the same restrictive ideologies as many of his counterparts in the region. "If you are so curious, I can introduce you to Israelis in a quiet way," Larsen replied. He began to arrange secret meetings in New York and Paris between senior Israelis and their Emirati counterparts.

First it was the foreign minister, Tzipi Livni, then the minister of defense, Ehud Barak and the minister in the Prime Minister's Office, Haim Ramon. Finally, at the UN General Assembly in New York in 2008, Larsen arranged a secret meeting between President Shimon Peres and the Emirati foreign minister, Sheikh Abdullah bin Zayed.

Two years later, when the al-Mabhouh affair erupted, Larsen received a phone call from the head of the Mossad, Meir Dagan. Larsen told me that he and Dagan knew each other well, and that Dagan knew about his connections in Abu Dhabi and wanted his help in delivering a message to calm the mood.[133] In the days after news of the assassination was made public, the Mossad was rocked by the decision to expose their agents in the media by Dubai's police commander, Dhahi Khalfan. Dagan spoke to Larsen several times and asked him to persuade the authorities in the UAE to stop the media campaign. The message went through and Khalfan significantly moderated his tone. As a next step, Larsen attempted to resuscitate the ties between Israel and the Emiratis. In 2011, after Tamir Pardo took over from Dagan as head of the Mossad, Larsen sought to persuade the Emiratis to receive him for a visit in Abu Dhabi. Following seven months of quiet diplomacy, the Emiratis agreed. The meeting took place in August, at the height of Ramadan. This was the first time the head of the Mossad had met with senior officials in the UAE since the al-Mabhouh assassination. Pardo met with the national security advisor at the time, Sheikh Hazza bin Zayed, one of the crown prince's five brothers. According to a senior Emirati official, the problem was not that the leadership in Abu Dhabi saw al-Mabhouh as any kind of martyr. Rather, they were furious that Israel had chosen to act of its own accord on Dubai's soil instead of asking the Emirati security services to arrest al-Mabhouh or simply waiting until he left the country and assassinating him somewhere else. Pardo's meeting in Abu Dhabi was difficult, but it reopened the direct lines of communication between the two sides and nudged them closer to a deal to end the crisis. A few months later, Larsen tried to arrange a secret meeting in Israel for the Emirati foreign minister, Abdullah bin Zayed. Following the usual internal power struggles in the Israeli government, it was decided that the Ministry of Defense would be in charge of the visit. This was partly to atone for its role in the cancellation of the drone deal that had so offended the Emiratis. Larsen's assistant, the French diplomat Fabrice Aidan, traveled to the home of Defense Minister Ehud Barak in Tel Aviv, where he called Sheikh Abdullah from his phone before handing it over to Barak. The conversation was positive; preparations for the visit continued and passport scans were submitted. But then the Emiratis withdrew at the last minute over concerns by Sheikh Abdullah that the visit would be leaked to the press.

Discussions on the deal to resolve the diplomatic crisis between the two countries were fraught. A senior official in the UAE described how, at one point, they demanded that Israel fulfill the canceled drone order as a condition for ending the feud, but quickly realized that Israel would be unable to meet the demand and backed down. "The Emiratis wanted an Israeli confession, at the very least through a backchannel, and for them to take responsibility for the assassination," Shapiro told me.[134] "In the end, they settled for less: an Israeli commitment that such things would never happen again on Emirati soil and a stated desire to return to focus on the shared efforts against Iran and regional terrorist groups." In addition to this promise, the company that signed the drone deal with the Emiratis returned some of the money they had been paid, and the Israeli government offered an additional incentive of increased security and intelligence cooperation. "It was an attempt to put everything that had happened behind them—al-Mabhouh and the drones—and to reach new security understandings between the two countries," recalled Shapiro.

A few months later, Larsen seized another opportunity to turn the page. In September 2012, Prime Minister Netanyahu and the foreign minister of the UAE, Sheikh Abdullah, came to New York for the UN General Assembly. The Norwegian diplomat offered to arrange a covert meeting between the two sides and received their permission to proceed. Netanyahu's speech at the UN that year was particularly dramatic. Like an end-times prophet, he took to the lectern in the General Assembly Hall holding a poster depicting a bomb. Using a thick marker pen, he drew a red line below the fuse and hinted that Israel would take military action if Iran crossed the threshold of 250 kilograms of uranium enriched to 20 percent purity. "Red lines don't lead to war; red lines prevent war," Netanyahu said in his speech. The next day, on Saturday morning, a diplomatic vehicle entered the underground parking lot of the Regency Hotel on the corner of 61st St. and Park Avenue in New York, where Netanyahu was staying. From the car emerged Foreign Minister Sheikh Abdullah bin Zayed. He strode across the parking lot and through the hotel kitchen, then rode the room service elevator up to one of the top floors, where a suite had been booked in anticipation of the meeting. Sheikh Abdullah was accompanied by his chief of staff, Mohamed Al Khaja, and Yousef Al Otaiba, the ambassador to Washington and the closest advisor to Sheikh Mohamed. Nine years later, Al Khaja would make history as the first United Arab Emirates ambassador to Israel. A few minutes before Sheikh Abdullah went up to the suite, Netanyahu returned from a stroll through Central Park with his wife, Sara, and he was in a good mood. Larsen told me that the al-Mabhouh affair was the first thing to come up in the meeting. "They started talking and I left the room," he said.[135] "The meeting lasted several hours and was held in good spirits." A source with a detailed knowledge of the meeting told me that once they had overcome the initial hurdle of the al-Mabhouh assassination, the two moved on to discuss Iran. Sheikh Abdullah had greatly approved of Netanyahu's speech. At the same time, the foreign minister of the UAE made it clear to Netanyahu that his country would not be able to offer any public thaw in relations with Israel without some kind of progress on the peace process with the Palestinians. Before that clandestine meeting, the crown prince had continued to harbor anger against Israel over the al-Mabhouh incident. Following the meeting, Sheikh Abdullah and Al Otaiba returned to Abu Dhabi, where they briefed Sheikh Mohamed and gave a positive report. Only then did the crown prince change his mind and agree to turn the page. The meeting in New York was one of the milestones that paved the way for the Abraham Accords eight years later. Larsen was among the guests of honor at the ceremony on the White House lawn.

It would take over a decade before Israel admitted responsibility for the al-Mabhouh assassination. The confession came on June 10, 2021. The outgoing Mossad director, Yossi Cohen, admitted in an interview with the Israeli journalist Ilana Dayan on her program *Uvda* (in English: *Fact*) that Israel was behind the assassination. "Sometimes operations are exposed," Cohen said with a thin, awkward smile. "When that happens, it's painful and it's unpleasant and it's embarrassing." Cohen noted in the interview that the incident had been a stumbling block for ties between Israel and the United Arab Emirates but confirmed that the difficulties had been resolved a few years earlier. He didn't apologize, nor did he express regret, but he did go further than any Israeli government representative before or since. "I can understand why the Emiratis felt offended," he said. Cohen's comments were out of step with the general tone in the Mossad in the years after the killing. In December 2010, when the then-head of the Mossad, Meir Dagan, gathered the diplomatic and military correspondents in the organization's headquarters for a background briefing on his last day in the role, he attempted to play down the diplomatic fallout from the assassination. A former senior official in the Mossad who was closely involved in the affair attempted to pass it off in a conversation with me as a minor bump in the road. "It was background noise in our relationship with them," he told me.[136] "Broadly speaking, the Emiratis used the affair as a bargaining chip to hold over Israel. In hindsight, it was a glancing shot across the bows, maybe not even that. At the end of the day, Mohamed bin Zayed made a strategic decision to build long-term ties with Israel. That decision led to the Abraham Accords. There were a million disagreements and incidents along the way."

When I visited Abu Dhabi in June 2021, I met with the foreign minister, Abdullah bin Zayed, for the first time. We sat on the sofa in his office for an hour. He wore the traditional Emirati *kandora* and *keffiyeh* headdress; I was in my Western suit. Abdullah bin Zayed is the youngest of the six brothers, but he has been in the role since 2006. He spoke softly and quietly and weighed every word before it left his mouth. I learned how strongly the feelings over the al-Mabhouh affair continued to burn within him, over a decade later. He explained that his biggest frustration was that the Israelis didn't understand then, and still don't understand today, just how offensive the incident was to the leadership of the UAE. "For us, we saw it as Israel giving us the cold shoulder," he told me.[137] "We felt that the Israelis did not really attach any importance to the ties with us." Sheikh Abdullah spoke about how the assassination caught the Emiratis by surprise precisely because it took place during a period of trust building between the countries. For the

Emiratis, he explained, it ran far deeper than the assassination itself. The Emirati ambassador to Washington, Yousef Al Otaiba, had expressed similar sentiments a few months earlier. "You think that killing someone from Hamas is okay anywhere, anytime," said Al Otaiba.[138] "Our problem was the fact that you didn't respect our sovereignty."

Senior Emirati and Israeli officials both admit that the diplomatic crisis was resolved in part by the passing of time. "Time has a way of solving things," said the Emirati foreign minister. "But without the al-Mabhouh affair, I think we could have achieved normalization much earlier. Maybe even five years earlier." But there were other circumstances that pushed the two sides back together. The events surrounding the Arab Spring, combined with the regional policies of the Obama administration and the talks with Iran, focused minds on both sides and made them realize that they had no choice but to put their differences behind them and work together. As soon as the crisis was resolved, in late 2012, both sides went back to addressing the issue at the top of both of their agendas: the Iranian threat. Israel and the United Arab Emirates were equally concerned about the negotiations that had just started between the United States and Iran and did everything in their power to prevent an agreement between the sides.

Iran

Donald Trump was agitated. We were sitting in the main lobby at Mar-a-Lago, and he was once again complaining about the Jewish voters who had given their votes to Joe Biden. "I'll tell you what," he began, and looked me in the eyes. "Had I not come along I think Israel was going to be destroyed. Okay. You want to know the truth? I think Israel would have been destroyed maybe by now." Trump was referring to Joe Biden's promises to return to the Iranian nuclear agreement—the same agreement that Trump had pulled out of three years earlier. "And guess what, now they're going to do it again. And if they do it again, Israel is in very deep, very grave danger. you understand what I'm saying?"

Trump was exaggerating, as was his way. Israel was not facing imminent destruction before he entered the Oval Office, and it isn't facing imminent destruction now he is no longer there. He is right, however, that his ascent to the presidency was the greatest gift the Netanyahu government could have asked for in the struggle against Iran. That holds equally true for the Emiratis and the other Gulf states—perhaps even more so. Pushing back against the Iranian nuclear threat and its regional destabilization was the shared interest that first brought Israel and the United Arab Emirates together 25 years previously. If the Obama administration's policy on Iran and the signing of the nuclear accord in 2015 brought Jerusalem and Abu Dhabi closer together, then Trump's Iran policy played an outsized role in the breakthrough that led to the peace treaty between the two countries. For the full picture, we have to go back to January 2009, when Barack Obama first stepped into the White House. One of the incoming president's campaign promises was to engage with Iran, which raised concerns in Israel. In Jerusalem, a transitional government was in power. The February 2009 elections had thrown up a constitutional abnormality; the largest single party by vote share was Tzipi Livni's Kadima, but more MKs had recommended Benjamin Netanyahu as prime minister, so the president gave him the first shot at forming a government. In the final days of Livni's tenure as foreign minister, she instructed the embassy in Washington to take an unprecedented step and reach out to the new ambassador of the United Arab Emirates, Yousef Al Otaiba, with a proposal for a joint Israeli–Emirati appeal to the new US administration over Iran. Jeremy Issacharoff was the deputy ambassador to Washington at the time. If Israel and an Arab country came together to send a message on Iran, the thinking went, it would have a bigger impact on the incoming administration.

The Emirati ambassador liked the idea. The leadership in Abu Dhabi was equally concerned about the potential outcome of negotiations between the United States and Iran. Like many Israeli politicians, the crown prince of Abu Dhabi and the de facto ruler of the United Arab Emirates, Sheikh Mohamed bin Zayed, described Iran to American diplomats in 2008 as an "existential threat." His position has only been reinforced since. The threat is partly to do with the size disparity: Iran is a country with a population of over 80 million people while the UAE has a paltry 1.5 million citizens.

But the bigger problem was their geographical proximity—only a few dozen miles of Gulf waters separate the two. A ballistic missile launched from Iran would take only 46 seconds to reach the UAE. There are also hundreds of thousands of Iranians living in the UAE. The overwhelming majority are residents and not citizens, but they are deeply integrated within the local economy and some have forged bonds of marriage with Emirati citizens. The diplomats in the US missions in Dubai and Abu Dhabi described the relationship between the UAE and Iran as akin to that between a bobcat and a caged lion. In an evocative cable to the US State Department in Washington in February 2009, they wrote, "[The UAE is] a potent fighter for its size, sharp of tooth and ready to defend its den, but fundamentally unprepared to provoke the bigger cat, wary in the knowledge that someday the lion may get out of its cage. The bobcat is less timid when it is certain that it has even larger cats on its side."[139] While for Israel, the nuclear program was the number one threat, the UAE's chief concern was Iran's hegemonic ambitions, conventional military power and attempts at regional destabilization using affiliated terrorist groups.

Back to Washington. After receiving the go-ahead from Al Otaiba, Issacharoff called Dennis Ross, who was in charge of Iranian affairs at the US Department of State at the time. He told Ross that he and the Israeli ambassador, Sallai Meridor, wished to meet with him the next day to express Israel's concerns over the new administration's policy on Iran. "One more small thing— Yousef Al Otaiba will be joining us in the meeting," Issacharoff informed a surprised Ross. Al Otaiba, who was still "new" in Washington circles at the time, was living in the Four Seasons Hotel. To ensure the meeting remained under wraps, it was held in his suite. For two hours, Issacharoff and Al Otaiba sat facing Ross, with each of them putting forward their country's position.

There was no notable coordination or preparation ahead of the meeting, but the longer it went on, the more it came to resemble an echo chamber, with the Israelis and Emiratis repeating each other's points and completing each other's sentences. "Without really meaning to, it showed the Americans how deeply our interests were aligned and our concerns shared," Issacharoff told me.[140] "That made an impression on them." Al Otaiba continues to believe that this 2009 meeting had a significant impact on the Obama administration's perspective.[141]

Israeli and the UAE's coordination on messaging continued to expand during the first year of the Obama administration. A delegation of senior US officials who visited Abu Dhabi in July 2009 heard the same message directly from Sheikh Mohamed himself. During dinner, which lasted for three hours, the de facto ruler of the United Arab Emirates made his point to the American officials in no uncertain terms. "Your negotiations with Iran will fail," he warned them.[142] "I fear we may be surprised. The Israelis are preparing a preemptive strike on the Iranian nuclear facilities, sooner than you think. Perhaps even this year. I am convinced that Netanyahu is preparing an attack in Iran. I agree with the assessment of the Israeli intelligence regarding the progress of the Iranian nuclear program." Bin Zayed noted that should such a scenario come to pass, the Iranians would respond by firing rockets and carrying out bombings against American forces in the region and its allies. "The United Arab Emirates will be a prime target for the Iranians," he told his American guests. A few months earlier, in a meeting with a different American delegation, Sheikh Mohamed said he had ordered his military chief to draw up attack plans against Iranian missile bases in preparation for an Iranian response to Israeli attacks. "This is the Middle East and we will do what we need to do...when the Iranians fire their missiles, we will go after them and kill them," Sheikh Mohamed warned.[143] A former senior official in the Obama administration told me that the White House's assessment at the time was that the Emiratis and the Israelis were in close coordination, and that bin Zayed was echoing what he was hearing from his allies in Jerusalem and vice versa.

The diplomatic crisis between Israel and the UAE over the 2010 assassination of Mahmoud al-Mabhouh, one of the leaders of Hamas, brought the diplomatic and intelligence cooperation on Iran between the two governments grinding to an almost complete halt. When the crisis was finally resolved, in late 2012, Israel and the UAE discovered that the scenario they feared most was coming to pass. In March 2013, a US military aircraft landed in Muscat, the capital of the Gulf Sultanate of Oman, quietly and without public notice. On board were Bill Burns and Jake Sullivan,[144] two of the senior advisors to President Obama, and they were on their way to an initial series of covert meetings with Iran hosted by Sultan Qaboos behind the backs of Israel, the UAE and the other allies of the United States in the Gulf. "I told Susan Rice [Obama's national security advisor] that if she wanted, I would give her the tail number of the plane too," Major General (Res.) Yaakov Amidror, then-national security advisor to Prime Minister Netanyahu, told me. "I told her that it was naive and even insulting on a professional level for them to think they could do something like that without us finding out about it…. I was disappointed that the Americans more or less deceived us." A senior official from the UAE testified that they felt the same sense of betrayal. During his first term, there were not many leaders closer to Barack Obama than Sheikh Mohamed, who now felt that the American president had stabbed him in the back.

In the second half of 2013, after Hassan Rouhani won the election for the Iranian presidency, Tamir Pardo—by now two and a half years into his tenure as the director of the Mossad —attended a meeting with Netanyahu. He carried with him a secret message from the Sultanate of Oman, a country unlike any other in the region. The secret ties between Israel and Oman date back more than 50 years, when Sultan Qaboos first came to power. It has a reputation as the Switzerland of the Middle East—partly owing to its natural beauty, but also because of its stated diplomatic policy of neutrality, the individual path it has forged for itself and its willingness to act as a discreet and effective intermediary. Two former senior Israeli officials told me that Pardo raised an idea with Netanyahu that sounded like pure fantasy. "The Omanis are offering to mediate in setting up a backchannel between us and Iran," Pardo told Netanyahu. The Omanis claimed that a channel of communication between Israel and Iran would ease the negotiations between the US and Iran. This proposal was radical and extraordinary. Iran was Israel's sworn enemy; Iranian politicians could often be seen calling to wipe Israel from the map and cries of "Death to Israel" were commonplace in protests in Tehran. For its part, Israel has sought to undermine Iran for years—sabotaging its nuclear program, assassinating scientists and threatening to bomb its nuclear reactors. Pardo and a few senior Mossad officials took the view that Israel should seriously consider the Omani proposal. Netanyahu's national security advisor at the time, Yaakov Amidror, strongly disagreed. "Talks between ourselves and Iran would have given legitimacy to the talks between America and Iran. Saying no was the right thing to do—and I still believe that with hindsight," Amidror told me.[145] Netanyahu took the side of his national security advisor over the head of the Mossad and rejected the Omani proposal.

As the secret negotiations between the US and Iran in Oman evolved into formal negotiations in Geneva and these led to the signing of the Joint Comprehensive Plan of Action (JCPOA) in late 2013, ties between Israel and the UAE became stronger still. During Obama's first term, the coordination between the two countries on Iran was at the working level. By the time he moved into his second term, and as the negotiations over the Iranian nuclear program progressed, that coordination went up a gear to the political level. "They were in constant dialogue," Dan Shapiro, at the time the US ambassador to Israel, told me. Despite this, the two countries adopted significant differences in approach. While the Israelis expressed their opposition in public in Washington and waged a public campaign against the nuclear agreement in the media and in the halls of Congress, the Emiratis preferred to convey their messages through more discreet channels. The best example of this came in March 2015, when Benjamin Netanyahu came to the United States to address the US Congress behind President Obama's back. The Israeli ambassador to Washington, Ron Dermer, issued a personal invite to his Emirati counterpart, Yousef Al Otaiba, to attend the speech. Al Otaiba, who didn't want to put himself in the middle of a conflict between the prime minister of Israel and the White House, politely declined. "I remember that Yousef told me at the time, 'don't put us in the same bracket with Israel when it comes to the opposition to the nuclear deal,'" Shapiro said. "I think they said something different to the Israelis." Netanyahu's speech before Congress failed to halt the JCPOA, which was signed in Lausanne in July 2015. Netanyahu and Mohamed bin Zayed's efforts may have fallen short, but they would be given a second chance not long after.

In early December 2016, I came to Washington for the Saban Forum: an annual event that brings together influential figures from across politics, civil society, business and the media in Israel and the United States. The forum is usually a glittering and celebratory occasion, but this time there was a heavy pall over the proceedings, especially among the American participants, the majority of whom were affiliated with the Democratic Party. Israeli-American businessman Haim Saban, the forum's founder who could usually be seen strutting around the event like a movie star at his latest premiere, was deflated. It was only a month after Hillary Clinton's election defeat to Donald Trump. Saban was a close confidant of the Clintons, one of the biggest donors to Hillary's campaign and a passionate campaigner on her behalf. For him, Trump's victory was also a personal defeat. For Prime Minister Benjamin Netanyahu, it could not have been more different. When he addressed the forum via satellite link from Jerusalem, he struggled to contain his glee. "I look forward to speaking with [President-elect Trump] about what to do about this bad deal," said Netanyahu. Trump's victory was a dream come true for Netanyahu, who despised Obama and fought with every ounce of his strength against the JCPOA. The president-elect had come out against the deal during the election campaign in even harsher terms than Netanyahu himself. "A disaster," "the worst deal ever" and "a nuclear Holocaust" were only some of the ways Trump described the nuclear accord before his election. In March 2016, at the American Israel Public Affairs Committee (AIPAC) summit in Washington, Trump promised that withdrawing from the JCPOA would be his number one priority should he win. All of this was sweet music to Netanyahu's ears. His national security advisor at the time, Jacob Nagel, and his foreign policy advisor, Jonathan Schachter, also participated in the Saban Forum. They slipped out of the hall between panels and speeches and joined the director of the Mossad, Yossi Cohen, who had come to Washington without drawing attention to himself. The three of them met up with General Michael Flynn, the soon-to-be national security advisor to the incoming president. The Israeli officials were unaware that Flynn had very recently been made the subject of a secret FBI investigation examining his ties with Russian government officials. Netanyahu didn't waste a second. He and his team coordinated positions on Iran with the president-elect before Trump even entered the Oval Office.

Two months later, in February 2017, Netanyahu arrived for his first visit to the Trump White House. A few days before the meeting, Trump had time to fit in a first round of sanctions against Iran in response to an Iranian ballistic missile test. One of Netanyahu's senior advisors who participated in the White House meeting told me that certain parts of that meeting were so far-reaching and sensitive that Netanyahu asked his team not to send a written summary of it through the classified computer systems of the Prime Minister's Office, and effectively kept the national security establishment out of the loop. Only very few people within the Israeli government received a verbal summary of what took place there, and the only documentation in existence is held in a folder in a safe in the Prime Minister's Office. It contains 13 pages of handwritten notes kept by National Security Advisor Jacob Nagel. "I think [there's] a change that is clearly evident since President Trump took office," said Netanyahu at the White House press conference with the US president. "I think it's long overdue, and I think that if we work together...we can roll back Iran's aggression and danger."

Despite Trump's public statements and his open hostility toward the Iranian leadership, he did not rush to abandon the 2015 nuclear accord. In April 2017, Trump had to declare before Congress through gritted teeth that Iran was meeting all of its obligations under the deal. A few days later, he placed further sanctions on Iran for reasons unrelated to the accord. In July, he repeated the trick, announcing that Iran was not in violation of the agreement but instigating fresh sanctions for their support of terrorism. Then-defense minister of Israel, Avigdor Lieberman, told me at the time that while Trump and his team wanted to withdraw from the deal, the secretary of defense, James Mattis, along with other senior officials in the US security establishment, claimed that such a move would result in the US isolating itself rather than isolating Iran.[146] The Israeli government was divided along similar lines: Netanyahu and Lieberman supported an American withdrawal from the accord, but the security chiefs were wary of such a move and warned about the possible consequences. "The IDF took the view that the JCPOA was a strategic turning point that allowed Israel to redirect its resources to confronting other threats, such as the Iranian entrenchment in Syria and thwarting Iran and Hezbollah's plans to conquer the Galilee," the former IDF chief of the general staff, Gadi Eisenkot, told me. "Following the nuclear accord, we were also able to return to our mission of covert targeted assassinations of elements involved with the Iranian nuclear program, instead of channeling all our efforts into drawing up plans for a military attack."

"We'll Break Their Bones"

In early 2017, soon after Trump entered the White House, Eisenkot requested an emergency meeting with a few of the senior officials in the US military, including the head of Central Command, responsible for US forces in the Middle East. In the meeting, held at a US base in Europe, Eisenkot warned his counterparts that Israeli intelligence had identified a dangerous shift taking place in Syria. The head of the Quds Force of the Islamic Revolutionary Guard Corps (IRGC), General Qasem Soleimani, had seen how the Russian and American coalitions were crushing the Islamic State group in Syria and spotted an opportunity for Iran to step into the vacuum that was being created. "Soleimani had a detailed plan," Eisenkot told me. "It included recruiting 100 thousand Shia mercenaries for pro-Iranian militias and moving them into Syria, setting up an intelligence gathering operation on Israel from Syrian territory, establishing a drone unit of the IRGC in every Syrian Air Force base and reaching an agreement with the Russians on setting up an 'Iranian wharf' at the Syrian ports of Tartus and Latakia." According to Eisenkot, Soleimani's plan included diplomatic, economic and demographic elements, which together would give Iran control over the Syrian economy and communication networks and even begin a process of "Shia-ization" of the local population by sending Iranian teachers to Syria. At that same secret meeting, Eisenkot informed his American counterparts that Israel was planning military action to counter the Iranian presence in Syria. He admitted that Israel had been so focused on the nuclear program that it had been caught on the back foot by Iran's quiet build-up in Syria. If until this point Israel had acted primarily to stop the transfer of Iranian weapons from Syria to Hezbollah, the new targets would now be the Iranians themselves. "I told them that we had decided to go all in on the Quds Force and break their bones," Eisenkot told me. Senior officials in the US military warned Eisenkot that such a step could spiral into war. "I told them we have no choice. I have the cabinet's approval and we are going to hit the Iranians where it hurts. We will attack them wherever we find them." True to his word, Israel began to drastically escalate its attacks in Syria soon after. Israel updated the Americans ahead of each attack, and the Russians were informed in real time. Within a few weeks, Iran began to suffer casualties and IRGC officers started returning to Tehran in body bags. For months, these attacks were carried out in a cocktail of stealth and ambiguity—until February 10, 2018. That morning, an Israeli Air Force helicopter shot down an Iranian drone that had crossed from Syria into Israeli airspace. In response to the violation, Israel bombed the base the drone had been launched from. During the raid, an Israeli fighter jet was shot down by a Syrian anti-aircraft missile and crashed in Israeli territory—for the first time in decades. The Israeli Air Force responded by taking out many of Syria's air defense systems. Twenty-five soldiers were killed in the Israeli retaliation, among them Iranians. From that day forward, the Israeli front against the Iranian presence entered a more visible stage.

During Trump's term, Israel attempted to persuade the Americans and Russians to work together on a diplomatic solution in Syria that would lead to the removal of the Iranian forces. In the first year of the Trump administration, the Russians and the Americans reached a few understandings on Syria—but these would only ever be partially implemented. "Russia became a politicized issue in the United States because of the election interference story, which meant we were unsuccessful in encouraging Russian–American cooperation in Syria," Eisenkot told me. "In one of the meetings, I told the Americans that the gaps between Roosevelt and Stalin in the Second World War were significantly wider than the gaps between Putin and Trump. But that didn't help. The suspicions and the resentment were so strong that it was impossible to make progress." The July 2018 summit in Helsinki between the two leaders also failed to produce a meaningful breakthrough beyond an increasing desire on Trump's part to remove his troops from Syria. In December 2018, Trump announced on Twitter that he had decided to withdraw from Syria. The message caught Israel and the other allies of the United States by surprise. Ultimately, however, most of the American forces stayed put, and Trump's policy shift remained confined to a tweet.

"Maximum Pressure"

Brian Hook met me in April 2021 at the Le Pain Quotidien café near the White House. Two armed bodyguards stepped out of the black jeep, opened the rear door and escorted him in. Hook had not held any US government position for more than three months by that time, but the Secret Service still considered there to be credible threats of Iranian reprisals against him. Tall and slender, with blond hair carefully combed to one side and glasses that completed a distinctly nerdy appearance, the 53-year-old Iowa lawyer was the one who translated the Trump administration's "maximum pressure" campaign on Iran into action. He was the man behind the 1,500 sanctions against Iranian individuals and institutions under the Trump administration. That made him one of the most despised individuals within the regime in Tehran. Consequently, his security detail continued to accompany him even after Biden replaced Trump in the White House.[147]

Hook's path to becoming one of the most influential figures in the Trump administration was a long and tortuous one. A classic Republican and an old-school conservative, he had worked in the US Department of State under Bush Jr. and advised Mitt Romney in his 2012 presidential campaign against Barack Obama. When Donald Trump declared his intention to run in the Republican Party primaries in 2016, Hook was among his critics. But when Rex Tillerson, Trump's designated secretary of state, invited him to a meeting two days before the inauguration ceremony, he answered the call. A few days later, he walked into the Harry S. Truman Building of the Department of State for his first day as director of policy planning, a key role that wielded significant influence. Hook quickly became one of Tillerson's most trusted advisors and his go-to man on a range of matters of strategic importance. One of which was Iran. At the same time, he developed very close ties with some of the leading figures at the White House, first and foremost the president's senior advisor, Jared Kushner.

In the first months after the transition of power, the Trump administration continued to attend the joint talks between Iran and the P5+1, the six global powers responsible for implementing the nuclear agreement (the five permanent UN Security Council members plus Germany). Hook was the US representative at the talks. In one of his first meetings, he also pulled the Iranian representative to one side for a one-on-one talk where he demanded the release of American citizens who had been arrested in Iran as bargaining chips.[148] "The main reason President Trump waited to withdraw from the nuclear accord is that the immediate matters that demanded his attention when he entered office were the elimination of ISIS in Syria and North Korea's increased ballistic missile testing," Hook recalled. "We were understaffed. Throughout the first months of the administration, I was almost the only political appointee in the government working on Iran. Iran was not the top priority at the time." That was about to change.

In September 2017, Trump came to New York to attend the talks at the UN General Assembly for the first time. In his speech before the assembly, he blasted the Iranian regime, labeling it a "corrupt dictatorship." He claimed that Iran had become a rogue state "whose chief exports are violence, bloodshed and chaos" and accused it of using its wealth to shore up the dictatorial regime of Bashar al-Assad in Syria. "We cannot let a murderous regime continue these destabilizing activities," said Trump. "We cannot abide by an agreement if it provides cover for the eventual construction of a nuclear program." The Iran deal, Trump continued, "is an embarrassment to the United States, and I don't think you've heard the last of it." Benjamin Netanyahu could not have been happier. At their meeting in New York the day before, Netanyahu told Trump that when it came to the nuclear agreement, it was time to "fix it or nix it." What Netanyahu didn't know was that a short time after he finished delivering his speech, Trump attempted to arrange a meeting with the Iranian president, Hassan Rouhani. "President Trump had made overtures to President Rouhani," Hook told me. "He asked the French president, Emmanuel Macron, to mediate between them and to arrange a meeting in New York." At the time, Macron had good ties with both Trump and Rouhani, and he decided to accept the challenge. He reached out to the Iranian president and proposed the meeting with Trump. Rouhani dismissed the offer without a second glance. "Macron came back with a negative answer. He told us that Rouhani didn't like the way Trump had spoken about Iran in his speech at the UN that day," Hook said. "Whatever Trump said that day at the UN pales in comparison to the vitriol and venom that Iran has been saying about the United States for the past 41 years. So we thought this was a little high-minded and wildly hypocritical for him to use that as an excuse not to meet." The next day, Rouhani delivered his response to Trump in his own speech. He referred to the US president as a "rogue newcomer to the world of politics," and called Trump's speech a display of "ignorant, absurd and hateful rhetoric" that was "unfit to be heard at the United Nations."

Trump couldn't stand the fact that he had to come before Congress every three months to declare that Iran was not violating the nuclear accord—the same accord he had sworn to withdraw from. Every time the date approached, he would go into a foul mood. In October 2017, he decided he could take it no longer. In a speech at the White House, Trump announced that he did not intend to declare before Congress that Iran was adhering to the terms of the agreement. But nor did he announce his intention to withdraw from it, leaving the door open for negotiations. Trump emphasized that he sought to introduce amendments to the JCPOA that would incorporate references to Iran's missile program, closer supervision of Iran's nuclear facilities and, most importantly of all, changes to the so-called "sunset clause" that would see the restrictions on Iran's nuclear program gradually lifted after 10 years. "In the event we are not able to reach a solution working with Congress and our allies, then the agreement will be terminated. Our participation can be canceled by me, as president, at any time," he said.

Trump's speech was a cause for celebration in the Prime Minister's Office in Jerusalem. Netanyahu felt like he was finally on track to achieve his goal of US withdrawal from the JCPOA. A few weeks after Trump's speech, a secret meeting took place at the White House between senior officials in the American defense and intelligence communities and their Israeli counterparts. The participants were members of an Israeli–American strategic forum on Iran. Code-named "Opal," the forum was established in the early days of Barack Obama's first term and convened regularly throughout most of his years in the White House. Their first meeting under the Trump administration took place in November 2017. The American side was led by the White House's national security advisor, H. R. McMaster, and the Israeli side by his counterpart in the Prime Minister's Office, Meir Ben-Shabbat. After two days of talks, the two sides formulated a joint strategy on Iran and decided to focus their covert and diplomatic efforts on the JCPOA, pushing back against Iranian destabilization in the region and its missile program and preparing for any large-scale regional military escalation with Iran.

At the same time as it was coordinating its position against Iran with Israel, the Trump administration was also continuing its talks on the JCPOA with the European powers. The thinking was that they would attempt to reach a side agreement with the E3—France, Germany and the UK—on introducing unilateral amendments to the agreement. Brian Hook led these efforts. He spent six months hopping between European capitals in an attempt to reach a compromise. "The president wanted to give diplomacy a chance and to see whether the agreement could be fixed," he told me. Weeks turned into months, and Trump grew increasingly impatient. His relationship with several of his key advisors deteriorated even further over differences of opinion on the subject. In March 2018, Trump fired his secretary of state, Rex Tillerson, via tweet. Tillerson was one of the most vocal opponents of unilateral withdrawal from the JCPOA and led the efforts to reach an agreement with the Europeans. A few days later, McMaster, the national security advisor, resigned and followed Tillerson out the door. The "establishment" camp in the Trump administration had lost two of its key figures. Trump replaced Tillerson and McMaster with two of the most prominent hawks on Iran to be found anywhere in the capital. As secretary of state, he appointed the head of the CIA, Mike Pompeo, and for McMaster's position as national security advisor, he appointed John Bolton—a man who had publicly called for the United States to work to overthrow the Iranian regime. As far as Netanyahu was concerned, these appointments represented a fantastic development.

Over the month of April 2018, the US and the European powers began to inch closer to a solution that would persuade the Trump administration to retract their threat to withdraw from the accord. Agreements had been reached on two of the three amendments Trump wanted to introduce: the need to supervise the Iranian nuclear warhead-compatible ballistic missile program and increased supervision over the Iranian nuclear facilities, especially facilitating unannounced inspections at suspicious sites. On the third and most important point that Trump sought to amend in the deal—its expiry date—the two sides reached an impasse. Trump demanded the extension of the accord's expiry date so that Iran would remain at a distance of more than a year from nuclear breakout for a period of time longer than the 10 years provided for under the existing deal. In the negotiations, Hook argued that the Iranians did not possess the leverage they claimed, and that they would not withdraw from the agreement even if the "sunset clause" was extended. The French, British and Germans disagreed. "They claimed that it would be a bridge too far in terms of unilaterally rewriting the nuclear accord," recalled Hook. "The Europeans argued that it would be unfair to make that kind of change to the deal without the Iranians sitting around the table too, but the Iranians refused to negotiate. I told them that the deal would expire anyway within a few years, so as allies, let's at least decide that we see the 'sunset clause' as void and hold Iran to that standard, and if Iran disagreed, the European countries would join us in applying additional sanctions on Iran until they agreed."

Extending the duration of the agreement remained a tricky point of contention, and the leaders of the European countries sought to buy more time. They scheduled individual meetings with Trump at the White House, one after the other. President Macron was first up. He arrived for a meeting at the Oval Office in late April 2018. The two men had a relatively strong relationship at the time, and Macron hoped he would be able to leverage it to persuade Trump not to withdraw from the deal. "We are conducting negotiations with Brian Hook—and we are close to a deal," he told the president. Trump, who hours earlier had referred to the nuclear agreement as "insane" and "embarrassing," looked at Macron and asked, "Who's Brian Hook?" The French president was stunned. He realized at that moment that Trump had never harbored any real intention of amending the existing accord and that any attempt to convince him not to withdraw from it was almost certainly doomed to failure. When I interviewed him three years later, Hook told me that he had not been in direct contact with Trump at the time and that he had reported to Secretary of State Tillerson. "That's why the president said what he said to Macron," he explained. Looking back, Hook maintains that it was European intransigence that ultimately prevented the JCPOA from being "fixed" and resulted in the US decision to withdraw from it. "They asked for more time for negotiations. We worked for six months and were unable to reach an agreement. I don't think the problem was a lack of time," Hook told me. "We gave the Europeans numerous opportunities to say yes. I told them that the consequences of a US withdrawal from the agreement would be far greater than a unilateral extension of the sunset clause. They could have saved the deal if they had agreed to extend that clause in perpetuity, but they felt it would be unfair to the Iranians. I think that was a mistake on their part. If they had agreed, Trump would not have quit the deal."

The Archive Heist

On April 30, 2018, as I left my home in Tel Aviv to make the short journey to the Channel 10 studios in Vered House in Givatayim, my phone pinged with a WhatsApp notification from the channel's CEO and chief editor, Golan Yochpaz: "Call me." A few minutes earlier, I had filed a report that Prime Minister Netanyahu had convened a meeting of the State Security Cabinet for a "diplomatic-intelligence update" on the Iranian nuclear agreement on very short notice. This was six days after the aforementioned meeting between Macron and Trump at the White House, and there was a sense that things were coming to the boil. When I called

Yochpaz, he informed me that he had just come off the phone with Netanyahu a few minutes earlier. This was highly unusual, to put it mildly. If the *Yedioth Ahronoth* daily newspaper was Netanyahu's "Great Satan," then *Channel 10 News* was the Little Satan, a status that could be traced back to a string of investigative reports it had published on the prime minister over the years. His animosity was such that Netanyahu consistently refused to be interviewed by Channel 10. If he was calling Yochpaz, it meant that something huge was happening. Netanyahu had told Yochpaz that he was due to deliver a speech that evening where he would expose new and dramatic intelligence that Israel had obtained on the Iranian nuclear program. He stressed the media value and political importance of the story and asked that the speech be carried live. The live broadcast was hugely important to the prime minister, and he held similar calls with the chief editors of the two other commercial Israeli television channels. The media heard about the impending drama before most of the cabinet.

Over two years earlier, in early 2016, a short time after the JCPOA came into force, Israel received an extraordinary piece of intelligence. According to the intelligence report, the Ministry of Defense in Tehran, led by the head of Iran's military nuclear program, Professor Mohsen Fakhrizadeh, had set in motion a plan to cover up the existence of Iran's project to create its first nuclear weapon—codenamed AMAD—by moving all the evidence to a secret location. Senior Mossad officials told me that all the intelligence coming in pointed to orders to gather and store all the documents and digital information on the nuclear activities from the last 15 years in a single nuclear archive. Beavering away in secrecy, the Iranians spent weeks transferring tens of thousands of documents from Ministry of Defense facilities dotted around the country to an unremarkable civilian warehouse in an industrial area on the outskirts of Tehran. Only a very small group of senior Iranian officials was informed of the plan, which was intended to prevent the documents from falling into the hands of inspectors from the International Atomic Energy Agency, whose authority to visit suspicious sites in Iran had been significantly expanded under the terms of the JCPOA. In his interview with the TV program *Uvda*, Mossad Director Yossi Cohen said that the moment he received the first indications regarding the Iranians' plan, he gave two immediate instructions: 1) to increase the surveillance of the document transferal process and 2) to begin planning an operation to steal the contents of the Iranian nuclear archive. Just after 10 PM on the night of January 31, 2018—two years after they first received word of the Iranians' intentions—a team of 20 Mossad agents moved into position near the target. As soon as the order to move came in, the Mossad agents disabled the alarm system, breached the doors and entered. Inside the warehouse were dozens of heavy safes. In his leaving interview, Cohen revealed that none of the team that broke into the warehouse was Israeli—they were all foreign citizens working on behalf of the Israeli intelligence agency. Over 100 Mossad agents were involved in the operation. The team on the ground cracked the safes and emptied them one after the other. They contained 110 thousand documents—half in hard copies and the other half on CDs. As the clock ticked toward 5 AM, the team loaded the stolen nuclear archive into a waiting truck and began to make their escape. A senior Mossad official told me that the raiders managed to get their hands on most of the materials in the warehouse. More than half a ton of materials were loaded onto the truck. "We didn't take the whole archive—that would have been too heavy," he laughed. In early February 2018, work began in the Mossad headquarters in central Israel to translate and pore over the documents, most of which were in Farsi. The organization's division dedicated to preventing the spread of non-conventional weapons to hostile actors put together a special team of 50 people, including experts from the IDF's Military Intelligence Directorate. It would take many months before all the information in the archive was translated and analyzed.

The moment the operation was successfully concluded and the materials had been spirited out of Iran, Prime Minister Netanyahu informed the White House of the heist. "I remember that Netanyahu called Secretary of State Tillerson and told him," Brian Hook told me. "I remember that Tillerson then called me into his office to brief me about the Israeli operation. It was a very sensitive issue at the time." A month later, on March 5, 2018, Netanyahu arrived in Washington for a meeting with Trump at the White House. Also at that meeting were Secretary of Defense Mattis, Secretary of State Tillerson and National Security Advisor McMaster. Netanyahu updated the four on the contents of the Iranian nuclear archive and provided a general summary of the findings after a preliminary analysis of the documents. At the same time, the Mossad passed all the documents it had obtained on to the CIA. Following the meeting with Trump, Netanyahu held a press briefing at Blair House. We asked numerous questions about Iran, but he gave nothing away about the drama of the last few weeks and his conversation with Trump about it in the Oval Office. A few days after his return from the White House meeting, Netanyahu convened the State Security Cabinet. "Trump told me that unless there is a dramatic change, he will withdraw from the nuclear accord with Iran within the next few weeks," Netanyahu told his ministers. He delivered the same message to the foreign ministers of France and Germany when he met with them in Jerusalem later that week. "Unless the accord is completely fixed, the United States will pull out of it," Netanyahu informed them.

"We can argue whether that is a good thing or a bad thing, but it's just the reality."

While it appeared that fate was smiling on him, Netanyahu had no intention of taking his foot off the gas. He planned to use the nuclear archive the Mossad had brought from Tehran to create a media spectacle that would generate further momentum for Trump's decision to withdraw from the accord. He gathered together the chiefs of the Mossad, IDF and Shin Bet—Yossi Cohen, Gadi Eisenkot and Nadav Argaman—and his national security advisor, Meir Ben-Shabbat, to discuss how the archive materials should be used. Everyone agreed that Israel's interests were not best served by keeping the materials secret or sharing them only with foreign intelligence agencies. They had to reach the press, where they could sway international public opinion. It's unlikely that any of the participants in that meeting thought their support for making the materials public would result in a prime-time theatrical performance. "Tonight, we're going to show you something that the world has never seen before," Netanyahu began. "Tonight, we are going to reveal new and conclusive proof of the secret nuclear weapons program that Iran has been hiding for years from the international community in its secret atomic archive." Microphone in hand and bursting with energy and adrenaline, Netanyahu looked like a lifestyle coach in full lecture mode, or an evangelist preacher delivering a fiery sermon to his flock. He danced from one side of the stage to the other, dramatically pulling away the black fabric behind him to reveal shelves stacked with folders designed to imitate the Iranian nuclear archive.

Netanyahu worked in secret on the "nuclear archive show" over several weeks. Aside from a small group of senior Mossad officials and close advisors—including the former national security advisor, Jacob Nagel, brought on board as an outside consultant—

nobody knew about the secret presentation or the set that had been prepared for the opening night extravaganza. Chief of the General Staff Eisenkot only found out about the planned event a few hours before it began. "After they delivered the archive, there was a discussion about whether it was right to leverage it through the media," he told me. "We said, of course. But I thought it would be used in a careful and sophisticated way. I never imagined it would end up as the Netanyahu Show on live TV. I didn't like that Yossi Cohen went along with it. I thought we should retain a certain ambiguity and not poke the Iranians in the eye with it."[149] Cohen, who came under criticism both inside and outside the Mossad for going along with Netanyahu despite knowing the archive was going to be used for a political stunt, would later claim in his defense that all the heads of the security establishment had supported the decision to publicize the archive raid. "It was important for us that the whole world see it and that the Iranians see that they could not get away with lies and cover-ups," he told Ilana Dayan in the interview.

Netanyahu saw the haul from the operation as the ace that would get him over the line in his push to convince Trump to withdraw from the nuclear agreement. When I asked Trump in our meeting at Mar-a-Lago three years later whether the nuclear archive was the deciding factor in his decision to walk away from the accord, he snorted derisively. "They showed me papers that were old. I looked at them and I said, 'Who drew these? Where do they come from now?'" he told me.[150] "I would have done that [withdraw from the JCPOA] whether Bibi existed or not. I was not convinced by him, just like he couldn't convince Obama in the opposite direction. I spoke to him about it. I spoke to many people about it. Many people didn't want me to do what I did. I felt you had to do it because I felt that you can't let these people have nuclear weapons." Trump's assurance that he would have walked away from the nuclear accord anyway is almost certainly accurate. His claim that the documents he was shown were old was also true.[151] On the other hand, his dismissive response in the interview may also owe something to the animosity that he built up toward Netanyahu during the final months of his term. At the time, he did not wave away the documents Netanyahu placed on his table. He even mentioned them in his speech on May 8, 2018, when he announced the withdrawal from the nuclear accord, using them as evidence that Iran was seeking to develop nuclear weapons. "That wasn't the only reason, but it did factor into the president's thinking when he made the decision," Hook told me.[152] "The nuclear archive accelerated the process and reinforced the president's existing determination to either drastically fix the deal or to withdraw from it."

Several years later, the debate surrounding the operation is still ongoing. On the one hand, there is broad consensus within the security and intelligence establishment—both in Israel and globally—that this was one of the most daring, creative and complex operations ever carried out. But alongside the professional assessment of the intelligence and operational achievements, divisions remain over whether what was found in the nuclear archive dramatically reshaped what was already known about the Iranian military nuclear plan and whether it offered a "smoking gun" regarding Iranian breaches of the 2015 nuclear deal. "It was a beautiful operation but it produced limited value," former Chief of the General Staff Eisenkot told me when we met two and a half years later.[153] Brigadier General "A,"[154] who was the head of the Non-Conventional Weapons Directorate within the Mossad at the time and led the analysis of the archive materials, sat next to Netanyahu at the press briefing the day after the nuclear archive was exposed and spoke at length about how the findings "reveal so much compared to what we knew in the past." He was right to say that the archive drastically expanded the international community's existing knowledge about the Iranian nuclear weapons program, but the bottom line of those 110 thousand documents was no different to what the Western powers knew back in 2003. "That was exactly why we worked so hard for so many years to reach a nuclear agreement that would halt the Iranian nuclear program," a senior European diplomat who served as head of the negotiating team for one of the major powers involved in the talks with the Iranians told me. Jacob Nagel and Yossi Cohen claimed that the archive exposed the fact that Iran had lied to the world when it denied having previously developed a military nuclear program and that it had even kept hold of all the documents from that period—in breach of the nuclear deal. This claim is true. However, the P5+1 signatories to the deal went into the negotiations knowing that the Iranians were lying, which was why there had to be an oversight mechanism that would make it harder for them to continue to do so.

The Withdrawal

On May 3, 2018, Netanyahu convened the State Security Cabinet ahead of what seemed to be an imminent US withdrawal from the JCPOA. None of the ministers had the expertise or the diplomatic-military heft to confront Netanyahu or to put forward a dissenting perspective—not that any of them had any desire to do so, anyway. But within the defense establishment, things were different. Mossad chief Yossi Cohen—who had fallen into complete lockstep with Netanyahu and considered the nuclear archive the crowning achievement of his service—argued that a US withdrawal from the agreement would be to Israel's benefit. But

Eisenkot and the other IDF top brass presented a far more nuanced picture. "We said that the US withdrawing from the agreement would not lead to it being canceled," Eisenkot recalled. "And we also told the ministers that if the Americans were to withdraw from the agreement, there would be advantages to that, but at the same time it would create new dangers for Israel." One of the points Eisenkot raised was that the US withdrawing from the nuclear accord would force the IDF to turn the bulk of its attention back to the Iranian nuclear threat and to allocate fewer resources to the northern front or the Gaza Strip. "They didn't like the army's position on the nuclear accord in that discussion," Eisenkot said. "There were arguments and voices were raised, but we continued to focus on the facts."

The following day, May 4, 2018, a transatlantic phone call took place. On the call were the new US secretary of state, Mike Pompeo, and his German, French and British counterparts. Pompeo informed the three that Trump was formally rejecting their proposed amendments to the nuclear accord. "The president told me that it's insufficient to make him change his mind," Pompeo told them. "Prepare yourselves for a statement in the coming days." For their part, the Europeans had resigned themselves to this outcome two weeks previously. They saw how Brian Hook was refusing to budge and figured that he too realized that Trump's mind was made up. In Berlin, London and Paris, there was a deep sense of frustration. "We knew that these negotiations were like playing roulette in the casino, and that even if we did reach an agreement, the odds were at least 50 percent that Trump would reject it. We really were close—but the Americans bolted 100 meters from the finish line," a senior European diplomat who had been on the call told me afterward.

On May 8, Trump faced the cameras in the Diplomatic Reception

Room of the White House, with hundreds of millions of eyes in the Middle East and around the world waiting for him to deliver his verdict. "We cannot prevent an Iranian nuclear bomb under the decaying and rotten structure of the current agreement," said Trump. "The Iranian deal is defective at its core. If we do nothing, …in just a short period of time, the world's leading state sponsor of terror will be on the cusp of acquiring the world's most dangerous weapon. Therefore, I am announcing today that the United States will withdraw from the Iran nuclear deal." As soon as his speech was finished, Trump signed the presidential decrees to restore the US sanctions on Iran that had been lifted in 2015 with the signing of the JCPOA. The congratulatory statements from Israel were quick to come—and the condemnations from Iran, likewise. In the European capitals, meanwhile, frantic discussions were held to find ways to hold the scraps of the accord together. Two weeks after Trump withdrew from the JCPOA, it was Pompeo's turn to stand in front of the cameras for a speech on Iran. In a long address, he outlined 12 American demands on Iran, from a complete freeze on all uranium enrichment to ending support for Hezbollah and releasing US citizens held in Iranian jails. Only if Iran met these demands, said Pompeo, would the United States lift the sanctions. But the demands were non-starters. What Pompeo was calling for, in effect, was for Iran to become Norway. It was never going to happen—and it didn't. The true goal of Pompeo's speech was to pave the way for the maximum pressure campaign the Trump administration employed to try and bring Iran to its knees.

Brian Hook was among the survivors of the dramatic shakeup within the US government during those weeks. Despite being a close advisor of Rex Tillerson, who had been fired, and being the head of the US negotiating team with the European powers on amending the nuclear accord that Trump had withdrawn from, he held onto his position. Jared Kushner, along with others in the White House who enjoyed working with Hook, encouraged the incoming secretary of state, Mike Pompeo, to retain his services. He agreed. Not only did Hook's standing not suffer under Pompeo; it even improved. In August 2018, Pompeo appointed Hook as his special representative for Iran. From this office, Hook put the maximum pressure campaign into practice, working with teams within the Mossad, IDF Military Intelligence Directorate and Israeli Ministry of Foreign Affairs. Meetings intended to tighten the sanctions on Iran—especially on its banking and oil sectors—took place in Washington and Jerusalem every few weeks. Hook, who led the economic campaign against the Iranians, started each morning by checking the exchange rate of the rial and other economic indicators. A profile piece published in *Vox* described how he personally called shipping magnates and even oil tanker captains around the world to warn them against transporting Iranian oil. On several occasions, he threatened that if they continued, they would be subject to US sanctions; other times, he proposed that they transport the Iranian oil to a different port instead, where it could be confiscated in exchange for a financial reward worth millions of dollars.

After he started working on the maximum pressure campaign, Hook met with Kushner and gave him an insight that would go on to shape a significant part of the administration's policy over the following two years. "Our files can be mutually reinforcing," Hook told Kushner. "Our partners in the Gulf and in Israel want us to reverse the Obama policy of accommodating Iran and are happy with the maximum pressure campaign. We can use that to strengthen the ties between them and to make progress on the president's peace plan." Kushner agreed. Hook then became part of the White House peace team. Their first major opportunity to collaborate came a few months later.

Secret Alliance

In late 2018, Hook traveled to the Gulf. When he arrived in Riyadh, the Saudi foreign minister at the time, Adel Al-Jubeir, proposed convening a summit of foreign ministers dedicated to peace in the Middle East. Unlike previous international conferences, however, this time the main talking point the Saudis proposed was not the Israeli–Palestinian conflict, but the Iranian threat in the region. Hook loved the idea and sold it to Secretary of State Pompeo. The Americans suggested to the Polish government that they host it in Warsaw. The Poles agreed, and in January 2019 invitations went out to dozens of countries, including Israel and six Arab nations (with most of the latter not having diplomatic relations with the former). And yet, as the date of the conference drew nearer, the Poles' enthusiasm waned. France and Germany announced that their delegations to the conference would not include their foreign ministers and even expressed criticism that the conference was intended solely to provoke Iran. The Iranian foreign ministry even summoned the Polish ambassador for a rebuke. In an attempt to balance the agenda, the White House announced that Jared Kushner would also be attending and that he would be providing a special update to all the participants on the progress of the "deal of the century." For Benjamin Netanyahu, less than two months out from the Knesset elections, this conference could not have come at a better time. As far as he was concerned, the summit was an opportunity to show off one of his singular strengths: his diplomatic prowess. He planned to make as much lemonade as possible from the bitter fruit of the elections.

A few hours after we arrived in Warsaw on February 13, 2019, I settled in at the lobby of the Intercontinental Hotel where Netanyahu was staying. Years of experience have taught me that keeping track of the comings and goings in the hotel lobby where the prime minister is staying in the hours after his arrival often yields an interesting story. So it proved on this occasion. Two Middle Eastern men in suits entered the lobby. They walked from one side to the other as if looking for someone. Then, one member of the Israeli foreign ministry team who had joined the prime minister on the trip unexpectedly approached and began to speak with them. When the three men disappeared into the elevator down to the parking lot, I hurried after them with my journalist friend, Tal Shalev. We reached the parking lot just in time to see a diplomatic car pulling up at the entrance to the elevators. A bearded man wearing a suit and fur hat stepped out of it. As he drew closer, I saw that it was none other than the foreign minister of the Sultanate of Oman, Yusuf bin Alawi, on his way to a meeting with Netanyahu. As I was filming in the underground parking lot, I went over to shake his hand and introduce myself; when he heard I was a journalist, he hurriedly disappeared into the elevator. That short clip alone earned a major headline in the evening news and set social media abuzz—especially within the Arab world. A few months before that encounter, Netanyahu had been invited to a meeting in Muscat with Sultan Qaboos. The Omanis had wanted to facilitate a secret summit between Netanyahu and the Palestinian president, Mahmoud Abbas, to renew the dialogue between the two sides. Abbas agreed, but Netanyahu did not respond, not even at that meeting in Warsaw. In the end, Sultan Qaboos realized that Netanyahu was deliberately being evasive because he had no real interest in such a summit.

That evening, while I was having dinner at a Warsaw restaurant with a few colleagues, the heads of the participating delegations were in a private dinner of their own. "We wanted the Europeans to hear from the Middle Eastern countries directly how they perceived the threats in the region," Hook said.[155] The highlight of the program was supposed to be a joint panel discussion featuring Netanyahu and the foreign ministers of Saudi Arabia, the United Arab Emirates and Bahrain. But the ministers from the Gulf states were reluctant to sit on a panel with Netanyahu in front of hundreds of participants. "It was politically impossible to convince them to sit with Netanyahu on the same panel, although we did manage to get them in the same room at the same dinner," Hook told me. When Netanyahu got up to speak at the dinner after the foreign ministers from the Arab nations, he immediately drew a laugh from those gathered. "I'm very disappointed. I thought I was the foreign policy hawk in the region when it came to Iran, but I've just discovered that I've been outmatched by our cousins," he said. Netanyahu and the other invitees at the dinner were surprised by how similar the positions of Saudi Arabia, the UAE and Bahrain were to Israel when it came to Iran—in some cases, they were even harsher. Netanyahu had no intention of keeping such a gift to himself, especially with elections just around the corner. The next day, as the summit drew to a close, the prime minister held a short press briefing, in which he mocked us over and over again for not doing our jobs properly and finding out what had really happened in the behind-closed-doors part of the summit. "Go look for the videos," he said. "My advisors have them all." We had no idea what Netanyahu was on about and assumed it was just his usual media bashing. As we were heading back to the hotel to get ready for our return flight to Israel, we received a WhatsApp message from the Prime Minister's Office with a copy of Netanyahu's speech at the event and a link to a video on the official YouTube channel of the Prime Minister's Office. None of the journalists on the bus bothered to open the message, except for Yoni Kempinski, a correspondent for *Israel National News*. "Guys, you have to see this," he said suddenly. When we clicked on the link, we understood which clips Netanyahu had been talking about. Instead of a video of the speech from the conference, what came up was a short clip from the closed dinner where the foreign ministers had spoken the evening before. The video, which had been lightly edited, included only the positive comments toward Israel that supported Netanyahu's own talking points. "We grew up talking about the Israel–Palestine issue as the most important issue.... But then...we saw a bigger challenge. A more toxic one. The most toxic one in our history. Iran," said the foreign minister of Bahrain, Sheikh Khalid bin Ahmed al-Khalifa. "Every nation has the right to defend itself when it's challenged by another nation, yes," added the minister of foreign affairs of the United Arab Emirates, Sheikh Abdullah bin Zayed, in response to a question about the threat to Israel from an Iranian entrenchment in Syria. The Saudi minister of foreign affairs, Adel Al-Jubeir, could also be seen speaking. "Everywhere in the region Iran is playing a destructive role," he said. "Look at the Palestinians: Who is supporting Hamas and the Islamic Jihad, and undercutting the Palestinian Authority? Iran." After the quotes had successfully found their way into the Israeli press, Netanyahu's advisors quickly deleted the video from the YouTube account of the Prime Minister's Office. "The video was uploaded by accident," they told anyone who asked. I'll leave it up to the readers to decide.

That same evening, after the famous dinner, Hook received a phone call from one of the Arab foreign ministers who had been on the stage. "You are welcome to come to our hotel and we can keep talking," the minister told him. When he arrived at the hotel, Hook found ministers from the UAE, Bahrain and Saudi Arabia sitting together and smoking cigars. They were very pleased with how the dinner had gone (they were significantly less pleased when the video was leaked the next day) and suggested to Hook that the summit should not be a one-off, but rather the start of a process in the region. Hook agreed. There were five follow-up meetings in the months after the summit, all focused on security challenges in the Middle East. South Korea hosted a meeting on protecting against cyber threats and the United States hosted a meeting on human rights. They met in Poland to discuss energy security, in Romania to discuss the threat posed by ballistic missiles and in Bahrain to discuss ways to protect shipping lanes in the Gulf. Senior officials from dozens of nations participated in every one of these meetings—most notably Israel and Arab countries. The presence of Israeli and Arab diplomats and security officials at the same table gradually became natural.

A few weeks after the Warsaw summit, Yousef Al Otaiba came to Hook's office. He presented him with intelligence that had fallen into the hands of the United Arab Emirates. It purported to show that the IRGC was planning a series of bombings against sensitive sites in the Gulf, with a potential impact on American interests. "If these bombings are carried out, it could result in a major escalation," Al Otaiba told Hook. A senior official in the United Arab Emirates told me that Al Otaiba proposed convening a meeting of security and intelligence officials from the US and the UAE to prepare for such a scenario and to attempt to foil the attacks.[156] "Great idea," Hook told him. "Do you mind if we bring the Israelis to this meeting too?" Al Otaiba called his national security advisor, Sheikh Tahnoun bin Zayed, for his thoughts. "I have no problem with the Israelis coming," he said. After the move was given the green light, Hook, Al Otaiba and the Israeli ambassador to Washington, Ron Dermer, began putting together the first meeting of this secret trilateral alliance against Iran. A total of 125 diplomats and security officials from the United States,

Israel and the UAE participated in the initial gathering at the Department of State building in Washington. Despite the number of participants, there were no leaks. The follow-up session took place in Jerusalem. A large delegation of Emirati diplomats and intelligence and security officials arrived at the foreign ministry under a veil of secrecy. A few months later, a similar Israeli delegation departed for Abu Dhabi to continue the talks. The Americans were surprised to discover that some of the Israelis and Emiratis already knew each other. "In those three-way meetings we talked about all the Iranian threats—nuclear, conventional missiles, cyber warfare, terrorism, espionage," Hook told me.[157] "After the first meeting, Ambassador Dermer told me, 'This is the path to ending the Israeli–Arab conflict.'"

Shortly after 3:30 AM on September 14, 2019, a series of powerful explosions tore through the Abqaiq oil processing facilities and the Khurais oil field to the east of Riyadh, both owned by Saudi Aramco—the national Saudi oil company. Within minutes, both sites were illuminated by columns of flame shooting into the night sky. Dozens of drones and cruise missiles were employed in the simultaneous attacks. The Saudi air defense units were sleeping on the job and failed to react in time, despite the anti-aircraft batteries that protect the sites and the attacks being launched from hundreds of miles away. The only course of action left for the Saudi soldiers at the sites themselves was to direct ineffective machine gun fire at the "kamikaze" drones as they nosedived toward the oil facilities in waves. The Saudis were caught by surprise and humiliated by the assault against the heart of their oil industry. It was the most serious attack on their territory in their history: a defining moment, a Saudi Pearl Harbor. The shockwaves reverberated throughout the global oil markets, far beyond Saudi Arabia itself. The Abqaiq oil facility is the largest of its kind in the world; the Khurais oil field is also among the largest. The attacks cut Saudi Arabia's oil production capacity in half overnight, from 10 million barrels a day to only five million; they also caused a 5 percent reduction in global oil production and a 20 percent increase in global oil prices—the largest spike since the 1980s. The price began to stabilize only after President Trump authorized the release of oil from the US Strategic Petroleum Reserve. The Houthi rebels in Yemen claimed responsibility for the attack, but the United States and European powers pointed the finger of blame at Iran. The US investigation found that the drones and cruise missiles had flown in from the north (the direction of Iran) and not from Yemen, located to the south of the stricken facilities. Israel believed that Amir Ali Hajizadeh, the commander of the Aerospace Force of the IRGC, was behind the attack. The effective and synchronized nature of the attack served as a warning for Israel too, which immediately began to prepare against the threat of similar attacks, based on a swarm of drones and cruise missiles being fired toward strategic targets in Israel by Iranian forces stationed in Syria or Iraq. For Yousef Al Otaiba, the Emirati ambassador to the United States, the Aramco attack was the exact scenario that had so concerned him. "We felt vindicated for going through the whole preparation process with the Americans and the Israelis," he told me. Three months after the attack on Aramco, the secret talks between the US, UAE and Israel reached their peak with a trilateral meeting between their top national security officials. On December 17, 2019, the White House hosted the national security advisors to President Trump and Prime Minister Netanyahu, Robert O'Brien and Meir Ben-Shabbat, and the director of national intelligence of the UAE, Ali Al Shamsi, for a joint meeting around the same table. The meeting was dedicated to discussing expanding cooperation on Iran—but the option of normalization between the UAE and Israel also came up. "The meeting was part of the process of building trust and relationships with the UAE," recalled Ben-Shabbat.[158] "That was already a semi-formal meeting in the White House. Just the fact that it was taking place was significant. It was a major milestone on the journey, but we didn't feel like we were there yet in terms of normalization. We realized it was the general direction of travel, but we weren't able to flesh out a timetable yet."

Nine months after the trilateral talks on Iran began, it seemed they were well on their way to achieving their strategic end goal: formalizing the relationship between Israel and the Gulf states. "The Obama administration's strategy on Iran alienated Israel and our Gulf partners and as a result the US had lost its unique authority to broker peace agreements," Hook claimed when we met in Washington in April 2021. "We were able to restore the trust with Israel and our Gulf partners by getting the Iran strategy right, and that really helped with the process of bringing Israel and the UAE closer together."

Trump Doesn't Pick Up

On August 25, 2019, I was on my way back to Israel from a family vacation in Italy. As I was waiting to board my flight from Rome to Istanbul, I received a phone call from Labor Party MK Merav Michaeli. Michaeli was one of the only members of the Knesset with extensive knowledge on Iran. She told me about a meeting she had attended with a Western diplomat who claimed that the Trump White House was due to start negotiations with Iran. This was the first time I had heard anything to this effect. If it was true, it was a hell of a scoop. I sent WhatsApp messages to a few people during the flight in an attempt to find out more. One of them was a European diplomat who had participated in the

G7 leaders' summit in the seaside vacation hotspot of Biarritz in southwestern France, on the Atlantic coast. "The Iranian foreign minister, [Mohammad] Zarif is on his way here," he wrote. "There are rumors of a meeting between him and Trump."

Zarif's journey to the summit had started two days earlier, when he met with President Macron at the Élysée Palace to discuss a possible deal to restart negotiations between Iran and the United States. That Saturday evening, Macron met with Trump and the other G7 leaders in Biarritz and told them about the meeting. Later, Macron said that Trump's reaction had been favorable and that he had received the go-ahead to invite Zarif for further talks on the sidelines of the summit. News of the expected arrival of the Iranian foreign minister at the leaders' summit reached the Prime Minister's Office in Jerusalem on Sunday morning. The evening before, security tensions had reached new heights following an Israeli Air Force attack on Iranian targets in Syria and a drone attack on a Hezbollah stronghold in Beirut that was being attributed to Israel. Now, along with the heightened alert over a potential further escalation by Iran or Hezbollah, there was this new front of an unexpected meeting between Trump and the Iranian foreign minister.

Netanyahu called the US ambassador to Israel, David Friedman, and pressed him to arrange an urgent call with the president so that he could ask him not to meet with Zarif. A frustrated Netanyahu tried every possible channel to get through to Trump—all to no avail. For hours on end, the US president was not taking his calls. A few days later, when I reported on what had happened behind the scenes during those hours, both the White House and the Prime Minister's Office described it as purely a matter of scheduling difficulties. But a few months later, when Trump's former national security advisor, John Bolton, published his book,[159] my original reporting was vindicated.

Bolton wrote that, on the morning of August 25, while he was at the Biarritz summit with Trump, he was exchanging emails with the secretary of state, Mike Pompeo. He inquired about the rumors that Zarif was on his way for an unplanned visit to the summit, but Pompeo knew no more than he did. Trump was in a meeting with the other leaders at the time, so Bolton sent him a note with the details of Zarif's arrival. The note he received back stunned him. Bolton's assistant, who was sitting with the president, wrote that Trump had already heard about it from Macron, and that the French president had even suggested facilitating a meeting between the two men. "The president would definitely like to do that,"[160] she wrote to Bolton. In his book, Bolton wrote that the note left him reeling, even preparing to resign should the meeting go ahead. Shortly after that, Bolton received another email from Pompeo, telling him that Netanyahu had called him and demanded to speak with Trump on the phone immediately regarding the rumored meeting with Zarif. At the same time, Netanyahu and Dermer called Bolton directly. "Tell Netanyahu I'm dealing with it," Bolton replied to Pompeo.

Bolton wrote that he hurried to the floor where Trump's suite was located. Jared Kushner was also there, engaged in a lively phone conversation with David Friedman. "Kushner told Friedman that he had no intention of allowing Netanyahu to speak with the president," Bolton wrote in his book. "When he ended the call with Friedman, Kushner explained to me that he had blocked Netanyahu's attempt to speak with Trump, as well as another attempt earlier that same day, because he did not think it was appropriate for a foreign leader to tell Trump who he should and should not be meeting with." The more Bolton looked into the situation, the more he realized that Trump had kept him and Pompeo in the dark. The only ones in on the secret were the secretary of the treasury, Steve Mnuchin, and Kushner, who were shepherding Trump around the summit. When Bolton finally managed to get into the president's room, Trump asked him whether he thought a meeting with Zarif was a good idea. Bolton immediately said no, and emphasized that this was not the time to relieve the pressure on the Iranians. According to Bolton, Kushner was actually in favor of the meeting, and felt that Trump had nothing to lose from it. "I don't mean to give the Iranians anything so long as there's no deal, but I think I will meet with Zarif in private. Maybe just a handshake," Bolton claims Trump said.[161]

A frustrated Bolton left the meeting and called Pompeo again. "So we have Mnuchin and Kushner, two Democrats, running our foreign policy," Pompeo said. In the end, Iran's supreme leader, Ali Khamenei, vetoed the idea and no such meeting took place. Later that day, at the press conference with Macron, Trump said that he felt the timing was not right for a meeting with Zarif, although he did make a point of saying he would be willing to meet with Rouhani in the future. By the time Trump was finally free to take the phone call from Netanyahu, it was no longer necessary. Bolton resigned two weeks after the Biarritz summit.

When I raised this story with Kushner, two years later, he claimed that a meeting with Zarif had never actually been on the cards for Trump. "Zarif came there to meet Macron. The French wanted to make their party more interesting and raised this option," he told me.[162] "Zarif didn't want to meet with Trump either because he thought that if he meets Trump, they'll kill him when he goes back to Iran." At the same time, Kushner did confirm that he thought at the time that it would be a mistake to let Netanyahu speak with Trump. The way he tells it, he even told the prime minister that Trump would not want to hear what he had to say. "I knew Trump was in a place where he knew what he wanted to do with Iran and how to negotiate with them," Kushner told me. "I thought that if Bibi talks to him on the phone and gives him a lecture about why he shouldn't negotiate with Iran it will cause more harm than good. I felt he didn't need Bibi's help and Bibi wouldn't make Trump change his mind anyway. Bibi insisted and said he wanted to speak to the president anyway. I told the president that Bibi wanted to talk to him, and he didn't react in a very enthusiastic way—so I told him, don't take the call."

Biarritz may not have culminated in a meeting between Trump and Zarif, but in Jerusalem they took the view that it was only a matter of time before negotiations between the US and Iran restarted. They turned their attention to the next global gathering, the UN General Assembly at the end of September, which both Trump and President Rouhani were set to attend. In early September, when I joined the press pool for Netanyahu's visit to London, he sought to play down the controversy and blamed the events in Biarritz on Macron. "I'm sure that if Trump enters into talks with the Iranians, he will be far tougher and more clear-sighted than has been the case previously," he said in the press briefing after his meeting with his British counterpart, Boris Johnson. Three weeks later, his confidence was almost put to the test.

Macron had twice attempted to arrange meetings between Trump and Rouhani, at the 2017 and 2018 UN General Assembly sessions, both times unsuccessfully. Undeterred, he tried again the following year. It was only a few days after the Iranian attacks on the Saudi oil facilities, and Macron hoped that his diplomatic initiative would lower the tensions in the Gulf. The French put together a four-point plan to be introduced at the summit between Trump and Rouhani. According to this plan, the United States would remove the sanctions it had placed on Iran since Trump had entered office—and Iran would once more be able to sell oil. For their part, the Iranians would make a commitment never to develop nuclear weapons and would implement the JCPOA in full. Iran would also agree to enter negotiations on a new and improved nuclear accord that would address their actions in the Middle East. Trump agreed to the principles of the French proposal. For two days, Macron, Boris Johnson and Angela Merkel pushed Rouhani to agree to a meeting with Trump, but he had a precondition: the US president would have to publicly announce the lifting of sanctions before the meeting could take place. Trump could not agree to such a condition. At the height of the drama, on September 25, 2019, Macron and Johnson were spotted with Rouhani in one of the hallways of the UN headquarters, urging him on camera not to miss the opportunity and to take the meeting. "You need to both be on the side of the swimming pool and jump at the same time," Johnson told him. The metaphor amused Rouhani, who burst out laughing. But his position remained the same: the US president must be the one to take the first step. Macron was on the verge of throwing in the towel. He took his advisors for pizza near the UN headquarters ahead of their return flight to Paris. During the meal, he decided to launch one last attempt—this time, to arrange a phone call between Trump and Rouhani. The American president agreed without hesitation. The Iranians, for their part, did not refuse outright. They allowed French technicians to come to the Hilton Millennium Hotel where Rouhani was staying and to install a secure line in the conference room next to the Iranian president's suite. The French believed they were within touching distance of a breakthrough. At around nine o'clock that evening, Macron came to Rouhani's hotel—but the Iranian leader refused to meet with him. When he got to the conference room, Macron was forced to call Trump and inform him that, just like previous attempts, this one had also failed. "Macron knew that Trump was always open to direct diplomacy with Iran," Brian Hook told me. "But the Iranian supreme leader, Khamenei, refused to give Rouhani permission to speak with Trump on the phone. Rouhani wanted to do it. None of the Iranian diplomats would agree to speak with us—because they have no leash and they know they might end up in Evin prison if they go outside their brief."

The Attack That Never Happened

Of all the changes to Israeli policy on Iran during Trump's time as president, none was more significant than the removal of the military option from the table. During President Obama's first term, Prime Minister Benjamin Netanyahu and Minister of Defense Ehud Barak poured over three billion dollars into preparing operational plans and capabilities for a military strike against Iran's nuclear facilities. The attack was never carried out. The negotiations between the US and Iran and the subsequent signing of the JCPOA in Obama's second term further diminished the political and diplomatic viability of any military option. Trump's election was supposed to herald the return of the Israeli military threat. After all, the new president would give Israel almost unconditional backing for such a move. However, things played out differently during Trump's term—on two fronts.

The Israeli decision to flesh out the military option was replaced by a hope that the Trump administration itself would attack the Iranian nuclear facilities at some stage, with the encouragement of their commander-in-chief. "There weren't really any operational discussions or moves regarding an Israeli attack on Iran during the Trump administration," the chief of the general staff in Israel during the first two years of Trump's tenure, Gadi Eisenkot, told me. "When Obama signed the JCPOA, we completely changed our attitude to [an Israeli military operation], and then later the

US withdrew from the nuclear deal and created an incentive the other way. One of the reasons is that we believed Trump when he said that Iran would not obtain a nuclear weapon, and another was that we never reached the stage where a discussion on the nuts and bolts of military action became relevant." A former senior official within the Trump administration corroborated Eisenkot's version and said that the question of a military operation targeting Iran's nuclear facilities had never been raised in talks between Israel and the US, as the Iranians never reached a point during those four years where such a discussion became necessary.

In October 2019, following the second consecutive round of elections, the former chief of the general staff and recent addition to the Knesset, Gabi Ashkenazi, was appointed head of the Foreign Affairs and Defense Committee. One of the first things he decided to investigate was the military's preparedness for a military operation against Iran. Ashkenazi discovered severe deficiencies and flagged the matter up to Netanyahu. After Netanyahu was ousted and a new government was formed in mid-2021, I heard the same assessment from a string of senior officials—including then-Prime Minister Naftali Bennett, then-Minister of Defense Benny Gantz and then-Minister of Foreign Affairs Yair Lapid—as to why Netanyahu had almost entirely failed to maintain the viability of the military option against the Iranian nuclear program while Trump was in office. They said that the former prime minister had expected Trump's maximum pressure campaign to bring the Iranians back to the negotiating table from a weaker position, lead to regime change, or cause the situation to deteriorate to the extent that Trump himself would order an attack on the Iranians. None of that materialized.

Senior officials in the Trump administration told me that, between 2017 and 2021, Israel and the United States resumed collaborating on a campaign of covert measures targeting the Iranian nuclear program; intelligence operations, targeted assassinations, sabotage and cyberattacks. Some were carried out in collaboration, others by Israel or the United States acting independently of the other. Wherever necessary, they informed each other ahead of time. Trump's special envoy for Iran, Brian Hook, told me that the administration gave Israel almost completely free rein on Iran. "They knew that we were in full support of whatever decisions they made in their sovereign capacity to counter the Iranian regime. There were no process fouls. There was no daylight between us. And the efforts that we took helped Israel and helped the US to deal with the common threat. We saw that we had a clear meeting of the minds on the Iranian threat," he told me. "We were keeping a very close eye together on Iran's breakout timeline on weaponizing. We were comfortable with the actions we took—and were prepared to take—to ensure that Iran never got a nuclear weapon."

For the first three years of Trump's term, he avoided almost any overt military action against Iran. He overlooked Iranian attacks on ships in the Gulf, bombings by Shia militias in Iraq, and even the strike on the Saudi oil facilities. The Americans did deploy aircraft carriers, heavy bombers and soldiers to the Gulf, but these were primarily intended as a deterrent. The most significant moment in the first three years of the Trump administration came in June 2019, when the Iranians shot down a US intelligence-gathering drone over the Strait of Hormuz. The Iranians argued that the drone had violated their airspace, while the Americans claimed it had been in international airspace. The US Department of Defense recommended an immediate response: taking out an Iranian missile boat in Gulf waters with advanced warning to give the crew members time to abandon ship. John Bolton and Mike Pompeo pushed for a far broader retaliation that included missile batteries within Iranian territory. The latter were able to persuade Trump, and the US military began to prepare accordingly. The Department of Defense, led by the chairman of the Joint Chiefs of Staff, General Joseph Dunford, warned Trump that such an attack could result in 150 Iranian casualties (a disproportionate response to the downing of a single drone) and potentially ignite a regional war. Trump wavered. He held discussions with members of Congress and senators. According to *The New York Times*, he even spoke on the phone with right-wing Fox News host Tucker Carlson, a vocal opponent of US military interventions abroad.[163] Carlson warned him that a strike against Iran would run counter to his promise to end the US's wars and could even cost him the next election. Mere minutes before the strike was due to get underway, Trump changed his mind and gave the order to stand down. In Jerusalem, there was surprise and disappointment that Trump had blinked at the last minute. All Trump could do was put out a tweet justifying his decision.

The last year of his term saw a shift in Trump's willingness to apply force against Iran. In December 2019, after a US citizen was killed in a missile strike on a US base in Iraq by pro-Iran militias, the United States retaliated with an attack on those same militia groups on the Iraqi–Syrian border, during which 25 Shia fighters were killed. In response, supporters of the Shia militias launched mass protests in Baghdad. Thousands of supporters made their way to the Green Zone in the Iraqi capital, where the foreign embassies are located. They forced their way in and besieged the US embassy for several hours, setting fire to guard posts and trying to climb the fences. For Trump, the assault on the American embassy was a step too far. He pointed the finger of blame squarely at Iran. Seeking a fitting response, the president referred back to a list of options for potential actions against the pro-Iran militias in Iraq that had been submitted to him two days before the embassy attack. One of the more extreme options was to assassinate the head of the Quds Force of the Islamic Revolutionary Guards Corps, General Qasem Soleimani. The Iranian general had been in the crosshairs of Trump administration officials since the president first entered office. On December 2, 2017, the then-head of the CIA, Mike Pompeo, sent a letter to Soleimani warning him that the United States would hold Iran, and him personally, accountable for any actions against US interests in the region.[164] But it was only after the rocket strikes in Kirkuk and the attacks on the US embassy in Baghdad that Trump decided to set the wheels turning on the plan to take out Soleimani. Six months previously, Trump had overlooked the drone incident and conveyed weakness. So, when the time came to respond to the rocket attacks on Kirkuk, he opted for the most extreme option on the table. In hindsight, Trump justified his decision by explaining that the US had intelligence indicating that Soleimani was planning a series of attacks on American targets in the Middle East—including four embassies. "He was a man who killed many American soldiers and badly wounded and maimed so many American soldiers," the former president told me in one of our conversations.[165] "I think he was trying to lead them to war. He was meeting with the people that got blown up with him [the commander of the Popular Mobilization Forces, Abu Mahdi al-Muhandis], and they were not meeting to discuss childcare. They had a lot of very bad intentions, and we knew that. So I felt very strongly that our country really had little choice."

Soleimani was considered one of Supreme Leader Ali Khamenei's closest allies, and the brains behind Iran's regional expansion. Soleimani's influence was so great that Iran's foreign minister, Muhammad Javad Zarif, even confessed that the general was often the one to dictate Iranian foreign policy behind the backs of the foreign ministry. He was Khamenei's point-man in Iraq, giving orders to the Shia militias (the Popular Mobilization Forces first and foremost) and spearheading efforts to push the Americans out. Soleimani was also the main point of contact for Hezbollah, Hamas and the Islamic Jihad. He was behind the Iranian entrenchment strategy in Syria and whipped up the Houthi rebels in Yemen in their war against Saudi Arabia. His power, knowledge and experience were such that his assassination had the potential to significantly reduce the ability of the Iranian regime to act outside its borders. Previous American administrations also had opportunities to go after Soleimani but demonstrated restraint in view of his political stature in Iran and the region. Over time, this contributed to a perception of invincibility that made the Iranian general careless with his personal security. He became a bona fide celebrity; social media was flooded with pictures and video clips of him visiting his foot soldiers in Iraq, Syria, Yemen and Lebanon. Soleimani's complacency played a major part in his downfall.

On the night of January 3, 2020, Soleimani arrived in Iraq from Damascus. A *Yahoo! News* investigation revealed that Israel had assisted the United States with intelligence regarding Soleimani's whereabouts and with tracking the cellphone that was on him when he landed in Baghdad. The head of the Military Intelligence Directorate, Tamir Hayman, confirmed in his retirement interviews that Israel gave information to the United States that helped with the assassination of Soleimani.[166] US military drones tracked his convoy, and at 1:30 AM, a few minutes after it left the airport, they launched the hellfire missiles they were carrying. Soleimani never stood a chance. He was killed on the spot alongside al-Muhandis, one of his most important allies in Iraq and the leader of the largest Shia militia in the country. The Iranians were stunned, and revenge was quick to follow. Five days later, they fired 16 missiles at US bases in Iraq. The Iranians stated that 80 American soldiers had been killed in the strikes, a claim that was entirely without foundation. At the same time, Trump's initial claims of zero casualties were also inaccurate. A month after the attack, the US Department of Defense released a statement that 110 soldiers had been wounded, many of them suffering from head injuries and concussions. The Iranian military response began and ended with this attack. Their strategic response to the assassination, however, was just beginning, as they swore to carry on the mission of the commander of the Quds Force and drive US troops out of Iraq. Former Chief of Staff Eisenkot told me that the assassination of Soleimani was in large part a consequence of Israel's actions to prevent an Iranian build-up in Syria. According to Eisenkot, over the course of 2019, Soleimani was forced to withdraw part of his forces from Syria for fear of Israeli attacks. Instead, he increasingly turned his regional focus to Iraq. This meant more powerful Shia militias in Iraq and increased tensions with the Americans. "On the one hand, Soleimani came into more direct conflict with the Americans," Eisenkot told me.[167] "On the other hand, the Americans saw that we were attacking the Iranians three or four times a week in Syria without them being able to defend themselves or retaliate, and that reduced their own concerns about striking the Iranians and taking out Soleimani."

Soleimani's assassination was supposed to represent the high-water mark of Israeli–American collaboration on Iran. Instead, it proved to be one of the lowest points in the relationship between the two countries under Trump. I discovered this in one of my interviews with the former president, when I asked him whether Israel had been involved in the assassination of the Iranian general. "I can't talk about this story. But I was very disappointed in Israel," he replied.[168] I thought I must have misheard and asked him to explain. "I can't mention that now, but I was not happy with Israel. Israel didn't do the right thing," he said. "People will hear about that at the right time." Trump's advisors were equally surprised at his words. When I tried to find out what Trump was referring to, I received a sweeping round of "no comments" from several former senior figures in the White House. There was a general feeling that the incident was an awkward subject for those on the American side who were privy to the full picture. Eventually, I managed to piece together the astonishing full details. Former senior American officials told me that Trump had expected Israel to take a more active part in the days surrounding Soleimani's assassination. Whether rightly or wrongly, he was upset by what he perceived to be ungrateful conduct by Netanyahu. "Trump was furious at Netanyahu and said that Israel was willing to fight Iran down to the last American soldier," a former American official told me.[169] "He put this incident in the same category as his disappointment and distancing from the NATO alliance." Several senior officials in the Trump administration admitted that the president's anger was not entirely justified. It was another example of Trump's tendency to adopt a stance on a subject based on partial information or an inaccurate reading of events. Even today, the Soleimani affair is engraved in Trump's mind as a low point in his relationship with Netanyahu. The number of people in the Israeli government who were familiar with the president's thoughts on this matter can be counted on one hand. Nor did Netanyahu's attempts to explain and to set the record straight a few months later yield any success. A former Trump aide said to me that in a brief conversation in the Oval Office on September 15, 2020, minutes before the signing ceremony of the Abraham Accords, Netanyahu whispered in Trump's ear that there was a misunderstanding regarding his position on the Soleimani assassination. Trump listened but remained unconvinced. He continued to believe that Netanyahu had manipulated him. A senior Israeli security official rejected the accusation that Israel had been unwilling to take part in the assassination of the Iranian general. According to him, in the discussions that took place between Israeli defense officials and their American counterparts, the Israelis had even offered to be the ones to act. It was the Americans, he claimed, who had insisted on being the ones to carry out the assassination.[170] Another senior Israeli official told me that other members of the Trump administration expressed a great deal of gratitude to Israel for its role in preparing for the Iranian response. Vice President Pence even called the national security advisor, Meir Ben-Shabbat, late one night to thank him for steps Israel had taken that had saved the lives of American troops in Iraq.

As the presidential election loomed closer, Israel increased its covert activities against Iran. Not only did the Trump administration not object, they even encouraged Israel. On July 2, 2020, there was a powerful explosion at the advanced centrifuge assembly facility at the Natanz uranium enrichment site. At first, the Iranians denied that any damage had been caused. Within a few days, however, the spokesman of the Atomic Energy Organization of Iran was forced to admit that the facility had suffered a heavy blow that would significantly set back Iran's ability to build new centrifuges. *The New York Times* reported that Israel was behind the sabotage. Six months later, on the same day I met Trump at his resort, there was another mysterious explosion at the same facility. Once more it resulted in heavy damage—and once more the Iranians accused Israel of sabotage. At the time of the second attack on Natanz, Joe Biden was president, and the US was in the middle of renewed nuclear talks with Iran in Vienna. Senior Biden administration officials told me Israel did not consult the

US ahead of the attack. The White House was furious. National Security Advisor Jake Sullivan protested to his Israeli counterpart Meir Ben-Shabbat during a meeting in Washington several days later. "You talk all the time about the need for close coordination on Iran. The Natanz attack is a good example of how this could have been helpful," Sullivan told Ben Shabbat. "If 'no surprises' is going to be a principle in the US-Israel relationship, it's got to be a two-way street."[171]

But the most significant blow to the Iranian nuclear program during the Trump administration had nothing to do with any of its facilities. That took place on Tehran's main highway on November 27, 2020, two and a half weeks after the US elections. General Mohsen Fakhrizadeh, the founding father of the Iranian military nuclear program and a prime target of the Mossad since the early '90s, was on his way for a weekend break with his wife at their holiday home outside Tehran. Shortly after the security vehicle that was leading his convoy left it to carry out a preliminary sweep of the house, Fakhrizadeh's car came under heavy machine gun fire from a commercial vehicle that was standing on the side of the road. Fakhrizadeh was severely wounded and later died in the hospital. His wife, who was sitting next to him, emerged unscathed. Reports in the IRGC-affiliated press claimed that the machine gun had been operated remotely and was destroyed in a powerful explosion moments later. Three months after the incident, *The Jewish Chronicle* reported that the Mossad was behind the assassination. According to the article, Israel had informed the Trump administration about the operation ahead of time, but there had been no American involvement.

The atmosphere in Washington, DC was very tense at the time. Trump was refusing to accept the election results, alleging fraud, and looking for any evidence at all that he could use to appeal to the Supreme Court. The chaos in the White House raised concerns within the American and Israeli security establishments that Trump was set to order an attack on Iran as part of his attempts to prevent the transfer of power to President-elect Joe Biden on January 20, 2021. Events in the United States fed back directly into the heightened tensions in the Middle East. The Iranians were concerned about an imminent US attack—and the Americans were preparing for Iranian bombings. Every few days, the Americans sent B-52 strategic bombers from the US to bases in the Gulf as a show of force and a deterrence. On November 17, *The New York Times* reported that at a White House meeting a few days earlier, Trump was presented with information indicating increased Iranian use of advanced centrifuges for enriching uranium. Reacting to the information, the president inquired about America's options. A few of his senior advisors emphasized that any American attack could lead to a significant escalation in the region. Three days after that report, I met with a very senior official in the Israeli defense establishment. He told me that the Israeli minister of defense, Benny Gantz, had ordered the IDF to prepare for a scenario involving a US attack on Iran before Donald Trump left the White House. He told me that the instructions from Gantz did not follow any specific intelligence or assessments that such an attack was in the pipeline. Rather, it had more to do with Trump's unpredictable character and the delicate situation in the weeks leading up to the transfer of power in DC. A month before Biden was due to take office, the chairman of the Joint Chiefs of Staff, General Mark Milley, came to Israel for a visit. Iran was at the top of his agenda for his meetings with Gantz and Netanyahu. Milley confided in a few of his Israeli interlocutors that he was concerned that Trump would order action against Iran before the end of his term. "When Milley visited, we spoke about the possibility that the president would take steps on

Iran before his term ended, but I didn't consider it to be particularly likely," Gantz told me.[172] In a book by the journalist couple Peter Baker and Susan Glasser, they revealed that Milley described how several of Trump's close advisors were agitating for such an attack.[173] Milley even claimed that Prime Minister Netanyahu pushed Trump to move against Iran following his election defeat. Milley's suspicions are easy to understand. Throughout Trump's term, stories spread about Netanyahu's supposed influence over the American president. But these stories, already exaggerated for the first three years of Trump's term, were downright inaccurate by his final year. After the elections in November, Netanyahu's influence on Trump was close to non-existent. As is clear from the open hostility Trump demonstrated toward Netanyahu in our conversations, it is hard to imagine a scenario in which he would have acceded to such a request from the Israeli prime minister. In our conversations, Trump confirmed that discussions did take place in which the option of attacking Iran came up but emphasized that he was opposed to the idea. "All of these reports are fake news," he stressed to me.[174] "There was no reason to strike Iran. Iran was at a point where if I had won the elections…which I did, but had I officially won, Iran would have had to deal with us within one week. That's why the stories are fake. It's all because of Milley. He was not much of a general and not much of a leader."

Success or Failure?

Looking back, Trump considers his withdrawal from the JCPOA in 2018 and the maximum pressure campaign against the Iranians over his four years in office to be one of his signature foreign policy achievements. He also sees it as one of his greatest contributions to Israel. The Netanyahu government embraced

Trump's approach to Iran, the prime minister encouraging his withdrawal from the JCPOA back in the days when his ties with Trump were still strong. The Israeli government also encouraged the maximum pressure campaign, and in some cases even helped to shape and push parts of it. In an interview with journalist Nadav Eyal,[175] the former deputy director of the Mossad, Ehud Lavi, said that Trump's withdrawal from the JCPOA had been "an Israeli strategic goal" the Mossad took on at the behest of the political echelon. However, what appeared at first to be a remarkable diplomatic success quickly boomeranged. The maximum pressure campaign did indeed significantly hinder Iran's ability to finance its regional proxies and fuel its plans to expand the influence of the Islamic Republic throughout the region, but it did not moderate Iran's nuclear ambitions—quite the opposite. In May 2019, a year after Trump's withdrawal from the JCPOA, President Hassan Rouhani declared that Iran would scale back the implementation of its commitments under the agreement. Or, to put it in non-political language, Iran would begin to violate the agreement and remove any restrictions or limitations on its nuclear program. In the 18 months that followed this statement, the Iranians restored their nuclear program to its pre-JCPOA state, and even significantly enhanced it by operating advanced centrifuges capable of enriching uranium at a much faster pace. Iran began enriching uranium to 20 percent, and then moved on to the unprecedented level of 60 percent, very close to the threshold needed to build an atomic bomb. At the same time, the Iranians started experimenting with producing uranium metal— the key raw material in creating nuclear warheads for ballistic missiles. At the time of Trump's withdrawal from the JCPOA, Iran's nuclear breakout time—the time needed to produce enough 90 percent enriched uranium for one nuclear bomb—stood at a year. Three years later, it was down to only three months. A September 2021 report by the American Institute for Science and International Security (ISIS) found that Iran would only need one month to produce enough 90 percent enriched uranium to build a single atomic bomb.[176] A report by the same institute in March 2022 set the Iranian breakout time at two to three weeks. The next report, in May 2022, concluded that Iran's breakout time had reached zero.[177] Lavi said that in hindsight, Trump's withdrawal from the JCPOA not only failed to serve Israel's interests, but actively harmed them. He stressed that the operation to steal the Iranian nuclear archives (which he led) was unprecedented in its scale and ambition, its ingenuity and ultimately in its success. Yet in the grand scheme of things, Iran's nuclear program had only escalated in the wake of Trump's withdrawal from the agreement.[178] "Our situation today is worse than it was when the agreement was signed. The Iranians did not halt their expansionist approach for a second; they are building rockets. The deal we made [with Trump] was not good. It brought us back to the start," Lavi said in March 2021. At the time of writing, the Iranian government is led by President Ebrahim Raisi, a far more hardline leader than his predecessor, Rouhani. Iran has not only advanced its nuclear program to an unprecedented level, it has also drastically restricted the International Atomic Energy Agency's (IAEA) monitoring and verification of its nuclear sites that were agreed upon as part of the 2015 deal. In June 2022, Iran removed 27 cameras from several of its nuclear sites, leading the director general of the IAEA, Rafael Grossi to admit that UN inspectors "were flying blind"[179] when it came to the Iranian nuclear program.[180] Negotiations between Iran and the global powers are stuck. A renewed diplomatic push at the end of June 2022 with a round of indirect talks between the US and Iran ended with no results, further reinforcing the assessment that the JCPOA is dead and cannot be revived, leaving the situation in a dangerous limbo. It is far from clear whether the supreme leader of Iran, Ali Khamenei, has any interest in returning to the nuclear accord or whether he prefers to continue his country's inexorable progress toward an atomic bomb. Lavi was one of the only decision makers during Trump's term who was willing to concede that US withdrawal from the JCPOA brought Iran closer than ever to a nuclear bomb—and put Israel in an incredibly challenging strategic position. Lavi's superior, former Mossad Director Yossi Cohen, and Prime Minister Netanyahu were not among those to express remorse.

The decades-long strategic alliance between Israel and the Gulf states against their mutual enemy grew stronger during the Trump years. But Iran was not the only reason these covert ties were gradually brought out into the light of day.

President Trump's advisors—Jared Kushner (right) and Avi Berkowitz (center)—
entered the White House with no previous experience in foreign policy or Middle
East affairs. Despite this, in their four years in the White House they achieved
the greatest breakthrough in the Middle East peace process in 25 years (photo:
uncredited).

Israeli diplomat Jeremy
Issacharoff (left) sitting
in a meeting between
then-Prime Minister
Itzhak Rabin and then-US
Secretary of Defense
William Cohen in
Washington in May 1995.
During that meeting, Israel
gave the US the green
light to sell F-16 fighter
jets to the UAE (photo:
uncredited).

For many years, Israeli diplomat Bruce Kashdan lived in the shadows. He spent 25 years in undercover postings in the Gulf on behalf of the Ministry of Foreign Affairs, and his name and face were barred from publication. His public service was finally revealed in the wake of the Abraham Accords. When Foreign Minister Yair Lapid flew to Abu Dhabi to inaugurate the new Israeli embassy, he brought Kashdan with him (photo: Barak Ravid).

In February 2019, an international summit was held in Warsaw, Poland. The summit was dedicated to discussing Iran, and among the participants were Israel and six Arab states. When I spotted suspicious activity in the lobby of then-Prime Minister Benjamin Netanyahu's hotel, I followed the security team into the parking lot. There, I found the foreign minister of Oman, Yusuf bin Alawi, who had come for a secret meeting with Netanyahu (photo: Barak Ravid).

At the time this photo was taken in one of the corridors of the Hôtel du Palais in the beach resort city of Biarritz, France, in August 2019, Benjamin Netanyahu was attempting to contact President Trump to ask him not to meet with the Iranian foreign minister. Trump didn't pick up, but eventually decided not to meet with the foreign minister of his own accord (photo: uncredited).

UAE Ambassador to Washington Yousef Al Otaiba (left) is one of the strongest, most connected and most influential people in Washington. He is also one of the architects of the Abraham Accords and the secret relationship between Israel and the United Arab Emirates (photo: uncredited).

All of President Trump's advisors gathered in the Oval Office on August 13, 2020 to listen to the historic phone call with Prime Minister of Israel Benjamin Netanyahu and Sheikh Mohamed bin Zayed, crown prince of Abu Dhabi. As soon as the call was over, Trump shocked the world when he announced the historic accords—via a tweet (photo: White House).

On August 31, 2020, a delegation of senior American and Israeli officials flew to Abu Dhabi for the first ever official public visit following the announcement of the Abraham Accords. This was to be the first flight to the United Arab Emirates by an El Al plane. I took this photo as the plane was crossing over the Saudi desert (photo: Barak Ravid).

H – The press pool fought for every available space on the flight. The journalists on board, here being briefed by Jared Kushner during the flight, were witness to this incredible moment in history (photo: United States Embassy in Israel).

Sheikh Zayed Grand Mosque in Abu Dhabi is one of the most spectacular and remarkable structures in the Middle East. Ironically, the vast carpet on which tens of thousands of worshippers pray every Friday was handwoven specifically for this mosque by Iranian weavers (photo: uncredited).

This image, which captured the departure of the Israeli delegation from Abu Dhabi in August 2020, quickly went viral. It is to a large extent the embodiment of the huge difference between Israel's "warm" peace with the United Arab Emirates versus the "cold" peace with Egypt and Jordan (photo: El Al Media Relations team).

US Envoy Avi Berkowitz prepares the documents of the peace treaty between Israel and the United Arab Emirates ahead of the signing ceremony on September 15, 2020 at the White House. He was only 31 when he mediated these negotiations, as well as those with Bahrain, Morocco and Sudan that followed (photo: uncredited).

A February 2019 interview I conducted with the foreign minister of Bahrain, Sheikh Khalid bin Ahmed Al Khalifa, was the first time a senior official from the Gulf states had spoken with the Israeli press on the record. Sheikh Khalid was one of the architects of the covert relationship between the two states (photo: Shai Spiegelman).

On October 18, 2020, Israel and Bahrain signed an agreement establishing full diplomatic relations. Minutes later, the Israeli diplomat Haim Regev approached the Bahraini foreign minister, Abdullatif bin Rashid Al Zayani, and handed him a formal request to upgrade the secret Israeli diplomatic mission in the country to an official embassy (photo: Barak Ravid).

In February 2020, Benjamin Netanyahu visited Uganda as the guest of President Yoweri Museveni (second from right). The primary goal of the visit was a secret meeting with the temporary ruler of Sudan, General Abdel Fattah al-Burhan (center). The architects of this meeting were Netanyahu's envoy, Ronen Levy, code-named "Maoz" (furthest left), whose name and face were barred from publication at the time, before he was appointed director general of the Ministry of Foreign Affairs in 2022, and the Sudanese diplomat Najwa Gadaheldam (second from left). In May 2020, Gadaheldam contracted COVID-19 and passed away. Five months later, Sudan announced the start of a normalization process with Israel (photo: uncredited).

On the morning of December 10, 2020, the White House peace team was putting the final touches on President Trump's announcement recognizing the Western Sahara as part of Morocco. The decision paved the way for the resumption of diplomatic ties between Morocco and Israel (photo: White House).

I sat with Donald Trump for an hour and a half in his Florida resort, three months after he left office. What he said in that interview changed everything I thought I knew about the relationship between him and Benjamin Netanyahu. "I haven't spoken with him since [the presidential election]," Trump told me. "Fuck him" (photo: uncredited).

Prime Minister Naftali Bennett was getting ready to leave his hotel for his meeting with President Biden at the White House on August 26, 2021 when a suicide bombing rocked Kabul Airport. The meeting was postponed and I, along with the other reporters in the traveling press pool, had to leave the White House grounds shortly after arriving (photo: Hadas Gold).

The director general of the Ministry of Foreign Affairs, Alon Ushpiz (left) with his Bahraini counterpart, Sheikh Abdullah bin Ahmed Al Khalifa, during Foreign Minister Yair Lapid's visit to Manama in September 2021. Four new Israeli diplomatic missions opened up in the space of a few months following the signing of the Abraham Accords (photo: uncredited).

The trilateral meeting between US Secretary of State Antony Blinken and the foreign ministers of Israel and the UAE in October 2021 in Washington was the first significant step by the Biden administration to strengthen the Abraham Accords (photo: Barak Ravid).

In November 2021, I visited Bahrain and participated in the Manama Dialogue. I drove on the King Fahd Causeway up to the border. This is the closest I have gotten to Saudi soil (photo: Barak Ravid).

On March 27, 2022, the Negev Summit convened in Sde Boker. Shortly after the historic event started, Foreign Minister Yair Lapid informed his counterparts from the US, UAE, Bahrain, Morocco and Egypt about a terror attack in the city of Hadera. They immediately agreed to issue a joint condemnation (photo: uncredited).

The press conference at the end of the Negev Summit was truly an unprecedented event. An Israeli foreign minister, US secretary of state and four Arab foreign ministers standing together on Israeli soil and calling to strengthen regional cooperation (photo: Barak Ravid).

In July 2022, General Aviv Kochavi made history as the first IDF chief of the general staff to hold an official visit to Morocco. The visit was a testament to how significantly security cooperation between Israel and many Arab states has grown since the Abraham Accords (photo: IDF spokesman).

In September 2022, Emirati Foreign Minister Sheikh Abdullah bin Zayed arrived in Israel for his first official bilateral visit. He spent five days in Israel and I had the pleasure of meeting him for a long and fascinating conversation (photo: uncredited).

From the Outside In

"You've reached Donald J. Trump. Please leave a message," said the voice on the other end of the line on the evening of July 19, 2021. The president's personal advisor hung up and called his cellphone. This time Trump picked up, speaking to me from his New Jersey golf course. That was my second conversation with the former president. I told him that the first anniversary of his phone call with Netanyahu and Mohamed bin Zayed where he announced the Abraham Accords was coming up in a few weeks. "We succeeded because we went in reverse—in the opposite route," he told me. "We didn't go to the Palestinians. We went to Mohamed [bin Zayed], who is so highly respected. It's an incredible thing that happened. If the elections hadn't been rigged, we would have many more countries already." Trump wasn't the first to try turning the map upside down—but he was the first to succeed. The idea for this approach came from Benjamin Netanyahu back in their first meeting at the White House. Netanyahu presented an "alternative" diplomatic vision, one that would go from the outside in—from the Arab world to the Palestinians. This wasn't the first time Netanyahu had raised this possibility. He tried the same move with President

Obama in May 2009, soon after he was elected. "I want to restart peace talks with the Palestinians immediately, but I also want to broaden the circle of peace to include others in the Arab world," Netanyahu said at the time. Obama was enthusiastic. "The other Arab states have to be more supportive and be bolder in seeking potential normalization with Israel," said Obama. However, the two leaders quickly discovered that while the idea looked good on paper, it was incredibly difficult to put into practice.

Attempts to advance toward normalization with the Arab world as an incentive for Israel to make progress with the Palestinians were at the heart of President Obama's peace initiative, which he launched on his second day in office by appointing former Senator George Mitchell as his Middle East envoy. Mitchell, who served as a key mediator in the historic Northern Ireland peace process and the resulting Good Friday Agreement, tried to shift the Arab countries in that direction starting in April 2009, a month before Netanyahu's meeting with Obama. On a visit to the Middle East, he met with 13 Arab leaders. He made a point of emphasizing that his efforts were based in part on the 2002 Arab Peace Initiative and asked for their support. "It is critical that Arab states consider actions that they can take, in the context of significant Israeli steps, to progress toward normalization with Israel," Secretary of State Hillary Clinton wrote to all the US missions in the region after Mitchell's visit. When Netanyahu met with Obama at the White House a few weeks later, he suggested that the US president focus his diplomatic efforts on Saudi Arabia. If the Saudis were to agree to normalization gestures, so Netanyahu claimed, the rest of the Arab world would follow—and public appetite in Israel for a diplomatic process with the Palestinians would increase. Obama took up the gauntlet. He flew to Saudi Arabia in early June, where he met with King Abdullah bin Abdulaziz Al Saud and put the idea before him.

The Saudi king listened but was underwhelmed. "King Abdullah told Obama that he presented the Arab Peace Initiative in 2002 and that he did not intend to change it," Dan Shapiro—at the time a White House Middle East policy specialist who accompanied Obama on the visit to Saudi Arabia—told me.[181] "The bottom line is, the king rejected President Obama's request." The Palestinians also didn't like Obama's move, perceiving it as an attempt to dilute the Arab Peace Initiative, which effectively gave them a veto over ties between Israel and the Arab countries in the region. When Abbas met with Obama at the White House a few days after the meeting with Netanyahu, he expressed disquiet over the pressure the president was applying to the Arab states in the region. "We told Obama not to ask the Arab countries to offer a carrot to Israel before Israel takes meaningful steps," Saeb Erekat told members of the president's staff whom he met with in Ramallah a few days later.[182] "I told Obama that it is unfair to ask the Arab states to make concessions without applying pressure on Israel at the same time." But despite the cool response from the Saudis and the Palestinians' reservations, the Obama administration decided to continue their pursuit of a gesture of normalization from the Arab world. Ahead of the Arab League meeting in late June 2009, the Americans began to apply extensive pressure on all the regional capitals for a commitment to steps that would thaw relations with Israel as soon as the latter took a meaningful step of its own, such as freezing settlement construction.[183] They were able to make some progress. Countries including Qatar, Oman, Morocco and Tunisia agreed to consider allowing Israel to reopen diplomatic missions in their capitals or to permit use of their airspace for flights by the Israeli national carrier, El Al.

However, faced with Saudi opposition and pressure from the Palestinians, those Arab countries that had considered steps toward normalization quickly retreated from their position. Even Netanyahu's Bar-Ilan speech in June, where for the first time ever, he expressed support for a demilitarized Palestinian state that recognizes Israel as the Jewish state, did not convince the Arab world to change its attitude. The announcement of a 10-month settlement freeze in November 2009 likewise failed to move them.

Disappointed to learn that the Saudis—and the rest of the Arab leaders in the region—were uninterested in taking steps toward normalization, Netanyahu lost any motivation he might have harbored for meaningful diplomatic progress with the Palestinians.

But despite the failure of the American initiative, Israel continued to seek out opportunities for normalization with the Arab world. When the chance arose, it came from an unexpected source. In 2009, the UN founded the International Renewable Energy Agency (IRENA). Several countries competed for the right to host the headquarters of the new organization. The last two standing were Germany and the United Arab Emirates, and both sought to enlist global support for their bid. Israel's natural inclination was to support Germany, but the decision was made in Jerusalem to attempt to leverage the opportunity for progress on a significant diplomatic push with the United Arab Emirates. The Israeli government told their German counterparts that they were considering backing the Emirati bid, explaining that they saw it as an opportunity to push for normalization with the Gulf states. At the same time, they made clear that their support was conditional: in exchange for Israeli support, the UAE would commit to permitting an official Israeli presence at the IRENA headquarters in Abu Dhabi. The Germans were persuaded to withdraw their candidacy and the Emiratis agreed to the Israeli request. In January 2010, a year after IRENA was founded and a few weeks before the al-Mabhouh story hit the headlines, the Israeli minister of national infrastructures,

Uzi Landau, attended the nascent agency's first summit. It was a rare visit by an Israeli minister to the United Arab Emirates. Despite this, the Emirati foreign minister, Sheikh Abdullah bin Zayed, refused to meet with him. "It is not a good time for talks with Israel," he told Kerri-Ann Jones, the assistant secretary of state for environmental and scientific affairs, who was attending the summit on behalf of the United States.[184] Bin Zayed agreed that Israel would be allowed to open a mission in Abu Dhabi, but caveated it by saying that, owing to security considerations, it should be located within the IRENA building and not in a regular office building. Landau and the other members of his delegation were kept under close surveillance. When they entered the country, they were not taken through the regular passport control that the other delegations went through, and none of the members of the delegation were issued a formal visa. The local security team asked them not to leave their hotel except for traveling to the summit itself, not to speak Hebrew among themselves and not to wander around with documents with Hebrew writing clearly visible. The Emirates even rescinded the invitation to the Israeli delegation to the official summit dinner, as it was not being held at the hotel. At the conference itself, the Israeli delegation sat with an Israeli flag, but when Landau spoke, it did not appear on the video screen broadcasting the summit, except for a few seconds at the end of his speech. Despite all of this, Landau's visit was unprecedented and regarded as a success. But the subsequent drama surrounding the assassination of al-Mabhouh halted any progress. The opening of the Israeli mission to the UN's IRENA headquarters in Abu Dhabi was delayed by several years. It was not until January 2014 that the wheels started turning once more. The new minister of energy, Silvan Shalom, attended the IRENA summit in Abu Dhabi and asked to restart talks to open the Israeli mission. This was the launchpad for renewed secret communication between the two countries, which lasted almost two more years. In November 2015, I received a tip-off that the negotiations were close to being finalized, and that the director general of the foreign ministry, Dore Gold, was expected to travel to Abu Dhabi to tie up the few remaining loose ends. When I approached the foreign ministry for comment, all hell broke loose. The ministry immediately turned to the Military Censor and appealed to it to prevent the publication of the story. On January 27, 2015, after Gold had returned from Abu Dhabi with an agreement to open the Israeli mission, the Military Censor granted me permission to publish. A few months later, the Israeli mission was opened in the IRENA building. The Israeli flag stood outside the offices and the state emblem appeared over the entrance.

While the Israeli diplomats posted there did devote some of their time to renewable energy, most of their efforts were dedicated to building diplomatic connections. The Emirati government had almost no contact with them, but the community of foreign ambassadors in Abu Dhabi was an excellent source of information on the goings-on in the country and on Gulf politics generally. Six years later, I flew with Yair Lapid as part of the first official visit by an Israeli foreign minister to the United Arab Emirates. Lapid inaugurated the Israeli embassy in Abu Dhabi on one of the top floors of the Etihad Towers. This new office was an official embassy like any other.

Iran's nuclear program and its tentacles reaching out into other countries in the region, coupled with a broader sense of dissatisfaction with the Obama administration's Middle East policy in Jerusalem, Abu Dhabi and other capitals created fertile ground for a thaw. But there was one more incident that helped to tip the scales.

On December 17, 2010, street vendor Mohamed Bouazizi set himself on fire on one of the main streets of Sidi Bouzid in Tunisia, in protest against the humiliation he had been subjected to by a government official. Two weeks later, he died of his injuries. Ten days after his death, with hundreds of thousands of protesters in the streets of Tunis calling to topple the regime, President Zine El Abidine Ben Ali gathered his family and fled to Saudi Arabia. The fire Bouazizi started that sparked a revolution in Tunisia quickly spread to Egypt, Libya, Bahrain, Yemen and Syria. In many other countries, rulers introduced whirlwind reforms in an attempt to ward off trouble. Israel and the Gulf states were shocked at the US response to events in the region—and especially in Egypt. Jerusalem, Riyadh and Abu Dhabi appealed to the Americans to lift some of the pressure from Mubarak and warned that his downfall would result in the rise of the Muslim Brotherhood. It didn't help. On February 11, Mubarak resigned and was arrested. The Muslim Brotherhood, which up until that point had been a proscribed organization, stepped into the power vacuum. A year and a half later, Mohamed Morsi was sworn in as president, and the Muslim Brotherhood's takeover of the country was complete.

Yaakov Amidror, Netanyahu's national security advisor from 2011 to 2013, believes that the Arab Spring, and especially events in Egypt, had an outsized impact on the shift in attitude toward Israel by many Arab states. Arab rulers, who watched anxiously as the Muslim Brotherhood took over Egypt, and ISIS and Al-Qaeda made significant inroads in Iraq and Syria, increasingly recognized the extent of their shared interests with Israel, which was also concerned about regional destabilization. The gradual retreat of the United States from the Middle East, which began during Obama's first term and continued into his second, and which opened the way for Iran to accelerate its regional expansion, further fueled this feeling. The signing of the JCPOA a few years later reinforced the trend. The latest failure to produce a diplomatic breakthrough between the Israelis and the Palestinians during Obama's first year in office also contributed to a sense of fatigue with the Israeli–Palestinian peace process within the Arab world. The Arab Spring caused many Arab countries to turn inward and pay closer attention to domestic affairs, with less energy to expend on the Palestinian cause as a result. "For many Arab leaders, the Arab Spring proved beyond doubt the need for political and economic changes and reforms," Amidror told me.[185] "They looked at Israel with envy, because we had managed to build such a successful and developed country. The Saudi prince, Turki Al Faisal, once told me at an event we attended in Washington that "with your money and our wisdom, we can change the Middle East." It was a joke, but it contained a grain of truth. These Arab countries realized that Israel was a genuine technological superpower that could help them implement the necessary changes. Before that point, the Arab world had distanced itself from Israel because of the Palestinians. Now they wanted to find a way to get closer to Israel despite the unresolved conflict with the Palestinians."

Further attempts to break the impasse between Israel and the Palestinians during Obama's second term were also unsuccessful. In 2013 and 2014, Secretary of State John Kerry negotiated with both sides in an attempt to secure a framework agreement. In his talks with Kerry and in the simultaneous backchannel talks with one of Mahmoud Abbas's close advisors, Netanyahu departed significantly from his baseline positions. He agreed to negotiations on the basis of the 1967 borders with territorial swaps and expressed a willingness to compromise on the key sticking points of refugees and Jerusalem. Abbas rejected the American initiative, in part because he didn't trust Netanyahu's intentions. In April 2014, this latest attempt blew up. Three months later, war broke out in Gaza. The 50-day conflict claimed the lives of 73 Israelis and 2,500 Palestinians and left a trail of devastation in its wake, taking the two sides back to square one. Regional shifts, the failure of Kerry's initiative and the Gaza War reinforced Netanyahu's belief in an "outside-in" approach. His national security advisor, Meir Ben-Shabbat, told me that the prime minister came to the conclusion that the Palestinians would not engage in any diplomatic process with Israel and the situation in Gaza could not be resolved, so he was therefore determined to seek out other opportunities in the region. "Netanyahu thought the younger generation in the Arab world was interested in tech innovation—and Israel's whole brand is the Start-up Nation," Ben-Shabbat said.[186] "He recognized that the countries in the region were fed up with the Palestinian veto; there was a sense of exasperation with their constant rejectionism. And then of course, there was the Iranian threat."

In September 2014, in his speech before the UN General Assembly, Netanyahu teased the policy that he would pursue over the next six years and that would eventually lead to the Abraham Accords. "I believe we have a historic opportunity," said Netanyahu. "After decades of seeing Israel as their enemy, leading states in the Arab world increasingly recognize that together we and they face many of the same dangers: principally, this means a nuclear-armed Iran and militant Islamist movements gaining ground in the Sunni world." Netanyahu explained in his speech that Israel and the Arab world could leverage these common interests to foster increased stability in the Middle East and to develop projects in water, agriculture, transportation, health and energy. As Trump would also tell me a few years later, Netanyahu argued that moving forward with peace in the region required working backward. "Many have long assumed that an Israeli–Palestinian peace can help facilitate a broader rapprochement between Israel and the Arab World," continued Netanyahu. "But these days I think it may work the other way around: namely, that a broader rapprochement between Israel and the Arab world may help facilitate an Israeli–Palestinian peace. And therefore, to achieve that peace, we must look not only to Jerusalem and Ramallah, but also to Cairo, to Amman, Abu Dhabi, Riyadh and elsewhere."

In the March 2015 elections, Netanyahu swept to a convincing victory, exceeding all expectations, including his own. Carried forward on a wave of euphoria, he decided to establish a narrow right-wing government with the support of only 61 of the 120 Knesset members. Trouble was not long in brewing; the government started falling apart, numerous members of the coalition began to rebel and a now vulnerable and exposed Netanyahu had to consider a change of direction. "We reached a crisis point where it became clear that we needed to expand the government," then-minister of tourism and Netanyahu's political fetcher and carrier, Yariv Levin, told me. "There was a lot of pressure coming through from the Obama administration at the time to take some kind of step, and there was an idea that a broader government would make it easier to withstand the great pressure the Americans were putting on us." Netanyahu's idea to extract himself from the situation was to form a national unity government with the center-left Labor Party. "At the end of 2015, Netanyahu told me in one of our conversations, 'Listen, I'm ready to move ahead with a national unity proposal which will be underpinned by a large regional summit,'" President Isaac Herzog, who was chairman of the Labor Party and head of the opposition at the time, told me.[187] "We talked about Egypt and Jordan, and the next names on our list were Saudi Arabia and the United Arab Emirates." Herzog didn't dismiss Netanyahu's proposal outright and began looking into whether his plan was at all feasible. He spoke with White House National Security Advisor Susan Rice and US Secretary of State John Kerry about the likelihood of putting together such a summit. A few weeks later, there was a sign that perhaps this endeavor was not mere fantasy. On February 21, 2016, a helicopter took off from Jerusalem in secret. On board were Netanyahu and his defense minister, Moshe "Bogie" Ya'alon. The helicopter made its way south, then cut across the Jordanian border and landed near the king's palace in Aqaba, on the shores of the Red Sea. In King Abdullah's palace, a secret diplomatic summit took place that also included President Abdel Fattah al-Sisi of Egypt and Secretary of State Kerry. Kerry presented a regional peace initiative that included recognition of Israel as a Jewish state and the renewal of negotiations with the Palestinians with the support of the Arab world. He asked King Abdullah to push President Abbas to agree to renew negotiations on the basis of the US initiative, and asked President al-Sisi to do the same with Netanyahu after the summit. Netanyahu did not agree to the proposal, claiming that he would struggle to receive support for the necessary diplomatic concessions within his fragile coalition. Instead, Netanyahu put forward an alternative proposal that included gestures on the ground for the Palestinians and a statement in his name making a positive reference to the Arab Peace Initiative. In exchange, the prime minister asked to convene a regional peace summit with delegations from Saudi Arabia, the United Arab Emirates and other Sunni states, following which negotiations with the Palestinians would be renewed.

I first heard about this secret summit a year after it took place. In February 2017, during Netanyahu's first visit to Washington in the Trump era, I met with a former senior official in the Obama administration. We sat down for lunch at the Tabard Inn, one of my favorite restaurants in the US capital. When the check came, he told me that in Aqaba, Netanyahu had once more refused to take any significant steps. I thought I might have misheard, so I asked him what he was talking about. "You haven't heard about the Aqaba summit?" He asked me. I tried to contain my excitement at the scoop that had just fallen into my lap. We paid the bill and went our separate ways. The moment I left the restaurant, I called another former senior official in the Obama administration and requested an urgent meeting. "Y'know, I was surprised it took you so long to find out about it," he joked when I told him I wanted to talk about the secret summit in Aqaba. Three days later, I published the story on the front page of *Haaretz*. It generated a lot of noise, revealing for the first time why Herzog had insisted on examining the viability of a national unity government with Netanyahu despite the widespread criticism the matter earned him, and casting Netanyahu as one who had spurned a historic diplomatic opportunity out of personal political interests.

No decisions were taken during the Jordanian summit, but it did have an almost immediate impact on Israel's domestic politics. The summit was the foundation stone on which Netanyahu and Herzog constructed their talks on a national unity government two weeks later. "As the summit was taking place, discussions were also ongoing about the diplomatic initiative that would bring two players who were already waiting on the sidelines into the field of play: the crown princes of Abu Dhabi and Saudi Arabia, Mohamed bin Zayed and Mohammed bin Salman," Herzog told me. "Netanyahu said to me, 'We will hit the ground running with a regional summit in Cairo.' I saw it as an attempt to make a historic move and said I was willing." The secret talks between Netanyahu and Herzog continued along two parallel tracks: political discussions about setting up a national unity government and policy discussions about launching the regional peace process.

One of the key men involved in both of these tracks was the former prime minister of the United Kingdom, Tony Blair. By then a private businessman, Blair was personally acquainted with all the relevant actors in the region. A few years earlier he had begun providing consulting services for Mohamed bin Zayed. In 2014, a year after the second coup in Egypt, when the Muslim Brotherhood government was toppled (with the encouragement of the United Arab Emirates, among others), Sheikh Mohamed dispatched Blair to "mentor" the new Egyptian president, Abdel Fattah al-Sisi. A year later, it was Blair who sought to bring Sheikh Mohamed on board with the regional initiative. "Over the last decade, I have believed that the road to resolving the conflict with the Palestinians travels through the Arab world," Blair told me.[188] "I had close relations with Sheikh Mohamed, and I started talking to him about the importance of relations with Israel and how it could benefit the United Arab Emirates. There was no hostility there, and it always seemed bizarre to me that they didn't have relations with Israel." In their conversations, Blair spoke with Sheikh Mohamed about Israel, its economy and its society. In one of the meetings between the two, Blair even showed the crown prince a video clip from the Tel Aviv Pride Parade as a way of highlighting the coexistence of its traditional and liberal values. Jerusalem and Tel Aviv: a bit like Abu Dhabi and Dubai. Sheikh Mohamed asked Blair on several occasions whether Israel would be truly interested in ties with the United Arab Emirates. "I'm talking to Emiratis and talking to Israelis and hearing the same things from both sides. We just need to find the way to make it happen," Blair replied. At the same time, Blair was having similar conversations with Netanyahu. He told him about Abu Dhabi and Dubai and encouraged him to push ahead with ties with the UAE. Netanyahu was enthusiastic, so Blair set up a backchannel between the prime minister's envoy,

Yitzhak Molcho, and Sultan Al Jaber, a close ally of Sheikh Mohamed and one of the most powerful men in the UAE. Back then, he was the CEO of the Abu Dhabi National Oil Company (ADNOC) and a deputy minister in the government. As of 2022, he is also the minister of industry and advanced technology and the UAE's special envoy for climate change. Blair arranged a series of meetings between Molcho and Al Jaber in London. Blair was present for the first meetings, but from there he left them to their own devices. "I told them that they had to find the way to a full relationship that would lead to peace and not to settle for security ties with no conflict," Blair said. Molcho and Al Jaber spoke about the nature of the relationship between Israel and the United Arab Emirates and about the regional summit initiative. Al Jaber was an enthusiastic supporter of the idea and loved Israel. He and Molcho built a backchannel between Netanyahu and Mohamed bin Zayed. In late 2014, when Molcho came to London to meet with Al Jaber, Blair told him there was a change of plans—this time Sheikh Mohamed bin Zayed would be attending too. Later on, the Al Jaber-Molcho channel led to phone conversations between Sheikh Mohamed and Netanyahu, and even a secret meeting.

But despite the covert talks between Molcho and Al Jaber, Blair remained unconvinced that the Emiratis were ready to take part in such a regional summit. He told Herzog they might compromise by sending a low-level delegate. Meanwhile, the secret talks between Netanyahu and Herzog about a national unity government and the regional summit continued. At the end of April 2016, late at night and under a veil of secrecy, the prime minister and head of the opposition flew to Egypt together to meet with President al-Sisi. Al-Sisi guaranteed the two men that if they set up a national unity government, he would organize a regional summit in Cairo and would work to encourage representatives from the

Gulf states to attend. A burgeoning "outside-in" regional peace process appeared closer than ever. In mid-May, the negotiations between Netanyahu and Herzog entered the home stretch—and came out into the open. The move generated a fierce backlash within the prime minister's Likud Party, but even more so within Herzog's Labor Party. The harshest criticism of all came from left-wing Labor MK Shelly Yachimovich, who likened Herzog to a dog chasing a weak bone thrown to him by Netanyahu. In the meetings where Herzog presented the move to senior officials in his party, he didn't reveal the confidential summit in Aqaba, the secret trip to Cairo or the diplomatic agreements he had formulated with Netanyahu. That may well have proven to be his greatest mistake. On May 17, with negotiations on the unity government reaching their climax, the president of Egypt decided to make an unprecedented intervention. In a broadcast on Egyptian television, he called on Netanyahu and Herzog to set up a national unity government for peace. "Al-Sisi said what he said after he had met with all the leaders in the Arab world.... The whole area was buzzing with the possibility of a really significant diplomatic process," recalled Herzog. Unfortunately for Herzog, the Egyptian president's statement may have been too little and too late. That evening, at the meeting between the two men at the Prime Minister's residence on Jerusalem's Balfour St., Netanyahu began to backtrack on his commitments to Herzog. "A minute before we made land, Netanyahu informed me during a conversation with Yariv Levin in his office that he was withdrawing the paper with the policy agreements," said Herzog. Levin confirmed this story. "I told both Netanyahu and Herzog that this was not why we had established a government and that this was not what the people wanted," recalled Levin. Herzog described to me the drama of those moments, with Levin bringing up names of members of the

Likud Central Committee from the settlement lobby who would come out against Netanyahu if he were to go for a national unity government. "Yariv Levin stood in front of Netanyahu and yelled at him, 'Bibi, they won't let you, Likud will oppose you.' Just like that, in the room, in front of me," recalled Herzog. Levin denied shouting at Netanyahu. "I told him that the public had chosen a right-wing government and not left-wing policies, and there was no chance that this agreement would get through the Likud or the public who had voted for us," he said. Netanyahu ultimately pulled out, and the meeting blew up. Yitzhak Molcho, who was in the United States at the time, was nonplussed by these developments. Late at night, the two spoke over the phone, a harsh conversation with raised voices. "You're making a big mistake," Molcho told Netanyahu. One of Molcho's friends, who heard from him about the events of that night, told me that the prime minister's envoy was stunned that Netanyahu had thrown all the understandings that had been reached into the garbage, along with the regional initiative. He recognized that politics had overcome statecraft and was said to be on the verge of tears. Over the week that followed, Molcho cut off communication with Netanyahu and wouldn't answer his calls. The morning after that fateful meeting, Herzog, Blair, al-Sisi and the other Arab leaders who had been involved in the initiative discovered that alongside the behind-closed-doors negotiations with Herzog, a whole other plot had been brewing. Netanyahu signed a deal with the head of the secular right-wing Yisrael Beiteinu party, Avigdor Lieberman, who brought his five members of the Knesset into the coalition in exchange for being appointed minister of defense. Netanyahu threw Herzog under the bus. As a result, the latter was widely panned, his political career dead and buried. "I don't think Netanyahu played me," Herzog told me three years later. "I think he wanted it at the time, but in the end his decisions were dictated first and foremost by his own political survival. I call it base-phobia." A few years after my conversation with Herzog, the shoe was on the other foot. He was elected president of the State of Israel—and a few days later Netanyahu was ousted from the prime minister's office after 12 consecutive years.

Coming Out

The UAE's ambassador to the United States, Yousef Al Otaiba, was sitting on the stage of the ballroom at the high-end Willard Hotel in Washington, DC. This was the closed part of the December 2016 Saban Forum, and the panel in question was discussing American policy in the Middle East. At the time, I knew Al Otaiba only through articles that had been published about him and from conversations with Israeli diplomats. This was the first time I had seen him in person. When they opened the floor to questions, I was given the opportunity to speak. "Mr. Ambassador, isn't it about time for your country to grow up and bring your relationship with Israel out of the closet?" I asked him. Al Otaiba didn't blink. "If you hadn't noticed, I'm sitting here at the Saban Forum on a panel with Israelis and talking in front of dozens of other Israelis. If that's called being in the closet, then we're doing a terrible job of keeping it discreet," he replied to the laughter of those present. At the end of the panel, I walked up to Al Otaiba and exchanged business cards with him. Neither of us could have imagined at that point how central a role the United Arab Emirates would come to play in my journalistic endeavors over the next four years.

Yet despite Al Otaiba's words, in early 2017, when President Trump entered the Oval Office, relations between Israel and the Gulf states were still mostly kept secret. It was only very occasionally that the tip of the iceberg appeared above the waves. In the first meeting between Netanyahu and Trump at the White House, in February 2017, Netanyahu not only presented his "outside-in" approach, but he also proposed a tangible example of it. Netanyahu attempted to achieve with Trump what he had been unable to with Obama. He once again raised the idea of a summit meeting of regional leaders at the White House or at Camp David. Netanyahu proposed that Trump invite the crown princes of Abu Dhabi and Saudi Arabia to the summit too. The public participation of bin Zayed and bin Salman at a summit with the prime minister of Israel would represent a historic breakthrough that would relaunch the peace process, Netanyahu claimed.

Netanyahu's national security advisor at the time, Jacob Nagel, confirmed to me that the subject was on the table during the first meeting between Netanyahu and Trump. "The opportunity to develop the relationship with the Sunni states in the Gulf informed a substantial part of our thinking during my time in the Prime Minister's Office," he said.[189] "We tried to break through that barrier in terms of the relationship with the Gulf states, and then use that to resolve the Palestinian conflict. We were of the opinion that as long as the Palestinians believed that the Arab states would pull their chestnuts out of the fire or keep sending them money, they would never come to the table. We believed that if the Palestinians understood that they no longer had the guaranteed safety net provided by the other Arab states, they might change their approach. I don't want to quote from conversations that took place behind closed doors between Netanyahu and Trump, but that is certainly something that the State of Israel said at the time—in public and in private."

Following up on Netanyahu's idea, the Americans made inquiries in Abu Dhabi and Riyadh, but were rebuffed. Bin Zayed and bin Salman were still not ready for such a dramatic shift. Despite this, the White House sensed that the window of opportunity may yet open further down the line. From his very first trip to the Middle East, a few months after Trump entered the White House, Jared Kushner already returned with new insights. He quickly realized that, alongside his engagement in finding a solution to the Israeli–Palestinian conflict, there was huge untapped potential in developing ties between Israel and the Arab world. "We spoke to the Arabs and we spoke to the Israelis and we found out that they hate the same people and like the same people and want the same things," Kushner told me. "Then we asked ourselves, why are they wearing the jerseys of rival teams? Why are they not on the same team? And we worked on it."

In mid-May 2017, Meir Ben-Shabbat was sitting in his office in the Southern Region headquarters of the Shin Bet in Ashkelon. He was closing in on three years in charge of the region tasked primarily with dealing with Hamas in Gaza. In the early afternoon, the phone in his office began to ring. "Meir, there's someone claiming to be the prime minister's secretary and she wants to speak with you," his secretary told him. Ben-Shabbat asked her to put the call through. "The prime minister wishes to meet with you. Please get to his office in Jerusalem by 10 PM tonight," said the voice on the other end of the line. A surprised Ben-Shabbat explained that he would have to receive the permission of his superior, Shin Bet Director Nadav Argaman, to attend the meeting. "Go to the meeting," Argaman told him. "Maybe he wants to offer you a job." Later that night, Ben-Shabbat walked into Netanyahu's office in Jerusalem. The conversation was brief. "I want you to be the head of the national security council," Netanyahu told him. "I haven't even introduced myself yet," replied Ben-Shabbat. "I've looked into you. I want to appoint you to the role," insisted the prime minister. Ben-Shabbat said he needed time to think. "There's something I need you to know—I don't like flying abroad, and I assume you'll want someone who's constantly going back and forth," he told Netanyahu as he was leaving the room. "Think about it, give me an answer by tomorrow," the prime minister responded. Ben-Shabbat returned to his home in the village of Merkaz Shapira, an hour's drive away, his mind reeling from the unexpected offer. "I took the whole night to think about it and told him I would rather not take the role," Ben-Shabbat told me when we met four years later.[190] "I thought there were other candidates better suited than me—and I don't enjoy traveling abroad. I felt uncomfortable, so I asked the head of the Shin Bet to convey my decision to the prime minister." Ben-Shabbat thought this would be the end of the story, but two days later, Friday at 3 PM, his home phone rang and on the other end of the line was the prime minister himself. Netanyahu had always had a gift for courtship. He asked Ben-Shabbat to come for another meeting that Sunday. "Meir, I understand your concerns, but I need you on the NSC," Netanyahu told him at the meeting. "Maybe you can start as acting head of the NSC for a trial period. If it's a good fit for both of us, you carry on, and if not, we'll go our separate ways as friends."

On August 7, Ben-Shabbat began his first day in his new job. One of Netanyahu's first decisions was to transfer all the responsibilities that had previously been held by his envoy and close confidant, Yitzhak Molcho, to Ben-Shabbat. Above all, this meant taking on the secret trips to Egypt, Jordan and the Gulf states.[191] "Netanyahu told me, 'I want to build ties with every country possible,'" remembered Ben-Shabbat. "We outlined the countries with potential alongside what we thought the odds of success were. I put strengthening the relationship with Egypt at the top of the list, in the context of Gaza and because they were the primary avenue to ties with other countries. We wanted Saudi Arabia and the Gulf states. But that would be harder. Despite that, we decided to work on everything together at the same time." A short time later, Ben-Shabbat flew to Washington for his first visit as national security advisor. There he met with his counterpart, H. R. McMaster, and with Jared Kushner, and together they went over the list of Arab and Muslim countries Israel wanted to attempt to normalize relations with. This became a recurring ritual every few months that continued with John Bolton (McMaster's replacement), Secretary of State Mike Pompeo and other Trump administration officials.

Throughout this time, attempts at normalization continued along several parallel tracks. In August 2017, as Ben-Shabbat was growing into his new role in the Prime Minister's Office, another key player in developing ties with the Gulf states was walking into his new office in the Ministry of Foreign Affairs in Jerusalem. For the first six months of the Trump administration, Dor Shapira served as the counselor for congressional affairs in the Israeli embassy in Washington, where he dedicated most of his time to attempting to advance pro-Israel legislation among American lawmakers. Upon his return to Israel, he was appointed director of the Coordination Department at the Director General's Office in the Ministry of Foreign Affairs. He quickly came to realize that behind the official title lay a far more alluring proposition: managing the foreign ministry's covert relationship with the Gulf states. He received a phone call from the Mossad during his first week in the job, informing him about an Israeli delegation that had flown to participate in the International Atomic Energy Agency (IAEA) summit in Abu Dhabi and got stuck at the airport. After a few minutes of confusion, he recovered and resolved the crisis with his designated contacts in Abu Dhabi—the first time he had spoken to them. Over the three years that followed, Shapira was part of a gradual process of drawing the Israeli–Emirati relationship into the public eye, with the support of the Trump administration.

Toward the end of 2017, the Emirati authorities granted entry permission to the Israeli envoy to the Gulf, Bruce Kashdan, for the first time since his expulsion in 2010 over the assassination of Mahmoud al-Mabhouh, the senior Hamas official. Israel had tried on several occasions since to receive Emirati approval for him to return to the country (and not only for a short visit) but their attempts had been rebuffed every time. Now the tide was turning—and permission was granted. At the same time, the Emiratis upgraded the status of the Israeli mission to IRENA in Abu Dhabi and allowed Israel to appoint a permanent diplomat for the first time. The foreign ministry took these steps as a sign that the Emiratis wanted to deepen the ties between the countries.

In February 2018, another small yet significant breakthrough took place. Following covert discussions between Israel, India and Saudi Arabia, the Saudis approved the use of their airspace for Air India flights traveling to and from Israel's Ben Gurion Airport, which shortened the flight time between Israel and India by over two hours and significantly reduced the cost of flights. This was intended by the Saudis as a gesture toward India, but it also contained a nod to Israel. In late March 2018, the first flight from India to pass over Saudi airspace landed in Israel. The inbound flight landed without incident, but when it was due to turn around for its return leg, Ben Gurion Airport staff struggled to coordinate the necessary permissions with the Saudi General Authority of Civil Aviation. The flight was delayed, and the impasse was only resolved following the intervention of White House officials with their Saudi counterparts.

The next breakthrough came from an unexpected source: the Judo International Grand Slam event in Abu Dhabi in October 2018. The year before, the Israeli delegation had participated in the tournament without any national symbols; the Israeli judokas competed without the Israeli flag, and when Tal Flicker won in the final of the under 66 kilogram category and went up to claim his gold medal, he stood on the podium and sang the words to "HaTikvah" to the tune of the anthem of the International Judo Federation (IJF). This time, the Emiratis agreed to the request by Israel and the IJF, and for the first time an Israeli delegation competed under the Israeli flag. The Emiratis opted to give equal treatment to the Israeli athletes rather than submit to Palestinian pressure and risk the cancellation of the tournament. Miri Regev, the minister of culture and sport at the time, seized the opportunity and joined the Israeli delegation, which raised the media profile of the event even further. Regev also generated a few unforgettable photos in Abu Dhabi, including one of her much-covered visit to the Sheikh Zayed Grand Mosque, wearing a traditional *abaya* robe and a head covering. When judoka Sagi Muki won the gold medal in his category and the Israeli national anthem played in the competition hall in Abu Dhabi, the Emiratis were astonished to witness an emotional Regev bursting into tears. In March 2019, an even larger Israeli delegation arrived to participate in the Special Olympics in Abu Dhabi. Eighty athletes and family members attended under the Star of David flag. "HaTikvah" was played a further four times around the competition venues in Abu Dhabi.

Shapira told me that the scale of bilateral activities with the UAE increased dramatically during that period. From 2016 to 2018, only four Israeli delegations visited the UAE. In 2019 alone, that number leapt almost fourfold, with 15 official delegations. "I visited Abu Dhabi and Dubai seven times in those years with my Israeli diplomatic passport," Shapira told me.[192] "All the signs pointed to a growing willingness to significantly upgrade ties with Israel."

The crowning achievement of Israel's diplomatic efforts in those years was the 2020 World Expo in Dubai. The Emiratis were obligated to welcome all the countries of the world to participate in the exhibition, but as of 2018 Israel was yet to receive any such invitation. Without it, the government was unable to assign budgets and move forward with planning the Israeli pavilion. A senior American official noted that the Israelis, supported by the Trump administration, pressured the Emiratis to issue a formal invitation. The Israeli ambassador to Washington, Ron Dermer, met his Emirati counterpart, Yousef Al Otaiba, no fewer than five times about the Expo issue alone. Al Otaiba, one of the architects of the covert relationship with Israel, was firmly in favor of an Israeli pavilion at the showpiece event. He leveraged his close personal relationship with the crown prince, Sheikh Mohamed, and with the national security advisor, Sheikh Tahnoun, to ensure the invitation was issued. In mid-2018, it finally happened.

Israel sought something deeper than traditional diplomacy. Social media provided unprecedented access to the Arab public around the world, especially to the younger generations. In February 2019, the Ministry of Foreign Affairs reestablished Israel's virtual "embassy" in the Gulf. In practice, this was a Twitter account engaging in public outreach with the people of Saudi Arabia, the UAE, Bahrain and more. "We saw that this Twitter account was becoming very popular," Shapira told me. "The number of views and replies from around the Gulf were incredible and grew week on week. We understood that something was happening here." By August 2021, the foreign ministry's Arabic-language Twitter account had amassed 450 thousand followers and become Israel's primary channel for conveying messages and swaying public opinion.

A former senior official in the Prime Minister's Office told me that Benjamin Netanyahu and Sheikh Mohamed held several secret meetings in 2018 and 2019. Netanyahu flew to Abu Dhabi on a private jet without a word leaking to the press. With him on these trips were National Security Advisor Meir Ben-Shabbat and Mossad Director Yossi Cohen. "These meetings were very warm and friendly—as well as very interesting in terms of the ground they covered and the partnerships that were discussed," said a former senior Netanyahu-era official.

Meir Ben-Shabbat told me that Netanyahu didn't press any of the Arab countries to take a step toward normalization with Israel. "He told us, 'These things have to happen when the leader feels like the time is right. If they do it too early, they might pay a political price or expose themselves to pressure that will cause them to walk it back. And if they do it too late, the moment will have passed.' He would say to the Arab leaders—we have a general interest in normalization. How we go about it depends on whether you feel like the moment is ripe."

On March 31, 2019, a week before the Knesset elections, Al Otaiba visited Jared Kushner at home. The two had become close friends, and on that Sunday, they were sitting in the living room when Al Otaiba made a major announcement. "Sheikh Mohamed is ready to move forward on normalization with Israel," he said. The plan was to make the move after the imminent elections in Israel, once a new government had been formed. Al Otaiba emphasized that in light of the political instability in Israel, Sheikh Mohamed wanted the Trump administration to act as a guarantor. "They didn't want it to become a domestic political issue in Israel. They wanted it to be a long-term move separate from the 'Yes to Bibi/

No to Bibi' internal disputes," he told me. "They told Jared that they trust the Trump administration to support them in taking this step in the right way."

The results of the April 2019 elections did not put wind in the sails of the Emirati initiative. Netanyahu was granted the first shot at forming a government, but he struggled to receive the support of the necessary 61-seat majority of Knesset members. A few days before Netanyahu's mandate to form a government expired, Kushner visited the Middle East. After holding talks in a few regional capitals, on May 29 he came to Jerusalem. Netanyahu was making last-ditch efforts to put together a government before the midnight deadline passed. By this point, he was so desperate that he made a pitch to the head of the left-wing Labor Party, Avi Gabbay, to join the government. In exchange, he offered to give the party control of the finance and justice ministries and to support the former Histadrut trade union and party leader, Amir Peretz, as the next president. The move failed, and at midnight Netanyahu dispersed the Knesset to prevent the mandate from passing to his political rival and head of the Blue and White party, Benny Gantz. Kushner was scheduled to meet with Netanyahu for breakfast the next day. In light of the political events, breakfast was pushed back to lunch, and when Kushner arrived at the Balfour St. residence, he realized he had walked into a wake. He asked to sit with Netanyahu alone, where he unveiled the UAE's normalization initiative, but Netanyahu's mind was elsewhere, already fixated on the imminent election campaign. "Within Netanyahu's team there were people who thought the offer was real and were excited, but others thought it would never happen and that we were dreaming. Regardless, the political situation in Israel was not conducive to progress," said a former senior White House official.

In July 2019, the UN climate conference was held in Abu Dhabi. A few months earlier, Likud stalwart Israel Katz had been formally appointed as foreign minister in the transition government that was in place following the first elections and into the second ones. Katz, who had been promoted into the role from the transport ministry, where he had registered several noteworthy achievements, fought a no-holds-barred battle for the foreign ministry appointment. After he stepped into the role, he quickly came to realize that not all that glittered was gold. Prime Minister Netanyahu was well on his way to dismantling the foreign ministry, slashing its budgets and ostracizing it from decision-making processes. Katz struggled to adjust to an underfunded ministry where success was often measured in terms of phone calls with other foreign ministers or the formulation of a strategy to address the relationship with China. He also struggled to hold diplomatic conversations in English. What's more, Netanyahu made no particular effort to assist him in being perceived as an influential figure on the world stage—quite the reverse. Netanyahu delivered a message to the Trump administration that Katz was not authorized to manage the relationship with the United States and humiliated him time after time. As a consequence, US Secretary of State Mike Pompeo refused to meet with Katz when he came to Washington and even afterward. Katz and his team were unaware of the message that had been delivered to Netanyahu only a few months previously on behalf of the United Arab Emirates, but Katz's political antennae identified the potential for progress with the Gulf states. He decided to take the opportunity of the UN climate conference to visit Abu Dhabi. The Emirati foreign minister, Sheikh Abdullah bin Zayed, did not meet with him on his visit, but Katz did meet with his deputy, Dr. Anwar Gargash, who was considered a prominent voice in shaping Emirati foreign policy.

Upon his return to Israel, Katz convened a meeting to discuss relations with the Gulf states. Dor Shapira and others in the foreign ministry told him they were seeing a window of opportunity to make a breakthrough with the UAE—and perhaps even with others in the region. Katz was enthusiastic. He arranged a meeting with Netanyahu where he sought his permission to attempt to move forward with a diplomatic initiative. Fully focused on the election campaign by this point, Netanyahu, who didn't take Katz seriously and didn't expect anything to come of it, gave him the green light. Katz and his team in the foreign ministry started to brainstorm ideas to advance accords with Gulf states that would fall somewhere beyond the status quo at the time and short of full peace and normalization agreements. "The prevailing idea that arose from these meetings was a non-aggression agreement: a one-page document in which the signatories agree not to engage in hostile actions against each other," Shapira told me.[193] "When we presented it to Katz, he said, 'Great, I want to sign it within a few months.' We all looked at him like he'd lost his mind."

In late September 2019, 10 days after the elections in which Netanyahu and Likud suffered a painful defeat, Katz traveled to New York. The prime minister, who was distracted by domestic politics and fighting to receive the mandate to form a government, remained in Israel. Katz had an opportunity to be Israel's representative at the UN General Assembly. In New York, he met once more with Gargash, as well as with the Omani minister of foreign affairs, Yusuf bin Alawi, and presented the non-aggression agreement initiative to them. The Arab ministers were unsure how to respond, especially in light of the possibility that within a few weeks a new government could be formed in Israel—one in which Katz would no longer be foreign minister, Netanyahu would no longer be prime minister and their Likud party would no longer be in the governing coalition. Katz's speech before the General Assembly was widely mocked for his poor English, which lacked the fluency and finesse of Netanyahu's. But his remarks also echoed the diplomatic move he was trying to advance. "We have no conflict with the Gulf states, and we have common interests in the field of security against the Iranian threat," he said. "Israel has a lot of capabilities in many areas including hi-tech, innovation, agriculture and water technology which can help the Gulf states, and the Gulf states have a lot of capabilities that can help Israel as well. I hope that this cooperation will lead to the signing of peace agreements between our countries, as we did with Egypt and Jordan."

Even after Katz returned from the UN, there were not many who took his ideas seriously, especially in view of the political impasse. However, that situation soon changed. In late October, the US secretary of the treasury, Steve Mnuchin, visited Israel. Katz, who was still seeking American support for his initiative, asked his aide in the foreign ministry to arrange a meeting. He hoped that this would be a way to bypass the Netanyahu/Pompeo channel and gain the ear of the White House for the non-aggression agreement initiative. His gamble paid off. Mnuchin liked the idea and promised Katz that he would raise it with the White House and the US Department of State. When he returned to the US, Mnuchin held true to his word. Katz attracted the attention not only of the White House, but also of the Prime Minister's Office. This quickly sparked an internecine war.

On November 6, Meir Ben-Shabbat convened a broad meeting in the Prime Minister's Office to discuss Katz's initiative. In addition to the representatives of the National Security Council and foreign ministry, also in attendance were members of the Mossad, IDF, Ministry of Defense and Ministry of Justice. A senior Israeli official who participated in that meeting told me that the Mossad officials were outspoken in their opposition to the initiative, and even claimed that it would harm Israel's relationships with the Gulf states. "It seemed that the Mossad was distressed by the fact that the initiative had not come from them," the senior official told me. The representatives from the Ministry of Defense and the IDF also opposed the move. They warned that the Emiratis would use a non-aggression agreement with Israel to demand that the United States supply them with F-35 fighter jets, which had not been provided to any country in the region aside from Israel until that point. "It could harm the qualitative military edge of our air force in the region," said the members of the defense establishment. Less than a year later, their warnings came true to the letter. For his part, Ben-Shabbat expressed doubts but did not dismiss the idea outright. "The bottom line in that meeting was that this was a nice idea, but unrealistic and aiming a bit too high," said Roi Sheindorf, the deputy attorney general for international law, who participated in the meetings.[194]

Despite the skepticism, both Katz and the National Security Council sought to push forward. Each of them began to prepare their own draft document, and they raced to be the first to finish. Ben-Shabbat wanted it to be detailed, while Katz preferred something simple and concise. Ultimately, they decided to prepare a draft agreement that was as general and short as possible.

On November 19, 2019, the deputy national security advisor to the White House, Victoria Coates, visited Israel. Coates was briefed about Katz's initiative by Mnuchin and wanted to hear more. When she met with Katz, he let her see the draft non-aggression agreement they had prepared. Coates promised to send out feelers in a few Arab states to assess their interest in such a step, and it was agreed that an Israeli delegation would go to Washington for further discussions two weeks later. "As soon as the meeting with Coates was over, Katz told us, 'Put together a delegation, invite everyone and fly to the US,'" Shapira told me.[195] When Coates returned to Washington, she summoned the ambassadors of the United Arab Emirates, Bahrain, Oman and Morocco to her office in the White House. She presented the Israeli initiative to them and showed them the draft agreement. She told them she knew that their countries had covert ties with Israel but emphasized that this was an opportunity to go one big step further along the road to full normalization. The ambassadors did not reject the idea outright, and some of them even expressed a measure of interest in it, but the political instability in Israel cast a giant question mark over the meeting. It was unclear whether the Israeli government had the mandate to sign such an agreement at a time when its future was far from certain.

On December 1, the Israeli delegation, led by Shapira, arrived in the US ahead of the talks with the White House. The participants were enthusiastic and looking forward to the meetings, but their hopes were dampened before they even started. The bucket of cold water came from none other than the Israeli ambassador to Washington, Ron Dermer. "It's a good idea, but it's a shame we didn't do it three years ago," said Dermer with unrestrained skepticism. He informed the members of the delegation that he had held a series of meetings on the subject a few days earlier with senior officials in the Trump administration, who had told him that the timing was not right for the White House, and that the Arab countries were not in the right place for it yet. Dermer explained that the Gulf states wanted to move slower, and that the Kushner-led White House peace team was focused on unveiling the Trump Plan and did not see the non-aggression agreements as a high priority. If this pessimistic outlook was not enough, Dermer also told the members of the delegation that he did not intend to attend the meetings at the White House the next day. "There was a feeling of disappointment, but we understood that we were laying the groundwork for something that might come in useful later, when the political circumstances were more favorable," Roi Sheindorf told me.[196]

When the members of the Israeli delegation got to the White House, Coates was waiting for them along with 20 US representatives from the National Security Council, Department of State, Department of Defense and the intelligence community. The immediate impression was that the Americans were taking the initiative seriously. "It's currently 12 PM, which means that in one hour's time Barak Ravid will report on Channel 13 that we are currently sitting in this room and discussing the non-aggression agreements," Coates said to laughter at the end of her opening remarks. Her prophecy was fulfilled two hours later. Dermer, who was not even involved in the discussions, was beside himself. He called Katz and angrily accused him of leaking. The publication of the story did not damage the move. Together, Israel and the United States started to promote the initiative. The Israelis thought their greatest chance of success lay with Bahrain, but the Americans, for their part, were pinning their hopes on the United Arab Emirates. Coates wrapped up the meeting and said that the Americans would raise the idea at the summit of the Gulf states that was due to take place the following week. "We left with an understanding that they knew what we were looking for and that they would start to make inquiries among the Arab states. [Coates] looked more optimistic than Dermer," Sheindorf told me.

While the talks with the Americans were ongoing, Dor Shapira met with the UAE ambassador to Washington, Yousef Al Otaiba. The two had met on several occasions in the previous two years and knew each other from Shapira's time as a diplomat at the embassy in Washington tasked with liaising with Congress. Shapira went over the draft agreement with Al Otaiba and sought his opinion. "Why a non-aggression agreement? There should be a peace treaty," the Emirati ambassador said. Shapira was happy to hear such a response, but then came the sting in the tail. "If we have a peace treaty, will you allow the Americans to sell us F-35s?" asked Al Otaiba. Shapira was not authorized to answer, but he made sure the message was delivered in his report to the other government ministries in Israel. Before they parted ways, Al Otaiba had one more message for him to pass on, regarding one of Netanyahu's election promises at the time: annexing the Jordan Valley and the settlements in the West Bank to Israel. "We want to upgrade our relations with Israel, but until you stop messing around with this annexation stuff, it won't happen," he said. A year and a half later, Al Otaiba told me that when he sent the draft of the agreement to Abu Dhabi, Sheikh Mohamed and the other senior officials gave him the green light to proceed, but the drawn-out political crisis in Israel and the elections taking place at the time prevented it.[197]

Shapira returned to Israel and delivered a positive and optimistic report to Katz. "On the way to Washington I was a skeptic who would have given us a 15 percent chance of success—by the time we returned I felt like we had a 40 percent chance," Shapira recalled.[198] "I was convinced we had grounds for discussion and partners for that discussion, and more than anything I felt that both sides understood the potential for such a diplomatic process together with Trump's political timetable." Within a few months, that potential began to be realized.

From Annexation to Normalization

In the early afternoon of Friday, January 31, 2020, Benjamin Netanyahu called the director general of the Prime Minister's Office, Ronen Peretz. The prime minister had returned from a week-long visit to Washington and Moscow only the day before. "Have you seen the reports about this virus in China?" Netanyahu asked Peretz, who was relaxing at home and trying to recover from the events of the previous week. Reports at the time about the mystery virus from Wuhan were accompanied more by question marks than exclamation points. The next morning, Netanyahu called Peretz again. "Two people in China have died from the virus," said the prime minister. "Who's the director general of the Ministry of Health?" Peretz brought Moshe Bar Siman Tov onto the call, along with Meir Ben-Shabbat. This was the first discussion in Israel about the coronavirus. None of the participants on the call could have predicted the extent to which COVID-19 would fundamentally change the world and the economic, technological and political revolution that would follow in its wake.

The following week, Channel 13 broadcast a series of reports I had put together entitled "Netanyahu of Arabia." They covered the secret relationship that had been formed with countries in the Arab world during Netanyahu's years in office. Just like that first call about COVID-19, I never imagined the degree to which that initial series of stories would act as a warm-up act to the main event (one that would define my professional career as a journalist for the next year) and the diplomatic earthquake that was soon to follow. One of the reports focused on the secret alliance between Israel and the United Arab Emirates against Iran. In it, I exposed a meeting that had taken place in the White House in January, a month earlier, between Meir Ben-Shabbat and the intelligence chief of the UAE, Ali Al Shamsi. I spent a long time trying to secure an interview with a senior government official from the UAE, to no avail. The Emiratis did not appreciate their cooperation with Israel against Iran being exposed. "I doubt anyone senior in Abu Dhabi would be willing to meet with you now," a senior Emirati official told me after the report was broadcast.

On February 6, I flew to Rome for a weekend with my family. We were taken aback by the strange sight of hundreds of people passing through thermal scanners at Fiumicino Airport. Those who showed up dark red on the screen were taken aside for a more thorough check. The next day, while we were strolling through the streets of the Italian capital near Piazza Navona, I received an email from the same Emirati official. "We wanted to invite you to an off-the-record meeting with the minister of state for foreign affairs, Dr. Anwar Gargash," he wrote. The meeting was set for February 15 in Munich on the sidelines of the annual Munich Security Conference. For me, this was an incredibly important professional milestone, but it was also a statement of intent for the relationship between the countries—a further step toward normalization.

The meeting took place in one of the conference rooms in the luxurious Kempinski Hotel in Munich. In addition to myself, there were five other journalists present in the room, from Germany, France, the United Kingdom and the United States.[199] A breakfast had been laid out that would have fed an entire battalion. When Gargash arrived, he wasted no time on pleasantries, launching straight into an overview of the strategic situation of the United Arab Emirates. As well as being one of the most engaging and intelligent people I have had the opportunity to speak with in my career, his analysis of the regional situation was very unexpected. As Israelis, our view of the region tends to be focused either on the immediate threats on our borders or on the Iranians. Gargash presented a sweeping regional analysis the likes of which I had almost never encountered in Israel, starting from the situation in Europe, passing through Libya and Turkey on the way to Sudan and Yemen, from there traveling across Syria and Lebanon before finishing up in Iran and the Gulf. More than what he did talk about, I was surprised by what his analysis omitted; there was not a word about the Palestinian situation or about Israel. When I asked him about the secret alliance between Israel and the United Arab Emirates against Iran, he laughed. "I think the Arab policy of the past 50 years of not engaging with Israel in any way has failed," Gargash told me. "There is slow progress with unofficial ties. But don't underestimate the importance of the Palestinian cause within public opinion in the Arab world. There will be progress in ties, but it won't be at the expense of the Palestinians." At the end of the meeting, we exchanged business cards, and I requested a visa to visit Abu Dhabi. "Maybe later," Gargash told me, and we parted ways with a smile.

In the March 2, 2020, elections, Netanyahu managed to recover from the blow he suffered six months previously, but it still proved insufficient. Against his expectations, he was unable to obtain the support of 61 members of the Knesset. The head of Blue and White,

Benny Gantz, was able to obtain the backing of more members of the Knesset to form a government than his rival. For the first time since 2009, Netanyahu failed to secure a mandate. But it was at this very moment, within touching distance of the Prime Minister's Office, that Gantz blinked. Netanyahu launched an aggressive and racist media campaign intended to delegitimize any government founded with the votes of the members of the Arab Joint List. He stood in front of the television cameras and, in black marker on a whiteboard, wrote out the election results as he saw them, erasing the voices of hundreds of thousands of Arab voters who had combined to give the Joint List 15 seats. Netanyahu's campaign, coupled with the opposition of two members of Gantz's party— Zvi Hauser and Yoaz Hendel—who refused to sit in a government supported by the Arab Knesset members, were enough to dissuade Gantz from even attempting to form such an alternative coalition.

At the same time, Gantz and his closest advisors were deeply concerned about the potential for a disaster with the COVID-19 response should Israel find itself spiraling into a fourth consecutive election cycle. "You don't understand the situation, everyone is going to die," one of Gantz's close advisors told me a few days after he was awarded the mandate. I was sure she was joking, but as the conversation continued, I realized she was completely serious. Even within Blue and White, not everyone was in agreement regarding the pandemic. "Yair Lapid said in internal discussions that the coronavirus is not a state of emergency, but a flu virus with public relations...that it's all part of a political trick by Netanyahu," recalled former Foreign Minister Gabi Ashkenazi.[200] Gantz and his team also considered it likely that in the fourth elections, Netanyahu and the factions that supported him would manage to overcome the 61-seat barrier. For all of those reasons, Gantz decided to enter into negotiations with Netanyahu on forming a power-sharing government led by the latter—violating the core election promise that had secured him the votes of over a million Israelis. On March 25, 10 days after Gantz received the mandate from the president, his party—the most successful center-left political project in Israel in over two decades—split up.

On April 20, Netanyahu and Gantz signed a coalition agreement on a national unity government. One of the key clauses in the agreement, which almost blew up the talks before the signing, regarded annexation of the West Bank. For three election campaigns, Gantz and his friends in the so-called "cockpit" of Blue and White maintained a deliberate ambiguity on annexation. They did not express outright support for it but neither did they reject it outright, hoping to avoid alienating an imagined electorate whose votes they feared losing. One of the most eyebrow-raising incidents in the third election campaign was a visit by Gantz and senior officials from his party to the northern Dead Sea area, during which they expressed support for annexation of the Jordan Valley, "in coordination with the international community,"[201] and promised to carry it out if elected. This directly contradicted things Gantz himself had said in public only a few weeks earlier and ran completely counter to what I heard from Gantz with my own ears a few days before that same visit. Former Member of Knesset Ofer Shelah told me that in discussions within the party before the March 2020 elections, he discovered that the former chief of the general staff and his partner, Yair Lapid, had simply not formulated any policy on the matter, and that they changed their minds along with the prevailing campaign winds and the recommendations of their strategic advisor, Israel Bachar.

Following long nights of debate, Article 29 of the coalition agreement was drafted. This article stated that, effective July 1, Netanyahu could bring any green light from the Trump administration on West Bank annexation to the security cabinet or the government plenary for discussion and to the government plenary or the Knesset for approval. "Yariv Levin pushed for the July 1 deadline," Gantz told me.[202] "He said that anything that doesn't happen quickly doesn't happen at all." Jared Kushner told me that the July 1 date had not been coordinated with the White House, and that President Trump was not even aware of its existence. "We treated this as a domestic political issue in Israel," said Kushner. "An ordinary diplomat would get offended, but I told myself—this is not my deadline. I don't care. When the deadline comes and nothing happens, Netanyahu will have to explain it to his public. We had a goal and we were focused on it." The coalition agreement also stated that any steps toward annexation must be coordinated with Gantz and take into consideration the view of the defense establishment and the peace treaties with Jordan and Egypt. "I assumed that the moment Bibi heard from all the professional bodies, it would temper him slightly in terms of his political courage and his fervor for annexation," Gantz told me. This assessment of Gantz's came with no small measure of risk. Ultimately, annexation was the only policy area in which the defense minister had no veto power. "It was clear to Bibi that we opposed annexation—and it was clear to us that he was in favor," Ashkenazi emphasized. "We told ourselves that when the moment came, we would work to stop annexation from within the government, hoping to be able to prevent it."

There was a string of political events that turned Netanyahu from a political leader who considered proponents of annexation to be Messianic weirdos, agreed to negotiate with the Palestinians on the basis of the 1967 borders with land swaps and warned of the dangers of a bi-national state, into a prime minister who made annexation his number one issue in a coalition agreement and who came to view it as the diplomatic move that would see his name written into the history books. Netanyahu emerged scarred from the negotiations with the Palestinians in 2013–2014, mediated by then-Secretary of State John Kerry. Whether he did it for perceived political gain, out of genuine desire to make progress or because he was dragged into it, Netanyahu agreed to unprecedented, far-reaching concessions. The fact that the Palestinians rejected the American initiative reinforced his belief that the most he would be willing to give did not and would never meet the least that the Palestinians would be willing to accept.

As the years went by, Netanyahu became more and more dependent on the extreme right wing. After the 2015 elections, he could have formed a unity government with Isaac Herzog, but he allowed himself to get carried away on a wave of euphoria from his great victory. He found himself leading a narrow right-wing coalition that was utterly in thrall to the votes of the settlement lobby and constantly having to correct his course further to the right to avoid being outflanked by rivals such as Naftali Bennett. In talks with the Obama administration pre-2015, Netanyahu used to explain that he needed them to give him something so that he could gain public support and overcome internal right-wing pressure. Brigadier General (Res.) Michael Herzog, who advised him during those years, told him in one of those discussions: "You're like the victim of a loan shark—however much you give the right won't help, and you'll only sink further and further."

Netanyahu's personal troubles also pushed him toward annexation. The corruption scandals, police investigations and ultimately the resulting charges left him increasingly concerned about his legacy. One consequence of his running war of words with the police and the attorney general's office was that he stopped trusting the voices of other expert authorities too, such as the team at the Ministry of Foreign Affairs, whom he considered to be lefties, and the military and Shin Bet security agency, whom he didn't trust. Netanyahu came to see all of them as part of a "Deep State" conspiracy seeking to topple him. The tighter the net closed around him, the more the prime minister hunkered down within his close family unit and was influenced by his son, Yair, who holds the most extreme of far-right views.

Last but not least, Netanyahu got drunk on power and the feeling that anything was possible in the wake of Donald Trump's ascent to the White House and the sense of victory following eight tough years working with the Obama administration. Ambassador Ron Dermer, one of the few people Netanyahu still accepted counsel from, told him over and over again that Trump's presidency represented a once-in-a-century opportunity to change the status quo on a series of supposedly dormant matters: the Golan Heights, Jerusalem and the annexation of the West Bank, among others. For Netanyahu, Trump's term was like an all-you-can-eat buffet—and he kept going back for more.

For their part, Gantz and Ashkenazi (the incoming foreign minister) began to sound a different tune on Netanyahu's annexation initiative from the very first days after the coalition agreement was signed. In public, the two of them spoke cautiously and retained an air of ambiguity, but in background conversations with journalists, they hinted that they had no intention of allowing Netanyahu to make his move on July 1. According to the agreement, Netanyahu did not need their approval to move ahead with annexation, but he did need a green light from the Americans. For its part, the White House had already explained to Netanyahu before the government was formed that any moves on annexation must have a wide political consensus in Israel and could not be a smash-and-grab.

Trump and Kushner's assessment of the situation was that after the unity government was formed, Netanyahu would deliver a speech that was pre-agreed with Gantz in which he would declare his formal acceptance of the Trump Plan in full, including not only annexation but also the establishment of a Palestinian state. Netanyahu had no such plans. "We didn't intervene in the formation of the Israeli government, but we did send a message to both Gantz and Netanyahu that we want to see a resolution," Kushner told me.[203] "We told them to get their acts together because they were wasting precious time when there is a supportive administration in Washington and when we can do many things.'"

On May 13, a few days before the new government was due to be sworn in, Secretary of State Mike Pompeo came for a lightning visit to Israel. For the first time in years, he met with Israeli politicians other than Netanyahu. From the prime minister, Pompeo heard about the desire to move ahead with annexation as quickly as possible. But when he met with Benny Gantz and Gabi Ashkenazi, he heard doubts and hesitation. The two raised significant questions about annexation and the potential ramifications for the peace treaties with Jordan and Egypt and argued that a unilateral step did not serve Israeli interests. "Our main goal was to explain to Pompeo that this was a government of national unity—a coalition—and not a one-man show," recalled Ashkenazi.[204] "I asked Pompeo who would appoint the replacement of his friend, Yossi Cohen. He said Netanyahu. I told him he was wrong, as any such decision required Gantz's approval as well. From that meeting on, the Americans began to take an interest in what we had to say too." Pompeo emerged from the visit confused. One of the US secretary of state's advisors told me at the time that Pompeo was surprised by the contrasting viewpoints he heard from Netanyahu, Gantz and Ashkenazi. "First of all, they need to reach an agreement between themselves," he told me.[205]

As the date of the swearing-in drew closer, the pressure from opponents of annexation around the world grew stronger. Fifteen European ambassadors came to the foreign ministry in Jerusalem together to submit a protest against the annexation clause in the coalition agreement and warned of the negative consequences of such a move for Israel's global standing. The Arab League convened a meeting and issued a unanimous statement opposing annexation. The Emirati foreign minister, Abdullah bin Zayed, published a rare statement aimed squarely at the Prime Minister's Office. "The statements of Israeli Prime Minister Benjamin Netanyahu, in which he referred to an implicit Arab acceptance [of annexation], contradict the reality," he wrote.[206] But the starkest warning came from King Abdullah of Jordan. "If Israel really annexes the West Bank in July, it would lead to a massive conflict with the Hashemite Kingdom of Jordan. "I don't want to make threats…but we are considering all options," the king said at the time.[207]

The conflicting messages Pompeo received on his visit, the growing international pressure, the troubled statements from the Arab world and the rapidly-worsening COVID-19 crisis in the United States—all of these resulted in the green light from the United States turning yellow. A senior White House official called me during those days and astonished me with his lukewarm tone on annexation. "We know that Netanyahu promised, but the US government does not consider July 1 to be a sacred deadline," he told me.[208] I asked him if Netanyahu had also received that message. "Yes," he replied. That message had been received loud and clear by Ron Dermer, who was being referred to as "Bibi's brain." Dermer spent those days in late April and early May explaining to anyone willing to listen in Jerusalem and in Washington that Israel had to carry out annexation at the earliest opportunity—

before the US elections in November—as he considered the Democratic candidate, Joe Biden, to be likely to win. Aware of the differences of opinion within the Trump administration and the increasing reluctance among senior officials in the White House and Department of State to support Israeli annexation of the West Bank, Dermer sought to speed up the process.

On May 17, the Knesset gathered to swear in the 35th government. Celebrations were muted. Netanyahu's speech was interrupted by hecklers reminding him of his charges of fraud, breach of trust and accepting bribes, but Gantz came under a much heavier barrage immediately after him. Netanyahu declared that it was time "to apply Israeli law" to the settlements in the West Bank. This was the new terminology in the new government's briefing notes, designed to paint the drastic step Netanyahu was planning in softer pastel shades that would incite less opposition.[209]

The reference to annexation in Netanyahu's speech was fleeting and went almost unmentioned within Israel, but in the Mukataa in Ramallah they heard it and took it as the cue that steps were underway against them. On May 19, President Abbas summoned the Palestinian leadership for an emergency meeting. He declared that, in light of the annexation clause in the Israeli coalition agreement and Netanyahu's speech during the swearing-in, the Palestinian Authority would immediately cease to uphold all of its agreements with Israel. This meant a freeze on security and civil cooperation between the sides. The prevailing belief in Israel was that Abbas's threats were empty, but the next day, his advisors informed the head of the Coordinator of Government Activities in the Territories (COGAT) unit, Kamil Abu Rukun, that this was not Abbas's usual "hold me back" speech. From that moment on, the Palestinians simply stopped picking up the phone. Some Palestinian officers even blocked their Israeli colleagues on WhatsApp.

Like the Israeli ambassador to the United States, the Palestinian president also understood that time was the name of the game. Abbas placed all his eggs in the basket of the approaching US elections. He kept his fingers firmly crossed for a victory by the Democratic candidate, Joe Biden, and hoped that if he could just delay annexation by a few months, a change of administration in the United States would take the matter off the table. That evening, a few hours after Abbas's dramatic declaration, Biden held a Zoom meeting with Jewish donors and underscored that the Palestinian president's hopes were not misplaced. "I do not support annexation. Israel needs to stop the threat of annexation and stop settlement activity, because it will choke off any hope for peace," said Biden.[210]

In the first weeks of the Netanyahu–Gantz government, the question of annexation almost never arose. Netanyahu continued to emphasize it among members of his party, with one eye still fixed on the July 1 target date, but Gantz and Ashkenazi didn't engage with it at all. When senior officials in the security establishment sought guidance from the political leadership on the scenarios they should be preparing for, they received no answers. With nowhere else to turn, Chief of the General Staff Aviv Kochavi was forced to base his decision-making on media reports. He instructed the army to prepare for a potential escalation in the West Bank and Gaza Strip starting July 1. In the meantime, the international community continued to apply pressure. Netanyahu received letters from the leaders of five of the most influential countries in Europe urging him against annexation.

On May 27, Ron Dermer attended a meeting with Avi Berkowitz at the White House. The US envoy to the Middle East proposed a string of measures that Israel would offer the Palestinians at the same time as the annexation. It would be a stretch to suggest that Dermer was enthusiastic about this proposal, but another issue that arose during the meeting gave him significantly more cause for concern. Berkowitz informed Dermer that, with a national unity government now in place, he intended to reach out to Gantz and Ashkenazi to hear their views on annexation. Dermer did not like this, to put it mildly, and asked Berkowitz that the White House not discuss annexation with the ministers of defense and foreign affairs, only with Netanyahu. One of Netanyahu's advisors explained to me that the prime minister didn't hold discussions on annexation with Gantz and Ashkenazi at the time, primarily because he had no intention of taking their views into account. "They weren't a factor as far as Netanyahu was concerned. We knew they were opposed to annexation, but it didn't affect us and didn't change our minds. But we also knew that what they say affects the Americans," Netanyahu's advisor told me.[211] Throughout those weeks, Netanyahu worked with Gantz and Ashkenazi as if there was no annexation—and discussed annexation with the Americans as if there was no unity government. Two and a half weeks after the government was sworn in, matters came to a head.

T-Minus One Month

On June 1, in the afternoon, Netanyahu was connected to a conference call. On the line were Israeli Ambassador to Washington Ron Dermer, US Ambassador to Israel David Friedman, White House Envoy Avi Berkowitz, and Jared Kushner. The goal of the call was to assess where things stood a month out from the deadline Netanyahu had set. Netanyahu spoke determinedly about his desire to move ahead with annexation.[212] "I thought we had already agreed on this," Netanyahu told Kushner. President Trump's most senior advisor was reticent. "We're not opposed to annexation, but it has to be done within the wider context of the Trump Plan," he told Netanyahu. They agreed that Berkowitz and Friedman would continue to talk with Dermer to see how they could make progress. That morning, Ambassador Friedman had met with Benny Gantz, but he failed to mention the planned conference call. Gantz and Ashkenazi only found out about it later that evening, when the existence of the conversation was reported in the press. They were furious. In the days that followed, they spoke with Friedman and senior White House officials, and protested that the talks had taken place with only one side of the Israeli government. They stressed that, as far as they were concerned, the days of Netanyahu's monopoly on matters of defense and foreign policy were over, and that if the Americans wanted things to happen, they would be well advised not to exclude them. "I spoke with Avi Berkowitz and told him, 'If you want to work with Netanyahu, be my guest, but nothing will move.' They received the message and made sure to talk with us from that point on," Ashkenazi recalled. Berkowitz told me that Ashkenazi was very angry and claimed that unilateral annexation would be a huge mistake. "Ashkenazi told me that we should be moving ahead with the Trump Plan and not with unilateral annexation," said Berkowitz.[213] The White House envoy informed Ashkenazi that the administration wanted any move on annexation to include gestures to benefit the Palestinians. The conversation was blunt, but Berkowitz and Ashkenazi came out of it understanding that they wanted the same thing.

Even though they hadn't participated in the conference call, Gantz and Ashkenazi began to recognize that the appetite for unilateral annexation within the White House was waning. The day before, protests over the murder of George Floyd had spread to the capital, with protesters almost reaching the White House perimeter fence, clashing with police and lighting fires. The Israeli illustrator Eran Wolkowski published a cartoon in *Haaretz* depicting President Trump staring out of the window of his office at the fires raging outside the White House as one of his advisors hands him the phone and says, "The Israelis are asking about annexation." It perfectly encapsulated how several senior White House officials felt about Netanyahu's attempts to plow ahead with annexation while completely ignoring the domestic situation in the United States. "When we saw it, we burst out laughing—especially because of how accurate it was," a senior White House official told me at the time.

The fight over annexation forced the White House to learn the names of people whose public statements almost certainly never crossed the radar of any American administration. One of them was David Elhayani, a resident of the Argaman settlement in the Jordan Valley who had been appointed to lead the influential Yesha Council settlers' lobbying group six months earlier. Tall, with a gleaming scalp, thick mustache and the air of a rugged cowboy from the Wild West, Elhayani was a different kind of chairman for the organization: a secular Likud-affiliated farmer of Sephardi heritage. The Trump Plan and the annexation initiative were the first major political events to land on his desk. After years in which the settlers had been the bête noire of Washington, the Trump administration opened the doors of the White House to them. They became guests of honor at the US ambassador to Israel's events and Republican members of Congress lined up to visit the settlements. The annexation move was supposed to be the realization of all the settlement lobby's hopes and most fervent dreams. But in practice, the opposite happened. Instead of reaching the pinnacle of their power and influence, the settlers' leadership fell into one of its worst internal crises since 1967, with deep cracks emerging. Strangely, Elhayani and a group of fellow council heads, primarily from the isolated settlements deep in the West

Bank, opposed the annexation initiative, as it formed part of the Trump Plan that also called for the establishment of a Palestinian state. Another group, led by the head of the Efrat local council, Oded Revivi, which included council heads from settlements in the blocs close to the Green Line, supported the move, seeing the Trump Plan as the most favorable one Israel had ever or would ever receive from a US president.

In early June, Netanyahu met separately with the members of both camps. The first meeting was with the opponents. Netanyahu brought with him the speaker of the Knesset, Yariv Levin—an outspoken supporter of annexation and a man to whose right flank stood only a brick wall. The two made an emotional appeal to Elhayani and his colleagues. They talked about the historic opportunity that had arisen, about how there was no choice but to agree to negotiations on the basis of the Trump Plan, and emphasized that the American position on annexation had toughened. "Your campaign against the Trump Plan is harming efforts to carry out annexation," Netanyahu and Levin told them. The meeting was long and exhaustive, but no agreements were reached. Netanyahu and Levin left the meeting annoyed, but they had no idea what was waiting for them around the bend.

Two days later, Elhayani gave an interview to *Haaretz* where he came out swinging against President Trump and Jared Kushner. "They are not friends of Israel, and they only care about winning the elections in the United States," said the head of the Yesha Council. The members of the Prime Minister's Office were stunned. When the interview was published on the *Haaretz* website in English, David Friedman—the settler's biggest ally in the US administration—was similarly taken aback. Within minutes, Netanyahu had come out against Elhayani's words in the harshest possible terms.

"It's unfortunate that, instead of gratitude, there is someone who is trying to deny this friendship, which has never been stronger," said Netanyahu in his statement.

The split within the leadership of the settler movement was further exposed a few days later, when Netanyahu met with the heads of the councils who supported annexation. The atmosphere was the reverse of the previous meeting. He appeared optimistic and received encouragement from those present. "Within the next few weeks, we will move ahead with annexation," Levin promised the participants. Netanyahu was more guarded. He talked about attempting to annex "as much as possible" but admitted that there were no agreements with either the White House or Blue and White. "We must not give Trump the impression that we are not interested," he emphasized.

As doubts began to creep in among the right wing on annexation, Netanyahu stressed in all his talks with the settlers and members of his party that Israel would not need to pay any price in exchange. In private and in public, Netanyahu promised that Israel would not agree to a Palestinian state, despite such a commitment featuring in the Trump Plan, and that the resolution on annexation that would be brought before the government or the Knesset would make no mention of the matter. His words reached the White House, where they were received with fury. A senior White House official privately accused Netanyahu of cherry picking only the parts of the plan he approved of and ignoring the inconvenient ones. "We didn't want the Israelis to cherry pick from the plan, but to accept it as a package and say they see it as a basis for negotiations," Kushner told me.[214] "Netanyahu said all that we agreed he would say—the problem was that he said several other things that we didn't agree on, like annexation."

On June 7, Netanyahu scheduled his first meeting on annexation with Benny Gantz and Gabi Ashkenazi. Upon entering the room, the ministers of defense and foreign affairs were surprised to find the meeting had grown into an unholy fusion of conflicting diplomatic and political interests. It started with the presence of the speaker of the Knesset, Yariv Levin; the head of the legislative branch invited to a work meeting of the heads of the executive branch which he was responsible for overseeing. As if that were not enough, Netanyahu had also invited the US ambassador to Israel, David Friedman, to this internal meeting of senior Israeli government officials—a meeting in which they were supposed to formulate a position on a critical aspect of national security policy. Adding to the blurred lines, Friedman found himself in the meeting attempting to mediate between the two rival camps within the Israeli government in order to pursue his personal ambition of ensuring annexation of parts of the West Bank. Early on in proceedings, Gantz expressed his surprise at Friedman's presence in the room. "With all due respect, what is the ambassador doing here?" he asked Netanyahu. A cowed Friedman left the room and waited in the office next door. Ashkenazi told me that Netanyahu opened the meeting by declaring his determination to begin with annexation on July 1. "Where do you stand?" he asked. Gantz and Ashkenazi responded that they were in favor of the Trump Plan, but only if it was implemented as part of a mutual and measured process. "We can't work like that," Netanyahu fired back angrily. Ashkenazi and Gantz replied that if he wanted, he was welcome to go ahead with annexation unilaterally, as the coalition agreement permitted him to do. Gantz told me that Netanyahu would not agree to show him any maps during that meeting, and that he tried every means possible to secure a commitment from the two former generals regarding the extent of annexation they would agree to.

"What percentage? What's your position?" insisted Netanyahu. Ashkenazi and Gantz told him that they would be willing to consider annexation of 3–4 percent of the West Bank, including the Gush Etzion settlement bloc to the south of Jerusalem and the city of Ma'ale Adumim to the east, but they repeated their view that the Palestinians must be offered concessions in exchange so that the move was not unilateral. "Where are the maps? We want to see them," they told Netanyahu. The prime minister refused, and the strange meeting came to an end without any agreements. Gantz told me that once the meeting was over, he went over to Friedman, who was still waiting. "If you think the question of annexation is going to go through with our support, you are mistaken," he told the US ambassador. "We won't allow extremist measures that remove any possibility of reaching a future agreement." Friedman emerged from the meeting thoroughly dispirited. With the Americans continuing to demand a broad consensus within the Israeli leadership as a precondition for their approval, it appeared that the July 1 deadline to begin annexing was set to come and go. "Friedman's presence in that meeting was absurd," Ashkenazi told me. "But he heard what we had to say, and he told Netanyahu, 'We cannot go to war with a divided house.'" As they were leaving the Prime Minister's Office, Levin chased after Ashkenazi and Gantz. "You're out of line," he told them. "You've known this was our position since the coalition negotiations," the two replied. "If you want it, go for it."

Following the meeting, Netanyahu was immensely frustrated. A few days later, I saw it for myself at the annual memorial for the victims of the 1948 Altalena Affair, in which soldiers from the newly formed IDF exchanged fire with members of the Irgun, a Jewish paramilitary group, who were attempting to dock in Israel on board the ship *Altalena*, carrying a cargo of weapons.

The situation escalated, and 19 people lost their lives. The modest annual memorial ceremony in Tel Aviv's small Nahalat Yitzhak Cemetery was even more intimate than usual because of COVID-19. Netanyahu had steadfastly and consciously refused to meet me or talk with me for over a decade, going back to March 2010. I don't think there was any particular trigger—I suspect the motive is primarily personal. The event at the cemetery represented a rare opportunity for me to quiz him directly. I assumed that few journalists would show up, and indeed it was only myself and Yoav Krakovsky from the Israeli Public Broadcasting Corporation. When the official ceremony was over, I approached Netanyahu and asked him whether he intended to begin with annexation on July 1. When he refused to answer, I asked again, and then once more. His chief of staff, Asher Hayoun, started yelling at me, and a few of Netanyahu's supporters who were nearby even threatened me with violence. Finally, Netanyahu answered. "Your problem is that you would not want to hear my answer," he told me—and walked away. The personal attack was an indication of the extent to which his annexation project was not proceeding according to plan. "Netanyahu was determined to carry out annexation, and his July 1 deadline was not political spin and was not empty words, but there were political forces trying to derail it," one of his senior advisors who was involved in the discussions at the time told me.[215] "Netanyahu understood that there were security implications, but he had made his peace with them. The situational assessments were that even if it didn't go smoothly, we would get through it and the prize was worth the pain."

As July 1 approached, Netanyahu finally internalized that his coalition partners would not present him with a blank check for annexation. When the German foreign minister, Heiko Maas, scheduled an urgent trip to Israel on June 10 to convey an unequivocal message against it, Ashkenazi stood by his side at the press conference and poured a bucket of cold water on the initiative. "There are no maps for annexation, there is no plan for annexation and there is no decision at the moment," Ashkenazi said to the TV cameras. The German foreign minister, who went from the press conference straight to a meeting in the Prime Minister's Office, could not get any sense from Netanyahu of his plan. Maas left Israel slightly more at ease. He could see that the move was nowhere near ready to go, and that the divisions within the Israeli government ran deep.

The man desperately trying to breathe life into the annexation proposal in those days was David Friedman. It was an unprecedented moment in the history of Israeli–American relations—the Israeli calf was less interested in suckling than the American cow (or at least its representative in Jerusalem) was in feeding it. Friedman went back and forth from Netanyahu to Gantz and Ashkenazi in an attempt to draft a compromise agreement that would enable annexation. A senior Israeli official who participated in those meetings told me that it was unclear whether Friedman was representing the position of the White House or pushing his own independent agenda. Friedman soon learned the hard way where Netanyahu's priorities lay. He came to the Prime Minister's Office for another meeting with Netanyahu, Levin, Gantz and Ashkenazi. Netanyahu and Gantz were already sitting in Netanyahu's office and addressing a burning issue: concerns that the High Court of Justice would strike down the amendments to the law that would enable Netanyahu to serve as "alternate prime minister" despite the indictments against him. After two hours of twiddling his thumbs on the sofa in the "aquarium"—the inner sanctum in the Prime Minister's Office—Friedman called it a day. Dispirited and frustrated, he left the building, never to return to those meetings.

Two weeks before July 1, Netanyahu was still trying to persuade Gantz and Ashkenazi to agree to any kind of move. He had accepted that full annexation was not going to happen but hoped to secure a "diet annexation" and to avoid as much as possible the "annexation zero" scenario. In a meeting with IDF reserves officers affiliated with the political right, he admitted that the internal divisions meant that annexation "would not happen in one stroke," but would require a few phases. Two days later, in a meeting with Gantz and Ashkenazi, he presented the two for the first time with the maps his team had been working on in secret for so many weeks. Netanyahu unveiled four maps, each representing a different annexation scenario: the maximum 30 percent annexation outlined in the Trump Plan, annexation of the Jordan Valley alone, annexation of the Jordan Valley and settlements and a restricted annexation of a few of the major settlement blocs. At no stage did Netanyahu state a preference for any one of the plans. "If we go for the widest annexation plan, which lands do we give in exchange from the State of Israel?" Ashkenazi asked Netanyahu. "The Trump Plan talks about giving land from the Negev desert." The prime minister dodged the question and didn't answer. For their part, Gantz and Ashkenazi said they opposed annexation of lands where Palestinians were living or any situation in which lands were annexed without the Palestinians on those lands being granted full and equal rights. "Any annexation must be part of a broader diplomatic process in which the Palestinians receive something in exchange—and not a unilateral step by Israel," they told Netanyahu. The prime minister fundamentally disagreed, and that meeting ended the same way as its predecessors.

While senior Israeli government officials continued to argue among themselves, international pressure continued to build. Every day, another foreign government—many from the Arab world—

released a public statement against annexation or delivered quiet messages warning of unspecified consequences. Unexpectedly at the forefront of the campaign against annexation was the United Arab Emirates—and no one more than its ambassador to Washington, Yousef Al Otaiba. When the Trump administration entered office in 2017, Al Otaiba was in his ninth year on the job. During the Obama administration, Al Otaiba had been one of the most influential and powerful foreign diplomats in Washington. That power and influence only grew stronger under Trump.

When Al Otaiba visited the White House for the unveiling of the Trump Plan in late January 2020 and heard Netanyahu talk about annexing parts of the West Bank, he didn't bat an eyelid. Even a short time later, when the Israeli prime minister announced that he would bring the matter of annexing the settlements to a government vote within a few days, he held firm to his belief that it was all part of Netanyahu's election campaign. From his conversations with the White House, he was confident that Jared Kushner and his team would not allow such a move to go ahead. It was only after the elections, when the topic of annexation found its way into the coalition agreement, that Al Otaiba began to ring the alarm bells within the halls of power in Abu Dhabi. He was strongly in favor of a gradual process of normalization, and every year he encouraged more and more small steps to bring the UAE and Israel closer together. Netanyahu's annexation initiative was on a direct collision course with this process and risked causing the collapse of the project to which Al Otaiba had dedicated more than a decade of his life.

Al Otaiba started pressuring the White House to oppose annexation from May 2020. He warned Kushner, Pompeo and Berkowitz that such a step would destroy any chances of normalization, harm the secret regional alliance the Trump administration was building against Iran, derail the two-state solution once and for all and undermine the stability of the Jordanian royal family. At the same time as the quiet messages, Al Otaiba also encouraged the Abu Dhabi leadership to speak out publicly against annexation—advice which was duly taken. The crown prince, Sheikh Mohamed, and foreign minister, Sheikh Abdullah, who usually refrained from making public statements on the Israeli–Palestinian issue, began to issue press statements and tweets every few days warning against annexation. But Al Otaiba wanted to take things a step further. He suggested to Sheikh Abdullah that he make a historic and unprecedented intervention by giving an interview on Israeli TV to deliver an anti-annexation message directly to the Israeli public. At first this suggestion was turned down, but one early morning in June, Al Otaiba received a phone call. He walked into the living room of his home to avoid waking up the rest of the household. On the line was Sheikh Abdullah. "Do it," the sheikh told him. "Do what?" replied Al Otaiba, still struggling to pull himself together from the early wake-up call. "You're constantly trying to get us to speak to the Israeli public directly on annexation," the foreign minister said. "So go on, do it. You're the ambassador to Washington. Write something and have it published in the Israeli media."

Al Otaiba was grateful for the green light but recognized that the success or failure of the move had been placed squarely on his shoulders. The only question that remained was how to go about it. Al Otaiba called his friend, the Israeli-American billionaire Haim Saban. He told him about the idea and the message that the UAE wanted to deliver to the Israeli public, and asked for his advice on where and how to publish the article. "Haim told me it has to be published in Hebrew in *Yedioth Ahronoth* and on Friday so that it gets the biggest exposure," Al Otaiba told me. Saban enlisted the help of his media advisor, Moshe Debby, who reached out discreetly to the editor of *Yedioth Ahronoth*, Neta Livne. At the same time, Al Otaiba sat down to write the op-ed. One of the people he spoke to quietly about its contents was the former US ambassador to Israel, Dan Shapiro. The two had grown close when Shapiro worked for the White House in the first two years of the Obama administration. The day before the piece was published, Al Otaiba sent it to Kushner and Berkowitz, to ensure there would be no surprises, and to ensure that it was not understood as a statement against the Trump administration. The two did not voice any opposition to the move. "The op-ed was Yousef's initiative. We knew it was happening but we weren't involved. [It] had a lot of influence," Kushner told me.[216]

On Friday, June 12, the article was splashed across the top half of the front page of *Yedioth Ahronoth*, with a further double-page spread on pages one and two. "Annexation will be a serious setback for better relations with the Arab world," ran the headline. The op-ed kicked up a political storm. Quite aside from the historic nature of a direct appeal in Hebrew to the Israeli public by the United Arab Emirates, the article took a wrecking ball to the main argument advanced by Netanyahu and his supporters, namely that the Palestinian issue was no longer relevant and that the Arab world did not oppose annexation. Netanyahu learned about the article only in the early hours of that Friday morning, and it took him by surprise. He was enraged by the Emirati intrusion. It is not unrealistic to suppose that at least part of his ire was due to the decision to publish the article in *Yedioth Ahronoth*, a newspaper that he considered a personal enemy. Netanyahu's communications with the publisher of *Yedioth*, Arnon "Noni" Mozes, had even resulted in a criminal indictment against the prime minister for breach of trust. A few hours after the article was published, as a new day was dawning in Washington, Al Otaiba received a phone call from the Israeli ambassador, Ron Dermer. Dermer was aggrieved and complained that Al Otaiba had not informed him ahead of time. He raised his voice, getting progressively more worked up until he was yelling at the Emirati ambassador. He sounded like a man channeling his boss's frenzied rage. "We had planned to carry out a limited annexation move, but now you've left us with no choice," Dermer threatened his counterpart. Dermer's outburst only served to convince the leadership in Abu Dhabi that the op-ed had served its goal. The UAE foreign ministry shared the article on social media, including tweets in Hebrew, and Al Otaiba recorded a video clip in which he explained why he had written the article and why the leaders of the UAE felt it was important to reach out directly to the Israeli public. Although the goal of the article was to halt the move toward annexation, the Ministry of Foreign Affairs in Jerusalem also saw a more positive side to it. Another message could be inferred from reading between the lines: the United Arab Emirates was ready for normalization.

Netanyahu didn't give up. He took those days to gauge the mood in Cairo and Amman. Gantz, Ashkenazi and senior officials in the security services warned that annexation risked endangering the peace treaties with Egypt and Jordan. "I remember speaking with the Jordanian foreign minister, Ayman Safadi, who told me that annexation would be a disaster for our relationship and have negative consequences for the peace treaty," Ashkenazi told me.[217] "The Egyptians were more restrained, but they also hinted that it would not be good for relations." The director general of the foreign ministry, Alon Ushpiz, told me that a special team compiled a document that was updated every few days regarding the diplomatic implications of annexation in the West Bank. Ashkenazi took the document with him to every meeting with Netanyahu on the subject. "The bottom line of the document was that annexation would set Israel back significantly," said Ushpiz.[218] "We didn't see how such a move could do anything but harm our relationship with Arab countries and nor did we think that the Middle East would take it lying down." Netanyahu felt the opposite. He sent his trusted confidant, Mossad director Yossi Cohen, who was in lockstep with him on the question of annexation, to talk with the Jordanians and the Egyptians. A few days earlier, in a meeting of the State Security Cabinet, Cohen had stood in front of the heads of all the other security and intelligence agencies and challenged their assertion that annexation might lead to an escalation in the security situation. In the third week of June, he met with King Abdullah of Jordan in his palace. "What would be your position should we carry out only a partial annexation? For example, if we only annex the settlement blocs?" asked Cohen. The king rebuffed him on the spot. As Cohen was on his way back to Israel, the Jordanian foreign minister was dispatched to the state television channel to deliver a public message. "Jordan opposes even a partial annexation that includes the settlement blocs of Ma'ale Adumim, Ariel and Gush Etzion, as such a move would split the West Bank and prevent the establishment of a Palestinian state," he said.

Trump's advisors were watching the events unfold, powerless to intervene. The election campaign was in full swing, COVID-19 was sweeping through the country, the Israeli government was unable to formulate a common position and, while all this was happening, calls were coming in every day from world leaders warning against annexation. One of the most categorical of these messages came from the United Kingdom. On June 12, Jared Kushner sent Avi Berkowitz and Brian Hook, the senior advisor to Secretary of State Pompeo, to meet with the British ambassador to the United States, Karen Pierce, to provide her with an update on the situation. Pierce caught the senior officials off guard when she warned them that if Israel were to annex parts of the West Bank under the justification of US support, the United Kingdom would respond by recognizing Palestine as a state. Such a move would almost certainly have created a domino effect in, for instance, France, Spain and other European countries. Berkowitz had also endured a tough conversation with senior German diplomats on annexation the day before. He asked them to deliver a message to the Palestinians. "I told them, 'Go to the Palestinians and tell them we are moving ahead with annexation. Ask them what they want us to get for them in return and we will try to do that,'" Berkowitz recalled.[219]

Ambassador Friedman, sensing that annexation was slipping away from his grasp, pressured the White House to act. He called Kushner and Berkowitz on a daily basis and asked them why they were not pushing the matter. In one of those conversations, which took place on an unsecured line, Friedman used cryptic biblical references to establish whether the president would be likely to allow annexation of parts of Hebron to Israel. "Do you remember what Abraham purchased in the story of Sarah? Can we do something with that?" he asked. A former senior White House official told me that in one of the conversations, Kushner explained to Friedman that circumstances had changed and that Trump had developed a severe personal antipathy toward Netanyahu. "You're six thousand miles away—and you're out of touch with things here. There's COVID-19, there's the elections. This is not the president's top priority right now," he told Friedman. "If you think that now is the time, we'll arrange a meeting and you can come and put your case to the president, but I'm warning you— it won't be an easy sell." Friedman decided to take him up on the offer regardless and asked for a meeting with the president.

Because of the COVID-19 situation, Friedman's own health and the fact that he was in an at-risk group, he was flown to Washington aboard a government jet. Ahead of the trip, Friedman begged Netanyahu and Gantz for an answer. "In three days' time I'm meeting with the president, and I need to come to him with a number [for the extent of the annexation that Israel wants to carry out]. I cannot go to the president without an agreement." But Gantz and Ashkenazi were unmoved, and the stalemate at the top of the Israeli government remained.

On June 24, President Trump convened a meeting with senior officials in his administration to decide whether to green-light annexation or not. The day before, Kushner and Berkowitz held a prep meeting with Friedman. "David was obsessed with getting permission for annexation, and Kushner and Berkowitz warned him again ahead of the meeting with the president," said a former senior White House official. Kushner's misgivings came almost flawlessly true. Trump was impatient and extremely short-tempered. Friedman, who was supposed to be leading the discussion, opened the meeting by giving the president a symbolic gift: a framed US flag that had previously flown over the embassy in Jerusalem. A former senior White House official told me that the president was unimpressed and looked at the deflated Friedman with disdain. As Kushner had anticipated, Trump immediately launched into a lengthy diatribe about Netanyahu's speech at the unveiling of the peace plan a few months previously. When Friedman finally received permission to speak and make his case, Trump once more cut him off within minutes. "David—why are we talking about this?" he asked. "Mr. President, this is an important matter—and we told them…" Friedman started, only for Trump to interrupt him again. "I have done more for Israel than any other president in history," he contended to those present in the room. According to a former senior White House official, Friedman admitted in that discussion that there was no consensus within the Israeli government on annexation, but he nonetheless tried his luck one more time. At that point, Trump's patience ran out. "You know what—if you want to do it, I have no problem with it. Mike, you decide," said Trump and pointed toward Secretary of State Pompeo. "But if anything bad happens, it's on all of you." The meeting dispersed with the majority of those present unenthusiastic at best about Netanyahu's annexation plan. On his way out of the room, Pompeo turned to the others and said, "If you ask me—I'm in favor." After the meeting, Friedman was anxious. "We have to do it properly because the president isn't entirely comfortable with it," he told Kushner and Berkowitz. Friedman understood that if something were to go wrong, if an outbreak of violence or international protests followed, he would be the fall guy. "I'll tell Dermer that the meeting ended 51:49," Friedman told Berkowitz before he left the White House, putting it in terms of a close Senate vote. "No, David, tell him it was 50:50, with the vice president having to cast the deciding vote," Berkowitz replied. Trump's advisors knew that Netanyahu would recognize the analogy and understand that they were meeting him halfway as a gesture of goodwill.

The only practical resolution to emerge from the meeting was that Berkowitz and Friedman would return to Israel to meet with Netanyahu and Gantz, to see whether there was anything else that could be done or whether it was time to take the matter off the table, at least until after the US elections in November. One of Kushner's takeaways was the need to prevent a recurrence of the misunderstandings that had led to the crisis surrounding annexation in January. "David was a very effective ambassador, but I wanted to make sure people don't hear what they want to hear," Kushner told me.[220] "I wanted Avi [Berkowitz] to be there to give me a full picture of what was going on in Israel so that we could avoid surprises."

Before Berkowitz left for Israel, Kushner spoke with Netanyahu over the phone to lay the groundwork. Netanyahu was angry and threatened to move ahead with annexation even without the support of the White House. "That will be the biggest mistake you could make," Kushner told him. "Trump will come out against you." Kushner figured Netanyahu was acting the way he was because of the political pressure he was under as well as his legal woes. He decided not to get involved in a confrontation, and to allow him to blow off steam. "I need to do something," Netanyahu insisted. "No, you don't," replied Kushner. "Adopt our plan. For the first time, you're on the right side and the Palestinians are being obstructionists. We have managed to give you the moral high ground, don't throw it away with annexation. You offered them maps, a state, economic rehabilitation—and they're running away and positioning themselves as an obstacle. Let them hang themselves. Relax and don't do anything." In our conversation on the topic, Kushner recalled, "I didn't think it was a big deal because they were planning on annexing areas the Israelis were already in anyway. But I wanted them to take steps for the Palestinians. But Bibi didn't want to do that. I told him the goal is to implement the plan, not annexation."

Four Days in June

Benjamin Netanyahu had no warning just how much the last week of June 2020 would affect his political situation. One of the things on his agenda that week was an application to the Knesset Finance Committee for tax refunds worth hundreds of thousands of shekels for expenses relating to his private home in the affluent town of Caesarea, at a time when hundreds of thousands of Israelis had lost their jobs in the wake of the pandemic. Coalition whip and Netanyahu ally Miki Zohar will go down in the history books of ill-advised political quotes for his claim in the committee hearings that the multi-millionaire prime minister was the victim of people attempting to "financially cripple" him. That Friday afternoon, police officers arrested Brigadier General (Res.) Amir Haskel at a small protest in front of the prime minister's house. Haskel's arrest sparked an unprecedented wave of protests against Netanyahu that lasted for nine months. At their peak, 30 thousand people protested outside the prime minister's official residence and thousands more took to bridges and intersections across the country.

This was the environment into which White House Envoy Avi Berkowitz stepped on June 27 for his meeting with Netanyahu. This visit was the toughest assignment of Berkowitz's three-and-a-half-year tenure in the White House. The 32-year-old's mission was to deliver a message to the US president's closest ally that the prime minister would be very unhappy to receive. The four days that followed in late June represented the lowest point of the relationship between Netanyahu and Trump's White House, but they would also make the biggest impact. Unlike his long-standing personal bond with Jared Kushner and his close relationships with David Friedman and Special Representative Jason Greenblatt, Netanyahu's relationship with Berkowitz was tepid. One of the prime minister's senior advisors told me that there was a poor chemistry between the two from the get-go. The deep cracks in the trust between Netanyahu and the White House in the wake of the events of January 28 were also still evident. Berkowitz found Netanyahu bitter and grumbling. The COVID-19 restrictions made the meeting even more difficult, with Netanyahu sitting at his desk behind a plastic see-through screen. It started off tense and deteriorated from there. "Stop leaking to Barak Ravid," Netanyahu rebuked Berkowitz right away. "What you just said is very offensive. I've done a lot for Israel," Berkowitz responded. Friedman intervened and attempted to placate Netanyahu, hinting to him that Berkowitz was the man holding the keys to his ambitions. One of Netanyahu's advisors who was present in the meeting with Berkowitz that Saturday evening told me that he had never seen Netanyahu so angry and behaving so undiplomatically. "It was really embarrassing," he recalled.

A former senior White House official pointed out that Berkowitz's primary goal for the visit was to reach a balanced agreement that would not look like a straightforward land-grab—something that could later be put before Kushner for his approval. Friedman, who recognized that Kushner would not endorse the annexation proposal without Berkowitz's seal of approval, changed his approach to the White House envoy and started showering him with affection. As far as Berkowitz himself was concerned, however, the man who had to give the kosher certificate for the plans was the mapping expert, Scott Leith, who was part of the delegation for the visit. He decided that if Leith viewed the Israeli proposal as a significant concession to the Palestinians, he would give Kushner a positive report. Should Leith give a negative opinion, however, then his report to Kushner would be pessimistic in turn.

Once the storm had eased, Netanyahu said that he was looking to annex 13–14 percent of the West Bank: the territory of all the settlements and the access roads to them.[221] Netanyahu also raised the matter of the Jordan Valley, which extends over a further 17 percent of the West Bank, though both sides knew this was not really on the table. Berkowitz emphasized that the president was reticent about any completely unilateral annexation, and that he was looking for a proposal that would advance his peace plan. He stressed that any Israeli annexation of the West Bank would have to be backed by favorable gestures toward the Palestinians. "We wanted to start implementing the plan on both sides—increasing the territory of the Palestinians, regularizing illegally constructed houses, giving them greater autonomy," a former senior White House official told me. "Netanyahu wouldn't agree to those steps, so we told him that we wouldn't allow annexation. We didn't want it to look like a unilateral land-grab. It would have destroyed everything we had built with the Arab world. We weren't expecting them to give one meter to the Palestinians for every meter they took, but we also didn't expect them not to give anything in exchange."

At one point during the meeting, Friedman left the room to bring a map. Berkowitz was left alone with Netanyahu, Knesset Speaker Yariv Levin and the director general of the Prime Minister's Office, Ronen Peretz. This was the window of opportunity he had been waiting for. "I don't know what David told you, but the meeting with the president went very badly," Berkowitz told Netanyahu. "Just so you understand the situation—it was 50:50 with a tiebreaker." Netanyahu didn't like what he was hearing. He lashed out at Berkowitz, voices were raised and the prime minister repeated his threat to Kushner from a few days earlier. "You're not keeping the promise you gave me," Netanyahu said. "If this is the situation, I might not have a choice but to move ahead with annexation without US support." Berkowitz told Netanyahu that if he did such a thing, the US would defend Israel in the UN but would be unable to help with subsequent proceedings at the International Criminal Court (ICC) in The Hague. The US envoy also added a warning: "The president will almost certainly tweet against you if you go ahead with annexation without his agreement." This jolted the prime minister. "The president will attack such a pro-Israel move so close to the elections?" He asked. Berkowitz replied in the affirmative. "The president doesn't really like you at the moment—and Jared also feels unfavorable toward you," he told Netanyahu. "You'll take your biggest friend in the world and make him your enemy. David won't be able to help you then. I can't tell you what to do, but I sincerely suggest that you don't do that." At this point, the door opened and Friedman walked in with a big smile and the maps in his arms, only to find a room full of long faces. Netanyahu, who understood the gravity of the situation he was facing, asked to speak to his team in private. "Is everything okay?" Friedman asked Berkowitz as they sat on the couch outside the conference room. "Of course," he replied. "Everything's good."

A senior official in the Prime Minister's Office told me that, in view of the American position, Netanyahu seriously considered moving ahead with annexation even without Trump's approval. One of the discussions that took place in those days focused on the price that Israel might pay. "There was a lot of pressure on the White House from the Arab states, to the extent that the Americans started to feel like there were more downsides than upsides to annexation," one of Netanyahu's advisors told me. He said the prime minister was surprised by how far the American position had shifted. "For a long time, we held discussions with the Americans about annexation and we felt like they would give us the go-ahead. We didn't think it would end up being worthless," Netanyahu's advisor told me. "That's why Bibi took it badly— and that feeling wouldn't leave him. He saw it as an American retreat. He had climbed up a tree in full view of the Israeli public and now he had a big problem climbing back down."

The next day, the prime minister's advisors sought to reduce the tension and proposed holding a further meeting, this time without Netanyahu. Ronen Peretz, Netanyahu's point-man on annexation, came to the meeting together with the head of the Civil Administration, Brigadier General Rassan Aliyan,[222] and showed the Americans maps that had been prepared for two scenarios under which Israel would annex 13 percent of the West Bank. The first map showed annexation of all the settlements, their territory and the roads surrounding them. The second map was for annexation of the Jordan Valley without the other settlements. In exchange for annexation, Peretz proposed that Israel would approve large-scale Palestinian construction plans in Area C and retroactively authorize illegal Palestinian construction on 0.2 percent of the land in the West Bank without changing the status of the territory or transferring parts of it to Palestinian control. "Our feeling was that the Americans were trying to please the Palestinians, who were opposing any process irrespectively, so why should we agree to it?" Netanyahu's advisor told me. Berkowitz was very disappointed with the plans the Israelis put before him. He had been expecting to hear far more generous proposals. "When I heard that, I understood the whole thing was not going anywhere," he recalled.[223] Frustrated, he called Kushner in Washington to provide an update: "We're not getting anywhere. We're wasting our time."

The next day, Berkowitz met with the defense minister, Benny Gantz. The latter, sensing that the Americans were wavering and the annexation bid was faltering, pressed home his opposition. He repeated his position that he would support such a move only if it were to take place in the context of the implementation of the Trump Plan. "July 1 is not a sacred date for annexation as far as I'm concerned," Gantz told Berkowitz. "The only sacred thing at the moment is bringing jobs back and dealing with COVID-19."

Moments after the meeting ended, Gantz publicized his position as a press release. A few hours later, Berkowitz met with Netanyahu once more and relayed to him that the offer his advisors had put forward came nowhere near to meeting the White House's expectations. "We're talking about transferring 5–6 percent of the West Bank to Palestinian control—and you're talking about less than half a percent," Berkowitz told him. Netanyahu attempted to explain his position, but Berkowitz told him that ultimately the person who would have to sign off on the deal was the US Department of State's mapping expert, Scott Leith, who was sitting outside the room. "Bring him in," said Netanyahu. Leith joined the meeting, and Netanyahu spent 10 minutes trying to persuade him that his threadbare proposals actually represented a huge Israeli concession. Leith, who knew every blade of grass in the West Bank, was unconvinced. He informed Netanyahu in no uncertain terms that his proposal was not serious—and soon found himself outside the room once more. Netanyahu continued to insist that he wanted to move ahead with annexation and Berkowitz once again warned him of the potential for an investigation into Israel at The Hague. "We'll cope with it," the prime minister replied. That second meeting also ended in a stalemate. When Berkowitz returned to his hotel room that evening, he was out of ideas. He called Kushner again and reported that they were at a dead end. Kushner and Berkowitz couldn't recall who first raised it, but one of the ideas the two came up with was to dangle the possibility of normalization with the United Arab Emirates in front of Netanyahu—something Yousef Al Otaiba had discussed with them many months previously. "Put it to Netanyahu; we have nothing to lose," Kushner said.

Berkowitz extended his visit by another day. On the morning of June 30, he proposed the idea to David Friedman. Recognizing that the annexation initiative was on its last legs anyway, the US ambassador thought it might not be a bad alternative. A few hours later, Berkowitz and Friedman came in for another meeting with Netanyahu—the third in four days—and raised the idea of normalization with the UAE as a substitute for annexation. Netanyahu was taken by surprise. "Is this real?" He asked. "I believe so," replied Berkowitz. "They won't do it," said Netanyahu. "And if they do?" Berkowitz asked. "If they say yes, then we'll think about it," the prime minister replied. The meeting concluded with Netanyahu asking that negotiations over annexation continue regardless. But Berkowitz told me that he left that meeting with the opposite observation: annexation was gone and normalization was here. "Jared was in favor, David was in favor and Netanyahu wasn't against it," he told me. The next day, July 1, the Prime Minister's Office was bombarded with questions from journalists about annexation and whether it was underway, based on the timeline that Netanyahu had set out in the coalition agreement. "The prime minister held a discussion with the security establishment regarding the application of sovereignty, and further discussions are planned over the coming days," the Prime Minister's Office replied in a press statement. Less than five people in Israel knew at the time that annexation was already dead in the water and that normalization was the new game in town.

"The target date in all of our heads at the time was July 1," recalled the national security advisor, Meir Ben-Shabbat.[224] "We were focused on that date, or one soon after, for the starter's pistol on annexation, but as the date approached, we understood there were still obstacles. There was a big security debate in the days leading up to July 1, with participants from across the security establishment, including Gantz and Ashkenazi. We talked about what would happen, what the consequences would be and how we should be preparing. It was at the forefront of all of our minds despite the difficulties with the Americans. After a few days, we recognized that there would be no annexation, and that instead there would be normalization with the United Arab Emirates."

The Rollercoaster

At 4 AM on July 1, Berkowitz landed at Newark Airport. He was burned out from a week of futile talks. The Trump Plan was in limbo, annexation was on life support and the tensions between Israel and the United States were only getting worse. After a four-hour layover in the airport followed by another flight, he reached Washington, DC exhausted and discouraged. On the way from Reagan Airport to his apartment, not far from the White House, Berkowitz received a call. On the other end was Yousef Al Otaiba. "You know, I have a crazy idea that might save the situation," the Emirati ambassador told him. "You know something, I've also thought about something crazy," Berkowitz responded. Very quickly they realized that they had the same idea in mind: normalization between Israel and the United Arab Emirates in exchange for taking annexation off the table. "Normalization was something the White House raised with us several months before, but we only started discussing this realistically in the context of annexation after Avi came back from Israel in early July," Al Otaiba told me.[225] "After the op-ed, I had no expectation anything was going to happen with this, but when I started talking to Avi on July 1, we brainstormed and all of a sudden things started moving." Berkowitz and Al Otaiba agreed that each of them would sound out their boss about the initiative. "I was really tired, but after the call with Yousef I felt for the first time in months that something positive could happen," Berkowitz recalled. He reported the call to

Kushner, who recognized that the half-baked idea they had thrown out to Netanyahu as a trial balloon the day before might lead somewhere. "Let's do it," he said. Berkowitz informed Friedman, who was also enthusiastic. A former senior White House official told me that the US ambassador expressed concerns at the time that, should annexation go ahead, the ICC in The Hague would issue an international arrest warrant against him and he would be unable to fly to Europe any more. So for Friedman too, normalization sounded like an excellent ladder with which to climb down from the tree of annexation. Once he had a firmer message from the Emiratis, he hurried to inform Netanyahu. The prime minister had not yet turned his back on his annexation initiative, but he was beginning to take the Emirati alternative more seriously. After the conversation with Berkowitz, Al Otaiba presented his idea to the senior government officials in the UAE. The response was laden with doubts. "The leadership [in Abu Dhabi] was concerned that we normalize and Israel will go forward with annexation later," recalled Al Otaiba. "I told them that we will condition it on stopping annexation and on US guarantees. They asked me if it could work and I told them it's worth a try."

On July 2, Al Otaiba met with Kushner and Berkowitz to start turning the abstract idea into a tangible process. Kushner proposed summoning Ambassador Dermer to the White House immediately to kickstart negotiations. "I would prefer to do it through you," Al Otaiba replied politely. The outcome was that Kushner and Berkowitz began to meet with Dermer and Al Otaiba concurrently but in separate meetings. One of the previously unreported details of the initiative is that for over a month of negotiations on the details of the agreement, Al Otaiba and Dermer never once spoke or met in person. This historic accord was reached entirely through indirect negotiations, with Kushner and Berkowitz ferrying messages and drafts between the sides. There were two main reasons for this: the first was the recent phone call during which Dermer had raised his voice at Al Otaiba over the *Yedioth Ahronoth* op-ed, and the second was the Emiratis' desire to ensure that all understandings were reached between the United States and the two sides individually. That way, should the Israelis decide to breach the agreement, it would be a violation of commitments they had given to the White House.

The broad outline of the agreement came together in a short space of time: the United Arab Emirates would fully normalize its relationship with Israel and, in exchange, Israel would commit to fully removing the option of annexation from the table. Reaching a consensus on the fine print proved far more challenging. During the negotiations, the Americans shuttled 115 drafts of the joint statement between the sides before they reached a mutually acceptable version. One of the sticking points was the use of the word "annexation." Dermer refused to allow the use of the term, as annexation constitutes a violation of international law. For his part, Al Otaiba argued that without the use of the word, it was unclear what the United Arab Emirates was receiving in exchange for normalization. Ultimately, they agreed that the joint statement would use the term "application of Israeli law," but that later statements published by the Emirati government would refer to "annexation." The next point of disagreement was over the description of Israel's shift on annexation. Dermer wanted the text to use the term "delay" or "postponement," to give the impression that it was something temporary and short-term. Al Otaiba wanted the words "halt" or "stop" to give the impression of a long-term outcome. Ultimately, they settled on "suspension."[226] After that, attention turned to the duration of this "suspension," which the United States, Israel and the United Arab Emirates never publicly outlined, and which doesn't appear in the joint declaration. A senior official in the United Arab Emirates told me that Al Otaiba initially sought a commitment from Israel that it would never annex certain parts of the West Bank. Dermer refused. Al Otaiba followed this up with a request that annexation be suspended for a period of at least five years. Dermer rejected this too. The compromise the two sides reached, through American mediation, called for the suspension of annexation for a period of at least three years. For the Emiratis, this was sufficient. In an old Jewish folk tale, a man promises his liege that he would teach his dog to sing, only to come up with repeated reasons for delays in the hope that if he could push the moment back for long enough, either the liege or the dog would die. The Emiratis similarly felt that within three years, either the liege or the dog of annexation would die. A former senior White House official noted that Kushner also insisted that the "suspension" would last for a period of three years, as he wanted to ensure that should Trump secure a second term, he would be able to threaten the Palestinians with approval for annexation should they prove unwilling to return to the negotiating table. "We told the Emiratis that we wouldn't do anything they were uncomfortable with," a former senior White House official told me. "If we won the elections then the Emiratis had our word, and if we lost then annexation was dead and buried anyway. We assumed so many things would change over three years that annexation would become irrelevant—either that or it would become uncontroversial."

At one point during the negotiations, while the Americans were passing drafts between the sides, Ambassador Dermer called Avi Berkowitz and tried to change the terms of the deal.[227] Dermer said that Netanyahu wanted normalization with three Arab states in exchange for suspending annexation. "If it's not three states, it's not worth our while," he told the White House envoy.

Berkowitz was gobsmacked and relayed the demand to Kushner, who couldn't believe his ears. "Tell Ron that one state is all he is going to get, and if he doesn't want it, he can go fuck himself," Kushner told Berkowitz. The White House envoy called Dermer and passed a lightly moderated version of the message on to him. "I'll put this gently: take what you're being offered," Berkowitz told the Israeli ambassador.

At an earlier stage in negotiations, Netanyahu had asked Kushner and Berkowitz to keep the talks a secret and not to bring Benny Gantz and Gabi Ashkenazi into the fold. After the accord was published, Netanyahu claimed it was the Americans and Emiratis who had also demanded that Gantz and Ashkenazi be excluded from the process. That was untrue. In reality, the Emiratis had specifically requested to update Gantz early on in the proceedings, to ensure the move enjoyed a broad consensus within the government. Ambassador Friedman took Netanyahu's side, however, and ultimately the White House decided to avoid getting involved in domestic political squabbles and agreed to the request. "Netanyahu told us that if Gantz and Ashkenazi found out, they would leak," a former senior White House official told me. "We felt that we couldn't afford to lose Bibi's support for the move, and it was less important to us whether Gantz and Ashkenazi were in the loop or not." One of Netanyahu's senior advisors at the time told me that while Netanyahu was indeed concerned about leaks, there were other considerations behind his request. "He didn't trust them, and this was his baby," Netanyahu's advisor said. "There was a lot of politics and a fight for credit involved." Even within Netanyahu's inner circle, very few people knew about the move. As the one in charge of the negotiations on the Israeli side, Dermer was the only one who was privy to all the details. Meir Ben-Shabbat knew some of the particulars, as did Ronen Peretz. More surprisingly, Yossi Cohen, the head of the Mossad, the agency responsible for managing the relationship with the Gulf states, was not involved in the discussions that took place in those days in Netanyahu's office or in the negotiations in Washington. According to Israeli and American officials, he was unaware of the move. Indeed, two hours before the agreement was published, a senior Mossad official called his counterpart in the Ministry of Foreign Affairs and asked him sheepishly whether he had heard anything about a normalization agreement with the United Arab Emirates.

Kushner and Berkowitz had managed to finalize an agreed draft of a joint statement on July 26, but it took two more weeks before the document was published. Until the end of July, only four people in the Emirati government were in on the secret: Ambassador Al Otaiba, who had led the negotiations, Minister of Foreign Affairs Sheikh Abdullah bin Zayed, National Security Advisor Sheikh Tahnoun bin Zayed and Crown Prince Sheikh Mohamed bin Zayed.[228] Two weeks before the statement was published, the circle of trust was expanded and a special team was set up that included 10 senior Emirati officials who made the preparations for the dramatic moment. In late July, Sheikh Mohamed sent an envoy to the leaders of the other six individual emirates to update them and receive their approval. It was over a week before they finally received the go-ahead from all of them.

Avi Berkowitz told me that those early August days were nail-biting. In fact, the whole period was a rollercoaster ride. Berkowitz opened every day with a discussion with his assistant, Scott Leith, on the odds of success of the move. Leith, who was well-versed in disappointment from previous negotiations in the Obama administration, never gave it more than 70 percent. Berkowitz was willing to go as high as 85.

On August 3, a week after the sides reached agreement on the wording of the joint statement, the White House was astonished to hear Netanyahu say in a weekly Likud faction meeting that his annexation proposal was not off the table. "It's in Washington's hands," Netanyahu told those present. One of Netanyahu's advisors told me a year later that the prime minister was going back and forth in his own mind over whether stepping away from annexation in exchange for normalization was the right move. "Bibi thought the Emiratis would agree to normalization anyway, even if it would take a few more years," an advisor to the former prime minister told me. "Such an opportunity for annexation was a one-off, but he ultimately realized that he would not have American support for it and didn't want to get into a fight with Trump and lose." In any case, Netanyahu's words at that faction meeting in the Knesset were a preliminary red flag for events that would follow a few days later. On August 6, a date was finalized for a conversation between Trump, Netanyahu and Sheikh Mohamed, after which the joint statement would be published. Apparently, the Emiratis wanted to hold the conversation on August 14, around midday in DC (evening in Jerusalem and Abu Dhabi), but the White House and Prime Minister's Office were reluctant. "We told them it was a Friday, which was a quiet news day in America," a former senior White House official told me. "We asked if we could bring it forward to August 13, and they agreed." Time was passing at a stubbornly slow pace, and Kushner and Berkowitz were counting down the days, concerned about what may yet be waiting for them around the next corner. They were physically and mentally drained. "I'm exhausted. Remind me never to take responsibility for peace negotiations again," Berkowitz told Leith on August 8.

On August 12, the day before the historic announcement, something happened that nobody was expecting, and which is reported here for the first time. The agreement was ready, the draft statement approved and the time for the trilateral phone conversation was on the schedules of the three leaders. But then, Netanyahu got cold feet. Ron Dermer called Berkowitz and told him the whole agreement was off. "The prime minister might be on his way to elections—and I don't know if we will be able to do this deal," he told the White House envoy, who couldn't believe what he was hearing. Dermer explained that a coalition crisis had arisen around the latest possible date to pass a new budget, August 25, and it appeared that the government was now days from collapse. Netanyahu therefore felt that the timing was inopportune to announce the deal with the United Arab Emirates.[229] Kushner was beside himself with rage. He could not understand how, after long weeks of secretive and delicate negotiations that concluded in a historic agreement, Netanyahu was about to throw it all away because of domestic political considerations. "It was a crazy moment," Berkowitz recalled. David Friedman, who had already traveled to Washington to be with Trump in the Oval Office during the telephone call, called the Prime Minister's Office in Jerusalem and spent several minutes yelling at various members of Netanyahu's staff. "Tell the Israelis there's no way we're calling it off. We're doing this—and they'll thank us for it," Kushner told his team. Friedman called Dermer again. "Ron, it's happening tomorrow. You have no say in the matter," he told him.

Netanyahu got the message. After a few suspenseful hours, the sides went ahead with the plan. There was, however, one important question that still needed an answer: the name that would be given to the accord. On the morning of the phone call between the three leaders, the senior director for Gulf affairs at the National Security Council, Brigadier General Miguel Correa, entered Berkowitz's office. Correa was a stern general who had spent the bulk of his service in the US Army Rangers. Before he took up his position in the White House, he was the military attaché in the embassy in Abu Dhabi, and the relationship with the United Arab Emirates was close to his heart. "The Abraham Accords," he told Avi Berkowitz. "The Abraham Accords…what?" The US envoy asked him. "That's the name for the agreement between Israel and the UAE," Correa replied. Berkowitz admitted that it was a good name, with deep historic and religious significance for all the parties involved. "I don't want to be the one to propose it because my name is Avraham," he told Correa. "Offer it to Jared and see what he says." The two entered Kushner's office, and Correa put forward his proposed name. Kushner looked over at Berkowitz and smiled. Berkowitz rushed to defend himself. "It's not my idea!," he said. "Avi, it's a great name," Kushner reassured him. When they went in to brief Trump ahead of the phone call, they told him about the name they had come up with. "The Trump Accords would have been a better name, but okay," the president told them.

On August 12, the defense minister and alternate prime minister, Benny Gantz, underwent back surgery. He was hospitalized at the Sheba Medical Center in Ramat Gan and a situation room was set up by his bedside to enable him to continue to carry out his duties. In the early hours of August 13, while he was still recovering from the operation, Netanyahu called him on the secure line. The second most senior politician in the Israeli government was caught completely off guard. "We're going to sign a normalization agreement with the United Arab Emirates today in exchange for suspending annexation," Netanyahu told him. Gantz understood that Netanyahu had once more lied to him and excluded him. "I give my blessing to anything that's good for the State of Israel," he replied after a moment's pause. Gantz told me he wasn't disappointed in Netanyahu, as he no longer had any expectations of him. "Bibi saw himself as Mr. Security. He had his own foreign ministry, otherwise known as the Mossad, and the head of the National Security Council in place of a government," Gantz told me in an interview I conducted with him exactly a year to the day.[230] "That's how Netanyahu works. It's the most Middle Eastern management style imaginable. You have two or three loyalists, and you run the country together with them."

Immediately after the conversation with Netanyahu, Gantz informed Gabi Ashkenazi. The foreign minister was enraged. In the two months leading up to that moment of high drama, there were people within the foreign ministry who had suspected that something was up. Whenever they tried to make inquiries with the Prime Minister's Office, they received no answer. I later discovered that a few officials in the foreign ministry heard about the plans from their sources a few days before the announcement but withheld the information from Ashkenazi. They feared that Netanyahu would withdraw from the agreement if he was forced to share the credit with his political partners-cum-rivals. After the conversation with Gantz, Ashkenazi called Netanyahu's national security advisor, Meir Ben-Shabbat, and went off at him. "Those were my instructions," Ben-Shabbat replied. "We didn't want to derail it." The next day, when Netanyahu claimed that he had kept Gantz and Ashkenazi out of the loop over concerns that the two former generals would leak the secret negotiations to the press, the foreign minister's outrage reached new heights. "Bibi exploited his position of authority inappropriately," Ashkenazi told me.[231] "You cannot sign a peace treaty with far-reaching diplomatic and security implications without any discussion. It cannot be one man's decision. We were facing a dilemma—to take offense or to think about the good of the country. We decided the right thing to do would be to welcome the development and to get on board with it."

Al Otaiba told me that he was exceedingly nervous in the hours leading up to the historic phone call on August 13, 2020. He had spent the preceding fortnight on his annual family vacation on a yacht moored off the coast of Sardinia. He returned a few days early to tie up the remaining loose ends. The evening before the phone call, he called Sheikh Mohamed to make sure he was ready for what was to come. The crown prince didn't flinch or turn his back on his decision. The Emiratis had kept the developments with Israel a closely guarded secret, even from most of their allies in the Arab world. The only Arab leader who was informed of the plans ahead of time was King Abdullah of Jordan—both because of his personal relationship with Sheikh Mohamed and also because of the outsized impact of annexation on Jordan. Sheikh Mohamed met with the Jordanian king two weeks before the statement and hinted that something was in the pipeline. Three days before the statement, a senior Emirati official called the office of the king and delivered a full briefing about the upcoming move. "The Jordanians were very happy and very curious," a senior Emirati official told me. The Saudi palace and the office of the Egyptian president were informed two hours before the White House statement. The Saudis were surprised but didn't object. If it were up to him, Crown Prince Mohammed bin Salman would have brought his own country on board with the initiative too. Notable by his exclusion was the Palestinian president, Mahmoud Abbas. The Mukataa in Ramallah found out about the diplomatic earthquake from Donald Trump's Twitter account.

A few hours before the phone call, I received a call of my own from a source closely aligned with the US Democratic Party. "The White House is going to give the green light for annexation today," the source told me. His premonition sounded outlandish and stood in stark contrast to everything I knew from my conversations with the White House at the time. But my source was insistent. I called one of my contacts in the White House, who didn't pick up. I sent a WhatsApp message and asked if a statement was forthcoming on annexation, and didn't receive a response. I sent an email. No reply. The radio silence made me think that perhaps my source's information was accurate. The more I tried to get answers from other sources within the Trump administration who didn't pick up, the stronger the feeling grew that something big was about to go down. As time passed, I began to wonder whether there had been a stunning reversal and the White House was indeed about to approve annexation. At around the same time, Israel's *Channel 12 News* put out a report stating that the US Department of State was set to announce that Israel would be allowed to carry out annexation. The report was discredited within minutes. I was busy calling everyone who was anyone, trying to find out what was going on, but no one was picking up.

At around 6 PM Israel time, the small group of co-conspirators in Washington, Jerusalem and Abu Dhabi gathered around their phones. The White House switchboard began to add the participants to the conference call. The first to join was Crown Prince Sheikh Mohamed bin Zayed. He was followed by Prime Minister Benjamin Netanyahu. Last but not least was President Donald Trump. But right at that moment, bin Zayed's line dropped. For 15 minutes, the White House unsuccessfully attempted to reconnect him to the call. "I was literally sweating in those moments," Al Otaiba told me. Finally, the White House managed to bring bin Zayed back— and the call began. Donald Trump was dialing in from the Oval Office, with a few of his advisors around him. The White House photographer captured those moments in a video clip which, at the time of writing, has never been published. As I watched the video, I could sense the tension in the room. There was visible emotion on the face of the president. Soon after the conversation began, he signaled to his staff a few times to keep an accurate record of what was being said. They assured him that everything was being recorded. The discussion was casual and informal. Each of the participants in turn offered his blessings for the accords and spoke about the historical nature of the occasion. "Mr. President, Mr. Prime Minister. I think what is happening now is one of the best news in 2020," said bin Zayed to laughter from Trump and Netanyahu. When the leaders bade their farewells at the end of the call, a rush of jubilation swept through the Oval Office. Trump's advisors stood and applauded for minutes on end.

As soon as the euphoria died down a bit, Berkowitz pressed send on the tweet from the president's account that heralded a regional realignment. Israel and the United Arab Emirates had agreed to normalization in exchange for the removal of the annexation initiative from the table. TV networks in Israel, the United States and the Arab world interrupted their coverage for the breaking news—and the political and diplomatic agenda had been irreversibly turned on its head. Minutes after the tweet went out, while I was still struggling to wrap my head around the enormity of the moment, I received a phone call from Berkowitz. "When I saw that you were calling and texting me like crazy, I understood we were successful in keeping it secret and that nobody knew what was going to happen," he said and laughed loudly. Yousef Al Otaiba later revealed to me that, in his private discussions with the members of the White House team, one of the challenges they had identified was how to keep the unfolding events secret from me. "We were concerned you would find out and screw everything," he told me. At the press briefing with Jared Kushner that same evening, I asked him about the goings-on behind the scenes in the days leading up to the announcement. "In Israel there is Barak

Ravid, and there is the Mossad," replied Kushner. "I know we did a good job keeping it secret, because not even you found out about it."

For Kushner and Berkowitz, beyond the historic achievement and the suspension of the annexation initiative, the diplomatic breakthrough also helped to ease the crisis in relations between the United States and Israel. "It was a very happy moment because relations [with Israel] were very tense at the time," recalled Berkowitz. "The president was very happy. Everyone was happy. The reactions in the press and in the international community were good. And most of all, we had answered the criticism that Trump didn't achieve peace in the Middle East. All of that was also a big asset for the president ahead of the November elections."

Looking back, many of those involved in the events of June–August 2020 admit that it was the initiative by the United Arab Emirates that set the wheels in motion. "We first spoke with the Trump administration about making a move with Israel back in 2019, almost a full year before Netanyahu started talking about annexation," the Emirati foreign minister, Sheikh Abdullah bin Zayed, told me when we met in Abu Dhabi.[232] "When COVID-19 started, us and the Israelis were both very concerned and took it very seriously. We saw the coronavirus as an opportunity to advance cooperation with Israel. Even at the time, we were saying in our internal discussions that any step we take toward Israel would have to go all the way."

Unlike the events surrounding the unveiling of the "deal of the century" in January—when Netanyahu had raised the subject of annexation—in May, when the elections were over, the Emiratis' assessment was that this time Netanyahu was serious and would follow through. For them, this was very bad news on several fronts, first and foremost because annexation would be a significant barrier to their core strategic goal of normalization with Israel. "We wanted to go the whole way to full ties, but when annexation was raised, we said to ourselves that we had to take it off the agenda, because otherwise we would not be able to get even halfway there," Sheikh Abdullah told me. "The Palestinian issue is important to us. There are hundreds of thousands of Palestinians living in the UAE, there's the religious aspect and the national one. At the end of the day, we are one big Arab tribe."

The Emiratis knew that Trump and his team did not support annexation, but they were feeling cornered by the presidential election and concerned that halting annexation would harm the president's standing with his evangelical base. "Everyone is against annexation, but nobody is putting forward suggestions for how to stop it," Kushner told Al Otaiba in one of their conversations in June, several weeks before the July 1 deadline. In Abu Dhabi, they understood that the solution had to be something that would gift Trump and Netanyahu the kind of historic achievement that would enable them to save face with their respective political bases. Sheikh Abdullah told me that he understood that the initiative had legs only after Al Otaiba's article, when public opinion polls showed that 70 percent of Israelis supported normalization with the United Arab Emirates over annexation of the settlements. "We were able to reverse the escalation on annexation and shift the narrative from something that would make things a lot more difficult to something that was very helpful," bin Zayed said. Al Otaiba added: "We gave the Americans and the Israelis a solution that benefited everyone and everybody was happy about. For us, we finally did something that was under consideration for a long time and would have maybe happened only five years later. At the same time, we found a way that prevented annexation, which could have been a disaster for the region."

Gantz and Ashkenazi believed that their opposition to annexation stopped the initiative and created the space for the Emiratis to come in with their normalization initiative. "If we hadn't entered the government in May, there would have been annexation by July," Ashkenazi told me. "The fact that we went into the government stopped that move in its tracks." Ashkenazi also believed that halting annexation signaled the death knell for the unity government. "Torpedoing the annexation initiative pushed Bibi further to the extremes. He was sick of the partnership with us, and we got the impression we were standing in his way," he said. In a conversation with me, Gantz claimed that his and Ashkenazi's position—that July 1 was not a sacred and untouchable date—won the White House round. "When the Americans saw that one route, that of annexation, was blocked, they made the most of the other available route: normalization," the defense minister said. The White House envoy, Avi Berkowitz, was inclined to agree. "They're right," he told me. "I used their reservations to tell Netanyahu that maybe he wants annexation, but his partners don't. They contributed to halting annexation."

As far as the White House was concerned, the stars had aligned perfectly. Kushner described it to me using the baseball analogy of the "suicide squeeze," when one of the players on third base begins to run toward the home plate even before the ball is struck. If the batter is successful, the player will reach home base safely and earn his team a point. If not, however, the player will certainly be tagged out. "We said we would let Netanyahu move ahead inch by inch on his annexation drive, because we hoped that would bring the Palestinians back to the negotiating table," he told me. "The Palestinians did not return to negotiations, but within the ensuing chaos, suddenly this opportunity came up to drag the cart out of the mud and to go in a different direction. In the UAE, they saw what was happening, and that encouraged them to take steps toward normalization and to be able to say that they held off the annexation threat. It's not how we imagined it playing out, and it wasn't an elegant solution, but at the end of the day it enabled the Abraham Accords to happen."

Neither Netanyahu's loyalists nor his detractors admit to this day that the former prime minister was forced to walk away from his plan to annex parts of the West Bank. Both sides revere him. They see him as an omnipotent sorcerer incapable of failure, a Machiavellian figure whose every step is part of a wider strategic master plan. If he succeeds—it proves the genius of the man. If he fails—it's a tactical diversion and equal proof of his brilliance.

All the testimonies I have collected and the information I have had access to while writing this book indicates that Netanyahu's annexation initiative was serious and genuine. As far as Netanyahu was concerned, July 1 was a plan of action, not another campaign line. The plan was staved off in January 2020, but Netanyahu was still pushing to implement it six months later. He saw this move as a political tool to win support from the right, and also as a way to cement his political legacy.

There were a few elements that combined to foil Netanyahu's plan. First was the opposition of his defense and foreign ministers, Benny Gantz and Gabi Ashkenazi, to his annexation initiative. When the background noise is cleared away, the two sides' positions become clear: Netanyahu is opposed to a two-state solution and as prime minister he strove to end the conflict through a calculated plan to destroy the Palestinian national movement. Gantz and Ashkenazi, on the other hand, support a two-state solution and hold a worldview that seeks to resolve the conflict through a political settlement with the Palestinian national movement.

The annexation initiative created a dividing line that the sides were unable to bridge. The issue was only brought to a conclusive resolution when one side had the upper hand. Netanyahu systematically isolated Gantz and Ashkenazi and assumed they would be unable to impact and stymie him. This was the result of him overestimating his own influence with the White House and underestimating theirs. Not to mention the diminishing light of Netanyahu's halo in the White House over the last year of Trump's term.

Another factor in the defeat of his initiative was the rampant spread of COVID-19 in the United States, which took up the White House's attention and became part of the political battleground in the run-up to the presidential election. Trump and his advisors felt that they had the votes of the evangelical right in their pockets already, and they didn't want even the slightest hint of a risk of a full-blown international diplomatic crisis that could hurt Trump's re-election bid.

On top of all of these was the fierce opposition from the United States' allies in the West and the Middle East. The United Arab Emirates was an unexpected leader of the Arab world's vocal and active opposition to annexation. The Emiratis were the most important regional ally of the United States in the Arab world up to that point, and they had the ear of those in the White House. Last but not least, it was the Emiratis who provided Trump's advisors with a *deus ex machina* and offered the administration a tow to drag it out of the crisis.

Looking back, when the position of the ministers of defense and foreign affairs are taken together with the internal concerns of the Trump administration, the White House's disillusionment with Netanyahu and the opposition of the international community to annexation, it becomes clear that the prime minister didn't stand a chance. It took Netanyahu himself longer than expected to reach the same conclusion. He fought for several weeks, but ultimately took a step back to assess the situation, after which he decided to cut his losses and abandon annexation in favor of normalization.

One of Netanyahu's senior advisors told me that for a while after the accords were signed, Netanyahu continued to harbor regrets over his decision. "Bibi has a habit of convincing himself of something, then getting excited about it as if it was what he actually wanted from the beginning and it's his biggest ever achievement," he told me. "But in hindsight, today he might have gone for annexation after all—and passed on the Abraham Accords. He would have wanted to go down in the history books as the one who fixed Israel's international borders and fortified the country's security situation, and not as the one who brought normalization agreements."

On the evening of August 13, while the commentators in the television studios continued to dissect the accords and the Tel Aviv Municipality lit up the city hall in the colors of the Emirati flag, I sent a WhatsApp message to the spokesperson of the foreign ministry in Abu Dhabi, Hend Al Otaiba, and requested an interview with the foreign minister, Abdullah bin Zayed, or the minister of state for foreign affairs, Dr. Anwar Gargash, whom I had met in Munich six months earlier. "Gargash will do it," she wrote back soon after. I was delighted. I didn't realize at the time how quickly things would move over the following days and weeks. The next day, I was signing into Zoom ahead of the interview. A few minutes later, Gargash was sitting in front of me in his office in traditional Emirati garb next to an Emirati flag. It was the first ever interview by an Emirati minister to an Israeli media outlet. "We are not talking about a very gradual and slow process. We want to move ahead with it ASAP," Gargash told me. On Sunday, August 16, three days after the announcement of normalization, the United

Arab Emirates lifted its ban on direct international phone calls to Israel. Shortly after the statement went out, Sheikh Abdullah called his Israeli counterpart, Gabi Ashkenazi. In Israel, they had planned to keep the two men's conversation a secret, and they were surprised when the Emiratis rushed to publish it through their official news agency. For anyone who was somehow yet to read the room, it was now clear that a new day was dawning. In the following days, there were additional calls between the Emirati ministers and their Israeli counterparts. "In the first call with Abdullah, my impression was that this was a strategic decision on the part of the Emiratis," Ashkenazi remembered. "They were hitting the gas and asking to move as quickly as possible."

The Fighter Jet Deal

Netanyahu presented the normalization agreement of August 13 as a personal achievement. He repeated his line about "peace for peace" ad infinitum, to further hammer home the scale of the achievement and to portray it as unrelated to the Palestinian issue, differentiating it from the "land for peace" formula endorsed by his political rivals to the left. This was spin. The accord with the United Arab Emirates was intrinsically linked to the Palestinian issue, and involved Netanyahu walking back his plan to annex swathes of the West Bank. Netanyahu's conduct throughout the process—excluding Gantz and Ashkenazi, the political spin—would come back to haunt him five days later. On August 18, the *Yedioth Ahronoth* journalist Nahum Barnea reported that one of the conditions for normalization imposed by Crown Prince Sheikh Mohamed bin Zayed was a US agreement to sell F-35 fighter jets to the UAE. The F-35 was one of the most advanced fighter jets produced by the US, and Israel was the only country in the Middle East it was sold to, which gave its air force unrivaled aerial superiority in the region. Israel had long opposed this deal as a threat to its qualitative military edge (QME), but Barnea claimed that as part of the accord, Netanyahu had given his tacit approval and kept it from the security chiefs who are mandated with determining whether an arms deal has the potential to harm Israel's QME.

The report sent shockwaves through the Israeli political system. Gantz and Ashkenazi justifiably seized on it as evidence that Netanyahu's decision to exclude them from the talks with the United Arab Emirates had been wholly irresponsible and unreasonable. Gantz argued that the fact that he and Ashkenazi had not been informed about the impending agreement ahead of time had harmed Israel's national security. "It's possible to make a peace deal while demonstrating responsibility for our security. It is forbidden to take risks with our security," Gantz said at the time, and noted that it was not in Israel's interests to have advanced fighter jets such as the F-35s passing around the militaries in the region. Ashkenazi joined in the criticism. "We are not familiar with any security-related promises, and if such promises exist, they were not done in coordination or consultation with us," he said. Netanyahu, for his part, denied that the accord included Israeli approval of any kind of arms deal between the United States and the United Arab Emirates, and even went so far as to claim that he had always opposed the sale of F-35s and other advanced weapons systems to Arab states that made peace with Israel.

As time passed, more and more previously hidden details came to light that suggested unusual conduct by the prime minister. Netanyahu's office put out a statement to say that the national security advisor, Meir Ben-Shabbat, had spoken with Israeli Air Force (IAF) Commander Amikam Norkin on June 2, 2020—some two and a half months before the normalization accords—to sound him out about the sale of F-35 jets from the United States to Arab nations. The conversation lasted less than a minute. Ben-Shabbat, who called Norkin directly without going through the defense minister's office, didn't provide the IAF commander with any context for his question. Norkin emphasized to Ben-Shabbat that he would oppose such a move but did not report the call to either the chief of the general staff or the defense minister's office.

"Every so often, the Americans would ask us about arms supplies to countries in the region, including F-35 jets," Ben-Shabbat told me.[233] "Every few months this question would come up—and that was what happened at the start of June, 2020. We were still looking at annexation at the time. The prime minister asked me for the military's view on this point and asked me to speak with the commander of the air force. I called Norkin, who said there was no change in his position and he was against it. I told the prime minister there was no point even discussing it, because Israel remained opposed to the idea. We knew that the United Arab Emirates was asking for F-35s. It was a request that came up constantly—and we opposed it every time. But my call with Norkin wasn't in the context of an agreement with the United Arab Emirates, which only came later. I used to speak with the generals all the time. It was not unusual. Had I thought it was unusual, I would have called the chief of the general staff or the minister of defense."

On July 7, a week after Trump's advisors first raised the option of a normalization accord in exchange for canceling annexation, Netanyahu spoke with US Ambassador David Friedman. According to Netanyahu, he expressed his unequivocal opposition to the sale of F-35 fighter jets to any other country in the Middle East, even in the context of peace agreements. The next day, Netanyahu wrote a letter to US Secretary of State Mike Pompeo to deliver the same message. It was not until three weeks later, when the final draft of the normalization accord had already been agreed between the sides, that Netanyahu remembered to inform his defense minister, Benny Gantz, of his position on the sale of the F-35s. But the letter that Netanyahu sent to Gantz used general language without any specific mention of the United Arab Emirates or the talks taking place at the time. On August 3, 10 days before the statement on the normalization accords, the Israeli ambassador in Washington, Ron Dermer, met with Pompeo and reiterated Israel's opposition to the sale of F-35s to any other states in the Middle East.

Netanyahu's reaction was not entirely false. The accords genuinely did not include a secret clause regarding arms deals, and the F-35s were not an Emirati condition for a deal with Israel. "We spoke about the F-35s with the US long before the Abraham Accords," Ambassador Al Otaiba told me. "We tried getting those jets for six years. We told the Americans we were flying 20-year-old F-16s. It was only natural that we also get the F-35 in order to have better capability. The bottleneck was always Israel's qualitative military edge, but we told the Americans that with the Abraham Accords, we are now friends with Israel, so it shouldn't be a problem."

At the same time, former senior officials in the White House, the UAE and Israel claim that Netanyahu knew full well about the F-35 discussions between the US and the UAE within the wider context of the normalization accords. They said that the Trump administration was persuaded by the arguments put forward by the Emiratis. The White House informed Israel that, following normalization, the UAE was officially on Israel's side, and therefore Israel had nothing to worry about should the United States decide to sell advanced fighter jets to the Emiratis.

"When the Americans began to talk about an accord with the Emiratis [in early July], Netanyahu sent a formal letter to Secretary of State Pompeo in which he wrote that Israel was very much interested in normalization with other countries in the region, but that it would not accept that such an arrangement would be in exchange for arms and systems that could harm Israel's QME," Ben-Shabbat told me. "Netanyahu wanted to avoid any doubts over this matter, and to rein in the US."

Gantz told me that when he saw the media reports about the fighter jet deal, he asked the director general of the Ministry of Defense (and former commander of the IAF), Amir Eshel, and the head of the Political-Military Bureau, Zohar Palti, to look into the reports and find out if there was any truth to them. According to Gantz, they came back a few hours later with confirmation. "I wasn't expecting answers from Bibi because his answers were not serious," Gantz told me.[234] "The conversation with the air force commander annoyed me, because it was proof that Netanyahu had looked into the matter, which was related to national security—but not through the proper channels."

Senior officials in the Trump administration and in the United Arab Emirates told me that, despite his denials, Netanyahu had indeed given his tacit approval for the move. The White House informed Ambassador Al Otaiba that the United States was planning to sell them the jets. "The Americans notified the Israelis that it's going to happen, and we understood that Israel gave their okay.... Netanyahu approved it without telling anybody, and when his coalition partners learned about it they were angry and it created a domestic political issue. We told the White House it's Netanyahu's problem. We had a deal and he needs to solve his own political problems." The former foreign minister, Gabi Ashkenazi, told me that he also learned this was the case when he started to look into the details in the wake of the media reports. "I later understood from the Emiratis that there was an initial Israeli agreement for the sale of the jets and that Netanyahu had lied," he said.[235]

Netanyahu's ducking, dodging and denials displeased the Emiratis, but the final straw came when Netanyahu said in a cabinet meeting that he would fight the sale of the advanced jets to the UAE in Congress. An infuriated Al Otaiba called Berkowitz and requested clarification because, as he saw it, Netanyahu had already given the deal his approval. The Emiratis decided to deliver the Israelis a warning shot to express their dissatisfaction and canceled at the last minute a scheduled trilateral meeting in New York between the Israeli, Emirati and US ambassadors to the UN which was supposed to take place in front of the cameras. "We decided that if the Israelis want to play games, we can do that too," a senior Emirati official told me. "We wanted to make it clear they could not back out from agreements, and that if they changed their minds, we would do the same."

In late August, Jared Kushner came to Israel to be part of an Israeli–American delegation on board the first-ever direct flight to the United Arab Emirates. He met with Netanyahu and made it clear that the fighter jet deal would go ahead. At the same time, Kushner met with Gantz and filled him in on the details. Kushner asked Gantz not to speak out against the deal. Gantz told me that he instructed the staff of the Ministry of Defense to assess the impact of the fighter jet deal on the IDF's qualitative military edge. Eshel and Palti flew to the United States in early September for preliminary discussions at the Pentagon. On September 21, 2020, Gantz went on a whirlwind visit to Washington, where he met with Secretary of Defense Mark Esper, National Security Advisor Robert O'Brien and with Kushner himself. Gantz conditioned his support on an American commitment to uphold the Israeli Air Force's QME even if the fighter jet deal went through. The Americans agreed. Two days later, a Ministry of Defense delegation came to Washington to finalize the terms of the agreement between Israel and the United States. The negotiations lasted for a month. According to a senior Israeli official, the most important element of the agreement was an American commitment that the F-35 jets to be sold to the UAE would be less advanced than the ones sold to Israel in terms of the systems installed in them. The Americans also agreed to further discussions with Israel before any further sales of F-35s to Middle Eastern countries. On October 21, Gantz departed for Washington once more to sign the accord. When he boarded the plane, he discovered that he was on the flight with White House Envoy Avi Berkowitz, on his way back from a visit to Bahrain with an Israeli–American delegation. Gantz invited Berkowitz to join him on the trip from New York to Washington. They spent the journey drafting the statement the White House had asked Netanyahu and Gantz to release—one of the only joint statements the two rival Israeli leaders published during the unity government. The White House agreed with them that the statement would be published on Friday, October 23, shortly after the start of the Jewish Sabbath. In the end, it was published alongside Trump's announcement of a third normalization agreement, this time between Israel and Sudan, which grabbed most of the headlines. The statement read: "The prime minister and the defense minister both agree that since the US is upgrading Israel's military capability and is maintaining Israel's qualitative military edge, Israel will not oppose the sale of these systems to the UAE."[236]

Senior White House officials told me that Gantz played a critical role in reducing the friction surrounding the F-35 deal, and that he prevented it from escalating into a serious diplomatic crisis with the United Arab Emirates. But the whole affair caused significant damage to the image of the peace treaty with the UAE among the Israeli public. Netanyahu's conduct reminded many Israelis of the so-called "submarine affair," in which he approved the sale of advanced submarines from Germany to Egypt behind the backs of the then-defense minister, Moshe Ya'alon, and the chief of the general staff, all without any discussion with the relevant professional authorities within the security establishment. The similarities between the two incidents only increased when Netanyahu claimed that he had not informed Gantz and Ashkenazi about the contacts with the UAE regarding normalization because he feared they would leak the information. In the submarine affair, he similarly claimed he had not informed the defense minister and army chief because of a "secret" that they were not party to. The diplomatic and public implications of the F-35 deal between the US and the UAE left Netanyahu facing extensive and justified criticism. At the same time, the charges already laid against him spawned conspiracy theories that were then amplified by the ongoing protests by opposition activists outside his residence on Balfour St. and on bridges across the country. They claimed that the accord with the UAE was not a "peace treaty" but a "corrupt arms deal" and a "business deal between tycoons." Not only was it not beneficial to the Israeli public, the argument went, but it was actively harmful to it. The same conspiracy theorists also claimed that the accord with the UAE was secret and being kept hidden from the public, despite it being published on the internet immediately after it was signed. Unfortunately, among parts of the Israeli public—and especially its left-wing supporters—some of these conspiracies are alive and kicking to this day.

From Declarations to Peace Treaty

On August 13, while the normalization agreements were being announced, Tal Becker was sitting in his office in the foreign ministry in Jerusalem. His official title was legal advisor to the Israeli Ministry of Foreign Affairs, but his brief extended far beyond that. He spent many years as a senior advisor to a succession of foreign ministers. He was very close to Tzipi Livni during her time leading the foreign ministry and oversaw the negotiations with the Palestinians on her behalf following the 2007 Annapolis Conference. In 2013, when Livni returned to the government as the justice minister with responsibility for negotiations with the Palestinians, Becker went back to work with her—this time on the peace initiative put forward by Secretary of State John Kerry. At the same time, Becker also earned the appreciation of Netanyahu, who as prime minister would often invite him to discussions and closed meetings on various delicate matters of foreign policy. Abroad, Becker held a reputation as one of the sharpest diplomatic and legal minds in Israel. He quietly built up a network of connections over many years that made him a valued partner in numerous regional and global initiatives. It was through this network that he received indications regarding the dramatic statement that was being constructed. In the immediate aftermath of Trump's tweet announcing the normalization accord between Israel and the UAE, Becker did two things. First, he let out a deep sigh of relief. He had been heavily concerned about Netanyahu following through with his annexation plans. He even warned those present in internal deliberations on several occasions about the dangerous consequences of such a move for Israel's international status and its legal position at The Hague. The second thing he did was take a seat at his computer and begin to prepare a draft peace treaty between Israel and the United Arab Emirates.

"I heard Netanyahu referring to it on TV as peace," Becker recalled.[237] "I thought to myself that on the one hand, that framing is correct, but on the other hand there are those who would say that it's not peace because there was no conflict between the countries. So I decided to draft a document that sets out what a peace treaty would look like for a country we weren't at war with. I asked my team for precedents of peace treaties between countries without prior conflict. They found a fair few of them, for example between Argentina and Japan. There was something positive about that, because when a peace treaty doesn't end a war, it's possible to apply a far broader definition to the peace and what it means."

Becker worked on a detailed draft of the peace treaty throughout the weekend that followed the announcement. First thing Sunday morning, he walked into the office of the foreign minister together with the director general of the ministry, Alon Ushpiz. Ashkenazi was still bitter and angry over Netanyahu's decision to keep him in the dark about the whole process. He listened to the proposal and didn't display any great enthusiasm for it. "I can't imagine the Prime Minister's Office will agree but go ahead. I don't care," Ashkenazi said. Becker approached a few people at the Prime Minister's Office, but they quickly dampened his enthusiasm. "The accord will be one page, very generic," they told him. "I can prepare a one-page agreement, but would you object if I were to try and advance a more detailed agreement?" he asked in one of the discussions. None of the participants sounded overly keen, but no one objected—so Becker kept pushing ahead. Two weeks after the initial statement on normalization, preparations began in Israel for a historic trip to Abu Dhabi by a joint Israeli–American delegation. Becker took his more detailed draft agreement with him on the trip. He asked to speak with Jared Kushner and put the idea to him. Kushner sent him to speak with Avi Berkowitz. "It will probably be a very broad one-page agreement," Berkowitz told him, and sent him to speak with his advisor, Scott Leith, from the US State Department. A discouraged Becker detailed his plan once more to Leith and explained the thinking behind it, despite his growing doubts about whether anything would come of it.

When the delegation landed in Abu Dhabi, Becker was dragged away to deal with another issue: preparing a memorandum of understanding on taxation. This was to be the first practical agreement between the UAE and Israel since the announcement. Becker's family tree has roots in Morocco, France and Australia, but the Israeli chutzpah shone through in a line he inserted into that memorandum, stating that the tax agreement was a precursor to a full peace treaty to follow between Israel and the United Arab Emirates. Becker showed the draft to Meir Ben-Shabbat a few minutes before he sent it to the Emiratis, and he didn't raise any objections. Becker was worried the Emiratis would be rattled by that line and ask to remove it, but they didn't object either. "As soon as it was in the small agreement, I knew there were legitimate grounds to push ahead with the big agreement," Becker told me. "Nobody in Israel was talking about who was preparing the agreement, so I went ahead and did it myself." Becker returned to Israel and fine-tuned the first draft he had prepared. He sent it to Ron Dermer, to the Prime Minister's Office and to the Ministry of Justice, but he was waiting for a sign that this was what the White House and the Emiratis wanted. Dermer eventually came back to him with American approval, but on one condition: the White House wanted to handle the negotiations over the text of the peace treaty.

The negotiations were relatively short and straightforward. "I included an article in the accord about how Jews and Arabs are both the children of Abraham and committed to coexistence," Becker recalled. "I thought they might struggle with that, but they agreed to the wording. That was the moment I realized that something completely new was happening." For 25 years, Becker had handled negotiations on behalf of the State of Israel with the Lebanese, Egyptians, Jordanians and Palestinians, but the talks with the Emiratis bore no resemblance to any of them. "They wanted what we wanted," he said. "Everything went very quickly. Negotiations with the Palestinians are like therapy sessions on a national scale. With the Emiratis everything was very practical. There's none of the trauma, none of the scars, none of the emotional baggage and none of the domestic political arguments."

I was there with Netanyahu on the flight to sign the peace treaty with the United Arab Emirates. The COVID-19 outbreak in the United States was at its highest peak yet, and the Israeli delegation was shocked by the fact that most of the US president's team wouldn't wear masks. While Netanyahu was on his way to the US, a particularly awkward flaw in his plans was unearthed. Under Israeli law, the only person authorized to sign international accords on behalf of the State of Israel is the foreign minister. Netanyahu, who considered the signing ceremony a personal celebration, had not invited Gabi Ashkenazi or Benny Gantz. The night before the ceremony, Ashkenazi received a phone call from the attorney general, Avichai Mandelblit. "You have to give Netanyahu power of attorney for him to be able to sign the accord tomorrow," he told him. Ashkenazi told me that he spent a while toying with the idea of refusing to do so. Despite his desire to troll Netanyahu, eventually the thought of the international embarrassment it would cause Israel convinced him to go ahead. "The fact that Netanyahu didn't invite me or Benny to the event while the other side sent their foreign ministers is exactly the kind of behavior over which he lost his position as prime minister," Ashkenazi told me. "He couldn't overcome his political urges, lost us as partners and acted irresponsibly. There's a limit to how many times you can do that. If Bibi had conducted himself differently with Benny and I, he would still be prime minister today."[238]

Once the power of attorney came through from Ashkenazi, a series of discussions were held to finalize the arrangements and the wording of the accords. The version printed on the morning of September 15 and placed inside the fancy White House folders ahead of the signing ceremony was almost identical to the draft Tal Becker had typed up on his home computer in the hours after the statement on August 13. It would have taken a microscope to spot the differences. "He who wields the pen determines what goes into the agreement—and gets to keep the pen at the end," Becker told me.[239] All the pens used to sign the Abraham Accords sit on his desk in his office in Jerusalem. After the signing ceremony, the prime minister called to thank him for his work. "You see," Netanyahu told him. "It's just as well we're not only talking about the ICC in The Hague. We'll have a lot more accords like this."

29 Days

A few hours after the announcement of the normalization accord between Israel and the United Arab Emirates on August 13, as President Trump and his advisors were wrapping up the press conferences and media briefings, the phone rang in the White House. On the other end was the Bahraini minister of finance, Sheikh Salman bin Khalifa Al Khalifa. Sheikh Salman, an economist and member of the royal family who had worked for several of the leading global banks and investment houses, was one of the most powerful people in the small Gulf kingdom. His father, who passed away in November 2020, was the prime minister of Bahrain for five decades. His eldest brother, Sheikh Ali bin Khalifa, served in the past as the deputy prime minister. But the secret to Sheikh Salman's power was his close relationship with the crown prince and his cousin, Sheikh Salman bin Hamad Al Khalifa. Sheikh Salman served as his chief of staff for five years before he was appointed to the finance ministry. When President Trump's senior advisor and White House envoy, Jared Kushner and Avi Berkowitz, pushed the speaker button, they heard a surprising message. "We want to be next," Sheikh Salman told them. Twenty-nine days later, pen was put to paper on another accord between Israel and a Gulf state.

Bahrain is a small kingdom in the heart of the Gulf region, with only 700 thousand residents. It was a British colony until as late as 1971. To its southwest sits its big brother, Saudi Arabia, and to the northeast lies its bitter enemy, Iran, which still harbors dreams of annexing it. One of the biggest reasons for concern over Iran is that the majority of the citizens of Bahrain are Shia Muslims, while the Al Khalifa royal family belongs to the Sunni minority. To protect itself, Bahrain is heavily reliant on its alliances with Saudi Arabia and the United States.

There is no better symbol of the close bond between Saudi Arabia and Bahrain than the King Fahd Causeway. The 15-mile-long causeway crosses the Gulf between Bahrain and the city of Khobar in eastern Saudi Arabia. The longest such structure in the Middle East and one of the longest in the world, it was inaugurated in 1986 after five years of construction at a cost of 800 million dollars. Over 400 million people have traveled across the 10-lane causeway since it opened, with more than 30 million crossing it in 2019 alone.[240] Bahrain is far more open to the West than Saudi Arabia, and the Bahraini economy is relatively free by regional standards. The causeway therefore made Bahrain a popular destination for millions of Saudi tourists seeking a more relaxed and liberal weekend getaway, contributing hundreds of millions of dollars annually to the Bahraini economy. In March 2020, the causeway was sealed off in the wake of the COVID-19 pandemic, a move which crippled the country's economy.[241] Unfortunately for Bahrain, it was not blessed with the vast oil and gas reserves of its neighbors. The kingdom suffered from a decade-long economic crisis and has been dependent on billions of dollars' worth of aid from Saudi Arabia, Kuwait and the United Arab Emirates.

The relationship between Bahrain and the United States dates back more than 130 years, when American missionaries settled in the territory. The American Mission Hospital and Al Raja School were founded by those missionaries at the turn of the 20th century—and both are still open today. In 1971, after Bahrain declared independence, a US naval base was established in Manama. In 1991, Bahrain signed a defense cooperation agreement with the United States that gave the US military access to all military facilities in the country. But the biggest boost to relations between the countries came in 2002, when the United States designated Bahrain a "major non-NATO ally." The Fifth Fleet of the United States Navy established its headquarters in Manama at around the same time, making it the central base from which US naval vessels patrolled the region. The United States is also Bahrain's primary trading partner after Saudi Arabia and the United Arab Emirates. The two have had a free trade agreement since 2006. In late 2019, trade between the US and Bahrain totaled four billion dollars a year.

The relationship between Israel and Bahrain was set in motion by the Madrid Conference 30 years ago and was almost entirely conducted behind closed doors. Bahrain participated in the conference and was a member of the working group established in its wake to promote regional talks on water, the environment and the economy. The Oslo Accords gave the relationship another nudge in the right direction. In October 1994, the minister for the environment, Yossi Sarid, became the first Israeli minister ever to visit Bahrain, as part of a large delegation that included Israeli journalists. During his visit, he met the Bahraini foreign minister, Mohammad bin Mubarak Al Khalifa, and the ministers of health and the environment. "The Bahraini foreign minister asked me to deliver a message of peace to the Israeli people and said that [the visit] was a first step to closer ties between the two countries," Sarid said in a speech he delivered to the Knesset.[242] A few days later, it was the turn of the Israeli foreign minister, Shimon Peres, to meet with his Bahraini counterpart on the sidelines of the Casablanca Economic Summit.

As with other Gulf states, the responsibility for managing the relationship on the Israeli side was divided between two government agencies: the first was the Foreign Relations Division of the Mossad, known as "Cosmi" (in one of his meetings with the US ambassador, King Hamad bin Isa Al Khalifa informed him, "We have secret ties with Israel through the Mossad").[243] The second was the Ministry of Foreign Affairs, and primarily the seasoned and secretive diplomat, Bruce Kashdan—one of the architects of the informal ties and who later developed a close relationship with several Bahraini foreign ministers. A US diplomat who met with Mohammad bin Mubarak Al Khalifa was surprised to learn that Kashdan had sat on the exact same couch the day before him. "We have had quiet, businesslike relations with Israel for some time," he told him.[244] The first meeting between Kashdan and the Bahraini foreign minister took place in 1998. The key point of contact during those years was the chief of staff of the foreign minister, Saeed Al-Faihani.[245] In early 2000, when Ehud Barak was prime minister of Israel and the peace process with the Palestinians was at a peak, a foreign ministry delegation headed to Manama in secret to discuss a draft agreement to formalize diplomatic ties between the countries that would include normalization and the presence of an official Israeli diplomatic mission in Bahrain. A senior official in the foreign ministry told me that soon after the delegation's arrival in Bahrain, the existence of the talks was leaked. The Bahrainis immediately halted all negotiations and demanded the Israelis leave the country. "We could have reached an agreement with them on diplomatic ties back then, over 20 years ago," the senior official in the foreign ministry who was involved in the talks told me.[246] "It was a matter of trust. For the Bahrainis, the leak threatened the stability of the government and was perceived as a breach of the trust between the sides. As far as they were concerned, if they were unable to trust the other side, they weren't interested in engaging at all."

The disengagement plan announced by Prime Minister Ariel Sharon in late 2003 and early 2004 gave a further boost to Israeli–Bahraini ties. A few months before the expected evacuation of Gush Katif settlements in the southern Gaza Strip, King Hamad told the US ambassador that he had instructed the new minister of information affairs that all new government press releases were no longer to refer to Israel as "the enemy" or "the Zionist entity." A few days after the evacuation, Crown Prince Salman relayed to the US ambassador that he was "encouraged" by the development, and even put out a supportive statement.[247] Two weeks after the disengagement was complete, Bahrain took an unprecedented step: ending its participation in the Arab boycott of Israel declared by the Arab League in 1951.

On September 5, 2005, the Bahraini finance minister sent a letter to the US administration in which he announced that all government offices had been instructed to end the boycott on Israel. Two weeks later, Bahrain informed the US that its dedicated Israel Boycott Office had been shut down. Senior Bahraini officials even took the economic attaché at the US embassy to the now empty building so he could see the closure for himself. The US diplomat confirmed that the telephone lines had been disconnected and that the six employees in the office had been transferred elsewhere.[248] The Bahrainis were primarily interested in ending the boycott not because of the disengagement plan, but because of their desire to sign a free trade agreement with the United States. The Americans conditioned such an agreement on the lifting of the boycott. The disengagement plan was simply another motivating factor, and the Bahraini government used it to sway domestic public opinion in favor of the move. Despite this, even the disengagement was insufficient to silence the internal criticism, and the Muslim Brotherhood and Shia parties in the parliament came out against it. But the government stood firm. It was the right thing to do, the Bahraini foreign minister told the US ambassador, adding that anyone who didn't want to was free to not buy Israeli products.[249] A few months later, the US embassy in Manama informed the State Department in Washington that Israeli goods were beginning to appear in local markets.[250]

The warming ties between the two countries at the time had less to do with the Israeli disengagement from Gaza than they did with a change in the Bahraini government. When Sheikh Khalid bin Ahmed Al Khalifa entered the foreign ministry in September 2005, he injected new life into the proceedings. He was a 45-year-old diplomat who had been elevated to his new office by the crown prince, Sheikh Salman, replacing a 70-year-old politician who had been in the role for 35 years. Sheikh Khalid brought with him a more "American" style. He had completed his bachelor's degree at St. Edward's University in Austin, Texas, and from there he was appointed almost directly to the Bahraini embassy in Washington, DC. He returned home to work in the office of the minister of finance, then was appointed as the spokesperson of the crown prince before topping it all off with a position as Bahraini ambassador to the United Kingdom.

When he took up his position as foreign minister, developing relations with Israel was one of his central policy objectives. He also had a partner on the Israeli side: then-Foreign Minister Tzipi

Livni. In September 2006, at the sidelines of the UN General
Assembly in New York, the two met in secret for the first time.[251]
A few months later, Sheikh Khalid even expressed his view on
relations with Israel in public through an interview with the
Bahraini *Al Ayam* newspaper, where he spoke favorably about
the Arab Peace Initiative, normalization with Israel and Jewish–
Muslim coexistence. "We need to get out of the bubble of the
Israeli conflict," he said in the interview.[252] When the Israeli envoy
to the Gulf, Bruce Kashdan, called him and praised him for the
interview, Sheikh Khalid asked him to ensure that it was translated
into Hebrew and published in the Israeli press.[253]

Sheikh Khalid sought openings for direct contacts with Israel.
In a meeting with the foreign ministers of the Arab League in
Cairo, he suggested sending a delegation of Arab foreign ministers
to Jerusalem as a message to the Israeli public. The idea met with
fierce resistance. The Syrian foreign minister, Walid Muallem, in
particular took a firm stand against any such move. The eventual
compromise was that only the foreign ministers of Egypt and
Jordan would visit Jerusalem. The US ambassador to Bahrain,
William Monroe, reported that when he met with Sheikh Khalid
on his return from Cairo, he found the foreign minister dispirited
and discouraged. "It was very disappointing because Egypt and
Jordan already have relations with Israel," he told the ambassador.
But he refused to give up, and told the ambassador that he would
be willing to speak with the Israeli press himself in order to deliver
a message to the Israeli public.[254]

That interview didn't end up going ahead. However, a few
months later, he met with Tzipi Livni once more, again on the
sidelines of the UN General Assembly. Though the meeting was
kept quiet, it still somehow found its way to the Israeli media.[255]
When the report was published in the English-language version

of *Haaretz*, all hell broke loose in Bahrain. Columnists lined up to denounce the foreign minister, and the parliament convened a special session. Sheikh Khalid remained calm. He attended the parliamentary session and took great pleasure in confronting his critics. "I have no intention of apologizing to anyone," he told the US ambassador.[256] One of the members of parliament from the Muslim Brotherhood subjected him to a verbal assault and called on him "to wash your hands seven times in water and then with sand" like after contact with unclean animals, because he had shaken hands with Livni. Sheikh Khalid was unruffled. "You who support Hamas should wash your hands from all the Palestinian blood on them," he said.[257] A few days later, Sheikh Khalid attended the Annapolis Conference and sat with Livni at the same table, to the further dismay of his critics.

He didn't stop there. A year later—back at the UN once more—he offered to establish a new regional organization that would include the Arab states, Israel, Turkey and Iran, based on the European Union model. This was entirely uncharted territory, and perhaps surprisingly, it was even able to garner a measure of support in the Arab world. The secretary-general of the Arab League, Amr Moussa, praised the proposal; Israel and the United States put out positive statements and Iran hurried to condemn it. The same members of the Bahraini parliament who had denounced Sheikh Khalid for meeting with Livni attacked him again. In a conversation with an American diplomat, the Bahraini foreign minister said that one of his goals for the new initiative was to renew regional discussions on the question of Israel. "The initiative will be a first step for many Arab states to build ties with Israel," he said.[258] Notably, Sheikh Khalid was not acting of his own accord. His proposal had been approved by the Bahraini government and had received King Hamad's blessing. In a meeting with the commander of the Fifth Fleet, Admiral William Gortney, the king expressed amusement at the responses to the Bahraini proposal in the wider Arab world. "The Arabs don't like it much either, but they'll get used to it," he said and burst out laughing.[259]

A few months later, upon Barack Obama's entrance into the Oval Office, Bahrain was given another opportunity to take the lead on building closer ties between Israel and the Arab world. The Americans, who tried to revive the Israeli–Palestinian peace process, asked the Arab states to put forward their own proposals to improve ties with Israel. Obama and his secretary of state, Hillary Clinton, essentially adopted the Bahraini philosophy wholesale, that closer ties between the Arab states and Israel would give the government in Jerusalem more confidence in making progress with a peace process with the Palestinians. In late June 2009, a few days after Prime Minister Benjamin Netanyahu delivered his Bar-Ilan speech, where he expressed his support for a demilitarized Palestinian state for the first time ever, Crown Prince Salman came to the White House for a meeting with Obama. The US president discovered that the Bahrainis had the potential to be the best possible partners for his plan.

Following his return from Washington, the crown prince met with Adam Ereli, the US ambassador. He was energized from his meeting with President Obama, Vice President Joe Biden and Secretary of State Clinton, and he informed Ereli that he was weighing up a number of possible moves that would facilitate the president's peace initiative. He said he had tasked his foreign minister, Sheikh Khalid, with finding the best way to reach out to the Israeli public—whether through the local press or even by giving a speech in Israel. A few days earlier there had been a rare sighting of a Bahraini plane landing in Israel's Ben Gurion Airport. On board were administrative staff from the foreign and interior ministries who had come to collect Bahraini citizens arrested for their part in the Gaza flotilla. Prince Salman said his father had approved the flight. "We could have picked them up from Egypt or Cyprus, but we wanted to send a positive message to Israel," he told Ereli. "We don't care about the criticism."[260]

The Bahrainis were indeed seemingly undeterred and continued to push for warmer ties with Israel. On July 16, 2009, the lead article in *The Washington Post*'s opinion section carried the signature of Prince Salman.[261] In the article, the crown prince of Bahrain spelled out everything that had hitherto been said only behind closed doors: "We should move toward real peace now by consulting and educating our people and by reaching out to the Israeli public to highlight the benefits of a genuine peace. Our job, therefore, is to tell our story more directly to the Israeli people by getting the message out to their media, a message reflecting the hopes of the Arab mainstream that confirms peace as a strategic option...."

The op-ed reverberated around the Middle East and the world, but Israel kept quiet. A week after the article was published, I attended an Egyptian National Day event at the ambassador's residence. Obama's Cairo speech and Netanyahu's Bar-Ilan speech were the two main topics of conversation among the gathered diplomats, politicians and journalists. Later that evening, Netanyahu delivered a speech and addressed the article: "I would like to express my appreciation for the Crown Prince of Bahrain, who wrote last week, and I quote: 'All sides need to take simultaneous good faith action if peace is to have a chance,' and that 'a real, lasting peace requires comprehensive engagement and reconciliation.' These sentiments are deeply valued. So too are valued the efforts of Arab states to advance peace initiatives. The spirit of such initiatives is an important change from a different spirit, the spirit of Khartoum four decades ago. And if these offers are not final offers, then I believe that this spirit can help create an atmosphere in which a comprehensive peace is possible."[262]

The White House was delighted with the crown prince's article. The US special envoy for the peace process, George Mitchell, visited Manama and heaped praise on Prince Salman, who in turn spoke of the overwhelmingly positive response he had received. "I published this article because we need to change something in the peace process," the prince told the US envoy. "Watching the progress in the peace process in recent years has been like watching paint dry." The crown prince explained that if other Arab countries would speak to the Israeli public, they would ease their fears and make Netanyahu's job easier. But he also explained to the Americans that they had to offer something in exchange to the Arab countries that agreed to take the plunge and seek closer ties with Israel. "We will want increased US trade and investment, because our public needs to see that we are gaining something from such steps," Prince Salman said. He went on to claim that this would create competition between the Arab states, all of whom would seek to improve ties with Israel in exchange for goodwill gestures from the United States.[263]

The crown prince's article managed to cause a stir in Israel. *Haaretz* journalist Akiva Eldar read it and decided to take up the challenge. "I saw the article as almost a personal message directed at me. I said, I'll try my luck. I sent an email to the Bahraini ambassador in Washington, Houda Nonoo, and asked her for an interview with the crown prince," Eldar told me.[264] A few days passed with no reply, so Eldar turned to his friend, Dan Shapiro, who was the head of the Middle East Department in the White House's National Security Council. After Shapiro revealed to him that the Obama administration had played a not-insignificant part in the publication of the article, Eldar decided to put him to the test. "Let's finish the job together," he said. Shapiro told me that the article was the most consequential gesture of normalization that the White House had managed to extract from the Arab countries they had spoken with, and that attempts had been made to use it to achieve further progress. Eldar told Shapiro that he had reached out to the Bahraini ambassador but hadn't heard back. Shapiro quickly called her and made it clear that the White House would be very happy to see the interview go ahead. A few days later, a reply appeared in Eldar's inbox. The Bahrainis invited him to interview their foreign minister, Sheikh Khalid bin Ahmed Al Khalifa, at the UN General Assembly in New York, two months later.

Eldar was a bit disappointed. He had hoped to interview the crown prince himself in Bahrain. Nonetheless, he accepted the offer. As the General Assembly drew nearer, however, Manama's charm offensive began to wane. The Bahrainis' interest cooled— and Eldar's planned interview was nixed. "I initially thought the Bahrainis were open, but when push came to shove they didn't say yes," Shapiro told me.[265] "That was another sign that even the Arab state that most wanted warmer ties with Israel was encountering obstacles." Eldar claimed that the Bahrainis were reticent not because they were having second thoughts, but because of Saudi pressure. That remains the most likely explanation. "I was later told that the Saudis didn't like the crown prince's article," he told me. "They didn't like the fact that someone was stealing the spotlight."

The Bahraini attempts to open up to Israel and publicly improve ties may have faltered, but beneath the surface, relationships seemingly drawn from the world of political dramas and spy thrillers began to coalesce. On July 13, 2009, three days before the crown prince's article was published in *The Washington Post*, a new limited company by the name of the Center for International Development & Trade was formally registered in Bahrain. The documents submitted by the company's founders listed its activities as marketing, promoting commercial opportunities for Bahrain and attracting investors. In reality, it was a front organization for a secret diplomatic presence in Bahrain run by the Israeli Ministry of Foreign Affairs. This was Israel's second such mission in the Gulf, following the one in Dubai that had opened three years earlier.

Talks regarding the diplomatic mission in Bahrain started in 2007–2008 with a string of meetings between then-Foreign Minister Tzipi Livni and her Bahraini counterpart, Sheikh Khalid. "They met on the sidelines of the UN General Assembly and talked about the possibility of setting up an Israeli diplomatic mission in Bahrain," the Israeli diplomat Josh Zarka told me. Zarka himself was tapped to open the new mission. "The Bahrainis thought it was the right thing to do. They understood that we needed to work together." When the Gaza War broke out in 2009, there was concern within the Ministry of Foreign Affairs that it would derail the talks with Bahrain. They were surprised to discover that their fears were unfounded and the Bahrainis didn't walk back their decision.

A few days later, the head of the secret mission in Dubai, Bruce Kashdan, called Alon Ushpiz, at the time the head of the Coordination Division at the foreign ministry, and informed him that they had received the green light to open the secret Israeli diplomatic mission in Manama. "Are you certain?" Ushpiz asked. "Yes," Kashdan replied. Ushpiz called his deputy, Gilad Cohen, and informed him of the latest developments. "You'll lead the project. Moments like this are the reason you come to work in the foreign office," he told him. The next day, they organized a confidential meeting in one of the conference rooms of the foreign ministry. Twenty people from the various relevant divisions signed NDAs and began making plans for the new mission. At the same time, Ushpiz spoke with Zarka and invited him to lead the new office. Zarka agreed.

The working assumption among the senior officials in the foreign ministry was that the reason the Bahrainis agreed was Livni's close personal relationship with her Bahraini counterpart; they may also have been swayed by the fact that Qatar—Bahrain's nemesis—cut off its ties with Israel in February 2009 and closed the Israeli mission in Doha.

In early 2009, Zarka moved to Manama to set up the secret mission. He traveled solo, leaving his family behind in Israel. Only a few dozen people in the Israeli foreign ministry and security services knew about his posting, along with a few senior Bahrainis. Also within the circle were the British and US ambassadors in Manama and the heads of the US Navy's Fifth Fleet, based in Bahrain. "I was doing two weeks in Bahrain, one week in Israel," Zarka recalled.[266] "We were there undercover, but the Bahrainis knew about my presence and treated me for all intents and purposes like an ambassador."

Zarka started setting up the new mission. The project was code-named "The Flying Camel." The keepsakes adorning the offices of the members of the foreign office who served there all bear a camel logo. The challenge was to find an office in a suitable location, one that would be acceptable to the Bahraini government, and then to find a construction company that could build a diplomatic mission without knowing that was what they were doing. "We had to meet the foreign ministry's security standards, but we couldn't say as much to the local contractor, to avoid giving ourselves away," Zarka remembered. "We had to be very creative in how we explained our unique construction requirements to the contractor." When the mission was finally ready to go, the foreign ministry team wanted to install a communication system that would enable them to send classified cables. In countries with diplomatic relations, this is as easy as sending the components via diplomatic post. This was not possible here. The Bahrainis allowed Israel to bring their equipment into the country, but wanted no part of the logistics. Senior foreign ministry officials told me that they racked their brains for days to find a way to deliver the sensitive technological equipment to Bahrain as securely as possible. The first idea was to send it on a flight via Ethiopia, but they quickly discovered that the Ethiopian airline would land in Kuwait on its way to Bahrain. They eventually decided there was nothing else for it, and Zarka would have to fly with the sensitive equipment in his hand luggage and never let it out of his sight. Zarka landed in Manama and reached the local customs checkpoint. As he was walking through, the customs officer asked him to step into a side room. He took the computer and tech equipment out of his bag and began to examine them. Zarka was concerned he might decide to confiscate them. He tried to get through to his contact in the Bahraini government, but he didn't pick up. He contacted the mission's security officer and asked him to get in touch with the local security services, but there was no luck there either. As the minutes passed, more and more customs officers entered the room to examine the unusual equipment that had fallen into their laps. At one point, there were no fewer than 15 customs officers gathered around the table. "We need to take this to be checked off-site," one of them finally told Zarka an hour later. Zarka refused. "This is my personal equipment. Check it here in front of me, and if there's anything illegal then tell me," he replied. After two hours, when the Bahraini customs officials had investigated every component of the computer and equipment, they told Zarka he was free to pack everything up and be on his way. "What was the issue?" he asked them. "One of the components of your equipment had 'Made in Israel' on it, and we thought that was forbidden. Have a good day," the customs officer replied. Zarka, who had already been preparing for the possibility that he would end the day in a holding cell and in the middle of a diplomatic incident, let out a sigh of relief, gathered his equipment and hurried out before the customs officer could change his mind.

It would be fair to say that the foreign ministry does not specialize in undercover work. The new diplomatic mission got off to an unsteady start. They had registered their Bahraini shell company and had even designed a website for it. The site introduced the company as a business consulting provider in the Gulf, with a second branch in Dubai—the mission headed up by Kashdan. Only, it then emerged that a simple online search using the WHOIS protocol was sufficient to reveal that the website's address had been purchased by the Israeli foreign ministry. The site was quickly taken down and a new one was built—this time without the fingerprints of the Israeli government all over it. Hiring local workers was also a challenge. When Zarka needed a driver, he came up with an idea—he hired the cousin of the Indian driver who worked for Kashdan in Dubai. Officially, he didn't know that he was working for the Israeli foreign ministry, until one day, a decade later, he became the driver of the Israeli embassy in Bahrain. "We were very careful," recalled Zarka. "There was a lot of responsibility on our shoulders—and a lot of concern. Our base assumption was that the Iranians knew about our existence. We were constantly thinking that nothing was happening to us because the Iranians had decided not to carry out a bombing or to kidnap one of us. It would have been a walk in the park for them."

In January 2013, the company changed its name to Advanced Gulf Enterprises. The change was a direct consequence of Kashdan's success in Dubai. He had built up such an extensive network of contacts that the fact that he was Israeli had become common knowledge in numerous social circles. The foreign ministry therefore decided that it needed to end the public connection between the Manama and Dubai offices.

The vision of the new company, so its website claimed, was to provide market penetration, consulting and marketing services for tech companies in the heart of the Gulf. It described itself as a service provider for non-oil sector clients in Europe and the United States interested in penetrating the Bahraini market. According to the website, most of its clients were tech companies in the medical, renewable energy, agriculture and IT sectors. The company even boasted of its extensive network in Bahrain.

Advanced Gulf Enterprises issued 400 shares worth a total of 20 million Bahraini dinar (approximately 53 million dollars), held by the two founders: Brett Jonathan Miller and Iddo Moed, supposedly South African and Belgian businessmen, respectively. Both were really diplomats in the Israeli foreign military with dual citizenship. The company's board of directors also included a British citizen by the name of Ilan Fluss. Fluss was also an Israeli citizen and diplomat. In 2018, the company appointed a new CEO, Nevo Barchad. He introduced himself as a Finnish businessman and even opened a fake LinkedIn account with a fictitious CV. The cover stories the Israeli diplomats in Bahrain created for themselves were not particularly impressive, but despite that, the existence of the Israeli mission was a closely guarded secret in Manama and Jerusalem. A very small group of senior Bahraini officials knew about it, and the censor's offices in both countries prevented journalists from publishing anything on the subject.

I discovered my first clue to the secret mission in Bahrain in 2013. It was a slow news day, so I was flicking through the foreign ministry chapter of the economic plan on the Ministry of Finance website.[267] To my surprise, I discovered that in 2010,

Israel had opened a new diplomatic mission in an unnamed Gulf state. The foreign ministry team members were rattled when I approached them for comment. It sent alarm bells ringing, and the foreign ministry even tried unsuccessfully to prevent the report from being published. A few years later, in a conversation with a former foreign ministry employee, I learned the full backstory of the new and mysterious diplomatic mission. In June 2019, when I visited Manama for the first time and met with the foreign minister, Sheikh Khalid, in his office, I asked him playfully how business was going for Advanced Gulf Enterprises. He stared at me in horror and quickly changed the subject. I later heard from a senior Israeli official that as soon as I left Sheikh Khalid's office, he rushed to warn his counterparts in the Israeli foreign ministry that the secret was out and in the possession of an Israeli journalist.

Life for the Israeli diplomats working in the secret mission was not easy. Beyond the security threats, they had to cope with the solitude of existing in the shadows. Very few people in Bahrain outside of the senior leadership knew that the foreign citizens working in this business consulting company were Israelis. A few members of Bahrain's small Jewish community were in on the secret and were among the only people who didn't work in the mission who were allowed to enter it. "We used to check in with them every so often to see how the Jewish community was doing," Zarka told me. Outside the mission's walls, the Israeli envoys would speak only in English and French. Phone calls likewise. One of the Israeli diplomats called his family in Israel and told them that he was posted in Turkey. His daughter asked what the weather was like there, and he replied that the heat was unbearable. Having read of the cold snap sweeping across Turkey just minutes earlier, his daughter grew suspicious and began to interrogate him. Her father, realizing that he had put his foot in it, explained that he had meant that the temperature within the embassy in Turkey was set uncomfortably high. But the most memorable story from the secret mission in Bahrain regarded a diplomatic couple who had a son together during their posting in Manama. For years, the child didn't know the truth about his place of birth. His parents were instructed to tell him that he was born in Jordan. As the boy grew up, he began to question the story. On one occasion, he even told his father that he was being evasive and hiding details from him about his childhood. In September 2020, following the declaration of the Abraham Accords, the father called his son and revealed the truth to him for the first time.

The mission was located in the heart of Manama's business district, to facilitate the diplomats' key role of building economic and commercial ties between companies from Israel and Bahrain. "We used to meet with local businesspeople and offer them business proposals in all kinds of countries, and once we'd reached a certain point with them, we'd offer opportunities in Israel," Zarka recalled. "There were some Bahrainis who responded positively and some who were unwilling to consider ties with Israel. Those who were willing, we connected to Israeli businesspeople and stepped out of the picture. A few of the Bahrainis wanted to pay us brokerage fees. In those cases, we told them there was no need because we had already received a commission from the other side." The Israeli delegation in Bahrain facilitated hundreds of business deals between Israeli and Bahraini companies over the course of a decade. At the same time, the Israeli diplomats maintained regular contact with senior Bahraini government officials on diplomatic affairs. A senior official in the foreign ministry told me that, in the years leading up to the Abraham Accords, the Bahrainis didn't want to meet with then-Foreign Minister Avigdor Lieberman or Netanyahu, preferring instead to hold talks with foreign ministry officials, offering them access to the highest levels of government in the kingdom.

Alon Ushpiz, who provided support for the two secret missions in Dubai and Bahrain as part of his role at the Director General's Office in the foreign ministry, insisted time after time on keeping the missions under the direct control of the director general to ensure that any life-and-death situations could be resolved with the necessary speed. "It was an operation in every sense of the word—especially when it came to security," Ushpiz said to me.[268] "But unlike military operations that last a few days or weeks, this one lasted years. We sent young people to participate in the most revolutionary innovation in the history of diplomacy, something that exists nowhere else on earth. We went from ragtag militia to finely drilled military—from one or two people wandering around the Gulf unchecked to two offices that opened up a brand-new career path."

A year after the inauguration of the secret embassy in Manama, the Arab Spring reached the shores of Bahrain. A wave of protests by Shia demonstrators against the ruling Sunni royal family swept the country. On one of the first days of the protests, Zarka found himself driving through a procession of thousands of Shia protesters. It doesn't bear thinking about how the situation would have unfolded had the protesters known who was sitting in the vehicle. King Hamad blamed Iran for stirring up the protests. This charge was not wholly accurate, but nor was it entirely baseless. Ever since the Islamic Revolution, the regime in Tehran has sought to portray Bahrain as essentially Iran's "14th province." The Iranians also supported the attempted coup in Bahrain in 1981 and encouraged the uprising that took place from 1994–1999. On the other hand, Dr. Yoel Guzansky, one of the foremost experts in Israel on Gulf politics and security, has argued that the House of Khalifa has used the Iranian threat and claims of "Shia plots" over the years to reject any discussion over meaningful reforms to the government and to silence arguments advanced by the Shia opposition that the country is run under a political system that favors the Sunni minority.[269]

When the protests erupted, King Hamad requested support from Saudi Arabia and the United Arab Emirates. The Saudis activated the mutual defense pact of the Gulf Cooperation Council and dispatched thousands of soldiers to Bahrain from its joint military arrangement, the Peninsula Shield Force. Some one thousand Saudi soldiers and 500 Emiratis came to Bahrain and helped quell the protests. This was no Peace Corps operation and there was no Supreme Court to petition: dozens of protesters were killed and thousands more arrested. Soldiers forcefully cleared the protesters from their main congregating site at Manama's Pearl Roundabout. The iconic monument in the center of the roundabout was torn down, and bulldozers destroyed all reminders of the site's existence. At the same time, Bahrain was caught up in the worst financial crisis in its history, and its Gulf neighbors had to step in with a 20-billion-dollar bailout to attempt to stabilize the local economy.

The other person who came in to support the House of Khalifa against the protesters was none other than the Israeli prime minister, Benjamin Netanyahu. In an interview on CNN, Netanyahu was asked for his thoughts on the Saudi military involvement in Bahrain. "I don't think it is surprising at all," said Netanyahu. "I think they are concerned with a possible Iranian takeover of Bahrain, which would put Iran effectively within spitting distance of the Arabian Peninsula."[270] The Saudis, and even more so the Bahrainis, were hugely grateful to Netanyahu for his intervention—especially in the face of increased pressure from the Obama administration on human rights. The Shia uprising, which ebbed and flowed until 2014, was one of the catalysts for the warming ties between Bahrain and Israel. The Bahrainis were concerned the Obama administration would take the same line with them as it had taken with the Mubarak regime in Egypt a few weeks earlier.[271] They asked Israel for help in conveying messages to the White House. These concerns were founded on justifiable fears. At the time, the Americans were indeed weighing up delivering a similar message to the House of Khalifa to the one they had delivered to Mubarak. Senior foreign ministry officials turned to their counterparts in the Obama administration and warned them of the potential domino effect that would enable Iranian penetration into the kingdom. Similar messages were delivered to senior members of the US Congress on both sides of the aisle who were considering supporting sanctions against Bahrain. "The king of Bahrain and the crown prince saw us as the ones who helped turn the tide with the Americans," a senior foreign ministry official told me. "They were somewhat right to do so, and that made us a valuable asset in their eyes. That led to a significant improvement in diplomatic relations with them."

Establishing closer ties with Israel and with the Jewish community in the United States were among the steps the Bahrainis took to soften the Obama administration's criticism over the violent suppression of the protests. One of the key figures in the warming ties was Rabbi Marc Schneier, a regular fixture in gossip columns in US tabloids. He is also referred to as "the celebrities' rabbi." In his day job, Schneier is the rabbi at a synagogue in the Hamptons. In the time that remains, he engages in promoting interfaith dialogue between Jews and Muslims. This hobby has made him a regular guest at the palace of the king of Bahrain over the last decade, and led to King Hamad appointing him as his special advisor on dialogue with the Jewish community. "I've known the king since 2011. The first time I met him at his palace in Manama, he talked about Iran and its terrorist activity. From 2013–2015, he led the Gulf states in designating Hezbollah as a terrorist organization, and in 2016 he told me that the only way to guarantee a strong and moderate Arab voice in the Gulf is with a strong Israel," Schneier told me.[272]

Despite these words, throughout those years the Bahrainis continued to work primarily behind the scenes. During the UN Climate Change Conference in Paris in November 2015, I wandered around the various pavilions together with my colleague, Raphael Ahren, who was working for *The Times of Israel*. The United Arab Emirates' pavilion piqued our curiosity, so we walked in. Walking in immediately after us was the Bahraini foreign minister, Sheikh Khalid, whom we recognized immediately. We approached him and introduced ourselves. Sheikh Khalid was genial, but politely declined our requests for an interview. A few months later, Israel's ninth president, Shimon Peres, passed away. Peres had been particularly close with the Bahrainis, and they sent a representative to the funeral. Sheikh Khalid surprised many people by sending a tweet eulogizing Peres. "Rest in Peace President Shimon Peres, a Man of War and a Man of the still elusive Peace in the Middle East [sic]," he wrote.

Someone else who maintained a close and warm personal relationship with Sheikh Khalid over the years was the former foreign minister, Tzipi Livni. They kept in touch both when Livni was away from the political arena and when she returned to it, often meeting at international summits and conferences. In February 2017, they met in Munich at the city's annual security conference. The Bahraini minister informed Livni that King Hamad had made a decision to move toward normalization with Israel. Sheikh

Khalid asked Livni—at the time a member of the opposition in the Israeli Knesset—to deliver a message to Netanyahu that Bahrain was interested in pursuing ties with Israel. She returned to Israel and hurried to inform the prime minister. A few months later, the king of Bahrain took a tangible step. At a meeting with Jewish leaders in Los Angeles, he announced the cancellation of the policy forbidding visits to Israel.

In December 2018, the Israeli Military Censor permitted the Israeli press to report for the first time on the existence of the normalization talks between Israel and Bahrain. As the diplomatic correspondent for Israel's Channel 10 at the time, I was working on a series of pieces on the secret relationship between Israel and the Gulf states, for which I interviewed dozens of people. On February 10, 2019, the first piece went out, focusing on Bahrain. The reaction I received proved to me that the Israeli public was curious about the Gulf. Two days later, I took off with the press pool for Netanyahu's trip to the summit on Iran in Warsaw. A few minutes after I boarded the plane, while it was still on the ground in Israel, I received a Facebook message in English from a woman I didn't know. She asked to speak with me about my segment on Bahrain. I gave her my phone number and she called me. To my amazement, she told me she was an Israeli who worked with the advisors to the crown prince of Bahrain, who had heard about the segment and wanted to receive a translation of it in English. The conversation took me by surprise and, as the plane was already starting to make its way toward the runway, I ended the call with the mystery woman with an agreement to stay in touch.

In the corridors of the conference center in Warsaw, I ran into Sheikh Khalid. We greeted each other. He still wasn't interested in giving an interview. At the time, he was not only Bahrain's number one diplomat, but also its most prolific tweeter. Anyone looking for evidence of the ongoing flirtation between Bahrain and Israel could find it on his Twitter feed. I followed him closely on the social media platform and saw how he was laying the groundwork in his home country for relations with Israel. A few weeks before the Warsaw Conference, when Israel exposed a series of Hezbollah tunnels under the northern border, Sheikh Khalid tweeted a condemnation of the organization and in support of Israel's right to destroy the tunnels. A few days later, he tweeted in favor of Australia's decision to recognize West Jerusalem as the capital of Israel and claimed that it was an implementation of the Arab Peace Initiative. When the representatives at the conference gathered for a joint photo-op, the Israeli journalists asked Sheikh Khalid whether he had met with Netanyahu. "It will happen when it happens," he replied. The next day, the photo of the leaders at the conference was published in the state-run newspapers in Bahrain, which noted in their captions that Prime Minister Benjamin Netanyahu of Israel appeared in the same picture as Sheikh Khalid. A few years earlier, the Israeli representative would have been cropped out of the image. The general feeling at the end of the Warsaw Conference was that it was only a matter of time before a breakthrough. The next major step came three months later.

The evening of May 19, 2019 was supposed to be a quiet one at work. I wasn't required for the evening news, so I was visiting friends. The meat was sizzling on the barbecue when I received a phone call from the United States. A senior White House official was on the other end. "In a few minutes we're going to announce that we're unveiling the economic part of the Trump Plan within a few weeks," he said. "But the really interesting part is that we're convening an economic workshop in Bahrain at the end of June." Before he could hang up, I managed to sneak in a question about whether Israeli government officials and journalists would be able to attend. "We're working on it. Stay tuned," he replied, and ended the call. I immediately called the network and managed to go on air via my phone before the end of the broadcast to report on the story. I barely remember the steaks that came off the grill that evening. All I could think about from that point on was going to Bahrain.

After the Warsaw Conference, I had tried a few times to get in touch with the Bahraini foreign minister. I sent him a direct message on Twitter every few days which was continually met with silence. After the announcement of the workshop, I wrote to him once more, offering to come to Bahrain and interview him while I was there. He didn't reply. My Israeli contact in Bahrain encouraged me not to give up, and to keep trying. "Trust me, it'll happen," she said. A month later, a Twitter DM notification popped up on my phone. When I opened the message, I was surprised to see that it was from Sheikh Khalid, who was getting in touch for the first time ever. "Hi Barak, I wanted to give you a heads up. We just told the White House to add your name to their press team attending the economic workshop in Manama. Looking forward to seeing you in my country," he wrote. We continued to exchange messages over the following days. This time, when I asked to interview him, he agreed.

The date of the conference kept drawing closer. Three days before, the White House published the economic portion of Trump's peace plan. At the heart of the plan was a 50-billion-dollar investment in the Palestinian economy, spread over a decade, as well as in Egypt, Jordan and Lebanon. Some of this money was to take the form of American financial aid, another part would be donations from Gulf states and a third part would be private sector investments. The White House shared a thick folder containing 100 projects, ranging from establishing a recognized land authority in the West Bank and Gaza to constructing a transit route between

Gaza and the West Bank that would include a train line and highway, and even building tourist resorts along the shores of the Dead Sea. The overarching goal of the project was to create a million new jobs in Gaza and the West Bank, reduce unemployment to a single-digit percentage and double the Palestinian GDP within 10 years. The Palestinians, who were invited to the Bahrain workshop, declared that they mean to boycott it. "The Palestinians cannot be bought off with money," said President Abbas's office.

In contrast to the Palestinians, numerous Arab states, including Egypt, Jordan, Saudi Arabia and the United Arab Emirates, announced their intention to send their finance and economy ministers. The desire to cooperate with the Trump administration overpowered any concerns about the Palestinian response and even the domestic criticism. The price to be paid for the participation of the Arab states in the face of the Palestinian boycott was that not a single Israeli government official attended the summit in Manama. The only Israelis present were a few businesspeople and journalists. Most disappointed of all was then-Finance Minister Moshe Kahlon, who had hoped to participate. But Kahlon, who is blessed with comic timing no less sharp than his political instincts, got his own back. The day the Manama summit opened, he met with the Palestinian minister of finance, Shukri Bishara, and put out a press release about it. The message was clear: you talk about the economy in Bahrain, and we'll work on economic collaboration here in Jerusalem.

That was how we found ourselves—journalists from six Israeli media outlets—packing our bags for Manama. The trip and the occasion were in themselves a small slice of history and a newsworthy story. It was the first time Israeli journalists visited the small kingdom in the Gulf since the delegation led by Environment Minister Yossi Sarid in 1994. The legendary producer

Shai Spiegelman, who joined me on the trip, recorded every minute of our journey: the moment we met up at Ben Gurion Airport, the layover in Amman and the boarding of the flight of the Bahraini national carrier, Gulf Air. The most powerful moment was during that flight, as we passed over the vast Saudi Al-Nafud desert. When we landed, we were taken to the VIP room at the airport. A waitress offered us orange juice while our passports were taken by the border officials. When the passports were returned to us, we made our way out of the terminal, where we met our colleagues from Kan—the Israeli Public Broadcasting Corporation—Moav Vardi and Gili Cohen, waiting on a bench before passport control. They had not been included on the White House's list but, displaying great courage, initiative and determination, had decided to come anyway on their foreign passports. The Bahraini border police immediately identified them as Israelis, but after a delay of a few hours, they were allowed in to cover the workshop.

The economic workshop was the official justification for the trip to Bahrain, but my personal goal was to take in as much as I could of the Gulf kingdom and to bring its sights and sounds back to an Israeli audience. On the morning of the second day, we headed out to the Souq Al Manama—the old market. One of the biggest question marks was how the local residents would respond when faced with cameras and microphones belonging to Israeli networks. We received our answer fairly quickly. Five minutes after Shai Spiegelman pulled out his camera at the entrance to the market, a police officer came over to us, asked if we had a permit to film and took us to the nearby police station.

As soon as we got there, the police officers asked to see our documents. When one of the officers noticed the nationality of our passports, his eyes shot up. He spent several minutes trying to decide how to report this to the senior duty officer in the next room. A few minutes later, the officer entered the room holding our passports. He looked like a man gripped by a piercing headache that he was unable to shake. We conversed with the officers in a mix of Arabic and English, and tried to explain to them what two Israeli journalists were doing filming in the *souq*. At this point, I decided to call the contact who had helped us to secure our visas—the spokesman of the Bahraini crown prince, Isa Al Hammadi. He inquired which police station we were being held at and promised to deal with the situation immediately.

A few minutes later, my phone rang. An unknown local number flashed up on the screen. When I answered, the person on the other end introduced himself as the assistant to the foreign minister, Sheikh Khalid. He said the foreign minister wished to meet with me in his office. I told him I was grateful for the invitation, but would unfortunately be unable to make the appointment as I was currently being held at a police station. He promised to take care of it. Five minutes later, the duty officer entered the room where we were waiting, handed over our passports, apologized and wished us a pleasant day. We parted ways with a smile. As we left the police station, we saw the officer who had taken us in at the market with two new victims in tow: our colleagues from Kan.

The foreign minister's assistant waited for me outside the police station and took me in his car to the minister's office, a few minutes away from the market. Sheikh Khalid waited for me at the entrance with a broad smile on his face. He shook my hand warmly and asked, "How was the police station?" He then turned and introduced me to the woman standing next to him. "This is Houda Nonoo, she was our ambassador to Washington." Nonoo was one of the most famous women in Bahrain. In 2005, she was appointed to the parliament by King Hamad, and in 2008 she became the first woman to be appointed to the prestigious post of ambassador to Washington, and indeed the first Jewish woman to be appointed as an ambassador on behalf of Bahrain. But the most interesting detail about Nonoo and her political and diplomatic career is that she is a descendant of one of the first Jewish families in Bahrain. Her grandfather, Ibrahim Nonoo, came to Bahrain from Iraq in 1888 and became a successful businessman.

Bahrain is the only one of the six Gulf states with an indigenous Jewish community. Today the community has only around 40 members, but at its peak it was estimated at approximately 1,500. Natan Aluf, who was born in Manama in 1918 and was among the leaders of the community, wrote in his book, *Bahrain—The Community That Was,* that the first Jew to come to Bahrain in 1880 was Eliyahu Yadgar, a trader from the city of Basra in southern Iraq who lost his assets and decided to try his luck somewhere new. "The people here are honest and innocent, and most importantly, they are worthy of trust," he wrote in a letter to his sons who stayed behind in Basra. Soon after, they joined him with their families. In the years that followed, more Jewish families emigrated from Basra, Baghdad and even Iran to Manama.[273]

The expansion of the Jewish community led to the construction of a synagogue in the heart of the *souq* in Manama.[274] At the same time, they needed to build a Jewish cemetery. Yadgar and a few other members of the community approached the mufti of Bahrain, Sheikh Jassim bin Mahza, and asked to purchase land for this purpose. Hostile to Jews, the mufti demanded an extortionate sum for the land and even chided the representatives of the community for their "Jewish tight-fistedness." The meeting went nowhere, and the next day the members of the community were horrified to wake up to antisemitic proclamations hanging on the outer walls of their homes. One of the older women in the community, who was close to Umm-Abdu'llah, the senior wife of the ruler, Isa Al Khalifa, led a delegation to the palace and recounted before her the recent events and the plight of the Jewish community. Umm-Abdu'llah took the representatives of the community to the office of Sheikh Isa. They recounted to him once more the story of the cemetery, the mufti's response and the antisemitic notices. Upon hearing their story, the sheikh was furious. He cursed the mufti and ordered his secretary to draft a formal missive to transfer a plot of land to the Jewish community at no charge. Yadgar hurried back to the mufti with the missive. Bin Mahza was taken aback. He apologized and instructed that the notices against the Jewish communities were to be removed at once. But this was not sufficient. Two weeks later, Sheikh Isa removed him from his post.[275]

Most of the members of the Jewish community in Bahrain were traders, but some of them—such as Natan Aluf—held management positions at Bapco, the local petroleum company that transformed the country's economy in 1932. Some of the Jews also worked at the British consulate or other British entities. On a visit to Mandatory Palestine, the British consul to Bahrain ordered fertilizer and sprinklers from the Agricultural Research Station in Rehovot in present-day Israel to grow trees for shade in Manama.[276] In 1942, a team from Solel Boneh, the civil engineering company founded by the Jewish labor movement during the British Mandate, arrived in Bahrain to build a new airport. The arrival of Jews from Palestine reinforced a powerful sense of Zionism among the members of the community. One of the results of this visit was the establishment of a union that represented all 650 members of the Jewish community in Bahrain in the 1940s in dealings with the emir and the British representatives in the country. This union would prove its worth a few years later—when the Jews of Bahrain faced their greatest crisis.[277]

On November 29, 1947, many members of the Jewish community in Bahrain were tuning into the BBC to hear live coverage of the vote in the United Nations General Assembly on the UN Partition Plan for Palestine. As in many other Arab countries, three days of protests were called against the decision. The first two days passed broadly without incident, but on the third day, December 4, a frenzied mob carried out a pogrom against the Jewish community. The protesters, led by Pakistani petroleum and dock workers, looted 15 Jewish homes, defiled the synagogue, beat several Jews and killed an elderly woman from the community. A few Muslim residents protected the Jews and hid them in their homes, but the local police didn't lift a finger to halt the rioters, Aluf wrote.[278]

In her book about the Jewish community in Bahrain, Bahraini Jewish member of Parliament Nancy Elly Khedouri quoted the British political advisor to the rulers of Bahrain, Sir Charles Belgrave, who wrote about the riots in his memoir, *Personal Column*.[279] Belgrave wrote that "the leading Arabs were genuinely shocked" by the riots and that many of them had given shelter to their Jewish neighbors.[280] Belgrave described in detail the damages from the pogrom and how he visited the injured in the hospital. "The police had more injuries than the Jewish victims," he claimed. Belgrave stressed that after the riots, there were no other violent attacks against the Jews who chose to stay in Bahrain rather than emigrate to Israel or other countries.

In the months that followed, Aluf wrote, the community lived in constant fear, many of them refugees in the homes of others. The fear increased as the day of Israel's declaration of independence neared. The community union turned to Sheikh Salman and the British representatives for their protection. They received comforting responses and, as promised, May 15 came and went without incident. Aluf wrote in his book about the events of the time from behind the scenes: "Two or three days before the declaration of independence, Sheikh Salman bin Hamad Al Khalifa delivered a message to the loyal and devoted tribe, wherefore bringing harm to the Jews would be seen in his eyes as bringing harm to his own name, and all four hundred members of the tribe swore that the ruler's decree would indeed guide their steps." On May 14, during prayers at the central mosque of Manama, Sheikh Salman called on the people not to hurt the Jews.[281]

But the problems did not end there. The Jewish community was constantly on edge. "The reports of the Arabs of the Land of Israel fleeing the cities and villages on the eve of the declaration of the new state spread far and wide, and increased the hatred for the Jews, who jumped at every whispering leaf carried on the breeze," noted Aluf. "To describe it in accurate words, every Jew in Bahrain, from young to old, felt detested." In July 1948, the union of the Jewish community received a demand from a group calling itself "The Union for Palestine" that was collecting donations for the refugees expelled from their homes. The demand was that the Jewish community donate its share. Many of those whose homes had been looted only a few months previously had no choice but to once again hand over their money. But that was not the end of the matter. "The Union for Palestine" demanded the Jewish community submit a "letter of surrender" stating its opposition to Zionism.[282] The heads of the union had no choice but to come together and draft a letter, in the broadest terms they could get away with. Emotions ran high within the community over the letter, but the move reduced tensions with the Muslim majority.

Despite this, many within the community began to consider leaving. "The Jews of Bahrain felt that the ground was burning beneath their feet and that the Garden of Eden in the shade of which they had found refuge for so many years had become hell," Aluf wrote. One of the primary destinations for emigration was the United Kingdom, of which Bahrain was a protectorate. Other destinations included the United States, India and Iran.[283] But starting in 1949, another opportunity for emigration entered the equation: Israel. Aluf and the community's rabbi, Shimon Cohen, got in touch with the Jewish Agency in Paris and Bombay to plan an operation to bring the Jewish community of Bahrain to Israel. Under maximum secrecy, a list was put together of candidates for immigration. The plans divided opinion within the community, with some members opposed to the idea and even trying to convince fellow Jews not to leave. The greatest fear was that someone would leak the plans for the operation to the authorities. Over a period of several months, dozens of Jewish families began their journeys from Bahrain, traveling first by ship to Bombay and then flying from there to Israel. A few hundred new immigrants arrived in Israel as part of this operation. Of the estimated 100–200 Jews who remained in Bahrain, the majority later moved to Israel following the Six-Day War in 1967.[284] The new ties with Israel gave a much-needed shot in the arm for the tiny community that remained, which could now be in direct and open contact with the State of Israel for the first time. The community is now attempting to once more swell its ranks.

Back at the meeting with Sheikh Khalid and Ambassador Nonoo, we sat in the office of the Bahraini foreign minister for an hour, covering a wide range of topics. The meeting was primarily intended to be an off-the-record introduction before the video interview to follow, in which interviewees tend to be more guarded and careful not to stray from their script. Before we wrapped up the conversation, Sheikh Khalid asked me whether the Israeli journalists who had come for the summit would be interested in a guided tour of the synagogue. Soon after, we were gathered in the heart of the *souq*, in an alleyway that leads to the synagogue, together with Ambassador Nonoo, who opened the door for us. I am not a religious man in any way, but I was nonetheless moved by the occasion. For my religious colleagues, this visit was one of the highlights of the trip to Bahrain. They returned the next morning, together with US Envoy Jason Greenblatt, for the *Shacharit* prayer.

The next day, I met with Sheikh Khalid once more in one of the suites of the luxurious Four Seasons Hotel in Manama, where the summit was due to take place. My producer, Shai Spiegelman, clapped once to let us know the cameras were rolling, and the interview began. The cliché that the importance of the event lies in the mere fact of its existence was all too true in this situation. It was the first time a foreign minister of a Gulf state was being interviewed for an Israeli media outlet. The fact that it was for TV, speaking directly to the Israeli people, made it even more special. But it was also newsworthy and interesting on its own merit, with the Bahraini foreign minister publicly calling to accept Israel as an integral part of the region. "Israel is a country in the Middle East. It is part of the heritage of this region historically. The Jewish people have a place among us. Communication must be a precondition to any conflict resolution. We have to talk," Sheikh Khalid told me. "The Israeli public needs to trust that there are countries in the region that do want peace and that do encourage the Palestinians to move forward and that do support them. We want the Arabs to feel that Israel is a country that belongs here. We may not have normalization or diplomatic relations—yet—but we know that Israel is a country that exists in the region and that its people want peace."[285]

After the interview went out, Sheikh Khalid instructed the Bahraini foreign ministry to share it via every possible platform.

The foreign ministry's Twitter account even shared the video of the interview. Sheikh Khalid's words reverberated around Bahrain, Israel and Washington. The foreign ministry in Jerusalem put out an official statement praising the interview, and Netanyahu addressed it at the opening of his weekly cabinet meeting. Further messages of support came from senior officials in the White House and US State Department. After the interview went out, I received another call from the same mystery woman, without whom none of it would have happened. "I told you it would go ahead," she told me.

Sheikh Khalid himself was very pleased with the interview, especially with the support he received for it from the royal palace and the White House. Three weeks later, he had a public meeting in Washington with the Israeli foreign minister, Israel Katz. The two had their picture taken together and shared the photo with the press. The man who orchestrated the image was US Envoy Brian Hook. It was his work behind the scenes to bolster the secret alliance between Israel and the Gulf states against Iran that had made this situation possible. Three months later, representatives of dozens of countries gathered in Manama once more for a conference on protecting waterways in the Gulf from the Iranian threat. This time, Israel attended with official representatives.

The Bahrainis were by now well on their way to normalization with Israel. It was no longer a question of if, but when. But the man who had done more than any other to reach this point did not remain in office long enough to see his signature added to the eventual accord. In January 2020, the king of Bahrain announced that Sheikh Khalid would step down from his position as foreign minister after 15 years and would become his new diplomatic advisor. In his place, the king appointed Abdullatif bin Rashid Al Zayani, the minister of the interior during the 2011 protests and more recently the head of the Gulf Cooperation Council (the umbrella organization that includes Saudi Arabia, the United Arab Emirates, Bahrain, Qatar, Kuwait and Oman). Before he left, Sheikh Khalid had time for one more powerful symbolic act. A few weeks after the statement about this impending reshuffle, he instructed the Bahraini ambassador in Washington to attend the celebratory ceremony at the White House where President Trump unveiled his plan to resolve the Israeli–Palestinian conflict. "We support the Palestinians but appreciate the Trump Plan and believe that its positive aspects are worthy of consideration," said Sheikh Khalid two days after the White House ceremony. This was a signal that Bahrain was willing to give the US president's plan a chance, and further still—that it was marching toward diplomatic relations with Israel.

When the Bahraini finance minister called senior White House officials six months later and asked to get on board the normalization train with Israel, it didn't come as a surprise. Kushner and Berkowitz decided to make the most of the existing momentum and push for an accord between Bahrain and Israel with all haste. As with the accord with the UAE, the deliberations took place within a small and restricted group of officials. On the Bahraini side, these were the crown prince and his close confidant, the finance minister. On the Israeli side, it was Prime Minister Netanyahu and Ambassador Ron Dermer. One of the key takeaways in the White House from the negotiations between Israel and the UAE was about Israel's domestic political situation. Trump's advisors had no desire to see a repeat of Netanyahu's conduct toward his defense minister, Benny Gantz, and foreign minister, Gabi Ashkenazi, from the previous negotiations, excluding them from the process and leaving them to find out about the agreement with the UAE at the last minute. The ugly domestic political saga in Israel had tarnished the historic achievement and painted the agreement with the UAE in partisan colors. When Kushner and Berkowitz visited Israel in late August, they met with Gantz and Ashkenazi and informed them about the breakthrough in talks with Bahrain. In the weeks that followed until the declaration of the accord, the White House kept the two up to date on the latest progress.

From Israel, Kushner, Berkowitz and their team flew to Manama. Before their visit to Bahrain, Kushner paid from his own pocket for a Torah scroll from a scribe in the United States. The scroll was intended as a gift for the king, Hamad bin Isa Al Khalifa, in recognition of his favorable attitude toward the Jewish community in the country. Berkowitz went into the meeting with the king with the Torah scroll in his arms. During that meeting with the king, and another one with the crown prince that same day, they made significant progress toward an accord with Israel. The Bahrainis had two requests in exchange: financial support from the US and patrol boats from the US Navy's surplus for their coast guard. Kushner and Berkowitz thought they would be able to reach an agreement there and then, but they decided to extend the talks for a couple of days to iron out the final details.

From Bahrain, the two continued to Saudi Arabia. The Americans wanted to ensure the Saudis didn't object to the normalization process by their neighbors. In their meeting with the Saudi crown prince, Mohammed bin Salman, Kushner asked whether Saudi Arabia would join the Abraham Accords. The Saudi crown prince told Kushner that the kingdom shared common interests with Israel but wanted to see how the agreement with the UAE went, and also to see progress on the Palestinian issue first.[286] Kushner then made two requests: for the Saudis to give the green light for Bahrain to follow in the footsteps of the United Arab Emirates and normalize relations with Israel, and to open Saudi airspace for flights from Israel to Abu Dhabi and Dubai. A former senior White House official told me that bin Salman agreed to both. This was a substantial breakthrough. The next day, the state-run Saudi Press Agency put out a brief statement with far-reaching implications. "We have approved the request received from the General Civil Aviation Authority in the United Arab Emirates, which includes the desire to allow flights coming to and departing from the United Arab Emirates to all countries to pass through the Kingdom of Saudi Arabia's airspace," the statement read. Beyond the boost this gave to relations between Israel and the UAE, it was also the single most meaningful gesture of normalization by the Saudis toward Israel to date. The impact of this gesture was felt in the hundreds of thousands of Israelis who began to flock to Dubai.

Further proof of the Saudi approval came the next day, when the Bahraini government put out a similar statement, confirming that it too would permit flights from the Emirates to Israel and back to pass through its airspace. Bahrain itself is a tiny island, but its airspace is significantly larger. The reasons for this date back to its days as a British protectorate. The British military placed its central radar station in the vicinity of Manama. In those days, airspace was determined by that radar station. The result was that Bahrain continues to control a large part of the airspace of neighboring Qatar to the present day, and it is entitled to permit Israeli planes to pass overhead, even in the face of Qatari objections. This shortened the flight time from Israel to the United Arab Emirates by 20 minutes. In addition to the practical changes, it was also a hint of the intensive secret efforts taking place between Bahrain and the White House to normalize relations with Israel. These efforts were revealed to the world within a matter of days.

The contacts between the senior White House officials and the Bahraini crown prince and his team continued into the first week of September. The date of the signing ceremony at the White House between Israel and the UAE had been set for September 15, and the White House wanted to finalize the accord between Israel and Bahrain beforehand. The feeling in the White House was that if two Arab countries showed up to the ceremony, the message that would send to the region and the wider world would resonate far more and contribute to a domino effect that would attract additional countries.

September 11, 2020 was a Friday, usually the only day of the week I permit myself to have a little afternoon nap. However, the White House was generating headlines almost every Friday in that period. At 4:26 PM, my phone beeped. It was a notification of a new WhatsApp message from a Bahraini contact. As soon as I read the message, I knew there would be no rest that day. "President Trump will almost certainly announce today that Bahrain is normalizing relations with Israel," the source wrote to me. Once I recovered from the initial surprise, I started trying to verify the story. I called every White House source, sent text messages and emails, but nobody replied. People who would usually answer immediately had gone to ground. Even my contacts in the Prime Minister's Office and the foreign and defense ministries had gone radio silent. After half an hour of trying, I managed to verify the information and published a report on the matter. Three hours later, President Trump held a conference call with King Hamad and Prime Minister Netanyahu, following which Trump tweeted out a statement on the new accord. Only 29 days after the statement on the accord between Israel and the UAE, a second normalization accord had been wrapped up.

In October 2020, a few weeks after the celebratory signing ceremony at the White House, I boarded an El Al flight from Ben Gurion Airport to Manama with an Israeli and American delegation. During that visit, the Israelis and Bahrainis signed an agreement establishing full diplomatic relations. As soon as the ceremony was over, I saw Haim Regev, the foreign minister's chief of staff, approach the Bahraini foreign minister, Al Zayani, and hand over a folder with the emblem of the State of Israel. The folder contained a letter from Foreign Minister Gabi Ashkenazi with a formal request to open an Israeli embassy in the country. A few weeks later, the secret diplomatic mission in Manama became a fully fledged and official embassy, with an Israeli flag and a sign on the door.

Maoz

It was the bread. Always the bread. Even in dictatorships, hunger drives the crowds into the streets. Omar Hassan Ahmad al-Bashir, the Sudanese president, learned that lesson on December 19, 2018. The day before, his government had decided to treble the price of a loaf of bread from one Sudanese pound (equivalent to two tenths of a US cent) to three. It was the third increase in the price of bread that year, and it was the straw that broke the camel's back. The protest began in the eastern city of El-Gadarif. Hundreds of residents took to the streets and clashed with the police. Six protesters were shot and killed, and the authorities decreed a state of emergency in the city. But the protests didn't end there, quickly spreading west to the capital, Khartoum, and other cities around Sudan. From there, it wasn't long before the focus changed. What had started as an economic protest over the cost of living escalated into demands for al-Bashir, who had ruled Sudan with an iron fist for 30 years, to be overthrown. Al-Bashir responded with force. A few weeks after the unrest started, he declared a state of emergency throughout the country, dismissed the civil government and transferred its authority to the army and intelligence forces under his command. In his desperation, the Sudanese dictator decided to take an extreme and previously unthinkable step: he turned to Israel.

The connection was poor. It's a common issue with calls to Africa—especially when one party is sitting in the Prime Minister's Office in Jerusalem and the other in the presidential palace in Khartoum. The two people on the call, which took place in early January 2019, couldn't be certain whether the other person could hear them properly. The language barrier further complicated matters; although both spoke Arabic, regional variations can often be so extensive as to render the language unintelligible to people from other regions, as in this case. One's Arabic was Sudanese, the other's Palestinian-Gazan. On one end of the line was the Sudanese dictator, Omar al-Bashir, and on the other was Prime Minister Netanyahu's envoy to the Middle East and Africa, known by his nom de guerre, "Maoz."[287] The call, which would have seemed like a flight of fancy even a short time previously, was brief: a few pleasantries, a short introduction and an agreement to set up a communication channel. "I want ties with Israel," al-Bashir told Maoz. "From today, I ask that you speak with Salah Gosh." If al-Bashir was the dictator, Gosh was the executioner. He was the director of Sudan's National Intelligence and Security Service under al-Bashir and served as his eyes and ears in Sudan. It was Gosh who organized the government militias responsible for some of the atrocities in Darfur, and he was even Osama bin Laden's point of contact with the Sudanese government in the '90s.[288] He was not the first murderer Maoz had dealings with, but he was undoubtedly the worst of them.

Until a few months earlier, Maoz had been dedicating most of his time to other clients—in the military branch of Hamas in Gaza. He was born and grew up in southern Israel, where he still lives today. When he enlisted in the Israeli Security Agency, the Shin Bet, around two decades ago as a handler, his first job was to recruit and manage assets in the Bedouin community in the south. He quickly rose through the ranks and gained a reputation for his exceptional ability to read people and situations, and to know which buttons to press to make people cooperate with him. When Meir Ben-Shabbat entered his role as head of the Southern Command of the Shin Bet, he recruited Maoz as his head of operations. A few years later, he was promoted to head of the Gaza Division. Maoz gained a reputation as the "Dr. Hamas" of the Israeli intelligence community, and by the age of 40 he was responsible for all intelligence-gathering and operations in the Gaza Strip. He was on the fast track to the top of the organization. But nothing prepared him for the twist in the tale that was to come.

In late 2017, after the government approved the appointment of Ben-Shabbat to lead the National Security Council in the Prime Minister's Office, he came calling for Maoz. "Come to the NSC. There's interesting stuff going on and you can make an impact," he told him. Maoz refused politely. He didn't feel he had achieved everything he wanted to in his current role and leaving it for the uncharted terrain of the gray and lifeless NSC felt irresponsible, verging on insane. Ben-Shabbat didn't give up. He pursued him doggedly for five months, calling him every few weeks until Maoz finally cracked. Prime Minister Netanyahu approached the head of the Shin Bet, Nadav Argaman, in person to ask him to loan Maoz to the NSC, and two weeks later he was standing in the Prime Minister's Office. Ben-Shabbat informed him that he wanted him to set up a Middle East Division within the National Security Council, with a special focus on building relationships with Egyptian intelligence on Gaza, and that he would be Netanyahu's envoy to the Arab world. A source in the NSC told me that Maoz was not overly enthused with the prospect. "Again with the Arab world? Give me something in Europe or America," he asked Ben-Shabbat. The national security advisor pondered for a minute, then replied: "You know what? Take Africa too."

It is difficult to overstate just how extraordinary al-Bashir's decision to approach Israel in January 2019 was. Sudan is not defined as an enemy country in Israeli law, yet the two nations have long regarded each other with open hostility, and they had no diplomatic relations. For many years, Hamas maintained a headquarters in Sudan, and it was a military and diplomatic ally of Iran and Hezbollah. The Iranians used it as a transit point for smuggling weapons into the Gaza Strip, and even built a huge arms manufacturing facility near Khartoum to build long-range rockets for Hamas and the Islamic Jihad. From 2008 to 2014, there were a string of aerial bombardments within Sudan on weapons convoys making their way to the Gaza Strip, on an Iranian weapons ship docked in Port Sudan and on a rocket factory near Khartoum. The Sudanese government blamed the attacks on Israel, although Jerusalem never claimed responsibility for them.

The hostility toward Israel began decades earlier. During Israel's War of Independence in 1948, Sudan sent reinforcements to the Egyptian army. In the Six-Day War of 1967, Sudan once more sent military reinforcements to assist the Egyptians against Israel. In the immediate aftermath of the war, the Arab League convened a summit in Khartoum, where the gathered Arab leaders signed the infamous "Three Nos of Khartoum" decree: no peace with Israel, no negotiations with Israel and no recognition of Israel. Sudanese law stated that Israel was the only country in the world Sudanese citizens were forbidden from traveling to. Sudanese people who entered Israel risked trial and lengthy jail sentences on their return. For decades, Sudan boycotted Israeli goods and forbade any contact with Israeli entities.

The shift began in late 2014. The combination of Israeli bombardments and heavy diplomatic pressure and financial support from Saudi Arabia and the UAE slowly shifted the Sudanese away from Iranian influence. As a first step, they expelled the Iranian cultural attaché from the embassy in Khartoum on suspicions of espionage and closed a number of Iranian cultural centers that were active in the country and accused of spreading Shia ideology. A few months later, Sudan joined the coalition established by the Saudis to fight the Houthi rebels in Yemen, and even sent military forces to join in the fighting. In January 2016, following the assault on the Saudi embassy in Tehran, Sudan cut off all diplomatic ties with Iran. The realignment was complete.

While it was cutting off ties with Iran, a fierce public debate arose in Sudan regarding normalization with Israel. The main goal was to bring about a thaw with the United States so that it would in turn lift the economic sanctions on Sudan. Supporters of normalization took the view that the road to Washington, DC passed through Jerusalem. Israel heard these voices. The Ministry of Foreign Affairs and the Prime Minister's Office approached the US administration and a few European Union member states and encouraged them to improve their relations with Sudan. Senior Israeli officials told me at the time that they had emphasized to the Americans and Europeans that they could not ignore the positive steps Sudan had taken and they should make an effort to reciprocate by, for example, wiping part of Sudan's huge foreign debt, which stood at close to 50 billion dollars.

After I published a few articles on Sudanese–Israeli relations, a few Sudanese journalists reached out to me. We followed each other on Twitter and started exchanging direct messages. That in itself was another sign of the changes taking place in the country.

Contacts with Sudanese journalists expanded and grew into a close professional relationship. In August 2017, one of my Sudanese colleagues sent me a link to a video clip on the YouTube channel of Sudania 24, the Sudanese public broadcaster. "You have to see this," he wrote. I clicked on the link and found myself watching an interview with the minister of investment in the Sudanese government, Mubarak Al-Fadil, in which he spoke out in support of ties with Israel. "We have no problem with normalization with Israel…. The Palestinians normalized relations with Israel…even Hamas speaks with Israel," said Al-Fadil, who was the chairman of the National Umma Party at the time.[289] He spent several minutes unleashing criticism at the Palestinians and praising Israeli democracy. It was a diplomatic earthquake. Al-Fadil came under extensive criticism for the interview, but also received no small measure of support. President al-Bashir may have spoken out against his views, but the taboo was broken. Normalization with Israel was no longer a dirty word in Sudanese politics.

To properly understand the background to the agreement with Sudan, it's important to first delve into Israel's relationship with another African country: Chad. Three weeks after Maoz took up his new position in the Prime Minister's Office, he was handed his first assignment by Netanyahu: opening a direct flight path from Israel to Latin America over Africa. Such a flight path would shorten the journey time by at least three hours. There was just one problem: it would require permission to enter the airspace of Chad, Sudan and Libya—three Arab and Muslim nations that had no diplomatic relations with Israel, two of which effectively acted as enemy countries. Chad was circled on the map as the most likely prospect. The huge, majority-Muslim Central African country had already had diplomatic relations with Israel in the past. The first president of Chad, François Tombalbaye, even visited Jerusalem in the 1960s. Then, in 1972, under pressure from Libyan leader Muammar Gaddafi, Chad cut off relations. "Renewing ties is much easier than creating new ones from scratch," Maoz told me in an interview we conducted in July 2021 following his retirement from the Shin Bet and the National Security Council.[290]

Israel has attempted to renew ties with Chad three times in recent years. In 2005, the foreign ministry tried and failed. A few years later it was the Mossad's turn, and it was equally unsuccessful. In 2016, the director general of the foreign ministry, Dore Gold, flew to Chad and met with President Idriss Déby at his presidential palace in a remote town in the Sahara desert. Against expectations, Gold's visit did not lead to renewed ties with Chad either. Each side pinned the blame for the failure on the other, and the resulting acrimony led to a two-year suspension of talks. Maoz started looking for communication channels with the leadership of Chad. He heard from former diplomats, businessmen and even rabbis who offered to act as intermediaries. The biggest challenge was deciding who was a serious prospect and who was a charlatan. Finally, in June 2018, one of his intermediaries connected him to Chad's national security advisor, General Djiddi Salah, who was a useful stepping-stone to the truly important contact: Colonel Abdelkerim Déby, the president's son and cabinet secretary. The younger Déby, only 27 years old at the time, had spent four years at West Point and his English was good. At their first meeting—a secret rendezvous in a European capital—Maoz was surprised to discover that he also knew a few words in Hebrew that he had picked up from Jewish friends in the United States. The next stage was direct phone contact between Maoz and President Idriss Déby himself. Then, Déby's son came to Israel bearing a letter from the president declaring his desire to renew ties. "I wanted to make sure we weren't setting ourselves up for humiliation, and I needed the letter to convince the Israeli foreign ministry that this was serious," Meir Ben-Shabbat told me.[291] After the visit and the letter came a phone call between Netanyahu and the president of Chad. Maoz told me that Netanyahu and Déby discussed the possibility of renewing ties and of a visit to Israel by the latter. At one stage, they even switched to speaking in French.

Chad was a French colony until 1960. Following independence, it became a corrupt African dictatorship. President Déby ruled Chad from 1990, after he ousted Hissène Habré in a military coup. A year later, he was appointed president, but he was only formally elected in 1996. Déby was elected for two terms, but in 2006 he changed the constitution to enable him to run again. Those elections were beset by widespread allegations of fraud. At this point, the country began to slide into one-man rule. In 2018, Déby changed the constitution once more. He removed the position of prime minister and changed the system of government to a presidential one that afforded him almost unrestricted power, declaring that he would be eligible to rule until at least 2033. The Freedom House NGO lists Chad as "not free" in its index.[292] The government has cracked down on opposition politicians, human rights activists and critical journalists, some of whom have been arrested or "disappeared." President Déby ran the country like a Byzantine court, and appointed members of his own tribe and family to the government, including 12 of his children. His fourth wife, Hinda Déby, was his personal secretary and the most powerful woman in Chad. One of her brothers was the president's chief of staff and three others were government ministers.

On November 11, 2018, Prime Minister Netanyahu flew to Paris. The official purpose was a ceremony to mark 100 years since the end of the First World War, together with dozens of leaders from around the world. But a secondary purpose was a clandestine meeting between Netanyahu and the son of President Déby, intended to finalize the details of his father's visit to Israel. The evening before that meeting, however, a special forces unit of the IDF was exposed by Hamas operatives in Khan Yunis in the Gaza strip. In the ensuing firefight, the commander of the unit was killed, and the remaining fighters were evacuated in a heroic mission. Hamas responded with rocket fire, Netanyahu cut short his visit and returned to Israel. The meeting was canceled.

The diplomatic process with Chad led to a power struggle within the Israeli government. The foreign ministry and the Mossad didn't like what Maoz and the National Security Council were doing. The head of the Mossad, Yossi Cohen, and the director general of the foreign ministry, Yuval Rotem, told Meir Ben-Shabbat and Netanyahu that President Déby was not serious, and it was a waste of their time. "We've been down this road before. He's already run away several times," Rotem said, according to a source who participated in one of the discussions. In September 2018, in an effort to get the foreign ministry on board with the move, Ben-Shabbat arranged a meeting between Rotem and the foreign minister of Chad at the UN General Assembly in New York. Even after that meeting, Rotem remained skeptical. He objected to the visit by the president of Chad and argued that there was no point inviting him before he declared his intention to renew ties in writing, and not only in general platitudes. "You're setting up the prime minister to fail," he warned Ben-Shabbat. But the national security advisor trusted his personal impression from his conversations with the Chadians and Maoz's gut instinct. Netanyahu eventually took the side of his advisors over the foreign ministry. Two weeks after the canceled Paris meeting, the president of Chad landed in Israel. "We seek to begin a new era of diplomatic ties," said Déby at the press conference with Netanyahu in Jerusalem. Just under two months later, in January 2019, I boarded an El Al flight at the crack of dawn to N'Djamena, the capital of Chad, for the first ever visit to the country by an Israeli prime minister. The head of the Mossad and the director general of the foreign ministry, both of whom thought (and perhaps hoped) that the trip would end in failure, did not join the delegation.

As the plane began to make its descent, I looked out of the window and saw why Chad has been given the unflattering nickname, "the dead heart of Africa." The Sahara desert covers the majority of its territory, it has no access to the sea and Lake Chad, its primary source of water, has lost 90 percent of its capacity since the late 1960s as a result of climate change, population growth and mismanagement of natural resources. The harsh climate, sandstorms, lack of water and locust infestations make it hard to develop agriculture and create extreme food insecurity and poverty. More than 80 percent of the population is below the international poverty line. N'Djamena, the most developed area in the country, resembles a dreadfully rundown version of Gaza. It's possible to count the number of incoming flights at its small international airport on one hand. The only destinations outside of Africa are Paris and Istanbul. Aside from the main road that connects the airport to the presidential palace and two or three more main thoroughfares, most of the movement around the city is along dirt tracks. As soon as I got off the plane, I was met head-on by the oppressive and dry desert heat. Not too far away, I could see two Israeli Air Force Hercules planes. They had brought with them armored vehicles and no fewer than 150 security guards, some from a special unit of the Shin Bet, who were armed to the teeth. Alongside them were hundreds of soldiers from Chad's special forces, who accompanied the Israeli prime minister's convoy. Evidence of poverty and neglect was visible at every turn on the road to the palace. As the gates of the presidential compound opened, they revealed a surreal vision: behind the high walls lay a beautifully maintained garden in bloom, with water fountains and an impressive building with marble floors and crystal chandeliers. The stark contrast between the streets of the capital and the presidential palace encapsulated everything we needed to know about Chad.

When Netanyahu landed in N'Djamena, the fine print had not yet been finalized on the agreement to rebuild diplomatic ties. Elections in Israel were less than three months away. A former senior official in the National Security Council told me that, during the meeting at the presidential palace, Déby promised Netanyahu that he would renew ties with Israel and build them up irrespective of the results and who was elected prime minister.[293] Outside the room where Netanyahu and Déby were sitting, the prime minister's advisors continued to negotiate with the Chadian president's son and his foreign minister on the wording of the draft agreement. The talks dragged on, and Netanyahu grew impatient, especially as his Shin Bet security team wanted to take off back to Israel before nightfall. Even when an agreement was finally reached, the signing was delayed. When the sides wanted to print out the final draft and submit it to Netanyahu and Déby for their approval, they discovered there was no working printer in the presidential compound. The signing was pushed back by more than an hour while a printer was located and brought in from one of the nearby government ministries. At long last, Netanyahu and Déby signed the accord. "We're making new inroads into the Muslim world," Netanyahu declared at the press conference following the signing, and hurried back to the airport to board the flight home. Maoz told me that Netanyahu spoke the truth. The renewed ties with Chad were a breakthrough that resonated around Africa and the entire Arab world. "To an extent, it all started there," he said. Ben-Shabbat agreed. "Idriss Déby was the first," he said.[294] "He came of his own accord, without the Americans pushing him. He did it all without knowing if he would be able to convince his public that it was worth doing. In hindsight, Chad was the first country in the Abraham Accords." In mid-April 2021, Idriss Déby died. He was reportedly killed in a battle with rebels in northern Chad, but the exact circumstances of his death remain unclear to this day. His son, Mahamat Déby, took his place and at the time of writing serves as the interim president.

When President Idriss Déby visited Israel in November 2018, Netanyahu told him of his desire to create a direct flight path between Israel and Latin America, crossing the airspace of Chad and Sudan. Déby offered to mediate with Sudan and placed his national security advisor, General Saleh, on the case. That led to the January 2019 phone call between Maoz and the Sudanese dictator al-Bashir, and the contacts between Netanyahu's advisors and the head of Sudanese intelligence, Salah Gosh. The prime minister, who wanted to use the flight to Chad to assess Sudan's resolve, asked his team to seek approval from the government in Khartoum to return from Chad via Sudanese airspace. Maoz called Gosh and relayed the request. "Go," he replied without a second's hesitation. A surprised Maoz asked whether it would be possible to receive official authorization from the aviation authority. "No need. Fly high and fast," Gosh told him. "There are no rockets?" asked Maoz. "Nothing. Don't worry," said the head of Sudanese intelligence. As the El Al plane approached Sudanese airspace, the pilots contacted the control tower in Khartoum. They identified themselves and asked permission to enter. There was no response from the other side. The plane continued on its way to Israel, with no questions asked.

Omar al-Bashir, the dictator who had ruled Sudan since the military coup in 1989, was among the most reviled leaders in the world. In 2009, an international warrant was issued for his arrest, after the International Criminal Court of The Hague charged him with crimes against humanity and war crimes in Darfur, where Sudanese forces massacred hundreds of thousands of people. In a first against a sitting ruler, the judges accused him of "intentionally directing attacks against an important part of the civilian population of Sudan; murdering, raping, torturing, forcibly transferring large numbers of the population and pillaging their property."[295] The call between al-Bashir and Maoz in early 2019 and the contacts with his head of intelligence didn't lead anywhere. A former senior official in the National Security Council told me that, aside from the general repulsion with al-Bashir, it was also clear that his continued rule was faltering, and that it may only be a matter of time until he was usurped. Within weeks, this assessment came true.

In early April, mass protests against al-Bashir resumed. They swelled until they eventually reached a point where the protesters were filling the square in front of the military headquarters and calling on the generals to remove the dictator. Within a matter of days, the military switched sides, from protecting the government to protecting the protesters. On April 11, 2019, there was a coup. Al-Bashir was overthrown, and the leaders of the military, headed by General Abdel Fattah al-Burhan, took power. The protesters, mostly young people who were not interested in replacing one military regime with another, stayed in the streets and demanded a civilian transition government to run the country. Over the course of several months, the generals negotiated with representatives of the "Forces of Freedom and Change." The result was a power-sharing agreement to divide the political power in the country between the military and a civilian government that would include representatives of the protesters for a period of 39 months, during which the country would transition from dictatorship to democracy.

Into this political drama stepped Nick Kaufman, a British-Israeli lawyer from Jerusalem, and Najwa Gadaheldam, a Sudanese diplomat. They had met by chance a year earlier in the business lounge at the airport in Addis Ababa. Kaufman left a 16-year career as a prosecutor in the Jerusalem District of the State Attorney's Office to pursue his true passion: international criminal law. He entered the small niche of defending people accused of war crimes at the International Criminal Court in The Hague. His Israeli guile and chutzpah—and his British passport—placed him in high demand, with clients ranging from the Gaddafi family in Libya, to Aleksandar Cvetković, accused (and later acquitted) of involvement in the Srebrenica massacre in Bosnia, all the way to the former vice president of Congo, Jean-Pierre Bemba.

Gadaheldam, a Sudanese-born mechanical engineer specializing in renewable energy, rose to become one of the most influential and powerful diplomats in Africa. She met the president of Uganda, Yoweri Museveni, while working at the United Nations Industrial Development Organization in Vienna. The two formed an instant connection. The Ugandan president sought her advice regarding his country's fraught relationship with Sudan, and she in turn offered to deliver a conciliatory message to al-Bashir. Her attempts at mediating between the two bore fruit. From that point, she became a close advisor to both Museveni and al-Bashir.[296] She was involved in the peace treaty discussions with South Sudan, sealing a deal for the release of Sudanese soldiers who had been kidnapped by rebel groups, and at one point Museveni even considered appointing her as his foreign minister, even though she was not even a Ugandan citizen.

When Gadaheldam entered the business lounge, huffing and puffing, Kaufman gave her a hand with her suitcases and offered up his seat. The two quickly struck up a lively conversation. She talked about her ties to Sudan and Uganda, and he mentioned the African clients he was representing in The Hague. Before they left, they exchanged business cards. They took to speaking every few weeks. Kaufman repeatedly asked her to help him get to Sudan and meet with al-Bashir to offer to represent him in The Hague, but protests that broke out soon after made it impossible. Al-Bashir's downfall a few months later further strengthened Gadaheldam's position, and she became a close confidant of the new interim ruler, General al-Burhan.

In 2019, when the Sudanese government changed leadership, Kaufman offered to visit Khartoum to meet with al-Burhan and discuss The Hague with him. "Najwa agreed and proposed another idea: to bring al-Burhan a letter from Prime Minister Netanyahu," Kaufman revealed to me.[297] He believed that the timing, months before the elections in Israel, meant that Netanyahu would agree to any Sudanese proposal, if only to help him register a diplomatic achievement he could then wave in front of the Israeli electorate. Kaufman even knew exactly whom to speak to. A few months earlier, he had been invited to a meeting at the Prime Minister's Office with Maoz, Netanyahu's envoy to the Arab world and Africa. Maoz wanted to utilize Kaufman's connections in the continent, specifically in Libya. "He gave me a laundry list of countries that were of interest to him," Kaufman said. In December 2019, he met with Maoz once more, and told him about Najwa Gadaheldam and her unrivaled proximity to the interim ruler of Sudan. Maoz liked what he heard, and Kaufman arranged a call for him with the Sudanese intermediary for a few days later.

Maoz told me that he and Gadaheldam hit it off straight away. It was she who suggested that he bring her the letter from Netanyahu for al-Burhan. Maoz agreed and suggested meeting in Uganda. "No, I need you to come to Sudan," she replied. He tried to explain that, for security reasons, that would not be possible, but she insisted. It was Kaufman who proposed a solution. He told the pair that he had been meaning to fly to Khartoum anyway to discuss al-Bashir's situation in The Hague with the new transitional government. He could deliver the letter from Netanyahu while he was there. Maoz approved, but added a cautionary note. "He said, if you go to Khartoum, it's at your own expense and your own responsibility. You are not there as a formal representative of the State of Israel, and if anything happens to you, we will not come to your rescue," Kaufman recalled.

On January 1, 2020, Kaufman boarded a flight to Addis Ababa, and from there another one to Khartoum. In his bag, he carried an official letter from Netanyahu to al-Burhan, offering a meeting to discuss the possibility of establishing diplomatic relations between Israel and Sudan. Gadaheldam was waiting for him at the airport, together with members of the Sudanese General Intelligence Service. They took him to the Corinthia Hotel in the capital, which had been built a few years earlier with funds donated by the Libyan leader, Muammar Gaddafi, as a goodwill gesture to al-Bashir. In the intervening years, Gaddafi had been overthrown and executed, and al-Bashir had been overthrown and jailed. January 1 is also Independence Day in Sudan, so the Sudanese intelligence agents accompanying Kaufman took him on a tour of the city and to a viewpoint over the Nile River that runs through it. When they returned to their car, they discovered someone had broken into it and stolen some of the equipment of the Sudanese security guards. Fortunately, Kaufman had not left the letter from Netanyahu in the vehicle. A few hours later, he and Gadaheldam met with al-Burhan. Kaufman gave him the short letter in Arabic from Netanyahu and received one in return expressing a willingness to meet, as agreed. When he returned to Israel, he delivered the letter to Maoz.

From there, the process accelerated. On January 6, Maoz flew to Entebbe in Uganda for a secret meeting with Gadaheldam and one of al-Burhan's senior advisors. Maoz outlined what Sudan stood to gain from ties with Israel, and pressed home the two countries' shared interests. The meeting was a great success. While the discussions were still ongoing, al-Burhan's advisor called Khartoum and put Maoz on the line with al-Burhan himself. This first call was also successful. They agreed to proceed to a leaders' summit facilitated by President Museveni. For the Ugandan president, this constituted a great diplomatic achievement. When Maoz arrived at the airport in Entebbe for his return flight to Israel, he found four crates of pineapples waiting for him—a gift from Museveni.

Al-Burhan's primary motivation for this unexpected about-face in long-held Sudanese policy was the severe economic crisis gripping his country, a result of years of crippling US sanctions targeting the regime of al-Bashir. Al-Burhan set himself a goal to get Sudan taken off the US Department of State's list of state sponsors of terrorism. One of the ways to achieve that was to improve ties with Israel. Netanyahu agreed to help. A week before the meeting in Uganda, he visited Washington, DC for the unveiling ceremony of the Trump Plan. He met with Secretary of State Pompeo and lobbied him to remove Sudan from the terror list. "The Sudanese are moving in a new and positive direction," Netanyahu said to Pompeo. "Al-Burhan wants to end his country's isolation." Pompeo called al-Burhan the day before the meeting in Uganda and invited him to Washington. For Sudan's interim leader, this was the proof he needed that the historical step he was planning was indeed the right move.

The meeting had been scheduled for February 3, 2020. The idea was that Netanyahu would arrive in Uganda officially, and al-Burhan would do so in secret. After the meeting, a decision would be made on whether to put out a statement or whether to keep it under wraps. The whole process encountered significant opposition within the Mossad, which had been in contact with Sudanese intelligence during the al-Bashir years. When members of the Mossad learned about the contacts ahead of the meeting between Netanyahu and al-Burhan, Director Yossi Cohen sent Netanyahu a letter complaining about Maoz and claiming that the move would be detrimental to ties with Sudan. Cohen even instructed his staff not to take part in the preparations for the trip and not to attend the discussions that were taking place within the National Security Council. By the time Netanyahu flew to Uganda, however, Cohen was already on board. Maoz and a few people from the National Security Council spent five days in Uganda preparing the meeting, together with Najwa Gadaheldam and al-Burhan's team. A few days before Netanyahu was due to fly, leaks started to emerge regarding the Sudanese angle to the trip, but the Israeli Military Censor came down hard and prevented any reporting on the subject in the press. A few hours after Netanyahu landed in Entebbe, the veil of secrecy was slowly lifted. It began with a tweet by a Sudanese journalist reporting that al-Burhan was also on his way to Uganda and continued with a brief statement about the historic meeting between Netanyahu and al-Burhan issued by the Israeli prime minister's press team shortly before the main evening news shows on television. "It was agreed to start cooperation leading to normalization of the relationship between the two countries," the statement said.[298]

In the hours that preceded that statement, however, things had not gone entirely smoothly. At one point, the meeting between Netanyahu and al-Burhan nearly fell apart in acrimony. The interim leader of Sudan expressed an interest in moving ahead with forming relations. "I have nothing against Israel," he said to Netanyahu. "Let me lay the groundwork among the people. The Sudanese do not hate Israel, and I believe we will be able to push it through." In exchange, however, he demanded that Israel leverage its influence in the White House and convince the Trump administration to remove it from the terror list, and for the international community to provide financial support for Sudan. Cohen grumbled his way through the meeting, and told Netanyahu that he did not think al-Burhan was serious. "We cannot promise you anything regarding the Americans," Cohen told the interim leader. A former senior official in the National Security Council said that Cohen continued his combative stance toward al-Burhan, until eventually Gadaheldam had to step in and demand that the Mossad director moderate his tone.[299] The atmosphere was tense, and she suggested to Maoz that something had to be done to avoid the meeting imploding. Maoz asked for permission to speak, and attempted to placate the irate Sudanese leader. "Don't worry, we'll do what we can to help with the Americans," he told him. The crisis was averted and the mood improved.

The meeting between al-Burhan and Netanyahu in Uganda was met with disbelief in Sudan. The head of the civilian government, Prime Minister Abdalla Hamdok, hurried to put out a press statement stressing that he had not been consulted or informed of the meeting, and that foreign policy fell under the authority of the civilian government and not al-Burhan. A spokesperson for the civilian government went further still and declared that Hamdok intended to request clarifications from al-Burhan regarding the summit meeting with Netanyahu. For his part, al-Burhan was not overly moved by the criticism. He said he had chosen to hold the meeting because it served Sudan's interests. "Al-Burhan is courageous beyond belief, a man who really cares about his people," a former senior Israeli official who met with al-Burhan on several occasions told me. He claimed that al-Burhan had been willing to proceed with normalization right after his meeting with Netanyahu, but opposition from Hamdok prevented it. But beyond the widespread criticism, the meeting also emboldened those in Sudan who supported normalization. Even at the time, however, in February 2020, Netanyahu and his advisors understood that any real breakthrough would have to be one part of a trilateral process with the United States that included removing Sudan from the terror list. Israel therefore began mediating between the government in Khartoum and the Trump administration.

On the evening of the meeting between al-Burhan and Netanyahu, I was interviewed on a popular evening news show on Israel's Channel 13. The presenter, Tal Berman, asked me about the significance of the meeting in Uganda, and I replied that it was the single greatest diplomatic achievement of Netanyahu's decade in power. For the first time as prime minister, he had held a public meeting with the leader of an Arab country with which Israel had no prior diplomatic relations and which was considered incredibly hostile. As far as he was concerned, it was vindication for his approach, which prioritized promoting ties with the Arab world over peace with the Palestinians. Netanyahu's advisors eagerly seized upon the interview, and the next day I found myself starring in the Likud's election campaign on social media. Netanyahu had avoided meeting with me entirely since 2010, yet to my surprise his supporters were suddenly embracing me. This didn't last long. A few days later, when I criticized Netanyahu over a different matter, his fervent supporters reverted to attacking me. One of them even asked me on Twitter: "Why did you have nothing good to say about Netanyahu's diplomatic breakthrough with Sudan?" I was quickly learning that, for an increasing number of Israelis, facts were becoming a luxury commodity.

A combination of the Israeli elections and the global pandemic meant that talks between Israel and Sudan were placed on the backburner. Maoz kept up the weekly talks with al-Burhan and his advisors, and gradually gained their trust. As a result, in March 2020, Sudan allowed El Al planes evacuating Israelis from South Africa and Latin America in response to COVID-19 fears to cross through its airspace. In April, US Secretary of State Mike Pompeo landed in Israel for a visit. Israeli officials told me that Netanyahu repeated to Pompeo his view that Sudan presented an opportunity, and encouraged him to look into the matter and to speak directly not only with Prime Minister Hamdok, but also with the head of the Sovereignty Council and de-facto head of state, al-Burhan. A few days after his visit to Jerusalem, Pompeo spoke with al-Burhan, who pressed the secretary of state on removing Sudan from the list of state sponsors of terrorism.

Progress was slow but steady. But then, in early May 2020, tragedy struck and threatened to put a major spanner in the works. Najwa Gadaheldam called Maoz and told him she wasn't feeling well, and that she was on her way to the military hospital in Khartoum. "It's probably the diabetes," she said. Within days, it became clear that she had caught COVID-19, along with several other advisors of al-Burhan. Unlike them, underlying medical conditions meant she was in a high-risk group. Her health deteriorated rapidly. Netanyahu called al-Burhan and told him that Israel wanted to help save the life of the architect of the relations between the two countries. The Prime Minister's Office called in

Gal Lusky, the founder of Israel Flying Aid (IFA), an organization that provides medical and humanitarian support in disaster areas around the world. Lusky and her team often work in countries that don't have diplomatic relations with Israel, including Sudan.

The plane leased by IFA was loaded with dozens of boxes of medicine and medical supplies. Maoz and two Israeli doctors were also on board. Israel was in lockdown, and Ben Gurion Airport was almost completely paralyzed, which meant the unusual flight immediately drew attention on flight-tracking apps. But nobody knew who was on board or what the purpose was. When the plane touched down in Khartoum, Maoz and the Israeli doctors headed straight to the military hospital. Dressed from head to toe in PPE to protect against the virus, they entered the unit where Gadaheldam was being treated. For the local doctors, this was their first-ever meeting with Israeli medical professionals. They stood around her bed together and attempted to stabilize her condition enough to transport her to Israel for treatment, but their efforts were in vain. Gadaheldam's saturation levels required external oxygenation and ventilation. A flight was out of the question. The Israeli doctors left equipment with their Sudanese colleagues with instructions for further treatment, and returned to the airport. The day after the delegation returned to Israel, the news filtered through to Jerusalem: COVID-19 had claimed the life of Najwa Gadaheldam. Perhaps counterintuitively, this tragedy dramatically improved the relations between the countries. "Al-Burhan saw this as a sign that Israel would not abandon its allies. He told us at the time, 'I'm with you until the end,'" Maoz recalled.[300]

The relationship with Sudan continued to cause tensions between the Mossad and the National Security Council, with both organizations fighting to claim the next breakthrough. This squabbling caused diplomatic incidents that cast dark clouds over the nascent relationship. A former senior official at the National Security Council told me about one case in which, after ties with Chad were renewed, the head of the Chadian intelligence agency—the Agence Nationale de Sécurité (ANS)—came to Israel for a visit. He mentioned that he had not spoken with anyone in the Mossad in years, and the team at the NSC decided to make the connection for him. During the talks between the Mossad and Chadian intelligence, the matter of Sudan came up. The head of the ANS offered to help, and told his counterpart, Yossi Cohen, about a man by the name of Mohamed Hamdan Dagalo, commonly known as "Hemeti." After the fall of al-Bashir, Hemeti was appointed deputy chairman of the transitional Sovereignty Council of Sudan—al-Burhan's number two. Before his rise to power, however, Hemeti had been the leader of a brutal militia responsible for mass murder and rape in Darfur. Over the years, Hemeti's militia took over gold mines and other large businesses in Sudan, and he became the richest person in the country. The ANS coordinated a meeting between the Mossad and Hemeti. The Qatar-affiliated *Al-Araby Al-Jadeed* news outlet reported that Yossi Cohen himself attended it.[301] Al-Burhan was surprised by news of the meeting between his deputy and the Mossad. A former senior official in the National Security Council said that al-Burhan expressed his deep dissatisfaction and demanded to know whether Israel was using his deputy to undermine him. It took a lot of work to mollify al-Burhan and assure him that he was the only point of contact for the prime minister of Israel.[302]

Progress in the talks between the United States and Sudan on removing Sudan from the terror list was also sluggish. That changed on August 13, 2020, when the normalization agreement between Israel and the United Arab Emirates was announced. In this new dynamic, the Trump administration was casting about for

428 | TRUMP'S PEACE | Maoz

additional countries that might join what would become known as the Abraham Accords. Senior Israeli and American officials told me that Israel then pointed the White House in the direction of Sudan. Israel suggested merging the discussions of Sudan's blacklisting by the US and its normalization talks with Israel. The Trump administration received a similar proposal from the UAE at the same time. Unlike Israel's accords with the United Arab Emirates and Bahrain, which the White House worked hard to facilitate, in this case it was Israel that pushed the United States and Sudan into each other's arms. Jerusalem's close ties with the Trump White House and the trust it had built up with Khartoum enabled Israel to resuscitate the faltering negotiations between the US and Sudan, and to put them on track for an agreement three months later.

When Pompeo visited Israel in late August 2020, Sudan occupied a prominent place on the agenda for his talks with Netanyahu. The US secretary of state had only minimal involvement in the accords with the UAE and Bahrain, and he wanted a notch in his own diplomatic belt. The White House and the Prime Minister's Office nudged him toward Sudan. The Israelis used their contacts with the Sudanese to arrange a direct flight for Pompeo to Khartoum. Before they took off, Pompeo's advisors received a thorough briefing from their Israeli counterparts, which even included tips on how to talk with the Sudanese leaders. In Khartoum, Pompeo met with al-Burhan, who was eager to make progress on both the terror list and the normalization accord. At the same time, he stressed to Pompeo that it would also require the approval of his prime minister, Hamdok. When Pompeo met Hamdok immediately after his meeting with al-Burhan, he offered him a deal: the US would remove Sudan from the terror list and offer financial aid to the beleaguered country in exchange for normalization with Israel.

Pompeo pushed for a snap decision. He told Hamdok that President Trump was ready to go straight away. Senior American officials told me that he even offered to call Trump and Netanyahu from the meeting room to seal the deal on the spot. Pompeo's overly aggressive approach intimidated and deterred the Sudanese prime minister; Hamdok wavered, and eventually told Pompeo that he was not yet ready to commit to such a step.

At the same time as Pompeo's visit to Sudan, a joint Israeli–American delegation departed for Abu Dhabi for their first visit since the announcement on normalization. Among those on board was Jared Kushner, who wanted to make the most of the remaining time before the November elections to rack up a few more diplomatic achievements for President Trump. Aryeh Lightstone, the senior advisor to Ambassador David Friedman, wanted to make progress with Sudan, and he proposed to Kushner that the United Arab Emirates be brought on board as part of those efforts. At the meeting with the national security advisor of the UAE, Sheikh Tahnoun bin Zayed, Kushner asked whether they would be willing to invite al-Burhan to Abu Dhabi so the sides could hold accelerated negotiations to break the existing deadlock between the United States and Sudan. The Emiratis were fully on board and even agreed to assist with the talks themselves. Kushner delegated the responsibility for leading the negotiations on the US side to Miguel Correa, from the National Security Council at the White House. That was where the problems started. Israel also offered to participate in the talks and to help them along, but Correa preferred to work alone. On September 21, he met with al-Burhan and the Sudanese foreign minister in Abu Dhabi. The talks quickly blew up. Senior Israeli and American officials told me that one reason for this was the gap between the reality of the economic aid package the US was willing to offer and the high expectations on the Sudanese side. Another comprised the cultural gaps and language barrier between the sides, which led to conflict between the negotiators—and ultimately to an impasse. Al-Burhan was furious. Maoz called the Sudanese leader and tried to placate him. He arranged a trilateral call with General Correa to smooth things over—but that went south too. The Israeli team reluctantly turned to Kushner and asked him to intervene. Together, they decided to inject the easygoing charm and smart political instincts of Lightstone into the negotiations with the Sudanese in order to counterbalance some of General Correa's rough edges.

After the talks collapsed, the Israelis and Emiratis tried to bridge the gaps, ease the tensions and frustrations and bring the sides back to the negotiating table. Senior Israeli officials told me that Israel and the UAE were at pains to emphasize to the Sudanese that they should accept the American offer, even if it was below their expectations, because they could be sure that any offer after the US elections would be far worse—if there would be one at all. At the same time, Israel and the UAE also asked the White House to sweeten the deal for the Sudanese as much as possible.

A month after the collapse of the talks in Abu Dhabi, the Israelis and Americans flew back to the Gulf together. This time it was to Manama to sign the agreement to formalize diplomatic ties. In between meetings, the question of Sudan came up again. Maoz and the director general of the Prime Minister's Office, Ronen Peretz, suggested arranging a negotiating session in Khartoum immediately after the visit to Bahrain to conclude things. Peretz and Maoz even offered to lease a plane at the expense of the Israeli government. General Correa didn't like the idea of Netanyahu's advisors joining the trip but, as they were his ride to Khartoum, he was left with little choice. On October 21, Maoz and Peretz took off for Sudan with Correa and Lightstone, in the hopes of returning with a deal. When they arrived at the presidential palace in Khartoum, Maoz and Peretz sat with al-Burhan while the American team negotiated with the Sudanese justice minister. After a few hours of negotiations, the talks were in danger of imploding once more—mostly around the question of who would make the first move.

The Sudanese wanted the United States to announce its removal from the state sponsors of terrorism list first. For their part, the Americans demanded that Sudan first announce normalization with Israel—or at the very least that the two statements be released simultaneously. Ultimately, the Americans gave in to Sudan. The amount of financial aid and grain supplies that Sudan would receive from the United States under the deal became another sticking point, as was the wording of the draft agreement between the sides and whether it would refer to "peace," "reconciliation" or "normalization." "You're making history here," Maoz told al-Burhan. "Don't get caught up in a few million dollars here or there, or whether we use this word or that word." He managed to convince al-Burhan, who summoned Prime Minister Hamdok into the room and ran through the details of the agreement with him. Hamdok gave it his blessing. Two days later, on October 23, 2020, in a phone call with Netanyahu and the leadership in Sudan, President Trump announced the agreement. "You think Sleepy Joe [Biden] could have made this deal, Bibi?" Trump asked Netanyahu in front of the cameras. The president was holding out for an endorsement from the prime minister of Israel on live TV two weeks out from the presidential election. Netanyahu sidestepped the question. Trump struggled to conceal his disappointment. He didn't forget this perceived slight.

The decision by Sudan's leaders to start normalizing relations with Israel was a very courageous one. The Sudanese government had to engage in a complete reversal of its previous open hostility to reconciliation and peace. Sudanese soldiers fought against Israeli soldiers in at least two wars. Israel killed Sudanese civilians in aerial bombardments on Sudanese territory—according to foreign reports—and even targeted the capital, Khartoum. In addition, al-Burhan and Hamdok sought normalization while leading a fragile transitional government that was attempting to rebuild a country on its knees following decades of brutal dictatorship. On the other hand, the Sudanese gained a lot from the normalization process with Israel. They were removed from the US list of state sponsors of terrorism, international sanctions on them were lifted, most of the lawsuits brought against Sudan in US courts were settled and they received an aid package totaling 700 million dollars plus food and fuel.

On January 6, 2021, while an angry mob of Trump supporters was storming the US Capitol in an attempt to prevent a joint session of Congress from formally declaring Joe Biden's electoral victory, US Secretary of the Treasury Steve Mnuchin was in Khartoum. In a small ceremony at the presidential palace, a representative of the Sudanese government signed a declaration expressing support for the Abraham Accords. That was the most the Trump administration could get from the Sudanese administration in the time they had left in office. Al-Burhan and Hamdok were already thinking about how to make sure that Biden didn't roll back Trump's commitments. The Israelis were equally concerned. They submitted a draft agreement on establishing diplomatic relations with Sudan, but the government in Khartoum didn't engage, stalling in the hopes of receiving an endorsement from the Biden administration. The Israeli government, fearing that the normalization process would fall apart unless it was anchored down, urged the Biden administration to invite Netanyahu, al-Burhan and Hamdok to an official ceremony at the White House to sign an agreement on establishing diplomatic relations in its very first weeks. The Biden administration did not heed the advice. One reason for this was their suspicions regarding Sudan's military leaders. When the Biden administration assumed office, they decided to strengthen the civilian government in Sudan and Prime Minister Hamdok over the military, in order to drive the transition to democracy. The Israeli government did not see things the same way. On January 25, 2020, Israel's minister of intelligence, Eli Cohen, made history when he became the first Israeli minister to visit Khartoum. He met with General al-Burhan and the Sudanese minister of defense, but not Prime Minister Hamdok or any other member of the civilian government. While the military was largely supportive of the normalization process with Israel, many members of the civilian government had reservations about it. Then-Foreign Minister Mariam al-Mahdi, for example, opposed abolishing an Israel boycott law when it was brought before the cabinet for a vote in April 2021. On the other hand, Nasreldin Abdelbari, who served as justice minister until the coup, was very supportive of the normalization process.

In the first months after Biden assumed office, Sudanese civilian officials told US diplomats in Khartoum that Israel was engaging only with the military and intelligence services and asked the Biden administration to intervene. According to a senior Israeli official, the State Department conveyed the message to Israel and explained that expanding contacts between the government in Jerusalem and the civilian faction of the Sudanese government could advance the normalization process. But a few weeks later, tensions were exacerbated when a Mossad-affiliated private jet landed in Khartoum. The officials from the Israeli spy agency came to meet with Hemeti, who had been trying to create his own channel of communication with the Israelis to promote his own domestic political agenda in Sudan. General al-Burhan was upset about the optics of the Mossad visit, which he saw as an attempt to undermine his authority.

Relations with Israel weren't the main source of tension between the military and the civilian government but it was a good litmus test for the growing political divide in the country. The trend was clear. Every month that passed brought more political instability. Several weeks before al-Burhan was supposed to hand over control of the Sovereignty Council to a civilian, everything came crashing down. The in-fighting between the military and the civilian politicians brought the democratic transition in Sudan to a halt. On October 25, 2021, a year after the phone call between Trump, Netanyahu, Hamdok and al-Burhan that turned over a new page in the US-Sudan relationship and launched the normalization process with Israel, the Sudanese military carried out a coup and took control of the country. Prime Minister Hamdok, who refused to support the coup and called for a popular uprising against the military, was put under house arrest, and several other key politicians were arrested. General al-Burhan dissolved the Sovereignty Council and announced a state of emergency. Shortly after, Sudanese civilians took to the streets of Khartoum and several other cities to protest. The Sudanese security forces responded with live fire against the demonstrators, killing several of them.

Just hours before the coup, US Envoy Jeffrey Feltman met with al-Burhan and Hamdok in Khartoum to try and find a solution to the standoff between the military and civilian wings of the government. Feltman told me that in a separate meeting on that same day, al-Burhan mentioned the possibility that elements within the Sudanese army might take matters into their own hands over tensions with the civilian government.[303] He warned al-Burhan that in case of a military coup, the US would respond forcefully, including by suspending all aid to Sudan and freezing many aspects of the bilateral relationship. Feltman departed Khartoum after the meeting, but by the time he arrived in Doha to catch a connecting flight back to Washington the first reports about the coup had started to emerge. He was stunned. A few days after the coup, the Biden administration announced it was freezing the 700 million dollar aid package to Sudan that it had received after the launch of the normalization process with Israel.

It is not completely clear to this day whether Israel knew in advance about al-Burhan's plans and whether it actively supported the coup. While Western governments unanimously condemned the military takeover, Israel kept silent—lending credibility to the perception in Sudan and in Washington that it was backing al-Burhan and the military. This wasn't far from the truth. In the year before the coup, the Israeli government continued to engage almost entirely with the military. Two weeks before the coup, a delegation of Sudanese military officials visited Israel and met with officials from the National Security Council and the Mossad. According to a senior Israeli official, the Sudanese officials gave a briefing about the political situation in the country but didn't mention any plans for a military takeover. In the days following the coup, the Biden administration asked for Israel's assistance. Secretary of State Antony Blinken called Minister of Defense Benny Gantz and asked that the Israeli government use its close relations with General al-Burhan to urge the military to restore the civilian government. Gantz was surprised Blinken approached him on this issue, because he wasn't involved in the relationship with Sudan in any capacity. Even after the normalization process with Sudan began, Gantz ordered the Ministry of Defense and the IDF not to engage with the Sudanese military until it was clear that the situation in Sudan was stable. But Gantz was not the only player in the Israeli security establishment. In the months leading up to the coup and even today, the relationship with Sudan has been handled by the National Security Council and the Mossad. Several days after the coup, officials from the two agencies visited Khartoum and met with their counterparts from the Sudanese military. The Israeli Prime Minister's office referred to it as a "fact-finding mission." But since that meeting, at least three more such visits have taken place. Sudanese military officials have also visited Israel at least twice since the coup. Most of the Mossad's engagement with Sudan during these months has been with al-Burhan's deputy, Hemeti. Last April, in an attempt to wrest back control of the contacts with Israel, al-Burhan appointed retired General Mubarak Abdullah Babiker as his special envoy for normalization with Israel. Abdullah Babiker visited Israel at around the same time for talks on the normalization of relations.[304] The continued engagement of the Israeli government with the Sudanese military and its silence over the coup reinforced the narrative that Israel supported the military takeover, damaging its standing among those within Sudan who supported the normalization process. "Israel has made a mistake," Sudan's outgoing ambassador to Washington told my colleague, Roi Kais.[305] "This is not the right way to enter Sudan. If you want the friendship of the Sudanese people, you need to enter through the door of the Sudanese people. Don't back the military that kills Sudanese civilians. The Sudanese people won't forget this."

Almost a year after the coup, Sudan remains in a deep political and economic crisis. All international efforts to mediate between the generals and the politicians have been unsuccessful and the attempts to reinstall the civilian government have likewise failed to bear fruit. Demonstrations against the military are still taking place every week around the country. Hundreds of civilians have been killed by the military during these protests. Thus, the coup in Sudan derailed the country's democratic transition, but it also suspended the normalization process with Israel. The Biden administration made it clear to the Israeli government that as long as the country remained under military rule, the US would oppose any renewed push for normalization, as such moves by Sudan's military leaders would lack credibility among the Sudanese people. The Biden administration urged Israel time and again to press Sudan's military leaders to end the coup.

At the time of writing, Israel remains silent. This conduct is morally repugnant and poor foreign policy. Sudan was neither as appealing a prospect as the UAE or Bahrain, nor as exciting and romantic as Morocco, but it was in dire need of Israel. In Sudan more than anywhere else, Israel could have played a unique role in the agriculture, health and water sectors, furthering its diplomatic interests while at the same time fulfilling the Jewish value of *tikkun olam* ("repairing the world") which, one would hope, will one day occupy a more central place among the priorities of policymakers in Israel.

The Moroccan Deal

The human element was the key component of all of the normalization agreements signed during Trump's term. In each of them, there were one or a few individuals who unexpectedly changed the course of history. The same was true with Morocco. It was hard to imagine how a single phone call between a former senior Mossad official, Ram "Rami" Ben-Barak, and Jewish-Moroccan businessman Yariv Elbaz, would act as the launchpad for a globetrotting process that culminated in renewed diplomatic ties between Israel and Morocco after a two-decade freeze.

In December 2017, Elbaz called Ben-Barak and asked him for an urgent meeting. Ben-Barak had been the director general of the Ministry of Intelligence until the year before. A former deputy director of the Mossad, he ran for the top job against his fellow deputy director, known by his first initial "N," and National Security Advisor Yossi Cohen. In December 2015, Cohen was appointed, in an evening full of drama befitting the finale of *Survivor* or *Big Brother* more than the appointment of a new leader of one of the most secretive and sensitive security organizations in the world. According to several reports, Prime Minister Netanyahu planned to appoint "N" to the role, but an intervention by his wife, Sara, tipped the scales in Cohen's favor.

Six months after he was overlooked, Ben-Barak resigned from the public sector after a career spanning more than three decades. He dipped his toe into the private sector and served as president of Fortify Solutions, a company managing security and agricultural projects in Africa. Elbaz, one of the most powerful figures in the food industry in Morocco, was the largest investor in the company. He had previously attempted to acquire Israel's Channel 10 and Sugat, a major Israeli food producer. He divides his time between homes in Switzerland, Morocco and Israel. Though he is not Israeli himself, much of his family lives there. The fluent Hebrew that spills from his tongue is a gift from his mother, who was a Hebrew teacher in Morocco. Elbaz would often visit Ben-Barak at his home in Israel's northern Jezreel Valley, where the two, who initially bonded over a shared love of horseback riding, would go out for long rides in the surrounding fields.

On one of those occasions, in late 2017, the Moroccan businessman told Ben-Barak an incredible story. The foreign minister of Morocco, Nasser Bourita, and his deputy, Mohcine El Jazouli, had approached him and asked for his support opening doors in Washington, DC on a significant diplomatic-security matter for the kingdom: the future of the disputed Western Sahara territory. Many readers may not even be familiar with this sparsely populated strip of land along the North Atlantic coastline, which was under Spanish control until 1975. When the Spanish left, Morocco stepped into the power vacuum, expelled some of the local residents (who fled to refugee camps in Algeria) and settled over 100 thousand Moroccan citizens in their place. In 1979, Morocco formally annexed the Western Sahara. The intervening years have seen cycles of violence and negotiations in the region, none of which achieved a breakthrough of any kind. Morocco steadfastly refused to grant independence to the Western Sahara and was willing to go only as far as autonomy. Throughout those years, no UN member state recognized the Moroccan occupation, and the European Union would regularly condemn Morocco for its actions.

Nerves were jangling in Rabat at the time. The new occupant of the White House well remembered Morocco's support for the presidential candidacy of his bitter rival, Hillary Clinton. Ten months after he entered office, communication between the palace in Rabat and the White House was almost entirely non-existent. Trump removed Morocco from any policy agenda, and the Moroccans, seeking a path back into the White House's good books, turned to Jerusalem. That was where Yariv Elbaz came into the picture. Senior officials in the Moroccan government assumed that the rich Jew with a home in Israel would have connections that could lead them to Washington. This assessment was entirely unsubstantiated. Elbaz knew nobody in Washington, nor did he have any connections in the Israeli government. The only person that came to mind was Ben-Barak. "When the king asks you to do something, you do it—but I have no idea where to begin, and I need your help," Elbaz told Ben-Barak.

Ben-Barak thought about it for a few minutes. "I have an idea. Tell the Moroccans the situation can be resolved, but it will need to be a deal that includes more than just the Western Sahara," he said. Using the instincts honed by his personal knowledge of the behind-the-scenes goings-on between Israel and Morocco, Ben-Barak proposed to Elbaz that in exchange for US support on the Western Sahara, Morocco would endorse Trump's plan to resolve the Israeli–Palestinian conflict and agree to renew diplomatic ties with Israel. The relationship between the two countries was informed by the long history of Morocco's large Jewish community. The Moroccans mediated between Israel and Egypt in the late 1970s, setting the two on the path to a peace treaty. In the 1990s, in the wake of the Oslo Accords, Israel and Morocco formalized diplomatic relations. Prime Minister Yitzhak Rabin and Foreign Minister Shimon Peres even visited Morocco in 1994 as guests of King Hassan II, where they opened the Israeli diplomatic mission in the country.

In 2000, following the outbreak of the Second Intifada, these ties were severed. The two countries closed their respective missions in Tel Aviv and Rabat. In the 20 years since, there have been a few covert meetings between the respective foreign ministers, as well as the occasional public one—such as Foreign Minister Silvan Shalom's trip to Morocco in 2003. Even though there were no diplomatic relations between the two, Israeli tourists continued to travel to the country on organized trips and through connecting flights from France and Italy. In recent years, the number of Israeli tourists to Morocco reached 50–70 thousand a year.

Ben-Barak made his suggestion without consulting anyone. He dangled the bait in the water without even being certain whether anyone would bite, but a week later, Elbaz came back to him with a positive answer. The Moroccans wanted to meet and to hear more. Ben-Barak realized he was in a bind. In his past life he had been a very senior official, but now he was a private citizen with no mandate to make diplomatic proposals on behalf of the government. He decided to turn to someone he thought would be able to help: Dore Gold. The two knew each other from Gold's days as director general of the Ministry of Foreign Affairs, when Ben-Barak had been his counterpart in the Ministry of Intelligence. In addition to Gold's diplomatic experience, he is also considered a close confidant of Netanyahu.

Ben-Barak and Elbaz arranged a meeting with Gold in his office at the Jerusalem Center for Public Affairs—the research institute he leads—in the city's Katamon neighborhood. They sat and went through the initiative at length with Gold and his deputy, Shimon Shapira. The two expressed enthusiasm and asked to participate. The next stage was a preliminary meeting with the Moroccan side in Berlin. Ben-Barak, Gold, Shapira and Elbaz arrived at the Intercontinental Hotel in the city and waited there for the Moroccan foreign minister, Bourita, and his deputy. The Moroccan officials were delayed and then delayed again, and at one point it appeared they might have gotten cold feet. Ben-Barak told me that he only learned later that Bourita had embarked on this journey of his own accord, without clearing it with the palace first and without receiving approval.[306] The foreign minister and his deputy were sitting in their hotel in Berlin and debating whether to attend the meeting with the Israelis or not. They finally arrived an hour and a half after the allotted time. Over the course of a meeting that lasted almost two hours, the doubts and hesitancy disappeared and the two sides went their separate ways, each to report back to their superiors before a follow-up meeting to decide whether to continue to pursue an agreement. Two weeks later, the four met again in London. This time, Bourita came with an unequivocal mandate from King Mohammed VI. "We can proceed," he said in the meeting.

From there, the ball moved into the court of the Israelis, who were tasked with bringing the Americans to the table. A few weeks passed with no news. Ben-Barak and Elbaz met with Gold and Shapira again. When they inquired about the lack of progress, Gold attempted to deflect the question. Shapira was less diplomatic. "Rami, let's put our cards on the table: you've gone from being an asset to an obstacle," he said. Ben-Barak was confused. "You know what Netanyahu's like," Shapira told him. "As long as you're involved, it won't go anywhere." Ben-Barak had announced a few weeks earlier that he was joining Yesh Atid, the centrist party led by Yair Lapid that was perceived as the main challenger to Netanyahu. That was enough to get him into Netanyahu's black books. "Dore Gold was afraid to go to Netanyahu and present the proposal to him and tell him that I was involved," Ben-Barak told me in one of our conversations.

Ben-Barak emphasized that he had no desire to become a problem, and that he was willing to step out of the picture immediately if it meant moving things forward. Elbaz followed the conversation with increasing horror. "You can't step out. The foreign minister of Morocco agreed on the basis of his personal trust in you," he said to Ben-Barak. The two understood that their collaboration with Gold had run its course and they needed to find a new way to reach the Americans. When Ben-Barak got back into his car for the journey from Jerusalem to Tel Aviv, he called one of his partners in the company and asked him to send an email to Elliott Abrams—a close friend from Ben-Barak's time in Washington.

Abrams was one of the leading foreign policy experts within the Republican establishment in the United States. He was a candidate for a senior position in the Trump administration but, following an unsuccessful job interview with the president, he found himself on the outside.[307] In the email to Abrams, Ben-Barak outlined the details of the "Moroccan deal" and asked for his assistance in arranging a meeting with President Trump's Middle East envoy, Jason Greenblatt. "Great idea," Abrams responded immediately. Within a few minutes he had spoken with Greenblatt, who was equally enthusiastic, and a quarter of an hour later Ben-Barak was staring at an invitation for a meeting at the White House.

The trip to the White House was supposed to be kept quiet. Aside from Elbaz, Ben-Barak and Abrams, nobody was meant to be in the know. Ben-Barak soon learned that Israel might be a small place, but Washington was even smaller. A few minutes after he took his seat in business class on the flight from Israel to the United States, he was joined by a high-profile fellow passenger: Yair Lapid, the chairman of the Yesh Atid party Ben-Barak had joined only a few weeks previously. "Where are you off to?" Lapid asked. "Business," replied Ben-Barak. But that was only the beginning. As he stood in line to check in at the front desk of the Four Seasons Hotel in Washington, Ben-Barak was astonished to see none other than Mossad Director Yossi Cohen enter the lobby with a team of people from the organization, some of whom had been under Ben-Barak's direct command. He stuck to his guns and mumbled something to them about being there on business. Worse was to come. The next day, he and Elbaz went to the White House for their meeting with Greenblatt. The meeting was delayed, and the two decided to pass the time with a guided tour of the historic building. When they returned to Greenblatt's office, they finally learned the reason for the delay. Out of the door stepped Ambassador Ron Dermer and Yuval Steinitz, the Israeli energy minister from Netanyahu's Likud party who a few years earlier had been Ben-Barak's boss at the Ministry of Intelligence. The two were taken aback at the sight of Ben-Barak. "What are you doing here?" Steinitz asked him. "Mingling," replied Ben-Barak. Dermer, his political antennae twitching, understood immediately that something was going on, and he called the Prime Minister's Office in Israel to inform them about Yair Lapid's man wandering around the White House.

When the meeting with Greenblatt finally got underway, they presented the proposed arrangement to him. Trump's envoy liked what he heard. He wanted to gather as much support from the Arab world as he could for Trump's Israeli–Palestinian peace plan, but he admitted that he was not overly informed on the details of the Western Sahara situation. "Let me check," he said. Greenblatt arranged a follow-up meeting with Ben-Barak and Elbaz in a month's time. The second meeting also took place in the White House, a few days before the annual gathering of the UN General Assembly. Throughout, no official state representative in Israel knew about the potential agreement. One reason was that Ben-Barak found every door he tried to walk through to be closed. Greenblatt brought all the relevant US administration officeholders to that second meeting, while Ben-Barak and Elbaz brought the Moroccan foreign minister, Nasser Bourita. The breakthrough there came from Elbaz, who suggested organizing a meeting between Bourita and Prime Minister Netanyahu on the sidelines of the UN General Assembly in New York a few days later. Bourita gave his approval. Greenblatt was raring to go and put Elbaz in touch with Maoz, Netanyahu's envoy to the Arab world. This was the end of the line for Ben-Barak's involvement, and the mantle was handed over to the Prime Minister's Office. On September 13, 2018, Elbaz and Maoz met for the first time. The next stage was a phone call between Maoz and Moroccan Deputy Foreign Minister El-Jazouli. Two weeks later, Netanyahu met with Bourita on the sidelines of the UN General Assembly. One of the prime minister's advisors who participated in the meeting told me that Israel proposed a two-phase process. The first phase would comprise setting up representative offices in Tel Aviv and Rabat and establishing direct flights between the two countries. In the second phase, the two countries would establish full diplomatic ties. "Bourita said that the king had given the move his blessing, but that they wanted our support with the Trump administration on the issue of the Western

Sahara," he told me.[308] Netanyahu promised to help. The meeting in New York was kept a secret for almost five months, until I heard about it in a chance encounter with a source who was not even directly involved, but had heard of it during a social event. It's a known aphorism in journalism that the best stories are stumbled upon by accident. When I revealed the details of the meeting on *Channel 13 News* on February 17, 2019, I had no idea of the full scale of the story, how convoluted and confidential the events behind it were and how much more was still to come.

The meeting between Netanyahu and Bourita was the start of a secret communication channel between Israel and Morocco. Leading the talks on Netanyahu's behalf were National Security Advisor Meir Ben-Shabbat and Maoz, who stayed in touch with Bourita and the senior advisor to the king of Morocco, Fouad Ali El Himma. This secret channel was established behind the back of the head of the Mossad, Yossi Cohen. When the secret talks between Netanyahu's advisors and the senior officials in the Moroccan government were exposed, the Israeli security establishment took to its internecine squabbles again. One of the triggers this time was a visit by Ben-Shabbat and Maoz to Morocco in November 2018 that had not been coordinated with Cohen and his team. A few days later, a report on the meeting was published in the Arabic-language press. Ben-Shabbat remains convinced to this day that Cohen was the source of the leak. "We told [the Moroccans] in the first meetings that daylight was the best tactic. We gave the example of Chad and emphasized that the reaction we got for renewing ties with them was not so bad," Netanyahu's advisor told me.[309] "But that leak still upset them a lot." That first meeting in Morocco jolted something among the prime minister's advisors. On a professional level, they were taken aback by the extent of the potential in renewing ties with Morocco.

On a personal level, they did not expect the genuine warmth and the immediate bond they felt with their counterparts. Ben-Shabbat and Maoz both have Moroccan heritage. One of the senior advisors to King Mohammed VI surprised Ben-Shabbat during the visit by taking him to visit the synagogue his father had attended in Casablanca. An emotional Ben-Shabbat was afforded the honor of being the cantor at the afternoon prayers. For him, this was one of the most powerful moments in the visit. "When we came back to Israel, I told the prime minister that I think we are completely ready to move forward with relations with Morocco," Ben-Shabbat told me.[310] "Netanyahu asked me what I was basing my judgment on. I told him that was my feeling from the mood in the street and the interactions with my Moroccan counterparts. I told the prime minister that the only thing left was to put in place the diplomatic conditions for renewing ties."

But the quarrel between the Mossad and the National Security Council was not over yet. A few days before the first round of the four-election cycle, in April 2019, I received an anonymous tip from a source within the Mossad. This was a first for me. The event the source described was so unusual that I knew straight away that it was a big story: contacts with Morocco and other Arab countries by Ben-Shabbat and Maoz had caused a conflict with Cohen. The head of the Mossad claimed the two were encroaching on his territory, and the Mossad even applied sanctions against Maoz and confiscated the operational passport he had received a few months earlier that enabled him to move around the Arab world more freely. When I approached the Prime Minister's Office for comment, Cohen was livid. Over the course of a 45-minute conversation, he switched between sweet talk and threats in an attempt to prevent the report's publication. The report was broadcast nonetheless on the evening news, two days before the election, and it kicked up a storm. Cohen launched an internal Mossad investigation to identify the source of the leak, and at the same time demanded of Netanyahu that he resolve the matter. Netanyahu did so, but not in the way Cohen hoped. He came down on the side of his advisors, Ben-Shabbat and Maoz, and even expanded their mandate to engage with the Arab world. "We didn't want to fight the Mossad," Ben-Shabbat told me. "We wanted to work together with them. I asked for the support of the prime minister at the very beginning, and everything we did was with his approval."

While the Israeli side squabbled over who would implement the diplomatic agenda, a new figure entered the relationship between the United States and Morocco—one who would be pivotal in the eventual breakthrough. Rabbi David Chananya Pinto was born into a Moroccan family with rabbinical heritage. He was educated in France and the United Kingdom and became famous not only for the network of religious institutions he founded in Israel and around the world, but also because of his involvement in Jewish mysticism and stories of miracles involving him and his family. His physical appearance and white beard, combined with his polished, French-accented English, cosmopolitan demeanor and charisma made him a mysterious and intriguing figure for many. Over the years, Pinto attracted Jewish celebrities to him, such as Bob Dylan, who came to study with him in the '90s.[311] Elbaz knew the rabbi and his family in Morocco and became one of his followers. He also discovered that one of his fellow followers was none other than Jared Kushner. The Kushner family's philanthropic foundation donated over 200 thousand dollars to the "Chevrat Pinto" organization and to the rabbi's *beit midrash* ("house of study") in Manhattan.[312]

Kushner visited Morocco for the first time in May 2019. One of the key stops on his visit was a meeting with Rabbi Pinto. They met at the Old Jewish Cemetery in Casablanca, where Rabbi

Pinto's great-grandfather, Rabbi Haim Pinto, was buried. A folk tale says that a visit to the site confers a blessing upon the visitor. Kushner came to the cemetery with his entire White House peace team. When he saw Rabbi Pinto in the cemetery, one of the most powerful men in the United States was reduced to being a self-conscious child faced with his teacher. He embraced the rabbi, kissing him on both cheeks, and the two walked arm-in-arm along the paths of the cemetery until they reached the grave they were looking for. Kushner bowed slightly and closed his eyes as Rabbi Pinto placed a hand on his head, recited a blessing and wished him luck in his efforts to bring about peace in the Middle East.[313] It was a very unusual sight. In hindsight, that moment in the cemetery in Casablanca was a milestone on the way to the renewal of diplomatic relations between Israel and Morocco, a year and a half later.

The pinnacle of Kushner's visit to Morocco was a meeting with King Mohammed VI in the royal palace. The dinner lasted long into the night, with waiters delivering a constant stream of food to the table. Sitting with the king and the crown prince at the table were Bourita and another key figure: the king's senior advisor, Fouad Ali El Himma—Kushner's counterpart and one of the most powerful figures in Morocco. During the dinner, the king raised the matter of the Western Sahara and requested American recognition of Moroccan claims to the region. This was the first time that senior White House officials fully recognized the depth of feeling within the Moroccan government on this issue, and how it could be used to advance Trump's policies in the Middle East. That evening, what had started out 18 months earlier as a private initiative between Ben-Barak and Elbaz became an official negotiation process between Morocco and the United States.

From that moment on, Israel encouraged the White House to move forward with the Moroccan deal. Beyond the regional diplomatic implications of an agreement between Israel and Morocco, Netanyahu had another, domestic political motive for pursuing this deal. Following his failure to establish a government after the April 2019 elections, Netanyahu was hoping for a diplomatic achievement that would catch the eye of the more than one million Israelis of Moroccan descent, and that would help him to win the second round of elections in September. Time and again, he tried to persuade the Moroccans to welcome him to Rabat for a visit, only to be politely rebuffed on every occasion. Then, he proposed an agreement for direct flights to benefit the tens of thousands of Israeli tourists who visit Morocco every year. This idea was also unsuccessful. After every such attempt, Netanyahu leaked hints about an impending breakthrough with Morocco to the Israeli press. The Moroccans did not like this one bit.

At the same time, the White House and the palace in Rabat grew steadily closer. Kushner handed the responsibility for the Moroccan deal to his deputy, Avi Berkowitz. Berkowitz discovered that power players in Washington were opposed to any change in long-standing US policy opposing recognition of Moroccan sovereignty over the Western Sahara. One of those people was National Security Advisor John Bolton. As part of the various senior positions he held in the George W. Bush administration, Bolton was involved in the UN-brokered negotiations to resolve the conflict in the Western Sahara. He became one of the most vocal voices opposing the Moroccan occupation of the region. In September 2019, Trump fired Bolton from his position due to irreconcilable differences of opinion between the two over Iran. This had the extra benefit of removing a major obstacle from the path toward a deal with Morocco.

In October 2019, Foreign Minister Bourita flew to Washington. He met with Secretary of State Pompeo and came to the White

House for meetings with Kushner and his wife, Ivanka, President Trump's daughter. A few weeks later, I was on board Netanyahu's flight to Lisbon. At the time, Israel was in the full throes of a political crisis. Both Netanyahu and Gantz failed in their attempts to form a government. Netanyahu offered Gantz a unity government in which the head of Blue and White would serve as the first prime minister in a rotation agreement, but Gantz hesitated. There was only a week left until the Knesset would be dispersed to pave the way for a third consecutive round of elections—Netanyahu's preferred course of action.

The main reason for Netanyahu's trip to Lisbon was a meeting with Pompeo. From Lisbon, the latter was due to fly for a meeting with King Mohammed VI, and the specter of the potential Moroccan deal was felt throughout. When asked, Netanyahu and Pompeo refused to address the matter, but there was a general sense that they hoped the conditions would be favorable for a diplomatic breakthrough—one which would also help Netanyahu rehabilitate his political status. In hindsight, they weren't even close. Pompeo was unable to deliver for the Moroccans on the Western Sahara and the king canceled their meeting after he had already landed in the country. With no Western Sahara, there was nothing to talk about, the Moroccan side emphasized. The Moroccans were deeply frustrated by the dissonance between the promises Netanyahu and his team were making and the reality. They also strongly disapproved of the spin Netanyahu was publishing about Morocco for domestic consumption.[314] In the palace, they decided to wait for the outcome of the third elections in Israel.

In February 2020, a few days before the elections, I aired a series of reports on Channel 13 entitled "Netanyahu of Arabia," all about the prime minister's secret engagement with the Arab world. One of the reports was a scoop on the Moroccan deal. The national security advisor, Meir Ben-Shabbat, turned to the Military Censor in an attempt to prevent it from being broadcast, but the chief officer of the unit, Brigadier General (Res.) Ariella Ben Avraham, approved the report with minor changes. In the Prime Minister's Office and the White House, there were concerns that it would definitively sink diplomatic efforts to make progress on a deal. In the end, the opposite happened. The report, which was widely shared in the United States and Morocco, highlighted Morocco's real priorities. In a discussion in the Foreign Affairs Committee of the Moroccan Parliament, several members leveled criticism at Bourita that he was trying to push for normalization with Israel while turning his back on the Palestinians. "The top foreign policy priority of Morocco is the Western Sahara—not Palestine," he replied. The message was clear—if the deal was genuinely on the table, Morocco would not hesitate to seize it with both hands.

The elections in Israel put the Moroccan deal on ice, but COVID-19 raised an interesting situation. In the wake of rising contagion during March, the government of Morocco decided to implement a nationwide lockdown and close the borders. A group of 30 Israeli citizens who were in the country at the time were trapped and unable to leave. They appealed to the foreign ministry in Jerusalem, which quietly reached out to the Moroccan government. One of the proposals was to send an El Al plane to retrieve them. Another option, should the Moroccans decide that discretion was the order of the day, was to send the private jet of Jewish-American billionaire Sheldon Adelson, who agreed to assist the operation.

The government of Morocco viewed the request favorably, and the sides began to coordinate and put together a list of the Israelis who wanted to leave. But then Israeli domestic politics got in the way, leading the Moroccans to abandon the talks. Foreign

Minister Israel Katz tweeted that he had received requests from the Jewish community of Morocco to assist dozens of Jews with dual citizenship to leave the country for Israel. "I have instructed the foreign ministry staff to give them every support in coming to Israel," Katz wrote. Senior officials in the Moroccan government saw the tweet and exploded with fury. It gave the impression that the government of Israel was evacuating Moroccan Jews because the Moroccan government was failing to take care of them. Katz deleted the tweet, but the damage was done. The Moroccans saw it as disrespectful to the king, who they insisted protected the Jewish community and treated them as citizens with full equal rights.

The government of Morocco refused to allow either the Israeli plane or Sheldon Adelson's private jet to land in the country. The Israeli citizens, who were scattered around a few different cities in the country, including some who were sleeping in tents on the beach in the city of Agadir, began to encounter difficulties. Some ran out of money, others ran out of medicine. Others still, including businessman Ilan Hatuel, who found himself stuck in Morocco while on a business trip and later established a situation room to coordinate among the Israelis in the country, reported psychological difficulties resulting from long periods of isolation and the fact that they were unable to leave the country for two months. In one of my conversations with Hatuel at the time, he asked me whom he could turn to for help with extracting the Israeli citizens from Morocco. I gave him the number of the chief of staff in the Israeli Prime Minister's Office, Asher Hayoun. Hatuel bombarded him with calls and messages until he received an answer. Hayoun put him in touch with Maoz. That was when things started to move. A few more weeks of quiet deliberations passed before Maoz was able to secure a deal: the Israeli citizens would leave the country on a commercial flight to Paris—and from there they would board

Adelson's jet back to Israel. The members of the group gathered in Casablanca for takeoff. When they landed in the French capital, Hatuel sent me a message. After a few weeks in which I hadn't published a word about the situation to avoid derailing the talks, I reported on the story in full on the evening news.

While rescue efforts were ongoing, a window of opportunity arose in early May 2020 to make progress with the Moroccan deal. Former White House Envoy Avi Berkowitz told me that despite the fact that the pandemic was exercising an unrelenting iron grip over the White House agenda, the president held a meeting on the subject. "Everything was ready," Berkowitz told me.[315] "The plan was for the president to give a statement supporting Morocco's position on the Western Sahara conflict. After that, Morocco was supposed to move ahead with a step of warming relations with Israel. The first phase we talked about was allowing direct flights."

The Moroccans were very concerned about leaks. They had not yet recovered from the initial reporting on the initiative three months earlier, and they were keen for the move not to be reduced to "Western Sahara for relations with Israel." Trump listened to his advisors' briefing on the situation with Morocco. "Wait, there's someone who always talks to me about Morocco," he told them when they were finished talking. "Who is it? Oh, I remember. Call Senator Jim Inhofe." The senior Republican politician and then-chairman of the Armed Services Committee of the US Senate was the most ardent supporter in Washington of the Polisario Front—the national liberation movement of the Sahrawi rebels, which had a stated goal of ending the Moroccan occupation of the Western Sahara. He was also very close with President Trump. "We didn't even know the Western Sahara issue was so important to Inhofe or that the President cared what Inhofe thinks about it," Berkowitz recalled. "We were on the brink of a deal with Morocco and didn't think this point through." While his advisors sat in the Oval Office, Trump spoke with Inhofe. "Mr. President, this would be a huge mistake. These people deserve freedom. They are Christians," Senator Inhofe told the president. The president's advisors who were listening in were confident that Inhofe's opposition would be insufficient to override their recommendation, but were surprised to discover that this wasn't the case. "Jim, you have my word, we won't do this without your permission," President Trump replied to the Republican senator. In that moment, Kushner and Berkowitz wished a hole would open in the ground and swallow them up. They had informed the Moroccans about the decisive meeting with the president and built up their expectations, and now they would have to call with bad news. "I had to apologize to Bourita, and the issue didn't come up again for a few months," Berkowitz told me.

Like the rest of the world, Morocco was caught off guard by the normalization accords between Israel and the UAE in August 2020. They were even more surprised by the headlines in the Israeli press in the following days naming Morocco as one of the Arab countries that was likely to be next in line to normalize relations with Israel. The prime minister of Morocco at the time, Saadeddine Othmani, from the Islamist Justice and Development Party (PJD), strenuously denied the reports in language lifted directly from the 1970s. "We refuse any normalization with the Zionist entity because this emboldens it to go further in breaching the rights of the Palestinian people," he said. His position was not an accurate representation of that of the king, however. The condition for normalization was and remained the "deal" for the Western Sahara. Still, Senator Inhofe continued to oppose it, and the president continued to rely on his political support.[316] Trump's advisors and the Moroccans both decided to hold off until after the US presidential election that November. Should Trump defy expectations and win, he would be able to do anything he wanted. Should he lose, on the other hand, he would be able to carry out the deal in the transition period before his successor was sworn in, and Inhofe would have no political leverage over him.

The elections threw those plans off track. Trump, who declared victory despite losing, dedicated all his time to finding ways to overturn the results. He fell into a vortex of conspiracy theories, court cases and outbursts at those around him. Following the accords with the United Arab Emirates and Bahrain and the seeds of normalization with Sudan, Kushner and Berkowitz felt that a fourth agreement was within their grasp, but they feared the post-election crisis wouldn't allow it. In November, two weeks after the elections, Berkowitz came to Israel for a farewell visit. Following a courtesy call with Netanyahu, Israeli National Security Advisor Meir Ben-Shabbat asked to speak with him in private. "What's going on with Morocco?" he asked Berkowitz. The latter replied that he didn't know if it was still possible to do anything, considering the post-election chaos in the White House. "The mission has not yet been completed," Ben-Shabbat said. "We're very close. We have to push and get Morocco done too. The time is right." Berkowitz promised to try. Early December provided a golden opportunity for a breakthrough.

Relations between Trump and Inhofe hit the rocks during negotiations over the National Defense Authorization Act. Trump demanded that Inhofe include an article applying sanctions against Facebook and Twitter, as part of his political war against the two tech giants. He also demanded that the senator remove an article from the bill to rename all US Army bases that honor Confederate generals, who were no longer seen as appropriate figures to glorify. Inhofe refused both demands. A furious Trump responded with a ferocious flurry of tweets against the senator. He claimed

Inhofe was harming the national security of the United States and threatened to veto the bill.

Trump's chief of staff, Mark Meadows, Kushner and Berkowitz spotted an opportunity. They held a quick strategy call and decided to bring the Moroccan deal to his table, in the hope that the president would see it as an opportunity to exact revenge on Inhofe. Their gamble paid off. Trump listened to them and gave them the green light. Kushner and Berkowitz spoke to Bourita and asked whether Morocco was still interested in the deal they had agreed to seven months earlier. Bourita replied in the affirmative. Within a couple of days, they had drafted an agreement: the United States would recognize Moroccan sovereignty over the Western Sahara and open a US consulate there. For its part, Morocco would renew diplomatic ties with Israel and hold bilateral meetings at the highest levels. Morocco also committed to permitting direct flights to and from Israel for members of the Jewish community and tourists, and to advancing economic and commercial ties with Israel. Last but not least, Morocco would seek to reopen the diplomatic offices in Rabat and Tel Aviv that had closed in 2002.

Israel played no part at all in these negotiations. When the agreement between the United States and Morocco was ready, the White House informed the Prime Minister's Office in Jerusalem about it. The White House told Netanyahu's aides that there would be a phone call between President Trump and King Mohammed VI, after which the US and Morocco would make the announcement. For Israel, it was a net positive: with the United Arab Emirates, they had agreed to a freeze on annexation; with Sudan, Israel had provided economic support. This time, Israel didn't have to concede a thing. It was all upsides. But, as the White House was astonished to learn, Netanyahu was not happy with the news. A senior Israeli official who is familiar with the details told me that Netanyahu didn't approve of some of the wording in the statement that Morocco was supposed to publish. He thought the gradual normalization the Moroccans had agreed to and the opening of diplomatic liaison offices in place of embassies was a step down from the agreements with the United Arab Emirates and Bahrain. Netanyahu was also disappointed that, unlike on previous occasions, he would not be invited to participate in the phone call between President Trump and King Mohammed VI. Netanyahu's pleas fell on deaf ears, and he had no choice but to take what he was given.

Ambassador David Friedman was also against the deal. He delivered a message to the White House both verbally and in writing, possibly on Netanyahu's behalf,[317] outlining his reservations regarding the draft agreement and claimed that it represented a "bad deal" for the United States. Friedman argued the White House should be using its leverage to demand that Morocco follow the same path as the UAE and Bahrain, with full normalization that included the mutual opening of embassies. "When Avi first presented me with the deal, I opposed it because it did not provide for full diplomatic relations between Morocco and Israel," Friedman told me.[318] "In response to my objection, President Trump tweeted out that the deal would include 'full diplomatic relations,' language which I understood to have been cleared with the kingdom. Based upon that revision, I rescinded my objection. I strongly endorse normalization between Israel and Morocco."

On December 10, President Trump publicly announced the Moroccan deal in a series of tweets from his account. Unlike the three previous accords, Trump did not convene a press conference in the Oval Office, nor did he celebrate the diplomatic achievement. There was no recognition of the moment on camera or in a speech, despite the change in US policy being far bolder than in any of the three previous accords. Trump was somewhere else by that point. The fact that he set aside his fight to overturn the election for long enough to sign the agreement was unusual enough. Almost no other issue managed to pierce the conspiratorial fog that enveloped the US president in his lame duck period.

Less than two weeks later, Kushner and Berkowitz landed in Israel for one final official visit to Jerusalem. Netanyahu organized a farewell celebration for them that included a tree-planting ceremony in the Grove of Nations in Jerusalem, alongside trees planted by heads of state from around the world. Netanyahu named the new addition "The Kushner Garden of Peace." At the subsequent good-humored press conference, Netanyahu projected his own political problems onto Kushner. "I remember, Jared, back in 2017, when President Trump first called upon you to advance these efforts, to bring peace to the Middle East. All the experts, you know, the so-called experts, belittled your appointment," Netanyahu told him. "By the way, I ask you not to take it personally. They do it to me too. Now I can say how wrong those naysayers were."[319] But behind the scenes, the meeting between Netanyahu and Kushner that day was rather less enjoyable. Netanyahu was disappointed in the agreement with Morocco that was due to be signed the next day. He urged Kushner to press the Moroccans harder to agree to the opening of embassies.[320] Kushner told Netanyahu the diplomatic liaison offices was the most he could get and urged him to let the process take its course. Eventually, Netanyahu agreed and signed off on the deal.

The next day, I found myself back at Ben Gurion Airport, boarding a flight to Morocco with Kushner and his team alongside an Israeli team led by Meir Ben-Shabbat, where they were to sign an agreement on renewing diplomatic relations. For 15 years, I dreamed of traveling to Arab states which were closed off to me as a journalist. Now, in the space of three months, I had visited three of them. This was a flying visit—we spent less than 12 hours on the ground. The first stop was the Mausoleum of Mohammed V—the most significant national heritage site in the kingdom— and from there we continued straight on to the palace. Journalists usually spend the vast majority of these visits kicking their heels. This time, Kushner and Ben-Shabbat were in the same boat. While the reporters waited in the official guest residence of the king of Morocco for the signing ceremony, Trump's senior advisor and Netanyahu's national security advisor waited in the palace for three hours for their meeting with King Mohammed VI.

The lavish guest house in the palace looked like something from a fairytale. The members of the delegations sat on brightly colored couches while waiters in traditional dress poured them fragrant tea and offered rosewater biscuits and chocolate. As dusk approached, Kushner, Ben-Shabbat and Bourita arrived for the signing ceremony. The most memorable moment in the press conference was Ben-Shabbat's speech, delivered in Moroccan Arabic. "A small expression of my feelings can be heard in the words I spoke in the Arabic of my mother," said Ben-Shabbat, his voice shaking. "Many Israeli citizens of Moroccan heritage dreamed of this day. Like me, many of the second and third generations of immigrants from Morocco living in Israel retain their bond to the heritage of their forefathers and carry on their traditions…. The warm relations between the royal palace and the Moroccan people with Moroccan Jewry is the bridge between the two countries and the foundations on which we will build peace between the countries." A few months later, when I met Ben-Shabbat at his home, he was still noticeably emotional as he recalled that visit. For him, the renewed ties with Morocco were more than a professional achievement: they were a personal moment, coming full circle. "With Morocco, we put this issue on the table and guided the Americans to it," he told me.[321] "In our region, negotiations and relations between countries are not guided purely by interests. There is a lot of importance attached to emotion—and that was a very important part of the process for both us and the Moroccans."

Following the ceremony, the speeches and the signing of the accords, the members of the delegation, senior Moroccan government officials and Israeli journalists hung around. It felt like a social gathering, where everyone was talking to everyone else. I asked Avi Berkowitz to introduce me to Nasser Bourita. When we approached him and Berkowitz mentioned my name, a smile broke out on Bourita's face and he ribbed me about the headache I had caused 10 months earlier, when I published the report on the impending Moroccan deal. I asked him whether he would be interested in granting me an interview, and to my surprise he immediately called one of his advisors over and asked him to coordinate it for that same evening. Bourita's advisor asked me to take a seat on one of the couches and wait. As I sat there, I saw the Israeli delegation depart back to the hotel, leaving me behind. They were followed by part of the American delegation, and eventually Bourita himself also left. The Moroccan minister's advisor, seeing that I was growing nervous, signaled to me not to worry. "He'll be back in a minute," he told me. An hour and a half later, a motorcade pulled up to the official guest residence in the palace. Kushner, Ben-Shabbat and Bourita walked in together, and were surprised to find me sitting in the entrance. "Don't worry, it's me he's lying in wait for," the Moroccan foreign minister said to laughter.

In the official guest residence, Bourita and I spoke about how long it had taken for the deal to mature. "King Hassan II, may he rest in peace, used to say that diplomacy was like agriculture. If you pluck a fruit from the tree before its time, it won't be ripe, and if you pluck it too late, you can't eat it anymore. The timing is important," he said. The Moroccans insisted on not being included under the umbrella term of the Abraham Accords. They explained to the Americans and Israelis that, unlike the United Arab Emirates, Bahrain and Sudan, all normalizing relations with Israel for the first time, Morocco had a long history of ties with Israel. "We were there long before," Bourita said. "We told our American friends— don't make everyone wear the same T-shirt. We were pioneers when it came to ties with Israel. It's a big occasion for us, but we're not starting from scratch. That's why, for us, it's not just a matter of formalizing relations—it goes far deeper than that. We are reviving a history of ties with Israel and want to build something that will stand the test of time."[322]

The director general of the foreign ministry, Alon Ushpiz, told me that the accord renewing ties with Morocco epitomized the Trump administration's relationship with Israel better than anything else. "Israeli citizens should stand and salute in honor of what Trump and his administration did," Ushpiz said.[323] "Take Morocco as an example—it happened five weeks before the transition of power in the States. In other administrations, people were already looking for their next job and sending out resumes, but in the White House they continued to work to achieve this deal. That was incredible and unprecedented in American terms. They were willing to exchange their most valuable assets to ensure Israel's well-being. That would not have happened without the president. That belongs to him."

A few weeks after the signing ceremony, Israeli diplomat David Govrin came to Rabat to reopen the diplomatic office that had lain dormant for two decades. "I received a call from the office of the director general of the foreign ministry, asking me whether I would be interested in going to Rabat to reopen the mission," Govrin told me. "It took me 10 seconds to say yes."[324] Two weeks later, Moroccan diplomat Abdel Rahim al-Bayoud came to Israel and reopened his country's diplomatic mission on HaYarkon St. in Tel Aviv. In early August 2021, less than a year after the historic agreement, I boarded a flight to Rabat once more. This time it was with Foreign Minister Yair Lapid, traveling to the dedication ceremony for the new Israeli mission. A few minutes before we headed back to the airport in Casablanca for our return flight, Lapid announced that he had agreed with Foreign Minister Bourita to complete the normalization process and upgrade the missions in Rabat and Tel Aviv to embassy status. The next chapter in the story of the two nations had been written.

"Fuck Him": Interview with Donald Trump

Miami International Airport was packed with Americans from the cold and rainy part of the East Coast traveling down to Florida in droves for spring break. My own trip was little more than a pit stop: 24 hours, in and out. After interviewing Jared Kushner for an hour and a half at his waterfront home in Miami Beach, I headed north for the crown jewel of the visit: a face-to-face interview with the 45th president of the United States, Donald Trump. Since leaving the White House, the former president had not returned to his apartment in New York's Trump Tower, preferring instead to spend most of his time at the Mar-a-Lago resort he purchased in 1985. Mar-a-Lago is the 24th largest mansion in the United States, extending over 62,500 square feet, with 128 rooms and a members-only club. During his term of office, President Trump hosted numerous foreign dignitaries there, including the president of China and the prime minister of Japan.[325]

On my way north, the skies darkened and it started to rain. I was welcomed at the entrance to the estate by a Secret Service agent. He flicked through my passport quickly and waved me through. The complex itself was quiet and sleepy. The exclusive members club is closed on Sundays, and the reception desk in the lobby was unmanned. The Grand Ballroom—all golden walls and crystal chandeliers—was deserted, the fireplace dark and the Steinway piano silent. I waited there for a few minutes, then Trump entered. He was wearing a black suit and white shirt (no tie) with his signature red MAGA cap on his head. I had seen him up close before on numerous occasions, at his meetings with Prime Minister Netanyahu at the White House and during his visit to Israel. I had even asked him questions at press conferences. But this was the first time I was sitting down with him one-on-one. I had no idea what to expect, aside from the unexpected.

He was friendly, but also impatient. "What's your book about?" he asked. I started to explain, but barely got a few seconds in before he interrupted me and launched into a diatribe detailing everything he had done for Israel, swerving off-piste every so often to attack his Democratic predecessor and successor over the Iran nuclear accord, grumble about the Jewish community in the United States and of course pivot time and again to what he termed the "stolen" election by his Democratic rivals. The longer our conversation went on, the more he returned to the theme of the "rigged election" he insisted he had actually won. Five months after the election and three months after the January 6 insurrection by his supporters, it felt like Trump was still reliving the defeat— genuinely believing that he had been heinously wronged—and that he was determined to return to the political arena.

"There's no president that ever did anywhere close to what I did for Israel," he said, unprompted, and began to check off a list of his achievements, including moving the embassy to Jerusalem and recognizing the city as the capital of Israel, recognizing Israel's sovereignty over the Golan Heights and withdrawing from the JCPOA with Iran. "[The JCPOA is] a disaster. Now,

Biden's going back into it because he has no clue. Israel fought it, and Obama didn't listen." I asked him how much of the decision to withdraw from the agreement in May 2018 was down to his relationship with Benjamin Netanyahu. His answer surprised me, and provided a sneak preview of the further revelations that lay in store during our conversation. "It was really my relationship with Israel—not with Bibi. It was my feeling for Israel," Trump said, and started talking about his childhood in New York, and his father, real estate mogul Fred Trump, whom he revered. "My father was very close to many Jewish people. Because it was Brooklyn real estate, Brooklyn and Queens, and he had many Jewish friends with a great love of Israel."

The former president's distinctive manner of speaking is unmistakable—and as with all of his public appearances and talks, here too, sitting in front of me in his own home, he flitted between subjects, chasing his train of thought from one station to the next. The stories of his father and his friends seemed to awaken some resentment in him toward the contemporary Jewish community of the United States. "A great love of Israel has dissipated over the years for people in the United States," he said. "I must be honest, it's a very dangerous thing that's happening. I told a few people that people in this country that are Jewish no longer love Israel. I'll tell you, the evangelical Christians love Israel more than the Jews in this country. I've never seen a turn like it in my life…. It used to be that Israel had absolute power over Congress. And today, I think it's the exact opposite." Unsurprisingly, the culprits for this in his view were Obama and Biden. That was why he was so frustrated that over 70 percent of American Jews voted for them in the presidential election. I asked him if he was disappointed. "I was surprised. I think it's a very serious problem for Israel," he replied. "The Orthodox Jews, by the way, like me very, very much.

I got 27 percent of the Jewish vote. How can you get 27 percent of the Jewish vote when I gave them so much—including Iran."

During the 2016 election campaign, he spoke a lot about peace between Israel and the Palestinians, I told him. It felt like that subject was really important to him. "My father wasn't Jewish, but he always had a great relationship with Jewish people, he had Jewish friends and Jewish lawyers," Trump told me. "Most of the people that I grew up with outside of college were Jewish. And my father would receive awards from Jewish organizations, including a development that he had in New York where he built a small temple. It was a complex in Beach Haven. And he had a lawyer named Bunny Lindenbaum, who was a very good guy." I wondered aloud whether his father had discussed Israel or the Middle East conflict with him when he was young. "No. My father was very close with many Jewish people. And in those days, Jewish people in the United States were pro-Israel. Today they're not. I mean, you look at *The New York Times*. *The New York Times* hates Israel. And [there are] Jewish people that run *The New York Times*, the Sulzberger family."[326]

It's difficult to square Trump's animus toward the majority of American Jews, his borderline antisemitic remarks during the election campaign when he told Jewish donors "I don't want your money" and his support for the white supremacist groups in Charlottesville whom he referred to as "very fine people" with the many Jews in his close circle: his daughter, Ivanka Trump, a convert to Judaism, his son-in-law Jared Kushner, lawyers Jason Greenblatt and David Friedman, who became his Middle East envoy and ambassador to Israel, respectively, and Avi Berkowitz, one of his closest advisors in the White House. He dedicated a few minutes to praising each of them in turn—especially Friedman, who was one of the most influential US ambassadors of all time, the man who led the process of legitimizing the Israeli settlement project in the West Bank.

"David Friedman was fantastic. He is, you know, a brilliant lawyer. Probably one of the highest paid lawyers in New York City, made millions of dollars a year," Trump said. He told me that when he offered Friedman the position of US ambassador to Israel, he left his law firm within 15 minutes, even though he would be forgoing 20 million dollars a year in doing so.

"David's made deals for me that were crazy. Crazy good. I told David, I'm not doing it to make you the ambassador. I'm doing it because I'd like to see if I could create peace in the Middle East. I have been told by everybody that it's not doable. Sheldon Adelson, who was a friend of mine, said it's not doable because the hatred is so great between the Palestinians and the Israelis. They learn from the first day they open books to hate each other, especially the Palestinians toward Israel. He told me the Palestinians say horrible things about the Jews. Sheldon was a great deal-maker, and even he said it's impossible."

That was the first time Trump brought up Sheldon Adelson during our meeting, but it wouldn't be the last. It was hard to miss Trump's admiration for the casino mogul. This had more to do with Adelson's business success and the vast wealth he had accumulated over the years than any political opinions or the hundreds of millions of dollars he poured into Trump's election campaign. "He started with nothing, and he was worth 35 billion by the time it was over," Trump gushed.

But unlike Sheldon, he did believe it was possible to achieve a peace deal, I said. "Yeah," Trump replied. "Look, you know the expression, what do you have to lose? So I thought it was worth a shot. It wasn't like I said it's going to happen. I said, what the hell do we have to lose by trying? I had all these very talented people. They happen to be Jewish, they happen to love Israel. They love being Jewish. Also, dealing with the Israeli–Palestinian issue wasn't a full-time job. And I said, let's give it a shot."

In his last three years in office, after recognizing Jerusalem as Israel's capital in December 2017, the relationship between the White House and the leadership in Ramallah hit its lowest point in two decades, since George Bush Jr. called for Yasser Arafat to be replaced. Prior to that, however, President Trump had a strong relationship with President Mahmoud Abbas. Perhaps surprisingly, Trump doesn't bear a personal grudge against Abbas, despite the personal attacks the latter aimed at him, including the infamous "may your house come to ruin" speech in front of the cameras. "I really liked him a lot," Trump recalled of his first meeting with Abbas at the White House in early May 2017. "We got along so well. And then he went back and started spewing things, essentially 'death to Israel.' It was just the opposite of our conversation in the White House. I know that on a personal basis, he liked me. But he felt politically it was good to leave and to say those things at home."

The most significant blow to the Palestinians came in January 2018, a month after the Jerusalem announcement that almost completely wiped out all communication between the Palestinian Authority and the White House. In a tweet, Trump threatened to cut aid to the Palestinians, and shortly afterward, he followed through. "I said, how much money are we paying them?" he remembered. "They said, 750 million dollars a year. I said, why would we give them anything when they've spewed hate? And then I spoke to people that represented our country years before over the course of many years. They got nowhere. They got absolutely nowhere. And they weren't negotiators. They were diplomats. But a diplomat isn't necessarily a negotiator. A diplomat is a person that knows how to give everything away. I said to them, have you ever just told the Palestinians that you're going to stop payment of any... and all money going to them? They said no. I said why not? They said they don't think it's appropriate. I said, well, when they say 'death to America,' 'death to Israel,' and we're giving them 750 million dollars, do you think that's appropriate? I said, then you're stupid people. Okay. So I used that card. I stopped the payment to the Palestinians."

I reminded Trump that, at one point, he had a good relationship with Abbas. "I thought he was terrific," he replied. "I thought he wanted to make a deal more than Netanyahu. And I will be honest, I had a great meeting with him. We spent a lot of time together, talked about many things. And he was almost like a father. I think he was so nice. Couldn't have been nicer. When Abbas left the White House, it was hugs and kisses, but when he went back home, he didn't say the right things. He said much more warlike things than what he said to my face. We had wonderful personal communication. I really liked him a lot. I still like him based on those meetings. The rest I just heard from the press."

Trump was sitting casually, leaning back and drinking his favorite drink, Diet Coke. The conversation flowed, and he moved on to talking about Benjamin Netanyahu. I had mentally settled in to hear a lengthy tribute to the Israeli prime minister, but he surprised me and claimed that Netanyahu had made a poor first impression on him. "My whole life is deals. I'm like one big deal," Trump said. "Whether it's that or buying things or negotiating for *The Apprentice*, it's just what I do. And after meeting with Bibi [the first time] for three minutes, I looked at him and said, 'You don't want to make a deal, do you?' And he said, 'Well, uh...uh... uh....' And the fact is, I don't think Bibi ever wanted to make a deal [with the Palestinians]." Throughout his adult life, he had always been sure that Israel was on the side of peace and the Palestinians were the obstacle, he said, but when he entered the Oval Office and met with Abbas and Netanyahu, he discovered a far more nuanced, perhaps even inverted, picture. "In the end, I found the Palestinians also very difficult, but I don't think Bibi wanted to make a deal," Trump said. "I don't know what it is. Maybe it's politics. I sat with Bibi and I told him I had a very good meeting with Abbas and we can definitely do a deal." And what did he reply, I inquired. "He said, 'Let's think about it. Let's not move too fast.' I stopped him in the middle of a sentence. I said, 'Bibi, you don't want to make a deal.' I can't speak for Israel. But I will tell you that, in my opinion, Bibi did not want to make a deal. That's why we went four years without a deal. I feel we could have had a deal with the Palestinians."

The decision to recognize Jerusalem as the capital of Israel on December 6, 2017 and to move the US embassy from Tel Aviv to Jerusalem made Trump the most popular politician in Israel. He seemed to take great pride in the fact that he was the one fulfilling the promise made by all his predecessors. He took satisfaction in recalling world leaders who had tried to discourage him and spoke lovingly of the embassy he had managed to open within six months at a cost of only a few hundred thousand dollars. On the other hand, he refused to accept that this decision almost certainly buried his chances of achieving a peace agreement between Israel and the Palestinians.

"Every president wanted to make that deal during the campaign. Then, when they got into the White House, they never made it," said Trump. "And I couldn't understand why. Because to me, it seemed very simple. But it wasn't. I would also talk about [the embassy move] as a talking point during the campaign. I mean, I had other things that frankly, were more important to me…. They cared about it in Israel, but they didn't care about it here. Some people did. Mr. and Mrs. Adelson did, Orthodox Jews did a lot, you know, and the evangelical community cared more than the Orthodox [Jews]. And as soon as I became president, I was called by heads of other countries who I became friendly with fairly quickly, and they all asked me not to do it. They said there'll be blood in the streets, it'll be a disaster. It got to a point where, when I thought they were calling about that, I delayed their phone calls. I said I would call back next week, and then I didn't. And that was it. I'd call them back after I made the decision. And then they said, well, we were calling you to tell you that we hope you don't make the decision on Jerusalem."

When I asked him whether, in hindsight, he would have done anything differently to prevent the crisis with the Palestinians, he demurred, preferring to talk instead about how quickly he opened the new embassy in Jerusalem. "That embassy wouldn't have been built for 30 years. It would have never happened. But we took an existing building and we renovated it. We did it for 500 thousand dollars, as opposed to two billion. They were going to spend two billion dollars to build an embassy like they did in London. It was the dumbest thing I've ever seen. I said, how the hell do you spend two billion dollars on a one-story building? We took an old building that we had in a better location. Good location, right? Would you say it's a good location?" he asked, not waiting for an answer before diving straight back in again. "And it's a nice embassy. We used the old Jerusalem stone. I have a friend in New York, Ron Baron.[327] The elevator wall in his office is Jerusalem stone. So he talks about his Jerusalem stone. It's very expensive in New York, but in Jerusalem, it's very inexpensive. So we used Jerusalem stone in honor of Ron Baron."

Trump brought up the Palestinians' anger over the Jerusalem declaration, before immediately pivoting to explain why the move was an important one. "For 25 years, you couldn't make a deal with them. Now, I know that the negotiators on the US side weren't the greatest in the world. And some were grossly incompetent, but some were not and [still] couldn't make a deal with the Palestinians," Trump said. "So once we couldn't make a deal with them, once you saw that this [has been] going on for 25 years—I thought to myself, what the hell do we have to lose? One of the primary reasons that you couldn't make a deal with the Palestinians was Jerusalem and the embassy. That was the number one point: you will never move the embassy. So I figured that if I move it to Jerusalem, it's now off the table. Do you understand what I'm saying?" I asked Trump if he didn't think it might have sent a message to the Palestinians that the United States doesn't recognize their aspirations in Jerusalem. "We were going to do something for them in a different part of Jerusalem, you know that," he replied. "I did say, look, Israel just gained a point. The next point is going to be theirs, they're going to get something very big that they want. I let them know that."

Whether he was trying to deflect the criticism or was simply bouncing from one topic to another again, Trump returned to the decision to cut US aid to the Palestinians after their furious reaction to the Jerusalem declaration. Attempting to justify his position, he reminded me how he cut 500 million dollars in US aid to Honduras, El Salvador and Guatemala, thereby allegedly forcing them to halt the flow of migrants through their countries to the United States. "I'm just trying to use an example," he said. But it didn't work out the same way with the Palestinians, I replied. "No, it didn't," he admitted. "It worked 100 percent with Honduras, and with Guatemala and El Salvador, but it didn't work the same way with the Palestinians. It was almost the same thing. It's very interesting what you said. Because with one it worked as soon as I stopped the payment. They said, we would love to have M-13 members back in our country. But on this one [the Palestinians], it didn't work. It softened them, but these are hardened people. There is great hatred. These are hardline people with tremendous hatred of Jewish people and of Israel. It's very interesting what you said, because it's almost identical—except for the total hatred."

Trump's analysis of events between Israel and the Palestinians in his first year in office is replete with contradictions. If he said that he realized very early on that Abbas was interested in a deal and Netanyahu wasn't, I asked, why was he harder on the Palestinians than he was on the Israelis? "Because I, like everybody else, was led to believe for years and years and decades that Israel wanted to make a deal and [the Palestinians] were impossible to deal with," he replied. "In the end, they really did say bad things. [Abbas] said great things to my face. But almost from the day he got back, one of the people in the White House said he was saying 'death to America' and 'death to Israel.' I said that's not possible. I had a great meeting with him. And they showed me the articles and they showed me the tape of him saying it."

The longer the conversation went on, the clearer it became to me that his first year in office had been marred by people in his inner circle regularly feeding him negative information about Abbas. Some of that information was true, but some of it had been twisted or given a pro-Israel or anti-Palestinian slant. Such was the case with the *New York Post* op-ed that called Abbas a "two-faced antisemite,"[328] which happened to find its way to the president's desk. "I scribbled on the article something to the effect of 'this isn't the way we talked,'" recalled Trump. "I asked [Abbas], 'Is this what you really think?' Our meeting was so different, you have no idea." Trump instructed his advisors to deliver a cut-out with his handwritten comments on it to the Palestinian president. Don Blome, the US consul general in Jerusalem, went to the Mukataa in Ramallah and delivered the envelope in person to a bemused Abbas.

Trump had never visited Israel before assuming the presidency, but he knew Benjamin Netanyahu from long before he threw his hat in the ring. He even recorded an endorsement clip for him ahead of the 2013 elections. "Choose Bibi—he's a winner," Trump urged voters in the video.[329] As I learned in my interview with the former president, he puts a lot of stock in comments made to camera. In one example, Netanyahu came to his defense at the White House press conference following their first meeting in February 2017: the president was taking heat for a sharp rise in antisemitism in the US, and Netanyahu addressed the cameras and said, "There is no greater supporter of the Jewish people and the Jewish state than President Donald Trump." Throughout Trump's four years in office, he and Netanyahu appeared to be in perfect lockstep—close, coordinated and committed to an unbreakable alliance.

The interview with Trump exposed a different picture. It's difficult to point to one specific incident, but at some point in the latter part of his term, a rift formed between the two men. It might have been the April 2019 Knesset elections, where Netanyahu was unable to secure victory despite the vocal support of the US president. It might have been the unveiling ceremony for the peace plan, in January 2020, which left Trump fuming after Netanyahu hijacked the event for a stump speech. Or it might have been his feeling that the Israeli prime minister's support for Trump's re-election campaign was insufficiently wholehearted. Whatever the reason, the result was that the Donald Trump I met at Mar-a-Lago in April 2021 was wound up and just waiting for an opportunity to unload on Netanyahu.

"I liked [Netanyahu] a lot," Trump began. "But we had an election in this country, which was rigged and stolen. Because we had guys like Mitch McConnell, who are stupid people, and weak and didn't fight for the president, or for the presidency. Nobody ever did more for Bibi Netanyahu than me. There's nobody that ever did more for Israel than me. And the first person to go to Joe Biden and congratulate him was Netanyahu. And not only did he do it, he did it on tape," Trump (falsely) asserted. "And if you look at the leaders of many other countries, such as Brazil, I mean, [Bolsonaro] waited months, frankly. Putin. Many other leaders. Mexico, because they, I think, they also felt the election was rigged. But there were so many other countries." I tried to interject to ask whether he was disappointed by Netanyahu's leadership, but it was hard to interrupt his stream of consciousness. "China would have waited, except what happened with regard to China was that COVID came in and now the relationship wasn't very good. But they would have waited too. Let me just say, nobody did more for Bibi in Israel than I did. Also money. I mean, you know, we gave a lot of money and I gave our troops…everything we did."

As an example of the kind of gestures he offered Netanyahu, Trump reminded me of his decision to recognize Israeli sovereignty over the Golan Heights a few days before the April 2020 elections. "If you look at the Golan Heights, that was a big deal," he said. "Somebody said the value of that deal was in the tens of billions of dollars. Like a piece of real estate." He mentioned how, during a debate with his advisors, he called Ambassador Friedman and asked him for a "five-minute lecture" on the Golan Heights and its strategic importance. "I stopped him after one minute," he said. "It's up high, so strategically important. I got that for them. People say that was a 10-billion-dollar gift." That was right before the elections, I reminded him. "I did it right before the election, which helped [Netanyahu] a lot. So he tied. Meaning he would have lost the election if it wasn't for me. He went up a lot after I made the decision on the Golan Heights. He went up by 10 or 15 percent."[330]

Above all, Trump was angry over the congratulatory message Netanyahu taped for Biden. It was Trump's wife, Melania, who first saw the tape and brought it to her husband's attention. "I liked Bibi. I still like Bibi. But I also like loyalty," he told me. "The first person to congratulate Biden was Bibi. And not only did he congratulate him—he did it on tape. Bibi could have stayed quiet. He made a terrible mistake. I was just disappointed in him on a personal level."

Trump recalled every word on that tape. He could not fathom why Netanyahu would bring up his great friendship with Biden. "Let me tell you, first of all, it was under Obama, not Biden, but you know, they were the Obama administration," Trump said angrily. "I remember Bibi coming over to the United States and begging Obama not to do that deal [with Iran]. All he got from Joe Biden was the Iran deal. That's all he got. How Jewish people vote for Biden or Obama, with what was done to them with that deal... Had I not come along I think Israel was going to be destroyed, okay? You want to know the truth? I think Israel would have been destroyed maybe by now. [Bibi and Biden] didn't have a friendship, because if they did, they wouldn't have done the Iran deal. And guess what? Now they're going to do it again. And if they return to the Iran deal again, Israel is in very deep, very grave danger. Do you understand what I'm saying?"

Trump returned to the theme of Netanyahu being the first to congratulate Biden and the tape at least five times during our meeting. The depth of his indignation was clear to see. "This was an election in dispute. It's still in dispute... So Netanyahu, before the ink was even dry, does a tape for Joe Biden?" Trump said disapprovingly. "And by the way, in Israel I'm the most popular person, because they understand. Now, you know, I don't get votes in Israel, so it doesn't matter. But they say my poll numbers in Israel are through the roof." I told him there were surveys showing him having 70 to 80 percent approval in Israel. One of his advisors, who was sitting with him, told him that Israel was jokingly referred to as "the reddest state in the Union."[331] "Who are the 20 percent? I'd like to know who the 20 percent are. That is so ungrateful, they are bad people," Trump was quick to reply. "Well, in Alabama I got more than 80 percent, I did better than that. And in other places I did better. And not only that, after [Netanyahu] did it, you know, he... I don't think he's gotten a phone call [from Biden] yet." I corrected him and pointed out that Biden did call Netanyahu, albeit only a month after he entered the White House. For the sake of comparison, Trump spoke with Netanyahu two days after he entered the Oval Office. "You see? It took a long time. He spoke to many other leaders before Netanyahu." At one point during our conversation, I had to interject to point out that Netanyahu was actually not the first one to congratulate Biden.[332] That did nothing to placate the former president, who cursed Netanyahu aloud. "It was early. Okay? Let's say this—he was very early. Like, earlier than most. I haven't spoken to him since. Fuck him."

It was no less than incredible to hear Trump talking like this about the person who, until a few months previously, appeared to be his closest ally among the world leaders. Throughout the interview, Trump had almost nothing good to say about Netanyahu. It was difficult to ascertain whether he felt the way he did about Netanyahu throughout his four years in the White House or the negative emotions were a response to Netanyahu's perceived disloyalty and lack of gratitude in congratulating Biden on his election win—a win that Trump still fails to recognize today.[333]

When we moved on to the subject of Iran, Trump told me about a good friend of his, a successful Jewish businessman whom he didn't name. In a meeting between the two, Trump asked him what he thought was the biggest thing he had done for Israel during his term. Moving the embassy to Jerusalem? Recognizing Israel's sovereignty over the Golan Heights? Or the Abraham Accords? The friend's response took him by surprise. "He said none of them," Trump recalled. "'By far the biggest thing you ever did was Iran. Breaking up that horrible deal was the biggest thing you've ever done.' I will tell you this, Israel cannot let that deal happen, because when they say 'death to Israel,' they mean it. These are religious zealots."

Netanyahu claimed that he was the one who talked Trump into withdrawing from the Iran deal, I told him. "Well, if he said so…" Trump replied sarcastically. I said Netanyahu claimed that he showed him the nuclear archives that the Mossad brought from Tehran and, in doing so, convinced him to walk away from the accord. Trump dismissed this version of events completely. "They showed me papers that were old. I looked at them and I said, who drew these? Where do they come from?" he said. "I would have done that [withdraw from the JCPOA] whether Bibi existed or not. I did that. I was not convinced by him, just like he couldn't convince Obama in the opposite direction. I spoke to him about it. I spoke to many people about it. I felt you had to do it because I felt that you can't let these people have nuclear weapons."

I asked him whether the question of giving Israel a green light for a military strike against the Iranian nuclear facilities had ever come up. He confirmed that the question had come up for discussion, but never went anywhere. "You know what, Israel has to defend itself," said the former president. "I think that if Biden signs this deal, it's a disaster for Israel. Now look at how [the Biden administration] is signing all of the things that I said you have to ask Iran for [in a new nuclear deal]. And they say Trump was right about those. That deal was a disaster. First of all, it was almost up. When you make a deal with a country, this isn't like leasing a store for 10 years. When you make a deal with a country, it has to be long term. This deal was a passport for Iran to legally have nuclear weapons. You can't let that happen."

On August 13, 2020, Trump stunned the entire Middle East when he declared via his Twitter account that he had secured a normalization agreement between Israel and the United Arab Emirates. In exchange for formal diplomatic ties with one of the most influential countries in the Arab world, Prime Minister Benjamin Netanyahu agreed to back down from his plan to annex parts of the West Bank. The deal was the single biggest breakthrough in the Middle East peace process in over 25 years. In a phone call with Netanyahu and Sheikh Mohamed bin Zayed of Abu Dhabi, Trump was visibly emotional. He asked his advisors who were also on the call to write down every word. When we spoke at Mar-a-Lago, Trump told me that he saw this moment as an accomplishment, but not one of the biggest of his term. "I have a great relationship with Mohamed [bin Zayed], and he did something that was terrific for his country, but also terrific for Israel," he said. "And the call was a great call, and it was very historic in a sense. Mohamed is a great leader and a wonderful person. He's very strong with his military and people really respect him. To get them as the first country, I think it was a great, great thing."

Trump believes that the main achievement of the Abraham Accords was that he was the first leader to make headway with the reverse Middle East peace process approach: first securing peace between Israel and the Arab world and only then peace between Israel and the Palestinians. "Everybody said you have to deal with the Palestinians first, and then you get the others. We did the opposite," he noted. "The Palestinians couldn't believe it, because for years they were blackmailing the other countries. And I went and tried to make a deal with the Palestinians, and I held up their money, and I did a lot of other things. But they're tough negotiators, to put it mildly. This is why people like Adelson said you can't make a deal with them. So I said, okay, the hell with them. Let's go the opposite route."

The former president was convinced that, given a second term, more countries would have joined the Abraham Accords within a matter of months. "I mean, we did a deal with four countries and it would have been five, six, seven, eight. We would have had them all, except the election was rigged and stolen... Saudi Arabia would have absolutely joined. A hundred percent. A hundred percent. They would have joined fairly quickly, had I won. I did win the election, but had the election not been rigged." I asked if he thought that, were he to call up the king of Saudi Arabia and ask him to normalize relations with Israel, the latter would have gone along with it. "I believe so. They would have done it in the first month. I have a great relationship with King Salman. I have a great relationship with the crown prince. They would have done it. And I have zero doubt that virtually every country that we're talking about would have done it... It was like a domino effect. They were all falling in and it was going to be a beautiful thing. And now Biden wants to go back to the Iran deal. And if you go back to the Iran deal, I think that this makes it very difficult."

Trump, who famously regularly clashed with his opponents in politics and the media, took great pleasure in the praise he received for the Abraham Accords, even from his most strident and vocal critics. He reminded me that President Biden said that he wanted to continue the process that had been started between Israel and the Arab world, and mentioned the favorable write-up he received from *The New York Times* columnist Thomas Friedman, as if it was a theater review. "You know, he's no friend of mine, but he gave it the most incredible review. He said, 'This is amazing.' In fact, he called up and he said, 'Is this for real?' He couldn't believe it. Tom Friedman, okay? Smart guy. He could not believe that we got that done. I thought we're going to get to that point [with the Palestinians]. And I thought that the Palestinians would have fallen in long before the remainder of the countries. I'm sure we would have had the Palestinians in the deal. But we didn't have time to get it done because of the election fraud."

There was only one Israeli politician other than Netanyahu whom Trump welcomed to the White House. The day before he presented his plan for the Israeli–Palestinian conflict, and a few weeks before the third elections in Israel, in March 2020, he met the head of the Blue and White party, Benny Gantz, in the Oval Office. Gantz was the only person to successfully prevent Netanyahu from forming a government twice in a row. "What happened and why wasn't he in this last election?" asked Trump. I replied that Gantz had in fact participated and even defied expectations in receiving eight mandates, and that he was still in government as the minister of defense. Trump listened, wide-eyed, before cutting in to launch into a monologue on the Israeli election system. "I gotta tell you, being a person that feels so strongly about Israel and loves Israel, your election process is a disgrace and an embarrassment to your country—just like it is in our country. We had a fake election." In June 2019, when Netanyahu was unable to form a government after the first election, Trump expressed his frustration in a call with journalists at the White House. He claimed Israelis had "messed up" and called on the citizens to "get their act together." He still felt the same way during our interview. "Now we're going into [election] number five. It's a disgrace. It's just a horrible thing."

I brought the conversation back to Gantz. "I thought he was great," Trump said. "I liked him a lot. A really impressive guy. He loves Israel. I just didn't know what happened to him. Because, you know, I heard that at a certain period in time, Bibi was going to leave and he was going to take over, then all of a sudden they went to a new election. The Israeli election process is as screwy as the US election process, but it's probably much more honest. Because our process is very dishonest. I think the Israeli process just happens to be like a 50:50 split, and you can't choose anybody. It's ridiculous."

He told me that his impression of Gantz, whom he referred to as "the general," during their meeting at the White House was that he was far more interested in making peace than Netanyahu. "I think it would have been a lot easier to make a deal with Gantz," he told me. "The Palestinians hate Netanyahu. They hate him with a passion. They did not hate Gantz. It's a big factor. I really liked the general. I said to Jared [Kushner] and David [Friedman] that if he became the guy—if he won—I think it would be a lot easier, because I don't think Bibi ever wanted to make peace. When I say that, I think he just tapped us along. Just tap, tap, tap. 'No, no, we want to, we want to.' You know, Bibi is Bibi. But I think Bibi didn't want to make peace. Never did." In his book, *Breaking History*, Kushner wrote that, following the unveiling of his Israeli–Palestinian peace plan, Trump was so frustrated with Netanyahu that he wanted to publicly endorse Gantz ahead of the March 2020 election. Kushner and then-White House Envoy Avi Berkowitz convinced Trump not to interfere and to wait and see how the Israeli elections panned out.[334]

Trump claimed that he wanted to unveil his plan for the Israeli–Palestinian conflict in early 2019, but then the first of the many rounds of elections was called. "And then you had the tie election. The first one... I mean, the second one," Trump corrected himself, like so many Israelis struggling to follow the political chaos. "And they said, oh, no, no, once [Netanyahu] gets in, we'll make a deal. I don't believe that. But they were saying once he gets in, we'll do it. And then there was another tie. This has gone on now for four or five elections. Two years, right? Two and a half years."

The plan was finally unveiled on January 28, 2020, five weeks before the third elections. At the ceremony at the White House, Trump formally accepted the two-state solution as US policy under his administration for the first time since his election. He was surprised to hear Netanyahu, speaking straight after him, thanking him for agreeing to allow Israel to annex parts of the West Bank and, according to his advisors, he felt that the prime minister had not shown any meaningful commitment to a deal with the Palestinians. "I didn't like his speech," Trump recalled. "I think I let it be known, though. At the time, you know, I didn't like it. I didn't think it was appropriate." Trump revealed to me that he never supported Israeli annexation of parts of the West Bank. "When he went in and said let's build, that people can go and build all this, all the real estate, all over the place, I got angry and I stopped it because that was really going too far. That was going way too far. You know, when he said let's take everything and just start building on it, we were not happy about that."

I asked Trump whether it was accurate that he asked Netanyahu to stop building in the settlements in the West Bank in their very first meetings. He confirmed the story. "I said, why are you doing this? You're forcing [the Palestinians] into a position where, from a position of pride, they can't do the deal. They can never do the deal," Trump said. "I got very angry with it, because I saw what he was doing. He was embarrassing them. You know, you have to give people their dignity. And he was taking their dignity away. Bibi did not want to make a deal. I'm telling you right now, even most recently, when we came up with the maps, it was all 'this is good, good, good.' Everything was always great. But he did not want to make a deal. Now, I don't know if he didn't want to make it for political reasons, or for other reasons. I wish he would have just said he didn't want to make a deal, because there were a lot of people who devoted a lot of work and time to it. But I don't think he would have ever made it. I think the general [Benny Gantz] wanted to make a deal. And the general had a much better relationship with the Palestinians. I assume that's true. Is that true? I mean, I think so. Do you think it's true? They hated Bibi so much. It was very hard to make a deal like that. Not everybody in Israel wants to make a deal. Do the people in Israel want to make a deal?" I replied that polling shows that the majority of the Israeli public supports a two-state solution with the Palestinians but doesn't believe it will happen. "If I were elected, if the election wasn't rigged, you would have had a deal," he replied.

Throughout Trump's term of office, Netanyahu was under criminal investigation for serious allegations of corruption. His trial began in May 2020 and is still ongoing. Trump was also being investigated, first over allegations of collusion with Russia during the 2016 election campaign, and later in his impeachment process in Congress for applying political pressure on the president of Ukraine, Volodymyr Zelenskyy, to investigate his political opponent's son, Hunter Biden. The day Trump revealed his Israeli–Palestinian peace plan, the prosecution filed charges against Netanyahu in the Jerusalem district court for bribery, fraud and breach of trust. A week after the plan was unveiled, the Senate began to debate Trump's impeachment—a process that ended with the Republican majority voting to acquit him. I asked him if he ever raised the matter of Netanyahu's criminal investigations in any of their meetings or phone calls. "I never talked to him about it, what's going on with it?" Trump replied. At this point, he asked to go off the record. For 20 minutes, he asked about the charges against Netanyahu, the potential ramifications of the investigation and the former prime minister's chances of acquittal.

I told him about the cigars and the champagne that, according to the indictment, he had been given as gifts from a billionaire friend, and the favors the friend had allegedly received in return. I brought up the negotiations with the publisher of *Yedioth Ahronoth*, Noni Mozes, to reduce the circulation of the rival *Israel Hayom*, the free daily bankrolled by Sheldon Adelson, in exchange for Mozes adjusting *Yedioth Ahronoth's* editorial line and making it more favorable toward Netanyahu. And the charges of favorable media coverage Netanyahu received in *Walla!*, allegedly in exchange for helping its owner, Shaul Elovitch, with another business deal. When I said that Netanyahu was potentially facing jail time, Trump couldn't believe his ears. He was astonished to learn that the chief of police and the attorney general, both of whom were appointed by Netanyahu himself, were the ones who investigated and indicted him, respectively. At one point, when the conversation tipped into the realm of gossip, Trump asked me to switch off my recording device.

When we went back to speaking on the record, I told him about the impact of the Abraham Accords among the Arab public in Israel, which was far more supportive of the initiative than its representatives in the Knesset were. That hurt them in the elections and made it harder for the opposition to block Netanyahu, I told him. "I saved his ass in many ways. I think I did," Trump said with a grin. "Man, it's very funny."

Almost an hour and a half had elapsed since the start of our conversation, and Trump's advisors were trying to nudge it toward its conclusion. "Here's the bottom line: nobody's done more for Israel than me, and I'm proud to have done it. I'm very proud... We'll see, maybe I'll have a second term. We'll see what happens." I asked whether he was planning to run again. "We'll see what happens. I'm not planning anything."

On the evening of July 19, 2021, my phone rang. On the other end of the line was the former president. He wanted to pick up our conversation from three months earlier at his Florida mansion. "Hello? Is this Barak? Hey, how's it going? How's Israel? What's happening in Israel?" he asked off the bat, imitating an Israeli accent. "Let's go, let's do 10 minutes. Frankly, after 10 minutes, there's not much you can say. It's not a complicated thing. The Iran deal is horrible. Going back to the Iran deal will be terrible." The aim of our conversation was to cover some ground that we had not managed to get to during our meeting. During the call, which lasted more than half an hour, Trump was calmer and less bitter than he had been at Mar-a-Lago three months earlier. He even tried to soften a few of the things he had said to me in that first interview—especially about Netanyahu. I was interested to hear how Trump saw the Abraham Accords now, a year later, but he wanted to talk about Iran. On that subject, he didn't tone down his rhetoric at all. "If Biden goes back to the nuclear deal with Iran, it will be terrible for Israel and for the Middle East," he said. "For Israel it will be a death sentence." I wondered if he didn't think that was going a bit too far. "No. That's what I think. That's my opinion. That's what I thought even before they signed the deal. If they sign it, it'll be a death sentence for Israel. I think for Israel it will be a disaster. It might also be a disaster for Iran." I asked him why. "Because people will fight back against them," Trump replied. I asked if he thought there would be a reaction if they continued with their nuclear program. "I don't know if they'll fight back against them before something happens with their nuclear program or after—that will depend on Israel and maybe the others. Going back to the nuclear deal is a death sentence for Israel, and very bad for Iran. They don't know it yet."

I could sense that Trump really wanted to talk about Iran, so I decided to skip the questions I had prepared on other subjects and circle back to them later, if I had time. In hindsight, it was a good decision. Trump lifted the curtain on one of the biggest secrets from behind the scenes between the United States and Israel following the assassination of the commander of the Quds Force of the Islamic Revolutionary Guards Corps, General Qasem Soleimani. From the outside, it looked like the height of coordination between Israel and the US in their fight against Iran, but I learned that it was actually a point of tension between the two. Below is our exact exchange on the subject.

Question: "I want to take you to January 2020, to your decision to kill Qasem Soleimani. Why did you decide to go for such a move?"

Trump: "He was a man who killed many American soldiers and badly wounded and maimed so many American soldiers. I think he was trying to lead them to war. He was meeting with the people that got blown up with him [the commander of the Popular Mobilization Forces, Abu Mahdi al-Muhandis], and they were not meeting to discuss childcare. They had a lot of very bad intentions, and we knew that. So I felt very strongly that our country really had little choice."

Question: "Was Israel involved somehow in this operation?"

Trump: "I totally know the story. I can't talk about this story. I was very disappointed in Israel over that event."

Question: "What do you mean?"

Trump: "I can't talk about it now, but I was not happy with Israel."

Question: "During the Soleimani assassination?"

Trump: "Israel didn't do the right thing. People will hear about it at the right time."

At this point, one of Trump's advisors who was on the call stepped in and steered the conversation onto a different subject. When I started digging around a few days later, I understood that Trump's frustration over the incident stemmed from an expectation on his part that Netanyahu and Israel would play a more active role. Trump was annoyed. He thought Netanyahu's response was ungrateful. Several senior officials in the Trump administration admitted that the president's anger was not entirely justified, but that incident remains a stain on his relationship with Netanyahu nonetheless.

A few days before my phone call with Trump, an article was published in *The New Yorker* claiming that, after the presidential election in 2020, Netanyahu pushed Trump to attack Iran. I asked the former president whether this was true. "No. It's fake news. Total fake news," he responded immediately. "There was no reason to attack Iran. Iran was in a situation where, if I had won the elections, and I did win the elections, but if I had won officially, Iran would have come to the table to make a deal within a week. There was no reason to attack—so these stories are fake." Trump claimed that the chairman of the joint chiefs of staff, General Mark Milley, was behind these leaks to the press. "It's all because of him," he told me. "Milley wasn't such a great general and he wasn't such a great leader. We would have reached a great deal with Iran straight after the elections. They thought we were going to win. Like a lot of people. And they were right. If we had won the elections officially, I think we would have reached a great deal with Iran within a week. There was no reason to attack them with the military. That's why Milley's claims that I wanted war with Iran are fake. There was no need. Because of the sanctions and all the other things that happened, they were ready to do a deal with us—and it could have been a fair deal for everyone." I asked him again whether he hadn't felt the need for a military solution to Iran. "No. These are fake reports. It's fake news by people whose approval ratings are lower than ever," he said. "There was no need to attack, because we would have won without going to war. It was also a lot better for Iran. We would have made a deal within a week. The sanctions were stronger than they thought. In the end, we would have made a deal with Iran that would have been good for everyone. There wouldn't have been a war because we didn't need one."

When he met with Netanyahu while he was in office, did Netanyahu ask him to attack Iran? I asked. "No. He didn't need to tell me. I talked about it with other people," Trump replied. "But there was no need. We would have got a good deal with Iran if the elections... Now there's a different situation because it looks like the Biden administration wants to go back to what I think is the stupidest and worst deal ever signed... That also puts Israel, more than anyone else, in terrible danger. Israel's existence was in danger—and it will be again if they go back to the deal. It's unfathomable." And did he not think the Israelis would exploit the post-elections lame duck period to attack Iran? I wondered. "No," Trump replied. "It was always possible, and in a way they did attack the Iranians if you look at what's happened in the last few years. But I didn't think that was going to happen." Trump's assessment was correct. Throughout his term, Netanyahu didn't invest efforts into fleshing out a military option against the Iranian nuclear program. He relied on Trump, who, from the sound of our conversation, didn't seem at all enthusiastic about the prospect.

At one point in the conversation, Trump interrupted his own train of thought and changed the subject. "I want to tell you something," he said. "I think it was the biggest mistake the United States ever made to get involved in the Middle East." In terms of military involvement? I asked. "Yes. With the military," he said. "George Bush and Cheney's decision [to invade Iraq]. Many people say that Cheney pushed him into doing it. I think it was the worst decision the US has ever made. Millions of people were killed. Not thousands. During the First World War, we had to be there, and the same in the Second World War, but this [Iraq] invasion was the worst decision by the United States." I told him that Biden was continuing what he himself had started and was withdrawing from the Middle East wars. Indeed, the United States was busy kicking its withdrawal from Afghanistan up a notch at the time, with Biden setting August 31 as the deadline for withdrawing the last US soldier. Two weeks before my conversation with Trump, US forces abandoned the Bagram Airfield—the largest military air base in the country, from which the Americans had conducted the fighting for over two decades. The US soldiers simply cut the power to the base and left in the dark of night, without telling a soul. The commander of the Afghan military forces in the base woke up in the morning to find it was completely empty. The US withdrawal caused morale to plummet within the Afghan military, and the willingness of its soldiers to fight the Taliban around the country evaporated. "Right, Biden is continuing it," said Trump. "The only difference, like you'll start to see, is that the Taliban wouldn't be behaving like this if I were president. We would have made a completely different deal. I don't want to get into it now. Maybe I'll talk about it in the future. But the Taliban would not have done what it's doing now and what it's planning to do in the future if I had been president." The collapse of the Afghan government in the weeks since my call with Trump was quicker than anyone expected. On August 14, Kabul fell to the Taliban, President Ashraf Ghani fled the country and tens of thousands of Afghan citizens, fearing the Taliban, rushed to the international airport, hoping for protection from the US soldiers who had been summoned at a moment's notice to evacuate the US embassy. Donald Trump played a critical role in the fall of Afghanistan. A year earlier, he signed an agreement with the Taliban, part of which included some of their leaders being released from prison. Like most of the American public, he didn't care about Afghanistan. If Trump had won a second term in the White House, he would have almost certainly acted more or less like Biden.

During my meeting with Trump at Mar-a-Lago in April 2021, he savaged Netanyahu. There was a great deal of uncertainty in the air at the time, and it was unclear whether a government could be formed or whether Israel was on its way to a fifth round of elections. In June 2021, a new and previously unimaginable government was formed that brought together disparate parties from a broad cross-section of Israeli political, ethnic and religious society. Our phone call took place a month later. I asked him how he felt about the results of the elections in Israel and the fact that Netanyahu was no longer prime minister. Considering how he had spoken about Netanyahu in our previous meeting, I imagined he would be pleased to see him dethroned. To my surprise, this time his tone toward Netanyahu was far softer. "You know, he was in the job for a long time," Trump told me. "I like the guy, but he was in the job for a long time. People were very angry at him when he was the first person to call and congratulate Biden." I reminded Trump that he was one of those people. "Yes. To be fair, I was not happy with it," he said. "Nobody, except for one or two Israeli prime ministers, did more for Israel than President Donald Trump. Look at the Golan Heights. People didn't talk about it because they said that was out of the question. And Jerusalem, and building the embassy at a record low price and in a better location than the one we had and that nobody thought we would use. But the biggest thing I did was not the Golan Heights or Jerusalem, it was terminating the Iran deal. That is the biggest thing I did." And did he think the fact that Netanyahu was no longer the prime minister of Israel was a good or bad thing for Israel? "Time will tell. We'll see. He was there a long time," Trump replied. "I like him. I think people were very unhappy with the fact that he was the first person to call Biden. Some loyalty. I was okay with it. It's his business. Not only did he call—he released a terrible video. It looked like he was begging for love. I said to myself, my, my, how things change. I was disappointed. In the end it hurt him a lot with the Israeli public. As you know, I'm very popular with the Israeli public. I think it really hurt him. What did Biden and Obama give him? What did they give Israel? The nuclear deal. A deal that in the end, I don't want to say it, but it will be the end of Israel. And now they want to do it again." At the time of writing, Trump is actively considering another run for the presidency in 2024 and Netanyahu is leading his Likud party in the November 2022 elections in Israel. In an interview with Newsmax last June, Trump said he was disappointed in Netanyahu but didn't rule out endorsing him in the future.[335]

During our conversation in July 2021, I reminded Trump that the first anniversary of the trilateral phone call that launched the Abraham Accords was coming up in a few weeks. I wondered how he felt about it now. "It was a great opportunity," he replied. "We decided we needed to do the opposite of what had been done in the last few decades. Because what they did didn't work. What happened was that we did it in reverse. Not the Palestinians, but the other way. We went to Mohamed [bin Zayed] who is highly respected. Mohamed is from the United Arab Emirates. They're great. Great things happened. If the elections hadn't been rigged, we would have got a lot more countries involved by now. What did upset me was that it looks like Biden's people, many of whom think the Abraham Accords were wonderful but they don't want to say it—it doesn't look like they're adding countries or trying to add countries to the list, even though it would be so easy to do. We would have got a lot more countries by now, and they're not doing anything to make it happen."

I asked him how he thought the accords would be judged in 50 or 100 years' time. "I think they will be judged very well," he said. "Nobody thought it was possible. To get the UAE, which is a leader, a very powerful leader, to get it as the first country, it was a great thing. Had the elections ended up the way they should have ended up, I think it would have gone down as a completed deal, because we would have added many countries to it. I don't know if Biden will be able to add countries. I don't know if he has the ability to do it." I asked him what advice he would give Biden on the Abraham Accords. "I would say, meet with numerous countries and you'll sign them up like hotcakes," Trump replied. "They're tired of fighting. The Middle East has been ripped apart so tragically for so many years, long before the US got involved." Trump's advisors cut in once more and reminded him that people were waiting for him for a meeting. I told him that I hoped to see him soon in Israel. "I'm looking forward to it," he replied. "Let me know what happens with the book. Bye, bye."

Biden's Peace?

On the night of June 13, 2021, Naftali Bennett was sitting in his small office in the Knesset. It was the most important day of his political career and perhaps the most dramatic day in Israeli politics in over a decade. Only an hour before, he had been sworn in as Israel's 36th prime minister. Bennett, a conservative right-wing hawk who stood at the head of the small Yemina party, did the unthinkable and joined forces with Yair Lapid, the leader of the centrist Yesh Atid party, to form a unity government that included parties from across the political spectrum. And to top it all off, for the first time in Israel's history, an Arab-Muslim party—Mansour Abbas's United Arab List (Ra'am)—joined the coalition too. To call it a political earthquake would not be an exaggeration. This chapter is based on interviews with a dozen senior Israeli, American and Emirati officials directly involved in the events. Some spoke on the record and others asked not to be named due to the diplomatic sensitivity of the matters in question.

Shortly after the vote of confidence, Bennett was sitting in his office with his chief of staff, Tal Gan-Tzvi, and his political ally, Ayelet Shaked. As the new reality began to sink in, the three engaged in a "how it happened" conversation. Outside, Bennett's long-time spokesman, Matan Sidi, was still taking in the unbelievable turn of events when his cellphone rang. It was an unknown number, but he answered it anyway. "Hi, Matan? It's Nate from the White House Operations Room. President Biden wants to talk to the Prime Minister," the person on the other end of the line said. Spurred into action by the call, the 26-year-old Sidi burst into the room. "Get out, get out of here now," he snapped at a shocked Shaked and Gan-Tzvi. An equally surprised Bennett asked what was going on. "Biden wants to talk to you in five minutes. We need a flag and a photographer here immediately," Sidi responded. Five minutes later, Sidi's cellphone rang again, and he handed it to Bennett. Biden was on the line. A Bennett aide told me that the call was very friendly. After conveying his congratulations, Biden asked Bennett about himself and his family, and the new prime minister told the president about his time living in Manhattan and taking the train to Biden's hometown of Wilmington, Delaware.[336] According to Bennett's aide, Biden then asked for a briefing about the new coalition. "Well, it's very diverse," the prime minister responded, before diving into the details. When the call ended, Bennett and his advisors sat in stunned silence. The penny had dropped. They were not in Kansas anymore.

The political shift in Israel was good news for the Biden administration, and the White House made no attempt to hide its satisfaction. When Biden assumed office in January 2021, it took him a month to return a call to then-Prime Minister Benjamin Netanyahu. With Bennett, the US president called him less than two hours after he was sworn in. During Bennett's one year in office, the Biden administration's main priority in its relations with Israel was the coalition's survival. White House officials never stated this bluntly, but it was clear from day one that they preferred

Bennett's broad coalition to the return of Netanyahu at the helm of a radical right-wing government.

While Bennett was settling into his new position in the Prime Minister's Office, his coalition partner Yair Lapid was starting his new job over at the foreign ministry. Less than a decade earlier, Lapid was a TV host and the anchor of a Friday night news show. Now he was one of Israel's most powerful politicians. Lapid had been angling for the foreign ministry for a long time. When he first entered politics, in time for the 2013 election, he won 19 seats and sought the finance ministry. He had no relevant experience and the joke at the time was that Lapid's only knowledge in finance was the advertising campaign he had done several years previously for a big bank. At the foreign ministry he was a natural fit—a confident English speaker with good people skills. During his years in the opposition, he focused on foreign policy and built relationships with world leaders like French President Emmanuel Macron and US politicians from both sides of the aisle, such as Senators Chuck Schumer and Lindsey Graham.

Lapid assumed office as the most powerful foreign minister in Israeli history since Tzipi Livni, who served between 2006 and 2009. Throughout most of Netanyahu's time in office, the Israeli foreign ministry had been weakened and sidelined. Though Lapid's predecessor, Gabi Ashkenazi, started rehabilitating it, his political rivalry and poor relationship with Netanyahu frequently posed an obstacle. In the nine months after the Abraham Accords were signed, Netanyahu impeded any progress in the relationships with the UAE, Bahrain and Morocco. In an act of naked self-interest, he banned all government ministers from traveling to these countries before he did. The result was an unbreakable logjam. Lapid realized this in his first week on the job, following a meeting with the senior hierarchy in the foreign ministry. "I told them at the end of the meeting that we are going to lead this thing," noted Lapid.[337] In a meeting with Bennett the next day, Lapid told him that his main priority in the immediate term would be pressing ahead with the Abraham Accords and rehabilitating the foreign ministry. Bennett gave him the go-ahead.

Lapid's first phone call on his first day in office was with the Emirati foreign minister, Sheikh Abdullah bin Zayed. "I want to come for a visit to Abu Dhabi to open the Israeli embassy as soon as possible," Lapid told his Emirati counterpart. "Come right away," Sheikh Abdullah answered. Two weeks later, Lapid landed in Abu Dhabi and inaugurated the small temporary embassy at the Conrad Towers, within walking distance from the Emirati foreign ministry building. One of the main goals of Lapid's trip was to begin building a personal relationship with his Emirati counterpart. Sheikh Abdullah had the same idea. "I will come to pick you up for dinner in my car," he told Lapid after they finished their working meeting. According to a senior Israeli foreign ministry official, when the Shin Bet security detail heard of this plan, they panicked—but they had no choice but to live with it. Sheikh Abdullah picked Lapid up from his hotel and drove him to Zuma, a restaurant on the other side of Abu Dhabi. When they ran a red light, Lapid jumped in his seat, only to realize that the whole road had been cleared for them. The Israeli official said the two ministers had sushi for dinner and were speaking about politics and their personal lives, when all of a sudden Lapid remembered something. "Isn't Germany playing England in the Euro football championship tonight?" he asked. "We have to watch," Sheikh Abdullah agreed. "Don't forget my brother is the owner of Manchester City," he said.[338] The two ministers spent the rest of dinner watching the game on the cellphone of one of the Emirati security guards.

One of the questions Lapid asked the foreign ministry experts when he assumed office was where the Biden administration stood regarding the Abraham Accords. As a presidential candidate, Joe Biden was quick to welcome the Abraham Accords shortly after they were announced by his political rival, then-President Donald Trump. But after Biden assumed office, the new administration's interest in the initiative seemed to cool. In closed meetings in his first few months in office, Biden's aides said they wanted to strengthen and expand the Abraham Accords, but in public the administration's spokespeople refrained from even speaking the name of Donald Trump's key foreign policy legacy.[339] This became apparent in an awkward press briefing on April 1, 2021, when veteran Associated Press reporter Matt Lee confronted State Department Spokesman Ned Price on this issue.[340] "What do you call these agreements?" Lee asked. "They're normalization agreements," Price replied. Lee didn't let it go. "But what is the name for them?" he asked. "Normalization agreements," Price reiterated. "No, there's a specific name that they all signed onto. I believe you know what it is," Lee insisted. Price didn't yield. "We call them normalization agreements. That's precisely what they are," he said. As the exchange went on, it became more and more uncomfortable. Lee wondered out loud why Price wasn't using the term Abraham Accords. "Can you say it for me, please?" he asked. "Of course I can say the term Abraham Accords, Matt," came the reply, "But we call them normalization agreements."

This was not an isolated incident. Several weeks later, President Biden had his first phone call with Sheikh Mohamed bin Zayed. An Emirati official told me Biden specifically mentioned the Abraham Accords during the conversation; the public readout issued by the White House, however, referred to them only as normalization agreements.[341] Two weeks later, during the war in

Gaza, then-White House Press Secretary Jen Psaki was asked in the daily briefing whether the administration was going to rethink the Abraham Accords. Her answer raised eyebrows across Washington, Jerusalem and Abu Dhabi. "We don't think [the Trump administration] did anything constructive, really, to bring an end to the long-standing conflict in the Middle East," she said.[342]

On June 27, two weeks after the new Israeli government was sworn in and two days before his trip to Abu Dhabi, Lapid traveled to Rome for his first meeting with US Secretary of State Antony Blinken. Three senior Israeli officials told me Lapid used the meeting to address the elephant in the room. "I know you are suspicious about this and that it's Trump's legacy, but we have a chance to promote peace and do big things," he told Blinken. The Israeli officials said the secretary of state treaded carefully, asked some questions and then said: "I don't know what I am supposed to call it and I don't really care. I know we want to strengthen the normalization process." Nevertheless, Lapid left that meeting with a nagging feeling that the Biden administration was not overly enthusiastic about the Abraham Accords.

Derek Chollet, the counselor of the State Department[343] and one of the Biden administration's top diplomats, rejected that characterization and claimed that any perception that the Biden administration had reservations about the Abraham Accords was a result of "hiccups during the transition."[344] He told me that when he was serving on Biden's State Department transition team, after the election and before the inauguration, the Abraham Accords were one of the few things in the inheritance they got from the Trump administration that they viewed very positively. "I think the Abraham Accords were one of the most positive things to have happened in the Middle East in quite some time," he said. "When we came into office, there was a lot of repair work to be done in several corners of the world. But the Abraham Accords were not something that we thought needed repairing. If anything, it was one of the things we wanted to build on from the previous administration. I don't ever recall a conversation we had, certainly not with Secretary Blinken, where we said don't use the term Abraham Accords. It wasn't a policy decision. But even after we used it repeatedly, we were still criticized for not believing in it. So, it was kind of damned if you do and damned if you don't."

In the weeks after Biden assumed office, when Secretary of State Blinken and his advisors tried to assess the state of the Abraham Accords, they discovered that the State Department bureaucracy was mostly out of the loop about what had been done and what had been promised as part of the different agreements: "It took time to sift through everything, but once we knew fully what we had inherited, we were off to the races."

Several other issues influenced the Biden administration's decision-making on the Abraham Accords during its first few months in office. First, it wasn't a priority in the new administration's foreign policy agenda, which was heavily focused on COVID-19, China and climate change. It wasn't even at the top of Biden's Middle East policy. The new president was focused on returning to the Iran nuclear deal and trying to stop the war in Yemen. Second, two months after Biden entered the Oval Office, Israel went through its fourth consecutive election campaign in two years. Gabi Ashkenazi, Israel's foreign minister at the time, told me the Biden administration was waiting for a new government to be formed in Jerusalem before it would start to push the normalization issue.[345] And third, it wasn't clear who in the Biden administration was even in charge of this file. Indeed, the matter was a source of internal tensions between the White House and the State Department. At one point, the White House considered appointing the former US ambassador to Israel under President Obama, Dan Shapiro, as a special envoy for the Arab–Israeli normalization process, but eventually decided against it. "The bottom line was that at that point in time the Biden administration wasn't into this issue," a senior Israeli official who was directly involved in the discussions told me. "They didn't walk into the room and say, 'We are going to own it.' We tried to spur them on but the State Department wasn't enthusiastic. The White House was more keen to engage but they had bigger concerns at the time. We moved from a situation where the Trump administration saw it as a core US foreign policy objective to a situation where the Biden administration was [just] thinking about it."

One of the big question marks surrounding the Abraham Accords during Biden's first few months in office was whether he would roll back Trump's controversial decision to recognize the Western Sahara as part of Morocco. Trump's move reversed decades of US policy regarding the disputed territory and made the US the only Western country to recognize Morocco's sovereignty there. The Biden administration's commitment to restoring the rules-based world order to which Trump had been so indifferent made this a real possibility. Both the Moroccans and the Israelis were very concerned. According to a senior Israeli official, preventing the US from walking back its recognition of Moroccan sovereignty over the Western Sahara was a top foreign policy priority for Israel during that period. Moreover, there had been almost no contact between the Biden administration and the Moroccan government in the first three months of the new administration, exacerbating Morocco's concerns. In mid-April, after several discussions at the White House and the State Department, Biden's top Middle East advisor, Brett McGurk, called the Moroccan foreign minister, Nasser Bourita, and gave him the impression that there would be no change in US policy on the Western Sahara. Ten days later, Secretary of State Blinken told Bourita that Biden would not reverse Trump's recognition of Morocco's sovereignty—at least for the time being.[346] At the same time, the US asked the Moroccans to support appointing a new UN envoy for the Western Sahara in order to try and resume talks on possible autonomy for the sparsely populated territory. The Moroccans felt better but were not completely reassured, holding the impression that the US position was still tentative. When the new Israeli government took office several weeks later, the US position on the Western Sahara was the main issue Bourita raised in his first phone call with his new Israeli counterpart, Yair Lapid.

On August 11, 2021, I boarded an El Al plane for Lapid's first trip to Rabat, and the first official visit there by an Israeli foreign minister in 20 years. The visit touched a deeply emotive chord within Israeli society and identity politics that went beyond diplomacy and foreign policy. More than a million Israelis have Moroccan heritage, and most of them vote for right-wing parties. This was an opportunity for Lapid to speak to that constituency. Lapid brought with him on the trip one of the senior members of his party, Meir Cohen, who was born in 1955 in a small house with no floor in the town of Mogador (Essaouira) on the Atlantic coast of western Morocco. At that time, Jews made up the majority of the town's population. Lapid's friend, musician Shimon Buskila, also accompanied them. His parents had come to Israel in the early 1960s, and many of his songs are in Darija (Moroccan Arabic). This was his first trip to Morocco. When we visited the synagogue in Casablanca and he performed his song "*Min Nhar Li Mchiti*," ("From the Day You Left") he almost burst into tears.

When Lapid arrived at the foreign ministry in Rabat, he found a conflicted Bourita. The Moroccan foreign minister confided in Lapid that he was struggling with a dilemma concerning huge fires that were raging in Algeria. Relations between the countries were strained over Algeria's support for the Polisario Sahrawi rebels in the Western Sahara. "Offer them help. When we had wildfires the Palestinians sent their firefighters to help us," Lapid told him. When they moved to discuss the Western Sahara, Lapid asked the director general of the foreign ministry, Alon Ushpiz, to join. Ushpiz, who is considered the "Mr. America" of the Israeli foreign service, had close personal relationships with many of President Biden's senior advisors. "How do we preserve US recognition of the Western Sahara as part of Morocco?" they asked him. Ushpiz proposed that Israel would urge the Biden administration to send a letter to the Moroccan government to reiterate their commitment to the policy on the Western Sahara. The Israeli foreign ministry raised the possibility of sending the letter with the State Department immediately after returning from the visit. "We told the US that the Moroccans were concerned about the Biden administration's position and warned that we were worried about the influence this could have on the future of the normalization agreement between Morocco and Israel," said a senior Israeli official. Several weeks later, Secretary of State Blinken sent his Moroccan counterpart a letter committing to upholding US recognition of Morocco's sovereignty over the disputed territory. The Moroccans even tried to use the opportunity to ask the US to open a consulate in the city of Dakhla in the Western Sahara and promote investments there. This was a step too far and the Biden administration made clear it was not going to happen. "The Biden administration didn't roll back Trump's decision because, at the end of the day, it meant supporting Algeria over Morocco. While Algeria was perceived by the US as a regional disrupter, Morocco was perceived as a stabilizing force. They did the right thing," said a senior Israeli official.

State Department Counselor Derek Chollet told me the Biden administration took a close look at the Western Sahara issue and how best to support the UN political process going forward. He admitted that sustaining the positive trajectory of the Israel–Morocco normalization agreement was a factor in the decision-making. "It wasn't the only concern. But certainly, that was a piece of it," he said. "We thought the net gain of what was achieved between Morocco and Israel was very positive."[347]

While Lapid was working on the Abraham Accords, Bennett focused on Israel's "old" peace partners in the region. In late June, two weeks after he was sworn in, Bennett boarded a helicopter. Thirty minutes later, he landed in the royal palace in Amman for a meeting with King Abdullah II of Jordan, his first ever meeting with an Arab leader. For the king, it was the first meeting with an Israeli prime minister in more than five years. To say that the relationship between the king and Bennett's predecessor, Benjamin Netanyahu, was bad would be the understatement of the century. The king saw Netanyahu as someone who was actively trying to undermine him and destabilize Jordan. Both Bennett and the king wanted to reset the relationship. Nevertheless, political tensions were still high, and the Jordanians asked to keep the visit a secret.

The meeting was a success. Right at the top, Bennett told the king that he was going to approve a deal for the sale of more water from Israel to Jordan, something Netanyahu had stalled on for a long time. This was very important for Jordan, which was facing a growing water crisis. "When the meeting ended, Bennett and the king agreed to turn the page from the Netanyahu era," a senior Israeli official told me. The king was very happy. A few days later, he traveled to the economic forum in Sun Valley, Idaho where he spoke with enthusiasm about Netanyahu's successor in several meetings, according to a person in attendance. Bennett and King Abdullah didn't agree on everything. Far from it. But from a starting position where Israeli–Jordanian relations were on the brink of implosion, the two leaders managed to defuse the tension and start rebuilding trust. For Israel's "new" peace partners, and especially for the UAE, this was a welcome development.

But Bennett's most important goal was his first meeting with President Biden. In early August, his national security advisor, Eyal Hulata, and his foreign policy advisor, Shimrit Meir, traveled to Washington to prepare the visit. As with Jordan, here too both sides wanted to start fresh and leave behind the sour memories Biden and many of his advisors held from Netanyahu's years in power. "We knew we couldn't erase history but wanted to try and establish trust with the Biden administration as fast as possible," a senior Israeli official told me. This was the first in-person meeting between Hulata and his White House counterpart, Jake Sullivan. Hulata made it clear to Sullivan that regardless of the disagreements about a possible nuclear deal with Iran, Bennett was not going to adopt the same tactics as Netanyahu. Bennett was determined not to repeat Netanyahu's mistakes with Obama, recognizing that a public fight with Biden on Iran would not provide the desired outcome and Israel would end up paying the price. Hulata told Sullivan that Bennett wanted Biden to say publicly during their meeting that he wouldn't allow Iran to achieve "nuclear weapons capability." A senior Israeli official told me Sullivan agreed to a more limited commitment and said Biden would stress that he would not allow Iran to acquire a nuclear weapon. "They thought the commitment we asked for would very quickly put them in a dilemma about using force," the Israeli official noted. Hulata raised the issue of the Abraham Accords with Sullivan and told him that Bennett wasn't sure if the Biden administration was comfortable with them and willing to advance the initiative, in view of the domestic political baggage surrounding Donald Trump and the foreign policy issues the Biden administration had with Saudi Arabia and the United Arab Emirates. "Can we call it the Abraham Accords or do we need to change the name?" Hulata asked Sullivan. Biden's national security advisor was quick to respond. "No, not at all. We have no problem with this," he said. The meeting between Bennett and Biden was set for August 26. But as the Israeli prime minister's trip to Washington drew closer, the US president became consumed with his biggest foreign policy crisis since assuming office.

On April 14, 2021, less than three months after he entered the Oval Office, President Biden walked into the Treaty Room at the White House and stood in front of the cameras to deliver a speech. President George W. Bush had stood in the same room several weeks after the September 11 terror attacks and announced the invasion of Afghanistan to wipe out Al-Qaeda. Twenty years later, Biden was about to announce his decision to withdraw US forces from the war-torn country. "It is time to end the forever war," Biden said. He set September 11, 2021 as the deadline for completing the pullout. As weeks passed, the situation in Afghanistan deteriorated. The Afghan government became increasingly dysfunctional, and every day saw the Taliban reclaim more and more of the country. On July 8, Biden announced that, on the recommendation of his military commanders, he was expediting the deadline for ending the withdrawal to August 31, almost two weeks earlier than expected. "Speed is safety," he said. When asked if a Taliban takeover was inevitable, Biden said no and stressed that the Afghan army had the capacity to face the Taliban. Events very quickly proved him wrong. Throughout July, the Taliban gained even more ground. On

August 10, CIA Director Bill Burns arrived in Israel. It was his first stop on a six-day trip around the Middle East. On August 15, while he was in Cairo meeting with Egyptian officials, news came through that Kabul had fallen. The Taliban were now in control of the Afghan capital. The CIA and the rest of the US intelligence community were highly criticized for an apparent intelligence failure over the swift Taliban takeover. The fact that Burns was on an overseas trip suggested the agency had failed to foresee that a collapse of the Afghan military was imminent.

Officials in Jerusalem and in capitals around the Middle East were concerned by the speed of the collapse. But they were alarmed even more by the message it sent about US engagement in the region as a whole. The Israeli government was careful not to criticize the Biden administration in public, as were the US's Arab partners in the region. In private, however, they were far more critical. Israeli and Arab officials told me the Afghanistan withdrawal strengthened the narrative that the US was leaving the Middle East to focus on a big power competition with China. "The US wants to disengage from the Middle East but will find that the Middle East will pursue it," one senior Israeli official noted at the time.

Derek Chollet pushed back on that claim. "For the last dozen years, people have been saying we're pulling out of the Middle East," he told me. "I always used to think, what is the baseline people use when they measure our presence in the Middle East? It shouldn't be the 150 thousand troops we had in the region in 2008. Our military presence today is still more than it was pre 9/11. We could not have conducted the withdrawal from Afghanistan without our vital partnerships in the Middle East, like the UAE and Qatar. The fact that we were able, at that moment of crisis, to work with those long-standing partners, was a testament to our relationships and our presence in the Middle East, not the symbol of our withdrawal."[348]

As Bennett and his advisors watched horrific scenes of thousands of terrified Afghans rushing to Hamid Karzai International Airport, hoping to board a flight out of the country, they realized their visit to the White House several days later was going to be totally overshadowed by Biden's "Saigon moment." No one thought things could get even worse. The flight to Washington on the prime minister's plane felt very different. In the previous 13 years I had flown more than 100 times on that plane with Benjamin Netanyahu. His absence this time around was even more striking than the fact that it was Naftali Bennett replacing him at the front of the plane. When Bennett came to the back to brief us, his nerves and excitement were palpable. After all, this would be his first time setting foot in the Oval Office. More than anything, though, Bennett looked exhausted. The preceding three months had been the hardest of his political career. One of Bennett's close advisors told me that in the days before the flight, Bennett spent most of his time preparing for the meeting and held several consultations with Minister of Foreign Affairs Lapid, Minister of Defense Benny Gantz and Mossad Director David Barnea. Iran was his top priority. During the flight, Bennett read a thick folder full of profile articles about Biden that had been published in the previous months in the US press. "Creating a personal connection with Biden was very important for Bennett and he wanted to learn everything he could about him," the former prime minister's aide said.

On Thursday morning, the traveling press pool left for the White House in advance while Bennett huddled with his advisors in his suite at the Willard Hotel—just down the street from the White House—to make last-minute preparations and put the final touches on the statement he was expected to give at the beginning of his meeting with Biden. An hour before he was due in the Oval Office, disaster struck in Kabul. At 5:50 PM local time (just before 11 AM on the East Coast), a suicide bomber detonated an explosive belt at the Abbey Gate of Kabul Airport. Seconds later, several gunmen opened fire on the thousands of people in the area. Thirteen American soldiers and 170 Afghans were killed in the blast and in the firefight that followed. The local affiliate of ISIS claimed responsibility for the attack. "When we heard the news, we knew we had a problem," one of Bennett's senior advisors told me. At 11:30 AM, 15 minutes before the meeting was due to start, one of the president's aides called the prime minister's legendary chief of protocol, Edna Halabani, and asked her to hold and not leave the hotel for the meeting. Biden was holding an emergency meeting with his advisors in the White House Situation Room at the time. Fifteen minutes later, another call came from the White House, asking them to keep holding. Thirty minutes later, the meeting was canceled. While this drama was unfolding, I sat in the White House Briefing Room with the rest of my traveling press colleagues. When we received the announcement that the meeting was off, we made our way out of the White House amid the chaos. *The New York Times* photographer Doug Mills captured that moment in a symbolic photo that ran on the homepage of the *NYT* website.[349]

After Bennett issued a statement condemning the Kabul attack, he sat with his advisors at the hotel, unsure if the meeting with Biden was going to be rescheduled. One of Bennett's top advisors told me they made it clear to the White House that they understood the situation and that Bennett would accommodate himself to Biden's schedule but stressed the prime minister was not going to wait the whole weekend in Washington. Three hours after the Kabul explosion, Shimrit Meir's cellphone rang: the president wanted to talk to the prime minister. According to one of Bennett's aides, the prime minister expressed his condolences while Biden apologized for canceling the meeting. "But I want to see you tomorrow. It's very important to me," Biden told Bennett. The prime minister and his team were relieved. Going back to Israel with no meeting would have been a terrible embarrassment for Bennett.

A day later, we went back to the White House. This time, the meeting took place. Biden took Bennett to his private dining room, where the two sat alone and spoke for over an hour. "It was two people with totally different views who met for the first time but clicked," one of Bennett's advisors who was with the prime minister in the Oval Office meeting told me. "Biden asked Bennett a lot of questions about the domestic political situation and about his eclectic coalition," another Bennett aide said. In the meeting, Bennett presented Biden with what he described as a "death by a thousand cuts" strategy against Iran. It involved countering Iran through a combination of many small actions across several fronts—both military and diplomatic—instead of a single dramatic strike. The Israeli prime minister was very happy with two things Biden said in his statements to the press after their meeting. First, Biden said he was committed to Iran never obtaining a nuclear weapon. Second, the president said that if diplomacy with Iran failed, he was ready to explore other options. Biden was also pleased with the meeting, primarily because it was "drama free," signaling that the relationship got off to a positive start, and also because Bennett told the president that although he was against a US return to the 2015 nuclear deal with Iran, he wasn't going to publicly campaign against it like his predecessor. Biden erased the big question mark Bennett had about the US position on the Abraham Accords.[350] "I am committed to strengthening it and I want to work on getting more countries on board," Biden told Bennett.

Expanding the Circle

As the first anniversary of the Abraham Accords approached, Israel, the UAE and Bahrain opened discussions on how to mark the occasion and how to make sure that the US would be involved. "We can't let September 15 pass without our four countries doing something to reaffirm our support," the undersecretary of the Bahraini foreign ministry, Abdullah Al Khalifa, told me when we met in Jerusalem several weeks prior.[351] Over two months, the three countries pressed the Biden administration to hold some kind of event to mark the day, but the White House and the State Department refused to be drawn into a commitment. Finally, a matter of days before September 15, the State Department invited the Israelis, Bahrainis, Emiratis and Moroccans for a virtual meeting with Blinken for the one-year anniversary. This was the first major gesture of support for the Abraham Accords by the Biden administration. "The Abraham Accords—the historic agreement signed between Israel and the governments of Bahrain and the UAE...show that peace is possible and worthwhile for the leaders who courageously pursue it—and for their peoples," State Department Spokesman Ned Price said in the daily press briefing on September 15, 2021, striking a new tone. From that moment, it was as if someone had flicked a switch. That same day, State Department officials participated in several events in Washington and in capitals around the Middle East to celebrate the Abraham Accords. "There was no shift in our policy," State Department Counselor Chollet told me. "That's just when people started noticing, to be honest. We knew it was the first anniversary and we wanted to just make it very clear where we stood. It wasn't like we were against it and then we were for it. We were always for it."[352]

At the same time in Israel, a strange internal struggle was taking place. September 15, 2021 was also the eve of Yom Kippur, the holiest day in the Jewish calendar. That morning, a few hours before the holiday started, Lapid and several other politicians issued statements to mark the first anniversary of the accords. Prime Minister Bennett, however, was silent. In the week leading up to the event, I asked the Prime Minister's Office several times if Bennett was going to do something to celebrate the anniversary and the answer was always negative. It seemed at the time that Bennett was distancing himself from the Abraham Accords— possibly because he saw them as the legacy of his predecessor, Benjamin Netanyahu. In his first three months in office, Bennett didn't give any public statement about them at all. After I posted several tweets on the matter that morning, I got an angry text message from Shimrit Meir. "Aren't you a bit too emotionally attached to the Abraham Accords?" she wrote. "Aren't you a bit too emotionally detached?" I replied. Only months later did I learn what really happened behind the scenes that day. Two of Bennett's aides who were directly involved in this episode told me that Eyal Hulata and his team drafted a statement for Bennett on the one-year anniversary, but Meir intercepted it and prevented it from being published. "It was a classic power play by Meir that made no sense," recalled a Bennett aide. It took several days for Hulata to find a way to bypass Meir and get Bennett to approve the statement. Shortly before Blinken's virtual meeting with his counterparts from Israel, the UAE, Bahrain and Morocco, Bennett finally issued the statement. "[The Abraham Accords] are a new chapter in the history of peace in the Middle East...Relations between the countries are only at their beginning and are already bearing much fruit," he said.[353]

When the Biden administration assumed office, it found that one of the loose ends that the previous administration hadn't had time to tie up was Sudan. The Sudanese signed the Abraham Accords declaration in the final days of the Trump administration, but never finalized an agreement with Israel on establishing diplomatic relations. In Biden's first few months in office, Israel sent Khartoum a draft agreement, but the Sudanese made it clear that they wanted to have it endorsed by the Biden administration and signed in a ceremony in Washington. Both the Netanyahu and Bennett-Lapid governments encouraged the White House to organize an official ceremony to seal the deal on the establishment of diplomatic relations between Israel and Sudan. Israeli officials told me they made it clear to the White House that a deal was nearly done, but that a White House ceremony could take it over the finish line—this would be very helpful for the Sudanese government and provide an easy win for Biden. The State Department and the White House tried to do just that and pushed it hard for several months. The efforts to hold a summit at the White House didn't bear fruit, but as the September 2021 UN General Assembly drew closer, the Israelis came up with another idea: holding a trilateral meeting between Biden, Bennett and Sudan's military and civilian leaders—General Abdel Fattah al-Burhan and Prime Minister Abdalla Hamdok—in New York. "We were kicking this idea around. Nothing had been decided because we needed to get the actual substance decided first, but we were thinking along that scale. We were reading the news too and we heard the chatter out there that we were somehow not fully on board with the Abraham Accords. And there would be no better way to lance that boil than to just demonstrate with something symbolically significant like that," a senior Biden administration official who was directly involved in the Sudan deal told me. But, in the end, this initiative didn't materialize either—mainly because it wasn't a high enough priority for Biden at that time. A senior Israeli official noted that the UN was a missed opportunity. "Had the meeting taken place we would have had a deal," he said. In mid-October, when Lapid traveled to Washington, he discussed Sudan again with Blinken and Sullivan and asked them to help get the deal over the line. But it was already too late. The domestic political crisis brewing in Sudan escalated a week later to a military coup. When the first reports of events in Khartoum reached Washington and Jerusalem, both sides knew the deal was dead. "The coup screwed everything. Within hours the Americans told us it was over. They really tried but it didn't work," a senior Israeli official recalled. A senior Biden administration official gave me a similar version of events. "We were really close and then when the coup occurred, everything just kind of stopped dead in its tracks. If there had not been a coup, we would be in a different place," he said.

On October 12, 2021, I traveled to Washington for a work trip. With me on United flight 91 from Tel Aviv were then-Foreign Minister Yair Lapid and his whole team and the Emirati ambassador to Israel, Mohamed Al Khaja. We were all there for the same reason: the first trilateral meeting between a US secretary of state and the foreign ministers of Israel and the UAE. This was another significant step by the Biden administration to lean into the Abraham Accords. For me, this flight was an information gold mine. I was the only journalist on board, surrounded by a dozen Israeli and Emirati officials on a 12-hour flight and I used every minute of it. The trilateral meeting between Blinken, Lapid and Sheikh Abdullah bin Zayed was the first in-person post-COVID event held on the eighth floor of the State Department, where the official diplomatic reception rooms are located. A big part of the trilateral meeting was dedicated to Iran. Lapid raised the need for a "Plan B" in case diplomacy with Iran failed. "There was a real discussion about developing a credible military threat against Iran...and when we discussed this Sheikh Abdullah didn't run out of the room. It showed us that the Emiratis see us as allies," a senior Israeli official who attended the meeting told me.[354] This became evident shortly after the meeting, when we were brought into the room for the joint press conference. Blinken, Lapid and Sheikh Abdullah sat next to each other in front of the cameras and spoke in one voice against Iran. It was a powerful and unprecedented moment. "The trilateral meeting in Washington showed the Biden administration how much they had to gain from the Abraham Accords," said Alon Ushpiz.[355] Chollet concurred. "It kind of injected a lot of momentum into our thinking because the conversation was so pragmatic and solution-oriented," he said.[356]

That evening, Sheikh Abdullah hosted Blinken and Lapid for dinner at the residence of Emirati Ambassador Yousef Al Otaiba in McLean, Virginia. When they entered the elegant house, which was arranged by the renowned interior designer Joan Behnke, Ushpiz told Lapid jokingly that he couldn't afford to have any Israeli ambassador see the place because it would start a revolt. When they went for a stroll in the garden on the bank of the Potomac River, Sheikh Abdullah explained that the UAE had bought the neighboring houses over the years in order to expand. "Like you do in the settlements," the Emirati foreign minister joked. "Your Highness, we don't have settlements that nice," Ushpiz responded.

Over dinner, when the ministers were eating truffle pizza and grilled branzino, Blinken raised an issue that was sensitive for Israel but even more so for the UAE: China. Several months earlier, US intelligence agencies discovered what they claimed was a Chinese military and intelligence facility under construction in the commercial Khalifa Port, 50 miles from Abu Dhabi. The Biden administration was stunned by the fact that its biggest rival was building a secret military facility on the soil of one of its closest military partners in the Middle East.[357] The US was alarmed because many of its most advanced weapons systems were positioned in the UAE—such as the F-35 stealth fighter jet. Under significant US pressure, the Emiratis halted the secret Chinese project. But the Biden administration remained suspicious. Even a year later, US officials told me they are still not fully reassured and are concerned that the Chinese might resume their activities at the compound. On the other hand, senior Emirati officials have said that the Chinese had acted without their consent and stressed that they shut it down and would never allow it to continue. The frustration and mistrust on both sides over the Chinese issue runs deep and could lead to an inflection point with ramifications for the US–Emirati relationship.

Back at the dinner at the Emirati ambassador's residence, while Blinken and Sheikh Abdullah were arguing over China's growing involvement in infrastructure projects in the region, Lapid interjected. "What about India?" he asked. Blinken and Sheikh Abdullah wanted to hear more. "They don't have manpower problems and they work on big infrastructure projects. Why don't we start working with them on something?" Lapid proposed. It was Wednesday. On the following Monday, Lapid was expected to host the Indian foreign minister, Subrahmanyam Jaishankar, in Jerusalem. The Israeli foreign minister said all four of them could hold a virtual meeting to talk through the idea. Both the US and the UAE were on board. "For the Biden administration this was a way to counter Chinese competition in the Middle East," the Israeli official said. The following week, Lapid and Jaishankar sat together at the foreign ministry in Jerusalem and held a Zoom call with Blinken and Sheikh Abdullah. The result was a joint forum called I2U2 (Israel, India, US, UAE). "I thought the way to strengthen the Abraham Accords was through multilateral cooperation. The more countries we get in the room the more successful it would be," Lapid told me.[358]

On July 14, the I2U2 convened for the first time on the leaders' level. This time, it was President Biden sitting with Prime Minister Lapid in Jerusalem. The result was a launch of two initiatives: construction of a series of big food parks to boost food security and the development of a huge project to produce clean energy through wind and solar power. In both cases, India would provide the land, the UAE and the US would invest the money and Israel would bring its technological expertise.[359] These are undoubtedly ambitious initiatives. It is unclear to what extent the words will turn into action and tangible results, but all parties acknowledge the potential is huge.

The Biden administration has made several secret attempts to expand the Abraham Accords. On October 13, 2021, a day before the trilateral meeting in Washington, Ushpiz arrived at the White House to speak with President Biden's deputy national security advisor, Jon Finer, in his office in the West Wing. Less than 15 years ago, Finer was a foreign correspondent for *The Washington Post* and covered the 2009 war in Gaza. Several months after President Obama assumed office, Finer joined the administration as a White House fellow, working for then-Chief of Staff Rahm Emanuel. His star rose rapidly. Soon, he moved to work as a foreign policy advisor to then-Vice President Biden, focusing on the Middle East, and later served as a senior advisor to then-Deputy National Security Advisor Antony Blinken. After Obama won a second term, Secretary of State John Kerry asked Finer to come work with him at the State Department. Over time, Finer became Kerry's closest advisor. I met Finer for the first time in 2014 when I was covering the nuclear talks between the US and Iran in Vienna and he was working with Kerry. I found him to be one of the most dedicated, hardworking and intelligent people I have ever met. When Biden assumed office, Finer was appointed as the deputy national security advisor, overseeing the whole national security interagency process. When Finer planned to travel to Mauritania in October 2021, it was clear to both the Biden administration and the Israeli government that this was an opportunity worth pursuing.

Mauritania, a poor country in North Africa, is not a major player in the Arab world but it was one of the countries that started warming relations with Israel in 1995 after the Oslo Accords. After several years of low-profile talks, both countries established diplomatic relations in a ceremony in Washington in 1999. Mauritania canceled the state of war with Israel that had been declared in 1967 and became the third Arab country to officially recognize Israel after Egypt and Jordan. Shortly after the agreement was signed, both countries opened embassies in Tel Aviv and Nouakchott, respectively. The Israel–Mauritania relationship lasted for more than a decade, only deteriorating when the war in Gaza broke out in January 2009. Under Iranian pressure, Mauritania suspended diplomatic relations, expelled the Israeli diplomats from the country and, in March 2010, announced it was cutting ties with Israel. The Mauritanians even allowed Iran to take over a hospital for cancer treatment that Israel built in Nouakchott (and which was about to be inaugurated) several weeks after the Israeli ambassador was expelled.

In its last few weeks in office, the Trump administration tried to reach some sort of breakthrough in Mauritania–Israel relations. Moroccan Foreign Minister Bourita also urged the Mauritanian government to consider a deal. A former Trump administration official told me the talks were moving in the right direction, but time ran out. So, when the Biden administration started thinking it terms of broadening the Abraham Accords, Mauritania was identified as a promising target.

Ushpiz came to the White House to brief Finer ahead of his trip to Nouakchott. "Tell them we want to go back to the pre-2009 status quo," Ushpiz told Finer. He said Israel wanted to re-establish full diplomatic relations, reopen its embassy in Mauritania and get back the hospital that had been given to the Iranians. "What are you willing to give?" Finer asked. Ushpiz told him that Israel had an assistance plan tailor-made for Mauritania waiting on the shelf. "Tell them that if we have a deal, we will implement the assistance plan," he said. Several days later, Finer landed in Nouakchott, met President Mohamed Ould Ghazouani and other senior ministers and raised the issue of normalization with Israel. The Mauritanians weren't enthusiastic but were willing to engage. President Ghazouani told Finer he wanted to resume ties with Israel gradually in several stages and not in one big leap. "We didn't want that at the time, but the discussion is still ongoing," a senior Israeli official told me.

Another country the Biden administration was trying to lobby to join the Abraham Accords was Indonesia. When Lapid assumed office as foreign minister he had identified Indonesia, together with Saudi Arabia, as the top priority for Israel's diplomatic efforts to expand the Abraham Accords. With around 280 million citizens, the majority of them Sunni Muslims, Indonesia is the most populated Muslim country in the world. It is also one of the few Muslim democracies, and among the world's 20 largest economies. Israel and Indonesia have had a secret relationship since the early 1960s. The Mossad, which was in charge of the relationship, brought Israeli experts to Indonesia to build farms as part of what was then called "agricultural diplomacy." Over the years, Israeli diplomats posted at the embassy in Singapore were also given responsibility over the relationship with Indonesia. In October 1993, history was made when Prime Minister Yitzhak Rabin visited Indonesia and met with President Suharto. The visit was the result of the new diplomatic momentum created by the signing of the Oslo Accords a month earlier. The Mossad spent weeks planning it in secret, and it was carried out as part of Rabin's trip to China. On the way back to Israel, the plane deviated from its official flight plan and landed in Jakarta. During the flight, Rabin came to the back of the plane and shocked the traveling press with the news of the new flight destination. Former Mossad Director Shabtai Shavit, who organized the visit, wrote in his memoir that one of the reporters was furious and threatened to file a lawsuit for kidnapping. During the meeting, Suharto told Rabin that Indonesia's relations with Israel would be linked to progress in the peace process with the Palestinians.[360] Over the next 25 years, this served as the organizing principle of the relationship between Israel and Indonesia. Behind the scenes, there were growing security, intelligence and economic ties, but any public aspect was always linked back to the situation on the ground in the West Bank and Gaza. The best barometer for that was tourism. At times of progress in the peace process, Israeli tourists were allowed in Indonesia and at times of tension, Israeli tourists were banned.

The Trump administration tried to break this cycle. As part of its push to get more Muslim and Arab countries into the Abraham Accords, the White House tried to get Indonesia on board. Its key partner was Luhut Binsar Pandjaitan, the minister for maritime affairs and investment and a key ally of President Joko Widodo. Luhut was a committed proponent of warming relations with Israel—partly as a way to improve ties with the US. In November 2020, a few days after the US presidential elections, Luhut visited the White House and met with Trump and Kushner.

According to a former Biden administration official, Trump and Kushner pressed for a deal that would include normalization with Israel. Adam Boehler, CEO of the US International Development Finance Corporation, who was also on Kushner's team, said the Trump administration offered Indonesia up to two billion dollars in development aid in return for joining the Abraham Accords.[361] But the Indonesians had another deal in mind. They wanted Trump to lower tariffs on textile imports from Indonesia in return for allowing direct flights from Tel Aviv to Jakarta and giving visas to Israeli tourists. By the time Trump left office no deal had been reached.

When the Biden administration assumed office, and later on when a new government was formed in Israel, Luhut tried to renew the push for a deal. He even reached out to former Trump administration officials and asked for help in opening a secret channel with Prime Minister Bennett and his advisors. When I attended the Manama Dialogue Conference in Bahrain in November 2021, I noticed that Eyal Hulata was sitting at dinner next to Indonesia's minister of defense, Prabowo Subianto. They had a lively conversation and exchanged business cards. Subianto was a key proponent of the Indonesian normalization with Israel. In recent years, he held several secret meetings with Israeli officials in Thailand and in other countries. After a photo of Subianto speaking to another Israeli diplomat at the conference in Manama went viral, he pushed back against his critics and issued a statement saying that speaking to Israeli officials was not prohibited when it served the national interest.

Unlike with Mauritania, in the case of Indonesia the new Israeli government agreed to take a step-by-step approach and try to get a deal on direct flights and visas for Israelis first. When Lapid saw Blinken in Washington in October he encouraged him to push for progress with Indonesia. Two months later, on December 13, 2021, Blinken arrived for a visit in Jakarta. He raised the issue of normalization with Israel in his meeting with President Widodo, Minister Luhut and with his Indonesian counterpart Retno Marsudi. While Luhut was supportive, Marsudi stridently opposed any move toward normalization.[362] Several days after the visit, I published a story about Blinken's normalization bid. The spokesman of the Indonesian foreign ministry confirmed the issue was discussed but stressed that Marsudi rejected the proposal. "The minister of foreign affairs conveyed Indonesia's consistency toward Palestine and that Indonesia will continue with the Palestinian people to fight for justice and independence," he said.[363] The story created an uproar in Indonesia. A senior State Department official told me that the government in Jakarta didn't appreciate it and neither did the Biden administration. "Indonesia is one of the heavier boulders we're trying to push up the hill. We've been working on that and we've made some quiet progress there. But sometimes, sunlight on this is not necessarily conducive to progress. The Abraham Accords were not negotiated in the open. We had some very candid conversations with the Israelis about how these kinds of stories in the press are not going to be helpful to our efforts to push for normalization because the Indonesians were not happy about that," he said. In the months that followed, some very small steps were taken in the relationship between Israel and Indonesia. At the time of writing, however, no breakthrough seems to be imminent.

Israel Steps Up

In November 2021, General (Ret.) Amos Yadlin visited Abu Dhabi. As the former head of Israeli military intelligence and later as the director of the Institute for National Security Studies

(INSS, Israel's leading think tank) he was a prominent voice in Israel's foreign policy and defense establishment. It was only natural that he would be invited for a meeting with then-Crown Prince Mohammed bin Zayed, whom he already knew. He found the Emirati leader in a foul mood and full of grievances and suspicion of the Biden administration over the Chinese military base crisis. When he returned to Israel, he called National Security Advisor Eyal Hulata. When Hulata was the head of the policy department at the Mossad, he would occasionally invite Yadlin to join the internal meetings to pick his brains. When Yadlin told Hulata about his trip to the UAE, the latter proposed that he come over and brief Bennett. The Abraham Accords were still not a significant issue on the prime minister's radar and Hulata sought to encourage him to get involved. During Trump's time in office and in the three years leading up to the Abraham Accords, Hulata was working on the normalization issue in the Mossad. One of his first trips abroad after Bennett's visit to Washington was to Abu Dhabi. He met MBZ and came back determined to organize a visit for Bennett in the UAE as soon as possible. "After getting the briefings from Hulata and Yadlin about their visits to Abu Dhabi, Bennett understood that he needed to build a relationship with MBZ," a senior Bennett aide told me.

Bennett's visit to the UAE was scheduled for December 12, 2021. I was supposed to join Bennett on the trip, along with several of my colleagues, but the day before, the prime minister's office announced they would not be taking any traveling press on the plane. The official reason for the cancelation was COVID-19 restrictions, but the truth was that Bennett didn't want the press there. The Israeli prime minister was recovering from a scandal around a vacation his wife and kids had gone on to the Maldives while he called on Israelis not to travel abroad because of COVID.

"We didn't need more criticism at that time," a Bennett aide noted. The Emirati crown prince didn't object to Israeli journalists joining Bennett's trip but didn't mind keeping the visit on a lower profile and maintaining tighter control over reports in the media either. A senior Israeli official told me the Emiratis were nervous about the Iranian response. Several weeks before, reports had appeared in the Israeli press about the possibility of posting Israeli military officers to military bases in the UAE. The Iranians sent angry communications to the Emiratis and warned them not to allow any Israeli military presence on their soil. The Emiratis then registered a formal protest with Israel about the press reports. A senior Israeli official told me they were trying to balance the normalization process with Israel and their risk management with Iran. "Some people in MBZ's close circle thought a visit by the prime minister of Israel at that time was not the right thing for them when it came to their situation with Iran," he said. A week before Bennett's trip, the Emirati national security advisor, Sheikh Tahnoun bin Zayed, visited Tehran for talks with his Iranian counterpart Ali Shamkhani. It was the highest-level visit to Iran by an Emirati official in years.

What appeared to be the beginning of an Emirati–Iranian rapprochement worried Bennett, but when he landed in Abu Dhabi the concerns disappeared. On that trip, Bennett made history as the first Israeli prime minister to make an official and public visit to the UAE. The Emirati foreign minister, Sheikh Abdullah bin Zayed, waited for him on the tarmac as he disembarked from the El Al plane, and he was treated to a welcoming ceremony at the airport with full honors. The next day, Bennett arrived at MBZ's private palace. After a short ceremonial meeting with their aides, MBZ suggested they speak privately. The two stepped out on a balcony overlooking the Gulf and engaged in a personal conversation. A senior Israeli official who was briefed by Bennett after the meeting told me MBZ spoke at length about his relationship with the Biden administration. He said he was concerned by the optics of the US pull-out from Afghanistan, frustrated by US policy on Yemen and Iran and complained about the American pressure regarding UAE–China relations. His main message was that he wanted more resolve and reassurances regarding US commitment. "Bennett was very impressed by MBZ's thinking and understanding of the West," the senior Israeli official recalled.

At one point in their four-hour discussion, throughout which they occasionally called in their advisors, MBZ told Bennett that the free trade agreement that both countries have been discussing was at an impasse. Bennett asked the director general of the prime minister's office, Yair Pines, to join the meeting. "I want you to invite an Emirati delegation to Israel, get a few rooms in a hotel in Tel Aviv and don't check out until you get a deal. Push it as hard as you can," said Bennett according to two Israeli officials. This moment secured Bennett a lot of credit with MBZ, who appreciated the prime minister's pragmatism and his efforts to get things done. Bennett set the deadline for signing the free trade agreement at the end of the second quarter of 2022. On May 31, 2022, the deal was signed in Dubai. "Bennett understood that we had to build a relationship with the UAE based on more than just the common threat of Iran," a senior Israeli official told me. "Bennett started shifting the relationship to a civilian-economic one too."

Whenever the Iranian issue did come up, MBZ was very careful. One of Bennett's aides said that the Emirati leader made it clear to his Israeli counterpart that he was not going to take an anti-Iran line. "They didn't want to mention Iran in the joint statement and asked us to refrain from saying the issue was even discussed," another Bennett advisor said. But behind the scenes, Bennett and MBZ discussed at length the indirect negotiations between the US and Iran on a possible return to the 2015 nuclear deal. A phone call between Bennett and Secretary of State Blinken about Iran several days earlier raised tensions between the US and Israel. The call itself was businesslike: Bennett raised his concerns about the nuclear talks with Iran and Blinken made it clear that the US thought diplomacy was the best way forward. Shortly after the call, Bennett issued a strongly worded statement in which he claimed that the US was being blackmailed by Iran and called for an immediate halt to negotiations. One of Bennett's aides even briefed reporters that the call was very difficult. Both Israeli and US officials told me Blinken waited to release his readout of the call out of respect for Bennett and was stunned when he saw what the prime minister told the press, especially when the talks with Iran were not even close to a decisive moment. According to a senior Israeli official, Blinken called Lapid later and told him how offended and frustrated he was by Bennett's behavior. "This shouldn't have happened," Lapid replied, and reassured his US counterpart that Israel hadn't changed its policy of not conducting a public campaign against the Iran deal. Three Israeli officials blamed Bennett's foreign policy advisor, Shimrit Meir, for creating the crisis. "Shimrit used very strong language in the readout because of domestic Israeli politics. She thought this was a way to deal with Netanyahu's criticism of the government's policy on Iran," a Bennett aide told me.

Back at the meeting between Bennett and MBZ, the Israeli prime minister raised an idea for how Israel, the UAE and other regional partners could work together to defend themselves against Iran and its proxies. "I call it MEAD," Bennett told MBZ. "Middle East Air Defense alliance." The vision, he explained, was to form a network of radars and sensors around the region that would be linked to different air defense systems and operate under the umbrella of the US central command. This way, Bennett said, all the countries that wanted to be part of this alliance would benefit from these assets and defend themselves together. This was a preliminary discussion that seemed theoretical. But several weeks later it became very real.

On January 17, 2022, around 10 AM, three loud explosions ripped through the Musaffah industrial district in the southern part of the city of Abu Dhabi. Several minutes later, another explosion was heard near Abu Dhabi International Airport. As fire trucks, ambulances and security forces raced to the scene, it became clear that the UAE was facing an unprecedented attack. "This was our 9/11," Sheikh Abdullah told me.[364] Details started to emerge quickly. Three kamikaze drones had hit an Abu Dhabi National Oil Company (ADNOC) refinery. Another drone hit an extension of the airport. Three people were killed and six wounded. One Zulfiqar ballistic missile was successfully intercepted by the Emirati military using the Thermal High Altitude Area Defense (THAAD) system. The UAE is one of the only countries with the US-developed system, and this was its first operational use anywhere in the world. Shortly after, Houthi rebels in Yemen claimed responsibility for the attack and said they also fired several ballistic missiles toward Abu Dhabi. The Houthis called the attack "Operation Hurricane of Yemen" and claimed it was a retaliation for the Emiratis' role in a successful offensive by the pro-government militia, the "Giants Brigade," against their forces in the Shabwa region in Yemen. "You don't understand, we don't have bomb shelters in every house in Abu Dhabi like you do in Israel. We never thought we would need it," Sheikh Abdullah told the Israeli foreign minister when he called shortly after the attack to convey his solidarity. When Blinken called Sheikh Abdullah several hours after the attack, the Emirati foreign minister had one request: that the US redesignate the Houthi rebels in Yemen as a terrorist organization. Less than a month after he assumed office, President Biden rolled back the Trump administration's decision on that matter, saying it hampered humanitarian assistance to the Yemeni people. Since then, the Houthis have escalated their attacks in Yemen and against other countries in the region. "The attack on civilian targets in Abu Dhabi fell squarely in that category [of terrorism]," a senior Emirati official said. Blinken condemned the attack, as did Jake Sullivan: "Our commitment to the security of the UAE is unwavering, and we stand beside our Emirati partners against all threats to their territory."[365] Two days after the attack, US Secretary of Defense Lloyd Austin spoke with MBZ. The Emirati leader had a list of requests for urgent US assistance in reinforcing Emirati defenses against missile and drone attacks as well as assistance in intelligence and targeting information for air strikes against the Houthis in Yemen. The Emirati director of intelligence, Ali Al Shamsi, arrived in Washington on the same day for a previously scheduled trip. Emirati officials said Shamsi pressed CIA Director Bill Burns and Sullivan on the redesignation of the Houthis and stressed that such an attack would not have been possible without Iranian support. A day later at a press conference, Biden confirmed he was considering redesignation. This raised expectations in the UAE. Senior Emirati officials were hopeful that the attack would be an opportunity to improve the relationship with the Biden administration and reinvigorate the strategic partnership that had been gradually eroded. Not long after, it became evident that the January 17 attack was indeed a watershed moment for the US–UAE relationship—but not for the better.

The Israeli government also saw the crisis as an opportunity. The Israelis wanted to show their new regional partner they were stepping up to help them in their time of need and, at the same time, project the benefits of the Abraham Accords to other countries in the region. "From the first moment there was a security principle in the alliance created by the Abraham Accords: the moderate countries in the region will take care of each other. So it was clear to us that we had to act fast," Lapid told me.[366]

For Prime Minister Bennett it was the realization of the threat his MEAD alliance had been designed to confront. Several hours after the attack, he sent a letter to MBZ. He conveyed his condolences and committed to working with the UAE against the Houthis. "We stand ready to offer you security and intelligence support in order to help you protect your citizens from similar attacks," Bennett wrote. "I have ordered the Israeli security establishment to provide their counterparts in the UAE with any assistance, should you be interested." The letter, however, caused a diplomatic incident. Shimrit Meir asked to put out a tweet about it and one of Bennett's media advisors thought this meant tweeting the original photo of the letter. Two Israeli officials told me the Emiratis did not respond positively to this. A senior Emirati official called Bennett's national security advisor and complained. The Emiratis appreciated the Israeli support but felt that making the letter public portrayed them as weak and dependent on Israel. "The tweet was a mistake, but the text of the letter was very good. Very quickly things turned for the better," said a senior Bennett aide.

Senior Emirati officials informed me that the first ones to show up in Abu Dhabi after the attack were the French, who have a defense agreement with the UAE and soldiers based in Abu Dhabi. The second to show up shortly after were the Israelis. A day after the attack, a delegation of Israeli officers from the Mossad and military intelligence landed in Abu Dhabi to assist with the investigation and the forensic work. "We really appreciated it," an Emirati official said.

The first Israeli official to speak to MBZ after the attack was Benny Gantz. The defense minister was also the first Israeli minister to meet with MBZ following the signing of the Abraham Accords. Shortly after the new Israeli government was formed, Gantz traveled to Abu Dhabi and discussed ways to strengthen security cooperation between the two countries with the Emirati leader. Unlike Bahrain and Morocco, who received Gantz for a high-profile public visit, the Emiratis wanted to keep it secret. It wasn't until six months after the visit that the Israeli military censor allowed the media to reveal its existence. An Israeli defense official told me that in their call on January 17, Gantz promised MBZ that Israel would offer all of its available resources to the UAE to defend itself. After the call ended, Gantz asked the director general of the Ministry of Defense, Amir Eshel, and the head of the Political-Military Bureau in the Ministry of Defense, Zohar Palti, to come to his office. "Give the Emiratis everything they need," he told them, according to a senior Israeli defense official.

In July 2021, Foreign Minister Lapid invited Amir Hayek, an economist and the former director general of the ministry of trade, for a meeting. He stunned Hayek and proposed that he become the first Israeli ambassador to the UAE. "Go home, think about it and let me know," Lapid told him. Hayek gave him an answer on the spot. "I don't need to go home. I'll take it," he said. On November 15, 2021, Hayek presented his credentials to the UAE vice president and the ruler of Dubai, Sheikh Mohammed bin Rashid Al Maktoum, and got to work. One of the first calls Hayek made after the January 17 attack was to President Isaac Herzog. Herzog's mother, Aura, had passed away a week before and during the shiva (the Jewish seven days or mourning) MBZ had called him to offer his condolences. "Now you need to call him," Hayek told Herzog, according to an official in the president's office. Herzog's call was also important because the Israeli president planned to visit the UAE at the end of January. Hayek stressed it was crucial to make clear to MBZ that there was no change of plans. On Friday evening, January 21, Herzog made the call. MBZ sounded angry. "I wanted to tell you that I am not afraid and I am still coming to see you," Herzog told the Emirati leader.

On the morning of January 24, a week after the first attack, explosions were heard in Abu Dhabi once more. The Houthis fired two ballistic missiles from northern Yemen. Both were successfully intercepted by Emirati air defenses and by US forces at the Al Dhafra Air Base. There were no physical damages and casualties, but the Dubai stock market cratered and cracks began to form in the general feeling of security and stability the UAE had enjoyed for many years. After the second attack, the Shin Bet, which is in charge of Herzog's security, wanted to cancel the visit that was one week away. Herzog overruled them and declared that he was sticking to the plan. After the trip was officially announced, the Houthis issued a statement and threatened to attack the Dubai Expo, where the Israeli president was due to visit. "When Herzog didn't cancel, the Emiratis were positively surprised. They were extremely happy," Benny Gantz told me.[367]

On January 30, Herzog and his wife Michal landed in Abu Dhabi. This was the first ever official visit by an Israeli president to the UAE and it came at a time of unprecedented turmoil in the country. "Visiting there and meeting him was really a dream come true," Herzog recalled when we met six months later.[368] "MBZ is a transformational leader. He is an extremely intelligent and very nice person. He inherited from his father the ability to plan 50 years ahead."

The welcoming ceremony at the presidential palace in Abu Dhabi was the most moving part of the trip. Herzog and MBZ walked into a grandiose white marble hall, its ceiling more than 50 feet high. An honor guard of soldiers in military uniform with rifles and others in traditional clothes, golden daggers in their belts and swords in their hands, was waiting in attention. As MBZ and Herzog arrived at a small stage in the middle of the grand hall, the military band started playing the Israeli national anthem, "HaTikva." The video of that moment opened all the evening news broadcasts back in Israel. "The acoustics in the palace are amazing and it was an unforgettable moment," Herzog told me.

After a working lunch with their teams, MBZ invited Herzog to continue the conversation at his private home, where he introduced the Israeli president to his children, after which they were left alone for another two hours. MBZ told Herzog of his deep disappointment with the US response in the two weeks since the first Houthi attack. "He was deeply offended," a senior Israeli official said. There was intelligence in the days leading up to the visit that suggested the Houthis might conduct another missile attack while Herzog was in the UAE. "Are you not afraid to be here?" MBZ asked Herzog. "How can I be afraid when I am in your house?" the Israeli president replied. Several hours later, shortly after midnight, air raid sirens were heard again in Abu Dhabi. It was the third Houthi attack in three weeks. One ballistic missile launched from Yemen fell outside of UAE territory and the other was intercepted by Emirati air defenses. The president's aides all ran in their pajamas to the operations room that was established on his hotel floor. The director general of the president's office, Eyal Shviki, went to Herzog's suite and knocked. Herzog, who was asleep and didn't hear the sirens, opened the door groggily. "We need to take you to a bunker right away," Shviki told him. Herzog said, "I am not going to any bunker. Good night," and went back to bed. In the morning he called MBZ to get an update on what happened. "How did you sleep?" the Emirati leader asked. "Really well," Herzog replied. "You weren't disturbed by the firecrackers?" MBZ inquired. "No. I don't know what you are talking about. You know I feel safe here," the Israeli president said and added that he was getting ready to travel to the Dubai Expo as planned.

Herzog's visit was a meaningful sign of political and moral support for the UAE by Israel, but behind the scenes something much bigger was taking place. The commitment Bennett and Gantz gave MBZ after the first attack on Abu Dhabi materialized into one of the biggest security cooperation efforts Israel has ever engaged in with an Arab country. Several days before Herzog's visit, a delegation of Israeli officials from the Ministry of Defense landed in Abu Dhabi. Two senior Israeli defense officials told me that in the initial conversations with the UAE in the immediate aftermath of the first attack, Emirati officials asked for the Iron Dome missile defense system, which has proved itself as the most advanced and effective system of its kind in the world. Over more than a decade, the Iron Dome intercepted thousands of rockets fired from Gaza, saving numerous lives and thereby preventing more devastating escalations. "We told them we weren't sure the Iron Dome was what they need and proposed to start by doing an overall threat assessment and building an air defense strategy for the UAE that fits their needs," a senior Israeli defense official said. The Emiratis agreed. The director general of the Israeli Ministry of Defense, Amir Eshel, personally oversaw the effort. Eshel, a retired general, had served as the commander of the air force and the head of the IDF Planning Directorate. He had the exact expertise needed for the project. He was joined by the head of the Political-Military Bureau in the Ministry of Defense, Zohar Palti, an ex-Mossad general who for years dealt with Israel's secret intelligence and security relationships in the Arab word. The two traveled to the

UAE several times after the attacks to understand the Emiratis' needs. Israeli defense officials said the assessment found that the Emiratis required missile defense, counter-drone technology and detection and early warning systems. "We were very quick to respond and very cooperative. We didn't just sell stuff to the Emiratis. We analyzed their needs and gave them what they needed as fast as we could and we think they appreciated that," a senior Israeli defense official told me.

The Israelis reached the conclusion that one of the systems that would be the best fit was SPYDER, an air defense system developed by Rafael, an Israeli defense technology company, and Israeli Aerospace Industries (IAI). SPYDER, which employs the same radar system as Iron Dome, can detect and intercept drones, cruise missiles and precision-guided munitions. While the Emiratis had the THAAD and Patriot systems to intercept ballistic missiles, SPYDER would fill the gap in their defenses. However, according to Western officials, there was a problem. The only SPYDER batteries Israel had in stock had been ordered and paid for by the Philippines. The Israelis reached out to the Ministry of Defense of the Philippines and explained the situation. They stressed the urgency and immediacy of the Emiratis' need, as they were still under threat of new attacks. The Philippines understood the situation and agreed to postpone the delivery of the SPYDER system they had ordered. The shipment was then diverted to the UAE. Another defensive system Israel proposed to the Emiratis was the Barak 8 surface-to-air missile, with the capability to intercept ballistic missiles and drones. On April 14, 2022, three months after the first Houthi attack on Abu Dhabi, a C-17 Globemaster of the UAE Air Force landed at the Nevatim Air Force Base in southern Israel. After an hour on the ground, it went back to Abu Dhabi. Over the following two weeks, seven more such flights took place.

This unprecedented airbridge transferred the SPYDER system and the Barak 8 to Abu Dhabi.[369] The Emiratis greatly appreciated the gesture. They felt that in their time of need, their new allies in the region—Israel—stepped up. They couldn't say the same about their old allies, the United States.

In the aftermath of the first attack on Abu Dhabi, MBZ held an emergency meeting with his military commanders to decide on immediate measures to defend the country from another attack. According to a senior Emirati official, the Emirati military informed MBZ that the best way to detect and intercept incoming drones with the UAE's existing capabilities was by having Emirati Air Force F-16s and Mirage 2000s in the air around the clock. For that to happen the UAE needed US Air Force KC-135 strategic tankers, which were deployed to the Al Dhafra Air Base in Abu Dhabi at the time. The US agreed to the Emirati request and the tankers refueled the Emirati fighter jets several times. But then something happened that shook MBZ. Several days after the second attack on Abu Dhabi, the military attaché at the US embassy arrived for a meeting with senior UAE military officials. Emirati officials thought he had come to discuss the Houthi attacks, only to discover that the meeting was over something completely different when the senior US military officer handed them the bill for the refueling of their jets. The Emiratis were deeply offended. For MBZ, this was further proof of his growing feeling since January 17 that the US had abandoned the UAE in its time of need. From that point on the US–Emirati relationship spiraled to its lowest point in decades.

On February 1, a day after the third attack, Secretary of Defense Austin called MBZ. Austin conveyed his solidarity and told the Emirati leader that Washington would continue to provide early warning intelligence and collaborate on air defense. He notified the Emirati leader that the US would send the Navy guided-missile destroyer USS Cole to the UAE and deploy F-22 fighter jets in Abu Dhabi. He also told MBZ he was sending the outgoing commander of US Central Command (CENTCOM), General Frank McKenzie, to the UAE for further discussions. The Biden administration thought at the time that the phone call went well and felt the response was robust. But on the Emirati side the perception was the complete opposite. "It took the US two weeks to send us military support but even then, it wasn't what we asked for," an Emirati official told me. A senior US defense official said the UAE asked the US for intelligence and other targeting data for airstrikes against the Houthis in Yemen. They didn't get it: "Some of the things the Emiratis wanted we didn't have." When General McKenzie arrived in Abu Dhabi on February 6, he was surprised to find that MBZ refused to see him. This was highly unusual. The Emirati leader would usually meet any number of US officials who passed through customs at Abu Dhabi International Airport. The fact that he didn't meet McKenzie was an unambiguous snub and a clear signal to the White House. "We couldn't believe it took the Americans 22 days to send someone to Abu Dhabi to show solidarity for the attacks," a senior Emirati official told me.

"Sheikh Mohamed was understandably upset," said Derek Chollet.[370] "I initially felt bad that so much time had elapsed, that he was feeling upset and we didn't have an indication that this was the case. Secretary Blinken had talked to ABZ soon after the attacks to express his concerns and ask what they needed. We certainly took it very, very seriously and felt that we responded in a way that we thought was responsive to our friends in need. Sheikh Mohamed did not feel that way."

The brewing crisis between the US and the UAE worried the Israelis. They heard from the Emiratis about their frustrations and noticed the Biden administration was at least partially oblivious to them. When Eyal Hulata visited the White House on February 9, he explained the Emirati position to his US counterpart, Jake Sullivan, and to Biden's top Middle East advisor, Brett McGurk. "The US didn't understand what the Emiratis were complaining about," a senior Israeli official told me. "Hulata told them that MBZ needed to know that the US stands by him in their time of need. They didn't only want US weapons. They wanted to know there was a US commitment to use weapons to deter any further aggression against the UAE."

When word of MBZ's snub of McKenzie reached the White House, McGurk asked the Emirati ambassador to Washington, Yousef Al Otaiba, what was the problem. By way of explanation, Al Otaiba told McGurk about the bill the US military attaché had tabled for the jet fuel. Biden's top Middle East advisor couldn't believe what he was hearing.

It was only then, three weeks after the Houthi attack, that the White House began to realize the extent of the crisis. Several days later, McGurk traveled to Abu Dhabi to try and bring the situation under control. He sat with MBZ for hours while he unpacked all his grievances about the US response to the Houthi attack, which he described as slow and weak. US and Emirati officials said MBZ told McGurk he never thought the US would treat the UAE this way after decades of security partnership. "Emirati soldiers fought shoulder to shoulder with American soldiers in Afghanistan and in other places after 9/11 and now when we have our 9/11 you are not here," MBZ told McGurk. The Emirati leader was also very frustrated about the time it took McKenzie to arrive in Abu Dhabi and the fact that the Biden administration had not accepted the UAE's request to redesignate the Houthis as terrorists. The State Department claimed that a redesignation would make the UN's and other aid groups' humanitarian work in Yemen much harder. This argument gave the State Department the upper hand in the internal debate inside the Biden administration on the issue. McGurk tried to calm MBZ and reassure him about US commitment to the UAE. McGurk told me two weeks after his trip to Abu Dhabi that he told MBZ McKenzie was unable to visit sooner because he was overseeing and advising the president on the operation that killed ISIS leader Abu Ibrahim al-Hashimi al-Qurayshi in Syria. "We met for many hours and discussed Yemen and many other Emirati concerns. We are already moving forward on several issues. I think they feel better," he said.[371] The Emiratis did not share this assessment. The crisis was about to escalate.

On February 24, 2022, the world changed. Russian President Vladimir Putin ordered his army to invade Ukraine. After 77 years of peace, war returned to European soil. The Biden administration had warned weeks before the war that the Russian military build-up around Ukraine, which included 150 thousand soldiers and thousands of tanks and artillery systems, would lead to an all-out invasion. Most of the US's Western allies, including Israel, didn't buy it. Even Ukraine's president, Volodymyr Zelenskyy, was skeptical. While the US was leaking its intelligence about Putin's war plans to the media, the Germans, French, British and Israelis all thought it was exaggerated and that the worst-case scenario was a limited Russian operation in eastern Ukraine to take over the Donbas region. But when the Russians did invade, their primary aim was to reach Kyiv as quickly as possible and attempt to cut off its government at the head. At the beginning, the Russian war plans seemed to be working. Several hours after the invasion, Zelenskyy shocked EU leaders who were speaking to him on a video conference call. "This might be the last time you see me alive," he told them.[372]

Secretary of State Blinken was working the phones on February

24 to mobilize the international community against Russia. One of the calls he made was to Foreign Minister Sheikh Abdullah bin Zayed. As the UAE was the Arab representative in the UN Security Council, Blinken asked Sheikh Abdullah to support a resolution recognizing Ukraine's sovereignty. The Emirati foreign minister was non-committal. Calls between Blinken and other Arab foreign ministers over the next few days garnered the same cool response. The Arab countries in the Gulf were in no hurry to rally behind the US and against Russia. "That was the moment the Biden administration realized that they had a big gap with the Arab world. We told them the reason was the feeling in many Arab capitals that the US was not committed," a senior Israeli official told me. When the UN Security Council voted to condemn Russia two days after the invasion, the UAE disregarded the Biden administration's lobbying efforts and abstained together with China and India. The Russians vetoed the resolution. The UAE's decision to abstain was directly connected to its disappointment with the US response to the Houthi attack on Abu Dhabi six weeks earlier. The Emiratis felt the US response to this crisis—including the push for sanctions and Security Council resolutions at the UN—was much faster and more forceful than when they were attacked. The Biden administration was deeply disappointed by the UAE's vote. Tensions were growing. Several days later, as the UN General Assembly was about to vote on a similar resolution, the Biden administration asked Israel for help. For decades, Israel had asked the US for assistance in lobbying countries ahead of important votes at the UN. Now it was the other way around. Blinken asked Lapid to speak to Sheikh Abdullah and urge him to vote in favor of the resolution condemning Russia. Lapid agreed and reached out to Sheikh Abdullah. Later that week, 141 countries voted in favor of condemnation. The UAE was among them. A few days later, in

early March, Biden wanted to speak to MBZ. The president's aides told the Emiratis he wanted to express solidarity over the Houthi attacks. MBZ wasn't in the mood to take the call. Firstly, because he felt Biden's call came six weeks too late. Secondly, because none of the Emirati requests since the Houthi attacks had been addressed by the US. "We told the White House that we would call them back," an Emirati official told me. When Ambassador Al Otaiba explained to Jake Sullivan why MBZ didn't take the President's call, the latter understood. "Let us know when you are ready," he said. It would take another four months until Biden and MBZ spoke.

The Negev Forum

The crisis over Ukraine and the deep skepticism in the Arab world toward the Biden administration created a window of opportunity. On March 21, MBZ announced on his Twitter account that he had arrived in the resort city of Sharm El-Sheikh in the southern tip of the Sinai Peninsula for a meeting with Egyptian President Abdul Fattah al-Sisi. This would have passed by unremarked, until it was discovered that Israeli Prime Minister Naftali Bennett was due to arrive at the same place at the same time. This was no coincidence. Within minutes the story was out: an unprecedented trilateral summit was to take place between the leaders of Egypt, the UAE and Israel. The idea for the summit first came up during Bennett's visit to Abu Dhabi several months earlier. When MBZ told al-Sisi about it, the Egyptian president agreed immediately. The Israelis were concerned until the last moment that the summit would be canceled if it leaked to the press. The prime minister's office asked the military censor to stop news stories about it until after the summit ended, but once MBZ's tweet went out, that became an impossible task. The military censor's office saw the tweet as a confirmation of the summit and lifted the gag order. Bennett, who was in the air when this happened, discovered that the cat was out of the bag when he landed in Sharm El-Sheikh. Eyal Hulata informed the director of Egyptian intelligence, Abbas Kamel, that now that word was out it was important to release a joint photo. The Israelis were concerned the Egyptians wouldn't be willing, but minutes later Kamel said yes and came back with several photos to choose from. The first picture showed the three leaders sitting in a meeting room with the flags of their countries behind them. It was a powerful image, and a historic one. The Biden administration only found out about the trilateral summit from the press. This was also significant. The message was that countries in the region were looking after their own interests; the Israelis, Egyptians and Emiratis didn't need US mediation anymore. One key issue that was discussed was the war in Ukraine and how Egypt, the UAE and Israel could minimize its ramifications on the region, such as the grain shortage. "It was pure normalcy. Three leaders from neighboring countries meet and talk about ways they can work together," a senior Israeli official told me.

The Sharm El-Sheikh summit was symbolic because the old and cold peace between Israel and Egypt was meeting the new and warm peace between Israel and the UAE. It showcased one of the key developments of the Abraham Accords that nobody had anticipated: improved relations between Israel and Egypt, as well as Israel and Jordan. "The Abraham Accords influenced the whole region. When I met MBZ in Abu Dhabi I understood that the Abraham Accords allowed Egypt and Jordan to take steps in their relationships with Israel they hadn't wanted to take before," recalled President Herzog.[373]

Over time, both Egypt and Jordan realized they had a lot to gain out of the Abraham Accords. In Jordan's case, this understanding turned into the biggest regional cooperation project ever undertaken between Israel and its neighbors.

On November 22, 2021, after long months of negotiations, ministers from Israel, Jordan and the UAE convened on the sidelines of the Dubai Expo together with the US climate envoy, John Kerry, and signed an "electricity for water" deal. For years this deal had seemed like a pipe dream. The vision originally came from EcoPeace Middle East, a regional NGO managed by Israeli, Palestinian and Jordanian peace and environmental activists. The logic was simple. Israel needs renewable energy but lacks the land for massive solar farms, which Jordan has. Jordan, meanwhile, needs water but can only build desalination plants in the remote southern part of the country, while Israel's coastline is closer to Jordan's big population centers. According to the plan, a huge solar farm to provide energy to Israel and the Palestinians would be built in the Jordanian desert and a desalination plant would be built on Israel's Mediterranean coast to provide water to Jordan. It was a clear win-win situation, but for years there was no funding for it and—more importantly—no political will. The Abraham Accords solved these two problems at a stroke. The UAE's renewable energy giant Al-Masdar decided to invest in the project, while the Emirati government gave its political backing to the Jordanians. A year after the agreement was signed, it was making slow and steady progress to overcome red tape, but Israeli, Emirati and Jordanian leaders all see the project as a priority and strategic investment.

For decades, Israel's main asset in the region was its strong alliance with the US. Arab countries who maintained official or clandestine relations with Israel knew that the road to Washington often went through Jerusalem. March 2022 was one such example.

But in many ways this time it was also the other way round. The Biden administration realized that the road to reconnecting with the region also passes through Israel, or, in this case, through a small kibbutz in the Negev desert called Sde Boker.

Secretary of State Blinken was fully consumed at the time with the Russian invasion of Ukraine. He was traveling from one European capital to another building up the Western coalition against Putin. The Israeli position on the war was nuanced. Sometimes too nuanced. While then-Foreign Minister Lapid condemned the Russian invasion, Bennett, who was the prime minister at the time, studiously avoided any criticism of Putin. The Israeli argument for this policy focused on the Russian military presence in Syria, concerned that a tougher line on Ukraine could push Russia to harm a key Israeli security interest and limit the Israeli Air Force's freedom of operation in Syria against Iran and Hezbollah. But on March 5, 2022, Bennett took his careful approach toward Putin one step further and traveled to Moscow to meet the Russian president in an attempt to facilitate a ceasefire. It was a move as bold as it was reckless. No Israeli prime minister had ever dived headfirst into an international crisis as a mediator. Bennett, a religious and observant Jew, traveled to Moscow secretly on Shabbat, which the Jewish religion doesn't allow except for life-saving purposes. Ahead of the trip, Bennett called Jake Sullivan to update him. The White House wasn't thrilled to hear about the plan. "Biden's advisors told us they didn't understand the logic and didn't think such a meeting would bear any fruit, but added that any effort was welcomed," a Bennett aide told me. "We used the second part to tell Israeli reporters that the Biden administration welcomed the meeting with Putin." Bennett arrived at the Kremlin with a small group of advisors. After several COVID tests and walking through a carwash-like disinfection tunnel, he entered the meeting with Putin, during which the Russian president embarked on a rambling monologue about how he had warned several times about NATO expansion. In turn, the Israeli prime minister put a written proposal on the table that included principles for ending the war. One of Bennett's aides who accompanied him on the trip told me the proposal, drafted by Eyal Hulata, was the basis for the whole conversation between the leaders. The crux of it was an immediate Russian withdrawal from the areas it invaded on February 24, a commitment by Ukraine never to join NATO and negotiations over the future of Crimea and parts of the Donbas that had been under de facto Russian control since 2014. Putin listened but was ambivalent and non-committal. At a certain point, he said something that seemed to be a message he wanted the Israeli prime minister to pass on. "Putin told Bennett he knows exactly where Zelenskyy is and could take him out at any minute if he wanted to, but he doesn't do it" the Bennett aide said.

Bennett's meeting with Putin raised significant question marks in Washington about Israel's policy regarding the Russian invasion. Lapid felt he needed to speak to Blinken face to face and explain the situation. Two days after Bennett's trip to Moscow, Lapid and Blinken met in Riga, Latvia. While the meeting managed to clear up some of the Biden administration's questions, it was also important for another reason. Lapid was concerned that as the war in Ukraine escalated, the Biden administration wasn't paying attention to the advances in the Iranian nuclear program and to the growing apprehension of its partners in the Middle East. "You really should come for a round of meetings in the region," Lapid told Blinken. Two weeks later, Blinken called Lapid. "I am coming to see you in Jerusalem next week," the US secretary of state said. When the call ended, Lapid and his advisors started to brainstorm. "Let's bring everybody here," said his diplomatic advisor, Yair

Zivan. "What do you mean everybody?" Lapid asked. "All the Abraham Accords countries' foreign ministers, for a summit with Blinken in Israel," Zivan replied. It was an unprecedented and ambitious proposal in an impossible time frame—but Lapid liked it. He called Blinken back and outlined the idea. "I told Blinken they need to show the US is committed to the region," Lapid told me.[374] "I said, 'We will get a remote hotel and sit down for an intimate and open discussion.'" Blinken was surprised but didn't rule it out. He asked if Lapid would be able to make it happen by Sunday—only five days away. "I said yes right away, with no real clue if I could deliver or not," Lapid recalled. Lapid's advisors also pitched the idea to the US ambassador to Israel, Tom Nides, and to Yael Lempert, the principal deputy assistant secretary for the Middle East. Both liked it and started to push for it on their side. On Wednesday, March 23, Lapid picked up the phone to his Arab counterparts. The first call was to the Emirati foreign minister, Sheikh Abdullah bin Zayed. "If you come the others will come," Lapid told him. Sheikh Abdullah said yes right away. The next call was with Bahraini Foreign Minister Abdullatif bin Rashid Al Zayani. "Sheikh Abdullah is on board. If I have you too everybody else will come," Lapid told his Bahraini counterpart. Al Zayani gave a tentative confirmation but stressed that he needed to check with the king. The third call was with Moroccan Foreign Minister Nasser Bourita. "Are you sure everyone is coming?" he asked. "Yes. Nasser, they are all waiting for your answer. Please, the white phone," Lapid replied, referring to the special phone in Bourita's office with a direct line to King Mohammed VI. Thirty minutes later, Bourita confirmed. Lapid then sent WhatsApp messages to Egyptian Foreign Minister Sameh Shoukry and Jordanian Foreign Minister Ayman Safadi and invited them to join as well.

With all three ministers on board, Lapid and his advisors now needed to answer one very practical question: where to host this summit? Alon Ushpiz shot down the idea of hosting it in Jerusalem right away. It was too sensitive politically. Holding the summit at the fancy Beresheet Hotel overlooking the Ramon Crater was also taken off the table because it was too extravagant and didn't convey the message they were trying to send. It was Yael Bar, Lapid's communications director, who proposed Sde Boker—an iconic kibbutz in the Negev desert and the burial site of one of Israel's founding fathers and its first prime minister, David Ben-Gurion. After he resigned in 1953, Ben-Gurion moved to a shack in the southern kibbutz. "The people of Israel will be tested in the Negev," he said two years later in one of his most memorable speeches. Ben-Gurion is buried alongside his wife, Paula, on a cliff overlooking the Zin Valley in Sde Boker. Bar thought this location represented the message the summit needed to project. Lapid approved. However, problems then started on the US side, as the US secret service objected to the location for security reasons. Nides and Lempert had to go directly to Blinken and ask him to overrule his security people. He did so. Shortly before midnight on Thursday, two days before the summit, the Ben-Gurion burial site was opened for the secret service advance team. The last issue was the hotel. The summit was planned to take place at the Kedma Hotel in Sde Boker. "It's a nice hotel but we were worried it wouldn't live up to the standards of the foreign ministers," an Israeli official told me. The hotel management had to clear the place from its guests on 48 hours' notice. On Friday night, while Lapid was having Shabbat dinner with his family, his phone rang unexpectedly. Foreign Minister Shoukry of Egypt was on the line with good news. "I am joining the summit," he told Lapid. Things were moving in the right direction. "It was amazing the summit was put together within days. If we had actually planned it six months in advance, I am not sure it would have happened," Nides told me.[375]

On Sunday morning, Blinken arrived at the foreign ministry in Jerusalem for his pre-summit meeting with Lapid. "Listen Tony," Lapid said to Blinken, according to Israeli officials. "In all my conversations with my Arab colleagues I hear deep concern about the US position on the Middle East. You are going to enter the room in Sde Boker and hear a lot of that. You should be ready." Blinken wasn't surprised. He understood completely what Lapid was telling him. In fact, this was part of the purpose of the whole event. In the afternoon of March 27, Lapid traveled to Sde Boker to welcome the Arab ministers. It was an unprecedented sight. Government jets from the UAE, Bahrain, Morocco and Egypt landed one after the other at the Nevatim Air Force Base and made their way in motorcades to Sde Boker. Lapid welcomed each of them on the red carpet at the entrance to the hotel and showed them in. The Negev Summit started. The atmosphere was festive but informal—exactly as Lapid wanted. In the evening, the ministers gathered for dinner at the hotel's restaurant. "I asked that the table be round and not too big," Lapid told me. "I wanted to create an atmosphere of intimacy." Blinken, who had a meeting with Palestinian President Mahmoud Abbas in Ramallah, was running late. "When he finally arrived, we all remarked that the folks from the Middle East were all on time and the Americans were late," Lapid remembered. "Everybody laughed."

But the laughs were soon interrupted by a dramatic development. At around 9 PM, while the ministers were having dinner, Yael Bar entered the room with a serious face. "I knew right away that something bad had happened because I had told my team not to interrupt us no matter what," Lapid said. After receiving the update, Lapid returned to the table. The other ministers could see instantly that something was wrong. "There was a terror attack in the city of Hadera, north of Tel Aviv," Lapid told them. "Several people were killed." The ministers were shocked by the news. There was a long silence. "I told them that if we don't put out a joint statement right away condemning the attack the summit is dead," Lapid recalled. Minister Shoukry was first to respond. "There is no question about it," he said. "We always condemn terror attacks and the targeting of innocent civilians. As far as I am concerned you can release a statement of condemnation for all of us." Shoukry's reaction was very important, as Egypt sets the tone for the Arab world on many issues. The same was true in this case. All the other ministers agreed immediately. Shortly after, a joint statement condemning the attack was published, along with a decision to continue the discussions as planned. A senior Israeli official described the rest of the evening as a friendly, frank and profound "intervention." The Arab foreign ministers all presented Blinken with their concerns about the Biden administration's policy in the region and the perception that the US was abandoning the Middle East. Sheikh Abdullah gave the example of the Houthi attacks on Abu Dhabi and the late and weak US response. "You got us all wrong," Blinken told the other participants. "We are not going away and we are committed to the region's security. It's true that the focus is on other places right now but that doesn't change our commitment." Lapid and the other ministers gave Blinken an earful about the rumors that the Biden administration was considering taking the IRGC off the US government's Foreign Terrorist Organizations (FTO) list as part of a deal with Iran on a mutual return to the 2015 nuclear agreement. "I can't imagine signing a deal that says targeting Israel is not allowed but targeting my American allies is," Lapid said, hinting at one of the prospects under discussion between the US and Iran in those days that included a US demand that Iran doesn't target Americans in the region. Minister Bourita told Blinken the Saharawi rebels' Polisario Front had become an IRGC proxy. The Bahraini foreign minister also spoke very negatively about the idea of taking the IRGC off the terrorist blacklist. "We understand the problem and your concerns. It is not a done deal," Blinken tried to reassure them. The evening didn't end with full agreement on everything, but it did give all the ministers a much clearer understanding of the other side's positions.

The next morning, I drove down to Sde Boker. The first day of the summit had been closed to the press but the second was more public. Dozens of television crews and a crowd of reporters from the Israeli and international press were lined up in front of the Kedma Hotel. Though I have witnessed similar events abroad when I covered the nuclear talks with Iran in Geneva and Vienna or at peace conferences in the US and Europe over the years, this was the first such event I covered in Israel.

When they first came up with the idea of the Negev Summit, Lapid and his advisors briefed Bennett and his aides. Bennett didn't object. One of Bennett's aides told me that Shimrit Meir said in the internal meetings ahead of the conference that she didn't think it was going to happen. As days passed and the summit started taking shape, Meir became more and more antagonistic about it. "While Bennett was supportive and saw the Negev Summit as a continuation of his trilateral meeting with al-Sisi and MBZ in Sharm El-Sheikh, Meir thought it was an attempt by Lapid to sideline Bennett," said a senior aide to the then-prime minister. A second Bennett aide told me that in an internal meeting at the prime minister's office a day before the summit, Meir referred to the event as "a classic Lapid public relations festival." According to Bennett's aide, Meir even mentioned that she spoke to several reporters and editors of Israeli television channels and told them the summit was a "nothing burger" and they shouldn't air it live. Two of Lapid's advisors told me they heard the same account a day after the summit. Eventually, however, the three main Israeli television channels gave the summit extensive coverage and aired large parts of it live.

During the statement the ministers gave at the end of the event, Lapid announced the key practical achievement: a decision to turn the Negev Summit into the Negev Forum and thus turn a one-off event into a permanent regional framework for cooperation. They formed six working groups on security, education, energy, tourism, water and food security. They also decided that a ministerial meeting would take place once a year—every time in a different desert. "I just want to say that Las Vegas is also in the desert," Blinken joked.[376] Another decision reached in the summit was to try and integrate more governments into the Negev Forum and its working groups—first and foremost the Palestinians. Minister Shoukry was the one who raised the issue and Blinken supported it. This was the first serious attempt to get the Palestinians to take part in the Abraham Accords. Israel wasn't very enthusiastic about this. Neither were the Palestinians. "It was a very good meeting and it was just further proof of the huge potential that is being realized and the further potential yet to be realized out of the normalization process in the region," Derek Chollet told me.[377] "Coming out of that, we were determined to find a way to further institutionalize it. Think of it like the G7, which started as the G5 in a moment of crisis in the mid-1970s, or the Arctic Council, which got started 15 years ago in a similar kind of ad hoc way, and both have become lasting institutions. We saw potential in making the Negev Forum bigger than just a set of individuals who might be in office at a given moment in time, turning it into something that could outlast us."

The closing ceremony of the Negev Summit was also an unprecedented sight. I was waiting with scores of other reporters in a big meeting room when the six ministers came out to stand together on the stage. All the ministers opened their speeches by condemning the Hadera terror attack. "Israel's founding father, David Ben-Gurion, who is buried two minutes away from here, once said history isn't written, history is made. What we are doing here is making history, building a new regional architecture," Lapid said in his remarks at the ceremony. Blinken, who stood next to him, concurred. "We are standing together in Israel. Just a few years ago, this gathering would have been impossible to imagine," he said. Sheikh Abdullah was the last one to speak after his Egyptian, Bahraini and Moroccan colleagues. "What we are trying to achieve here today is changing the narrative, creating a different future and building a better hope for us and for our kids and grandkids," he said. He then looked at Blinken and added: "Tony, your presence here means a great deal, the United States not only being here but encouraging us to do more."[378]

Sheikh Abdullah's remarks were a sign that Blinken's messages of reassurance had not fallen on deaf ears. It was a good start for Blinken's next stop. The US secretary of state wanted to use the trip to the Middle East to mend relations with MBZ, who was still deeply hurt by the Biden administration's lackluster response to the Houthi attacks. Blinken had his own grievances though. A few days before he traveled to the region, Syrian President Bashar al-Assad made a surprise visit to Abu Dhabi. It was the first time Assad had visited an Arab country since the outbreak of the Syrian civil war 11 years earlier. The Biden administration was caught off guard by the visit and learned about it from the media. This added more tension to the already strained relations between the US and the UAE.

MBZ was on holiday in Morocco at the time, so Blinken decided to add Rabat to his itinerary in order to meet the Emirati ruler. Blinken and MBZ's brother, Sheikh Abdullah, used the Negev Summit for a one-on-one conversation. It served as good preparation for the meeting with MBZ at his private residence in Rabat, which lasted three hours and was mostly between the two of them alone. It started with a discussion of the tensions in the relationship but quickly moved on to issues like the Houthi attacks on the UAE, Iran, Syria, the Abraham Accords and the Russian invasion of Ukraine.[379] Blinken told MBZ the US remained committed to helping the UAE defend itself against threats from Yemen and elsewhere in the region, but, more importantly, he apologized to the Emirati leader. "We dropped the ball and I am sorry for that," Blinken told MBZ and admitted that the Biden administration took too long to respond to the Houthi attacks. "It was a positive meeting that helped move the relationship between the UAE and the US back on the right track, where it belongs," Ambassador Al Otaiba told me.[380]

The meeting in Morocco was definitely a start, but it would take more time for MBZ to put this episode behind him. After the president of the UAE, Sheikh Khalifa bin Zayed, died on May 13, 2022, the Biden administration decided to convey a message about its relationship with the UAE and its new president, Sheikh Mohamed, by sending one of its biggest delegations ever to offer condolences, led by Vice President Kamala Harris and including Secretary of State Blinken, Secretary of Defense Austin, CIA director Bill Burns and a dozen other senior US officials. The Emirati leader greatly appreciated the gesture but was still looking for a more tangible US commitment. According to both US and Emirati officials, behind the scenes, the Biden administration started discussing more seriously with the UAE a possible strategic agreement that would give the Gulf country specific US security guarantees. The "Strategic Framework Agreement" was an Emirati idea, but Brett McGurk liked it and tried to get it across the line. The Biden administration sent the Emiratis a draft agreement which included a security component but also covered economic, trade, science and technology issues.

On July 16, MBZ met President Biden for the first time in Jeddah, on the sidelines of a summit between Biden and the leaders of nine Arab countries. It was the first time MBZ and Biden had spoken since the January Houthi attacks. Emirati officials told me MBZ laid out to Biden the reasons for his disappointment in the US. The Emirati leader spoke softly and politely but was very direct in his criticism, repeating the charges of abandonment in the UAE's hour of need that he had made to McGurk in the immediate aftermath of the attacks.

Biden was visibly taken aback by MBZ's remarks. He shook his head in disappointment and looked at his senior advisors. "Why wasn't I made aware of this?" Biden asked his team. The president then told MBZ he wanted to fix it. He invited him to the White House and told his team to push forward with the "Strategic Framework Agreement." It was a difficult meeting, but both sides left with a positive feeling.[381] As of January 2023, there was still no deal. The maximum security commitment the Biden administration was willing to give didn't reach the minimum the Emiratis were willing to accept. Nevertheless, for the Biden administration the relationship with the UAE remains of great importance, especially at a time when US ties with Saudi Arabia are cold and unstable.

Islands in the Strait

On the evening of November 22, 2020, Avi Scharf was sitting

in his living room in Modi'in. At 7:30 PM, the senior Israeli journalist's phone beeped, and a notification popped up from the Flight Radar flight-tracking application. When he looked at the screen, he saw that the small business jet owned by the businessman Udi Angel had taken off from Ben Gurion Airport, heading east. Scharf has been a "plane spotter" since his army days. When his eyes are not glued to the radar on his phone app, they're scanning the skies for interesting planes. In the years I worked with Scharf at *Haaretz*, he drew me into this fascinating world, and I'm grateful that he did—it has led me to more than one scoop over the years. Angel's plane was of particular interest to Scharf. On several occasions, it has been put into service by senior Israeli officials for secret trips to neighboring countries.

When he woke up at six the next morning, the mystery flight from the evening before popped back into his head, and he quickly checked the app to see what had become of it. Scrolling back, he saw how the plane had curved away to the south over the Jordan Valley. On the radar, at first it looked like any other flight by a businessman to the port city and tourist destination of Eilat, at Israel's southern tip, but instead of dropping its altitude as it approached Ramon Airport on the outskirts of the city, it had carried on further south, far above the Red Sea. Somewhere over the Egyptian resort town of Sharm El-Sheikh, the pilot reduced his speed and height and banked sharply to the east, entering the airspace of Saudi Arabia and landing at the airport in Neom, Saudi Arabia's "City of the Future." Five hours later, the plane was back on the ground at Ben Gurion Airport.

At 07:01 AM, Scharf tweeted about the unusual flight. It was clear there was a big story waiting to be told here, so I started messaging any and all of my contacts who might know what it was. One of my sources got back to me and confirmed that the prime minister himself, Benjamin Netanyahu, had been on board the flight together with the head of the Mossad, Yossi Cohen, for a secret meeting with the Saudi crown prince, Mohammed bin Salman, also known as MBS. Usually, such flights take place under the strictest secrecy. The Mossad even knows how to prevent such trips from showing up on flight-tracking apps. This time, the existence of the flight was public information. There was also one other difference. When I sent my report to the Military Censor's Office ahead of publication, past experience led me to assume that it would be rejected on the grounds of potential damage to Israel's foreign relations.[382] But, to my surprise, a few minutes later the story was cleared for publication. That was another sign that the most important passenger on board—Benjamin Netanyahu— wanted this story published.

When the story was published, first on *Walla! News* at nine o'clock in the morning before it was picked up by other Israeli media outlets, it raised eyebrows around the region and the world. Stories about the secret ties between Israel and Saudi Arabia would more usually appear in media outlets affiliated with Qatar, as part of the propaganda campaigns waged between the small emirate and the vast kingdom; on rare occasions, certain details would sneak into the US media first. But the fact that this time it had come from Israel was a new development. This was not the first meeting between Netanyahu and the Saudi crown prince, but it came at a critical moment—two weeks after Joe Biden's victory in the US elections. The Israeli prime minister, riding the wave of the peace treaty with the United Arab Emirates and the normalization accords with Bahrain and Sudan, had made a last-ditch effort to achieve a similar breakthrough with the Saudis. It was an ambitious attempt with very little chance of success. MBS was slightly perturbed that his UAE counterpart, Sheikh Mohamed bin Zayed, had not consulted with him before deciding to normalize relations with Israel, but he supported the move as a positive step for the countries in the region. MBS opened Saudi airspace for flights from Ben Gurion Airport to Abu Dhabi and Dubai, gave the green light for Bahrain to proceed with its own normalization process with Israel and even helped to further the agreement between Israel and Sudan.[383] If it had been left up to him, he would have taken his own country down the same route, but his father, King Salman, had the final say on matters concerning Israel and the Palestinians. Netanyahu therefore returned from his trip to Neom empty-handed.

On January 5, 2021, two weeks before Trump left office, the Saudi city of Al-Ula hosted a summit between Qatar on one side, and Saudi Arabia and the other Gulf states on the other, which resulted in a joint statement ending their hostilities. The agreement brought to a close a three-and-a-half-year long economic boycott of Qatar by Saudi Arabia, the United Arab Emirates and Bahrain. The Trump administration played a central part in escalating the initial crisis between the Gulf states—and an equally large part in ending it. Kushner, who mediated between the sides, was present at the summit where they signed the reconciliation agreement. That was his last visit to Saudi Arabia as a senior government official. He was on his way back to the United States when the January 6 rally began. The rally ended in the notorious Capitol riots by Trump supporters seeking to stop the certification of the election results, one of the darkest days for democracy in the history of the United States.

In his final days before the swearing-in ceremony for the new president, Kushner met twice with Biden's prospective national security advisor, Jake Sullivan, to brief him on the Abraham Accords and Saudi Arabia. During those meetings with Sullivan, Kushner proposed a Middle East policy framework for the new administration. First, Kushner advised Sullivan not to chase after Iran. "Tell the Iranians that you're busy with China, COVID-19 and climate change, that you don't have time to meet with them and that they can call you if they want," Kushner told Biden's advisor. The second part of the framework directed the new administration to reach out to Saudi Arabia. "Sit with MBS, tell him that normalization with Israel is your priority and you'll work with him on a plan to get there," Kushner said. The third part touched on the Palestinians. Kushner recommended that Biden's advisor make it clear to the Palestinians that the new administration would restore the aid that Trump had cut and would help them extract concessions from Israel, but only if the Palestinian leadership engaged with the Trump Plan in good faith. Sullivan listened politely but took a different view on all three points. At least at that time.

Former President Trump, Jared Kushner and other senior officials in his administration remain convinced that, had they won a second term, Saudi Arabia would have joined the Abraham Accords within six months. It is an assessment shared by Netanyahu and his team. A former senior White House official told me that, as Trump's term came to an end, "the groundwork had been laid for a normalization agreement between Israel and Saudi Arabia." He claimed that the Saudis knew it would be a historic achievement for Biden, but they wanted the White House to treat them with respect. The former Israeli national security advisor, Meir Ben-Shabbat, agreed with this reading of the situation. When we spoke, he said the Saudis were 70 percent of the way there on normalization with Israel.

It's difficult to say whether this estimate was accurate. What was clear is that the Saudis were not happy about Netanyahu allowing the leak of the secret meeting with MBS. Two senior Israeli officials told me this created a serious crisis in the clandestine relations between Saudi Arabia and Israel which lasted many months. According to a senior Israeli official, "The Saudis felt Netanyahu violated their trust and dramatically decreased the level of engagement with us." "Saudi Arabia was a major foreign policy goal for us, but Bibi screwed everything with this leak," said a second senior Israeli official.

Joe Biden's victory in the 2020 presidential elections was very bad news for MBS, who was rooting for Trump. Biden had declared during the campaign that Saudi Arabia should be treated as a "pariah state" for the brutal murder of *The Washington Post* columnist Jamal Khashoggi by its agents in the Saudi consulate in Istanbul on October 2, 2018. In Donald Trump's White House, MBS had been a close ally—Benjamin Netanyahu likewise. After the Khashoggi murder, both Trump and Netanyahu issued weak condemnations and followed them up with defenses of MBS that sought to absolve him of all responsibility.

For the Saudis, the policy shift in Washington was felt within days. Two weeks after assuming office Biden announced that the US was to end all support for offensive military operations in Yemen by the Saudi-led coalition. "The war in Yemen must end," Biden said. The immediate consequence was a halt on the sales of precision-guided bombs and missiles to Saudi Arabia and US logistical support for Saudi airstrikes, such as mid-air refueling of fighter jets. Ten days later, Biden reversed Trump's decision in his last days in office to designate the Houthi rebels in Yemen as a terrorist organization. On February 25, 2021, Biden had his first phone call with King Salman. The White House made it clear at the time that King Salman was Biden's counterpart and communication would therefore be with him, rather than his son, the crown prince. After talking about the need to end the war in Yemen and stressing the US commitment to help Saudi Arabia defend itself against

Houthi attacks, Biden raised the issue of human rights with King Salman. Ahead of the call, the Saudis released several Saudi-American human rights activists who were under arrest. The White House readout of the call said Biden welcomed the move but told King Salman he wanted to see further progress on human rights and the rule of law—code for the Khashoggi murder. The next day, Biden authorized the publication of a CIA report stating that MBS himself had authorized the kidnapping and murder of the journalist, who was one of the most vocal critics of the regime in Riyadh. Releasing the report had been one of Biden's campaign promises. The report didn't say anything that wasn't already known. It just made it official. It also made it clear that the Khashoggi murder was set to overshadow the relationship.

In late September 2021, Biden's national security advisor, Jake Sullivan, traveled to Saudi Arabia. He was the most senior American official to visit the kingdom since Biden entered office. "Jake understood pretty early that in order to stabilize the situation in the Middle East, the relationship with Saudi Arabia needed to be fixed," said a senior Israeli official who met Sullivan ahead of the trip. The visit centered on the fraught relationship between Riyadh and Washington, but also touched on Saudi Arabia's relationship with Israel. Senior Israeli and American officials told me that, during the meeting between Sullivan and MBS in Neom, Biden's senior advisor raised the possibility of a normalization accord between Saudi Arabia and Israel and for Saudi Arabia to join the Abraham Accords. Seemingly, Sullivan had finally taken on board at least part of the briefing he had received from Kushner nine months earlier. MBS was cautious but didn't rule it out. He handed Sullivan a long list of Saudi demands for the United States. What MBS wanted had little to do with Israel or the Palestinian issue but rather with the US–Saudi relationship. Some of his demands regarded the sensitive and politically explosive matter of the crown prince's standing in Washington following the assassination of Khashoggi. It was clear after Sullivan's visit that normalization between Saudi Arabia and Israel was on the cards but only following a US–Saudi normalization process. Another conclusion was that any normalization with Saudi Arabia would happen slowly and include many small, incremental steps.

One such option came up during Sullivan's visit when the Saudis raised an issue the White House had not previously looked at: the islands of Tiran and Sanafir. The two islands in the Red Sea are small but strategically significant. They control access to the Straits of Tiran, an important naval passage to the ports of Aqaba in Jordan and Eilat in Israel. Saudi Arabia gave Egypt control of the islands in 1950 in the context of the conflict with Israel. The closing of the straits by Egypt and the blocking of the passage to Israeli ships en route to Africa and Asia was a major spark for Israel's decision to go to war in 1967. The islands were demilitarized following the 1979 Israeli–Egyptian peace treaty. The US-led multinational force of observers (MFO), tasked with monitoring the implementation of the peace treaty, established a permanent presence on one of the islands and conducted patrols to ensure freedom of navigation through the straits.

The status quo on the islands was preserved for more than 35 years. But in April 2016, a dramatic shift took place. During a visit to Egypt, MBS signed a deal with President al-Sisi to transfer the islands to Saudi sovereignty. In return, Saudi Arabia committed to investing more than 15 billion dollars in the Egyptian economy. The agreement was met with public protests in Egypt but was ratified by parliament in June 2017 and approved by the Supreme Constitutional Court in March 2018. The Egyptian–Saudi deal also needed input from another key player in the region: Israel.

Ceding the islands to Saudi Arabia would undoubtedly affect Egypt's peace treaty with Israel. Several questions arose: How would the demilitarization of the islands be preserved? Would the Saudis commit to freedom of navigation in the straits? What would happen to the multinational observers? In 2017, Israel gave its qualified approval to the deal over the islands, pending an agreement between Egypt and Saudi Arabia on continuing the work of the MFO. The Saudis committed to upholding all the Egyptian guarantees in its peace treaty with Israel, though several loopholes remained, mostly surrounding the MFO.[384]

The issue died down for a few years, but came up again in the fall of 2021 because the Saudis wanted to convert the two largely uninhabited islands into tourist resorts. But that would not be possible while the MFO was there. To solve the matter, they needed a new deal with Israel, Egypt and the US. For the Biden administration and the Israeli government this was the opportunity they had been waiting for. The Biden administration started negotiating the deal quietly behind the scenes. Brett McGurk was tasked with leading this sensitive diplomatic effort. If successful, it had the potential to serve as a first step on the road to normalization between Saudi Arabia and Israel. But the cool relationship between the Biden administration and the Saudi government posed challenges to the initiative. When Biden finished his first year in office, tensions with Saudi Arabia went from being a foreign policy issue to a domestic one, largely due to one reason: oil. As the world recovered from the COVID-19 pandemic, demand for oil increased. At the same time, supply remained low. The result was an increase in oil prices around the world. For the US, which is the biggest global consumer of gasoline, this meant a rise in fuel prices and a domestic political headache for Biden. As oil prices continued to rise in January 2022 to more than 90 dollars a barrel, the White House desperately sought ways to reverse the trend. According to a former US official, Biden decided to do what he had been avoiding doing for a year: engage directly with MBS. The president had no choice. He needed the Saudis to increase oil production together with other members of the OPEC group of oil-producing countries. In early February, when the White House tried to coordinate the call, MBS didn't want to take it. "The crown prince's message was: President Biden said his counterpart was King Salman, so he should call him," a former US official who was briefed on the issue told me. Several days later, Biden called King Salman and asked him to increase production. MBS, who was sitting in the room with the king while the call took place, made sure Biden did not get a positive answer. Two weeks later, when Russia invaded Ukraine, the energy crisis dramatically escalated, upending the White House's calculations. Repairing the relationship with Saudi Arabia and getting more Saudi oil on the market became a much more pressing issue.

MBS knew Biden was in a bind and planned to exploit it to his advantage, making the most of the unexpected leverage he had over the American president and ensuring that everybody knew about it. On March 3, *The Atlantic* published a wide-ranging interview with MBS. In it, the crown prince bluntly declared that he didn't care what Biden thought about him and suggested that alienating Saudi Arabia would only harm America. "It's up to him to think about the interests of America," MBS said.[385] The same week, two of Biden's most senior advisors—Brett McGurk and US Energy Envoy Amos Hochstein—traveled to Riyadh for a meeting with MBS and his two brothers, then-Deputy Minister of Defense Prince Khalid bin Salman and Minister of Energy Prince Abdulaziz bin Salman. When McGurk and Hochstein returned to Washington, the White House started discussing something nobody thought would happen during Biden's term: a presidential visit to Saudi Arabia.

In every engagement with the Saudis during those months, Biden's aides raised the issue of normalization with Israel while the Saudis raised the issue of the Red Sea islands. The White House discussed this with the Israelis too. These negotiations were kept secret for more than six months. "We started discussing this with the US in late 2021. The Saudis wanted our approval for their plan for the islands and we wanted Saudi normalization steps. This launched a long back-and-forth process between the parties," an Israeli official told me.

In May 2022, I visited Washington for an *Axios* all-staff retreat. On one of the nights there, I met a long-time contact at the bar of the St. Regis Hotel. Over drinks—a vodka martini for me, cognac for him—he told me about the secret negotiations, the emerging deal and the fact that Biden wanted to announce it during a visit to Saudi Arabia, part of which included attending a summit with nine Arab leaders. This was quite the dramatic scoop, but it needed confirmation. The next day, I met an Israeli diplomat for breakfast near Dupont Circle. When I raised the issue of the secret US mediation between Israel and Saudi Arabia over the islands, he looked stunned. "Leave me out of this," he said and quickly changed the subject. It was clear there was a story there. Over the next few days, I managed to confirm different parts of the story from four other current and former US and Israeli officials.

The broad strokes of the deal were as follows:
- Israel would agree that the MFO would leave the islands.
- Egypt would agree for the observers to move to new positions in the Sinai Peninsula.
- Israel, Egypt and Saudi Arabia would agree to replace the MFO with advanced cameras on the islands to monitor them and en-

sure they were demilitarized.

- Saudi Arabia would commit to keeping the islands demilitarized and to maintaining full freedom of navigation for all ships through the straits.
- The US would be the guarantor of the new arrangement.

There was another part to the deal: Israel wanted Saudi Arabia to take two significant normalization steps. The first was allowing Israeli airlines to cross Saudi airspace for eastbound flights, which would dramatically shorten flights to India, Thailand and China. After the Abraham Accords were announced, Saudi Arabia began to allow Israeli airlines to cross its airspace for flights to the UAE and Bahrain and promised the Trump administration that they would extend this to all eastbound flights from and to Israel. However, this was never implemented, partly out of their anger over the leak of Netanyahu's meeting with MBS. But the Israelis wanted the Saudis to take an even more significant step and allow direct flights from Israel to Saudi Arabia for Israeli Muslims seeking to go on pilgrimage to the holy cities of Mecca and Medina.

When I published the story about the secret negotiations around the Red Sea islands on May 23, it received a lot of attention both in the US and in the Middle East. Saudi Foreign Minister Prince Faisal bin Farhan was asked about the story during the World Economic Forum in Davos, Switzerland. He didn't deny it. "We have always seen normalization as the end result of a path," he said. "Normalization between the region and Israel will bring benefits but we won't be able to reap those benefits unless we are able to address the issue of Palestine."[386] I published the story as Biden's aides, McGurk and Hochstein, were about to travel to Saudi Arabia to continue discussions about Biden's possible visit, oil production and the Red Sea deal. Biden's aides consulted with

Israeli National Security Advisor Eyal Hulata on how to mitigate the fallout from the story. This was no easy feat, as the Saudis were deeply unimpressed. When McGurk and Hochstein arrived in Riyadh, the Saudis protested that the secret negotiations were now out in the open. "The publication of the story was very painful for them and as a result the negotiations got stuck for quite some time," a senior Israeli official told me. But the fact that the story was out also created an opportunity for the White House. Biden was trying to push back on criticism from within the Democratic Party about his possible trip to Saudi Arabia. The president needed Saudi Arabia to increase oil production in order to try to bring gas prices down ahead of the midterm elections. He also needed it to be able to push for a wide range of sanctions on Russian oil amid the ongoing war in Ukraine. The president's critics argued that while Biden might achieve an oil deal with the Saudis, he would also give international legitimacy to MBS and break his campaign promises about holding the crown prince accountable.

During their visit to Saudi Arabia in late May, McGurk and Hochstein reached a deal with MBS and his close aides on increasing oil production. According to *The New York Times*, in the first phase of this deal the Saudis would get the OPEC+ group of oil-producing countries to increase production by 400 thousand barrels a day in July and August, instead of in September as was planned.[387] The US hoped that would be sufficient to stop oil prices from going up. On June 2, the Saudis delivered. The move paved the way for Biden's visit to the kingdom, but the White House didn't acknowledge it straight away. A day later, when he was asked about the possible trip to Saudi Arabia, the president claimed the goal of the trip was not oil, but an attempt to push for peace between Israel and the Arab world. From that moment, the White House tried to change the framing of the trip from oil to Arab–Israeli peace, making the prospect of progress in relations between Saudi Arabia and Israel the sweetener for the president's controversial move. "Biden needed to cross the Rubicon with the Saudis and to justify his trip domestically. Saudi normalization steps with Israel were the deliverable he needed," a senior Israeli official said. "The Saudis wanted to get something because they felt they were paying a price for Biden's visit. The Red Sea islands were also a deliverable for them. This also worked great for us because we wouldn't have been able to make progress with the Saudis without US involvement."

For several weeks, the White House refused to confirm the trip to Saudi Arabia; when it finally did, Biden and his aides were non-committal when asked in public whether the president would meet with MBS. The will-he-won't-he speculation underscored the tension for Biden between realpolitik at a time of tensions with Iran and sky-high oil prices, and his desire to put human rights at the forefront of US foreign policy. For his part, the Saudi crown prince heard the statements from the White House and felt the president wasn't treating him with the respect he was due. On June 14, a month before the trip, the White House finally acknowledged that Biden was expected to meet with MBS in Saudi Arabia. The plan was for the president to also visit Israel and the Palestinian Authority. In an attempt to shift focus away from the meeting with MBS, White House officials emphasized another angle: "The president will fly directly from Israel to Saudi Arabia for the first time," they said, presenting it as progress toward Israeli–Saudi normalization.[388]

Biden hoped that the Red Sea islands deal he was working on would be the first step in what White House officials described as "a road map for normalization" between Saudi Arabia and Israel. Biden's aides envisioned it as a long-term process that would materialize step by step. A key part of that road map had to do with security cooperation and the vision of a Middle East air and missile defense alliance that Bennett and other Israeli officials were pushing for. In January 2021, four months after the Abraham Accords were signed, the US Department of Defense announced a major policy change: it moved Israel from the responsibility of the European command area to that of the central command (CENTCOM), which included the Middle East. The combination between this move and the normalization agreements opened the door to unprecedented security cooperation between Israel and Arab countries in the region. "The move to CENTCOM was like a home run," a senior Israeli official told me. "Militaries have their own dynamics—exercises, meetings, visits. Once it started rolling it just grew more and more." On September 30, 2021, then-Foreign Minister Lapid visited Bahrain to cut the ribbon on the Israeli embassy in Manama. The visit took an interesting twist when, in addition to his meetings with the king and crown prince, Lapid received a last-minute invite to the nearby headquarters of the United States Fifth Fleet in Manama. The Fifth Fleet is part of CENTCOM, responsible for naval activity in the Persian Gulf and the Red Sea, especially regarding Iran. At the end of his visit, Lapid stood in front of the cameras alongside his Bahraini counterpart, Abdullatif bin Rashid Al Zayani, commander of the Fifth Fleet, Admiral Brad Cooper, and US Chargé d'Affaires *ad interim* Maggie Nardi, with an imposing US warship in the backdrop. It was a clear message to the regime in Iran and the realization of one of the great promises of the Abraham Accords: to build security cooperation between the United States, Israel and the Gulf states. The Iranians were furious and passed on threatening messages to the Bahrainis, which only caused the Bahrainis to double down. In February 2022, an Israeli Air Force jet landed in Manama carrying then-Minister of Defense Benny Gantz. It was an unprecedented flight, an unprecedented visit and another clear message to Iran. "The Bahrainis wanted it to be as public as possible," a senior Israeli defense official told me. After meeting with the king and the crown prince, Gantz signed an official defense cooperation agreement with Bahrain. It was the second such agreement Gantz signed with an Arab country, following a November 2021 agreement with Morocco. "Since June 2021, there have been more than 200 meetings between Israeli military officers and defense officials and their counterparts in Arab countries—some of which had diplomatic relations with Israel and some of which did not," Gantz told me.[389] One such meeting took place in March 2022 in Sharm El-Sheikh. CENTCOM's outgoing commander, General Frank McKenzie, invited the Israeli military chief of staff, General Aviv Kochavi, for a secret meeting with his Saudi counterpart, Air Chief Marshal Fayyadh Al-Ruwaili, and the commanders of the militaries of Egypt, Jordan, the UAE, Bahrain and Qatar. According to the *Wall Street Journal*, they discussed expanding cooperation on early warnings against threats from drones operated by Iran and its proxies in the region.[390] "The move to CENTCOM was a big deal," said Gantz. "It allowed us to gradually build a regional architecture that differentiated between Iran, Syria and Lebanon, who are hostile toward Israel, and all the rest who have some kind of open or clandestine security relationship with Israel." One element of these security relations was arms deals with Israel. According to Gantz, in the first two years since the Abraham Accords were signed, Israel's defense exports to the Arab world (including to countries that didn't normalize relations) totaled more than three billion dollars, from air defense systems to the UAE to attack drones and cyber systems to Morocco.

Israeli officials hoped that Biden's upcoming visit would

lead to a breakthrough in the Middle East Air Defense alliance. White House officials also spoke about plans for the president to discuss a vision for "integrated missile defense and naval defense" among the US, Israel and several Arab countries, including Saudi Arabia. Both envisioned a regional network of radars, sensors and air defense systems in Israel, Saudi Arabia, UAE, Bahrain, Egypt and Jordan connected through CENTCOM that would be able to provide early warning and intercept attacks. It was a creative and bold idea; however, as Biden's trip to the Middle East got closer, it became clear that the political conditions were not yet ripe to move it forward.

As the White House was preparing Biden's trip, a political earthquake rocked Israel. On June 20, Prime Minister Naftali Bennett and his political partner, Foreign Minister Yair Lapid, recognized that their increasingly desperate attempts to hold their fragile coalition together were growing impossible and decided to cut their losses. Rather than be dragged into it against their will and lose more political support in the process, they called a press conference and announced they were dissolving the Knesset and moving for early elections, only a year after forming the unity government that ousted Netanyahu. The announcement triggered the rotation agreement between Bennett and Lapid, which stated that if the Knesset was dissolved and an election called, Lapid would become the acting prime minister. The White House, which made every effort to ensure the Israeli unity government's survival, stressed that Biden's trip would go ahead as planned, but followed the political developments in Jerusalem with growing concern.

Two weeks before Biden arrived in the region, there was still no deal on the Red Sea islands. Diplomats and lawyers from the US, Israel, Saudi Arabia and Egypt worked on a complex choreography of agreements, understandings and letters that would allow the agreement to be inked ahead of the president's visit. It wasn't easy. Because Saudi Arabia and Israel don't have diplomatic relations and can't sign bilateral agreements officially, the countries involved tried to use creative legal and diplomatic solutions to indirectly finalize a deal. The idea was that Saudi Arabia would sign an agreement with Egypt and send a letter to the US, outlining the latter's commitments as the guarantor. The US would then give Israel a letter with guarantees, mainly on the issue of freedom of navigation. "The trick here was for Saudi Arabia to sign an agreement with Israel without signing an agreement with Israel," said a senior Israeli official. Ten days before Biden was due to arrive, a crisis erupted in the sensitive negotiations. The Saudis got cold feet and refused to provide commitments in writing. "They claimed they couldn't do it because Israel leaks everything," another senior Israeli official told me. "The Saudis said, 'We'll give a secret commitment and then find it in the press.'" The US made a last-minute effort to resolve the crisis. McGurk and Hochstein traveled to Saudi Arabia a few days before the president's trip to finalize the understandings and agreements behind it. Following talks with MBS and his brother Khalid bin Salman, they managed to convince the Saudis to give a written commitment. "The Americans did the heavy lifting, got the Saudis on board and solved the crisis," a senior Israeli official noted.

On July 13, 2022, Biden landed in Israel. This was his 10th visit to the Jewish state. "I am home," he told President Herzog, who greeted him on the tarmac at Ben Gurion airport. His first visit took place 49 years earlier, when he was a young senator from Delaware. His meeting in 1973 with then-Prime Minister Golda Meir, a few weeks before the Yom Kippur War, has become a go-to story that he has told dozens of times over the years as an example of his pro-Israel record and long relationship with

Israeli leaders. "When the photographer was taking pictures... she said, 'Why do you look so sad?' and I said, 'Well, Madam Prime Minister, you've painted such a dismal picture,'" Biden recounted.[391] "She said, 'Don't worry. We have a secret weapon in our battle in this area.' I said, 'What's that?' She replied, 'We have no place else to go.'" Biden's number one goal during his visit was to stress to the Israeli people that support for Israel was in his *kishkas* and that he cared deeply for its future. "You need not be a Jew to be a Zionist," the president said at the welcoming ceremony.[392] Biden also made his case two hours later on a visit to Yad Vashem, where he laid a wreath at the Hall of Remembrance. On the other side of the hall sat 95-year-old Auschwitz survivor Giselle (Gita) Cycowicz and 87-year-old Rena Quint, who survived Bergen-Belsen. Biden walked toward the two women, dropped to one knee and spoke to them for more than 20 minutes. It was an iconic moment. The leader of the free world expressed his respect to two Holocaust survivors live on television and gave them his full attention as if nobody else was there. This gesture—as well as Biden's strong statements on Iran the following day—did the trick: polls conducted after the visit showed more Israelis expressing confidence in the US president.[393]

Biden's meeting with Prime Minister Lapid on July 14 focused on Iran and Saudi Arabia. Israeli officials said Lapid told Biden the Iranians were playing for time and the US should set a deadline on the nuclear talks. Biden told Lapid in private that he would not wait forever for the Iranians to respond to the US proposal. At the press conference after the meeting, he reiterated this point in public. After their meeting, Biden and Lapid signed the "Jerusalem Declaration" on the strategic relationship between the countries. One of the clauses in the declaration covered Iran. "The US stresses that integral to this pledge is the commitment never to allow Iran to acquire a nuclear weapon, and that it is prepared to use all elements of its national power to ensure that outcome," the declaration reads.[394] Lapid was very satisfied with what he heard from Biden. "The president has put himself in the top 10 percent of his administration when it comes to being tough on Iran," he told me.[395] Since then, there had been no breakthrough in the nuclear talks with Iran. The Iranians didn't agree to the US proposals and the negotiations reached an impasse. The outbreak of the protests against the Iranian regime in mid-September 2022 in response to the death of 22-year-old Jina Mahsa Amini (who was arrested for not wearing her hijab in accordance with the government's standards) significantly cooled the willingness of the Biden administration and European powers to cut a deal with Iran. The Iranian decision around the same time to supply attack drones to Russia for its war in Ukraine led the Biden administration to state publicly in late October that a nuclear deal was not on the agenda and that Biden was ready to use military means as a last resort to prevent Iran from acquiring a nuclear weapon. On the sidelines of a November 4 election rally in California, Biden told a woman who attended the event and protested against the Iranian regime that the 2015 nuclear deal with Iran was "dead," but stressed that the US would not formally announce it.[396] When the video of the exchange surfaced more than a month later, it was the strongest confirmation yet that the Biden administration believed there was no path forward for the Iran deal. Biden met Lapid and Herzog a day before his trip to Saudi Arabia and expressed to both men his discomfort and frustration with his upcoming visit and meeting with the Saudi crown prince. "Biden said he knew the visit to Saudi Arabia was important, but he was in two minds about it because in his worldview what MBS did, with the murder of Jamal Khashoggi, was unacceptable," a senior Israeli official told me.

The Israeli view was markedly less ideological. "Our argument to the Americans in the months before the visit was simple: MBS could be the leader of Saudi Arabia for the next 50 years, so no matter what we think about him, we have to live with it," said another senior Israeli official. During the meetings in Jerusalem, Lapid and Herzog encouraged Biden to go to Saudi Arabia and fix the relationship with the kingdom. "Saudi Arabia is the key to the entire region. At the end of the day, they are your partners. Go there and show you are the boss," Herzog told Biden according to a source briefed on their meeting.

On the evening of July 14, while I was on the train from Jerusalem to Tel Aviv, I got a call from a senior Israeli official. "We have a deal," he said. Shortly before he called, the Israeli government had approved the parameters of the agreement with the US, Saudi Arabia and Egypt on moving the MFO from the two strategic Red Sea islands to the Sinai Peninsula in return for new security arrangements and a Saudi pledge to the US that it would uphold the commitments of the 1979 Israel–Egypt peace agreement, namely maintaining freedom of navigation in the Straits of Tiran for Israeli shipping. "We needed a lot of creative diplomacy to do it, but eventually we received all the guarantees we needed, and it was communicated to us indirectly through the US," a senior Israeli official told me. Now it was Saudi Arabia's turn to deliver. On July 15 at 2 AM, several hours before Biden was due to fly from Tel Aviv directly to Jeddah, the Saudi General Authority of Civil Aviation sent out a tweet: "We announce the decision to open the kingdom's airspace for all air carriers that meet the requirements of the authority for overflying."[397] Although the word "Israel" wasn't mentioned, the meaning was clear, as Israeli airlines were the only ones prohibited from using Saudi airspace. It was a historic decision that was met with praise from

Biden, who stressed its importance as a momentum-building step for Israel's further integration into the region, and he vowed to do all he could to keep advancing it. "You have to admit the airspace thing is cool," White House National Security Advisor Jake Sullivan said to the traveling press as the president made his way from Tel Aviv to Jeddah. "This is a first step but a big step." With this significant achievement for Biden, the ground had now been laid for his visit to Saudi Arabia.

On Friday afternoon, July 15, Air Force One landed at Jeddah International Airport. The only officials there to greet him on the tarmac were the governor of the Mecca region and the Saudi ambassador to Washington. This snub was a calculated message from the Saudis. After a short drive, the presidential limousine, known as "the Beast," stopped at the entrance to the Al-Salam Palace. Crown Prince Mohammed bin Salman was waiting for Biden on the red carpet to welcome him. When the president walked out of the car, he didn't shake MBS's hand but gave him a fist bump. This was intended as a US signal to the Saudis, but first and foremost to the public back home. It didn't work. While Biden had hoped it would be perceived as a downgrade from a handshake, many saw it as being friendlier. The fist bump became the center of media coverage and made Biden the target of an avalanche of criticism from within his own party.

Biden's meeting with King Salman was largely ceremonial. The more significant working meeting was with MBS. The crown prince didn't like hearing Biden hedging when he was asked ahead of the trip whether the two would meet. The fist bump didn't help to break the ice either. But what brought the tensions and suspicions out into the open was the Khashoggi murder, which Biden raised at the very top of the meeting. "I said very straightforwardly: for an American president to be silent on an issue of human rights is inconsistent with who we are and who I am. I'll always stand up for our values," Biden stressed after the meeting.[398] The Saudi crown prince told Biden that he was not personally responsible for the murder of Khashoggi. Biden replied that he thought he was. MBS said that what had happened to Khashoggi was "regrettable" and that Saudi Arabia had taken all the necessary legal steps to address it, including an investigation, indictments and convictions. MBS also told Biden the kingdom had taken steps to prevent such "mistakes" from happening again. In an attempt to counter Biden's arguments, the Saudi crown prince also raised the abuse suffered by prisoners of the US-run Abu Ghraib prison in Iraq and the US response to the killing of Palestinian American journalist Shireen Abu Akleh during an Israeli military raid in the occupied West Bank two months earlier. "The US made many mistakes of its own," MBS told Biden. "What did the US and other countries in the world do about Shireen Abu Akleh?"[399] The highly charged exchange between Biden and MBS in the meeting and the fact that Biden voiced his criticism minutes later in front of the cameras on Saudi soil, as well as the mutual attempts by both sides to make sure their spin dominated the press reports about the conversation, didn't help in creating trust and turning the page between the two countries and their leaders.

Nonetheless, Biden did raise the matter of normalization with Israel in the meeting. "The issue came up quite a lot in the conversation and Biden made it clear that it was in everybody's interest to move toward normalization," a senior Israeli official who was briefed on the meeting told me. Senior US officials who attended the meeting said the Saudis agreed to start discussions on direct flights from Israel to Jeddah for approved airlines for Muslims in Israel wanting to participate in the following year's Hajj pilgrimage. It was the second step Saudi Arabia had taken toward normalizing relations with Israel during Biden's trip to the region. Direct flights from Israel to Saudi Arabia could serve hundreds of thousands of Muslims in Israel who have had to travel for the Hajj through Jordan, making the trips longer and far more expensive. Agreeing to discuss this issue for the first time was a significant gesture by the Saudis. Israeli officials told me that completing the arrangements for such direct flights would take a long time to nail down. While these lines are being written, it remains unclear whether this will happen in time for June 2023, when the pilgrimage takes place.

One of the key motivations for Biden to travel to Saudi Arabia was to meet with the leaders of eight other Arab countries who attended the summit organized by the Saudis. The president wanted to push back on the narrative that had taken root in many countries in the Middle East that the US was abandoning the region. This perception opened the door for other world powers like China and Russia to expand their influence. When Blinken visited Israel in March 2022, President Herzog described the situation to him with a metaphor about kids whose parents went on a long vacation. "The kids learned how to manage," Herzog told him. "And when you leave, other empires come."[400] Biden's speech was meant to send the message that the parents were back. "Let me state clearly that the United States is going to remain an active, engaged partner in the Middle East," Biden said in front of the Arab leaders.[401] "We will not walk away and leave a vacuum to be filled by China, Russia or Iran." Shortly after the speech, Biden wrapped up his visit and traveled back to Washington. While the White House tried to frame it as a success, many questions remained, first and foremost whether the president had been successful in his attempt to recalibrate relations with Saudi Arabia. Another was whether the Saudis would implement the understanding about increasing oil production. Ahead of the visit to Jeddah and after the trip, the price of oil slowly dropped, and the White House was optimistic. A few days after Biden returned from Saudi Arabia, his top Middle East advisor, Brett McGurk, told a group of think tank experts close to the administration that the Saudis and the Emiratis "have more to give" when it came to oil production. The White House was focused on the OPEC+ group meeting on August 3. "It's crucial," McGurk told the group. As days passed, worrying signs appeared. Less than a week after Biden's visit, the Saudi crown prince held a phone call with Russian President Vladimir Putin. The call was about the same issue Biden had pressed the kingdom on: oil production. "The importance of further coordination within the framework of the OPEC+ group was emphasized," the Kremlin said in a statement.[402] More than anything else, the call looked like a signal from MBS that he was not in Biden's pocket. The second worrying sign came on August 3, when the OPEC+ group agreed to increase oil production by only 100 thousand barrels a day— half of what Biden's advisors thought the Saudis had promised. A month later, the group of oil-producing nations backtracked entirely and announced a cut of 100 thousand barrels. The White House was stunned. According to the understandings they had reached ahead of Biden's visit, the Saudis were supposed to increase production, not the other way around. Everything seemed to be going against the plan. As the October OPEC+ meeting got closer, the White House scrambled to make sure the Saudis were ready to come through on their promises. McGurk and Hochstein traveled to Saudi Arabia in late September for talks with MBS and his senior advisors. They came out of the meetings reassured, but several days later they realized the Saudis had changed course and were planning to proceed with another production cut. In a last ditch effort, the Biden administration tried to press the Saudis to reconsider. At the request of the Biden administration, senior Emirati and Iraqi officials traveled to Riyadh to try and convince the Saudis to reconsider. The national security advisor of the UAE, Sheikh Tahnoun bin Zayed, told MBS that such a move could create a deep crisis with Washington. But all the warnings and lobbying efforts were to no avail. At the OPEC+ meeting on October 5, Saudi Arabia and Russia passed a resolution for a dramatic oil production cut of two million barrels per day—the most dramatic shift in two years.

Biden was furious with the Saudi volte-face, which represented a personal humiliation for the US president. Some of the members of Congress and senators who had previously spoken out over Biden's trip to Jeddah were now publicly saying "we told you so." The White House announced the president had decided to reassess relations with Saudi Arabia, and the Pentagon canceled a planned meeting with the Saudis on missile defense. White House officials claimed the oil production cut was part of a deal between Saudi Arabia and Russia to help the Russians in their war effort in Ukraine. Some Democrats in Congress even claimed it was a Saudi conspiracy to harm Biden and the Democratic Party in the midterm elections. Saudi officials fired back and said that the US's outrage had nothing to do with Russia, but was due to domestic political concerns about rising gas prices ahead of the midterms.

Two years after Biden assumed office and despite his visit to Jeddah, US–Saudi relations remain fraught at best, and it will take a lot of diplomatic work to get them back on track. At the time of writing, it is unclear whether the Saudi crown prince even wants to try.

Epilogue

On November 8, 2022, I landed in Abu Dhabi. It was my third time in the UAE since the Abraham Accords were signed two years before, but it was the first time I was visiting on my own and not as part of an official delegation. But there was another reason for my excitement: I had been invited together with several colleagues to speak at a conference organized by the Emirates Center for Security Studies and Research (ECSSR) about the results of the Israeli elections a week earlier. This was the first ever conference about domestic Israeli politics being held in an Arab capital with Israeli participants. It was a moving moment for me, not only because I was speaking for the first time in front of an audience in Abu Dhabi, but also because the ECSSR and its founder, Dr. Jamal Al-Suwaidi, played a pivotal role in building the relationship between Israel and the UAE. The atmosphere among the 150 Emiratis who gathered at the Rixos Marina Hotel for the conference was one of excitement and curiosity but also of concern regarding how the success of the ultra-right-wing coalition in the Israeli elections could affect their relationship. While the Israeli speakers spoke like Israelis do—bluntly and directly—

the Emiratis in the audience were incredibly restrained in their questions. At a certain point, Dr. Ebtesam Al-Ketbi, the president of the Emirates Policy Center, asked to speak. Al-Ketbi, who is one of the most respected and influential scholars in the Arab world, didn't beat around the bush. "I think the elections have proved the rise of populism, anti-Arab feelings and Jewish Salafism in Israel," she said. "How will this reflect on the Abraham Accords, that are based on tolerance between religions? The accords will remain untouchable politically, but we in the UAE fought against extremism. Israel needs to do the same."[403]

Two months earlier, the Emirati foreign minister, Sheikh Abdullah bin Zayed, arrived in Israel for his first-ever bilateral visit. He spent five days in the country and met almost all the leaders of the different parties who were busy preparing for the elections. When we met in the garden of the Emirati ambassador's residence, Sheikh Abdullah was very happy about his visit to Israel and the state of relations on the one hand, but concerned about the possibility that right-wing extremists and Jewish supremacists, such as Itamar Ben-Gvir and Bezalel Smotrich, would become senior ministers were Benjamin Netanyahu and his coalition partners to win the election and form a government. A few weeks after we met, I heard from several sources that Sheikh Abdullah raised these concerns directly with Netanyahu during their meeting in Israel. Netanyahu listened to the Emirati foreign minister, but after winning the election he nonetheless appointed Ben-Gvir as the minister of national security, in charge of the Israel Police and Israel Border Police units in the West Bank, and Smotrich as the minister of finance. Smotrich also received unprecedented authority over Israeli settlements in the West Bank. The foxes had been assigned to guard the henhouse.[404]

The Abraham Accords were Netanyahu's foremost foreign policy legacy. When he returned to office in December 2022, he found them in a far more advanced and developed state than where he had left them. Two years on from the Abraham Accords, it is clear to all that they were a resounding success. For the first time since its founding, the State of Israel has been afforded legitimacy in the region, entering the Gulf proudly through the main entrance as a legitimate partner and not a secret mistress. The peace between Israel and the UAE was warm from the very first day. Since the treaty was signed, around half a million Israelis have visited Abu Dhabi and Dubai, according to Israeli government estimates. That's a huge number—made even more remarkable in the context of two years in which COVID-19 restrictions severely limited international travel. Israelis rushed to add Dubai to the top of their lists for weekend breaks or vacations during the Jewish holidays. Once there, they were welcomed with open arms, as if relations between the two countries had always been this friendly.

The accords have already had a positive impact on the lives of millions of people throughout the Middle East. The last two years have seen dozens of agreements signed between Israel and the UAE on the economy, energy, science, agriculture, academia, cybersecurity and medicine. Entrepreneurs travel freely to sign deals, and the trade balance between the countries has shot up by hundreds of percentage points within a matter of months. According to the Israeli Central Bureau of Statistics, in 2020 trade between Israel and the UAE stood at around 190 million dollars. In 2021 it grew to 1.22 billion dollars, and in the first 10 months of 2022, it had already surpassed that and reached more than two billion dollars in goods alone.[405] Israeli and Emirati officials expect this trend to continue to grow and reach five billion dollars annually within a few years. Bahrain is showing a similar, albeit more moderate, trend. Trade in goods between Bahrain and Israel has increased from seven million dollars in 2021 to close to 20 million dollars in 2022. The potential in the deal with Morocco is enormous and is already being converted into action. The Moroccan government's goal is to reach 200 thousand tourists from Israeli annually, in comparison to 50 thousand two years ago.

Since they were signed in late 2020, the peace and normalization agreements with the UAE, Bahrain and Morocco have also proven to be sturdier and more resilient than many expected. The Abraham Accords are an inseparable part of Donald Trump's legacy, and they continue to endure in the wake of his departure from the White House. They survived numerous hurdles, first and foremost the change in administration in the United States in January 2021. The accords also weathered a change of government in Israel. For years, Benjamin Netanyahu sought to present himself as someone in "A Different League"—as one election slogan put it—whose ousting would facilitate a collapse in Israel's security, economy and diplomacy. None of that happened. In the first nine months after the accords were signed, Netanyahu impeded any progress in the relationship with the UAE, Bahrain and Morocco out of personal political interests and a desire to claim all the credit for himself. Immediately after the new Israeli government was established in June 2021, the accords were given a new lease on life, with dozens of ministerial visits and opening of embassies and missions. This was proof, if any was needed, that these countries did not sign an agreement with Benjamin Netanyahu but with the State of Israel, and that, on their part, this was a strategic decision entirely distinct from any fleeting interests or temporary alignment of political circumstances.

The definitive evidence of the durability of the accords could be found in May 2021, when ties with the UAE, Bahrain, Morocco and Sudan remained resolutely unaffected by a round of fighting in Gaza. Despite 10 days of Israeli strikes against Hamas and the Palestinian Islamic Jihad in the Gaza Strip, and in the face of public criticism within the Arab world and protests in several Middle Eastern capitals, not one of the signatories to the Abraham Accords so much as threatened to sever ties again, recall their ambassador for consultations or expel Israeli diplomats. The accords went on as before—and even expanded in the months after the ceasefire. This was evident once more in the short round of fighting in Gaza in August 2022.

The Abraham Accords also contributed to a significant positive change in Israel's relationship with Egypt and Jordan. The fact that four additional Arab countries had normalized relations with Israel gave the king of Jordan and the president of Egypt the justification and the political backing they needed to thaw the otherwise cold peace. For the first time in many years, there were public meetings between Israeli foreign ministers—first Gabi Ashkenazi and then Yair Lapid—and their Egyptian and Jordanian counterparts. Netanyahu's successor, Naftali Bennett, visited Sharm El-Sheikh after more than a decade in which no Israeli prime minister had openly set foot in Egypt. Moreover, the Egyptians joined the Negev Summit with the signatories to the Abraham Accords, and Jordan is weighing up joining too.

The accords contributed to the political transformation in Israel in mid-2021. The warm peace with the United Arab Emirates, the formalized relationship with Bahrain and the normalization with Morocco somewhat mitigated the hostility, suspicion and mistrust among a significant part of Israel's Jewish population toward anything that looks or sounds Arab. No one showcased this better or more humorously than Hamada Odeh, a young Arab Israeli, and his friends, who dressed in traditional Emirati garb and wandered around the streets of Tel Aviv pretending to be tourists from Dubai. Excited passersby waited in line to have their pictures taken with the group, only to find out a few minutes later that they were actually from the nearby Arab city of Kafr Qasim.[406] Israel's Arab society also went through changes following the accords. Arab citizens of Israel suddenly had easier access to the wider Arab world, with more cultural, academic, employment and business opportunities as a result. The 15 members of the Arab Joint List, the Arab-majority party, misjudged the mood of their public and voted against the Abraham Accords in the Knesset. A survey by the Konrad Adenauer Foundation and the Moshe Dayan Center at Tel Aviv University, published on December 6, 2020, found that 62 percent of the Arab public in Israel supported the normalization accords, while 35.5 percent opposed them.[407] The prevailing views among the Israeli Arab public on the Abraham Accords contributed to a shift in perspective among some of the Arab politicians, chief among them the head of the United Arab List (Ra'am), Mansour Abbas, who decided his party should be partners in any new potential coalition, which ultimately led to its split from the Joint List. Abbas told me he warned his colleagues in the Arab Joint List not to vote against the Abraham Accords, because it would be perceived as a vote against peace. He proposed that they abstain or walk out of the room during the vote. His opinion was rejected. Abbas said this vote and the aforementioned polls were some of the reasons that pushed him to split from the Arab Joint List and run independently.[408] These changes in Jewish and Arab society in Israel paved the way for an Arab party to join the governing coalition for the first time in Israeli history. Abbas and his party won four seats in the 2021 elections and became prominent partners in the coalition. Even though this coalition survived only a year, it was a historic progressive landmark in Israeli politics.

From the outside, the Abraham Accords looked like the crowning achievement of a diplomatic relationship between a US administration and an Israeli government and a personal relationship between their leaders, Donald Trump and Benjamin Netanyahu. The latter exploited this point mercilessly in the various and numerous election campaigns. The reality was different. Behind the scenes, Trump and his senior advisors were completely fed up with Netanyahu, and Trump grew increasingly frustrated and angry with the prime minister as time passed. By the end of his first year in office, Trump had made his mind up that Netanyahu had no interest in making progress on peace with the Palestinians. Later, Trump came to feel that Netanyahu demonstrated a lack of gratitude to him over Iran and other issues. In the last year of Trump's term, his negative feelings toward Netanyahu reached their apex. On more than one occasion, the president's senior advisors felt that Netanyahu and his ambassador to Washington, Ron Dermer, were treating the president like a useful idiot and boasting about their ability to make him do their bidding. They even said as much to Dermer. This view also came across strongly in my conversations with the former president. Even when Trump tried to tone down his outbursts against Netanyahu, his disappointment—whether justified or not—was clear. In November 2022, Trump announced he was planning to run in the 2024 presidential elections. In the two years that passed since he left the White House he hasn't spoken to Netanyahu. A scenario in which Trump returns to the White House would compel the two leaders to mend their relations.

When the accords were announced, they were subjected to no small amount of criticism in both Israel and the United States. Paradoxically, it came primarily from the left—the camp that in normal times would stand on the side of diplomacy and peace treaties. Their primary cause for opposition was no more profound than the fact that the Abraham Accords were associated with Donald Trump and Benjamin Netanyahu. The two politicians are so toxic to the liberal camps in the United States and Israel that there is no capacity to apply any sort of critical thinking to their legacy, and to express support even for those moves that align with liberal values. The most common criticism leveled by the Israeli and American left against the Abraham Accords is that they were not "peace treaties," as there was no war between Israel and the UAE or Bahrain.[409] While it is technically true that there was never a direct conflict between Israel and those countries, there is no question that, over the course of decades, they were part of the group of nations that consistently took an openly hostile line against Israel in international forums and supported states, organizations and entities that fought against it. The F-35 fighter jet deal brought another wave of condemnation that painted the accords as no more than a corrupt arms deal that would jeopardize Israel's security. A deal between the Eilat Ashkelon Pipeline Company (EAPC) and a private company in the UAE, signed after diplomatic ties were formalized, fomented yet more criticism, this time amid claims that the Abraham Accords were a mere "oil deal between tycoons" that would provide no benefits to the citizens of Israel and even risked polluting the waters of the Gulf of Eilat. Criticisms surrounding Netanyahu's conduct on the fighter jet deal and the agreement signed with the EAPC were justified, but the attempts by critics to use them to stain the Abraham Accords were inappropriate and made in bad faith. The accords were not an arms deal. They did not jeopardize Israel's security—they strengthened it. The oil deal was unconnected to the Emirati government, and when it was suspended by the new Israeli government at the end of 2021, the Emiratis made clear it would not harm bilateral ties. Even if there were businesspeople who made money from deals between the countries, these deals opened up new opportunities for trade and employment, with a positive economic impact for all citizens of Israel.

Another criticism of the accords was that they were a distraction from the bleeding wound of the Israeli–Palestinian conflict, and that they got Israel no closer to a solution. The Abraham Accords came at the height of the biggest diplomatic crisis between the United States and the Palestinian Authority since the Second Intifada. This crisis also had diplomatic, economic and reputational consequences for the Palestinians. A string of punitive measures adopted by Trump, spurred on by a few of his more extremist advisors and with Netanyahu's encouragement, had an outsized impact. But the responsibility lies also with the Palestinian leadership. President Mahmoud Abbas failed to identify the changing winds in the US, the Middle East and the world when it came to the Palestinians, their fatigue with the frozen peace process and the need for the superpowers to focus their attentions on more pressing international affairs. The boycott of the Trump administration utterly failed to serve the Palestinian cause and only worsened the desperate situation of the residents of the West Bank and the Gaza Strip. At times, the leaders of the Palestinian national movement appeared to be repeating the grave mistakes of their predecessors from the 1930s and 1940s: the internal divisions, a misplaced trust in the wider Arab world and an inability to see the diplomatic signs that led up to the Nakba of 1948. The same symptoms were present in 2017–2021.

The Abraham Accords were not designed to resolve the Israeli–Palestinian conflict, nor were they a means to crush Palestinian aspirations for independence. To a great extent, the accords were only possible because of the long-standing impasse in the Israeli–Palestinian peace process. The leaders on both sides—Netanyahu and Abbas—were mirror images of each other. They both preferred to maintain the status quo and avoid making any decisions that would lead to a diplomatic breakthrough. This status quo no longer served the interests of the United Arab Emirates, Bahrain, Morocco and Sudan, so they decided to move on. The fact that the Abraham Accords stopped Netanyahu from carrying out his annexation initiative in the West Bank prevented a severe escalation that could have resulted in a third intifada and preserved the prospects for a future two-state solution.

At the same time, the Abraham Accords cannot be used as an excuse to permit the Israeli leadership to ignore the conflict with the Palestinians and the disastrous implications it has for Israeli society. The lack of a resolution remains an existential threat to Israel's future as a Jewish and democratic state. At the time of writing, in December 2022, two years after the Abraham Accords, this threat has only increased and the situation on the ground has deteriorated to what the Israeli defense establishment says could be a third intifada. The UAE, Bahrain and Morocco spoke of how their relations with Israel would give them the opportunity to exert greater influence on Israeli policies regarding the Palestinians. They applied this pressure during the May 2021 Gaza war and again a year later when tensions flared at the Temple Mount/Haram al-Sharif compound in Jerusalem. The resolve by these countries to press the Israeli government on the Palestinian issue will be put to the test in the coming years, especially as a new hardline Israeli government settles into power. It is yet to be seen whether it will grow into something more effective and tangible than political slogans and repeated talking points.

While the Abraham Accords showed a willingness among governments in the region to normalize relations with Israel regardless of the impasse in the Israeli–Palestinian peace process, public opinion in the Arab world is still very much supportive of the Palestinians. This basic truth became evident to many Israelis during the FIFA World Cup in Qatar. Fans from around the Arab world who arrived in Qatar used the international attention around the games to demonstrate their solidarity with the Palestinians. This created numerous tense encounters between Israeli journalists and fans from different Arab countries who either refused to speak to the Israeli press in order not to "normalize" it or used the opportunity to state their views on the Israeli occupation of the Palestinian people live on television. At the same time, the fact that dozens of Israeli journalists and more than 10 thousand Israelis visited Qatar during the World Cup was unprecedented, especially considering the Qatari government's opposition to the Abraham Accords. Five or 10 years ago, the protests against Israelis would have been far greater.

Nevertheless, two years after the Abraham Accords, one of their big challenges remains garnering popular support in the Arab world. Public opinion polls conducted by the Washington Institute for Middle East Policy about the Abraham Accords in March and August 2022 set off alarm bells in Washington, Jerusalem and several capitals in the region. The poll showed a significant decline in popular support for the accords in countries in the region.[410] While in the polls conducted in November 2020 and in July 2021, 47 percent and 44 percent of Emiratis, respectively, said they had a positive view of the Accords, two polls conducted in March and August 2022 showed that Emirati public support for the accords fell to 25–26 percent. A similar trend exists in Bahrain. In November 2020 and July 2021, 45 percent and 41 percent of Bahrainis, respectively, said they viewed the accords positively. In the polls conducted in March and August 2022, that number dropped to 20 percent and 23 percent. In November 2020, 41 percent of Saudis said they had a positive view of the Abraham Accords. By July 2021, that number went down to 36 percent; in March and August 2022, Saudi public support was at only 20 percent. On the other hand, on the question of support for cooperation in business and participation in sports activities with Israel, the polls showed quite significant and steady support that hasn't declined in the two years since the Abraham Accords were signed. In some countries it has even increased. Thirty-seven percent of Bahrainis said they support business and sports cooperation with Israel, and 43 percent of Emiratis expressed a similar view. Most surprisingly, in the August 2022 poll, 42 percent of Saudis said they supported doing business or participating in sports events with Israelis—the highest number since polling started in July 2020.[411] "The challenge we face is to show the fruits of peace to the public. If the people in the Gulf countries don't see the benefit they get from the Abraham Accords, the support will continue to decline," President Herzog told me.[412]

The Biden administration, which entered office in January 2021, was ambivalent about the Abraham Accords. On the one hand, the president and his senior advisors expressed their public support for the accords and declared their intention to build on them. The new president also didn't cancel the controversial F-35 fighter jet deal, didn't retreat from his predecessor's recognition of Moroccan sovereignty in the Western Sahara and followed through on the aid package promised to Sudan as part of its normalization with Israel. On the other hand, for several months official Biden administration spokespeople consistently refused to refer to the agreements as the "Abraham Accords," a name that is associated with Donald Trump, preferring instead to speak of "normalization agreements." On the face of it, this may seem like meaningless pedantry, but it sent a negative signal about the Biden administration's willingness to push other countries to normalize relations with Israel with the same determination that the Trump administration did. Further down the road, the Biden administration's attitude toward the Abraham Accords changed significantly for the better. The US leadership in establishing the Negev Forum was the first significant step. This was followed by the deal on the Red Sea islands that the Biden administration brokered between Saudi Arabia, Israel and Egypt, leading to the first normalization steps by Saudi Arabia toward Israel. Regional integration between Israel and Arab countries in the Middle East in the fields of security, economy and infrastructure is one of the key principles in the Biden administration's national security strategy; however, as of December 2022, no new countries have joined the Abraham Accords. Israeli officials believe that a greater US push and more engagement by the Biden administration could bring four or five more Muslim and Arab countries to sign normalization agreements.

Looking forward, Saudi Arabia remains the holy grail of the normalization process. Benjamin Netanyahu, who returned to the Prime Minister's Office in December 2022, has stated publicly on several occasions that peace with Saudi Arabia is his main foreign policy priority for his sixth term in office. Netanyahu rightly claims this will put an end to the Arab–Israeli conflict, while leaving the Israeli–Palestinian conflict unresolved. Many other Muslim and Arab countries will likely follow Riyadh. But the fact that Netanyahu is leading an ultra-right-wing coalition that includes anti-Arab racists and Jewish supremacists who envision building the Third Temple in place of the Al-Aqsa Mosque could make this far more challenging, to put it mildly. The cold relationship between the Biden administration and the Saudi government is another stumbling block. Any normalization between Israel and Saudi Arabia would likely have to be preceded by normalization between the US and Saudi Arabia. On the other hand, all the senior

Israeli officials I spoke to agreed that full Israeli–Saudi relations are not a matter of if but when. They all concur that it is unlikely to happen before the generational shift in Saudi Arabia is complete and MBS becomes king. But until then, both countries continue to take incremental steps in that direction. "I hope that in my time as president we will establish relations with Saudi Arabia," Herzog told me.

Whatever happens, the Abraham Accords are not the end of the road; they are the start of a process that must move forward. "We are witnessing a historic shift in the relations between the Jewish world, Israel and the Arab and Muslim world," noted President Herzog. "The Abraham Accords allowed this to surface and created a new reality of mutual respect and partnership...when you look at it on a historic timeline, think where we can be 50 years from now."

The existing accords must be strengthened and protected from extreme steps and policies that could destabilize the region and unravel the regional normalization process. While these lines are being written and the new Israeli government is taking its place, this is a serious concern. The accords must also be expanded. New agreements with additional countries are within reach. This must be a core mission for any and every Israeli government for the next decade.

As someone who grew up in Israel in the 1980s and during the First Intifada, spent the Gulf War in a bomb shelter, was an adolescent at the time of the Oslo Accords and the assassination of Prime Minister Yitzhak Rabin and served as an officer in the army during the Second Intifada, peace, integration into the wider region and acceptance within the Arab world always felt like a horizon that got further away the more you ran toward it. That is why the Abraham Accords were such an exciting experience for me—the fulfillment of a years-long desire. For my daughter, Yuval, and my son, Uri, spending Hannukah in the Emirates or learning Arabic in Morocco has become an entirely normal prospect. The Abraham Accords will give them and many children like them in Israel and the Middle East a better future. Thanks to the accords, their present is already a brighter place.

On a personal note, this book covers 17 years of journalism, most of them for *Haaretz* and many spent covering Israel's ties with the Arab world. The majority of the book is based on the work I did for Channel 10 (which later became Channel 13) from 2017–2021, and for the *Walla! News* website and for *Axios*. Its seeds were planted in late 2018, when I began to work on my reporting series, "The Secrets of the Gulf," which aired on *Channel 13 News* in February 2019. It continued with a second series, "Netanyahu of Arabia," which aired a year later. That's one of the reasons why the Abraham Accords, which started in August 2020 and created a domino effect, became for me the journalistic story of a lifetime. The accords also came at a time when I was reaching career highs, as well as my deepest professional lows, when my tenure at *Channel 13 News* came to an end. I decided to write this book to tell the most complete version of the story of the road to the Abraham Accords that I can, but also perhaps to facilitate my own personal re-emergence from that dark place. I am grateful for the chance to do it.

Barak Ravid
Tel Aviv
December 2022
Kislev 5783

Acknowledgements

Before I started writing this book, I had my doubts about books generally. I didn't know if people still read them, and whether they would be interested in the story I wanted to tell. My friend, Naomi Toledano, who was the spokeswoman at the Israeli President's Residence at the time, was the one who first gave me the idea, back in October 2020. I was unconvinced, but she put me in touch with Dov Eichenwald, editor-in-chief of the Yedioth Books publishing house. "I'm certain he'll be interested," she told me. My first call with Dov was very short. We'd never met, but he believed in the story. "Start writing," he told me. Without their initiative and encouragement, this book would have never seen the light of day. A whole host of family and close friends came with me on this journey. First and foremost, my wife, Adi, who read every chapter the moment I was done writing it, and who contributed her wisdom and supported me the whole way. For that, I am incredibly grateful. My daughter, Yuval, and my son, Uri, were also an active part of the writing process. They were fully in the loop on the people I met and interviewed, without once leaking a thing in school or at family events. Above all, they were understanding and tolerant of the time it took me to write this book. A huge thank you to my parents, Israel and Batya Ravid, who supported me in my professional career—through setbacks, smears and stress. A special thank you also to my in-laws, Benny and Hanna Pri-Zan, for their vital family support throughout the period I wrote the book. My friend, the journalist Yiffat Givon, has spent years by my side covering Israel's relationship with the Arab world. Yiffat edited the "Netanyahu of Arabia" reports with me for *Channel 13 News*, as well as many other reports on diplomatic events in recent years. She is one of the best editors in Israeli journalism. I was lucky she agreed to edit the Hebrew version of this book, and I am grateful to her for every comment, caution and change she made. I am also grateful to Benny Mizrahi, my proofreader, who contributed so much of his experience and wisdom. I also want to thank Sahar Zivan, who demonstrated great talent and sensitivity to the subject matter in translating this book into English. His work has enabled this book to reach out from Israel to the English-speaking world. Sofia Kouropatov of Pelican Editing did great work in editing the English edition of this book. Her insights and questions made this book better and I am grateful for that. Many thanks to my journalist friends, Nadav Eyal and Tamar Ish-Shalom, who provided support and feedback. A special thank you to Tami Litani, whose support and feedback were worth their weight in gold. I also want to thank my journalist friend, Noa Landau; my historian friend, Shay Hazkani, for his encouragement and enthusiasm; the former chief editor of *Channel 10 News*, Golan Yochpaz; the head of the news division at *Walla!*, Lior Landenberg; editor-in-chief of *Walla!*, Eran Tiefenbrunn and his predecessor, Maayan Dagan. I am grateful to my editors and colleagues at *Axios* for their support and help: Mike Allen, Jim Vandehei and Roy Schwartz, Nick Johnston, Sara Kehaulani Goo,

Alison Snyder, Laurin-Whitney Gottbrath, David Lawler and Jonathan Swan. Foreign ministry spokesman Lior Hayat and his deputy, Tal Naim, provided invaluable assistance with coordinating interviews with Israeli diplomats who served in the Gulf. State Department spokesman Ned Price and US Ambassador to Israel Tom Nides were extremely helpful, for which I thank them. I also want to thank the dozens of interviewees in the book who gave me their time, opened their hearts and told me their stories. I wish to express my deepest admiration to all those who were involved in building and maintaining relations between Israel and the United Arab Emirates, Bahrain, Morocco, Sudan and Saudi Arabia over the last 30 years, especially around the Abraham Accords. Israeli, Arab and American patriots, each and every one of them. They turned from evil, did good, sought peace and pursued it.

Notes

1 During his time in office, Trump gave two interviews to the right-leaning Israeli daily newspaper, Israel Hayom, owned by the late Sheldon Adelson and his wife Miriam. The Adelsons were among the biggest donors to Trump's 2016 and 2020 election campaigns. Those two interviews, in 2017 and 2018, were conducted by Boaz Bismuth, the then-editor-in-chief of the newspaper. He also interviewed Trump on two occasions during his 2016 election campaign.

2 The Hebrew version of this book was published in Israel a year later, in December 2021.

3 On May 14, 2022, Sheikh Mohamed bin Zayed was appointed president of the United Arab Emirates, a day after the passing of his predecessor, Sheikh Khalifa bin Zayed.

4 Interview with a former senior White House official who asked to remain anonymous, June 2021.

5 Flynn stated during his interrogation that Kushner was the one who had led the efforts to block the vote. Robert Mueller, *Report on the Investigation into Russian Interference in the 2016 Presidential Election* (Washington, DC: US Department of Justice, 2019), 167–169, https://www.justice.gov/archives/sco/file/1373816/download

6 The spokesman of the Egyptian president published a statement saying that Trump had asked al-Sisi to suspend the vote in order to give the new US administration an opportunity to address the Israeli–Palestinian conflict and not to take any steps that would make things difficult for Trump and his team as they entered office.

7 Mueller, *Report*, 168.

8 Conversation with a Western diplomat on December 26, 2016.

9 Yael Feldboy passed away on May 16, 2022. For three decades, she was the point of contact at the US embassy in Israel for dozens of Israeli journalists. She was a friend and confidant, and an outstanding professional who mediated between the Israeli press and US diplomats. May she rest in peace.

10 In early 2015, the American government published data on entry passes given to visitors to the White House. The figures revealed that Dermer only visited the White House once in 2014, for a meeting with one of Obama's advisors. Barak Ravid, "White House Records Reveal Rift between Ambassador Ron Dermer and Obama Advisors" [Hebrew], *Haaretz*, April 15, 2015, https://www.haaretz.co.il/news/politics/.premium-1.2614209

11 Arbess denied introducing himself as an associate of Trump's advisors, but senior Palestinian officials said at the time that this was the reason he was afforded a meeting with Abbas.

12 Interview with former White House Middle East Envoy Jason Greenblatt, Zoom call, May 2021.

13 Interview with former President Donald Trump, Mar-a-Lago, April 2021.

14 Interview with a former senior advisor in the Trump administration, April 2021.

15 Interview with former White House Middle East Envoy Jason Greenblatt, Zoom call, May 2021.

16 On June 13, 2021, Bennett was sworn in as prime minister, ousting Netanyahu after 13 consecutive years in power.

17 Conversation with a senior Israeli minister, a member of the State Security Cabinet, February 13, 2017. On that same day, the cabinet gathered to make plans ahead of the prime minister's trip to Washington. There, Netanyahu told the ministers about his first call with Trump, which had taken place a few weeks earlier.

18 Interview with former White House Middle East Envoy Jason Greenblatt, Zoom call, May 2021.

19 Phone interview with the former senior advisor to the president of the United States, Jared Kushner, April 2021.

20 Interview with former President Donald Trump, Mar-a-Lago, April 2021.

21 Interview with a former senior advisor to Prime Minister Benjamin Netanyahu, January 2021.

22 Conversation with a former senior advisor to Prime Minister Benjamin Netanyahu, January 2021.

23 Peace Now, "Greenlighting De Facto Annexation: A Summary of Trump's Impact on the Settlements," November 9, 2020, https://peacenow.org.il/en/greenlighting-de-facto-annexation-a-summary-of-trumps-impact-on-the-settlements

24 Interview with a former senior advisor to President Donald Trump, May 2021.

25 On March 12, Greenblatt paid his first visit to Israel and the Palestinian Authority. Over five days, he met with senior figures in the diplomatic hierarchy on both sides, though most of his meetings took place with the Israelis.

26 Interview with former White House Middle East Envoy Jason Greenblatt, Zoom call, May 2021.

27 During his meeting with Netanyahu in Jerusalem, Trump said to the cameras—unprompted—that he had not mentioned the word "Israel" to the Russian foreign minister. Embarrassed, Netanyahu quickly stepped in and declared that intelligence cooperation between the United States and Israel had never been better.

28 As a senior Israeli official told me at the time.

29 On September 17, 2019, Tillerson participated in a closed conference at Harvard University and talked about how he had learned to approach any dealings with Netanyahu "with a healthy dose of skepticism." He described a few occasions in which Netanyahu presented Trump with misleading information to convince him that Israel was the good guy and the Palestinians, or whoever the other side was, were the bad guys. "It bothered me that a close and important ally was treating us that way," Tillerson said. Christina Pazzanese, "Tillerson's Exit Interview," *The Harvard Gazette*, September 18, 2019, https://news.harvard.edu/gazette/story/2019/09/rex-tillerson-details-his-frustrations-on-iran-israel-russia-and-his-revamp-of-the-state-department/

30 Friedman wanted to join Trump for his meetings in Bethlehem. Abbas, who considered Friedman a settler, refused point-blank. According to a former senior White House official, this enraged Friedman. The same official also said that Friedman did not like the—reasonably successful—efforts by the president of the World Jewish Congress, Ronald Lauder, to lobby Trump and persuade him that Abbas was a partner in peace.

31 In his book, *Sledgehammer*, published in February 2022, Friedman acknowledged that he suggested Netanyahu prepare a two-minute clip with Abbas's speeches. After the tape had ended, Friedman quoted the president as saying, "Wow, is that the same guy I met in Washington last month? He seemed like such a sweet, peaceful guy" (David Friedman, *Sledgehammer: How Breaking with the Past Brought Peace in the Middle East* [New York: Broadside Books, 2022], 75–76).

32 According to a former senior White House official.

33 According to a former senior White House official.

34 Interview with the former senior advisor to the president of the United States, Jared Kushner, Washington, July 2021.

35 The Temple Mount, or Haram al-Sharif in Arabic, is where the Al-Aqsa mosque is located today and where the Jewish temple was located two thousand years ago. It is the holiest site for Jews and the third holiest for Muslims after the cities of Mecca and Medina in Saudi Arabia.

36 The US intelligence community, including the CIA, warned that a decision to move the embassy could destabilize the Middle East and create a wave of anti-American protests in the region.

37 Netanyahu raised the matter of the embassy in his first meeting with Trump at the White House in February 2017, but he did not conduct a public campaign on the issue. Among other things, Netanyahu worried that he would be asked to "pay" for the embassy move in the form of concessions to the Palestinians. In May 2017, following US media reports that he was reticent about moving the embassy to Jerusalem, Netanyahu's office took the unusual step of publishing parts of the summary of his meeting with Trump. In it, he asserted that moving the embassy would not lead to bloodshed, as those opposed to the move claimed.

38 Erekat provided the details of the meeting in question at the Doha Forum in December 2018. At the same time, Kushner denied some of the particulars, including the claim that he had shouted at Erekat.

39 According to a former senior White House official.

40 Jared Kushner, *Breaking History* (New York: Broadside Books, 2022), 142–143.

41 Netanyahu issued a statement on July 30, 2022 after excerpts from Kushner's book were published.

42 Dermer gave his version of the events around Trump's Jerusalem announcement in an interview to the Jewish Institute for National Security of America podcast. Ron Dermer and Michael Makovsky, "Ep. 10: Operation Breaking Dawn, Kushner's New Book, Remembering Russell & Scully," *Politically Incorrect* (podcast), August 8, 2022, https://jinsa.org/diplomatically-incorrect-episode-10/

43 Interview with a White House official, Washington, July 2018.

44 Interview with a White House official, Washington, July 2018.

45 President Bush gave his speech, the result of an Israeli diplomatic campaign against Yasser Arafat, on June 25, 2002, a few weeks after Operation Defensive Shield in the West Bank. During the speech, Bush expressed support for a two-state solution, but called on the Palestinians to choose new leaders who were not involved in terrorism. "Full Text of George Bush's Speech," *The Guardian*, June 25, 2002, https://www.theguardian.com/world/2002/jun/25/israel.usa

46 Meeting with the former senior advisor to President Trump, Jared Kushner, at the White House on July 18, 2018.

47 Friedman wrote in his book that after Trump's announcement, Tillerson tried to slow down the process and issued a memo ordering the State Department to carry out a full assessment on moving the embassy, which could have taken years to implement (*Sledgehammer*, 107–108).

48 Friedman wrote in his book that he managed to bypass Tillerson and the State Department by working behind the scenes with Vice President Mike Pence and by speaking directly with President Trump and getting a green light for moving forward with opening the new temporary embassy (*Sledgehammer*, 109–113).

49 Congressman Ted Deutch, together with a group of other Democratic lawmakers, complained publicly that they had not been invited. Friedman claimed he did invite some Democrats but they could not or chose not to attend.

50 Heather Nauert, the spokesperson for the US State Department, was forced to disavow Jeffress and Hagee, claiming that they were personal guests of Friedman and that the State Department in Washington had not had any input regarding the decision to invite them.

51 Eliza Relman, "Jared Kushner's 28-Year-Old Protégé is His Right-Hand Man in the White House," *Business Insider*, April 5, 2017, https://www.businessinsider.com/jared-kushner-avi-berkowitz-trump-2017-3

52 According to a former senior White House official.

53 The buyers of the ambassador's residence were Sheldon and Miriam Adelson, Friedman's allies in the campaign to move the embassy to Jerusalem. According to a report in the Israeli financial daily newspaper *Globes*, the Adelsons bought the residence for an Israeli record sum of 67 million dollars.

54 The decision to close the consulate further exacerbated the disconnect between the US and Palestinian administrations. Contacts between the Palestinian Authority and the staff of the Palestinian department in the embassy resumed only in May 2021, after President Joe Biden's secretary of state, Antony Blinken, announced that the United States would reopen the consulate. At the time of writing, it has yet to reopen, but in June 2022 the State Department rolled back the Trump administration's decision and separated the Office of Palestinian Affairs from the embassy to Israel, re-establishing the direct line of communication with Washington.

55 Friedman's memoir, written at the end of his tour as ambassador, was entitled *Sledgehammer* after the event in question.

56 Friedman, *Sledgehammer*, 160.

57 A former senior White House official told me that over the first two years of Trump's tenure, Netanyahu attempted to distance himself as much as possible from the talks on piecing together the American plan.

58 Interview with former National Security Advisor Meir Ben-Shabbat, Merkaz Shapira, August 2021.

59 Interview with a former White House official, September 2021.

60 In early 2012, the then-outgoing director general of the Yesha Council, Naftali Bennett, unveiled a policy program that included annexing all of Area C—some 60 percent of the entire West Bank. Bennett, who was taking his first steps in the political system at the time, gave his program the Orwellian name "The Stability Initiative." As the years passed, Bennett talked about this initiative less and less. In 2021–2022, Bennett served as prime minister of Israel, but he did not make any efforts to advance the annexation plan in that time.

61 Trump's recognition of the Golan Heights as part of Israel was an impulsive move by the president, carried out without any serious discussions. Trump himself described in several speeches the moment when he made the decision. During a discussion with a few of his advisors, he put Ambassador Friedman on the line. Trump then asked Friedman to explain to him in five minutes why the Golan Heights were important. "I told them, give me a short history lesson," Trump recounted. After Friedman gave his explanation, Trump asked him for his opinion on the immediate recognition of the Golan Heights. Trump described how Friedman "was surprised like a wonderful and beautiful baby." A few minutes later, he tweeted out his decision. US Secretary of State Pompeo, who was visiting Israel at the time, was also caught out by the news. Two hours before Trump's tweet, I had interviewed Pompeo and asked him about the Golan Heights. Nothing in the answer he gave suggested that Trump was two hours away from making history.

62 Interview with a former White House official, September 2021.

63 During Israel's first election cycle in this period, in April 2019, Trump devoted a lot of time to helping Netanyahu win, including recognizing Israeli sovereignty over the Golan Heights two weeks before the vote. Ahead of the repeat elections in September 2019, Trump avoided any direct interference of this nature; three days before the vote, however, under heavy pressure from Netanyahu and Ambassador Dermer, the US president agreed to send out a tweet saying that he had spoken to Netanyahu about the possibility of establishing a mutual defense treaty between the United States and Israel—a highly controversial proposal in the defense establishments of both countries. "We'll talk about it after the elections," Trump wrote. The initiative led nowhere.

64 Interview with former Defense Minister Benny Gantz, HaKirya military headquarters, Tel Aviv, August 2021.

65 One of Netanyahu's senior advisors told me that there was poor chemistry between Netanyahu and Berkowitz from the get-go. At least one of the reasons for this was the generational gap between the 70-year-old prime minister and the 30-year-old US envoy.

66 Eshel was also appointed as head of the IDF's Planning Directorate in 2008. In this role, he was involved in formulating Israel's security needs as part of any permanent accord with the Palestinians. In May 2020, Gantz appointed him director general of the Ministry of Defense.

67 Interview with former Minister of Defense Benny Gantz, HaKirya military headquarters, Tel Aviv, August 2021.

68 Interview with former Foreign Minister Gabi Ashkenazi, Kfar Saba, August 2021.

69 Interview with the former senior advisor to the president of the United States, Jared Kushner, Miami Beach, April 2021.

70 Interview with former Foreign Minister Gabi Ashkenazi, Kfar Saba, August 2021.

71 Interview with former National Security Advisor Meir Ben-Shabbat, Merkaz Shapira, August 2021.

72 Interview with former Minister of Defense Benny Gantz, HaKirya military headquarters, Tel Aviv, August 2021.

73 Unusually, the percentage of land in the West Bank that would be assigned to each side's sovereignty was not stated within the plan itself, only in verbal statements by a few senior members of the Trump administration and in the unpublished understandings between the sides.

74 The "Triangle" area in Israel includes several Arab cities and towns with a combined population of more than 100 thousand citizens.

75 One of Netanyahu's senior advisors told me that the American view was that these 15 settlement enclaves were not viable in the long term, but they did not want to say as much for political reasons. "The Americans thought that these settlements would be like a balloon on a string, and that every vehicle coming and going would require a military convoy, meaning it would not be possible to live any sort of normal life within them. Over time, they believed, rather than expanding, people would abandon these settlements and they would simply die out," Netanyahu's advisor said.

76 Interview with the former senior advisor to the president of the United States, Jared Kushner, Washington, July 2021.

77 Jared Kushner noted in his book that, as he was walking with Trump back to the Oval Office after the ceremony, the president expressed disappointment over Netanyahu's remarks and said: "Bibi gave a campaign speech, I feel dirty" (*Breaking History*, 319).

78 In his book, Friedman makes no reference to this briefing or these comments. He downplays the efforts he made with Netanyahu to push for swift annexation and portrayed the incident as a series of misunderstandings between himself and Kushner, and Netanyahu and his advisors (*Sledgehammer*, 193–196).

79 Friedman met with both Netanyahu and Gantz ahead of the launch of the plan and told them the Trump administration would recognize Israeli sovereignty in the parts of the West Bank the plan allocated for Israel. Friedman claimed that Jared Kushner agreed in exchange for an announcement by Netanyahu that he accepted the Trump plan as a basis for negotiations with the Palestinians (*Sledgehammer*, 186–187). My conversations with Kushner and Berkowitz did not support this version of events.

80 Kushner offered the interview to Bremmer for his *GZERO MEDIA* website at the same time as Netanyahu was traveling from Washington to Moscow to bring home Naama Issachar, a young Israeli woman who had been detained for months in Russia as a bargaining chip and who was pardoned as part of an agreement between the two sides. As soon as Netanyahu landed in Moscow, Kushner's interview was one of the first things he saw. Interview with Ian Bremmer, "Kushner on Israeli Annexation Plans: Not Now," *GZERO MEDIA*, January 30, 2020, https://www.gzeromedia.com/jared-kushner-interview-israel-palestine-middle-east-peace

81 Kushner, *Breaking History*, 319.

82 Phone conversation with the former US ambassador to Israel, David Friedman, August 1, 2022.

83 According to a statement by Benjamin Netanyahu sent to me by his spokesman Ofer Golan on August 4, 2022.

84 Dermer spoke about this issue for the first time after Kushner's book was published (*Politically Incorrect* podcast, August 8, 2022).

85 A former senior White House official told me that Kushner and then-White House Envoy Avi Berkowitz told Trump not to interfere and see how the Israeli elections played out. See also Kushner, *Breaking History*, 321.

86 Aluf Benn, "Rice's Visit in the Shadow of Martin Luther King," *Haaretz*, October 16, 2007, https://www.haaretz.com/2007-10-16/ty-article/rices-visit-in-the-shadow-of-martin-luther-king/0000017f-ea8f-dc91-a17f-fe8f35800000

87 Interview with former President Donald Trump, Mar-a-Lago, April 2021.

88 Walker, who passed away in London in 2018 at the age of 89, became an iconic and celebrated figure in the UAE. James Langton, "British Diplomat Who Mapped the Borders of the Emirates Dies Aged 89," *The National*, July 23, 2018, https://www.thenationalnews.com/uae/british-diplomat-who-mapped-the-borders-of-the-emirates-dies-aged-89-1.753231

89 The most serious charge leveled against the migrant worker industry in the UAE is human trafficking, including widespread sex trafficking of women from Eastern Europe and Southeast Asia. See Ayesha Shahid, "Trafficking of Women in the UAE: A Critical Assessment of the UAE's Obligations under International, Regional and Domestic Legal Frameworks," https://pureportal.coventry.ac.uk/en/publications/trafficking-of-women-in-the-uae-a-critical-assessment-of-the-uaes

90 The US embassy in Abu Dhabi delivered the news of the state of mourning in the country in a cable sent the day after Sheikh Zayed's passing. Cable from Ambassador Michele Sison, "UAE Mourns the Death of Its Leader," November 3, 2004, available at *WikiLeaks*, https://wikileaks.org/plusd/cables/04ABUDHABI3966_a.html

91 Cable from Ambassador Michele Sison, "UAE First Lady: Behind-The-Scenes Player," October 6, 2004, available at *WikiLeaks*, https://wikileaks.org/plusd/cables/04ABUDHABI3527_a.html

92 Cable from Ambassador Richard Olson to President Obama ahead of the president's first meeting with bin Zayed, "Scenesetter for the President's Meeting with Shaykh Mohammed bin Zayed," August 31, 2009, available at *WikiLeaks*, https://wikileaks.org/plusd/cables/09ABUDHABI862_a.html

93 Interview with a senior advisor to Crown Prince of Abu Dhabi Mohamed bin Zayed, May 2021.

94 Cable from Ambassador Michele Sison to the State Department, "UAE Succession Update: The Post-Zayed Scenario," September 28, 2004, available at *WikiLeaks*, https://wikileaks.org/plusd/cables/04ABUDHABI3410_a.html

95 Cable from Ambassador Richard Olson ahead of the visit of Treasury Secretary Timothy Geithner to the United Arab Emirates, "Scenesetter for Treasury Secretary Geithner's Visit to the United Arab Emirates," July 9, 2009, available at *Wikileaks*, https://wikileaks.org/plusd/cables/09ABUDHABI701_a.html

96 Interview with a senior advisor to Crown Prince of Abu Dhabi Mohamed bin Zayed, May 2021.

97 According to Freedom House, the voter registry for the October 2019 elections grew to 337 thousand members, up from 224 thousand in 2015, but still far short of the entire voting-age citizen population. Five hundred candidates ran for the 20 elected seats. Voter turnout was only 35 percent, similar to the 2015 elections. See more here: Freedom House, "United Arab Emirates," https://freedomhouse.org/country/united-arab-emirates/freedom-world/2022

98 Cable from Ambassador Richard Olson to the State Department in Washington, "Strong Words in Private from MBZ at IDEX—Bashes Iran, Qatar, Russia," February 15, 2009, available at *WikiLeaks*, https://wikileaks.org/plusd/cables/09ABUDHABI193_a.html

99 Cable from Ambassador Michele Sison to the State Department in Washington, "UAE Minimizing Influence of Islamic Extremists," November 10, 2004, available at *WikiLeaks*, https://wikileaks.org/plusd/cables/04ABUDHABI4061_a.html

100 Olson, "Strong Words."

101 In November 2021, Mohamed bin Zayed (also known as MBZ) visited Turkey as part of an attempt to warm relations and boost trade. In February 2022, Erdoğan visited Abu Dhabi for the first time in almost a decade. Although relations have improved since the two visits, MBZ has not changed his suspicious attitude toward Erdoğan.

102 Interview with a former senior Mossad official who asked to remain anonymous, April 2021.

103 Yossi Beilin, "Oslo Successes" [Hebrew], *Haaretz*, September 17, 2013, https://www.haaretz.co.il/opinions/.premium-1.2121460

104 Interview with the Israeli ambassador to Germany, Jeremy Issacharoff, Zoom call, December 2020.

105 Interview with the Israeli ambassador to Germany, Jeremy Issacharoff, Zoom call, December, 2020.

106 Congressional Research Service, *Israel's Qualitative Military Edge and Possible U.S. Arms Sales to the United Arab Emirates* (Washington, DC: Congressional Research Service, October 26, 2020), 10, https://crsreports.congress.gov/product/pdf/R/R46580

107 Israeli Ministry of Foreign Affairs, "Cabinet Communique on the Sale of U.S. Aircraft to Saudi Arabia," Jewish Virtual Library, September 13, 1992, https://www.jewishvirtuallibrary.org/cabinet-communique-on-the-sale-of-u-s-aircraft-to-saudi-arabia

108 Over the years, the Emirates Center for Strategic Studies and Research (ECSSR) has become a semi-autonomous research institute, but it still represents the policy positions of Mohamed bin Zayed. "UAE Think Tank Director Speaks Out On Iran, Iraq, and the UAE," May 10, 2006, available at *WikiLeaks*, https://wikileaks.org/plusd/cables/06ABUDHABI1948_a.html

109 Interview with Shimon Sheves, February 2019.

110 Interview with Shimon Sheves, February 2019.

111 Interview with the envoy of the Israeli Ministry of Foreign Affairs to the Gulf, Bruce Kashdan, Jerusalem, May 2021.

112 Interview with the deputy director general for strategic affairs at the Ministry of Foreign Affairs, Josh Zarka, Jerusalem, April 2021.

113 Interview with the deputy director general of the Asia-Pacific Department at the Ministry of Foreign Affairs, Gilad Cohen, Jerusalem, April 2021. A few months after the interview, Cohen was appointed ambassador to Japan.

114 Interview with the director general of the Ministry of Foreign Affairs, Alon Ushpiz, Jerusalem, September 2021.

115 Cable from Ambassador Michele Sison to the State Department in Washington, "Emirati Businessman Looking to Invest in West Bank and Gaza," February 22, 2005, available at *WikiLeaks*, https://search.wikileaks.org/plusd/cables/05ABUDHABI834_a.html

116 Cable from Ambassador Michele Sison to the State Department in Washington, "MBZ on Iraq, Extremism, Palestinians, Saudis," September 25, 2005, available at *WikiLeaks*, https://wikileaks.org/plusd/cables/05ABUDHABI4045_a.html

117 Interview with the director for Jordan, Lebanon and Syria in the Ministry of Foreign Affairs, Liron Zaslansky, Jerusalem, June 2021.

118 Interview with the deputy director general of the Asia-Pacific Department at the Ministry of Foreign Affairs, Gilad Cohen, Jerusalem, April 2021.

119 Interview with the director for Jordan, Lebanon and Syria in the Ministry of Foreign Affairs, Liron Zaslansky, Jerusalem, June 2021.

120 Interview with the head of the Department of Coordination at the Office of the Director General at the Ministry of Foreign Affairs from 2017–2021, Dor Shapira, Jerusalem, June 2021.

121 In a cable to the State Department in March 2008, after Al Otaiba was appointed ambassador to the United States, Quinn wrote a profile on Al Otaiba that referred to him as "the right-hand man to Crown Prince Mohamed bin Zayed." Martin Quinn, "The UAE's Young New Ambassador—MBZ's Right Hand Man Gets Ready To Take On Washington," March 27, 2008, available at *WikiLeaks*, https://wikileaks.org/plusd/cables/08ABUDHABI392_a.html

122 Interview with the director for Jordan, Lebanon and Syria, Ministry of Foreign Affairs, Liron Zaslansky, Jerusalem, June 2021.

123 Mughniyeh, former head of the military wing of Hezbollah, was assassinated in 2008 via car bomb in Damascus. Hezbollah blamed the killing on the Mossad, but Israel never claimed responsibility. His dominant position in Hezbollah meant that his assassination dealt the organization a severe blow. Qasem Soleimani was the head of the Quds Force of the Islamic Revolutionary Guard Corps in Iran. He was taken out in a US drone strike during a visit to Iraq in January 2020. His assassination had a critical impact on the IRGC and its destabilizing influence in the region.

124 Interview with a former senior Mossad official, Tel Aviv, April 2021.

125 Ireland, the United Kingdom, Germany, France and Australia responded with protest measures against Israel. In those countries where Israel had a Mossad representative, they were expelled, and where they didn't, another Israeli diplomat was expelled instead. In some of those countries, the Israeli ambassador was summoned for a rebuke.

126 Interview with the envoy of the Israeli Ministry of Foreign Affairs to the Gulf, Bruce Kashdan, Jerusalem, May 2021.

127 A few months before the al-Mabhouh assassination, Israel had opened a secret office in Manama, the capital of Bahrain, along the lines of the one in Dubai. For more information on this story, see the chapter "29 Days."

128 Interview with the director general of the Ministry of Foreign Affairs, Alon Ushpiz, Jerusalem, September 2021.

129 Interview with the director for Jordan, Lebanon and Syria in the Ministry of Foreign Affairs, Liron Zaslansky, Jerusalem, June 2021.

130 Interviews with the United Arab Emirates ambassador to the United States, Yousef Al Otaiba, Washington, April 2021 and Zoom call, May 2021.

131 Interview with a senior Western diplomat who asked to remain anonymous, March 2021.

132 Interview with a former senior official in the Ministry of Foreign Affairs who asked to remain anonymous, December 2020.

133 Phone interview with former UN Special Coordinator Terje Rød-Larsen, March 2021.

134 Interview with the former US ambassador to Israel, Dan Shapiro, Tel Aviv, January 2019.

135 Phone interview with former UN Special Coordinator Terje Rød-Larsen, March 2021.

136 Interview with a former senior Mossad official, Tel Aviv, April 2021.

137 Interview with the United Arab Emirates minister of foreign affairs, Sheikh Abdullah bin Zayed, Abu Dhabi, June 2021.

138 Interviews with the United Arab Emirates ambassador to the United States, Yousef Al Otaiba, Washington, April 2021 and Zoom call, May 2021.

139 In a joint cable from the US embassy in Abu Dhabi and the consulate in Dubai bearing the signature of Ambassador Richard Olson, the US diplomats urged the new administration to address the UAE's concerns regarding the negotiations between the United States and Iran. Olson even wrote that he agreed with the position of the government in Abu Dhabi that the talks with Iran should address Iran's behavior in the region and not focus solely on its nuclear program: "The Bobcat and the Caged Lion – Thoughts on the UAE and Iran," February 2, 2009, available at *WikiLeaks*, https://wikileaks.org/plusd/cables/09ABUDHABI126_a.html

140 Interview with the Israeli ambassador to Germany, Jeremy Issacharoff, Zoom call, December 2020.

141 Interview with the United Arab Emirates ambassador to Washington, Yousef Al Otaiba, Zoom call, May 2021.

142 In a cable sent to the State Department in Washington, the US ambassador in Abu Dhabi reported bin Zayed's statements. The heads of the American delegation—Assistant Secretary of Defense Alexander Vershbow and Assistant Secretary of State for Political-Military Affairs Andrew Shapiro—attempted to placate the crown prince and even claimed that they did not consider an Israeli attack on Iran to be an immediate threat. Bin Zayed remained unconvinced: "(S) MBZ Hosts Gulf Security Dinner with ISA ASD Vershbow and PM A/S Shapiro," July 22, 2009, available at *WikiLeaks*, https://wikileaks.org/plusd/cables/09ABUDHABI746_a.html

143 Report by Ambassador Richard Olson, "Strong Words in Private from MBZ at IDEX – Bashes Iran, Qatar, Russia," February 25, 2009, available at *WikiLeaks*, https://wikileaks.org/plusd/cables/09ABUDHABI193_a.html

144 When Joe Biden entered office in January 2021, he appointed Burns as head of the CIA and Sullivan as national security advisor.

145 Interview with the former national security advisor, Maj. Gen. (Res.) Yaakov Amidror, Ra'anana, December 2019.

146 Interview with former Minister of Defense Avigdor Lieberman, September 2017.

147 Hook remains a target of Iranian retaliation and continues to receive a security detail from the US government. As part of the indirect negotiations with Iran in the first half of 2022, the Biden administration asked the Iranians to commit to not targeting Hook and other former US officials for their role in the assassination of Quds Force Commander Qasem Soleimani. The Iranians refused.

148 Hook represented the United States at the talks on the prisoner exchange that was finalized in Zurich in December 2019. The Iranian diplomat dispatched to Zurich refused to shake his hand or even acknowledge Hook's presence. He instead addressed the Swiss intermediaries and spoke to Hook through them.

149 Interview with former IDF Chief of the General Staff Gadi Eisenkot, Tel Aviv, August 2020.

150 Interview with former President Donald Trump, Mar-a-Lago, April 2021.

151 The documents in the Iranian nuclear archive primarily included documentation on the military nuclear program up to 2003, when it was frozen.

152 Interview with the United States special representative for Iran in the Trump administration, Brian Hook, Washington, April 2021.

153 Interview with former IDF Chief of the General Staff Gadi Eisenkot, Tel Aviv, August 2020.

154 The identity of current and former Mossad officials is subject to a gag order under Israeli law unless they choose to identify themselves after retiring. "A" is the first letter of the first name of the officer.

155 Interview with the United States special representative for Iran in the Trump administration, Brian Hook, Washington, April 2021.

156 Interview with a senior official in the United Arab Emirates, April 2021.

157 Interview with the United States special representative for Iran in the Trump administration, Brian Hook, Washington, April 2021.

158 Interview with former National Security Advisor Meir Ben-Shabbat, Merkaz Shapira, August 2021.

159 Bolton's book, *The Room Where It Happened* (New York: Simon & Schuster, 2020), was published in June 2020. Bolton was highly critical of Trump in the book.

160 Bolton, *The Room,* 378.

161 Ibid., 380.

162 Interview with the former senior advisor to the president of the United States, Jared Kushner, Washington, July 2021.

163 Peter Baker, Maggie Haberman and Thomas Gibbons-Neff, "Urged to Launch an Attack, Trump Listened to the Skeptics Who Said It Would Be a Costly Mistake," *New York Times*, June 21, 2019, https://www.nytimes.com/2019/06/21/us/politics/trump-iran-strike.html

164 It was the Iranian leader's chief of staff who first published the response to the letter. He noted that Soleimani refused to read it, claiming there was nothing for Iran and the United States to say to each other.

165 Phone interview with former President Donald Trump, July 2021.

166 In an interview for Israeli media outlet *Walla!* on October 1, 2021, Hayman said that the Military Intelligence Directorate had exposed sensitive information regarding Soleimani's plans to carry out attacks on American targets in the Gulf. In an interview with the *N12* outlet on the same day, Hayman said that the Soleimani assassination represented the high point of Israeli–American intelligence collaboration on Iran. See: Amir Bohbot, "Killing Soleimani, Iran and the Actions that Surprised Hamas: The Head of the UN in a Special Interview with *Walla!*" [Hebrew], *Walla!*, October 1, 2021, https://news.walla.co.il/item/3462526; Nir Dvori, "Major General Tamir Hyman in an Interview with *N12*: "The Position of Head of the MID Made Me 'Anti-Iranian' in an Extreme Way" [Hebrew], *N12*, October 1, 2021, https://www.mako.co.il/news-n12_magazine/2021_q3/Article-61e326e9b313c71026.htm

167 Interview with former IDF Chief of the General Staff Gadi Eisenkot, Tel Aviv, August 2020.

168 Phone interview with former President Donald Trump, July 2021.

169 Interview with a former senior advisor in the Trump administration, April 2021.

170 Interview with a senior official in the Israeli defense establishment, Tel Aviv, October 2021.

171 Conversation with a senior Biden administration official who participated in the meeting with Ben-Shabbat and had direct knowledge of the US reaction to the Natanz attack, Washington, April 2021.

172 Interview with former Minister of Defense Benny Gantz, HaKirya military headquarters, Tel Aviv, August 2021.

173 Peter Baker and Susan Glasser, *The Divider: Trump in the White House 2017–2021* (New York: Doubleday, 2022).

174 Phone interview with former President Donald Trump, July 2021.

175 The interview was published on the front page of *Yedioth Ahronoth* in early March 2021. Nadav Eyal, "The Former Deputy Head of the Mossad in a Rare Interview: 'The Situation Today With Iran is Worse'" [Hebrew], YNet, March 5, 2021, https://www.ynet.co.il/articles/0,7340,L-5893846,00.html

176 The report determined that producing an atomic bomb and fixing it to a long-range missile warhead would take the Iranians longer. The assessment of the Israeli intelligence community in 2022 was that the Iranians were between a year to two years away from building a nuclear missile warhead.

177 The report stated that "Iran has effectively broken out slowly by accumulating 60 percent enriched uranium." David Albright, Sarah Burkhard and Andrea Stricker, *Analysis of IAEA Iran Verification and Monitoring Report – May 2022* (Institute for Science and International Security, June 6, 2022), https://isis-online.org/isis-reports/detail/analysis-of-iaea-iran-verification-and-monitoring-report-may-2022

178 Netanyahu and those around him rejected the claims and accused Lavi of being bitter that he had been overlooked for the position of director of the Mossad. Yossi Cohen rejected the criticism and claimed that Iran was no closer to nuclear weapons than it had been before Trump's withdrawal from the JCPOA.

179 "IAEA Chief Rafael Grossi, a Diplomat on the Frontlines," *France24*, September 2, 2022, https://www.france24.com/en/live-news/20220902-iaea-chief-rafael-grossi-a-diplomat-on-the-frontlines

180 The Iranian government's decision to remove the cameras was in retaliation for a resolution by the IAEA board of governors, led by the US, France, Germany and the UK, that criticized Iran for failing to cooperate with the IAEA investigations.

181 Interview with the former US ambassador to Israel, Dan Shapiro, Tel Aviv, January 2019.

182 Upon his return from the United States, Erekat met with members of the PLO's Negotiation Support Unit (NSU) and briefed them on the meeting with Obama. A summary of the meeting was published in *Al Jazeera* as part of a massive leak of 1,700 NSU documents in January 2011: Al Jazeera Investigations, "Meeting Minutes: Saeb Erekat with NSU on US Meetings – The Palestine Papers," *Al Jazeera*, n.d., http://www.ajtransparency.com/en/projects/ thepalestinepapers/20121820584945393913.html

183 Cable from Secretary of State Hillary Clinton, "Demarche: Arab League Ministerial," June 17, 2009, available at *WikiLeaks*, https://wikileaks.org/plusd/cables/09STATE62909_a.html

184 In a cable by US Ambassador Richard Olson, summarizing the IRENA summit, he wrote that the Emiratis had treated the presence of an Israeli delegation as a highly sensitive matter, and emphasized that they were in Abu Dhabi for IRENA and not for a bilateral meeting: "Progress Made with the International Renewable Energy Agency, but Long Road Ahead," February 21, 2010, available at *WikiLeaks*, https://wikileaks.org/plusd/cables/10ABUDHABI89_a.html

185 Interview with former National Security Advisor Yaakov Amidror, Ra'anana, December 2018.

186 Interview with former National Security Advisor Meir Ben-Shabbat, Merkaz Shapira, August 2021.

187 Interview with the chairman of the Jewish Agency, Isaac Herzog, January 2019. In July 2021, Herzog was sworn in as president of the State of Israel.

188 Interview with the former prime minister of the United Kingdom, Tony Blair, Zoom call, May 2021.

189 Interview with the former national security advisor, Brigadier General (Res.) Jacob Nagel, Givatayim, January 2019.

190 Interview with former National Security Advisor Meir Ben-Shabbat, Merkaz Shapira, August 2021.

191 Molcho was gradually winding down his activity as Netanyahu's envoy after eight consecutive years. One of the main causes was the police investigation into the so-called "submarine affair" that ensnared several close associates of Netanyahu, with accusations of improper conduct in a deal between Israel and Germany for the purchase of naval vessels. Molcho was questioned under caution as part of the affair, but ultimately the police recommended closing the case against him due to "insufficient evidence to indicate criminal activity." Tamara Zieve, "Police Recommend Indicting Netanyahu Lawyer in Submarines Affair," *Jerusalem Post*, November 8, 2018, https://www.jpost.com/israel-news/ police-recommend-indicting-netanyahu-lawyer-in-submarines-affair-571373

192 Interview with the head of the Coordination Department at the Office of the Director General at the Ministry of Foreign Affairs, Dor Shapira, Jerusalem, June 2021.

193 Interview with the head of the Coordination Department at the Director General's Office at the Ministry of Foreign Affairs, Dor Shapira, Jerusalem, June 2021.

194 Phone interview with the deputy attorney general to the government for international law, Roi Sheindorf, April 2021.

195 Interview with the head of the Coordination Department at the Director General's Office at the Ministry of Foreign Affairs, Dor Shapira, Jerusalem, June 2021.

196 Phone interview with the deputy attorney general to the government for international law, Roi Sheindorf, April 2021.

197 Interview with the United Arab Emirates ambassador to Washington, Yousef Al Otaiba, Zoom call, May 2021.

198 Interview with the head of the Coordination Department at the Director General's Office at the Ministry of Foreign Affairs, Dor Shapira, Jerusalem, June 2021.

199 Munich was also where I first met the spokeswoman of the UAE foreign ministry, Hend Al Otaiba. A brilliant and remarkable woman, she held a central role in the normalization process between Israel and the United Arab Emirates as it came to fruition throughout 2020. Al Otaiba is also the scion of a family with a long history of public service in Abu Dhabi. Her father, Mana Al Otaiba, was the first minister of petroleum and mineral resources of the United Arab Emirates and a close confidant of the founder of the state, Sheikh Zayed. Her brother, Yousef, is the Emirati ambassador to Washington. Another brother, Tareq, is a senior advisor to the national security advisor, Sheikh Tahnoun. In July 2021, she was appointed as the UAE's ambassador to France.

200 Interview with former Minister of Foreign Affairs Gabi Ashkenazi, Kfar Saba, August 2021.

201 During the visit, Gantz called the Jordan Valley "Israel's eastern protective wall." Jacob Magid, "Gantz Vows to Annex Jordan Valley 'in Coordination with International Community,'" *Times of Israel*, January 21, 2020, https://www.timesofisrael.com/gantz-vows-to-annex-jordan-valley-in-coordination-with-international-communtiy/

202 Interview with former Minister of Defense Benny Gantz, HaKirya military headquarters, Tel Aviv, August 2021.

203 Interview with the former senior advisor to the president of the United States, Jared Kushner, Miami Beach, April 2021.

204 Interview with former Minister of Foreign Affairs Gabi Ashkenazi, Kfar Saba, August 2021.

205 Interview with a senior US State Department official, May 2020.

206 Netanyahu and his team were briefing journalists at the time that the Arab states didn't care about annexation. Several pro-Netanyahu journalists and media outlets bought this spin. The story reached its peak when the May 26, 2020 edition of the pro-Netanyahu *Israel Hayom* daily ran with a front page declaring that "under the radar" the Arab states were indicating they would accept annexation of the West Bank. Bin Zayed's statement was published by the official Emirati news agency. Raphael Ahren, "Emirati Foreign Minister Condemns Israel's Annexation Plans," *Times of Israel*, May 10, 2020, https://www.timesofisrael.com/emirati-foreign-minister-condemns-israels-annexation-plans/

207 The king's quotes are from an interview with *Der Spiegel* magazine. His comments raised significant alarm bells in Washington and shifted the American attitude toward annexation. Interview by Susanne Koelbl and Maximilian Popp, "The Danger of People Starving to Death is Greater than the Danger from the Virus," *Der Spiegel*, May 15, 2020, https://www.spiegel.de/international/world/jordan-s-king-abdullah-ii-the-danger-of-people-starving-to-death-is-greater-than-the-danger-from-the-virus-a-4b220928-7ff9-4219-a176-ec380ec16cf3

208 Senior White House officials were immensely frustrated by what they saw as Netanyahu's complete lack of consideration regarding the calamitous pandemic crisis swirling around the White House and Trump in particular. This was one of the main reasons they cooled off on annexation.

209 In one of Netanyahu's background press briefings at the time, he emphasized that he did not use the word "annexation" because the territory in question was not land belonging to another country.

210 Biden's advisors deliberated at the time whether to take more active measures against annexation. On the one hand, they were concerned that the annexation would go ahead and place them in a difficult position on Israel, but on the other hand, they were wary of conducting themselves like Trump and engaging in their own independent foreign policy during an election campaign.

211 Interview with a former senior advisor to Prime Minister Netanyahu, Tel Aviv, January 2021.

212 According to a former senior White House official.

213 Interview with former White House Middle East Envoy Avi Berkowitz, Miami Beach, April, 2021.

214 Interview with the former senior advisor to the president of the United States, Jared Kushner, Washington, July 2021.

215 Interview with a former senior advisor to Prime Minister Benjamin Netanyahu, Tel Aviv, January 2021.

216 Interview with the former senior advisor to President Trump, Jared Kushner, Miami Beach, April 2021.

217 Interview with former Foreign Minister Gabi Ashkenazi, Kfar Saba, August 2021.

218 Interview with the director general of the Ministry of Foreign Affairs, Alon Ushpiz, Jerusalem, September 2021.

219 Interview with former White House Middle East Envoy Avi Berkowitz, Miami Beach, April 2021.

220 Interview with the former senior advisor to the president of the United States, Jared Kushner, Miami Beach, April 2021.

221 According to a former senior White House official.

222 Aliyan was later promoted to major general. As of August 2022, he serves as the head of the Coordinator of Government Activities in the Territories (COGAT) unit, the Israeli Ministry of Defense body in charge of civilian affairs in the occupied West Bank.

223 Interview with former White House Middle East Envoy Avi Berkowitz, Miami Beach, April, 2021.

224 Interview with former National Security Advisor Meir Ben-Shabbat, Merkaz Shapira, August 2021.

225 Interview with the United Arab Emirates ambassador to Washington, Yousef Al Otaiba, Zoom call, September 2021.

226 The exhausting debates over specific terminology and the resulting compromises didn't dissuade Donald Trump from convening a press conference a few hours after the agreement was published and announcing that annexation was "off the table." This was in contradiction to Netanyahu's insistence that annexation was "not off the table." Ambassador Friedman, who sat in the White House Press Briefing Room and heard Trump's statement, hurried to explain that annexation was "off the table now, but is not off the table permanently."

227 According to a former senior White House official.

228 According to a senior Emirati official.

229 A few days later, they reached a compromise that pushed the final date for passing the budget back from the end of August to the end of November. But the postponement had no significant bearing on Netanyahu's decision to avoid passing a budget in order to get out of honoring his commitment to the rotation with Benny Gantz. The government fell apart in November, when Netanyahu once more refused to pass it, meaning Israel went three years without an approved state budget.

230 Interview with former Minister of Defense Benny Gantz, HaKirya military headquarters, Tel Aviv, August 2021.

231 Interview with former Foreign Minister Gabi Ashkenazi, Kfar Saba, August 2021.

232 Interview with Emirati Foreign Minister Abdullah bin Zayed, Abu Dhabi, June 2021.

233 Interview with former National Security Advisor Meir Ben-Shabbat, Merkaz Shapira, August 2021.

234 Interview with former Minister of Defense Benny Gantz, HaKirya military headquarters, Tel Aviv, August 2021.

235 Interview with former Minister of Foreign Affairs Gabi Ashkenazi, Kfar Saba, August 2021.

236 Prime Minister's Office, "Joint Statement from Prime Minister Benjamin Netanyahu and Minister of Defense Benny Gantz," October 23, 2020, https://www.gov.il/en/departments/news/spoke_pmo231020

237 Interview with the legal advisor of the Israeli Foreign Ministry, Tal Becker, Jerusalem, May 2021.

238 Interview with former Minister of Foreign Affairs Gabi Ashkenazi, Kfar Saba, August 2021.

239 Interview with the legal advisor of the Israeli Foreign Ministry, Tal Becker, Jerusalem, May 2021.

240 Based on data from the King Fahd Causeway Authority (*Akhbaar24*, December 18, 2019, https://akhbaar24.argaam.com/article/detail/471760).

241 The causeway was reopened in May 2021. I drove along it when I visited Bahrain in November 2021. Unfortunately, I could only go as far as the border with Saudi Arabia, but not cross it.

242 Knesset speech [Hebrew], December 5, 1994, Jerusalem, https://knesset.gov.il/tql/knesset_new/knesset14/HTML_27_03_2012_06-21-01-PM/19941205@19941205007@007.html

243 Cable from the US ambassador in Manama, William Monroe, "King Discusses Regional Issues with Ambassador," February 16, 2005, available at *WikiLeaks*, https://wikileaks.org/plusd/cables/05MANAMA230_a.html

244 Cable from the US embassy in Manama, "Bahrain: Preparing for the Sharm Al Sheikh Summit," August 10, 2005, available at *WikiLeaks*, https://wikileaks.org/plusd/cables/05MANAMA1163_a.html

245 In 2017, Al-Faihani was removed by royal decree from his position as president of the National Institute for Human Rights and from his ambassadorship. The king held him responsible for the decline of Bahrain's image on matters of human rights.

246 Interview with a senior official at the Ministry of Foreign Affairs, Jerusalem, April 2021.

247 Cable from Ambassador Monroe, "Crown Prince Concerned About Sectarian Spillover From Iraq to Bahrain," August 29, 2005, available at *WikiLeaks*, https://wikileaks.org/plusd/cables/05MANAMA1256_a.html

248 Cable from Ambassador Monroe, "Israeli Boycott Scrapped," October 3, 2005, available at *WikiLeaks*, https://wikileaks.org/plusd/cables/05MANAMA1434_a.html

249 Cable from Ambassador Monroe, "New Foreign Minister Emphasizes Desire to Enhance Bilateral Relations," October 11, 2005, available at *WikiLeaks*, https://wikileaks.org/plusd/cables/05MANAMA1469_a.html

250 Cable from Ambassador Monroe, "Bahrain: Implementation of Boycott Statutes," May 10, 2006, available at *WikiLeaks*, https://wikileaks.org/plusd/cables/06MANAMA831_a.html

251 Cable from Ambassador Monroe, "Bahrain FM Discusses AL Middle East Peace Ministerial Proposal," September 8, 2006, available at *WikiLeaks*, https://wikileaks.org/plusd/cables/06MANAMA1638_a.html

252 Cable from Ambassador Monroe, "Foreign Minister Discusses Arab Peace Initiative, Iraq, Iran," April 4, 2007, available at *WikiLeaks*, https://wikileaks.org/plusd/cables/07MANAMA319_a.html

253 Monroe, "Foreign Minister Discusses Arab Peace Initiative, Iraq, Iran."

254 Cable from Ambassador Monroe, "Foreign Minister Emphasizes Need to Reach Out to Israeli Public on Peace," May 1, 2007, available at *WikiLeaks*, https://wikileaks.org/plusd/cables/07MANAMA404_a.html

255 Aluf Benn, "Livni Met in the United States with Bahrain's Foreign Minister" [Hebrew], *Haaretz*, October 7, 2007, https://www.haaretz.co.il/misc/1.1448145

256 Cable from the US Ambassador in Manama, J. Adam Ereli, "FM Defends His Meeting with Livni," October 24, 2007, available at *WikiLeaks*, https://wikileaks.org/plusd/cables/07MANAMA968_a.html

257 Cable from Ambassador Ereli, "FM Clashes with MPs over Livni Meeting," November 28, 2007, available at *WikiLeaks*, https://wikileaks.org/plusd/cables/07MANAMA1067_a.html

258 Cables from the US embassy in Manama: "Bahraini Proposal for a Regional Organization That Includes Israel and Iran," October 3, 2008, available at *WikiLeaks*, https://wikileaks.org/plusd/cables/08MANAMA677_a.html;"Bahraini FM Will Seek the Secretary's Support for His Regional Initiative," October 14, 2008, available at *WikiLeaks*, https://wikileaks.org/plusd/cables/08MANAMA705_a.html

259 Cable from the US embassy in Manama, "King Hamad on Iran, Iraq, Regional Integration, Russia, China and India," November 12, 2008, available at *WikiLeaks*, https://wikileaks.org/plusd/cables/08MANAMA765_a.html

260 Cable from Ambassador Ereli, "Bahrain's Crown Prince Discusses Peace Process, Steps Bahrain is Prepared to Take," July 6, 2009, available at *WikiLeaks*, https://wikileaks.org/plusd/cables/09MANAMA409_a.html

261 Cable from Ambassador Ereli, "Bahrain's Crown Prince Discusses Peace Process, Steps Bahrain is Prepared to Take," July 6, 2009, available at *WikiLeaks*, https://wikileaks.org/plusd/cables/09MANAMA409_a.html

262 Prime Minister's Office, "Prime Minister's Speech at the Egyptian Ambassador's House on the Occasion of Egypt's 57th National Day," July 23, 2009, https://www.gov.il/en/departments/news/speechegypt230709

263 Cable from the US embassy in Manama, "Bahraini Crown Prince's July 28 Meeting with Centcom Commander Petraeus, Special Envoy Mitchell, and NEA Acting Assistant Secretary Feltman," August 4, 2009, available at *WikiLeaks*, https://wikileaks.org/plusd/cables/09MANAMA456_a.html

264 Interview with Akiva Eldar, Tel Aviv, December 2018.

265 Interview with the former US ambassador to Israel, Dan Shapiro, Tel Aviv, January 2019.

266 Interview with the deputy director general for strategic affairs at the Ministry of Foreign Affairs, Josh Zarka, Jerusalem, April 2021.

267 "The Budget Revealed: Israel Had Opened a New Diplomatic Mission in the Persian Gulf" [Hebrew], *Haaretz*, May 12, 2013, https://www.haaretz.co.il/news/politics/.premium-1.2017722

268 Interview with the director general of the foreign ministry, Alon Ushpiz, Tel Aviv, September 2021.

269 Yoel Guzansky, *The Gulf States in a Shifting Strategic Environment* (National Institute for Security Studies, 2012), 65–67.

270 Prime Minister's Office, "PM Netanyahu's Interview with Piers Morgan of CNN," March 17, 2011, https://www.gov.il/en/departments/news/interview_cnn170311

271 According to a senior foreign ministry official.

272 Interview with Rabbi Marc Schneier, Tel Aviv, December 2018.

273 Natan Aluf, *Bahrain—The Community That Was* (Israeli Ministry of Defense Publishing House, 1979), 21–22.

274 Ibid., 25–26.

275 Ibid., 34–38.

276 Ibid., 58–59.

277 Ibid., 100–110.

278 Ibid., 111–122.

279 Nancy Elly Khedouri, *From Our Beginning to Present Day*, 2nd rev. ed. (Al Manar Press, 2008), 87–94.

280 Khedouri mentioned the families of Brigadier Ali Mirza and Salahuddin Ahmed bin Hassan Ebrahim among those who offered protection to their Jewish neighbors. She also mentioned the Qannati, Khonji and Kanoo families, who hosted Jewish families in their homes after the pogrom. Shikha Ayesha bint Rashid bin Mohammed Al-Khalifa also gave shelter to a Jewish family in her house (ibid., 89–93).

281 Aluf, *Bahrain,* 123–128.

282 Ibid., 130–135.

283 Ibid., 161.

284 Khedouri wrote in her book that "the Jewish families who left were not forced to leave. They did so out of their own free will" (*From Our Beginnings*, 296). She added that after the emir, Sheikh Isa bin Salman Al-Khalifa, passed away, his successor, King Hamad bin Isa Al-Khalifa, invited the male members of the Jewish community to a meeting and assured them that they had nothing to worry about and that the government would continue the same policy of religious tolerance (26).

285 The full transcript of my interview with the Bahraini foreign minister can be found here: https://www.documentcloud.org/documents/6171743-Interview-With-Foreign-Minister-of-Bahrain.html

286 Kushner, *Breaking History,* 411.

287 Maoz's real name (Ronen Levy) and photograph were revealed for the first time in January 2023 when it was announced that he would be replacing Alon Ushpiz as the director general of the Ministry of Foreign Affairs. Lazar Berman, "Foreign Ministry Director General Resigns, Key Intelligence Official to Step In," *Times of Israel,* January 23, 2023, https://www.timesofisrael.com/foreign-ministry-director-general-resigns-key-intelligence-official-to-step-in/

288 See Mark Leon Goldberg, "The Test," *American Prospect,* February 17, 2006 https://web.archive.org/web/20071113195215/http://www.prospect.org/cs/articles?articleId=11167

289 Sudania 24 Television, "Sudanese Minister: Normalization with Israel No Big Deal," MEMRI, https://www.memri.org/tv/sudanese-investment-minister-normalization-israel-no-big-deal-arabs-peddled-palestinian-cause

290 Interview with Prime Minister Netanyahu's envoy to the Arab world and head of the Middle East and Africa Division at the National Security Council from 2018–2021, "Maoz," Tel Aviv, July 2021.

291 Interview with former National Security Advisor Meir Ben-Shabbat, Merkaz Shapira, August 2021.

292 According to the Freedom House index from 2021, Chad is 26th in the world for lack of civil and political freedoms: Freedom House, "Freedom in the World 2021," https://freedomhouse.org/country/chad/freedom-world/2021

293 Interview with a former senior National Security Council official who asked to remain anonymous, May 2021.

294 Interview with former National Security Advisor Meir Ben-Shabbat, Merkaz Shapira, August 2021.

295 *The Prosecutor v. Omar Hassan Ahmad Al Bashir* (The Hague: International Criminal Court, July 2021), https://www.icc-cpi.int/sites/default/files/CaseInformationSheets/AlBashirEng.pdf

296 For more on the relationship between Gadaheldam and Museveni, see: "Museveni's Powerful Sudan Fixer Dies after Contracting Coronavirus," *Monitor*, June 11, 2020, https://www.monitor.co.ug/uganda/news/national/museveni-s-powerful-sudan-fixer-dies-after-contracting-coronavirus-1894206

297 Phone interview with Nick Kaufman, February 2020.

298 The statement also stressed that Netanyahu believed Sudan was "headed in a new, positive direction, and he expressed his views to the Secretary of State of the United States of America." Prime Minister's Office, "PM Netanyahu and Chairman of the Sovereignty Council of Sudan, Lieutenant General Abdel Fattah al Burhan, Met Today in Entebbe, Uganda, on the Invitation of Ugandan President Yoweri Kaguta Museveni," February 3, 2020, https://www.gov.il/en/Departments/news/evebt_meeting030220

299 Interview with a former senior National Security Council official who asked to remain anonymous, May 2021.

300 Interview with Prime Minister Netanyahu's envoy to the Arab world and head of the Middle East and Africa Division at the National Security Council from 2018–2021, "Maoz," Tel Aviv, July 2021.

301 In the report, published on August 21, 2020, they wrote that the meeting with Hemeti had been organized by senior officials from the United Arab Emirates, and that Sheikh Tahnoun bin Zayed, the national security advisor, had participated in it. According to the report, the sides discussed the potential for diplomatic ties between Israel and Sudan.

302 Interview with a former senior National Security Council official who asked to remain anonymous, May 2021.

303 Phone interview with Jeffrey Feltman, November 2021.

304 *Asharq News* reported that Abdullah Babiker was a senior officer in Sudan's military intelligence who later worked as the head of the Foreign Relations Department within the Ministry of Defense. According to the report, al-Burhan tasked Babiker with finalizing the normalization process. Maha Taleb, "Sudan Sources to Al-Sharq: Al-Burhan Assigns a Former Military Officer the File of Normalization with Israel" [Arabic], *Asharq News*, April 5, 2022, https://asharq.com/ar/328OBTNszSAHib8PcW5s8A-%D8%A7%D9%84%D8%B3%D9%88%D8%AF%D8%A7%D9%86-%D8%A7%D9%84%D8%A8%D8%B1%D9%87%D8%A7%D9%86-%D9%8A%D9%83%D9%84%D9%81-%D8%B9%D8%B3%D9%83%D8%B1%D9%8A%D8%A7%D9%8B-%D8%B3%D8%A7%D8%A8%D9%82%D8%A7%D9%8B/

305 Interview with Roi Kais, "Sudan's Ambassador to the US in a Message to Israel: 'Do Not Side with the Sudanese Army'" [Hebrew], Kan, March 13, 2022, https://www.kan.org.il/item/?itemid=123858

306 Phone interview with the former Mossad deputy director, MK Ram Ben-Barak, March 2021.

307 In January 2019, Abrams was appointed as the United States special representative for Venezuela, a role he held for two years. In the final months of Trump's presidency, Abrams also replaced Brian Hook as the special representative for Iran, holding both positions concurrently.

308 Interview with a senior advisor to Prime Minister Netanyahu, Tel Aviv, May 2021.

309 Interview with a senior advisor to Prime Minister Netanyahu, Tel Aviv, July 2021.

310 Interview with former National Security Advisor Meir Ben-Shabbat, Merkaz Shapira, August 2021.

311 Dylan visited Rabbi Pinto in France in 1994 and 1996. Michael Gray, "Bob Unloads His Head in Paris," Bob Dylan Encyclopedia: A Blog 2006-2012, July 18, 2012, http://bobdylanencyclopedia.blogspot.com/2010/07/bob-unloads-his-head-in-paris.html

312 More information about the relationship between Kushner and Pinto can be found here: Josh Nathan-Kazis, "Jared Kushner and the White-Haired Mystic Whose Dad 'Got a Ride' From a Dead Sage," *Forward*, January 29, 2017, https://forward.com/news/361035/jared-kushner-and-the-white-haired-mystic-whose-dad-got-a-ride-from-a-dead/

313 Video clips of Kushner's visit to the cemetery were shared across social media and quickly went viral, especially within the ultra-Orthodox community: "WHILE IN MOROCCO: Kushner & Greenblatt Visit Rabbi Pinto, Daven at Kevarim (VIDEO & PHOTOS)," *The Yeshiva News*, May 29, 2019, https://www.theyeshivaworld.com/news/israel-news/1734909/while-in-morocco-kushner-and-greenblatt-visit-rabbi-pinto-daven-at-kevarim-video-photos.html

314 As a senior Israeli official told me at the time.

315 Interview with former White House Envoy Avi Berkowitz, Miami Beach, April, 2021.

316 In the 2016 election, Trump received 65 percent of the votes in Inhofe's home state of Oklahoma. Since Trump assumed office, Inhofe praised him publicly on numerous occasions, mainly for his willingness to increase military spending. Inhofe even shifted his own positions and supported Trump's decision to withdraw the forces from Afghanistan and Iraq. In 2018, following the death of Senator John McCain, Trump endorsed Inhofe's appointment as the chairman of the powerful Senate Armed Services Committee.

317 In his book, Kushner confirmed this account and wrote that Netanyahu and Friedman echoed each other in their reservations about the deal (*Breaking History*, 443).

318 Phone conversation with the former US ambassador to Israel, David Friedman, August 1, 2022.

319 Ministry of Foreign Affairs, "PM Netanyahu Meets with US Senior Presidential Advisor Jared Kushner," December 21, 2020, https://www.gov.il/en/departments/news/pm-netanyahu-meets-with-us-senior-presidential-advisor-jared-kushner-21-december-2020; full video here: IsraeliPM, "Prime Minister Benjamin Netanyahu and Special Advisor to the US President Jared Kushner in Joint Statements" [Hebrew], YouTube, 11:17, December 21, 2020, https://www.youtube.com/watch?v=NLw17KdrZFI

320 Kushner wrote in his book that Moroccan Foreign Minister Nasser Bourita was frustrated by the Israeli position and even threatened to call off the signing ceremony (*Breaking History*, 442).

321 Interview with former National Security Advisor Meir Ben-Shabbat, Merkaz Shapira, August 2021.

322 Several months later, when Secretary of State Antony Blinken held a virtual event to mark the first anniversary of the Abraham Accords, Bourita was present. Today, Morocco sees itself as part and parcel of the accords.

323 Interview with the director general of the Ministry of Foreign Affairs, Alon Ushpiz, Jerusalem, September 2021.

324 Phone conversation with the head of Israel's diplomatic liaison office in Rabat, David Govrin, August 2021.

325 On August 8, 2022, the FBI raided Mar-a-Lago, executing a search warrant. Federal agents found a trove of classified documents Trump had taken with him when he left office. Some of the documents were marked as top secret and several were even more classified and sensitive. According to *The Washington Post*, some of the documents were related to top secret information about the US nuclear arsenal. Devlin Barrett, Josh Dawsey, Perry Stein and Shane Harris, "FBI Searched Trump's Home to Look for Nuclear Documents and Other Items, Sources Say," *Washington Post,* August 11, 2022, https://www.washingtonpost.com/national-security/2022/08/11/garland-trump-mar-a-lago/

326 The current publisher of *The New York Times*, Arthur Gregg Sulzberger, is not Jewish and neither was his father, Arthur Ochs Sulzberger, who held senior positions at *The New York Times* until 1997. Nevertheless, they are the descendants of Adolph S. Ochs, the son of Jewish immigrants from Germany who bought the newspaper in 1896. Josefin Dolsten, "The Sulzberger Family: A Complicated Jewish Legacy at *The New York Times*," *Times of Israel*, December 20, 2017, https://www.timesofisrael.com/the-sulzberger-family-a-complicated-jewish-legacy-at-the-new-york-times/

327 Baron is a Jewish businessman from New York, the founder of Baron Capital, an investment management firm with tens of billions of dollars in assets. Trump was a client of Baron's.

328 Five weeks after Trump's announcement on Jerusalem, pro-Trump and pro-Netanyahu columnist Michael Godwin published an op-ed in the *New York Post* on Abbas's response to the American move: "Abbas Proves to Be Nothing but a Two-Faced Anti-Semite," *New York Post*, January 16, 2018, https://nypost.com/2018/01/16/abbas-proves-to-be-nothing-more-than-a-two-faced-anti-semite

329 The clip was the initiative of an Israeli right-wing activist and PR industry professional, Jonny Daniels: Guy Katsovich, "Watch Trump Support Netanyahu: 'He's a Winner and Highly Thought of by All'" [Hebrew], *Globes*, January 16, 2013, https://www.globes.co.il/news/article.aspx?did=1000814756

330 It's unclear whether Trump's decision on the Golan Heights improved Netanyahu's situation in the polls by 10 to 15 percent as Trump claims. But a survey by the Israel Democracy Institute a week before the elections found that 66 percent of Jewish Israeli citizens agreed with Trump that US recognition of Israeli sovereignty over the Golan Heights would strengthen Netanyahu's position in the elections. Tamar Herman and Or Anbi, "Half of the Public Does Not Believe in Election Polls" [Hebrew], Israeli Democracy Institute, April 1, 2019, https://www.idi.org.il/articles/26442.

331 This quip appeared in a column by Israeli journalist Chemi Shalev on the day of the US elections in 2020. Shalev wrote that, based on a survey by Mitvim, 70 percent of Israelis would prefer to see Trump win, compared to only 30 percent who preferred Biden. Among Jewish Israelis, the findings were even more stark: 77 percent and 23 percent, respectively. A separate survey by Ipsos found that Israel was the country where the president enjoyed the highest approval rating—orders of magnitude above any other nation. Chemi Shalev, "The Reddest State of All: Netanyahu Made Israelis Adore Trump" [Hebrew], *Haaretz*, November 3, 2020, https://www.haaretz.co.il/news/world/america/us-election/.premium-1.9286223

332 US television stations called the election for Biden on the morning of Saturday, November 7. Minutes later, the leaders of Germany, the United Kingdom, France and Canada, among others, put out statements congratulating the president-elect. Netanyahu waited until the following day to release a written statement congratulating him, as well as the tape which Trump has still not forgiven him for.

333 When Trump's remarks were published in the Hebrew edition of this book in December 2021, Netanyahu issued a statement claiming he had no choice but to congratulate Biden. "I highly appreciate President Trump's big contribution to Israel and its security. I also appreciate the importance of the strong alliance between Israel and the US and therefore it was important for me to congratulate the incoming President," Netanyahu said. Barak Ravid, "Netanyahu Responds to Trump's 'F**k him,' Defends Congrats to Biden," *Axios*, December 10, 2021, https://www.axios.com/2021/12/10/netanyahu-responds-trump-fuck-him

334 According to a former senior White House official.

335 Sandy Fitzgerald, "Trump to Newsmax: Won't Commit to Supporting Netanyahu's Reelection Bid," Newsmax, June 30, 2022, https://www.newsmax.com/newsmax-tv/donald-trump-benjamin-netanyahu-israel/2022/06/30/id/1076763/

336 Interview with a senior aide to former Israeli Prime Minister Naftali Bennett, Tel Aviv, July 2022.

337 Interview with former Prime Minister Yair Lapid, Tel Aviv, August 20, 2022.

338 Sheikh Mansour bin Zayed, the minister for presidential affairs in the UAE government, bought the Manchester City Football Club in 2008.

339 *The Washington Free Beacon* reported that there were written guidelines inside the State Department at that time not to use the term Abraham Accords in talking points, documents and statements. Adam Kredo, "State Department Shuns Term 'Abraham Accords,'" *Washington Free Beacon*, June 4, 2021, https://freebeacon.com/biden-administration/state-department-shuns-term-abraham-accords/

340 See the full transcript here: US Department of State, "Department Press Briefing—April 1, 2021," April 1, 2021, https://www.state.gov/briefings/department-press-briefing-april-1-2021/

341 According to the White House statement on May 4, Biden "underlined the strategic importance of the normalization of relations between the United Arab Emirates and Israel. He expressed his full support for strengthening and expanding these arrangements." The White House, "Readout of President Joseph R. Biden, Jr. Call with Abu Dhabi Crown Prince Mohamed bin Zayed," May 4, 2021, https://www.whitehouse.gov/briefing-room/statements-releases/2021/05/04/readout-of-president-joseph-r-biden-jr-call-with-abu-dhabi-crown-prince-mohamed-bin-zayed/

342 See the full transcript of the White House briefing here: US Embassy in Israel, "Press Gaggle by Press Secretary Jen Psaki," May 18, 2021, https://il.usembassy.gov/press-gaggle-by-press-secretary-jen-psaki/

343 The counselor is one of the most senior positions in the State Department, Chollet serves at the rank of under secretary as a senior policy advisor to the secretary of state on a wide range of issues and conducts special diplomatic assignments. US Department of State, "Derek H. Chollet," https://www.state.gov/biographies/derek-h-chollet/

344 Phone interview with Counselor of the State Department Derek Chollet, August 23, 2022.

345 Phone conversation with former Foreign Minister Gabi Ashkenazi, June 2021.

346 According to a senior Moroccan official.

347 Phone interview with Counselor of the State Department Derek Chollet, August 23, 2022.

348 Phone interview with Counselor of the State Department Derek Chollet, August 23, 2022.

349 See the photo here: Gili Cohen, Twitter post, August 26, 2021, 8:51 PM, https://twitter.com/gilicohen10/status/1430981176974532614?s=20&t=JGwJjcbT2RLDG42EH67Wwg

350 According to a senior US official.

351 Conversation with the undersecretary for political affairs of the Bahraini foreign ministry, Abdullah Al Khalifa, Jerusalem, August 8, 2021.

352 Phone interview with Counselor of the State Department Derek Chollet, August 23, 2022.

353 Ministry of Foreign Affairs, "PM Bennett Comments on the First Anniversary of the Abraham Accords," September 17, 2021, https://www.gov.il/en/departments/news/pm-bennett-comments-on-the-first-anniversary-of-the-abraham-accords-17-september-2021

354 Conversation with a senior Israeli official, Washington, October 14, 2021.

355 Interview with the director general of the Israeli foreign ministry, Alon Ushpiz, Tel Aviv, September 7, 2022.

356 Phone interview with Counselor of the State Department Derek Chollet, August 23, 2022.

357 The story was first published by the *Wall Street Journal*: Gordon Lubold and Warren P. Strobel, "Secret Chinese Port Project in Persian Gulf Rattles US Relations With U.A.E.," *Wall Street Journal*, November 19, 2021, https://www.wsj.com/articles/us-china-uae-military-11637274224. CNN reported later that US intelligence detected that Chinese signals intelligence ships that were disguised as commercial vessels used the facility at the Khalifa Port: Katie Bo Lillis, Natasha Bertrand and Kylie Atwood, "Construction Halted on Secret Project at Chinese Port in UAE After Pressure from US, Officials Say," CNN, November 19, 2021, https://edition.cnn.com/2021/11/19/politics/china-uae-us-construction-port/index.html

358 Interview with former Prime Minister Yair Lapid, Tel Aviv, August 19, 2022.

359 See the White House statement summarizing the meeting: The White House, "Joint Statement of the Leaders of India, Israel, United Arab Emirates, and the United States (I2U2)," July 14, 2022, https://www.whitehouse.gov/briefing-room/statements-releases/2022/07/14/joint-statement-of-the-leaders-of-india-israel-united-arab-emirates-and-the-united-states-i2u2/

360 See excerpts from Shavit's book published in the Israeli press: Shabtai Shavit, "This is How Rabin's Secret Visit Unfolded: From the Book *The Head of the Mossad*" [Hebrew], YNet, March 10, 2018, https://www.ynet.co.il/articles/0,7340,L-5148655,00.html

361 Boehler spoke about the proposed deal in an interview with Bloomberg a month after Luhut's visit to Washington. Ivan Levingston, "Indonesia Could Get Billions in US Funding to Join Israel Push," *Bloomberg*, December 22, 2020, https://www.bloomberg.com/news/articles/2020-12-22/indonesia-could-get-billions-in-u-s-funding-to-join-israel-push#xj4y7vzkg

362 According to two senior US and Israeli officials who had direct knowledge of the issue.

363 See statement here: Antara, "We Will Always Stand by the Palestinians," *Jakarta Globe*, December 24, 2021, https://jakartaglobe.id/news/we-will-always-stand-by-palestinians-indonesia/

364 Conversation with Emirati Foreign Minister Sheikh Abdullah bin Zayed, Herzliya, September 16, 2022.

365 The White House, "Statement by National Security Advisor Jake Sullivan on Houthi Attack Against UAE," January 17, 2022, https://www.whitehouse.gov/briefing-room/statements-releases/2022/01/17/statement-by-national-security-advisor-jake-sullivan-on-houthi-attack-against-uae/

366 Interview with former Prime Minister Yair Lapid, Tel Aviv, August 19, 2022.

367 Interview with former Minister of Defense Benny Gantz, Tel Aviv, August 23, 2022.

368 Interview with President Isaac Herzog, Tel Aviv, July 28, 2022.

369 In late October 2022, satellite imagery which was shared on Twitter showed Barak 8 launchers and their radar system deployed at Al Dhafra Air Base, south of Abu Dhabi. Emanuel Fabian, "Citing Satellite Image, Analysts Say UAE Deploys Israeli-Made Air Defense System," *Times of Israel*, October 29, 2022, https://www.timesofisrael.com/citing-satellite-image-analysts-say-uae-deploys-israeli-made-air-defense-system/

370 Phone interview with State Department Counselor Derek Chollet, August 23, 2022.

371 Phone interview with White House Middle East Coordinator Brett McGurk, March 1, 2022.

372 "'This Might Be the Last Time You See Me Alive,' Zelensky Warns EU Leaders," *Times of Israel*, February 25, 2022, https://www.timesofisrael.com/liveblog_entry/this-might-be-the-last-time-you-see-me-alive-zelensky-warns-eu-leaders/

373 Interview with President Isaac Herzog, Tel Aviv, July 28, 2022.

374 Interview with former Prime Minister Yair Lapid, Tel Aviv, August 19, 2022.

375 Phone conversation with the US ambassador to Israel, Tom Nides, April 2022.

376 On January 9, 2023 the first meeting of the Negev Forum took place in Abu Dhabi. All six working groups convened and started discussing regional projects. One hundred and fifty diplomats and officials from the US, Israel, the UAE, Bahrain, Egypt and Morocco participated. This was the biggest meeting between Israel and its Arab neighbors since the 1991 Madrid conference. The decision was made that a ministerial meeting of the Negev Forum will take place in Morocco by the end of March 2023.

377 Phone interview with Counselor of the State Department Derek Chollet, August 23, 2022.

378 See the full remarks at the closing ceremony of the Negev summit here: US Department of State, "Secretary Antony J. Blinken Joint Press Statements at the Conclusion of the Negev Summit," March 28, 2022, https://www.state.gov/secretary-antony-j-blinken-joint-press-statements-at-the-conclusion-of-the-negev-summit/

379 According to a senior Emirati official with direct knowledge of the meeting.

380 Phone conversation with the United Arab Emirates ambassador to Washington, Yousef Al Otaiba, March 30, 2022.

381 The account of the meeting between Biden and MBZ is based on conversations with two Emirati officials.

382 Since the establishment of the State of Israel, the freedom of the press has been limited by a system of military censorship. Any news report that deals with national security matters, including contacts with countries that don't have diplomatic relations with Israel, has to be sent by the media outlets to the military censor for vetting. Over the years, the number of news reports that are censored have decreased dramatically, but the system still exists to this day.

383 Jared Kushner wrote in his book that when he met MBS in Riyadh in early September 2020 the crown prince told him that Saudi Arabia had common interests with Israel, but stressed that he wanted to let the region process the normalization between Israel and the UAE and see if progress could be made with the Palestinians before warming relations (*Breaking History*, 411).

384 In an interview with Egypt's CBC television channel in April 2016, Saudi Foreign Minister Adel al-Jubeir said the agreement with Egypt on the islands doesn't include direct Saudi–Israeli contacts but added that the kingdom is committed to the commitments that Egypt accepted related to the islands. Dan Williams, "Israel Gives Blessing to Egypt's Return of Red Sea Islands to Saudi Arabia," *Reuters*, April 12, 2016, https://www.reuters.com/article/us-egypt-saudi-islands-israel-idUSKCN0X9106

385 The Saudi crown prince signaled in the interview that he was open to moving away from the historic alliance with the US in favor of China. "Where is the potential in the world today? It's in Saudi Arabia. And if you want to miss it, I believe other people in the East are going to be super happy," MBS said. Graeme Wood, "Absolute Power," *Atlantic*, March 3, 2022, https://www.theatlantic.com/magazine/archive/2022/04/mohammed-bin-salman-saudi-arabia-palace-interview/622822/

386 See the Saudi foreign minister's comments here: "Saudi Foreign Minister Reiterates Kingdom's Position on Israel," *Arab News*, May 24, 2022, https://www.arabnews.com/node/2088851/saudi-arabia

387 Mark Mazzetti, Edward Wong and Adam Entous, "US Officials Had a Secret Oil Deal With the Saudis. Or So They Thought," *New York Times*, October 25, 2022, https://www.nytimes.com/2022/10/25/us/politics/us-saudi-oil-deal.html

388 See the full remarks of White House officials' briefing on Biden's trip to the Middle East here: The White House, "Background Press Call by a Senior Administration Official on the President's Trip to The Middle East," June 13, 2022, https://www.whitehouse.gov/briefing-room/press-briefings/2022/06/14/background-press-call-by-a-senior-administration-official-on-the-presidents-trip-to-the-middle-east/

389 Interview with former Minister of Defense Benny Gantz, Tel Aviv, August 23, 2022.

390 Michael R. Gordon, "US Held Secret Meeting With Israeli, Arab Military Chiefs to Counter Iran Air Threat," *Wall Street Journal*, June 26, 2002, https://www.wsj.com/articles/u-s-held-secret-meeting-with-israeli-arab-military-chiefs-to-counter-iran-air-threat-11656235802

391 The White House, "Remarks by President Biden During a Menorah Lighting in Celebration of Hanukkah," December 1, 2021, https://www.whitehouse.gov/briefing-room/speeches-remarks/2021/12/01/remarks-by-president-biden-during-a-menorah-lighting-in-celebration-of-hanukkah/

392 The White House, "Remarks by President Biden at Arrival Ceremony," July 13, 2022, https://www.whitehouse.gov/briefing-room/speeches-remarks/2022/07/13/remarks-by-president-biden-at-arrival-ceremony/

393 A poll by the Israeli Democracy Institute showed a rise in the proportion of respondents who believed Biden would take Israel's security into account during negotiations with Iran, up from 15 percent before the visit to 34 percent after among Jews, and from 20.5 percent to 26 percent among Arabs. Tamar Hermann, Or Anabi and Yaron Kaplan, "President Biden's Visit, in Retrospect," The Israel Democracy Institute, August 8, 2022, https://en.idi.org.il/articles/39524

394 The White House, "The Jerusalem US-Israel Strategic Partnership Joint Declaration," July 14, 2022, https://www.whitehouse.gov/briefing-room/statements-releases/2022/07/14/the-jerusalem-u-s-israel-strategic-partnership-joint-declaration/

395 Interview with former Prime Minister Yair Lapid, Tel Aviv, August 19, 2022.

396 See the video with Biden's remarks here: Damon Maghsoudi, Twitter post, December 20, 2022, 6:16 AM, https://twitter.com/DamonMaghsoudi/status/1605084721016209411

397 ksagaca, Twitter post, July 14, 2022, 11:56 PM, https://twitter.com/ksagaca/status/1547716582545076224

398 The White House, "Remarks by President Biden on his Meetings in Saudi Arabia," July 15, 2022, https://www.whitehouse.gov/briefing-room/speeches-remarks/2022/07/15/remarks-by-president-biden-on-his-meetings-in-saudi-arabia/

399 According to Saudi officials, MBS told Biden that different countries have different values and if the US only has alliances with countries that share all its values, it will be left only with NATO countries. Reem Krimly, "All Legal Measures Taken Over Khashoggi Killing: Saudi Crown Prince to Biden," *Alarabiya News*, July 16, 2022, https://english.alarabiya.net/News/gulf/2022/07/16/All-legal-measures-taken-over-Khashoggi-killing-Saudi-Crown-prince-to-Biden

400 According to a senior Israeli official with direct knowledge of the issue.

401 The White House, "Remarks by President Biden at the GCC + 3 Summit Meeting," July 16, 2022, https://www.whitehouse.gov/briefing-room/speeches-remarks/2022/07/16/remarks-by-president-biden-at-the-gcc-3-summit-meeting/

402 Mark Trevelyan, "Putin Discusses Oil Market with Saudi Crown Prince Who Hosted Biden Last Week," *Reuters,* July 21, 2022, https://www.reuters.com/world/putin-saudi-crown-prince-underline-importance-opec-framework-kremlin-2022-07-21/

403 See the full ECSSR conference here: TheECSSR, "Symposium | Prospects for Israeli Politics Following the Knesset Elections," YouTube, 3:20:07, November 24, 2022, https://www.youtube.com/watch?v=p00ZkMnPG2M

404 On January 3, a few days after the government was sworn in, Ben Gvir visited the Al-Aqsa mosque compound. His visit generated widespread condemnation, mainly from the Abraham Accords countries.

405 This number includes commercial goods and services. It does not include software sales, estimated at a further 500 million dollars during this period, and defense sales, which are confidential but estimated to be worth more than two billion dollars during 2022.

406 Odeh told the 103 FM radio station the next day that the responses from Israeli Jews were very positive. "The Israelis Who Disguised Themselves as Tourists from Dubai: 'We Felt That the Citizens Wanted Peace'" [Hebrew], *Maariv*, December 6, 2020, https://www.maariv.co.il/news/israel/Article-806655

407 According to the survey, the primary reasons given for supporting the accords were financial (26 percent), a hope that Israel would no longer be a foreign element in the region (11.7 percent) and even a desire that they would forge a greater understanding of Arab culture among Jewish Israelis (7.4 percent). On the other hand, the primary reason given for opposing the accords was a sense that the agreements would come at the expense of a solution to the Palestinian issue (22 percent). See the full poll results here: Arik Rudnitzky, "Public Opinion Poll among Arab Citizens in Israel," Moshe Dayan Center for Middle Eastern and African Studies, December 6, 2020, https://dayan.org/content/public-opinion-poll-among-arab-citizens-israel

408 Phone interview with the head of the Ra'am party, MK Mansour Abbas, January 2022.

409 This claim did not hold up so well in the case of Sudan, which was an active participant in several wars and terrorist attacks against Israel.

410 Dylan Kassin and David Pollock, "Arab Public Opinion on Arab-Israeli Normalization and Abraham Accords," Washington Institute Fikra Forum, July 15, 2022, https://www.washingtoninstitute.org/policy-analysis/arab-public-opinion-arab-israeli-normalization-and-abraham-accords

411 See the data here: "TWI Interactive Polling Platform," Washington Institute Fikra Forum, June 30, 2022, https://www.washingtoninstitute.org/policy-analysis/twi-interactive-polling-platform

412 Interview with President Isaac Herzog, Tel Aviv, July 28, 2022.

Index

About the Author:

Barak Ravid is the Middle East correspondent for *Axios* and the diplomatic correspondent for *Walla!* in Israel. He is based in Tel Aviv.

Ravid began his career in journalism in 2005 as a diplomatic correspondent for the Israeli *NRG* news website. From there, he moved to the *Haaretz* daily newspaper, where he spent a decade as a diplomatic correspondent and columnist. In 2017, he was appointed as the chief diplomatic correspondent of *Channel 13 News*, a position he held until 2020.

Over the last 17 years, Ravid has covered Israel's national security and foreign policy extensively, as well as US policy in the Middle East. He has reported from more than 30 capitals in five continents and covered five Israeli prime ministers and four US presidents.

Over the course of his career, Ravid has published hundreds of exclusive stories on the Middle East peace process, Israel's relations with the Arab world, the Iran nuclear crisis and the US–Israeli relationship. In 2019 and 2020, Ravid published two series of detailed reports on the secret relationship between Israel and the Gulf states. The Abraham Accords were signed a few months later.

Ravid is a frequent guest on US television networks. He has given numerous interviews on CNN, Fox News, MSNBC, CBS and Newsmax. He has a large social media presence, with more than 215 thousand followers on Twitter, and his newsletter, "Axios from Tel Aviv," is sent out to 30 thousand subscribers every week.

Ravid holds a bachelor's degree in Middle East history from Tel Aviv University. He is married to Adi Prizan-Ravid, and they have two children—Yuval and Uri.

About the Translator:

Sahar Zivan was born in Leicester, in the United Kingdom. He holds a bachelor's degree in Italian studies from the University of Bristol and a master's degree in translation and culture from University College London (UCL). He translates from Hebrew and Italian into English, and his previous works in translation include Claudio Fava's *The Silenced* and Andrea Schiavon's *Five Rings and One Star—The Story of Shaul Ladany* (both Polaris Publishing). He lives in Haifa, Israel.